NO BELLS TO TOLL

Barbara Bode

NO BELLS

TO TOLL

Destruction and Creation
in the Andes

CHARLES SCRIBNER'S SONS • NEW YORK

Charles Scribner's Sons
Macmillan Publishing Company
866 Third Avenue, New York, NY 10022
Collier Macmillan Canada, Inc.

Library of Congress Cataloging-in-Publication Data
Bode, Barbara.
No bells to toll: destruction and creation in the Andes/Barbara Bode.
  p. cm.
Bibliography: p.
Includes index.
ISBN 0-684-19065-6
1. Huaylas, Callejón de, Region (Peru)—History. 2. Earthquakes—Peru—Huaylas, Callejón de, Region—History—20th century. 3. Earthquakes—Peru—Huaylas, Callejón de, Region—Religious aspects. 4. Huaylas, Callejón de, Region (Peru)—Description and travel. 5. Bode, Barbara—Journeys—Peru—Huaylas, Callejón de, Region. I. Title.
F3451.A45B63 1989
985'.21—dc19   88-32914 CIP

Macmillan books are available at special discounts for bulk purchases for sales promotions, premiums, fund-raising, or educational use. For details, contact:

Special Sales Director
Macmillan Publishing Company
866 Third Avenue
New York, NY 10022

10 9 8 7 6 5 4 3 2 1

Printed in the United States of America

To
Cirila, Domitila, and Jesusa,
women of the Andes,
and
to the memory of
Don Juan

*Do you know? Underneath it all, we are children
playing around the sun. . . .*

*Humberto de Jesús,
Lima, Christmas 1970,
to his friend Hugo Ramírez Gamarra,
in Recuay, a town in the
Callejón de Huaylas*

CONTENTS

Contents   xi

ILLUSTRATIONS

MAPS

1. South America, Showing Peru and the Department of Ancash

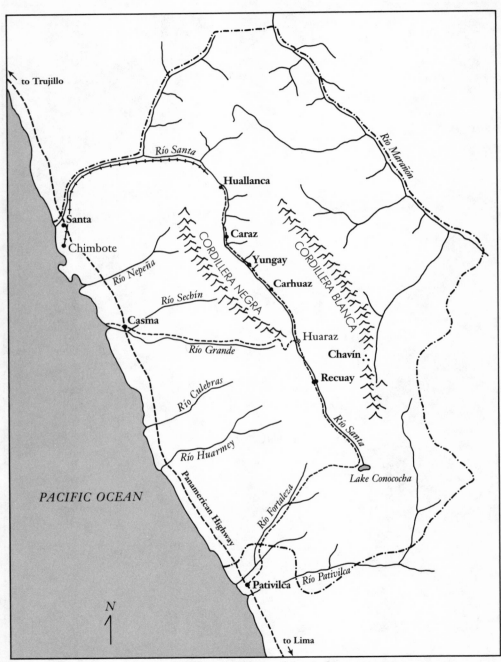

to Trujillo

PACIFIC OCEAN

Río Santa

Huallanca

Santa

Chimbote

Caraz

Yungay

CORDILLERA NEGRA

Río Nepeña

CORDILLERA BLANCA

Carhuaz

Río Sechin

Huaraz

Casma

Chavín

Río Grande

Recuay

Río Culebras

Río Santa

Río Huarmey

Lake Conococha

Panamerican Highway

Río Fortaleza

N

Pativilca

Río Pativilca

to Lima

Río Marañón

2. **Department of Ancash**

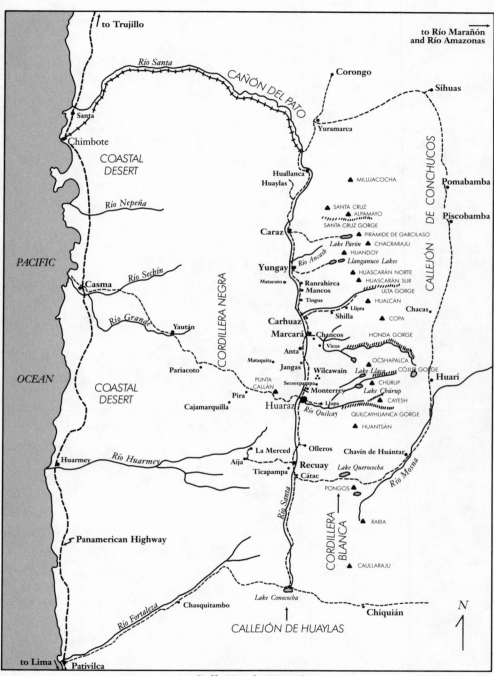

to Trujillo

to Río Marañón
and Río Amazonas

Río Santa

CAÑON DEL PATO

Corongo

Sihuas

Santa

Yuramarca

Chimbote

COASTAL
DESERT

Huallanca
Huaylas

▲ MILLUACOCHA

Pomabamba

Río Nepeña

▲ SANTA CRUZ
▲ ALPAMAYO
SANTA CRUZ GORGE

Piscobamba

PACIFIC

Caraz

Lake Parón ▲ PIRÁMIDE DE GARCILASO
▲ CHACRARAJU
▲ HUANDOY

CALLEJÓN DE CONCHUCOS

Río Sechín

Casma

CORDILLERA NEGRA

Yungay

Río Ancash

Llanganuco Lakes

Matacoto ●

▲ HUASCARÁN NORTE
▲ HUASCARÁN SUR

Ranrahirca
Mancos

ULTA GORGE

Tingua

▲ HUALCÁN

Río Grande

Yaután

Llipta
Shilla

Chacas

▲ COPA

Carhuaz

Marcará

Chancos

HONDA GORGE

Anta

Vicos

OCEAN

COASTAL
DESERT

Pariacoto

Mataquita

Jangas

Wilcawaín

Lake Llaca

OCSHAPALCA

Huari

CÓJUR GORGE

CHURUP

Cajamarquilla

Pira

PUNTA
CALLÁN

Secsecpampa

Monterrey

Lake Chúrup

CAYESH

Huaraz

Río Quilcay

Llupa

QUILCAYHUANCA GORGE

▲ HUANTSÁN

Huarmey

Río Huarmey

La Merced

Olleros

Chavín de Huántar

Aija

Ticapampa

Recuay

Lake Querococha

Río Mosna

Panamerican Highway

Cátac

PONGOS ▲

CORDILLERA
BLANCA

▲ RARIA

▲ CAULLARAJU

Lake Conococha

Chasquitambo

Chiquián

N

Río Fortaleza

CALLEJÓN DE HUAYLAS

to Lima

Pativilca

3. Callejón de Huaylas

4. Profile of the Cordillera Blanca as Seen from the Valley Floor

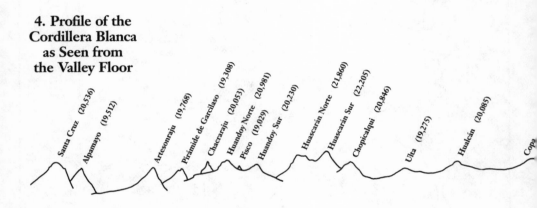

Santa Cruz (20,536) · Alpamayo (19,512) · Aresonraju (19,768) · Pirámide de Garcilaso (19,308) · Chacraraju (20,053) · Huandoy Norte (20,981) · Pisco (19,029) · Huandoy Sur (20,230) · Huascarán Norte (21,860) · Huascarán Sur (22,205) · Chopicalqui (20,846) · Ulta (19,275) · Hualcán (20,085) · Copa

Northern Half

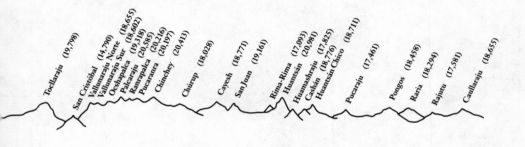

Toclaraju (19,798)
San Cristóbal (14,790)
Vallunaraju Norte (18,655)
Vallunaraju Sur (18,602)
Ocshapalca (19,318)
Palcaraju (20,585)
Ranrapalca (20,216)
Pucaranra (20,197)
Chinchey (20,413)
Churup (18,038)
Cayesh (18,771)
San Juan (19,161)
Rima-Rima (17,093)
Huantsán (20,981)
Huamashraju (17,825)
Cashán (18,776)
Huantsán Chico (18,711)
Pucaraju (17,461)
Pongos (18,458)
Raria (18,294)
Rajutu (17,581)
Caullaraju (18,655)

Southern Half

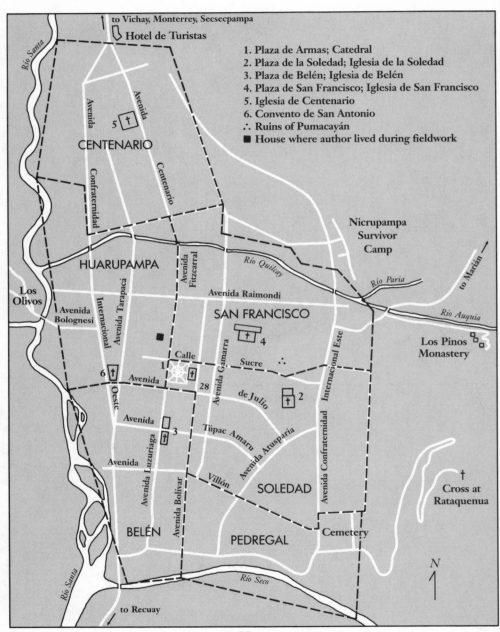

to Vichay, Monterrey, Secsecpampa
Hotel de Turistas

1. Plaza de Armas; Catedral
2. Plaza de la Soledad; Iglesia de la Soledad
3. Plaza de Belén; Iglesia de Belén
4. Plaza de San Francisco; Iglesia de San Francisco
5. Iglesia de Centenario
6. Convento de San Antonio
∴ Ruins of Pumacayán
■ House where author lived during fieldwork

Río Santa

CENTENARIO
5

Avenida
Avenida
Confraternidad
Centenario

Nicrupampa
Survivor
Camp

to Marián

HUARUPAMPA

Río Quilcay

Río Paria

Río Auquia

Los
Olivos

Avenida
Bolognesi

Avenida Internacional

Avenida Tarapacá

Avenida Fitzcarral

Avenida Raimondi

SAN FRANCISCO
4

Los Pinos
Monastery

Calle
1
6
Avenida
Oeste
28

Avenida Gamarra

Sucre
∴

de Julio
2

Avenida Internacional Este

Avenida
3

Túpac Amaru

Avenida Atusparia

Avenida Confraternidad

Cross at
Rataquenua

Avenida

Avenida Luzuriaga

Avenida Bolívar

Villón

SOLEDAD

BELÉN

PEDREGAL

Cemetery

Río Santa

Río Seco

to Recuay

N

5. Huaraz

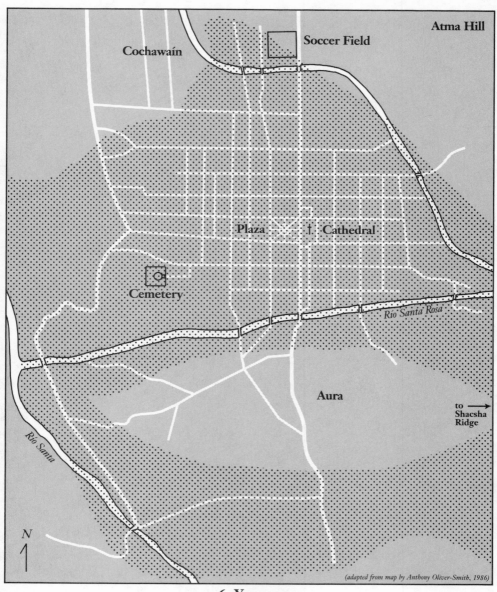

Atma Hill

Cochawaín

Soccer Field

Plaza ☩ † Cathedral

Cemetery

Río Santa Rosa

Aura

to
Shacsha
Ridge

Río Santa

N

(adapted from map by Anthony Oliver-Smith, 1986)

6. Yungay

AUTHOR'S NOTE

I lived this experience largely in Spanish. All survivors' statements I recorded in Spanish in my field notes. Or they were transcribed in Spanish and Quechua from the tapes I made. For the most part, Reyna Alberto Quito translated from Quechua to Spanish. I have made all translations from Spanish to English. Likewise, all translations from sources published in Spanish—newspaper items, pamphlets, books, poetry—are mine.

PROLOGUE: MAY 31, 1970

On May 31, 1970, an earthquake struck Peru. Tremors were felt in most of the country, but it was the Department of Ancash, 40,000 square kilometers of coastal lands and mountain ranges, that was ravaged that Sunday afternoon at 3:23. In Ancash, intense shaking occurred in the sierra, in a narrow 125-mile-long valley between two Andean ranges, the Cordillera Negra and the Cordillera Blanca, a valley called the Callejón de Huaylas. Within the Callejón de Huaylas, the towns of Yungay and Huaraz were hardest hit. Yungay was obliterated by an ice-and-mud avalanche from the 21,860-foot north peak of Huascarán, triggered by the earthquake. Six thousand people were buried, many alive, in the town center. Thousands more in Yungay's environs, including Sunday visitors and market vendors, were buried by the avalanche or swept away down the valley river, swelling the losses in the Yungay community to 18,000. Most of Huaraz, including all of its urban center ("casco urbano"), collapsed from the shaking alone. Twenty thousand were killed, 10,000 buried under the rubble of the casco urbano. All told, the valley may have lost a fourth of its population of 300,000. It is possible that 75,000 people died on May 31, 1970, in the Callejón de Huaylas.[1]

CAST OF CHARACTERS

ABEL — member of the predisaster "high society" in Huaraz

ABUELA — "Grandmother"; mother of Jesusa; Don Juan's mother-in-law

ALBINITO — sacristan in Centenario in 1980

DON* ALEJANDRO — guardian of the two Llanganuco Lakes

DON ALEJANDRO — old man of San Francisco barrio

DOÑA* ANATOLIA — rich woman who owned much of the land on which the Nicrupampa survivor camp was built

DOÑA ANGELITA — shopkeeper in San Francisco barrio

DON ANTONIO — shopkeeper in Centenario where I bought staples

ATUSPARIA — lawyer from Huaraz living in Lima; named for his famous ancestor, the Indian leader of Marián

FATHER AUSCARIO — the German priest at Centenario

CÁCERES — man engaging in philosophical discussion with Atusparia

CAGLIOSTRO — high CRYRZA official

CALIXTO CAMPOS — majordomo of Uchcupat'sa, mountain cross of Secsecpampa

---

*"Don" and "Doña" are terms of respect.

CHEPO — survivor of Yungay

CIRILA — survivor of Yungay

CLAUDIA — rescuer of the images of San José and the Virgin

CUCHA — my landlords' daughter; teacher in Casma

DELIA — devotee of the Virgin Mary Helper

ABDÓN DEXTRE — poet from Huaraz

DINA, SANTIAGO, and OMAR — Cirila's daughter, son-in-law, and grandson

DOMITILA — Evangelical in Nicrupampa camp

DON JUAN DURÁN — leader in the hamlet of Secsecpampa

EDWINCITO AND LUCHO — Domitila's sons

DON ALEJANDRO ESPINOSA and HIS WIFE DOÑA PAJITA — owners of the house I lived in on Nueva Granada on the pampa

PADRE ESPINOZA — the priest of Soledad

ESTHER — woman living near the Plaza de San Francisco

VÍCTOR FIGUEROA — a leader in the Nicrupampa survivor camp

FLAVIO and ELENA — Evangelicals who lived in San Francisco barrio

FLOR, CONSUELITO, and MACHI — little girls of San Francisco barrio

PADRE GUIMARAY — secular priest of Huaraz

HELIODORO, ROSA MARÍA, WASHI, PERPETUA, SHANTI, MARGARITA — Don Juan's children

HILARIO — Benedictine monk at Los Pinos

JESUSA and NICOLÁS — Don Juan's sister-in-law and her husband; catechists in the hamlet of Secsecpampa

JUAN MANUEL — English teacher of Huaraz

JULIÁN — chauffeur of Huaraz

GENERAL LUIS LA VERA VELARDE* — the chief of CRYRZA during 1972

WALTER LEYVA — sculptor from Lima who restored the Lord of Solitude shortly after the earthquake

---

*In Spanish, often two surnames are used. The first is of the father, and the second of the mother. Therefore, for example, Roberto Blanco Salazar would be addressed as "Señor Blanco."

PADRE MAGUIÑA — the priest of San Francisco

MARIANELA — young woman who guarded the Lord of Solitude

PADRE MAX — secular priest from Huaylas

THE MENACHOS — shopkeepers in Nicrupampa

BENJAMÍN MORALES — glaciologist; director of the Santa Corporation and survivor of Huaraz

NORABUENA — protector of *La Belenita*, and other images at Belén

THE OLIVERAS — family in San Francisco barrio who lost five children in the earthquake

PACO — former hacienda owner in the Callejón

DON PEDRO — villager from Matacoto

PETER — the disc jockey at Radio Huascarán

PILATOS — the image maker

PRESIDENTS OF PERU:

    GENERAL JUAN VELASCO ALVARADO, 1968–1975

    GENERAL FRANCISCO MORALES BERMÚDEZ, 1975–1980

    FERNANDO BELAÚNDE TERRY, before and after military rule

    ALAN GARCÍA PÉREZ, since 1985

PADRES QUINTANA, EFRAÍN, and HIDALGO — the Spanish Franciscans at San Antonio in Huarupampa barrio

CLEMENTE QUISPE — native of Huanmarín; lived in Nicrupampa camp

RAFAEL AND JULIA — children of Jesusa and Nicolás

DR. RAMOS GUARDIA — physician and survivor of Huaraz

REYNA — survivor of Huaraz; my assistant

PADRE ROMERO — the priest at Soledad during the early sixties

RUBÉN — survivor of Yungay; Cirila's companion

PADRE SORIANO — the priest-archaeologist

TEÓFINES — accountant in Huaraz; owner of *La Guinda*

VÍCTOR VALENZUELA GUARDIA — teacher, composer, survivor of Huaraz; mayor of Huaraz after 1980

MARÍA DE VALENZUELA — teacher, poet, survivor of Huaraz

PADRE WASHI — priest in Yungay in the aftermath; priest of Soledad in 1980

MARCOS YAURI MONTERO — poet and novelist; survivor of Huaraz

PREFACE

Life at the edge of glaciers . . . Trial by ice marked the rise of modern human beings. . . .

John Pfeiffer

I can still close my eyes and see a glacial night, jagged ice-covered needles of rock thrusting into a sky made luminous by the light of a full moon and, almost at dead center, the concave ice-blue contours of Mount Huascarán, drawing the landscape of a continent up to its treacherous summit.

I can still see highland Indians crossing the bridge over the Río Quilcay—men in dark ponchos bent under their burdens, women in bright-colored skirts and shawls—silhouetted against the glistening white of the Cordillera Blanca.

I can still see creased and dust-beaten faces, hear wind-driven silences, and feel the deep Andean dusks settle in upon the Callejón de Huaylas.

It was eighteen years ago that the earth shook that glacial

outpost in Peru and the mountain fell; eighteen years since I stood, pregnant and full of hope, cooking over a stove in a carriage house in New Orleans, hearing the news of that remarkable cataclysmic event that would soon stake its claim as the worst natural disaster in the history of the New World.

As a graduate student in anthropology with a year's fieldwork still ahead of me, I wanted to go right then to that glacial valley in Peru, to learn, but also to help, translate, console, to repay in some measure the knowledge and enlightenment and consolation I had experienced in previous fieldwork in Latin America—in Chile, Guatemala, and Costa Rica. But I knew I could not go there then. With a child, I would have to choose more traditional fieldwork, a more traditional subject, an assignment easier for me, in a place I knew and had worked in before.

But the child did not live, and I was free, awesomely free, shaken like the glacial valley I had heard about on the radio that first day in June 1970. I needed to do something extraordinary to catapult myself out of my personal tragedy.

So I went to that Peruvian valley, the Callejón de Huaylas, in October 1971 and spent a year there that forever marks my life. This book is about that valley, that event of May 31, 1970, and my connection to the place, the tragedy, and the people.

Though my original fieldwork plans were rather narrow and specific—to find out what changes, if any, occurred in survivors' religious beliefs as a result of the disaster—they soon broadened into an attempt to understand everything about the event and its aftermath. Like the survivors, I was swept up into all the currents of thought, feeling, and action that found their focus in the disaster. Survivors themselves were grappling with making sense of the event and its complex aftermath, and my quest became to try to comprehend and describe their quest to interpret what had happened and what was happening to them.

This book, then, is essentially about the meaning of an extreme event, meaning forged by survivors in the rubble of their devastation. It is about a great natural disaster and about "natural" survival, human beings overcoming what it does not seem possible to overcome. But it is also about the clash of cultures, highland and lowland, victims and reconstructors. It is about an instance of the revolutionary enterprise that has for some years both racked and revitalized Latin America and that found a fertile ground for experimentation in the destroyed valley.

As I think back over the year of the aftermath I spent in the Callejón de Huaylas, in the shattered town of Huaraz, a metaphor comes to mind that captures the essence of that year. That central metaphor is "palimpsest." The term is used in anthropology to describe an aspect of prehistoric art, the cave and rock paintings of the upper Paleolithic, some 15,000–35,000 years ago, when our ancestors found themselves squeezed between glaciers advancing from the north and the Mediterranean Sea. The ancient painters often made their drawings on top of previous ones. A bison might be superimposed on an elk. Surfaces were used and reused by overpainting or overengraving. This phenomenon of palimpsest gave cave art a transparent quality, like an X ray. If, as some scholars think, the Cro-Magnon hunters were making statements about their world, they did not bother to obliterate earlier statements. It is believed that however their predecessors communicated with one another, this early art reveals the blossoming of symbolic thought as we know it. Man had begun to mark the real world, to interpret it through imagery. Symbols set loose a rush of images that changed forever the relationship of human beings to the world.

The idea of palimpsest helps to understand the mental aftermath of the disaster. Survivors dwelt among varying superimposed spheres of thought simultaneously. New ideologies blew in on the winds of change stirred by the disaster, and other meanings were constructed out of old myths. Ideas were traced one upon another, and new formulations of meaning did not displace others. Rather, meanings assigned to the tragedy were layered. The layers were not opaque but transparent.

My experience in the aftermath drew me close to our Paleolithic forebears. I began to realize that we are all cave painters, sketching out the meanings of our lives, and then others come along and have their say. Indeed, viewed in the light of the long sweep of human evolution, we are practically contemporaries of the Cro-Magnon hunters, "recent descendants of Ice Age people, still striving to devise strategies for survival." That is what this book is about, the mental "strategies for survival" that gave meaning to survivors who suffered their own "trial by ice." We all undergo trial by something, and so we, too, are survivors, creating our lives through a series of cumulative images, never really being able to erase the past. We all live in an aftermath of plagues and wars, floods and cattle frozen in drifting snow, as well as personal conflict and tragedy. Most important, we live in the aftermath of that first time our ancestors saw more in a cloud than the cloud itself.

DURING the year I spent in the Callejón, not a day went by without my feeling I was in an extraordinary place at an extraordinary time. Not before or since have I been so acutely conscious of the bare fact of life. Though deeply engaged in purposeful work, at the same time, I felt no need of a raison d'être. I remember thinking often that it was a place where it was enough just to watch a day transpire. It was still pitch-black on the valley floor when the morning sun crept unevenly over the Cordillera Blanca, highlighting now one jagged peak, now another. And at the end of the day, as the sun slipped behind the Cordillera Negra, darkness came swiftly to the devastated towns, while the glaciers towering above them remained basking in the long dusk provided by a sun sinking just beyond the mountains, yet no longer visible from the depths of the valley.

The changing patterns of light, shifting from peak to peak in the Andean succession, are only one of the features of the setting that lend themselves to the metaphor of palimpsest, of one poly-chrome painting translucent above another. Others abound. Planted fields, spread like a patchwork quilt over the mountain slopes, only thinly sheathe the earth's strata, visible in the pitch of the mountains against the sky. On the high plains, tiny, isolated dome-shaped straw huts merely suggest the human occupation that overlies the planet's great geologic age. Eucalyptus trees that shield the fields from wind shed their layered bark, and the trunks of the *quinual* trees, twisted and bent by winds that scour the bases of the glaciers, are glazed with a transparent orange bark that can be peeled away like the thin layers of a Greek pastry.

As shallow as human existence seemed in comparison with the marks of geologic time, there was, too, everywhere, the ghost of a long human past. Through the valley there still walked people who in physiognomy, dress, and manner were much like the peoples who lived there long ago. The hillock, Pumacayán, at the edge of Huaraz, was an Inca mound that now supported a small chapel. The five terraces that contained the niches of the contemporary Yungay cemetery were built on a temple mound from the Chavín era of 800 B.C. The big Christian crosses guarding the fields were implanted in ancient cairns, to which modern Indians crossing the cordilleras never failed to add a stone to ensure their safe passage. Guitarrero Cave, where some of the oldest textiles of Peru have been found, sheltered survivors of the earthquake, as it sheltered hunters 10,000 years ago.

In the aftermath, there was ruin upon ruin. Beside enigmatic boulders deposited by ancient uncharted glaciers lay those that still had reference points in history and legend, making the valley a geologic boneyard of mammoth rocks. Evidence of past disasters —from the 1725 avalanche from the glacier of Huandoy, which erased the town of Ancash, to the inundation of part of Huaraz in 1941 by freezing waters from a glacial lake, to the avalanche that buried Ranrahirca in 1962—was there to be seen in a boulder lodged in the fork of a tree or in hardened silt. Behind these more recent disasters lay fragments of events, myth, legend, and history more remote, from the deep, unrecorded past before the Incas, from Inca times, and from the confrontation of the Inca Empire with the rolling swell of the Spanish Conquest. "The landscape [was] alive with remembered events."

Like *bricoleurs*, survivors rebuilt the shattered tombs of Huaraz's cemetery with stones from the destroyed cathedral. Chapels that had withstood the earthquake were used as granaries, and new granaries ordered by reformists were being built by villagers who secretly waited to turn them into their village chapels. I remember so many libations of corn beer poured over *Pachamama* ("Mother

Earth") during political meetings held on mountain slopes and in
town plazas, meetings designed to strip away such ancient customs.
I cannot forget the monstrance that was held aloft in a ceremony
inside the ruins of a church. The roof of the church was completely
gone, and the gold of the Host's receptacle was blinding in the
sun's rays that struck between the freestanding walls. In like manner, five centuries earlier the golden symbol of the Inca supreme
being, the Sun, was held aloft in procession, searing the glance
of followers.

The layers were all there, in dress, in beliefs and customs, in
physical artifacts, and in the geologic record, of both slow and
uniform changes in the great Andean system as well as of catastrophic events. Like the outer bark of the *quinual*, the present was
translucent. The past was luminous under the impact of the extreme
event of May 31, 1970. The shaking earth itself had stirred up the
past. To be there in the aftermath was to feel the weight of the
strata of history and myth and layers of thought, all not yet congealed into "the modern world." The valley was both permanent
and fragile, ancient and new.

THIS phenomenon of extreme collective tragedy—the way it illuminates the past and brings the routines of normal times into the
spotlight—is a key to understanding what has been called the special
"vulnerability" of transitional societies to disaster. In ordinary
times, Third World societies, touched by modernization that has
not yet consolidated its position, where Western technology is not
yet taken for granted as right, good, and inevitable, are breeding
grounds for ideological debate. When disaster of extreme proportions strikes such a society, it becomes a battleground of ideological
conflict.

In the earthquake's aftermath, the conflict was due to the valley's transitional status. In spite of the incipient changes occurring
prior to the earthquake, it was still a valley where history and myth
intermingled and where evil was not relative but absolute. With
the disaster, the chorus of voices for change and development intensified. A preexisting tension between two conflicting notions of

progress—one perceiving it as decadence, the other as refinement of an antiquated system—broke out into open warfare. Intersecting various currents of thought about the nature of progress, the disaster was left wide open to varying interpretations.

The process of interpretation must have been similar in the past, even in 1725 when the hamlet of Ancash disappeared in the Huandoy avalanche. There was probably the same tone of inquiry, of advancing several hypotheses, of holding simultaneously what seemed like contradictory explanations for the tragedy. It is possible that messiahs emerged to point to new ways perceived to be capable of correcting the inadequacies of the old ways. But if prophets of change arose, they arose within a system that, relative to the contemporary scene of radical change and intense communication, was fairly coherent and fairly isolated.

The aftermath of the earthquake and avalanche of 1970 was different. The valley swarmed with ideas from external cultural systems. Now there were hydrogen bombs and moonwalkers and transistor radios to hear about them on. And so, in this place where evil and punishment were still plausible and past ages still alive, the new voices created anxiety among survivors over whether change and modernization had been a cause of the disaster or were preordained to be its result. The valley was vulnerable to the metaphor of creation. Yet modern technology had not yet given people any real control over their lives. And after the earthquake the voices of change came too loudly and too fast for survivors to preserve even an illusion of control. They floundered, shattered doubly by the disaster and the intensity and extensiveness of the proposed overhaul of their valley.

To many, the ultimate tragedy was that their world could not be restored to what it was. They clung tenaciously to their old ways, seeking some sense of continuity, some comfort in the commonplace, in a world suddenly turned surreal. They held on to their own aesthetic. "They should build a city in intimate relation with us," a survivor said. Long before the modernizing reconstruction of the aftermath, historian Jorge Basadre wrote: "Peru is not merely a social and political problem . . . Peru has an architectonic, an aesthetic frame . . . The geographical setting, the quality of light, the intensity of color, the tones of the landscape, the racial heritages, make aesthetic fulfillment essential to any political fulfillment."

If only this had been recognized by the Revolutionary Military Government. If only they had perceived that what for them was a political mission of hope would not work for the victims of the disaster, who first had to grieve over their destroyed world. Instead, they saw the opportunity for social revolution through an act of nature.

Change does not take place in an instant simply by negating the past. Human life entails so many continuities on so many levels that it resists simultaneous destruction and creation. Innovation and ideological adjustment occur over time through a process analogous to palimpsest. This is exactly what was happening in the Callejón aftermath as successive lines were drawn and terms reached, only to be superseded by still other terms. Only, the process was painful to the extent that it was not recognized that we are all still much like our Cro-Magnon ancestors, stepping in and out of dark caves, leaving our message on top of others that were left before and underneath those that will inevitably be left upon ours. Instead, ideologues saw some final truth in their beliefs, as if they did not know that our modern world, too, will one day be ancient, as if they did not know that bells must toll.

THIS book is about more than a single disaster in the Peruvian highlands. Within the last three and a half years alone, the Cocos plate under the Pacific jerked forward, making Mexico City reel violently. A thick mudflow buried a Colombian town. A poisonous cloud of gases rose from the bottom of a volcanic lake in Cameroon, suffocating more than 1,700 people. And rocks along the Motagua Fault slipped, initiating a quake in El Salvador. These events are nowhere mentioned in the book, but much of what is written here resonates with reports from the scene of those events. In Mexico, people knelt and prayed, a gas station attendant said, "God is sowing his people," and the names of Tepeyolohtli, the Aztec god of earthquakes, and Coyolxauhqui, the goddess of magic and damage, were heard in the streets of the capital. Two months after the Mexican earthquake, on the night of November 18, 1985, on public radio, I heard that the Mexican government had expropriated 7,000 properties, including some not even damaged, and that the political tremors were expected to "last beyond the bulldozers and jackhammers," just as they had in Peru. Survivors called the mud shroud left by Nevado del Ruiz over Armero in Colombia a collective cemetery that should be named the Land of the Dead, much like the town of Yungay's Beach of the Dead in the Peruvian valley. On November 19, 1985, public radio reported that the Colombian government saw the disaster as a "national event" and lamented the fact that it could not "absorb the shock" and consequently did not act rapidly enough. In the same way, Lima, at first, could not, would not, believe that Huaraz was leveled and Yungay had disappeared. Farmers near the banks of Lake Nyos in Cameroon attributed the noxious gases to gods inside the volcano, who most surely would again concoct the deadly mixture.

Even our own national disaster, the explosion of the space shuttle *Challenger* on January 28, 1986, brought rationalization and metaphor. A journalist asked, "Who's to blame? We need to know 'Why?' to absorb the shock of disaster. We need demons and villains in the face of disaster of such magnitude." And the president said the astronauts had "touched the face of God."

JUST as the ghosts of ancient humanity, of all the epochs the Callejón had passed through—from pre-Incaic to the modern revolutionary aftermath—and the ghosts of past disasters moved in the valley, when I came, it was not without my own ghosts. These ghosts, too, were cultural and geophysical, fashioned of the lore and the silt of growing up in the Mississippi delta and textured with the events of my personal history, the palimpsest of my life.

My connection to survivors was marked by one special ghost, the specter of personal tragedy, the loss of a child that had occurred months before I went to the Callejón. My quest was in part to learn about survival from survivors. There were parallels between their aftermath and my own. I remember, for example, how tragedy had instantly illuminated the layers of my life, how I had recounted to friends events of my past, which had before languished in the penumbra of memory, and how I clung to these events. I remember how the dead child had become the measure of my life, next to which nothing was truly bad, how my life seemed divided into a "before" and an "after," just as survivors of the earthquake seemed to measure theirs.

My fieldwork in the Callejón was in part an attempt to propel myself worlds away from my personal tragedy, to globalize it by living it through within a much larger context. Earthquake survivors, too, broadened their sights, projected their personal and community tragedy against a world screen, made it into an event that would forge world peace. The destroyed Huaraz was "a small wound for humanity" that would bring nations together in brotherhood.

I did not often tell people about my loss, though my closest friends in the valley knew. Abel, my friend in Huaraz, sensed something without my telling him and said to me one night, "You have suffered an earthquake inside you." Because of cultural differences, some I told interpreted my tragedy as a blessing, for babies are believed to fly directly to play with the angels. Some I didn't tell misinterpreted my reactions. Once, in a gathering of people, when I saw, framed and sitting on a table, the baby picture of a young girl killed in the earthquake, I began to cry. A man said tenderly, "Look, she is crying for our sorrows." I could not tell them why I was crying, and besides, what he said was also true. At Christmastime, in the market, a woman asked a vendor for a doll for her little girl. "There are no longer any dolls," replied the vendor. The woman pressed herself against me. "Gringuita, do you have children?" "No," I answered. "Why, because you don't like the noise they make?"

To some I told, the marks of my own survival lay in unspoken layers, as theirs with me. It was this way with Cirila of Yungay, who lost two sons. I would go with her to the spot on the Yungay avalanche where she had made an altar for them. We rarely spoke on these occasions. An enormous empathy that could not be translated into words bound us together.

Most often, as I had planned it, my tragedy was dwarfed by the immensity of the event and aftermath there. I dreamed survivors' dreams—that another earthquake would come, that Huascarán would "devour us all"—sometimes with fragments from my own fears and past. Though I had spent All Soul's Day in Huaraz, I dreamed that night that I was in Yungay. All I recall is a small white coffin, used for children, in the upper right-hand side of the image in my mind. Early in my stay in the valley, I dreamed I wore two layers of clothes. At a certain time, I would be forced to reveal the under layer, though I feared doing so. Perhaps the under layer was my own sorrow and personal search for survival.

Doing anthropological fieldwork means becoming like a child again, open to the new and different. But I was especially vulnerable, and my own vulnerability coalesced with that of survivors. I was raw, the subject matter was raw, and the people were raw. Though I was seeking a way out of personal tragedy, I was not seeking distraction from it but rather the understanding of tragedy and survival at a broader, deeper human level. On March 18, 1972, I wrote in my notes: "It seems there are essentially two ways to live, to distract oneself from the major themes of life or to deal with them head-on." If you don't lay claim to tragedy, it will claim you.

I had chosen the right place at the right time. There was little distraction from life's major themes. Nor were they considered in the cold light of the intellect alone. I remember Doña Angelita trying to explain to me why she remained in Huaraz in the midst of destruction: "I go to Lima and they take me out in the afternoon. We go here and there, seeing new things. I dissimulate in Lima. Here there is no dissembling."

I had doubts when I was there in the valley, doubts about seeing accurately, portraying accurately, and interpreting accurately, the fears of any anthropologist, magnified by the vastness of the Andean setting, the event and its aftermath. This was my own doing, for I could not narrow my scope to one facet of the disaster. I refused to try to hold separate such analytic constructs as religion, politics, and economics or to expunge human feeling from the disaster. The event had been like a dam burst open. All that lay quiescently cloaked in the routines of a taken-for-granted world—religion, politics, emotions, ideologies—had broken through the barrier of ordinary life.

Once, when I confessed that I felt overwhelmed by it all, the words of a survivor helped. He said I was there to bear witness to their experience, to be their messenger to the outside world. Yes, I could try to do that. So rarely do we gain any intimacy with the lives of people in the far-flung regions of the world. We know them only superficially, in a quick news item or a flash on a television screen. We see a child being dragged from the mud, or a burst of flame. What do we know of the months after, the thoughts inside survivors' heads? Perhaps, in this instance, I could bring us closer by trying to tell their story. Though events—and ways of defining them and surviving them—may take a thousand different forms, suffering, survival, and trying to understand unite the valley survivors to all people.

"THERE exists a relationship among all things," a man from the Huaraz barrio of Soledad who had a small hardware store told me. "Beauty, greatness, even bad things, all are related. Necessarily, beauty brings ugliness. That's the way it is. It is all a complex that each person has to get beyond."

Almost daily, a mountain ballad poured out over Radio Huaraz: "Take care, God, of those who remain, / in this immense sea of pain." True, the imprint of suffering lay over the land. But slowly I came to understand what the shopkeeper was saying and to glimpse from time to time that place we all have to "get beyond." I learned, though I still forget, how to live without a false sense of control over life, that, as Rubén said when I probed him about the choice of location to rebuild the new Yungay, "there is no safe place." The razor-sharp peaks of the Cordillera Blanca themselves represented vulnerability, lack of stability, insecurity. Yet they instilled a sense of the excitement of the earth in formation, of the earth still untamed and wild. There is no safe place anywhere, though in our everyday life we tend to lose sight of the insecurity and lose, too, the excitement, as well as the peace of acceptance that the man from Soledad barrio alluded to. In the valley—with its stone upon stone, adobe upon adobe, collective tragedy impressed upon personal tragedy—I came to feel in the end, if only for fleeting moments, that bare core where small hurts and unspeakable horrors, along with the glacial caps and the winnowed wheat, dissolve into one and are accepted.

I also came to feel that neither suffering nor happiness is boundless. When life is not safe and concerns with survival and mere existence take over, as they did for people of the valley, and in some measure, for me that year, there is a way in which the space reserved for sadness gets filled up, and there is no room for many of the subtler worries that occupy us when we are not faced with extreme difficulty. So, too, with happiness. A bud pushing its way through the alluvial silt of Yungay might, if only for an instant, fill the space of happiness.

WHEN I look at the aftermath now, it is as a curator of a cave painting trying to lift all the layers into view. But at the time I left the valley, it was different. The re-creation of the event that has come with the writing did not yet exist. I would grasp the whole and then lose it again. Sometimes I felt unable to make generalizations at all.

Not long before my departure, I talked for some hours with the shopkeeper from Soledad barrio who helped point me to that place where good and evil are related, and happiness is pregnant with sorrow, that place of "acceptance." Afterward, he drove me back to my room in the destroyed center of Huaraz. When we arrived, we sat for a long time in silence in the cabin of his truck, looking out into the dark. Suddenly he said: "So now soon you are leaving; by now you must know, tell me, what are we like, what do we believe?" A wave of premature nostalgia for the valley, for Huaraz, swept over me. I felt incompetent, unable to summon the scientist in me. I had spent a year there, and I could not tell him.

At that moment, all I seemed to know were many stories: who was where when the earthquake struck, what they thought, what they did, stories of individuals with names. I began to cry uncontrollably. He tried to comfort me. He said something like when one sees so much happen as they had, he tries to orient himself rightly, that faith is a gift. Everything is a gift. Through the windshield of the truck I saw a man, his poncho flung over him, his silhouette darker than the night, striding across the ruins.

The people of the Callejón wanted us to know them. The last day I spent in the valley, in a dimly lit, windy shack, a woman tugged at my skirt with the wish, almost command, that I return home and tell what I had seen. If only the world knew, they would not be condemned "to live like shadows without footprints." The world, by then, had already begun to forget that event in the high mountain valley of Peru, and in the succession of crises that beset us, the forgetting is near complete. For me as well as for them, I have needed to put together the story of their struggle to make sense of the earthquake that shook them from their moorings on May 31, 1970.

Charlestown, Rhode Island
December 28, 1988

Part 1

THE EVENT

*This is not the terror felt by someone
running from a furious bull, a threatening knife. . . . This is a cosmic terror, an instant danger, the universe
caving in and crumbling away. And,
meanwhile, the earth lets out a muffled
sound of thunder, in a voice no one knew
it had. The dust raised by the houses as
they came crashing down settles little
by little. And we are left alone with
our dead, with all the dead, not knowing how we happen to be still alive.*

Pablo Neruda, *Memoirs*

One

CALLEJÓN DE HUAYLAS

Brushed by a tremor, suddenly the pin-
nacles of the Andes awaken. . . .
                José Santos Chocano,
                    El Hombre y el Sol

ISOLATED by some of the world's most rugged mountains, the valley is so narrow that they call it an "alley," the Callejón de Huaylas. Barely five miles at its widest and one hundred twenty-five miles long, the valley is wedged between two chains of the Andes known as the Cordillera Blanca and the Cordillera Negra, the White and Black ranges. From the valley bottom, to see the horizon the eye must look halfway up the sky.

Myth tells that long ago the valley shook so violently that great avalanches swept down to the sea, scouring the mountains and leaving only taper-thin, denuded pinnacles of an intense blue color. These sharp peaks stood so high that on its nightly rounds, the moon scraped them, sprinkling upon them its astral snow. Over immense stretches of time, this snow became the glaciers of the Cordillera Blanca. Rivers born in the glaciers then brought forth the idyllic pastures of the Callejón de Huaylas.

At lower altitudes, one is part of the world. In the Andes, most of the world is below, and one feels closer to the stars, adrift in the universe, part of the primordial ferment when the earth was formed, torn apart, and re-formed. Thoughts of telluric fury are never entirely banished.

Yet, in this vastness lies an infinite silence. Sun and shadows play on the peaks and valleys. The wind whispers *soledad*. Aloof, the mountains arouse this haunting solitude. At 15,000 feet, a solitary horseman gallops across cold and bleak plateaus. At the edge of a frost-glazed lake at dawn, her vista rimmed by the ice-glow of the glacial summits, a small girl tends her flock.

The very word *Ande* conjures up all the sadness, the loneliness, and the beauty of the world. It is as if the mountain peaks themselves, by some magnetic force, had drawn these qualities up from the earth below and assembled them in rich concentration in the high Andean valleys. In the north central Peruvian highlands, 270 miles north of Lima and 10,000 feet above it, lies the valley of Huaylas, the most tragically beautiful of them all.

FROM an ancient plateau eroded over millions of years, the Central Andes were shaped. Some 13 million years ago, the plateau lifted to 14,000 feet above the level of the sea, and rivers cut out deep furrows. Powerful plutonic intrusions pushed the enormous bulk up another 7,000 feet, forming the core of granodiorite that, with erosion, became the crown of the Cordillera Blanca. The final contours of the Blanca range were carved during the last glaciation of the Pleistocene, the Great Ice Age that began about 2 million years ago. Because they are young geologically, the mountains of the Cordillera Blanca have not been worn and weathered into rounded stumps like older ranges of the world. Rather, in their youth, they are razor edged, still rising rapidly by geologic measure. The range rose again, between two and three feet, on Sunday, May 31, 1970.

Glaciated, covered by permanent snowfields, the Cordillera Blanca dominates the valley. Its glaciers, in contrast with those of the great Asian and European ranges, which cover broad, sloping areas, are attached directly to the summits and steep rock walls of the mountains. Inclined at dizzying angles from forty-five degrees to nearly ninety degrees, they are extremely unstable and break off from time to time. Prevailing winds from the Amazon rain forest drive turbulent clouds up the eastern wall of the cordillera, where, impeded in their passage, they drop their moisture on the granite peaks, constantly adding layers of snow to the already voluminous glaciers. Overhanging ice cornices are continually sculpted by these winds and stand out in bold relief against the midday azure sky.

Some thirty of the major peaks of the Cordillera Blanca reach altitudes of over 20,000 feet, making it by far the highest tropical range in the world. In fact, the range lies so close to the Equator that the snow line does not begin until one reaches an altitude of nearly 16,500 feet, high above the tallest peaks of the Rockies. Below 11,800 feet, snow rarely falls, and frosts are uncommon below 9,800 feet. So near the Equator, the sun rises abruptly and sinks suddenly, and its violet reflection on the snow turns into the ice blue of a glacial night.

On the Cordillera Blanca, *quinual* trees, their trunks twisted by winds that roar along the steep cliff walls, bend over the shores of hundreds of morainal lakes nestled in deep U-shaped gorges called *quebradas*. Because of heavy rains or unstable ice cornices that snap and tumble into the morainal lakes, these lakes constantly threaten to spill over their banks and flood the valley towns below.

In contrast to the Cordillera Blanca, the Cordillera Negra is older. It is the remains of the last major stage of volcanic extrusions that occurred during the Pliocene. Being of greater age, the Negra range is more subdued, with a broad, gently undulating crest. It rises in dark folds, shot through with minerals, up to 17,000 feet, its massive hulk breaking the warm Pacific air currents, thus acting as a shield against the melting of the glaciers and perpetual snows of the Cordillera Blanca. There are no glaciers or snowfields on the Negra. As the sun sets over the Pacific, the dark massiveness of the range, like a swatch of billowing velvet, is outlined against the rose glow of the western sky.

Cutting a path between the two great ranges, the Río Santa begins in trickles from Lake Conococha, at the south end of the Callejón, gathering volume as it flows northward through the valley until it finally breaks through the Cordillera Negra at the Cañón del Pato (Duck Canyon) and plunges down to the ocean near Chimbote. The steep granite walls of the Cañón del Pato, carved out over the millennia by the tumultuous waters of the Santa, rise 3,300 feet from the level of the river. Here the Cordilleras Negra and Blanca almost touch.

From Lake Conococha, at nearly 14,000 feet, the valley floor slopes down for 100 miles to the town of Huallanca, at 4,600 feet, where the Santa makes its sudden westward swing to the Pacific. The principal valley towns, going south to north from 11,000-foot Recuay through Huaraz, Carhuaz, and Yungay to 7,500-foot-high Caraz, hug the banks of the Santa. A cord could be stretched taut through these towns lining the troughlike valley bottom. Only to the east of the Río Santa does the valley open out sufficiently to sustain towns and cultivation at valley-floor level. With the exception of Huaylas, an important town of size nested high on the thorn steppes of the Cordillera Negra, and Aija, in the folds above Recuay, mainly small hamlets are perched on the steep east-facing slopes of the Negra, above the narrow floodplain of the river.

It is eight miles as the crow flies between Yungay, at an altitude of 8,500 feet, and the highest peak of the Cordillera Blanca, the 22,205-foot southern summit of Huascarán, a difference of almost 14,000 feet, one of the steepest grades in the world. Nowhere else, not even in the Himalayas, do towns of substantial populations, like those of the Callejón, exist in such propinquity to glaciers of such magnitude.

PERHAPS 20,000 years before the dawn of the Christian Era, hunters and gatherers moved into this Andean valley and occupied caves up to altitudes of 15,000 feet or more. These first inhabitants of the Callejón roamed the cordilleras hunting deer, guanaco, and aquatic birds that populated the high morainal lakes.

By the year 2000 B.C., the potato was being cultivated, and a thousand years later, the first pan-Andean culture of Chavín, based on the feline cult of the puma, began to spread out from the valley of Conchucos, which lies to the east of the Callejón de Huaylas. From the principal ruins at Chavín in the valley of Conchucos, a foot trail, still used today, leads to a 16,000-foot pass across the Cordillera Blanca and down through the Quebrada Honda ("Deep Gorge"). The path then follows the course of the Río Marcará, one of several rivulets that begin as trickles in the pristine heights of the Cordillera Blanca and flow westward into the Santa.

In prehistoric times, the Andean cultural pattern was one of regionalism and local styles, followed by drives toward political and cultural unity, succeeded again by the breakdown of unity and a return to localized cultures. Faithful to this cyclical pattern, when

Chavín's influence waned in the Callejón de Huaylas, the stylized, angular designs of jaguars, condors, and serpents that archaeologists have typed "Recuay" began to flourish. Then, around A.D. 600, a second attempt at unity brought the Tiahuanaco style in masonry and pottery from the south highlands to the Callejón. Near the town of Huaraz, at the ruins of Wilkawaín, is found a three-story temple, ornamented with a projecting cornice and a row of carved stone puma heads, which bears the mark of Tiahuanaco.

Finally, the Incas, demigods, sons of the Sun, emanating from Cuzco, also in the south highlands of Peru, achieved political and cultural unity along the sweep of the Andes, and their language, Quechua, suppressed all earlier languages. The Incas conquered the Callejón de Huaylas sometime after A.D. 1460, at the time of the Emperor Pachacuti. Although the imperial Inca religion left little lasting effect on the peoples they subdued, much of the popular religion, which penetrates deep into the Andean substratum and which the Incas saw fit to incorporate rather than destroy, still prevails in the Callejón. This religion of the people is concerned with the powers of the earth, of springs, stones, and mountains. It was believed that the supernatural power of a mountain varied in proportion to its height. All snow-capped peaks were important deities and were called *Apu* ("Lord"). The pinnacles of the Cordillera Blanca have Quechua names.

The Inca Empire was splendid but short-lived. When it had not yet endured a hundred years, the Spaniards came. Hernando Pizarro was the first Spaniard to lay eyes on the beauty of the Callejón when he passed that way in early 1533, shortly after the capture of the Inca emperor Atahualpa, in Cajamarca.

We hear little of the valley during the three centuries when most of the New World was ruled by the Spanish crown. But it was the scene of important battles for independence. Liberators San Martín and Bolívar were both there. After the particularly fierce Battle of Yungay in 1839, fought at the site of the confluence of the Río Ancash with the Santa, the political unit, or department, was named Ancash, meaning "blue" in Quechua. Ancash contains within its borders the highest mountains of Peru, the valleys of Huaylas and Conchucos, and the coastal deserts and fishing port of Chimbote.

Through all these centuries, generation upon generation of the

original inhabitants of the valley remained in some form of sub-
jugation, first to the Incas, then to the Spaniards during the colonial
period, and finally to the European-dominated peoples of the Republic of Peru. Only in relatively recent years has Peru been stirred
by a broad revolutionary enterprise. Ideas of land reform and freedom of the highland Indians from the yoke of domination have
finally taken root.

A strange and unsettling landscape separates the Cordillera Negra
from the Pacific coastline. Seemingly interminable sand dunes
stretch down to the shore, where ocean and desert—one of the
driest in the world—meet, emitting quivering currents of heat.
Telegraph poles along the coastal highway cut a black path through
the desolate landscape of sand, lizards, and snakes more like worms.
Large, rugged wooden crosses, decorated with the symbols of
Christ's Passion, and glass-enclosed altars are planted here and there
in the desert sand, its infecundity relieved only by small, irrigated
patches of corn, truck crops, gourds, and the *atilecia* plant, which
thrives in the winter coastal fog and turns to a black stubble in the
summer heat. Near the junction that opens out into the Supe valley,
just south of the Pativilca road that winds tortuously up into the
Callejón de Huaylas, cane huts, nakedly exposed to the barren glare,
cluster around a sign reading Pampa Middle World.

This desert wasteland separates the noise and amenity of Lima
and small towns that hug the shoreline from the silent, austere
Andean valleys. At 3,000 feet up the western slopes of the Cordillera Negra, the town of Chasquitambo, with its bulrushes, pal-
metto, and papaya, is the last outpost of warm coastal lands. From
that point on, eucalyptus, cactus, and alders lead up to the puna,
the bleak and cold Andean tableland.

On the puna, near frost-glazed Lake Conococha, suddenly the
saw-toothed peaks of the Cordillera Blanca rise up and stretch northward the length of the Callejón: Caullaraju peak, which in Quechua
means "beginning of the snow," Rajutu, Pongos, Pucaraju; Huantsán, Cayesh, Huamashraju, Chúrup, Rima-Rima, Ranrapalca, Vallunaraju, over the town of Huaraz; Copa, Hualcán, Chopicalqui,
over Carhuaz; culminating in the 22,205-foot south peak of Huascarán above Yungay; Huandoy, Chacraraju, over Caraz; and dropping down to 20,000-foot Alpamayo, famed for its elegance of form,

its comely cone-shaped pinnacle dominating the view from Huaylas at the northern end of the valley.

Because of clouds, it is rare to see all at once these glacial peaks of the Cordillera Blanca. But one January afternoon in 1972, on an ascent to the valley from the coast, as our jeep came up over a ridge near Conococha, the Cordillera surprised us, each individual summit, for practically its entire length, ablaze in the glow of a fiery sunset.

THERE is a sense of containment in the Callejón. The Cordillera Negra is a powerful barrier, isolating the valley from the coastal desert. From Conococha, there is only one road to follow north to the valley's end, passing through the main towns to Huallanca, where before the earthquake a narrow-gauge railway paralleled the westward flow of the Santa down to the coast at Chimbote. After the earthquake destroyed the railway, the Pativilca route, through Conococha, had to serve as both entrance to and exit from the valley.

Like an easement into the Callejón, there is one other route besides the Pativilca, a route that rises from Casma on the coast, goes over a pass at Punta Callán on the Cordillera Negra, and descends directly into Huaraz. But the Punta Callán passageway, steeper and more tortuous than the Pativilca road, is often closed for long periods during the rainy season, from October through April.

Along most of its length, the Cordillera Blanca is impassable, with only a few footpaths at some 16,000 feet. Beyond the Blanca chain and to the east of the valley of Conchucos, the drop into a lowland region known as the "eyebrow of the tropical forest" (*ceja de la montaña*) is precipitous. And then, beyond the *montaña*, lies the vast Amazon jungle of Brazil.

THE Callejón de Huaylas is inhabited mainly by people of ancient ancestry, descendants of the pre-Columbian cultures, Indian in features, in style, and in custom. Admixture with European stock is evident in the physical makeup of the residents of the larger towns at valley-floor level. And even when biologic mixture is minimal, in the towns people have adopted many Western ways and clothes. The towns, then, are largely mestizo, of mixed European and Indian heritage. On the mountainsides of both the Cordillera Blanca and the Cordillera Negra are nestled small hamlets called *caseríos*. These hamlets are essentially Indian, composed of people closer genetically and culturally to the ancient Peruvian populations.

Neither the llama nor the alpaca, so familiar in the southern highlands of Peru, has inhabited the Callejón in recent times. The only remaining camelid is the smaller vicuña, now seen only rarely and at extremely high elevations. The most prominent game animals are *venados*, or white-tailed deer, which graze in small herds on the slopes of the Cordillera Blanca, and *viscachas*, small rodents about the size of ground squirrels, which scurry among the rocks and along the cliff faces. From the wool of ubiquitous sheep, women spin thread, which is then dyed in brilliant colors from minerals of the earth and woven by both sexes into clothing, shawls, ponchos, and blankets.

Of carnivores, the puma, fox, and a small mountain cat are still extant in the region. From time to time, the huge condor is seen soaring gracefully between the sheer mountain walls, hovering over the glacial lakes, or sailing down toward the valley floor.

Vegetation in the Callejón is typically high Andean, with mountain grasses, rainy-green dwarf shrubs, and prickly cactus. Alder, willow, and acacia grow along the banks of the Río Santa, and stunted alders in the deep gorges of the high slopes of the Cordillera Blanca, but trees are scarce except for the gray-green eucalyptus.

The highest and coldest zone utilized in the valley is the puna, or *jalca*, which means "wilderness" in Quechua. Puna is flat, windswept tundra between roughly 13,000 and 15,000 feet, which has probably changed little in 10,000 years. Up there, only *ichu* grasses grow, and the ground seems perpetually frozen. Still, sheep graze on the puna, ranging as high as three miles above sea level. Foot trails meandering along the mountain slopes and crisscrossing the puna connect clusters of small, temporary grass huts used by shepherds.

The upper limit of agriculture is about 13,000 feet. Below that, steep plots of alfalfa, wheat and barley, and the ancient biblical carob tree, *algarrobo*, create a patchwork pattern on the mountainsides. From middle to high elevations, native Andean tubers, *oca* and *olluco*, are cultivated. The potato, native to the Andes, grows in a great variety of colors: black, yellow, purple, and marbled. Swatches of the valley floor and foothills are covered with the violet flowering potato plants, the tiny yellow flowers of Spanish broom, cherries, wild currants, and arrays of fragrant herbs. Ultimately, the aroma of eucalyptus absorbs them all and pervades the Callejón. Corn is grown at lower elevations, though it, too, can be found up to 10,000 feet, when cultivated, as an Andean scholar put it, "as you would a rose."

Setting the valley apart from all others in the world is the unique giant cactus, called the *Puya de Raimondi*. Secluded, found only in certain remote parts of the mountain range, the *Puya* lives for over a hundred years, reaching a height of twenty feet or more before flowering, seeding, and dying.

THE valley floor of the Callejón de Huaylas combines open countryside and towns going back far in time, even to before the ascendancy of the Incas in the fifteenth century. The actual towns destroyed in the earthquake had been built of adobe bricks largely in the eighteenth century. Since both countryside and urban centers were of the earth, they blended one into the other with no abrupt boundaries, though, no doubt, this was truer after the earthquake, when the towns were only crumbled clay.

The sun on the land, on wheat fields, and on the clay of adobe structures bathes the whole valley in an amber warmth. Everywhere grains of wheat and barley, used in the preparation of flours and gruels, lie drying in the sun. Bread, always round, comes hot and crisp from clay brick ovens, and the *chicha* (corn beer) is strong, with a heady spume. Along the main road and mountain paths, little red and white flags, frayed by sun and wind, announce the sale of *chicha* and bread. Whenever *chicha* or *aguardiente* ("firewater," an almost pure alcohol) is passed around, people always pour a little on the ground and toast *Pachamama*, as their ancestors have done for perhaps 2,000 years.

In the markets, sheep's heads for making soup glower from wooden tables, and when there is meat, it is usually dried and brittle, called *charqui*, hanging on rope lines out in the sun. Guinea pigs (*cuyes*) are the real luxury food, eaten on special occasions in a hot red pepper sauce. Before they meet this fate, the *cuyes* rustle about gobbling up whatever kitchen refuse falls on the dirt floors. They make a whispering sound, like the *ichu* grasses on the windy puna.

It is this beautiful, austere, precariously poised, and gentle valley, luminous in the glacier-studded rareness of the Andean air, that the earthquake ripped apart.

Two

THE LONGEST NIGHT

> *May was spreading its fingers timidly be-*
> *tween the doors and windows. Shadows*
> *and reflections played in the strange shapes*
> *of a late afternoon drawing near. Life*
> *rambled on with a gentle transparency*
> *. . . and then . . . the most horrendous*
> *cataclysm which humanity can remember*
> *occurred.*
>
> Hugo Ramírez,
> *Ancash, Vida y Pasión*

AT THREE O'CLOCK IN THE AFTERNOON, Sunday, May 31, 1970, virtually all Peru was poised for the World Soccer Championship being played at Aztec Stadium in Mexico City. The games were transmitted via satellite, and on the coast, people watched on their television sets. In the Callejón, they listened on transistor radios. Mexico was playing Russia, and by 3:23 the game was ten minutes away from completion, and the two teams were locked in a scoreless tie. By the time Peru beat Bulgaria on June 2 to advance in the World Cup matches, the whole country had been plunged into mourning.

At three o'clock, some valley inhabitants were lolling over their lunches in restaurants. Others were traveling from one town to another to visit friends and relatives. Men of the upper class sat in town squares having their shoes shined. A group of nuns on a

Sunday excursion were in the train running through the Cañón del Pato. Some *Huaracinos* (natives of Huaraz) were getting ready to attend the Corpus Christi procession. As was their custom on Sundays, Quechua-speaking Indians from mountainside hamlets had come down to the towns to buy and sell in markets and socialize in canteens and outdoor food stalls.

On the outskirts of Huaraz, in the minutes just before the first earth shock at 3:23, a priest was feeding about thirty doves in the patio of the small archaeological museum that he directed. Seconds before the earth's rumble became audible, the doves suddenly took flight. Then the museum walls fell all around the priest, and the monolithic sculptures from the ancient ruins of Chavín and Wilkawaín danced on the gelatinous ground. The priest heard shouts and cries coming from Huaraz in the distance. Then there was silence.

Crouched in his fields on a hillside above Huaraz, an old man saw the town collapse before his eyes: "It was as if a large hand swept across the town, tumbling the houses like a mere deck of cards."

In Huaraz, the earthquake began without prior warning as a gentle swaying motion. Accompanying this mild horizontal movement was a muffled humming sound. A young woman described how she first felt her bed swaying back and forth. Then a crack appeared in the wall, and a vase vibrated on a table. Then all the glasses leapt, and adobes began to fly. It became difficult to walk in the side-to-side motion, but she made her way to the front door, which opened out onto the street. By then hard shaking had begun, and she saw that the whole of Huaraz was swaying with the earth. At the end, vertical movements abruptly replaced the horizontal rocking, and all of Huaraz foundered at once. Ironically, while there was still movement, the young woman experienced some sense of stability. In that final, prolonged heave of the earth and during the frozen seconds that followed, she thought destruction was total, that everyone had died, that perhaps the world was ending.

A graveyard silence engulfed her. Then she began to see motion, people passing silently, without bearing, like zombies. White-haired, caked in dust, they were unable to recognize each other. When they began to speak, it was to ask, "Who are you?" "I am so-and-so."

Fearing that a piece of mountain would topple into a lake and disgorge its contents, survivors searched the gorges with their eyes for signs of alluvion[1] from one of the many glacial lakes high above Huaraz. None came, though they were apprehensive for days, listening, unable to see, living in "an atmosphere of dust," unaware of the Huascarán avalanche and all that had happened north to Yungay.

THE earth shook so violently that Sunday afternoon in 1970 that it jarred loose a huge chunk of ice and rock from the glacial peak of Huascarán Norte. Ricocheting between the mountain's flanks, the avalanche sped downslope at 200 miles an hour, sucking up thousands of boulders, many weighing hundreds of tons, and hurling them against the mountainsides. Barely four minutes after the first earth shock, the avalanche, preceded by and cushioned on a deafening air blast, buried the town of Yungay, and all but a few hundred of its inhabitants and Sunday sojourners, under a billion cubic feet of water, ice, rock, and mud.

Passing this way over a century ago, though farther south in the Andean range, Charles Darwin wrote in his journal that were an earthquake to strike the glaciers, they would fly apart like chaff from a wheat stalk. Now, from the base of the Huascarán glacier, an Indian farmer witnessed the first movements of the ice as it broke from the summit. When he was a boy, Don Alejandro used to chop blocks of ice from the same glacier—Glacier 511, the Leprince Ringuet glacier, as it was to be named by scientists—and carry them on his back down to Yungay to sell. Now he thought the world was ending. The avalanche sailed down Llanganuco gorge as if on the wings of a condor, he said. "It carried away people, animals, and birds." He saw it carry off the mountainside hamlet where he lived, and all his family.

The avalanche flared out over Ranrahirca and hurled itself over a 600-foot ridge that divides Yungay from Ranrahirca. The ridge had always been felt to be Yungay's safety valve, its protector against an avalanche from Huascarán. A narrow, unscathed rib of land, called Aura, extends out from the ridge, and on this rib deserted intact houses and eucalyptus trees remain. Here a man stood with his young son, waiting for a bus, at 3:23 that Sunday. As the avalanche sailed past them, its rock projectiles clashing in midair, setting off sparks like lightning, he, too, thought the world was ending, leaving him and the boy alone, stranded in the universe on a green slip of land.

A lobe of the Huascarán avalanche swerved north along the Río Santa, carrying houses and bodies from Yungay. Moving like a slug, it deposited parts of Yungay along its path and lapped up small settlements on the Santa's banks. It climbed 200 feet above the river floodplain, up onto the foothills of the Cordillera Negra, where it left an indelible mark that can be seen from the road going north from Yungay to Caraz.

At the north end of the Callejón, near Huallanca, the Santa, choked by boulders fallen from the mountainsides, had suddenly dried up just after the earthquake, and then, an hour later, upon arrival of the debris-laden waters, the river swelled to sixty-five feet above its prequake level and ran full for four hours before beginning to subside. Reaching the valley's end, Huascarán's avalanche deposited all it had amassed in its path, including room-size boulders and hundreds of bodies, at the gates of the hydroelectric plant below the Cañón del Pato. The valley's current was extinguished. Rocks choked the canyon, demolishing the small train and splitting the rails, thus blocking the northern exit from the valley, and killing the nuns on holiday.

Only a score of Hiroshima-size bombs, dropped throughout the valley, could have destroyed so much so quickly. All along the 125-mile-long valley, roads slumped into gullies, and fissures appeared in the foothills. Dark moss outcroppings in the mountain gorges combined with crumbling shale to turn the rivulets flowing into the Santa black. Thermal waters, drained of their rust color, gushed pale and hotter than usual. After the earth's last heaves, a dust cloud rose to 18,000 feet, shrouding the valley. The temperature dropped to near freezing. Through sixty-four strong aftershocks, survivors huddled together during the cold and moonless night. The Callejón de Huaylas was cut off from the rest of the world. It was, as one survivor called it, "the longest night in the Southern Hemisphere of the world."

IRONICALLY, on the morning of May 31, 1970, a Peruvian geophysicist, Mateo Casaverde, accompanied by a French scientist, Gerard Patzelt, arrived on an official mission to install a seismograph somewhere in the Callejón. They went to see Benjamín Morales, director of the Santa Corporation, which is a government agency concerned with geophysics and glaciology and designed to keep vigil over the glacial moraines and lakes. Benjamín, a native of Huaraz, was only a boy when Lake Chúrup came down on Huaraz in 1941. At that time, he vowed he would learn all he could about glaciers and as a young man came to study in the United States and spent time in Alaska and in Europe observing glaciers. The Santa Corporation and Benjamín were thus supremely important to the security of the valley.

On that Sunday morning of the disaster, the three men, Casaverde, Patzelt, and Benjamín, had decided that the appropriate place for the installation of the seismograph was at one of the corporation's camps, located in Cátac, at 12,000 feet in the southern part of the Callejón. Benjamín reasoned that from Cátac they could obtain a profile of the earth's movements from the coast up over the cordilleras and down into the rain forest. The visiting scientists agreed to leave at once for Cátac, and as far as Benjamín knew, that's where they were headed. But it was Sunday, and the two men were suddenly drawn in the opposite direction, to lower, warmer altitudes, and they went instead to Yungay.

Meanwhile, Benjamín had been planning to attend the opening of a sports club, San Francisco, two blocks from the Plaza de Armas in Huaraz. About noon, though, "without any justification," he said, he decided to excuse himself from that commitment and instead left for the Chancos baths at the mouth of Honda gorge in the foothills of the Cordillera Blanca, where his mother was spending a short holiday. Upon arriving at Chancos at 12:45 P.M., he was invited to lunch with his mother and her companion. "Incomprehensibly, almost discourteously," he declined the invitation and instead convinced his mother to go with him to Caraz. At 2:00 P.M., they ran into his brother, sister-in-law, and their two daughters in Caraz, and they all decided to lunch together. Unexpectedly, friends of his brother arrived and invited them all to a *pachamanca*, which is a method of cooking food on hot stones under the ground. Again, dumbfounding himself, Benjamín declined this new invitation.

Seized by a strange uneasiness, I take my mother and nieces to Yungay, where we arrive around 2:30 P.M. Finally, we decide to have lunch at Los Claveles, which was a pretty restaurant. The first match of the world soccer championship in Mexico was on the radio, and everybody was commenting on the game. Almost everyone in the restaurant was from Huaraz, and we chatted from table to table. We got up from the table at three o'clock, a little past. I don't know why we ate more rapidly than is our custom, but my restlessness hadn't disappeared.

Yungay was famous for an ice cream called Niza, and we went to get some in the plaza. And who do I see on the plaza but Mateo, the geophysicist, and the Frenchman! And I say to myself, Gosh, these fellows are on a pleasure trip instead of installing that seismograph in Cátac. And I was going to go up to them, but I held back. We had said we'd pick up someone in Chancos at four o'clock, and if I started talking, I'd be late. So I said instead, "Let's go." But my mother and the kids wanted to buy bread. "I'll buy you all the bread you want in Huaraz, but let's get going," I said stubbornly. I astonished myself by my persistent refusal to please my mother, by going to buy the famous breads of Yungay, or to visit a relative she hadn't seen in a long time.

At 3:15, after crossing rapidly over Ranrahirca, we arrived at Mancos, at the very foot of Huascarán. My mother is very religious, and she wanted to go into the church to pray. We stopped in the doorway a moment, and I noticed that some canes about fifteen feet long were hanging dangerously from the roof of the church, and I hurried the family back into the car.

We rapidly left the town of Tingua behind, and about 3:23 I was crossing the bridge over the river that comes down out of Ulta gorge at the foot of Huascarán Sur. I began to comment on the dust whirls whipping up in the foothills. I kept driving. We were about to enter Toma and I see an adobe brick fall from a house. As I saw more adobes and masonry coating falling along the narrow street, my anxiety grew. Then I felt the movement, and I knew we were in the midst of an earthquake.

I pressed the gas pedal down to the floor and shot through the narrow street like a rocket to get to open space. After 100 yards, I couldn't drive anymore. The noise in those moments was terrifying. It was like many tanks passing nearby or like we were in the middle of an elephant stampede.

I got out of the car and grabbed my watch and began to count the seconds. The earthquake continued. The hills were falling, the lands sliding, tons of rocks coming down from the mountains and my fear increasing with the growing darkness of the atmosphere, the dust making it almost impossible to breathe.

The shaking hadn't even stopped, but spontaneously, as if to calm my mother and myself, I began to explain what an earthquake is like. I explained the geologic mechanism that produces earthquakes. Imagine! They wanted to cry, but they didn't. And I kept expounding, and my mother began to pray. And then when it stopped more or less, I continued toward Carhuaz, but I couldn't pass through Carhuaz because the city had fallen. We turned back in the direction of Yungay. I thought about my brother in Caraz.

I didn't think about Huascarán, that it might have . . . People along the road would say, "Alluvion from Huascarán! Don't go toward Ranrahirca." But I continued. In Toma, with help, we cleared a passage to be able to continue with the car. People helped, did what they were told, as if they were automatons. A terrible uneasiness crept over me when I saw stretches of road that had sunk and the enormous fractures.

It was already five o'clock when we passed through Mancos. It was deserted. People had fled into the mountains. I still didn't know the reason. There was so much dust, you couldn't see a thing. Visibility was less than 150 feet.

I kept driving until suddenly I had to slam on the brakes because there ahead was a black wall across the road. Shaking, I backed up and got out of the car. Everything was dark. I examined the soft barricade in front of me. It was about thirteen feet high, and from it cropped out parts of houses, trees, and even human remains.

I realized then that I was looking into the bed of a seismic avalanche from Huascarán that had covered Ranrahirca. The thought that the entire city of Yungay might have disappeared did not even occur to me.

A glacial cold enveloped us. I suspected there was a lot of ice, but the material looked black. I didn't see rocks or ice; everything was black, not exactly black, but a dark gray. I couldn't get too close because I would sink in it. It was mud, pure mud at the edges. With a stick from the edge of the alluvion, I scraped one of the big blocks and saw that it was all ice. Most of the blocks were ice, huge blocks of ice. There was no longer any doubt that the alluvion had come from Huascarán. Toward the other side, toward Yungay, I couldn't see a thing, and still I could not imagine that Yungay was buried. How could I?

It was of course impossible to get to Caraz. Dispirited, I turned back toward Carhuaz, conscious that from that moment on the grave responsibility for the technical side of the disaster rested on my shoulders. I knew I would immediately have to take steps to secure the hanging glaciers and the lakes that, affected by the tremendous quake, could produce still another catastrophe like the avalanche off Huascarán. We were over the earthquake, but a new stage was beginning of painful uncertainty about the 265 glacial lakes, with their unstable batters and the possible fractures in their already fragile dams.

When we neared destroyed Carhuaz, it was already too late to build a shelter. With other survivors, we gathered in the garden of a house. That night was the longest and most horrible in history. It was a night of more than sixty aftershocks, each seeming stronger than the one before. All night, the movements kept on. There and then, we were all afraid, really afraid, panic-stricken, because we could not see. A dense dust cloud imprisoned us. The house had not totally fallen, and it could fall at any moment and strike our car. We were inside the car. Often we had to turn the car lights on after a strong shock to see if the house was about to fall. It didn't, only an adobe here, another there. Though overcome by a terrible fatigue, still we could not sleep. The memory of the awful images we had seen, and the darkness and the shocks, unbalanced our already weakened nerves.

Now I no longer thought about any theory of earthquakes; no, not during that night. I absolutely didn't think about technical questions. I thought about those who were with me—my mother, my brother's children, about the atmosphere that seemed like it was going to asphyxiate us, and about my brother and my sister-in-law, who were on the other side, in Caraz, and I didn't know what had happened to them. The night passed that way, without sleep. My mother was praying, and she made the women who were there pray, too, the rosary, the Our Father. My mother prayed, and I don't know if maybe I even prayed with her. I don't remember. But if I didn't accompany her, anyway, I respected what she was doing.

Finally, day came. The first thing was to make a refuge for my mother and the children. I knew there was no way they could move from Carhuaz for a week or more. We made a shelter with eucalyptus branches. We looked for blankets in a fallen house. Then I walked over the rubble to the center of Carhuaz to find supplies and water. There was no drinkable water, so I went to a spring for water. That work took me all day long. I had to make many trips with buckets. In those circumstances, I think the first thing one does is look after the integrity of his family. You see people, in good or bad shape, and you say, "How are you?" but you keep working for the well-being of your family. That was all of Monday. In the afternoon, I did go again to Ranrahirca to try to see my brother on the other side. But it was impossible to see because there was so much dust.

No one on this side of the avalanche knew yet anything about Yungay. A lot of us were there at the edge of the alluvion, trying to see to the other side of Ranrahirca, but nothing, no one could see. That was Monday.

It was in the afternoon of Tuesday, June 2, when the first helicopter from the coast was able to break through the dust cloud and land in Caraz. By Tuesday, Benjamín, having secured his family in Carhuaz, was making his way on foot to Huaraz. He had reached the fork in the road where the western prong veers off to Anta. Benjamín had accepted in his mind the possibility of his brother's death when he heard him and his sister-in-law calling to him from the helicopter, which had found a hole through the dust. They had been so desperate to find their children that the pilot, who had landed in Caraz, agreed to try to fly them to the other side of the avalanche. Reunited, only now did Benjamín learn what had happened north of Ranrahirca.

After having seen the destruction of the earthquake, I could believe anything. So when my brother told me about Yungay, I said, "*Caracho*, what bad luck!" In those moments since something so big as the earthquake had happened, something as big as the avalanche could happen. It wasn't like it was just the avalanche, because it was an appendage of something bigger. To see the destruction . . . I don't know how many people died. . . . Well, they died. Now, let's get to work, I said to myself. There was no time to wail then. Those of us who had work, who had responsibility, who didn't have time to be . . . It was better that way.

After the *pachamanca* in Caraz, Benjamín's brother and sister-in-law had gone to a house that was almost swallowed in a crack that opened in the earth. They started out on foot toward Yungay, where they could see the black mass of the alluvion, which by then was churning down the Santa, overflowing its banks. They ran toward the foothills and just managed to climb up on a big rock as the debris glided around the rock. A doctor running alongside them tripped and was caught up in the slime.

Benjamín's friends at Los Claveles restaurant in Yungay died in the avalanche, but the scientists who had come to the valley to install the seismograph, whom Benjamín had spotted on the plaza when he was buying ice cream, survived.

After lunching in Yungay that fatal Sunday, Casaverde and Patzelt headed down toward the Yungay cemetery. This was about 3:10 P.M. With a Hasselblad 1000-F camera, Casaverde took some photographs of the Huascarán, which was partially covered with clouds. Through the lens he could clearly see horizontal cracks in part of Huascarán Norte. "Strangely enough," he recalls, "I commented to Patzelt that the Huascarán constituted a serious danger and at any moment it could come down." Just as they settled into their 1968 Chevy truck to return to Huaraz, the earthquake began. The vertical movement of the earth was the most intense and made the truck jump up and down. Adobe houses were crumbling into pancakes, the asphalt road was buckling, and pockets of earth exploded on the Cordillera Negra.

The two geophysicists got out of the car. A low-frequency noise rumbled in their ears. They looked toward Huascarán and saw a giant dust cloud, the color of clay. It was descending. The time was 3:24. Looking around, they saw that the only place that offered relative security was the cemetery, which is built on a pre-Inca mound in circular tiers of diminishing circumference. They ran the 100 yards or so to the bottom rung. The burial niches had opened in the shaking. When Casaverde looked back toward the Cordillera Blanca, he saw "a giant wave of mud, a light gray color." This wave contained no dust. The clay-colored dust cloud had remained behind Yungay, hovering above the gorge that opens into Ranrahirca. He knew that the dense gray wave would strike Yungay.

Climbing in unison with a woman and three small children, the two men gained a foothold on the second rung of the cemetery, but the way to the third was obstructed. With a thunderous roar, like a whiplash, the gray wave struck the second tier and rushed past their feet. Now the sky blackened with the pulverized adobes of Yungay, which had been lifted on the avalanche. Then silence and cold entombed Yungay. By 4:30 P.M. only the barest outline of the sun shone through the dense dust. During two nights and two days, the geophysicists took refuge among the tombs, without coats or food, until the mud hardened enough to be walked on.[2]

MEANWHILE, in Huaraz, the towers of the cathedral on the Plaza de Armas had toppled, and all around the plaza, whatever walls remained standing threatened to drop onto the square. Still, in the hours after the earthquake, survivors made their way over the rubble to huddle together and keep warm by bonfires they built around their central square. They carried their dead and piled them up on the grass in the plaza. Late that night, monks from Los Pinos, a monastery in the foothills, came down and hauled away bodies back up the mountain and buried them in a common grave near the monastery.

The tombs of the Huaraz cemetery had broken open, and the dead had to be reburied, this time along with earthquake victims, in three large communal graves that survivors began to dig. But there were too many dead—the numbers would rise to 10,000—and after three days, the remaining cadavers were burned in bonfires on the plaza as fear of an epidemic loomed. Many of the dead were never accounted for. During eight months, one woman searched the rubble for her little girl until a man told her he had seen the child in one of the common graves at the cemetery.

That first long night, the one valley hospital, in the Belén section of Huaraz, was a groaning sanctuary for wounded too numerous to count. A woman who escaped injury because she had been picnicking with her family in an orchard made her way over the ruins to the hospital to offer her help. On her way, she met a town dentist whose whole family had died and who stumbled zombielike over the ruins asking anyone he ran into to kill him. The man's skin hung loosely from his bones, and the woman shook him, shouting, "React! You are alive; you could at least give injections at the hospital. Come to help. I, too, am alone," she lied. "Only a few of us are alive, and we must help."

When she reached her destination, the hospital's disheveled

director greeted her tiredly with the words "Señora, we have no water. We are lost. The hospital is falling down."

"It won't fall any more than this," she answered him, out of a strength and authority that strangely impelled her. She set about collecting eucalyptus branches, lashing the hospital corridors with them, scattering the branches about. She did this to fumigate the hospital and keep the injured from getting the grippe, she said. There was no water, no current, no light. Only small candles illuminated the crammed corridors, candles picked from the rubble of stores survivors passed as they made their way to the hospital.

Only five of the staff of twenty-three doctors managed to reach the hospital. Those who had survived tended first to their own families. The hospital staff was called on a loudspeaker, but as a nurse said, she went but had to come back to her family. The physician most responsible for holding things together that first night, Dr. Ramos Guardia, attributed his being able to function to the fact that most of his family was in Lima that Sunday. Shouting to the one son who had remained at home with him, "Survive!" he made the arduous trek across the ruins to the hospital. The first thing he did was to catch water from the broken pipes. "Without water, we'd have had to throw in the towel," he told me.

For three nights and four days he never left the hospital. By the hundreds, the wounded amassed in the corridors. The doctor stuffed his pockets with antibiotics and aspirin. He passed out aspirin to everyone, with elaborate instructions as to when to take the tablets, "in order to distract them from their wounds." He knew there was no way to heal their wounds with the resources available. Though he himself often wanted to flee the tottering building, he knew he must above all avoid panic. So with each new aftershock, he held tight, laughed, and said aloud, "Though I may die here, I'm not moving." Words heard in the corridors were not complaints about one's own injuries, he said, but rather cries of "Doctor, my brother . . . Doctor, my child . . . my mother . . . Have you seen her?" Accompanying him in his odyssey was a quiet North American monk from Los Pinos.

It was four days before planes penetrating the dust cloud dropped supplies of food and medicines, many falling onto the mountain slopes, never to be retrieved by survivors. By the time chickens dropped were found, they had rotted. More days passed before parachutists jumped to the valley floor with provisions.

After two weeks, Argentine medics and nurses landed at Anta, a small airstrip hurriedly prepared outside Huaraz. The valley's only airstrip, at Caraz, was inoperable, covered by the Huascarán debris flow. The Argentines brought a water purifier, which they set up in the Río Santa. Eventually, the Russians dropped a giant geodesic dome from a plane and inflated it in the valley. Many said that in that "hospital" the Russians performed "the most incredible operations." The unbearable frustration and helplessness of being faced with an impossible task the night of May 31, 1970, and the immediate days that followed led most of Huaraz's surviving medical staff to leave the valley, never to return.

Normal chains of authority in the valley were ruptured. Both the prefect and subprefect (like our governor and lieutenant governor) were killed in the earthquake. The mayor of Huaraz survived but could not cope with the disaster and soon left. Before he left, on the day after the earthquake, the mayor did manage to send for miners from Ticapampa to help dig out the dead and wounded. Twenty miners arrived, but an official of the Civil Guard intercepted them and incomprehensibly ordered them to march in a field on the outskirts of the center. Realizing that the guard "had lost his mind," the mayor took him to the hospital. The guard never fully recovered. A man from outside was sent to replace the mayor, but people said he lacked true affection for Huaraz. Lawyers, teachers, leaders, and police had been killed or were injured or were engaged in their own search for family members.

In the center of Huaraz, banks and pawnshops had split open, liberating neatly packed bundles of bills as well as transistors and jewelry that people had pawned. Survivors dug in the rubble of food stores for supplies. Scores of peasants from the surrounding mountainsides came down into Huaraz. Some helped to dig out the buried. Others looted in the dark. It was days before guards were designated and ordered to shoot at anything or anyone moving after dark. This brought a hush to the night in the destroyed central part of Huaraz that was to last for years.

Strangely, within twenty-four hours after the disaster, the strains of a popular ballad, "Los Cubanos," could be heard on the plaza. The earthquake had jammed the transmitter of Radio Huascarán, one of two local valley stations, and had scattered the phonograph records usually played by Peter, the local disc jockey. Peter managed to find only one record intact in the rubble, "Los

Cubanos," and he played it over and over again, with his transmitter locked on "Emergency."

On the Plaza de Armas that first night, one man, who had lost seven members of his immediate family, got a gun and had to be restrained from shooting himself. This was the only suicide attempt after the disaster that I heard about. On the plaza, Huaraz's leading poet, Marcos Yauri Montero, wrestled through the night with the image of his two children crushed beneath Santa Elena, a religious school located on the square. Lovers surprised in an embrace had been catapulted from their room and impaled on a flagpole that hung over the plaza. There they remained for three days and nights.

The old-time photographer with his tripod camera and hood stayed in the plaza, where he had been photographing a child seated on a life-size stuffed donkey as the earth began to shake. The old priest who had been feeding the doves on the outskirts of Huaraz when the disaster struck made his way to his house, where he discovered that all sixteen of its occupants had perished. He then pushed on to the plaza and collapsed from exhaustion in the central fountain, which became his bed for many nights after.

Those huddled together in the Plaza de Armas of Huaraz did not know about the ninety-two survivors clinging to the top of Yungay's tiered cemetery. If Benjamín could not imagine an avalanche so big that it would bury the entire town of Yungay, even less could others. Days would pass before wardens of the morainal lakes could make their way across the mountains from Llanganuco with news of the full extent of Huascarán's havoc and the threat that still existed there.

Ramírez Gamarra, poet and survivor from the town of Recuay, remarked in his journal that the towns of the Callejón de Huaylas had a telluric destiny to fulfill. It had been done.

Three

NOW HUARAZ IS
ONLY A PAMPA

*When I first came from the province of
Recuay here to the city of Huaraz,
Huaraz was very pretty to me. There
existed many people, a cathedral and con-
vents. All seemed marvelous to me. I felt
happiness inside myself. There were long
rows of houses, streets. . . . And now,
those things no longer exist. The cathedral
has fallen. Only the dome remains. They
have cleaned up every last little bit of
rubble, all that fell down in the city. Now
Huaraz is only a pampa.*

boy in a survivor camp

O N TUESDAY, June 2, 1970, Benjamín Morales walked
from Carhuaz to his native Huaraz, a distance of
twenty-two miles. It took him six hours. He said that
people along the road told him that Huaraz had been completely
destroyed and thousands were dead, but he could not believe it.
His house, near the Plaza de Armas, was strong, with columns.
Surely it had not fallen. Besides, his eyes were riveted on the
glaciers of the Cordillera Blanca, shrouded in the dust cloud, but
he could trace their jagged profile in his mind. His immediate
destination was the Santa Corporation at the north end of Huaraz
in the barrio of Centenario, where he would have to begin to face
the possibility of further avalanches from the jarred glaciers.

As he reached Avenida Centenario, he felt relieved. The barrio
had suffered perhaps 40 percent damage; not bad, he thought. But

the Santa Corporation office was a madhouse. Hundreds of people pressed into the building around the shortwave radio, the only radio in touch with Lima. Instantly, he took over and set about dealing with the issue of the glaciers, still denying whatever he heard about the center of Huaraz. Anyway, it was assumed by others that he had already seen the *casco urbano*, and in the chaos there was neither the chance nor the spirit, he told me, to dwell on what had already happened. His energy was absorbed in what might still come. He slept in his office that night, and only on the afternoon of Wednesday, June 3, did he first see the ruins of Huaraz's center.

He crossed the bridge over the Quilcay onto Avenida Raimondi. Not a house was left standing on Raimondi. Getting closer to the center, he saw the dead being carried out by the dozens.

> The more I penetrated the city, the more my anguish grew. There had been no exaggeration. It was real. The destruction was total. With each new tremor, rafters would fall and kick up more dust. It was hard to know when I was walking on what had been a street or a house. The fact is I was walking on rubble ten feet high above the level of the ancient streets. I was stepping on adobes, timber, cane, cement, furniture, iron, tiles. Even the dead were draped like macabre tapestries in my path. I ran into many grief-stricken friends who were excavating the place where the recently inaugurated Club San Francisco had been. Save a few, all those attending that fiesta that I had so mysteriously decided not to attend had died there. Everywhere I heard the same questions: "Have you seen my mother, my children, anyone of my family?" And the same urgent summons: "Please help me to dig her out; perhaps she is still alive!" Or, "Listen, by the voice I think it is my child. Help me!"

After helping to dig out the dead and the injured, Benjamín finally made his way to the area of his home. He found only an amorphous heap, indistinguishable from the sea of rubble. He could not even salvage one chair. Now, three days after the earthquake, with people still crying out from under the ruins, he said to himself, What is a house, after all?

IN the mountain hamlet of Secsecpampa, high above Monterrey but still considered to be within the orbit of Huaraz, lived Don

Juan, who was to become my friend and principal Indian informant, his wife, and eight children. As the peasants of the uplands sometimes had to do, Don Juan was working on the coast, near Cachipampa, as a laborer when the earthquake struck.

As the earth began to shake, Don Juan automatically looked up into the face of the immense mountains rising from the desert, among which is nestled his village. The mountains seemed to be rolling over, he said, and thundering down onto the desert strip. They spat forth boulders that clashed and broke up into pieces. Around him, the coastal roads sank, and offshore the ocean swelled. Muddy water squirted from holes that opened in the desert floor. Birds fell to the ground, took flight, and were forced again to the ground. Even fat hens lumbered into the air, their wings standing on end, and fell. Dust choked Don Juan and the other peasants looking up into the mountains, leaving them in a thick darkness. Not until Monday, at noon, could they begin to try to reach their homes.

Some sixty men began to climb up through the pass at Callán and into the Callejón, a distance of sixty-two, mostly vertical, miles. Don Juan imagined his wife and children dead. Desperation to reach their families drove all the men forward on a march that they would not have thought possible under normal circumstances. Exhausted, hungry, thirsty, some did not make it. One man was struck and killed by a rock at Uchupampa. Because he was old, the younger men took pity on Don Juan. "Here, poor old man, let me rub your feet. You won't make it. You'll die," they would say to him, breaking off a piece of potato they had rummaged from the ground to give to him. At nightfall, on Wednesday, June 3, the men descended into the valley.

Don Juan found his wife and children crying in the mountains of Secsecpampa. Thinking they would never see him again, they had found a spot where there were no rocks and where a hillock would protect them. When they saw him, they shouted, "Neighbors, he is alive!"

The next day, the family came down the mountainside to see Huaraz. When they reached the edge of the center, the smell of death overcame them, and they turned back. Looting had begun by then. "Poor people, who had never had radios or watches," Don Juan said in a tone that was neither accusing nor excusing. A neighbor from a nearby hamlet was caught stuffing her stocking with cash and checks from the strongbox of a bank and was shot three times.

DESTRUCTION of Huaraz's urban center was virtually total. Of a rural and urban population of 65,000, about 20,000 people lived in the four sections, or barrios, that made up the urban center, the oldest part of the city, called the *casco urbano* (literally, "urban helmet"). Some 10,000–15,000 more lived in newer barrios that spread out from the urban center toward the north and southeast. The remainder, the rural population, inhabited the mountain hamlets.

Half a billion cubic feet of adobe bricks buried the *casco urbano* and half its population of 20,000. Another 10,000 died in the rest of Huaraz. Over 90 percent of the structures in the center collapsed. On the Plaza de Armas alone, beneath the ruins of the religious school, Santa Elena, hundreds of children who had been performing in plays and skits in honor of the mother superior were entombed.

Memories of the first days in the center of Huaraz are filled with images of feeling buried under tons of crumbled adobe, of surfacing only to walk "over the bones of brothers," past men, women, and children, mute and numbed, crossing the rubble. The earth appeared to have splintered or to have "shattered like a crystal." All that was heard in the night was the creaking of eucalyptus trees and the hushed fall of snow masses from the summits.

As days passed, lean-tos were put together, and when tents were finally dropped from helicopters, they stood unevenly upon the rubble or in nearby potato fields, sagging, lighted by candles. Mothers could be heard inside coaxing their silent children to eat. Gradually, the center was abandoned altogether, and survivor camps grew up in the foothills. Asleep in these camps, people would dream the city was still there, still the same, only to awaken to each new dawn and find their dreams turned to nightmares, that Huaraz was rubble, that there was *nada* ("nothing"), that "all were dead." With this constantly renewed consciousness, they would cry and want to be numb again. With the coming of government troops and a curfew imposed on the destroyed center, survivors, though drawn to the rubble, became afraid to come down, even to try to retrieve any of their own things, lest they not be recognized and so, perhaps, shot.

After dusk, nothing stirred in the center, but during the first weeks and months after the earthquake, people hallucinated, seeing and hearing "living corpses." In Andean belief, the dead are visualized as living corpses whose spirits cling to earth for a year. One night, I was told, after survivors had already taken refuge in the foothills, two native guards who had been assigned to the ruins heard a religious procession coming down Calle Sucre, which runs east to west, bordering the Plaza de Armas. A band was playing drums, flutes, and trumpets. All the musicians and instruments emitted light, so that the procession took on the appearance of a luminous mass moving across the ruins. When it reached the plaza, the mass turned into a lone man wearing a poncho. The guards went mad and had to be taken away.

Another time, a guard making his rounds of the ruins saw a man approaching him. The man's face was hidden by his scarf, and a hat was pulled down over his eyes. At first, he only asked the guard to direct him to Calle Comercio; then he insisted that the guard accompany him. Feeling there was something strange about the man, the guard touched him and found that the man "was all bone."

Even after a year had passed and the rubble had been removed, a man driving his truck across the center one afternoon sensed that a spirit, trying to hitch a ride, had boarded his truck from behind. The dead did not enjoy their confinement to the ruins.

CLOSE to the first anniversary of the disaster, bulldozers from the coast finally managed to crawl up to the high valley. They ripped through the ruins and carried away most of the rubble. Only a few of the less stricken buildings were left standing. Because the government paid the contractors for the rubble, measured by the cubic yard, they were reluctant to allow anyone to salvage a beam or a brick. They made 11 million *soles* (more than $250,000) off the rubble.

Using torches to illuminate the devastation by night, they bulldozed around the clock, unearthing such specters as a microbus buried with twenty-nine passengers. Dynamite blasted the remains of the cathedral. Only its cupola was left standing as a historical landmark. Then, just as abruptly as the bulldozers had come, they departed, back down to the coast, and Huaraz's center lay still and abandoned for over another year.

Survivors, who had been growing desperate after a year amid

the ruins, at first saw this sudden and aggressive movement as a signal by the national government that reconstruction would soon get under way. They felt deceived when it became apparent that there was no intention to follow through. As plans for reconstruction remained on the drawing boards in Lima, they began to sense that the horrendous *remoción de escombros* ("removal of ruins") had been only a showpiece, ill conceived by the new Revolutionary Military Government.

Since the *casco urbano* had been blanketed by curfews and survivors forbidden to occupy their land, to move an adobe from it, or now to lay an adobe upon it, there was nothing to do but wait. The rains and cold of several more seasons would come and go before even the first permanent house went up. Slowly, survivors began to call the removal of ruins a second earthquake. The scraped and leveled urban center of Huaraz became known simply as the pampa, which, in Quechua, means "a plain." The Huaraz pampa was a flat and empty dust-swept hollow.

IN the region of Huaraz, the pinnacles of the Cordillera Blanca are especially bold. An old man told me that Huaraz was named by the ancient Peruvians. He said that as they emerged over these peaks from the east, the sun was just rising over their shoulders. So they called the place spread out in front of them at the foot of the mountains "Dawn." "Yes," he said, nodding, "Huaraz is where day is produced, to be enjoyed, and it carries that name."[1]

The Río Quilcay, which flows down the Cordillera Blanca and empties into the Santa, divides Huaraz into two parts. To the north, the relatively new barrio of Centenario extends on either side of Avenida Centenario toward the two mountain ranges. This barrio received the full brunt of an alluvion that swept out of Cójup canyon and down the Quilcay on December 13, 1941. Enormous boulders, scattered along both sides of the Quilcay and throughout Centenario, attest to this.

Survivors of the 1941 alluvion had moved from those more rural outskirts of Centenario barrio to the opposite side of the Río Quilcay, to the old part of Huaraz, the part most completely destroyed in 1970. Now, many survivors of 1970 moved back across the Quilcay, repopulating Centenario. Both survivors of the earthquake and people who entered the Callejón to do business after the disaster opened small shops and makeshift restaurants that turned Avenida Centenario into the principal commercial street. The Centenario church of the German Fathers of the Sacred Heart was the only Catholic church of the city left standing after the earthquake.

To the south of the Río Quilcay lie the four barrios of the old city—or urban center—namely, San Francisco, Soledad, Belén, and Huarupampa. Each barrio had its own church and its own *plazuela* ("little square"). Special *huaynos*, the sometimes plaintive, sometimes playful sierra ballads, are dedicated to each barrio, and each barrio was said to have its own particular character. San Francisco, near the Quilcay, was quiet, almost monastic, people said, its tree-lined alameda a place for lovers. Belén, to the south, had the most beautiful colonial church and a fine sculptured plaza. Since it is higher than other parts of Huaraz, people would exclaim in Quechua, "*Alalac*, Belén!" ("How cold, Belén!").

To the west, along the banks of the Santa, is Huarupampa. The most rural of the four main barrios, it sprawls along to the Río Quilcay, and its few streets open into a square where a bust of liberator Simón Bolívar stands, facing the Cordillera Negra.

To the east, near the Cordillera Blanca and high like Belén, is the Barrio de la Soledad, the barrio of solitude. *Soledanos*, as residents of this barrio are called, consider themselves to be the head of all the barrios and the heart of the city.

The same rivalry that exists among the towns of the Callejón exists among the barrios of Huaraz. They thrive on it. The first question asked when one meets a stranger is "What barrio are you from?" People say the answer reveals much about the person. They felt that if the barrios were eradicated in the reconstruction or people were forced to live in other than their native barrio, they would be disoriented and their history, lore, and character would be lost.

In general, the urban centers of sierra towns are a commercial and residential conglomerate. They are urban, with shoemakers and bakeries and hotels, and houses built close to one another. Yet the towns remain rural, the houses built with corrals and inner patios for storing grain and keeping animals.

Everyone said Huaraz had been a charming and beautiful colonial town, with balconies and imaginative adornments unique to each house, though the doors were painted in colors identifying each barrio. These charming houses of the urban center were of

old adobe construction, supported by eucalyptus beams, subject to
dry rot and termites, and topped by cumbersome tile roofs. Streets,
really cobbled lanes built for horses, were so narrow that a car could
barely pass. People would demonstrate how one could reach out
the car windows and touch the houses on either side. These narrow
streets became a trap for the inhabitants of Huaraz's center.

All four of the old barrio churches were destroyed in the earthquake. Afterward, San Francisco's temple became a tiny adobe
structure. Belén's church, its finely carved altarpiece once famous
throughout the Callejón, was now a simple wooden building. There
was no plan to rebuild the Huarupampa church. The Spanish Franciscan priests, also located in Huarupampa, took over the parish.
The Spaniards' church, San Antonio, became a makeshift building,
its windows pieced together with fragments from its own shattered
stained glass. A piece of stained glass reading *Banco de Crédito* ("Bank
of Credit"), salvaged from the rubble of the bank, had been fitted
into a lower left window. Soledad's temple, after the earthquake,
was a mud-floor, wattle-and-daub structure with a corrugated tin
roof.

I came to know Huaraz through the barrio of Centenario, for the
colectivo (a collective taxi that takes five passengers) in which I arrived
in the valley for the first time skirted the pampa and took a road
near the Río Santa. It was getting dark and raining hard that afternoon when the car pulled up to the Hotel de Turistas, the tourist
hotel at the northern extreme of Centenario.

Under those circumstances, the name of the hotel seemed lu-
dicrous. There were only five other guests, all officials of some
kind, who were living in the hotel, as there were few places to find
lodging. I walked into the hotel through the frame of a glass door
no longer there. The walls were cracked, and glass and fallen tiles
lay strewn around. It was like a bombed-out building, desolate and
lonely, where footsteps echoed in the corridors.

After settling into my room, I walked down Avenida Centenario through deep mud, jumping over holes, and went into one of
the little mud-floor, tin-roofed shanty restaurants that had sprung
up along Centenario to accommodate relief personnel who poured
into the valley after the disaster. I ordered a cup of tea and was
invited to join a table at which were seated an American Peace

Corps volunteer who was in charge of installing pipes for potable water in another town, some bereted and bearded Peruvians with Communal Development, a Brazilian (I never learned what he was doing there), and a Belgian woman who I later learned drove a mean jeep and worked in the Nicrupampa survivor camp. The conversation in progress was about how materials should be dispensed; how to get corrugated tin slabs, which were used to build temporary shelters, up the mountainsides; the idiosyncrasies of various nearby villages; and a missionary who had run off with a nurse. With my head throbbing and my heart pounding from the altitude, I excused myself and walked back to the hotel through the cold darkness. During the night, the circular neon lighting fixture on the ceiling of my room, probably shorted out, kept flashing on and off. I lay there feeling ill from the altitude, watching the flickering light as it illuminated each fissure in the walls, and wondered how I could possibly stay in the Callejón.

My fears dissolved somewhat when the sierra morning broke into a hot sun and the ice-capped peaks that the evening before had been shrouded in rain clouds rose sharp and clear from the valley's edge. I saw Huascarán for the first time. Soaring 22,000 feet above the Pacific Ocean and 14,000 feet above the valley floor, the mountain, an imperturbable precipice of silence, dominates the Callejón. When I was finally able to break my gaze, my eyes searched the dark folds of the two cordilleras, and like hundreds of mirrors, the tin slabs of provisional shelters glittered in the sunlight.

I walked down Centenario, the aroma of eucalyptus and the strains of *huaynos* in the air. An Indian band, playing trumpets, flutes, and drums, and dancers had come down from the higher villages and were moving up and down the avenue carrying a statue of the Virgin Mary. Dilapidated cars and panel trucks shuttled passengers and produce back and forth, whipping up the dust. Cows, donkeys, and sheep shared in the bustle of Centenario. As annoying as the ubiquitous dust was—people held handkerchiefs to their mouths or lifted their ponchos or shawls over their faces —I came to love Centenario, especially at dusk, when the activity was greatest. At sunset, the dark crests of the Cordillera Negra cast deep shadows across the valley floor. Herds were being driven home through the streets, peasants were making last-minute purchases and hurrying up the mountain paths to reach their hamlets before nightfall, and *colectivos* were bound on their final trips to towns up and down the valley. The setting sun would catch each speck of dust whipped up in the scurry, enveloping the barrio in a dense pink haze.

Centenario was like a frontier boom town. Unfamiliar as this Andean sierra world was to me, it was still within the range of an ordinary world. When I crossed the Río Quilcay south, however, going through the marketplace and coming out onto the pampa, where Old Huaraz had been, there was nothing that could have adequately prepared me for what I saw and how I felt.

SIXTEEN months had intervened since the earthquake, but I might have guessed that barely a fraction of that time had passed. In sharp contrast to the bustle of Centenario, nothing moved on the pampa. The event was everywhere present, and disaster wrapped its arms around me.

I looked across to the towering cupola on the Plaza de Armas, which had purposely been left standing when the cathedral ruins were blasted and the rubble of Huaraz hauled away. This skeletal remnant of "before" stood out against the blue sky, asserting the absence of the city that had surrounded it. I sat on a bench in the Plaza de Armas, accompanied only by the old-time hooded photographer who had been there the Sunday of the earthquake. As if rooted to the plaza, he had stayed on, with his tripod camera and his life-size donkey, barely taking in 100 *soles* ($2.50) a week, which before the earthquake might have been a Sunday afternoon's earnings.

Were it all gone, had every last ruin been removed, it would not have been so strange. There would be no sign of the past. But the few remaining houses, one of which I came to live in, the few half buildings, a freestanding facade with a marquee reading Ice Cream and Pastries, an exposed section of beautiful tile flooring projecting from the ground, all of which had miraculously escaped the insistent bulldozers, seemed to whisper that this had been a city. Surreal and eerie now, this space had been Huaraz.

Sitting there on that bench in the plaza, my first day in the Callejón, I wondered how survivors survived at all. How did the few I could see now, figures small in the distance, traversing the narrow streets over the unoccupied pampa, manage to live with their memories? Hundreds of houses had lined these streets, shading them, embroidering them in the shadows of wrought-iron grillwork. What did survivors say to each other? What were they thinking? Did they despair and withdraw or go back to the fields and dig the potato from the shivering earth?

Like the hooded photographer, I felt moored to the plaza. As the day waned, mule trains passed beneath the cathedral's cupola. Nearby, a little girl was switching her piglets, an Indian family sat on the ground eating breads they picked from a carrying shawl, and a dog was climbing the stairs of the ruins of a house, stairs that dropped off into nowhere. In the surrounding low hills and on the outer fringes of this devastated area, I could see the survivor camps, made up of tents, pasteboard structures they called *módulos* ("modules"), and corrugated tin shelters. Ringed by these encampments, the pampa was like the ghost of a city embattled.

During the course of my stay, such peculiar things happened on the pampa as armed guards standing watch all night over a large buried wooden box that, when excavated the following morning, turned out to be soap powder. I would sometimes see bizarre scenes, like those one might expect in a Bergman film. Walking up to the barrio of Soledad one afternoon, I saw a man dressed in a black coat and tie, with a stiff white collar, most unusual attire for the Callejón, especially at this time. He was peering over the top of a freestanding wall on which the words Funeral Parlor were painted in black letters. A comforting sight was a big red Salvation Army truck that stood in the middle of the pampa. In white letters across its side was written: "Sent by the City of New York, with Love."

FOR months after I arrived, Huaraz had still, within its own torn integrity, a kind of internal consistency. But when I returned from a brief January break in Lima, the regional offices of several national ministries and the Commission for the Reconstruction and Rehabilitation of the Affected Zone (CRYRZA) had moved into the valley. Alongside the burros and cattle that wandered on the pampa were bulldozers and shiny new jeeps. It was disconcerting to see the confrontation of heavy machinery with an Indian band of drummers and flutists or a small procession carrying a religious image on one of the narrow streets that crisscrossed the pampa. The embattled city had been occupied.

After a few weeks, however, the reconstruction crews retired to the outskirts of Centenario to build their own living and working quarters, leaving the pampa once again deserted. From time to time surveyors came to mark out proposed new streets with a white chalky powder. The rains would wash the powder away, and the process would have to be repeated.

For a week or ten days in early February, the silence of the pampa was temporarily broken by a lone bulldozer leveling the ground. By then I was living in a house that had remained standing only because the Señora had thrown herself in front of the advancing machinery during the big "removal of ruins" that took place in May 1971. She had shouted that they would have to run her down before she would let them take her house, and they relented.

With the ominous roar of the bulldozer that February, threatening again to take down the few remaining ruins, including my house, I experienced in minute proportion the anxiety people felt during the infamous "removal." It had been for them so thorough an assault that they had been exiled from their land with neither brick nor beam to rebuild with.

In August 1972 both Centenario and the pampa became a veritable puzzle of deep trenches in preparation for the laying of water and sewage pipes. It became dangerous to cross the pampa at night. The trenches were deep, and there was still no lighting. More than one person was lost in those trenches, which remained empty for a long time.

Though during my year in the valley the pampa continued to be spectral and surreal, toward the very end of my stay there were signs of life. The municipal building on the Plaza de Armas was nearing completion, and on the edges of Huarupampa and San Francisco a few model concrete houses were going up. Now when I walked around the square, it was under the arcade of the new town hall. I imagined people there, and shops. Now, in the third year since the earthquake, a tenuous hope was beginning to penetrate the desolation of the pampa.

Four

YUNGAY, BEACH OF THE DEAD

*The clowns of the circus were painting on
a red smile, as if their upper lip hung from
their ears, and the children were applaud-
ing a tired pirouette dancer and a sorry
tight-rope artist.*

Hugo Ramírez,
Ancash, Vida y Pasión

WITHIN FIFTEEN SECONDS of the earth's shaking, the
snow at Huascarán's summit burst into a brilliant
cascade of white crystals. A million cubic meters of
ice fell freely from the pinnacle, driving into Glacier 511 on the
north face of the mountain. The impact set in motion 24 million
more cubic meters of ice from 511. Now 3,000 feet wide, a mile
long, and 100 feet deep—"a wall of debris as high as a ten-story
building"—the avalanche began the nine-mile trajectory to the valley floor. Geologists estimated a speed of 250 miles an hour during
part of the trajectory and an average velocity of well over 100 miles
an hour.

Because of its rapid movement downslope, the ice mass was
partly converted to water by heat and friction, a geologic process
never before recorded. The rapid descent was due to the steep

slope, some seventy degrees, from which the avalanche originated, and to the great vertical drop, nearly 14,000 feet, down the nine-mile path to the Río Santa.

Near its source, the ice, cushioned on an air mass, flew across ridges of unconsolidated morainal material without disrupting them. Then, in its sweep down the Llanganuco valley, which begins at the lakes between Huascarán Norte and Huandoy, to Ranrahirca, the ice flow began to pick up morainal rock. Preceded by a turbulent air blast, it moved with a deafening noise. At its highest velocity, which occurred in mid-course, thousands of boulders were hurled 2,000 feet back and forth across the steep valley. Friction from the boulders colliding in midair made them look from below like red fireballs. Whole hamlets and an estimated 1,800 people along the path of the fertile Llanganuco valley were swept up into the fulminant avalanche. Reaching the Callejón bottom, the massive flow of ice, rock, mud, and water—twenty-seven times greater than an avalanche that buried Ranrahirca in 1962—spread out over the already interred town and then impounded the Río Santa.

With its high velocity and enormous force, it did something no one thought was possible. A tongue of the avalanche leapt over the 600-foot ridge, called Shacsha, that separates Yungay from Ranrahirca. Because of this ridge, Yungay had always been considered one of the safest towns of the valley. Scarcely four minutes had elapsed from the first stirring of ice and snow at the pinnacle until the avalanche reached the cemetery on the edge of Yungay near the Santa.

The forward-moving nose of the flow carried victims and debris from Ranrahirca and Yungay down the Santa to Huallanca, but an estimated total deposit of more than 70 million tons remained to rebury Ranrahirca and to bury Yungay.

Heavy under its own weight, the viscous mass settled quietly over Yungay, some 20 feet deep at the central plaza and up to 200 feet at its maximum depth. Only the tops of four lone palm trees on the plaza protruded from the surface. Everywhere blocks of ice emerged from the blackish pastelike matter. It seemed only a second, one survivor said, from the moment Huascarán exploded "like a white rose scattering its petals to the air" until Yungay was covered by an immense black mantle.

So extraordinary was this avalanche that geologists Ericksen,

Plafker, and Fernández wrote: "Conceivably, such an event may not occur again for thousands of years."

IN Yungay, only some 200 people survived. Ironically, the life that stirred was at the town cemetery and at a circus. The cemetery is a circular terraced hill, constructed on a pre-Inca ruin, its burial niches built into its five tiers. There ninety-two people scrambled to safety on the upper tiers. On the fringes of town, at the opposite side of Yungay from the cemetery, mostly children attending the circus that afternoon were spared. The circus had been set up on a soccer field. The cutting edge of the alluvion ran just past a goal.

With few other exceptions—the narrow slip of land called Aura extending out from the Shacsha ridge, where the man and his son had been waiting for a bus that Sunday, and another high place called Cochawaín, at the edge of the center—Yungay, which people called the jewel of the Callejón, lay cold and still under the mud and ice.

As time passed and the sun melted the ice and dried the mud, cadavers emerged. The scattered boulders that Huascarán had hurled down seemed larger as the mud subsided around them. Eventually, baked by the sun, the alluvionic debris turned into a gray-white powder, cratered and pocked like the surface of the moon. The lunarlike plain became known simply as the playa ("the beach"). The avalanche had surpassed in magnitude the eruption of Vesuvius in the year A.D. 79 that buried the city of Pompeii. Like that ancient city, the Yungay playa was also left undisturbed.

ABOVE Ranrahirca, at an altitude of 8,600 feet on the Cordillera Negra, with a bearing of fifty-five degrees into the face of Huascarán, lies the village of Matacoto. At three o'clock on the afternoon of May 31, 1970, a group of men were preparing to install a new door on the church of their patron saint, John the Baptist. They had taken the image of the saint down from its niche and placed it on a platform so that their patron could witness the festivities celebrating this occasion.

At this moment, the shaking began, slowly at first, then violently until everything fell, church and houses. Dust from the crumbling adobes and landslides from the surrounding mountains masked the village. Then the noise began, a different noise from the slow rumble of the earthquake, a deafening noise, more like that of a thousand airplanes, that grew louder with each passing second. Without being able to see through the blinding dust, people knew that Huascarán was plummeting headlong down the Llanganuco valley. Though the thought that the avalanche could climb up the Cordillera Negra and reach Matacoto never occurred to them, nevertheless, everyone, except one elderly man, fled up into the mountains, even as fissures in the earth opened and shut along the slopes.

The one man, Don Pedro, knelt and prayed, and then he began to feel his way down the foothills to try to see the avalanche he knew was careening down the Cordillera Blanca toward the Santa. He could still see nothing, and the augmenting roar, coming closer and closer, sent him running back up toward Matacoto. By his own account, he reached the village plaza only two or three steps before the alluvial debris swept onto the plaza, depositing there a tremendous boulder the size of a house, before it stopped.

A turbulent wind knocked Don Pedro to the ground, leaving him wounded and bloody. Alone, everyone else in the upper mountains, he began to cry, thinking of a hamlet directly opposite Matacoto on the Cordillera Blanca, where a close companion lived. He knew now that that hamlet had been effaced. As best he could, he made himself a bed next to the mud and the huge boulder that sat in the plaza. By dawn, villagers were making their way down again to Matacoto. They began to dig out the dead who had been trapped in the earthquake.

Still, and for three days longer, the Matacotans could not see either Yungay or Ranrahirca and did not suspect that Yungay was buried. The bridge over the Río Santa was gone; they were cut off completely. In their minds, however, they held one image, indelibly engraved on January 10, 1962, when an avalanche off Huascarán destroyed Ranrahirca. Because that 1962 avalanche had not been triggered by an earthquake, little dust had obstructed the Matacoto villagers' view. From their vantage point on the Cordillera Negra, they had watched the inhabitants of Ranrahirca running toward the banks of the Santa in a desperate effort to cross the river before the avalanche that flew at their heels reached them. But the Ranrahircans found that the bridge had already been carried away in the turbulence of the river. They embraced each other as the avalanche tossed them into the Santa and swept them downstream. In 1962, the force of the avalanche had not been strong enough to defy gravity, and the Cordillera Negra remained untouched.

Now, in 1970, after three days, as the atmosphere began to clear, the Matacoto survivors saw that Yungay was buried. In disbelief, their eyes gazed upon the scar at Huascarán's north summit, "where ice was missing." Though a sadness even greater than that of 1962 filled their hearts, they knew that had a lobe of the avalanche not been diverted to Yungay, had all of it come down through Ranrahirca, as it had in 1962, this time the hamlets of the Cordillera Negra would have totally disappeared.

A day or two after the avalanche, the Matacotans noticed with astonishment that the huge boulder that had come to rest in the midst of their town appeared smaller. As one day followed another, their suspicions were confirmed. The "boulder" was no boulder at all. It was a block of ice that had broken from the face of Huascarán and, spearheading the avalanche, had traveled eleven miles, leaving Ranrahirca in its wake and continuing to roll across the Río Santa until it had climbed 230 feet up the side of the Cordillera Negra, coming to rest in the middle of their town plaza.

THE ninety-two people who took refuge on the cemetery mound were dwarfed by a colossal concrete image of Christ, sixty feet tall, that stands on the highest tier, arms outstretched toward the Cordillera Blanca. This Christ image had been erected by the people of Yungay in 1962 in gratitude for having been spared when the avalanche from Huascarán's same Glacier 511 buried neighboring Ranrahirca and its 4,000 inhabitants. Later that year, in eerie portent, a *National Geographic* article stated: "No one knows when the mountain will again conjure the fatal formula that sends ice and snow crashing into the valley. Mighty Huascarán . . . keeps counsel only with itself. They say the Huascarán is a villain who may yet have more to say."

A survivor described his flight toward the cemetery as a man running from the angry bellows of a thousand stampeding bulls. As the avalanche engulfed those still racing toward the mound and those who had barely reached the lower tiers, their cries ceased like the snuffing out of a candle. Striking the base of the cemetery, survivors said, the avalanche reared up into a wall of ice, rock, and mud twice the height of the cemetery hill itself. The Christ image swayed. A unanimous scream went up from those who had gained precarious purchase on the upper tiers as they waited for the wall of debris to curl down upon them. But suddenly the massive wall deflated and slipped around the cemetery, leaving it like an atoll in a high sea. Through the night, as aftershocks caused rock masses from the mountains to drop off into ravines with crunching sounds that echoed in the dark, the image of Christ would also move, threatening to fall on the handful of survivors.

The night passed like an apocalypse. Their clothes ripped from them, the ninety-two shivered in the ashen cold, some wrapped in the vestments of the dislodged dead, unable to see anything around them but the oceanic mantle of ice and mud. Some threatened to hurl themselves down into the oozing mass in a futile attempt to search out family who had not reached the cemetery in time. When total darkness came, their intense feeling of having survived "alone" was relieved in some measure as they began to see a few lights flickering dimly in hamlets on the Cordillera Negra. By the following morning, for sustenance they had begun to suck the gummy liquid of the prickly pear that grows on the cemetery knoll. With daylight, the oceanic mantle was still palpitating, as one man said, "like a lion panting after having devoured its prey."

Later, as the sun began to penetrate the dust-laden clouds, they noted an area behind the cemetery hill that appeared not to be as deep with mud. It led to the area north of the cemetery, called Cochawaín, that had not been buried. An anguished discussion ensued over whether to remain on the hill until help might arrive or to risk an escape. Survivors from a nearby hamlet and those of Cochawaín who had escaped the earthquake began to extend eucalyptus trunks over the mud to provide a walkway to those stranded on the cemetery hill, who, in their turn, laid down coffin boards from the broken niches. After long deliberation, the majority elected to undertake the exodus. A few, among them the two geophysicists, chose to remain.

Even after the decision to leave had been made, still they vacillated as they watched the improvised bridge of trunks and coffin boards shift unsteadily at the slightest movement. They hesitated to leave behind the injured who could not walk. On the other hand, they knew it would be days before the debris would harden enough to be safely traversed.

Finally, a youth grabbed up three small children and took the first steps out onto the walkway. One of the children fell into the alluvial mud. As all looked on, the child began to sink "as if swallowed up in the jaws of a wild beast." As the mud began to smother the child's cries, another youth stepped out onto the trunk and managed to yank the child out by his hair. The child's being saved, even at the last moment, animated the others and gave them courage. One by one, they began to cross the makeshift bridge, looking down into the sea of mud, from which protruded naked bodies, some decapitated, and arms and legs. The nearby river's banks were strewn with the dead borne on the avalanche.

At Cochawaín, those who escaped from the cemetery were united with the survivors of that high ground and a mound of cadavers that had been cast ashore or pulled from the surrounding debris. Observing that a Peruvian flag was still flying on that spared patch of Yungay, they set about to deal with their wounds and fractures and to try to improvise a way to carry the gravely injured off the cemetery. Eventually, Indian peasants from the Cordillera Negra hamlets and survivors from Mancos, a town south of Ranrahirca, who found a route over the mountains, would reach the group at Cochawaín with food and blankets.[1]

That first night, a handful of *Yungaínos*, who outran the avalanche to the outskirts of the center, and pockets of survivors from nearby towns and hamlets made their way to an area called Pashulpampa, just north of the city. There, in the lee of a hill called Atma, which eventually rises to 13,000 feet, they felt shielded from Huascarán. They began to build cornstalk lean-tos. As the months and years went by, the gentle foothills of Atma would become the site of tents, straw-mat shacks, the prefabricated shelters of the camp called Yungay Norte, and finally, of the new city of Yungay.

PEOPLE told me that when the avalanche had passed, the clowns and the children gathered themselves up, with whatever equipment they could salvage. Since they could not cross the alluvion, which would remain for some time like quicksand before the sun baked it solid, they climbed first a nearby foothill and from there made their way higher into the Cordillera Blanca. Bedraggled from their march across terrain that still quivered like an animal recently killed, after about a week the circus survivors descended from the mountains into Huaraz. A woman said she had seen them come through

Huaraz and they were sadder than almost anything or anyone she
had ever seen before. She recalled that the night before the earthquake, the circus was in Huaraz and she had gone to see them
perform. She mimicked a clown who kept saying, "How pretty,
isn't it?" Late that night, the circus performers moved on to Yungay
and set up their tent on the soccer field. "Circus people are so long-
suffering," the woman said with a sigh, "so sad, and yet they try
to make us happy."

In mid-July 1972, the same circus returned to Huaraz for the
first time since they had played there the night before the disaster.
I could see the circus people setting up their tent right outside my
window on the pampa. Of animals, they brought only two little
brown bears, which were kept in a cage outside the tent. For the
rest, the animals that always crossed the pampa—sheep, pigs, donkeys, cows—simply strolled in and out, under the tent, as if walking
onstage and offstage. Adults and children filled the tent at every
performance, but as each day passed, the already worn tent became
even more tattered by the afternoon winds. One morning I noticed
a big tear. On that afternoon, the wind and dust blew more and
more furiously, loosening the tent from its moorings. I watched
from my window as the circus people struggled to right the tent
and anchor it down. But with each new rip the winds penetrated
the tent, until finally, after one great heave, it tumbled down on
top of everyone. They repaired the tent as best they could, and
late into August I could hear from inside my room the plaintive
sounds of the circus trumpet emanating from the tent.

I first saw the Yungay playa on November 8, 1971, a year and a
half after the avalanche. It was quiet, a sepulchral quiet, and the
air was like a soft caress. A sign on the road that wound around
the playa into Yungay Norte, the survivor encampment, read that
animals and vehicles must stay on the road and not traverse the
alluvial plain itself.

Hundreds of small wooden crosses, some painted blue, some
white, and some black, some crudely carved in memory of parents
or children, with wreaths hung on them, were stuck into the hardened debris. The crosses marked the places where survivors reckoned that relatives had lived or where they were when the debris
wave hit. Some of the wreaths had been freshly placed; others had

already withered in the midday sun. A large black wooden cross dominated the others. It was dedicated "To all the parents, from all the orphans," the children who had been at the circus.

My eyes followed the alluvial material up to the empty space in Glacier 511. A sun ray bouncing off the glacier filtered through the tiny crosses, creating latticework shadows on the gray-white powder. A dilapidated bus named *Mala Noche* ("Bad Night") stopped along the road. Descending from the bus, an Indian woman wearing a derby felt hat that identified her as a native of the nearby town of Mancos trotted barefoot across the sun-baked sea of rock and mud, all the while spinning yarn. She carried in her shawl a tiny wreath, which she placed on one of the small wooden crosses. I looked back toward the Christ figure and up again to the top of Huascarán.

Still in November, I traveled again to the playa, this time with two Protestant missionaries. It was the first time I would go up toward Huascarán's peak. From the playa, we turned off on the narrow road to Llanganuco, where two glacial lakes, Huarmicocha and Orkococha, nestle at 12,000 feet, between Huandoy and Huascarán. The road to Llanganuco passed through green countryside, which was like an unsevered artery coursing its way up the mountain, connecting the valley floor to Huascarán. All around, on the foothills and over the valley floor, lay, some nine feet deep, the chalky alluvial powder.

The rainy season had begun, but the weather held out, since we had gotten an early start. It was cold and crisp, and the lakes shone like brilliant emeralds in the sunlight. Against the blue-green water was the orange-colored papery bark of the gnarled trunks and branches of *quinual* trees.

Don Alejandro, a man perhaps in his late fifties, was the warden, or guardian, of the two lakes. He lived alone in a little shack behind a cabin used by engineers of the Santa Corporation, which oversaw the morainal lakes and kept tabs on the hazardous buildup of ice on the summits. Don Alejandro's duties were to check the water levels in the lakes and watch the glaciers for changes in configuration, alerting the Santa engineers below if there was danger.

When we got down from the jeep, Alejandro greeted us with a broad smile. Short and stocky, he was wearing an Indian *chulo*, the colorful woolen cap with flaps that cover the ears and a point at the crown. We handed him our letter of introduction from Benjamín Morales, the director of the Santa Corporation. He could not read it, but held it reverently as it was read to him, and then he tucked it into his pocket. Alejandro welcomed visitors to break the loneliness of his solitary vigil, but he liked them to come officially, with proper documents.

We had brought a lunch and sat down by the table in the cabin to eat. Don Alejandro would not sit down with us; rather, he preferred to take the food we shared with him out back to his shack. From time to time he returned with a bucket of water from the lake, a fresh fish, or water he had boiled for our tea.

Risking feeling like an intruder, I went to talk to him, having to duck in order to enter his tiny doorway. It was black and smoky inside as he hovered over a grate, frying fish. He seemed so utterly alone there, near the top of Huascarán. In halting Quechuized Spanish, he told me he was from the hamlet of Washua, one of the many small *caseríos* on the slopes of Huascarán. Then he added impassively, "The avalanche carried away my house and my wife. Not a trace did it leave. There was air, wind, much wind, uprooting the trees. It came with such a noise, such a big noise. Two carloads of picnickers from Mancos were buried, along with gringos, not very old and not very young. One never knows up here if or when he will return to his house."

Don Alejandro and I did not talk anymore about the avalanche on that first visit. Rather, he told me about remedies for the cold of the mountain that works its way into the body.

The missionaries and I climbed about halfway to the snow line, at some 14,500 feet. Orchids bloomed among the rocks. We slid back down, gathered up our luncheon remains, and got into the jeep. One of the missionaries told Don Alejandro he would bring him a Bible on the next trip. Alejandro nodded assent and smiled his great broad smile as we drove away.

On our descent to Yungay, the alluvial debris flanking us, carrying us down into the outstretched arms of the Christ image, the missionary said, "They built the Chirst in gratitude, yes, but they built it not as we Protestants would build it, with hands facing inward, in a position of welcome, of receiving. They built it with hands facing outward, telling Christ to stop any avalanche, and he failed."

The majority of survivors who spoke of the Christ figure did not think that he had failed but that he had miraculously saved himself in the final moment, as the alluvion lapped at the cemetery, and had also saved them, wherever they were, miraculously. Rather than arrogantly commanding Huascarán to hold back, as the North American missionary had implied, Christ's hands were meant to bless Huascarán. Andean people often make soft benedictory gestures with their hands when they mean to appease.

IT had been Alejandro and another guardian of the glacial lakes who, four days after the disaster, on June 4, 1970, managed to reach the Santa Corporation in Huaraz, traveling along the ledges and paths of the high cordillera like the circus people, and bring the alarming news that an enormous piece of rock was obstructing the drainage of Lake Orkococha. The lake was swelling ominously. The wardens had also brought the news that the entire Czechoslovakian mountain-climbing expedition—fourteen climbers—one Chilean climber (the gringos Alejandro had referred to), and fifteen people from Mancos who were picnicking with the mountaineers, had perished. Not many days before the disaster, a Czech climber had fallen to his death, and as was the custom of the valley people, the Mancos townspeople had gone to offer their condolences to the foreign alpinists.

It was not until Friday, June 5, that the helicopter *Alouette III* landed near Huaraz and Benjamín Morales was able to fly over Yungay and Ranrahirca. The helicopter landed first on the soccer field at the edge of Yungay. The debris was still soft. Taking off again, they flew up toward Huascarán and landed on the banks of Lake Orkococha, right by the side of what had been the camp of the Czechoslovakian mountain climbers. Floating in the lake were blue sleeping bags, a jacket, and pieces of supply cases. Benjamín retrieved the jacket and a sleeping bag and put them in the helicopter. Then they measured the height between the surface of the lake and the top of the debris and calculated that 15 million cubic meters of water were damming up, sufficient to produce a new disaster. It would not take much time for the water to reach the top and overflow.

By Sunday, June 7, mountain climbers from New Zealand, Chile, the United States, and Japan, who had landed at Jorge Chávez Airport in Lima, were quickly dispatched to Llanganuco to cut an escape channel. Benjamín remembers wondering what further harm could befall the valley below even if Orkococha did burst. There were camps of survivors being set up on the edges of Ranrahirca, and a new alluvion could take that path or a path through Indian hamlets that had not been erased on May 31. But, mainly, Benjamín knew that, psychologically, it was important that *nothing* further happen. All in all, ten brigades were organized to visit the lakes and glaciers that were most threatening the valley.

Awareness of the glacial lakes had increased a thousandfold from ordinary times. People would tell me how they lived with eyes peeled on and ears tuned to the high cordillera. It was the custom that church bells be rung to warn them of an alluvion, but now no bells were left hanging to ring.

BY the next time I went to Llanganuco, well into the rainy season of 1971–72, grass was pushing its way up through the alluvial debris, as if asserting life on the playa. The mountains were loose from the rains, and many small mud slides, called *huaycos*, along the road made the climb difficult. We passed hamlets with round thatch-roof houses built in the Inca style and black cows sniffing out a blade of grass on the whitish alluvial silt. One hamlet had been bisected by the avalanche. Ours was the only vehicle on the road. Occasionally, a train of burros being packed over to the valley of Conchucos would nudge us close to the mountain wall.

At the pass, which is the entrance to the north peak of Huascarán, all of a sudden an enormous rock face was towering above us, perpendicular to our jeep, now just a speck crawling alongside the rock slab. In crevices of the rock slab, *machay*, a plant used to decorate big wooden crosses that guard the mountain passes, was growing.

It was nearing dark as we drove up to the Santa Corporation's cabin. The lake waters were a deep blue. The cabin looked minuscule, like a matchbox lying between the sheer rock faces of Huascarán and Huandoy. I realized how hemmed in we were when a shapeless fog suddenly swept up from below and became densely packed as it was channeled between the two imposing mountain slabs.

I was eager to see Don Alejandro again. I had begun to think of him as my intercessor with the mountain. He again showed great pleasure with our letter from below, giving us permission to spend the night in the cabin. After dark, I went out to take him some beans we had cooked. I called from the fence outside his shelter. As he approached in the swirling fog, I could only hear his voice and see the barest outlines of his stocky body. Not until we stood very close together could I see his face, its furrows even deeper with worry. He said he was spending the night outdoors because there were "audacious people" below. He could see their flashlights flickering around the bends on the mountain paths. I asked him what their purpose was, and he said they were driving cattle across the pass to the valley of Conchucos. They were "bad people" trying to get their cattle out before the agrarian reform would take over their haciendas. They might enter the cabin to harm us. I kept the news Alejandro had given me from my companions and fell asleep wrapped in heavy blankets in a rocking chair in front of the blazing fire.

After a cleansing night of rain and fog, the dawn was brilliant, the lakes once again blue-green in the morning sun. Don Alejandro and I sat on two straight-back chairs, looking into the great mountain. We sat erect, as it did not seem proper to slouch in the face of Huascarán. My tape recorder rested on my lap, but neither of us paid any attention to it.

Alejandro told me that Huascarán is *cerro imán* ("magnetic mountain"). Through underground tunnels, Huascarán is linked to Cuzco, the ancient Inca capital, magnetic center of the universe. He spoke of the power of the mountain's magnetizing force. My eyes scanned the rock face of Huascarán Norte up to the top of the continent. Indeed, it felt as if we might fall off the globe were it not for the sheer spine of the mountain confronting us, rising yet another 10,000 feet above where we sat, already 12,000 feet above the level of the sea. No other glacial summit in the world towers so close over human settlements.

On the return trip to Yungay, we gave a lift to a man who had been with the Czechoslovakian mountain climbers minutes before the earthquake began. He had gone to ask the Czech doctor, a member of the team, to come to treat his sick child. The doctor promised to come along later, and the man returned to his house. Just as he reached his house, he saw the two Llanganuco lakes curl up, "form into two balls, and the earth opened between them. Then

it was like the sky and mountains falling all around. There was no
shouting, nor could I see because of the dust. We were not conscious
of anything anymore. It seemed like the end of the world. We were
paralyzed. We were half-dead."

Finally, he asked his wife, "Have all these things happened
only up here?" and they started down to Yungay. "Down there,"
he told us, "they were all buried, the naked dead. Only in the
cemetery and the circus did they save themselves. . . . There is
nothing on the mountainside now, not even salt. That is why I
must go down."

Back on the road that winds through the playa, we were hailed
down by a man in a crumpled uniform. He was familiar to my
companions as the guard they called *el loco* ("the crazy one"). As
soon as he had settled in the jeep, he began speaking as if under
great pressure to tell his story. He had returned to Yungay from
the coast five days after the avalanche to find that his entire family
had disappeared. "The dogs were eating the dead," he said, and so
he took upon himself the task of burying 6,892 cadavers that had
emerged from the mud, all the while searching for his own family.
He had counted them, writing the names of those he recognized
in a little notebook. In what is no doubt an exaggeration caused by
his gruesome ordeal, he told us he had reckoned that 51,000 "souls"
were in Yungay that Sunday and that, besides, the alluvion had
carried off twenty-two hamlets in its downslope path. He recited
the names of the hamlets, as he had done perhaps a hundred times
before, as if by keeping track of them, appointing himself their
historian, he could prevent their being forgotten.

Yungaínos respected him, though it was common knowledge
that he had never recovered from the experience. He remained
nearby, wandering across the playa on foot and hitching rides back
and forth on the road that traverses it, retelling over and over again
his story. When we neared the edge of the playa, he asked to get
out and continued his pilgrimage on foot across the avalanche. After
he had gone some distance, he turned around and waved as he
shouted back at us, "This is Yungay, just this!" The survivor camps
did not exist for him. He had sentenced himself to the holy ground,
to watching over the dead. Often he and the Christ image were
alone on the playa.

———

ONE group of survivors had settled in tents, then in corrugated tin shelters, at Tingua, a village south of Ranrahirca and Mancos. It was strange to see there, at some distance from the playa, a sign on the road that read Welcome to Yungay. Most of those who considered themselves "true" *Yungaínos*, from the town itself, went just north of the playa, to Pashulpampa, where they were now living in the one-quarter-inch-thick pressboard shelters called *módulos*. The barrackslike camp was named Yungay Norte. This camp was considered to be the "true" Yungay, and its occupants did not like the qualifier "North." At first the camp numbered only some 200 or so, but by 1971, its population had grown to almost 2,000. People from surrounding hamlets, especially Indians from the upper parts of the mountains, had come down, and entrepreneurs of the disaster had come from outside the valley to set up small businesses. A market was located along one side of the road, and small shops and improvised restaurants made of straw mats or woven split cane along the other side. The *módulos*, where people slept, were in the foothills of Atma hill, where "true" survivors, the *Yungaínos*, wanted Yungay to be rebuilt. Those encamped in Tingua or elsewhere would simply have to move back.

The feeling was that there must be only one Yungay, though geologists and other experts from outside the valley were arguing that there should be a number of settlements located at various places that were considered by them to be safe from avalanches. The *Yungaínos* wanted to be as close as possible to the alluvial scar. With the passing months, and years, the feeling grew that Yungay should even be rebuilt in the very same place. There was an overwhelming desire to live with the dead, to be able readily to go and mourn over the small crosses on the *playa de los muertos*. Sweeping his arm across the panorama of the playa, one survivor exclaimed, "Here there is life!"[2]

IT had not been long after the avalanche, as soon as it was realized that the dead were already buried by several feet of alluvial debris, that the playa was declared *Campo Santo* ("Holy Ground") and was made a national cemetery. It was envisioned that a chapel would be built near the four exposed tops of the palm trees and would become a national monument.

When I first saw the playa, it was still strewn with huge boul-

ders, one weighing 14,000 tons, another 7,000 tons. There were
only the palm crowns, a tiny rustic chapel constructed of palm
fronds, the vast gray whiteness dotted with small wooden crosses,
and exposed sections of a bus and a truck that had been surprised
that Sunday in mid-passage. And there was not a blade of grass.
Later, in 1972, as the national airline SATCO began official bi-
weekly flights to the Callejón, boulders from the playa were dy-
namited and fragments transported in trucks to Anta to make the
airstrip. These blasts on the mute playa disturbed survivors, who
said that all should be left as it was, every last rock, as a witness
to that day. Besides, some jeered, Huascarán might get angry at
the destruction of its boulders and toss down more.

By the end of the rainy season, in May 1972, as it became
clear that Yungay would never be rebuilt in its exact same place,
the vision that roses, jasmine, and lilies should be cultivated in
perpetuity on the playa began to take shape.

ONE late night, during the heavy rains, the *colectivos* had stopped
running, and I was not able to hitch a ride from Yungay Norte
back to Huaraz. Finally, after I had been in the road for almost an
hour, a bus came along. I sat in front, right behind the driver. As
we crossed the playa, lightning striking all around us, suddenly the
driver proclaimed loudly: "Don't think you've been spared because
you are alive after the alluvion. Right here and now we are all going
to die. When Huascarán is bitter, it does not respect even Yungay."

I wondered if it would respect the dead of the Holy Ground,
and I wondered where the crazed guard had taken refuge in the
storm. I never lost the feeling that I was pressing my luck every
time I went to Yungay and always breathed easier when we came
out on the other side of the playa. These thoughts must have occurred to others, for invariably, as bus or jeep or *colectivo* began to
cross the playa, chattering would stop, and everyone would fall
silent. During the silences of those crossings, though, almost always
someone would express one of these thoughts, usually in a whisper,
sometimes jarringly, as on that stormy night. To some extent, it
was like that in the whole valley. The atmosphere was one of
expectancy. The inescapable presence of the event made merely
being there, alive, a kind of living on the edge.

Five

IN THE GRAVEST OF
LANDSCAPES

*Often, here at 10,000 feet, destruction
everywhere, walled by icy spires and massive folds, I think of your phrase "In the
gravest of landscapes."*

from a letter to a friend in Spain

I HAD NOT KNOWN the Callejón prior to the disaster. In the
months before I left for the field, I tried to find out as much
as I could about what it was like afterward. But this was not
easy. Even after I arrived in Lima, I could learn very little of what
was happening in the valley, now sixteen months later. It seemed
that the news from there had dissipated along with the cloud of
dust that had hung for weeks over the valley following the earthquake.

In October 1971, after about ten days in Lima, I left at dawn
one morning in a car shared with four Andean peasants who carried
blankets ready to throw over them when we reached the high altitude. The eeriness of the coastal desert strip from Lima to Pativilca
was dispelled briefly in Barranca, where we stopped for breakfast.
There the noise, expansiveness, and urban decay of small coastal

towns erupted out of the midst of the desert wasteland. At Pativilca, we turned upward toward the Callejón. Before long, we began to meet cattle, sheep, and goats on the narrow dirt road. At Chasquitambo, some 3,000 feet high, we took in the last breath of warm coastal air. From there on, we retreated further and further into silence and austerity, where few amusements distract from the land around and where poverty is of a different sort from that of the coast. It comes from the starkness of the land rather than from the decaying profusion of man-made objects.

Because the Pativilca road was single-laned, the chauffeur had to make intricate maneuvers in order to get around the big trucks, all with names like Condor of Chavín or Lord of Solitude, making their way down to the coast. Occasionally, our back wheels hung at the edge of a cliff.

By the time we reached the puna at 14,000-foot Lake Conococha, it was late afternoon and raining. One by one, in the thinness of the atmosphere, the passengers nodded off to sleep. My head was thick and fuzzy, but I tried to stay awake, uneasy, keeping a close eye on the chauffeur, who never spoke a word. We descended from the puna into Cátac, at 12,000 feet.

Nothing was left of the adobe town of Cátac. It had become a small encampment of corrugated tin buildings that I learned were as hot as irons in the noonday sun and turned into cold slabs in the frosty sierra nights. Survivors used these buildings as shops, where you could buy supplies like soap, candles, and matches and drink coffee from tin cups. They preferred to sleep in sheltered places and caves in the foothills. A fellow passenger commented, "Not even pigs sleep in these *calaminas*," as the tin structures were called.

All the towns we passed through from Conococha to Huaraz looked deserted. Signs of destruction were everywhere, in rubble heaps and in wide gaps in the walls of dwellings lining the narrow streets, all giving a feeling of desolation and abandonment. When we reached Huaraz, at dusk, the driver diverted from the main road across the pampa to a road along the Río Santa and deposited me on the steps of the Hotel de Turistas in Centenario.

A bout of altitude sickness in the first days after my arrival brought about a felicitous meeting with one of the four FAO (the food and agriculture branch of the United Nations) engineers who had come to the valley as part of the relief effort. Ted had heard that a gringa was sick in the Hotel de Turistas. So he appeared in my room at the hotel carrying a box of instant mashed potatoes. In those early days, it was hard to find a place to eat, to know what to eat, and a box of golden nuggets could not have been more welcome. The FAO engineers, one Italian, one Chilean, one Bolivian, and Ted, North American, became a mainstay in emergencies, especially if I needed to travel, because they had jeeps and themselves would ply the valley in connection with their various projects.

I remained in the tourist hotel for less than a week. With the help of a man from Lima who worked with Communal Development, a small group that had established itself in the valley after the disaster, I was able to find a room in what had been a wealthier household in the higher parts of the barrio of San Francisco. From there I explored the other towns on the valley floor, and the hamlets on the mountainsides, in an effort to choose an appropriate place to work. My thinking back in the United States had been to find a hamlet somewhere in the foothills, probably of Huaraz. The population should be small and circumscribed, I reckoned at that time, where I could study what changes attributable to the disaster might have taken place in the religious beliefs of survivors.

IT was with Ted that I made my first trip through the Callejón, trying to imagine what it must have been like before the disaster. What must have been a fairly unbroken line of adobe houses and countryside was then a line of toppled walls, wooden beams fallen like chopsticks, and survivor camps of corrugated tin and pasteboard dwellings, sent by the Organization of American States (OAS). Some camps were along the road itself, though most were set up off the valley floor in the foothills. The fields of corn and avocado looked, perhaps by contrast with the disintegrating materials, more fertile than they would have seemed before.

In the last century, the Italian scholar and traveler Antonio Raimondi, for whom the *Puya* cactus is named, coined a saying about the major towns of the Callejón:

> Recuay, *ladronera* ("den of thieves")
> Huaraz, *presunción* ("conceit")

Carhuaz, *borrachera* ("drunkenness")
Yungay, *hermosura* ("beauty")
Caraz, *dulzura* ("sweetness")

Though I never quite understood the charm it held for the people of the valley, it is the verse they most eagerly recite to strangers. It reflects their sense of humor and ease at laughing at themselves and the playful rivalry among the towns. As we traveled through the valley, I felt the disaster had given the saying an irony, especially true for Huaraz, the once haughty capital, and for Yungay, which, despite a competitiveness among the towns, the other towns recognized as the exquisite jewel of the Callejón.

Traveling north from Huaraz, at 10,000 feet, we came down first into Carhuaz, at 8,800 feet. Carhuaz was still filled with rubble. A lonely bulldozer chopped away at it. None of the other towns had undergone the infamous "removal of ruins" that took place in Huaraz to mark the first anniversary. Church towers had fallen, and their dislodged bells lay on the ground.

On the dusty, unpaved road, it was two hours to Yungay, at 8,500 feet. I have already described my first impressions of the playa. Indelible still in my mind are the hundreds of wooden crosses, casting their tiny shadows on the vast, hardened whiteness, framed by the sunlit beam of frozen Huascarán.

It took us another forty minutes to descend from the camp at Yungay Norte to 7,500-foot-high Caraz. On the road between Yungay and Caraz, my eyes were fixed on the mark engraved on the slopes of the Cordillera Negra, where the avalanche had overflowed the Río Santa channel. Caraz gave me different feelings, as if I had plunged from the upper chambers of the world. It was warm, even felt tropical. *Caracinos* joke, saying Caraz is "coast." Though heavily damaged also, compared to the other major towns Caraz seemed intact. Since I had already spent several weeks at the other end of the valley, I remember the odd sensation it was to walk on a sidewalk, to look inside a building and see a chandelier, to see activities conducted in expected places. I had grown accustomed to ruins and to the unexpected, to the face that would loom above a freestanding wall on the pampa, to donkey trains passing under the cupola of Huaraz's cathedral.

Still, the signs of disaster were there, in sights like the black "igloos" of hardened foam plastic that Germany had sent to Caraz's homeless. These shelters climbed the hillsides like giant beehives. People commented, "These 'igloos' are so warm. Why have they put them here, and the tin slabs not even pigs will sleep in at the cold end of the valley?"

Many sights along that road through the Callejón are impossible to forget. There were the upturned tombs of the cemetery near Anta. And there was the topiary art, carefully molded figures of dogs and ducks, clipped in the cypress trees of a tiny town called Toma, the fantasy of the gardener accentuated by the broken walls and rubble heaps nearby.

During those early weeks of attempting to absorb so much, I was constantly assessing towns for their appropriateness as a place in which to concentrate my fieldwork. In addition to towns along the valley floor, I made short trips up into the mountains, to *caseríos* with names like Paria, Amashca, Huánchac, and Marián and to major survivor camps like Nicrupampa and Tingua.

Before I became fully conscious of the rational and objective reasons that favored it, I had become emotionally attached to the "presumptuous" high city at the southern end of the Callejón and decided to settle there, in Huaraz. The pampa would become my vantage point from which to view the whole valley, from which I would travel back and forth and up and down, always returning to the pulseless heart of Huaraz. This was the first major change in my fieldwork plans. I could find no town or hamlet that all by itself seemed the right place to limit my work. Life in the valley flowed back and forth and up and down. The main road, the only road connecting the major towns of the valley floor, and the countless mountain paths were part of a whole. The valley itself was the protagonist.

AFTER about six weeks in the room in the barrio of San Francisco, I managed to rent a room in a house right on the pampa, in the barrio of Huarupampa. It was one of the four or five houses in the *casco urbano* that had survived the "removal of ruins" of May 31, 1971. My landlord said, "How could we lose everything of thirty years' work?" as he told me how his wife had knelt in front of the bulldozers and refused to move.

The house, a two-story adobe structure, was badly damaged.

I lived in one of two rooms that had remained intact on the second floor. The roof and walls of the other rooms had caved in. I reached my room via a staircase covered by a precarious roof. The outer wall of the staircase had become detached from the house, coming to rest about a foot away from its normal juncture with the roof. I could see the sky as I walked upstairs, usually wondering what kept the outer wall from falling completely and how the roof stayed in place. No one would inhabit a second story anymore, and people were astonished that I would do such a foolhardy thing, especially since mine were quarters that had been occupied by the nephew-priest of my landlords, who was killed in the earthquake and whose spirit might return to his room.

The simple whitewashed room had lovely qualities. Its window faced the Cordillera Blanca, and, invariably, the first thing I would do upon awakening in the mornings was to look out at Huascarán. It was sheer magic to wake up in the middle of the night and steal a look at the glaciers by the light of a full moon or to see a blizzard over San Cristóbal in the early morning. Each morning I could be sure that an immense drama would unfold in the skies that day.

One June evening at six o'clock, I was moved to record the play of light on Huaraz's peaks that I observed from my window:

> Above the trees, the foothills of the mountains are a deep mauve. A wisp of white cloud hovers between the south face of Huascarán and Chopicalqui. A puff of cloud floats over the pyramidlike point of Chopicalqui, and another cloud stretches to Hualcán. Copa is clear, and San Cristóbal dark against the fading blue of the sky. The sun is hitting Vallunaraju. Ocshapalca is black except for a sliver of glistening snow. Rima-Rima is almost dark now, like the far side of the moon. Hanging over the gorge between Rima-Rima and Chúrup is a very big, fluffy pink cloud. The deep gorges of Quilcayhuanca and Paria appear fathomless. The clouds have now lost their incandescence and look gray and lifeless against the sky, which has begun to smolder with a soft glow.

So much happened in the sky and on the pampa, there was always something to see from my window. I got to anticipate when a certain peasant would drive his oxen by my window. I grew fond of a certain black pig that lolled about outside; then I found out he was being fattened up for slaughter and had to accept his demise. I would watch family scenes take place in patches of rubble, a toddler undressed and redressed and, with great giggles from his parents, tied onto a burro. On moonless nights, as I sat by the window, I could see the big beams of the Expreso Ancash bus headlights bear down on the blackened expanse like a plane landing on a secret, darkened airstrip. To the east, on top of Rataquenua hill, by night, a neon cross illuminated a corner of the pampa.

Across the patio, downstairs, was one of the few functioning ovens of Huaraz. I would awaken in the small hours and hear the rhythmic kneading of the dough, and if I looked out the door, I saw the bakers working by candlelight and the oven fire being stoked. The kneading sounded like the low drumroll of an Indian band accompanying a religious procession on Good Friday. And late at night the chirping of the guinea pigs, which inhabited the patio, would keep me company in the solitude of that room on the pampa.

By day, donkeys would enter the patio laden with straw and wood for the oven. Early in the mornings, men would arrive on tricycles to fill their baskets with bread for the market. A steady stream of people came to buy the day's bread. I would drop down a little basket from the balcony, and my landlord would fill it with fresh hot bread for my breakfast.

I slept on a straw mattress, in a sleeping bag with a heavy woolen blanket on top. There were four hooks on which to hang my clothes, a table in front of the window, at which I wrote field notes at night by candlelight, and another low table by a cot. I felt secure in this room, especially when I could hear my landlords, an elderly couple who always spoke to each other in Quechua, chatting over their coffee in their kitchen downstairs.

WATER and sewerage lines had broken in the earthquake, and this was almost the biggest material problem for everyone. Sections of dislocated pipes protruded from the ground and coiled like snakes on the pampa. Although there was one spigot downstairs in the patio where I lived, it often failed, and we would have to go in search of water from springs or distant pipes. For days at a time there simply would be no water, and we husbanded precious droplets of rain or water that had been hoarded in thermos bottles. Whatever water came out of the scattered faucets was dirty, often actually black to the eye, and had to be boiled for a long time, especially since water boils more slowly at high altitudes.

Those few of us scattered on the pampa used washbasins and slop buckets, which would all be emptied just outside the ruined houses. Directly across from our house was an open refuse spot, used also as a public bathroom. There simply were no facilities, and people squatted where they could. Water and sewage problems did create hazardous health conditions, epidemics, and many infant deaths, particularly in the crowded survivor camps. In Nicrupampa, for example, more than a thousand people shared six outhouses at first, until they soon became unusable. Then everyone simply had to use the land and the brooks and irrigation ditches that emptied into the Quilcay or the Santa.

These conditions, as oppressive as they might sound, were ameliorated by the translucency of the atmosphere. As one of the FAO engineers said, "Take this level of unsanitary conditions in which people are forced to live now in the aftermath and move it down to hot coastal country, where organisms thrive more readily, and the surviving population would be wiped out."

There is not much wood at that altitude, and people cooked mainly with kerosene. In the rainy season, when the trucks could not make it up from the coast, long lines of people waiting to buy kerosene twined across the pampa to the market and the few other outlets. Often there was no kerosene to be had.

Besides the valley people themselves, who could make do somehow during these periods, there were still relief workers from several countries in the Callejón. They had to be fed, and some of the shanty restaurants in Centenario—*quinchas* made of walls of laced reeds and plastered mud, or structures built of corrugated tin slabs—were ingeniously operated. One proprietor, for example, had rigged himself up a stove that functioned, as he explained, on the principle of a steam engine. He carried water in buckets from the Quilcay, gathered what ingredients he could, improvised, scribbled his imaginative menu on a blackboard, and in general provided respite to foreigners in the valley.

My cooking for the year was done on a Primus stove with a single burner, which I finally mastered the art of lighting. The

Primus has a receptacle in which alcohol, in the form of a crude rum (sold, much to my surprise, at the bank), has to be heated while you pump the stove just at the precise moment to get a flame going. When the Primus broke, I borrowed a kerosene stove. Frequently, my lack of expertise with kerosene cooking caused small conflagrations, and I spent more than a few nights in despair over the amount of time sheer basic living—marketing, washing clothes, and cooking—took.

Mostly, I boiled liquids and filled thermos bottles—a standard bit of material culture in the valley—and lived on gruels, boiled potatoes, and bread. As a special treat, I learned to drop a piece of chocolate into oatmeal. Because digestion is sluggish at that altitude, you cannot eat anything heavy for hours before retiring, and fats of any kind are bad. We would have herbal teas at night, and bread. Tea brewed with coca leaves is wonderfully soporific. The last thing someone would say upon parting, as the sharp Andean night set in, was "Drink something hot for the cold."

THE native people of the Callejón de Huaylas are, for the most part, bilingual in Spanish and Quechua. Quechua, the language of the Incas and their descendants, is spoken by at least 8 million people in the Andean highlands. The Quechua of the Callejón is one of several dialects, the most prestigious of which is generally thought to be that of Cuzco, the old Inca capital. Quechua replaced many other Indian languages no longer spoken and to which we have no access. The Ancash dialect of the Callejón no doubt carries remnants from the languages of peoples more ancient than the Inca, who occupied the valley, peoples of the Chavín, Huari, and Wilkawaín cultures. More than Cuzco Quechua, the Ancash dialect is sprinkled with Spanish words to which Quechua suffixes have been attached. For example, instead of the Spanish *Quedémonos*, for "Don't go" (literally, "Let us stay"), people will say, "*Quedakushun*," using the Spanish root and adding Quechua suffixes.

Since I am fluent in Spanish, this process helped me. I had studied Quechua intensively before going to Peru, but it was the Cuzco dialect, and though I generally knew the content of conversations, I would have been lost had I not been able to use Spanish. And I would have been lost without the help of Reyna Alberto

Quito, who became my friend and companion as well as assistant. Like everyone from the towns, Reyna was bilingual in Spanish and Quechua. I met her through the FAO engineers, for whom she was working as a secretary. Our relationship deepened over the months until, during my last few months of fieldwork, we were together part of almost every day. Reyna would transcribe the tapes I was making, many of which were at least partially in Quechua. I often went for the late-afternoon snack of oatmeal, tea, and bread to her house, which was also extensively damaged. Around the table with her mother, five sisters, and nephews, we laughed and cried and spent long hours during which I learned from them much about life in the valley before and after the earthquake.

Occasionally, toward the end, Reyna and I would go out to visit informants at night. Though we carried flashlights and clung to each other, we often sank in mud or stumbled into holes and trenches. I, and certainly Reyna, never really got used to walking across the dead city, especially at night. Our laughter at our awkwardness, as natural and spontaneous as it was, sounded crushing as it echoed in the dark. Reyna never walked alone on the pampa at night. Memories would flood back, she said, of houses and people she had known, and she would begin to imagine again the lighted houses or someone coming out to talk on the street. When she left me at my stairway, I would watch her as she ran home, to the far side of Huaraz, just off the pampa, where houses still stood. All I could really see was the tiny bouncing beam of her flashlight, and she mine, as I waited; we had special signals to indicate that all was well.

During my stay in the Callejón, I met no one native to the valley who did not speak Quechua, though some were more comfortable in Spanish. On the valley floor, in the towns, both Spanish and Quechua are used by the mixed Indian and European population, who are called mestizos. Even here, however, Quechua appears to have a firmer grip than Spanish. My landlords, for instance, who would not have classified themselves as Indian, nevertheless spoke Quechua most of the time. So did Reyna and her family.

The satellite villages of the Callejón are mainly populated by descendants of the ancient Peruvian civilizations. Old people in hamlets near the valley floor may speak only Quechua, and in the higher altitudes, in villages at, say, 12,000 to 14,000 feet, everyone may be monolingual in Quechua. I remember a hamlet high on the Cordillera Blanca where only the teacher, who had come from Huaraz, spoke Spanish.

Foreigners in the valley, prior to the earthquake, included the Spanish Franciscan priests of Huarupampa barrio, the German priests of Centenario, and American Benedictines. The Franciscans had been expelled from the valley at the time of Independence, in 1826, but the order returned to Huaraz around 1900. The German priests had been in Huaraz only some twenty years. On a hill above Huaraz is Los Pinos, the Benedictine monastery and school. From their hilltop vantage point, the monks looked down in horror at the collapse of Huaraz, where they lost one of their members. Hundreds of earthquake victims are buried at Los Pinos. From a shortwave radio at the monastery, the earliest messages of destruction were relayed around the world.

One evangelical sect had been firmly rooted in Huaraz before the disaster. Its elderly North American founder still made visits to the Callejón. Mormon missionaries had also been established in the valley for several years.

More rugged in terrain and more isolated, the Callejón has never known the tourists that frequent the southern Peruvian highlands, visiting Cuzco and Machu Picchu. But there is another group of foreigners who are not strangers to the valley. These are the serious mountain climbers of the world; they come in expeditions during the dry and cold Callejón "summer," from June through August, when Lima and the coast are enveloped in mist and it is winter there. The summits of the Cordillera Blanca offer a challenge to mountaineers second only to some of the Himalayas.

From their camp high on the Cordillera Blanca, a Japanese mountaineering team captured on film the first movements of the 3,000-foot-wide and mile-long wall of ice and rock as it began its fatal journey downslope on May 31, 1970. They also saw the avalanche take the fourteen Czech climbers at their base camp near the snow line of Huascarán Norte.

In the 1972 dry season, Canadians, Japanese, Italians, and Americans made assaults on Huantsán, Hualcán, and Huascarán. The climbers took lodging in the Monterrey Hotel, five miles north of Huaraz. This hotel-spa, having withstood the earthquake, had become a refuge from the broken world outside. In the Inca tra-

dition, there are public baths at Monterrey, and the people of the
Callejón would travel there to bathe in the thermal waters. I would
go to Monterrey every ten days or so, when I longed for some
comfort and momentary escape from the disaster. After a hot mineral bath, I would sit by the fire in the hotel writing field notes
and listening to the stories of climbers who had gotten close to the
glaciers and who saw them in a different light than survivors below.

SHORTLY after the earthquake, the Callejón was inundated with
emissaries, both secular and religious, from the four corners of the
globe. Poles, Russians, the French, Cubans, North Americans,
Argentines, the Dutch—everyone came to study scientifically the
seismographic event and the geologic wonder it had produced, to
proselytize new religions, or simply to help. According to reports,
Russian doctors who had never been on horseback rode up the
mountainsides to treat peasants who had never seen a Russian. The
American Peace Corps was supplemented by some twenty-five
young people, who for weeks after their arrival would sit stunned
and in culture shock. It is one thing to move into a culture very
different from one's own and another to enter into a setting of
massive destruction.

By the time I arrived, most of the foreigners had gone, though
it was still possible to come into a hamlet and have kids surround
me shouting, "Do you want to see the Russian?" People from many
different countries, remnants of the world's task force, and Peruvian
nationals still labored under the trying conditions, still sat in the
shanty canteens trying to figure out what to do next and how to
do it. Although envoys from all over the world had come and gone,
or lingered still, a sense of cut-offness continued to exist in the
valley.

A feeling of isolation had been deep since the outset. Remember that the Caraz airport was buried by the debris flow and it took
almost two weeks to complete the strip at Anta so that supplies
could be flown into the valley and the injured evacuated to hospitals
on the coast, among which was the medical ship *Hope*, which had
docked offshore at Chimbote. Because the valley was wrapped in
a blanket of dust, four days passed before helicopters were able to
fly over and drop goods and paratroopers onto the mountain slopes.

Now, sixteen months later, the first year's flurry of attention
had ended. Those relatives from the coast who had made the Her-

culean trek on foot up the landslide-strewn roads from Pativilca
and Casma had returned to the lowlands. Bulldozers had carted off
the rubble of Huaraz but did not return. With plans for reconstruction stalled and only a token contingent of CRYRZA located
in the valley, the alienation from the rest of the country grew even
more intense. It was as if the valley were a spaceship, hanging
there, disconnected from the world below. One of the Franciscan
priests described survivors as "unhinged." It was as if time, too,
had stopped on May 31, 1970, and when I entered the Callejón, it
was into another time dimension. The rest of the earth turned on
its axis and revolved around the sun, but the valley remained perfectly poised and still, awaiting reentry into the workings of the
universe. Sometimes it seemed as if some nuclear war had left us
all, survivors and the remaining outsiders, stranded up there. Was
anyone alive below, and would they remember to look for us?

Contributing to the isolation, the winter rains blocked off the
valley entirely for weeks at a time. With few vehicles circulating
and none going up and down the mountains to the coast because
the roads were closed, Huaraz was more desolate than ever. There
were lines for sugar and no eggs at all. You had to get papers from
the PIP, the Peruvian secret police, in order to be allotted a ration
of kerosene or gasoline.

With the tenacious rains, isolation, and mourning renewed
with each fresh loss—a young engineer struck by lightning, vehicles
plunging over the mountainsides, someone brought down off a
mountain dead—depression pervaded the valley that winter season
of 1971–72. "*Yo tengo pena*," they would say in Spanish, or in
Quechua, "*Llaquinami*" ("I have pain, grief, sorrow, affliction"). The
birds were suffering, the rocks, the shattered religious images, the
mountains, I was told. "The sun and the moon share our pain,"
one man said. Another word that described the feeling of individuals, and of the collectivity, was *Quelamihuaqarqan*, which in Quechua means that the spirit is fragile and the body uneasy. There is
no interest in eating or drinking, and besides, the body feels a
premonition of something ominous. This feeling, some said, had
begun even days before the earthquake and continued still.

YET there was joy and laughter, laughter different in the highlands
than on the coast, quieter, turned inward, stifled by hands that
rush to cover the mouth. It is a myth, almost a cliché, that Andean

peoples are "closed," suspicious, even disagreeable. Underneath a taciturn exterior, braced against the *penas* of the Andes—hail, frost, scarcity of food, and premature death—lies a cauldron of mirth and humor. It revealed itself even in the aftermath of disaster.

I was privy to this mirth, especially in the women, and if I had other lives, I would choose to live one as a Quechua woman. Their multiple brightly colored skirts swished across the pampa and up and down the mountain paths, and listening closely, you could hear the tinkle of their jewelry. I would praise their thick black braids, and they would answer in kind about my blondness —*shumaq peka* ("pretty head"). We would talk of exchanging heads and giggle at each other, sometimes from one hilltop to another, for no reason at all, except perhaps the recognition of something shared beneath such different exteriors. I would turn a corner at the market, and they would laugh as they sat over their little knolls of potatoes and ask if I wanted to have their suckling babes. Sometimes they would threaten an older child who was misbehaving with "Do you want the gringa to take you?" Everywhere I was called *mamita*, as all females, from very young on, are considered mothers. As I approached hamlets in the foothills of Huaraz, I would hear shouts passed from woman to woman in their fields, "*Gringa karamushqa!*" ("The gringa is coming!")

Irony and pluck would appear out of the blue. Like the green shoots that pushed their way through the alluvial debris of Yungay, they would pierce the timorous uneasiness of *Quelamihuaqarqan.* For instance, the sardonic story circulated that a man shaving ice for snowballs alongside the road in Yungay Norte, when asked what he was doing, replied, "Here, avenging myself on the Huascarán." During the worst of the rainy season, people made jokes: "We are going to have to put up a tent over the whole Callejón."

There was the joy of new beginnings, the first time that there was school again, with desks scattered about under the eucalyptus; or that a movie was shown in Huaraz in a corrugated tin building named Soraya, for the owner's lost daughter; or that carnival could take place again after a suspension of all festivities for a year.

By February 2, 1972, the carnival season had begun. Bands had played the night before, and I had awakened to see fireworks cascading outside my window. The marketplace was filled with an atmosphere of fiesta. Colored paper cutouts hung from the stalls.

Elaborate arrays of snake and lizard skins and herbal remedies were set out by "witch doctors," Indians up from the eastern *montaña* rain forest. Natural dyes in dazzling hues were piled in neat little mounds. Sheep's heads stared up from tables, challenging their purchase and preparation in a "head broth" (*caldo de cabeza*). Two little girls stood at the edge of the market, coaxing a performance from a puppy they had trained to dance. A woman switched a donkey through the narrow lane between market stands, dodging small boys who splashed water on each other. "They're starting to play," she muttered.

Again, the day the first fallen church bell in Huaraz was hoisted and rung was a day of jubilation among the ruins. Not a church bell in all the valley had remained in its belfry, and the Soledad bell, too, lay on the ground. It was decided that Soledad's bell should be the first to ring out after the earthquake. The Indian peasants, who had always claimed a special closeness to the Señor de la Soledad ("Lord of Solitude"), would raise the bell. They came down from the mountainsides with candles, flowers, drums, flutes, and trumpets.

The work was directed by a tiny wrinkled old woman who lived in a tin shelter back of the church. She was dressed all in black and wore a cream-colored hat with a black band. It was amazing to see such energy spring from the diminutive woman. She darted here and there, up and down the knoll on which the Soledad temple stood, summoning now one Indian band, now another, silencing some and directing others to play, commanding a horn to be blown or a drum to be beaten.

She called for ropes to hoist the bell and stones to hammer into the ground a frame of logs from which the bell would hang. "Straighter, straighter, straighter. No, farther back, back, back," she shouted in Quechua as they tried to stand the frame in the ground. She ordered the Soledad priest to find some kind of ladder. "You know we have nothing," he said. "The earthquake has leveled us." Finally, some men brought a donkey to serve as a ladder. "Everyone has to collaborate." The woman chuckled. "Now, pull, pull, pull!"

"Do you see what they are doing?" she yelled at me over the blaring bands. "In the earthquake, the bell fell down. Now it's going to be almost two years. We have to put our bell in place.

This bell is the most renowned and important bell from before. It is from before! Let us have some *chicha*." And the liquor was poured into tin cups from a bucket, and the band played loudly, and the bell was hoisted from the donkey's back.

"It will give so much joy to hear our bell," she said. And then the workers stepped forward to name their hamlet. "We are from the *caserío* of Atipayán! . . . from Marián . . ." and on and on, they cheered.

"Ring the bell," the crowd demanded. But there was no clapper. It had disappeared, and so they hit the bell with a stone as the band played, drums, trumpets, a *huayno*, and the *chicha* flowed.

When I went up to visit the old woman six weeks later, she was still talking about the bell. "That bell is so beautiful, so unique. It is not like other bells. There is nothing to equal that bell in all of Lima!"

"How is it so different?" I asked.

"It has another sound, I don't know how to say it, but lovely, lovely, not like other bells."

Then she told me there had been two bells, one in each tower of the Soledad church, and that the monks from Los Pinos had carried one of the bells off. "As soon as the country people have finished harvesting their fields, we will go to take our bell back. Why should they have taken it off after the earthquake? Did they think we would not go to reclaim it? Didn't they know that we would long for it?"

At times, merriment unexpectedly and almost imperceptibly moved toward hysteria, and then joy and conviviality would abruptly give way to screams and weeping. This happened once in the house I first lived in, where a daughter had been killed in the earthquake. The phonograph was blaring popular ballads— "Amor por Ti"; "El Condor Pasa"—and everyone seemed to be enjoying themselves until, without prior warning, as if struck by some fulminating pain that quickly spread, everyone broke down and cried.

DURING my year there, I went only a few times to Lima, and then only of necessity. Once, in the rainy season, late at night, coming down the mountain was more like gliding, the *colectivo* sliding in mud, propelled by gravity, descending amid a dizzying blitz of dark mountains, rain and fog swirling all around us. We passengers were wrapped in blankets against the cold air streaming in through cracks in the rear of the car. We had all nodded off to sleep and were suddenly awakened by the otherwise-stoic chauffeur shouting, "The brakes are gone; grab on to one another!" To prevent our going over the side, he crashed the car against the mountainside.

Shaken, we all got out and stood silently in the mud. The men eased the car out of its lock on the mountain, and the chauffeur set about patching the brake line with chewing gum and adding brake fluid. *Colectivos* often travel in pairs, and the one that had slid around us as we lay against the mountainside now waited to act as a buffer should our brakes fail again on the descent. We started up, slowly at first, but it was not an hour before our car overtook the *colectivo* ahead and began traveling rapidly, as if to get the descent over with. No one ever countermanded a sierra chauffeur. More than being scared for my life, I felt we were losing altitude too fast, landing too abruptly out of the wet winter sierra night into the hot summer desert morning. Racing through the coastal towns along the Pan American Highway, civilization clanged, searing my spirit.

The transition was too quick. In Lima, I became a mere earthling, sitting at a sparkling outdoor café, walking and talking in an ordinary way. I remember being in a Lima church where the women wore slacks and halters in bright lightness of spirit. Strangely, I longed to be again in the heart of darkness, in the gravest of landscapes, where earth, altitude, and cataclysm had attuned people to cosmic forces, primed them for large questions, bent them to mystery. I longed to meander not on city streets but along mountain paths closer to other galaxies, to see the deep purple hues playing on Huascarán, to hear the mute toll of clapperless bells, to be again in the charged, humbled, and silent valley.

The silence of the valley was not just an absence of sound. Rather, it was symphonic, a heard silence made up of ice-blue glaciers, softly moving *ichu* grasses, gold-speckled dusks, and thunderous mountains bursting like orchestral cymbals.

I first became aware of the symphonic silence while coming down on one occasion from the 14,000-foot pass at Punta Callán on the Cordillera Negra to Casma on the coast. As the *colectivo* crossed the puna, I felt like I was flying, enveloped in the Cordillera Negra, alone in a great concert hall hewn out of rock and earth.

My ears were stopped up, but as we descended, they popped, and a popular ballad that had been playing all the while on the car radio invaded my consciousness, calling attention to the silence that had been stored up inside me, the silence that would soon give way to verdant villages in the foothills and then spiraling black smoke mingling with the smell of fish in the oil-slicked ocean, silence drowned in the noise of the urban coast.

In spite of the comforts and pleasures of Lima, to which part of me was drawn, I always hated going down the mountain, feeling that great symphonic silence I held deep inside slowly ebbing away. In contrast, on the ascent from the coast to the Callejón, I was always filled with anticipation of the silent crescendo that would begin to build inside. It was as if I were returning to a place where light could be shed on the problem of evil and where the most elusive secrets of life might be deciphered, secrets such as how the world was formed and how it might end, what human life on earth was all about.

Only on my last descent, fieldwork done, emotionally exhausted by the farewells and the packing, encumbered by boxes of notes, tapes, film, did I settle back, peaceful, perhaps only numb, emerging in stages from the gravest of landscapes, accepting reentry into my ordinary world.

Six

A DEEPER IMMERSION

*I cannot be here at this time without ask-
ing myself daily the most basic questions
of life and death, reality and fantasy, the
way the world is and ought to be.*

from my field notes

FIELDWORK IN THE CALLEJÓN was different in many important ways from fieldwork I had done previously elsewhere, because it was done at the unique juncture of an extraordinary time and place. An overwhelming event had happened to everyone who was there on that Sunday afternoon in May 1970, and everyone who entered the valley subsequent to that day participated in it. For us all—Russian doctor, North American fisheries expert, radical priest, Marxist revolutionary, Jehovah's Witness, Japanese seismologist, American anthropologist—the reality of the earthquake was central, an axis around which all else turned.

Usually the ethnographer has to probe to get at the subject of his study. He has to try to figure out the significant features of his subject, whether kinship or trading patterns or religious rituals, to people going about their daily lives in a "normal" world. How can he elicit both speech and action that are crucial to his understanding without getting caught in the epistemological dilemma of wondering whether he is inventing the features of his study or truly discovering them as they exist among the people? In short, is he asking valid questions? Are the people merely being polite, trying to accommodate the ethnographer, answering something—anything—to his inept questions? Anthropologists are never entirely free of this predicament because it is inherent in human beings studying themselves. But this problem, by and large, was minimized in post-earthquake Peru by the rawness and accessibility of the subject.

From the moment I arrived in Huaraz, I heard people talking daily about the earthquake and its aftermath. I didn't have to initiate discussion of the subject matter I had gone to try to understand. In their absorption with the event, survivors moved back and forth from the concrete to abstract philosophical planes. This was true whether I was listening or asking questions or not. For instance, one dusk, half-asleep, crowded into a corner of a *colectivo* returning to Huaraz from Yungay, with peasants talking, switching from Spanish to Quechua, I caught the sentence "It seems to me the truly human no longer exists." Freed by their immersion in the disaster, I could fade into the background, simply listening and watching. That is what I did for the first two months.

Ironically, rather than probing, I had to try to damp down the multitude of perceptions constantly coming in, in order to maintain an equilibrium myself. It was easy to be dazed by the event and the deprivations of the aftermath. I had to give in to the tragedy, to let it come inside me, for this was a necessary part of understanding survivors' responses to the disaster. However, practically, I also had to learn to hold it at bay or my work would have been severely jeopardized. This is just one of the tightropes I had to walk.

The hardest thing in the world for an anthropologist to do in the field is to relax, to stop attending to every minute detail. In other places, other fieldwork situations, I had been able to relax from time to time. Going to the market or even doing my washing or other chores of daily living had provided a break from the strain of fieldwork.

In Huaraz, withdrawal in daily chores was not possible. When I first went to buy buckets and washbasins, I was told that some were better than others because they were aseismic, not prone to destruction by earthquakes. Months later, in the same market, a woman looked at me and said, "You must be the wife of one of the Czechs who were lost on Huascarán." The walls of the thermal watering places where I bathed, in Monterrey and Chancos, were cracked, and even by the fire in the hotel at Monterrey, climbers' conversations never veered long from imagining the event that left the scar in Glacier 511. The little post office in Centenario where I picked up my mail was about to collapse.

Then there was the frequent reflection of survivors upon my living on a second floor of an adobe house, in the room that had been occupied by the beloved priest whose soul must surely linger there. There was no electricity, which did not disturb me at all, though it meant much to my landlords, who often reminded me that theirs had been a house with a dozen outlets, resplendent with light "before the earthquake."

Toward the latter part of my stay, the house was declared unsafe and was marked for demolition by the reconstruction unit, CRYRZA. This resulted in frantic activity on the part of my landlords to shore up the house in order to argue that it should not be bulldozed. As Indian bricklayers, summoned from the mountain hamlets, began sorting through the clay, cane, and straw, dismantling walls and mixing new adobe bricks, the delicate balance that had been achieved over the two years since the earthquake was upset. One day as I headed down the stairs, heavy tiles from the precarious roof fell just ahead of me.

No choice of housing would have removed me from the all-engrossing event. Had it been possible for me to live in a *módulo* in one of the camps, I probably would have found it near unbearable because of the crowded conditions and the epidemics that constantly plagued these camps. And in my little room I was at least there on the pampa, the scene of Huaraz's greatest destruction, perhaps, it was thought, still inhabited by thousands of *almas* ("souls"), a central place in a frayed land whose ghost might yield up some secret I could find nowhere else.

Besides the practical aspects of living, many other factors conspired to make the task of keeping my center amid the vortex of disaster a difficult one. They ranged from constantly expressed feelings of foreboding at changes in the weather to small landslides

that oozed out of the high gorges through the long rainy season of
1972 and even to dreams about future earthquakes that I began to
experience along with survivors.

In later phases of the work, the geophysical edge I lived on,
along with survivors, became almost secondary to the edge of a
politically charged atmosphere as the reconstruction, fueled by
ideas of revolution and reform, seized upon the tremulous landscape
for exercises in world building. Though I felt myself to be, and
was recognized as, an advocate of the people of the valley, their
positions were not always clear, and at the same time that I tried
to navigate the choppy waters of their conflicts about reconstruction, I could not alienate myself from the representatives of the
nation, who now occupied the valley, especially Huaraz, with ideas
and conflicts of their own.

All told, the event itself, and all that attended it, imposed a
deeper immersion in fieldwork than I had known before.

Curiously, in the aftermath I found that I even passed easily
from the role of ethnographer to the role of informant. For example,
on the second anniversary of the disaster, foreign newsmen appeared in the valley and sought me out to ask, "What is it like . . . ?"
During my year there, two film crews arrived and embarked on
the impossible task of trying to record the aftermath in a few brief
days. The cinematographers, too, searched me out as a witness,
an intermediary.

Wary, I joined one of the crews on a day's shooting in April
1972. We traveled to Yungay, and I watched as their camera panned
the panorama of the avalanche, coming to rest on a glass-covered
picture set up on a stone in the lean-to chapel on the playa where
Yungay's cathedral was buried. The print depicted souls in purgatory, flames leaping about them. The Virgin and the Christ child
floated above on a cloud. Angels wept as they lifted the souls out
of the flames. Withered flowers and stubs of candles lay on the
stone in front of the picture.

The rainy season was ebbing, rain falling now in downpours
followed by a bright sun. The air was fresh and moist from the
heavy rains of the day before, and the tiny crosses and the new
blades of grass that shot up now through the debris hung heavy
with dew droplets. To the south, though, the twice-buried town
of Ranrahirca remained a lunar surface.

Next, the cinematographers wanted to film a survivor. Survivors were all around, sitting by the roadside in Yungay Norte, washing clothes in the brooks in the Tingua camp. But the film crew wanted to stage a scene of a boy fishing in the Santa. This would show an orphan going about his life. We found a young boy who was living at the New Restaurant in Tingua. The boy seemed very sad and really didn't want to fish. But in spite of my misgivings, they urged him down to the river and provided a net. Happily, another little boy joined us, and at the river's edge the boys ripped off their clothes, jumped in the river, and began swimming and laughing, now wanting to be photographed. There were no fish to catch.

From Tingua, in the crew's van, we drove to the Huaraz cemetery, where they wanted to film a family at a graveside. It was late in the afternoon by the time we reached the cemetery. Unexpectedly, I was feeling more uneasy about this than about the staging of the boys swimming in the Santa, and I was relieved to see the one family group who remained at a grave wander off as the sky began to fill with threatening clouds. A young girl was selling flowers at a stand, and the film-crew chief induced her and some children playing nearby to be filmed walking through the cemetery. Assigning me the task of directing the scene because I spoke Spanish, he offered to take the flower girl's place and positioned himself behind her stand.

It was all so strange. No one was around anymore, yet there stood this tall gringo holding up a bouquet of flowers as I took over his role as director of the film and the flower girl turned into an actress. I became caught up in the enterprise while all the time questions concerning "life" versus "art" swam in my head. The crew was happy with the way the scene turned out, and we packed up and went back to the Monterrey Hotel, where they were staying. Later, a landslide came down on the road, cutting me off from Huaraz, and I had to spend the night at the hotel. All evening I felt at odds with myself, watching the CRYRZA reconstruction people playing cards at the dining-room tables, hearing the partying of the foreigners, and knowing what it was really like back there on the pampa that night, in the little Tingua "restaurant," on the Yungay playa, and in the survivor camps.

THE earthquake affected all aspects of everyone's lives. Having left few closed walls, it brought much of the conducting of their lives out into the open, literally as well as figuratively. Because so much was on the surface and people were constantly reacting to situations and to each other in light of the event, I had always their model before me. In the abstract, the disaster, as tragedy, was universal. Nevertheless, it occurred in a definite time and place. Because of the universality of tragedy, there were human emotions, empathetic responses, I shared with survivors. What I had to learn were the local nuances of emotional response, when one cries, when one keeps silent, when one makes jokes or gets angry, and I had to learn the particular phrasings of the more abstract questions about life and death that people pondered.

Here is just one example from my field notes of the way in which, unsolicited, I had always the model of people's reactions before me:

This afternoon Reyna and I set out to attend a meeting in the barrio of Belén. To locate anything in Huaraz, where familiar landmarks of orientation have been erased, is always a problem, and we wandered around lost for about half an hour near the wide-open field where a seminary had been, our only guide to where this meeting was to take place. An icy, dust-laden wind whipped across the unshielded land, sending us for protection and perhaps further directions into one of the prefabricated shelters at the edge of Belén.

An old lady was cooking over a wood fire. Reyna and I were both strangers to her, but her first remark after we went through the customary arm-patting greetings was "How painful it is to live in a house that does not belong to one (¡Qué penoso es vivir en casa ajena!)! And so near the river, it is so cold!" Reyna agreed there was almost nothing worse than living en casa ajena. (Ajena means "foreign, different, somebody else's"). I thought how all Huaracinos were living in strange and unfamiliar corners. The city itself has lost its core and has been relegated to its largely effaced borders and to the mountain folds.

The old lady began to cry over the loss of a daughter, who she said was tall like me. Reyna comforted her by saying she must know her daughter was near God and it was better, as she was not suffering what the survivors were suffering. The old lady then pointed to her grandchildren kicking a ball around in the dust storm: "Look at the little creatures. What does it matter to them? They just go on playing." Reyna said, "It's better. They'll know soon what life is like."

This scene contains both universal and particular elements. Besides the universal aspect of the sadness at personal loss of loved ones, we see, also, what may be a universalistic response of survivors to disaster: that it is worse for the survivor than for those who die in the catastrophe.[1]

The particular brought out in this scene is the distress people felt in living in a structure that did not belong to them. This was a pervasive theme, overshadowing what, to North Americans at least, would be more significant, namely, the inadequacy of the dwelling itself and its lack of all facilities. That it did not belong to one—that one had not fashioned it out of the earth with his own hands, that one was cast into an immediate environment not of his own making—was extremely troubling to the people.

Moreover, the threat of total change hung over their heads. For many months, Huaraz itself was blueprinted for relocation. Geologists had declared its old location unsafe. To move from their place, their *sitio*—to leave their dead and their market, and the broken images from their churches—was anathema to survivors. When finally their protest was too big to quell, it was declared that Huaraz would remain "in its place." To survivors, it would not be Huaraz were it not "in its place." Like the opposite of reification, where an abstract idea is treated as if it had concrete and material existence, the material town was imbued with all the power of abstraction. To be "in its place" was to be right and good. It was hoped that streets, too, could remain in their places and could retain their own names. "We would be very sad and confused if streets were called by other names," people said.

The anthropological value of studying people's reactions to each other and to their surroundings under the circumstances of disaster might be questioned. It could be argued that one learns only how people behave in times of stress. However, stress is only stress in relation to what is perceived as "normality," and so I learned, also, a lot about ordinary living, ordinary reactions. Survivors were constantly engaged in trying to recapture the ordinary world. In the telling and retelling, that world became more explicit than it had ever been. Its lines were carefully drawn, its materials

cataloged, its essence savored in memory. The image was ideal
perhaps, romanticized in its loss; nevertheless, it was sharply
drawn.

SOMETIMES doing fieldwork feels like being in constant search of
someone. I would walk up to a mountain hamlet only to find the
person I was looking for had gone down into Centenario, or I would
look for someone at his market stall and learn he was planting on
the mountainside. The day I wandered around Cochawaín looking
for Padre Washi, Yungay's priest, illustrates the looking for, the
waiting, that are so frequent. It also illustrates the sense of eerie
disorientation that was so profound in the postdisaster setting, one
I shared with survivors.

Cochawaín is the area of high ground to the north of Yungay
that was not buried by the debris avalanche. It was to Cochawaín
that survivors on Yungay's cemetery had escaped. I went there one
gray day to look for the elderly priest who was now practically
Cochawaín's only resident. I wanted to ask whether there had been
a rise in religious marriages after the disaster.

The wind hissed. Clouds cloaked the glacial peak of Huascarán, though I could feel its presence beyond them. I looked
through the windows of the chapel the *padre* had built and into the
tent where he lived, next to the chapel. He was not to be found.
I sat on a curb on the tiny plaza called San Martín de Porres. Streets
cut by the avalanche ended abruptly. Streetlights, mere inert fix-
tures now, were still standing, like the headless columns in a De
Chirico painting. I felt isolation in the extreme. A lone sheep grazed
nearby, and the red petals of a poinsettia quivered in the wind
against the gray background. I marveled at the numbers and names
engraved on plaques on the few remaining abandoned houses. I
always felt a twinge of pain in identification of this kind.

After a long time, I walked down to the survivor camp at
Yungay Norte, where I found Padre Washi in Cirila's roadside
restaurant. When I asked about religion after the earthquake, he
said tiredly, "The saints are gone, but the tradition continues."

From him and other priests I learned of the "sacramentaliza-
tion," as they called it, that took place after the disaster. Especially
from the mountain uplands, Indians descended upon the valley.
"They would get all dressed up in their best clothes, find godpar-

ents, and demand that their babies be baptized or that the marriage rite be performed," the weary priest said. Without these rites, they believed that if one died he might not go to heaven or that further disaster might ensue because they lived that way.

This placed a heavy burden on the few priests left functioning in the valley, who, besides giving the concrete help that was needed from them, grappled with decisions about what sort of community ceremonial actions should be taken. At Masses for the dead, for example, survivors wanted to hear individual names recited, a task that soon became impossible. Finally, the priests of the valley concurred that there would be one Mass a week offered for all the dead.

The Yungay priest spoke sparingly, and I remember thinking how futile it would be to press for any quantitative data on sacraments after the disaster. I choked on the mere thought of the word "data." As I was leaving, someone shouted, "Huascarán is coming!"

Cirila shouted back, "It doesn't matter. For me, any day."

Again, at the end of my fieldwork, I made a lame effort to record some statistics that might show the number of sacraments performed in each parish in the predisaster years and to compare this with figures from the two postdisaster years. As the priests would try to find the records or present me with weathered, earthquake-beaten ledgers, my original feelings of futility returned. How could I control for so many factors: the number of those who left the valley, the number of people who came to the valley from outside after the disaster, even the number of dead and injured. The population had changed radically.

I recall sitting in the priest's office in Belén. He placed a large book on my lap, opened to the date May 31, 1970. Beneath the date appeared a note that the parish priest had died in the earthquake and that henceforth, as the "church" moved from one makeshift shack to another, it was "very difficult to keep up the books at this time."

BESIDES the transparency of life in the aftermath and the power of a shared extreme event, another factor made this experience different from my previous fieldwork. Usually the anthropologist has to explain herself in some way soon after arriving in the field. Where

does she come from? What on earth is she doing there? This was
not necessary in the Callejón aftermath. I wasn't odd in a valley
through which hundreds of foreigners had passed during the year
following the disaster. Though most had left, they were remembered, their nationalities recalled by the color of the clothes they
wore. (The Russians were in green, people told me, and the Ecua-
dorians wore orange jumpsuits.) The Cubans were still building
clinics, and Dutch and German volunteers and the augmented U.S.
Peace Corps were circulating the roads in their jeeps. Religious
personnel from outside plied the mountain paths.

I was at first assumed to be a member of one of the relief
organizations. When I said I wasn't, I was simply accepted as one
who had come to *acompañar*, to "be with" the survivors. The "being
with" was appreciated as much, perhaps more, than substantive
aid, and since it was also true that that is why I had come—as well
as to do fieldwork—I never had to deny this.

When I spoke of the study I proposed to make, this, too, was
accepted, especially once it was realized that the study was not to
be "at the flight of a bird," as they said, but, rather, that I had
come to live there for an extended time.

Soon after the disaster, besides relief and religious workers,
there had been an influx of *sociólogos*, a catchall term for census
takers and social scientists of all types and all levels of profession-
alism. Using long questionnaires, they would extract their answers
and disappear as new batches, up from the coast, took their places,
asking the same questions. People told me they would be awakened
in the middle of the night by these intrepid data gatherers calling
into their tents, rousing the living in order to count the dead. Some
of this was no doubt necessary, but the manner and redundancy
with which it was carried out was distressing to the people. So the
odd thing was not that I had come to the valley after the earthquake
but that I had no questionnaires and had come to stay and to listen.
There was a pressing need on the part of survivors to be heard, to
be listened to, not interrogated and enumerated.

However, some survivors indicated that they preferred not to
speak of the disaster in a personal way. There were instances also
when it was I who could not speak of someone's personal tragedy.
Often the two naturally coincided. In each case, great and unusual
personal loss had been sustained. Hardly anyone had not lost a

relative or a close friend. Those first terrible days after the disaster were spent in recounting the losses, one to another, and the person whose family had remained intact was the exception. But many lost several relatives, some almost everyone. There were some from whom the 1970 disaster snatched a whole second family that had been created in the interim between either the 1941 alluvion in Huaraz or the 1962 avalanche at Ranrahirca and the earthquake. For instance, one man, scrambling with his second wife and second set of children up onto the terraces of the Yungay cemetery, saw the debris wave carry them off, just as, in 1962, the alluvion over Ranrahirca had swept away his first family.

But besides their own accounts, people narrated the stories of others, their losses, their reactions. Therefore, I heard about these cases of extreme bereavement from those more fortunate or more recovered from their own trauma.

Actually, I often did hear, at a first encounter, the accounts of severe losses directly from those who had sustained them. At that point, I was still only a sympathetic stranger, and their stories spilled out like a record that needed to be set straight. As I saw these people more and more, though, I became a friend, and then, intuitively, it would usually seem best to allow the record, after that initial catharsis, to remain silent, known but not discussed. Time with them was spent in talking of other things or in activities engaged in together. "Come over," they would say to me, "to distract." I remember one long, rainy afternoon I sat reading *Don Quixote* to a family.

ONE of these persons who had been unusually traumatized was Cirila Luna, the owner of the restaurant in Yungay Norte, who had said, "For me, any day," when someone shouted in jest that Huascarán was coming down. Cirila had been picked up and carried on top of the avalanche down to the Río Santa. No one else survived this way.

When the earth began to tremble that Sunday, Cirila, with her two young sons, was in front of her house making plans for the sale of piglets. When the rabbit and guinea-pig cages began to roll across the courtyard, she drew her children to her. Alive or dead, the three would be together. The earth seemed to calm for an instant, and then came the noise, like an explosion that never ended but only drew nearer. The three ran, hanging on to each other, stumbled, and then the wave hit. Cirila lost consciousness, and when she awoke, she was near the river, buried, survivors of Cochawaín pulling her by the hair, placing a rope around her mud-caked body. Having swallowed debris, she could not speak, nor could she open her eyes. Above all, she could not cry. All her joints had come undone. She was held together by the mud, unspeakable pain engulfing her.

Three more days she lay there, drifting in and out of consciousness, consumed by pain, wishing to die, kept alive by the thought that her sons would surely come to look for her. Instead, through the nights a stranger came from time to time to where she lay alone, hearing moans coming from Cochawaín. The stranger burned cane near her to give her some warmth. She could move only the middle finger of her left hand to signal she was still alive.

In the first helicopter to land, Cirila was taken to Chimbote and then to Lima, where she spent the next five months in the hospital. During all this time, the idea that her children were still alive never left her. Little by little, her injuries healed, and when she was able to walk again, she began to make pilgrimages to all the coastal hospitals where any survivors had been taken in search of her sons or any word about them. Sobbing, she wandered aimlessly through Lima's streets. She would look at rows of soft drinks on counters in the market, thinking if only she could just share a soda with her sons. Cirila herself told me none of this.

She did tell me about her return to Yungay, in December 1970. Beaten down further by hardships in a squatter settlement on the coast and having despaired of finding her boys, she gave up her search and, as she put it, came back to live out her life near her dead sons "on the giant cemetery of Yungay." She told me that she now imagined that her survival was due to her body having been cradled by the bodies of her sons as the three were swept up in the debris wave. She placed crosses on the spot where she figured out the avalanche must have struck them. From then on, her pilgrimages were made to the playa to put wreaths on the crosses. I accompanied her a number of times. We never spoke of the day of the avalanche in any detail. She knew I knew, and that was enough.

I tried once, early on, to speak of the day, but her sadness was so profound that, for then at least, it could not bear touching.

"When I think of that day," she said softly, "I could die this minute." I put my arms around her and whispered that I would never mention her own tragedy again.

With long deep-black braids and high Indian cheekbones, Shilli—her Quechua name—is as beautiful and indomitable as the mountains themselves. As a little girl, alone, she had crossed the high pass over the Cordillera Blanca from the valley of Conchucos and found work as a servant girl with a family in Yungay. She never learned to read or write, yet as a young woman she managed to own and operate a small restaurant in the center of Yungay. Now, when she returned in December 1970, solemn but still so very much alive, she built her restaurant of woven split cane in the survivor camp of Yungay Norte. Through long afternoons and evenings, she presided there, giving good food and her own natural warmth to her fellow survivors. To help her, she took in a boy who was orphaned in the earthquake and who, like herself thirty years before, had walked across the 16,000-foot pass from Conchucos into the camp at Yungay.

Whenever I visited Cirila—she lived in back of her restaurant—we would embrace one another and chat. We laughed a lot. She had a marvelous style, a robust humor, that belied the fact that deep down inside her, it was still the same day, still May 31, 1970.

ALL of Yungay's survivors had suffered extreme loss. I remember one rainy afternoon. I was sitting at the head of a large table in Cirila's restaurant, five men in the other chairs around the table. These men, a few of them teachers, one a dentist, had lost their entire families. They spent most of their time drinking and walking up and down on the road outside her restaurant. These widowers were known in the camp as the *chupamaros*, a combination of the slang usage of *chupar*, meaning "to drink alcohol," and *Tupamaros*, an epithet for "revolutionaries" taken from the name of the Peruvian Indian rebel of the eighteenth century Túpac Amaru, who had become a symbol of the Revolutionary Military Government then in power. The men described themselves as *malogrados* ("wasted, failed, come to naught"). "It doesn't matter if another day comes or not," they would say. The desperation in these men's eyes was hard for me to handle. The "distraction" of my visit filled only a

thimble. As we stood outside waiting for a *colectivo* to take me back
to Huaraz, one of the men said, "Tell me what I can do now." He
meant in the very next moment.

Once I spent a few days in *módulo* 183 in the camp at
Yungay Norte during a brief period when my friend and fellow
anthropologist Tony Oliver-Smith and I were in the valley at
the same time. One of the teachers occupied one side of the
prefabricated dwelling, Rubén and his only surviving child the
other. Rubén's blustery, rough-hewn humor matched Cirila's
stalwart mountain spirit, and he had become her companion.
Together they helped sustain the anguished widowers who made
their home at her restaurant. Rubén had lost his wife and three
children as well as his parents and brothers and sisters. Pepe, the
surviving son, had gone to the circus the day of the avalanche.
Rubén introduced the thirteen-year-old to me as "a survivor of
the alluvion." The boy lay on a cot holding a transistor radio. He
was waiting for the soccer game between Argentina and Peru to
begin at 9:30 P.M. We didn't need his radio. We heard the game
on the neighbor's. With a quarter inch of pressboard between
módulos, every move, rustling, snoring, even breathing, could be
heard. In the day, with the cutout windows and doors open, everything could be seen. Pepe, fully dressed, wrapped in a blue blanket,
fell asleep listening to the game. I heard him steal away early in
the morning.

The ditch water was dirty, and only one faucet was functioning
for the whole camp of nearly 2,000. The spigot was located in the
marketplace, and after going there to splash water on my face, I
went down to Cirila's for breakfast. Someone who had died in the
night was being carried down through the camp, covered with a
blanket.

That night, around the dinner table at Cirila's, candles flickering against the flowered oilcloth table covering, Rubén held forth
about the past glory of Yungay in the nineteenth century, the days
of his great-grandfather. He spoke of great *caballeros*, aristocratic
gentlemen of Yungay, riding into Caraz on their steeds; and of a
great lady who had rheumatism and was carried around on a platform by bearers. He went on to describe the magnificent crimes
that had been committed in Yungay during its glorious epoch. He
told of a woman who cut off the testicles of her betrothed, who

had betrayed her with her own sister. In this vein, the evening passed. Tony said he had not heard such extravagant stories when he had first done fieldwork in Yungay in 1966.

Months later, near Eastertime, I sat talking with a man called Chepo in Cirila's restaurant. One of the widowers, Chepo had lost his entire family: his wife, his three children, his parents. On the day of the avalanche, he had set out for Lima at 3 P.M. with a truckload of pigs. His wife was to drive another truck down, but she told him to get started. On the road, the other side of Ranrahirca, the car began shaking. He turned back, and then he saw "Huascarán coming down."

It was Tuesday before he could begin to grope his way across the avalanche area. As he passed someone, he would ask about his family, and each time that person would answer that he thought he had seen one of his daughters. But someone else would say no, it was another girl. "If only one had survived," Chepo kept repeating to me.

At this point, Rubén entered the restaurant. Commenting on a religious image he had seen on Palm Sunday, he asserted, "The Christ of the Palm Branches [*el Señor de Ramos*] used to be stronger, more miraculous. Now he's the same as Chepo." Roaring profanely, he went through to the back to see what was cooking.

"We live to offer prayers to our dead," Chepo continued. "And to dream . . . and dreaming, dreaming, dreaming, I caress my wife." In a Calderonian way, that dreaming was his real life; his waking life was unreal. "Life is false," he went on, "but no one is psychotic here. We wake, we drink, we dream."

Whenever I left Yungay for the trip back to Huaraz, I felt a strange jumble of emotions. One was an intense sensation of the ephemeral quality of life, an anxious feeling. But on the other side of that was a feeling of catharsis, a kind of cleansing, a peaceful feeling. I think the latter was due to the fact that, while on one level time was passing in Yungay and life was going on, on another level, there was no motion. We were all outside of time, relieved of history. Yungay's fight against relocation, its fight to remain just north of the playa, close to its dead, had rallied survivors during the first year of the aftermath. But now, in the second year, as it became certain that that battle had been won, Yungay seemed quiescent, waiting on the outskirts of history. In Yungay, I felt we were in some deeply universal space where all was becalmed. The worst had happened, and there could be no deeper sorrow. That space was death, though, and when Rubén would recall the past glorious events of Yungay's history, he was luring himself and us and the town back to life.

ON the cold, wet night of December 16, I went down to Doña Angelita's little store in Huaraz's San Francisco barrio, where she sold bread and a few staples. Women would gather there in the evenings, sitting in straight-back chairs lined up against one wall, knitting. Usual topics of conversation were the cold and how Huaraz was now "pure pampa." That particular night, a woman said, "We feel so threatened, so afraid. Everything is destroyed; it has all terminated." Pointing to a woman I had not met before, she added, "She has lost five children." I learned that the children were between the ages of nine and sixteen and that two daughters remained. Besides the five children, the grandparents and one of her brothers living in the same household had perished, as well as other relatives living elsewhere.

Finally, the woman herself, Señora Olivera, spoke: "All the children stayed at home in order to study for Monday. A friend had taken me in a car to the baths at Monterrey. That's how I was spared. My husband was crushed, too, but he survived." She asked me if I wanted to come home with her right then.

"Home" was a half-finished house on a bluff behind the barrio of San Francisco. They had been building the new house at the time of the earthquake. Its large frame and many rooms were now superfluous. The remaining family members occupied a corner of the lower level. One room was filled with straw. Tree trunks to be sold for use in bread-baking ovens lay in the patio.

Señora Olivera put a kettle on for tea and then said, almost in a whisper, "At times one does not know how to go on living. It has affected my heart. It is the pain of a mother." I somehow knew that that would be the last time she would speak of her personal tragedy. Her husband, who worked as a clerk in the court, came in, and we had bread and tea.

After that first night, from time to time I would pass by to chat about the smallest things with them. Or they would come to my room, and we would have hot chocolate. Once Señora Olivera showed me how to stuff potatoes, and a few times we packed a lunch and walked up into the mountains. "*Paseos* [walks, excursions] are good," Señor Olivera would say.

Both of them were in a great deal of psychic pain, and as I saw them over the months, I realized that their "survival" was full of conflict. For example, I ran into Señora Olivera and her daughter at the market a few days before New Year's Eve, 1971. They invited me to come over on New Year's Eve and seemed delighted when I accepted. They began to plan the dinner and the hot chocolate we would have as midnight approached. They would even find a way to provide some music.

The house was quiet and darkened when I arrived at about ten o'clock on New Year's Eve. As I entered the patio, three big dogs, usually tied up, came at me, and I screamed, which made them bark even more ferociously. Señora Olivera came running out and restrained the dogs. She took me into a room where we sat in the dark on a bench against the wall. I explained to her that dogs were what most frightened me in the Callejón. Everywhere, but especially along the mountain paths, dogs are trained to snarl at intruders and are an effective burglar deterrent. I told Señora Olivera that I was particularly shaky because I had recently been bitten in Tingua, and although we could not locate the dog, I had elected not to go through the ordeal of rabies shots. Rabies was prevalent in the area. I eventually learned the proper Quechua words to shout in order to hold the rapacious sierra dogs at bay and to throw stones at them, but dogs remained a kind of nemesis in my fieldwork.

Anyway, there we were on New Year's Eve, sitting on a bench in the dark whitewashed room, a survivor of extreme loss comforting *me*. When I calmed down, I began to wonder what had happened to our proposed fiesta. Señora Olivera told me that the cold of the night had entered her husband and he had already gone to bed. He had decided that with eight family members dead in one household, they could not celebrate New Year's Eve, though it was now the second one to pass since the earthquake. One wears black in bereavement for a year for one family member. How long, she asked herself out loud, must they remain in mourning for the loss of so many? "*Es por el duelo que se debe guardar*" ("It is because of the state of mourning that we must keep"), she kept repeating, excusing herself from our plans. "But," she mused aloud, "the earthquake was so extraordinary, perhaps the usual custom should not apply."

All this was going around in her head, locking her between the desire to begin to recover from an event that broke all bounds and the dictates of her culture with its prescribed response to death. I slowly came to understand that this conflict was the reason for my not being completely comfortable even in "being with" this family. Their conflict made for double messages to me: "Come and take away our grief. But you can't; no one can."

With my flashlight, I made my way back to my room, but found it hard to fall asleep. I felt lonely and scared, suddenly sure I would get rabies. But most of all, I felt disturbed, agitated, yet unable to put my finger on the reasons why I was so at odds with myself. Maybe I was ashamed to feel so many concerns for myself when so much material and emotional devastation lay around me.

Thinking of the way Señora Olivera treated me that night, when I was frightened and confused, brings back a quality in survivors I experienced on many occasions and that affected me a great deal: the tenderness that existed in too many places to name. Disaster, when it does not embitter the soul beyond repair, engenders compassion.

LOSSES were not commonly so unspeakable as among the handful of "true" Yungay survivors and among some families of Huaraz, like the Olivera family. When loss had not left psychic wounds too sensitive to touch, wounds that still needed to scar over, people wanted to talk about what had happened.

After the first months, when I simply listened, I began to ask questions. Many were questions that had become familiar, since I had heard people asking them of each other and of themselves. Along about February 1972, I began to make tapes, though most use of the tape recorder took place in the last months, when I was more secure with it and with informants and knew the result would be as natural and as uninhibited as if the machine were not there. One advantage of taping in this bilingual setting, where people spoke Spanish and Quechua, was that it did not matter how much Quechua was spoken or whether I got it all or not. I knew Reyna, in transcribing the tapes, would translate for me. When the recording phase of fieldwork began, I could, for example, just set the recorder in a family's courtyard, having many voices coming in, the younger members speaking Spanish, usually, and the older ones Quechua. Sometimes the younger people would help in interpreting between me and the monolingual Quechua speakers, and this was all on tape for later study. In short, I did not have to restrict or guide conversations much or be too preoccupied with the accuracy of the instantaneous interpretation from Quechua to Spanish, as the whole thing would get a second going-over with Reyna. By the time I left the Callejón, I had over seventy hours on tape.

I felt there had been some natural cycle to the fieldwork when, shortly before I left, I made the final tape. Three generations were present in my room on the pampa: the *abuela* ("grandmother"), who was the mother-in-law of Don Juan of Secsecpampa, my principal Indian source; the *abuela*'s daughter, Jesusa; and Jesusa's daughter, Julia. The grandmother spoke only Quechua. The younger women were both bilingual. Interjecting very little into this conversation, I sat back, listening to the dialogue among the women—Reyna, mestiza of the town, and the three Indian peasant women—as they brought into sharper focus some of the more important issues we had all been working on in previous months.

No fieldwork is ever "finished." Yet it seemed, with that last full and rich tape, made virtually without my having to say a word myself, that a phase of what I then thought would be renewed and prolonged encounters in the Callejón had reached a kind of completion. I had begun the fieldwork by simply listening; then there was a period of asking, probing, searching; and now it was ending with my withdrawal into listening again.

I know now that I was not able to return frequently, as I planned then, to follow the aftermath through the years, that it would not be until the ten-year anniversary of the disaster, May 31, 1980, that I would stand again on the playa of Yungay or look out over the center of Huaraz. The year of the aftermath, from October 1971 to September 1972, recorded here, thus stands encapsulated.

Part 2

WHY DID IT HAPPEN?

A bad earthquake at once destroys our oldest associations; the earth, the very emblem of solidity, has moved beneath our feet like a thin crust over a fluid. One second of time has created in the mind a strange idea of insecurity, which hours of reflection would not have produced.

Charles Darwin,
The Voyage of the Beagle

Seven

THE RASHOMON FACTOR

I am becoming more and more convinced that the "objective event," if it happened anywhere, happened only on the seismograph.

from my field notes

I N THE WELL-KNOWN SHORT STORY "Rashomon," an incident occurs in a bamboo grove off the Yamashina road in Japan. Several people witness the incident, and each tells a different version of what happened. Like those wayfarers in the Japanese story, survivors of the earthquake gave what appeared to be conflicting interpretations of many facets of the disaster.

The earthquake that shook Peru at 3:23 P.M. on May 31, 1970, is a documented event. It registered 7.7 on the Richter scale. Its epicenter was located at 9° 24' south latitude, 79° 18' west longitude, fifty kilometers off the coast of Ancash; its hypocenter twenty-four kilometers deep under the sea. It lasted forty-five seconds. Yet, beyond the brief, measurable flutter of the seismograph, the disaster became an event of the most varied meaning for all whose lives it touched.[1]

Rumbling through an area of 65,000 square kilometers, it snuffed out 75,000 lives, injured 50,000, and demolished some 186,000 buildings, roughly 80 percent of all the structures in the area. On the coast and in the sierra of the Department of Ancash, it left 800,000 people homeless. In the Callejón alone, thousands were adrift both physically, their material possessions gone, and emotionally, spiritually, even cognitively, their familiar world destroyed.

The disaster also touched the lives of hundreds who took part in the relief and reconstruction. Many went to the scene knowing little of where they were going or what to expect. They included Russians who spoke no Spanish and urban Latin American nurses, who in normal times would have suffered culture shock in the sierra. A nurse from Buenos Aires, along with a small medical corps, landed in a military plane at Anta outside Huaraz on June 6, 1970: "An airstrip of small stones had been improvised. It was still not finished when we landed. . . . I tell you the truth, now I realize I didn't even know when the earthquake had occurred. . . . None of us knew much about what we were going to do. We knew we were going to help in an earthquake, but nobody knew where or how or what or anything. We crossed the Andes without heat in the plane, wrapped in newspapers."

Besides relief personnel, earth scientists from many countries hastened to the scene to measure ground effects and to reconnoiter the glacial crevices from helicopters. They were soon calling the event one that "ranks high among the world's catastrophic natural disasters." The destruction wrought by the Yungay avalanche they termed "almost unbelievable, possibly surpassing in magnitude such catastrophic events as the Mt. Pelée eruption of 1902 on the Island of Martinique and the eruption of Vesuvius in the year A.D. 79 that buried the city of Pompeii."

As the worst natural disaster on record to strike the Western Hemisphere, the earthquake was reported widely in the world press.[2] The *New York Times* gave extensive daily coverage for the solid month of June 1970. Reported by the media, knowledge of that terrible minute in Peru must have made many people all over the world pause over it for at least that long. I know I thought about it for days at the time as news reports gradually revealed the enormous dimensions of the earthquake and avalanche. It was not till many months later, however, that I knew I would go to the Callejón de Huaylas.

WHEN that time came, I read the ethnography of the Callejón and surveyed the social-science literature on disaster.[3] This was the "homework" I felt obligated to do, although I knew I wanted to be as free of theoretical constructs as possible, with no preconceived hypotheses to affirm or reject, open to the facts as I would see them. I wanted to know everything about the human response to disaster of this magnitude. But I also knew that I needed to have some focus to my work, and I phrased my research proposal around what happens to people's beliefs about nature, man, and the supernatural in the face of such an extreme event.

Because of the nature of the event itself, it was not possible to set up a formal research strategy. I had, though, tentatively planned to choose a small hamlet on the mountain slopes in which to study religious change wrought by the earthquake. By the time I was ready to leave for the field, the disaster had long ceased to capture the imagination of the world press, and even in Lima, when I first arrived in Peru and started asking questions, no one could say what it was like in the Callejón those sixteen months after the earthquake. It was strange to be going to do fieldwork in a destroyed valley, where I could not imagine where or how I would live, could not even look on a map and count on a town's being there.

The turns my work would take began to develop shortly after I arrived in the valley. To the eye alone, it was obvious that while the earthquake had reverberated up and down the mountainsides, badly damaging many indigenous communities, it was at the level of the valley floor, in the towns, that most destruction and loss of life had occurred. I also became aware that the relationship between the towns and their satellite villages was crucial and that confining the research to one or the other environment would result in serious omissions. My tentative plan to limit my study to one peasant hamlet, then, no longer seemed appropriate. Moreover, aside from the fact that in the first weeks I had become attached to Huaraz, it made sense to make my base there, in the leveled center, on the pampa, and from there to walk up to the satellite hamlets and occasionally to travel north from Huaraz to Yungay or Caraz or Huaylas and south toward Recuay and Cátac.

Furthermore, it was becoming apparent that postdisaster circumstances were extremely complex, much more so than I had ever
imagined. The earthquake was far from being an isolated event. It
could not be seen as the sole cause of social changes that were
occurring in the valley. Nor could it be considered a simple turning
point in the growth or decline of religious fervor. By the time I
arrived, the disaster had already become deeply entangled with at
least two major processes of change in Peru. One was the Revolutionary Military Government of Gen. Juan Velasco Alvarado,
which had seized power in October 1968. The other was the "theology of liberation," a synthesis of various lines of thought that had
been brewing in Latin America as a result of the Catholic Reform
movement launched by Pope John XXIII and Vatican Council II
in the 1960s.

As a matter of fact, one of my earliest field notes reads "Where
I look for religion, I find revolution." That was long before I came
to understand the intricate ways in which religion and revolution
had joined hands and how the two were affected by the earthquake
and, in turn, were affecting both the interpretation and the man-
agement of the disaster. Nevertheless, I was not long in the valley
before the vague feeling began to possess me that I was attending
something more than just the aftermath of a "natural" disaster.

IMMEDIATELY after the earthquake, the Revolutionary Military Government had placed a moratorium on all land transactions in the
valley towns. Therefore, virtually nothing had happened by the
time I arrived. People were poised on the mountainsides, in survivor
camps, waiting to rebuild but not allowed to do so. No one could
buy or sell land or occupy his own land or lay even as much as an
adobe brick upon it. These restrictions cast a pall on the valley. At
the same time, however, the atmosphere was charged with an air
of expectancy, an anxiety about how the physical problems of the
valley would be resolved, where and how the towns would be
rebuilt, and whether or not the churches would be reconstructed.

One thing, though, was becoming clear. The major decisions
would be made by the national government—outsiders—and not
by survivors themselves. Consequently, the political atmosphere
was strained, and at that point, the mood was one of uneasy containment. From the encircling mountains, thousands of eyes were

looking down on the scourged and barren pampa. The valley lay motionless and tensely quiet.

BUT underlying the tautness and uncertainty were the questions Why? Why did it happen? Why here? Why now? During those first months of fieldwork, during which I mainly listened, these questions kept recurring, like the varied repetitions of a fugue. Finally, it was the question Why? that would give shape to my work. Since survivors were asking Why? of themselves, of each other, even of me, I would try to learn the ways in which they were answering it.

I began to use the word "explanation" in my thinking to myself: How do these people explain the disaster? And I was soon using it in its largest sense: how people perceived and understood the event as well as how they accounted for it. To what causal factors did they attribute the disaster? What meanings did they see in it or give to it? In short, I would try to discover all that made the event comprehensible to them, all that—in the dictionary definition of "explanation"—"removed it from obscurity."[4] This concentration on the ways in which survivors were explaining the tragedy would, I felt, lead me deep into the heart of it, closest to my innermost goal of describing the event in some total way, of understanding the human response to a disaster of such magnitude. My quest, then, reflected theirs. Survivors, too, wanted to understand the disaster in some comprehensive way. They needed to come to terms with it in order to be able to go on. For them, there was the goal, too, of striking at its ultimate cause.

One thing was becoming clearer and clearer to me. There was no such thing as "the event in itself"—a phrase that had gone round in my mind—something I might be able to capture and describe. The disaster was too linked to what preceded it and what followed it for me to be able to isolate it and analyze it as one would a rock crystal extracted from its matrix. The word "linked" began to be important.

The ruins that sprawled around us were real enough. The pampa of Huaraz and the avalanche scar of Yungay were not only real but stark and overpowering. But no one had formulated a single, encompassing description of what had happened or an overall evaluation of the aftermath we were living in. The scientific literature contained only bald statements and the numbers—like the probable speed of the avalanche or the millions of cubic meters of adobe bricks or ice, mud, and rock that had fallen. Even the scientific data sometimes conflicted. But, anyway, the survivors themselves cared little about the numbers. It was the quality of the event, which had no length or breadth or weight, that mattered to them.

Those who had actually experienced the disaster had done so from only one small vantage point. The totality of the event and the setting in which it had occurred were too monumental to witness or even to grasp from one spot. Its scale defied the intellect and taxed the imagination. The survivors had to look at it through a prism, decompose it into its various hues, and examine one color at a time. Doing this, perhaps they might later be able to blend the separate shades into a chromatic whole, making sense of the event.

MUCH has been said about the impact of disaster on man. But human beings also have an impact on disaster. Imagine an unpopulated earth. The physical shock caused by the earthquake would have occurred in some nameless place. The avalanche would have leapt a nameless hill, spilled out over a nameless plain, and coursed its way down a nameless river. Along with all other such events in a vast universe, the great Peruvian earthquake would have been a timeless and meaningless sputter. Even had the earth shaken a tract of jungle inhabited only by monkeys, they would have winced and howled and scrambled to the highest treetop. But then the event would leave their minds, to survive only in the logs of seismographic stations and the memories of a few geologists.

Human beings don't seem able simply to "leave the event alone." From death and chaos in one's midst, some meaning must be teased, some purpose must be found, some semblance of order restored. Like mountain climbers seeking an overarching meaning to life and finding it not on the peak but only later in reflection, survivors began to ponder the disaster. It began to take on a shape, and meanings began to grow. In its re-creation, the event was becoming a human artifact. Truly "natural" disasters occur perhaps only in that proverbial spot in the woods where the tree stands alone.

This proclivity in human beings for finding meaning arises from the fact that we connect events. We build a causal chain, one link following inevitably after another. And then we tend to justify our construction. In an effort to understand the great Lisbon earthquake, Candide rationalized timidly, "There is no effect without a cause. Everything is necessarily linked up and arranged for the best."

This notion of cause and effect appears to have emerged with the capacity for and use of language, with culture itself, back in the Paleolithic. The thought process of linking events in order to explain one by another undoubtedly evolved in tandem with the increasing plasticity of the human animal, who enters the world more nearly instinctless, more bungling and more uncertain of how to behave than the infant of any other species. Indeed, this uncertainty made culture necessary, for without it, the human creature, lacking the instincts and programming of other animals, would have been lost in a sea of jumbled stimuli. Out of this necessity, complex and varied cultures, elaborate statements about the nature of things, have, over the millennia, developed.

But all the glory of culture has not been achieved without a price, for in attempting to replace uncertainty with certainty, through efforts to make sense of his world, man has lost the freedom to experience the world directly. We see it through a screen, which obscures and distorts "the event in itself." When survivors linked the Callejón disaster to political events or to daily occurrences that preceded it, and indeed even to those that followed it, its boundaries invading both past and future, the earthquake as a concrete, distinct physical event was lost.

ONE of the consequences of the causal chains that human beings build is that explanations of an event that appear to be multiple and even contradictory may not be so at all. Rather, the explanations may reflect different levels of causation. The same event may be assigned a series of causes, each producing another, each more remote than the other. A woman in Huaraz, for example, reasoned, obviously enough, that she had escaped death in the earthquake because she was in an open plaza where there were no adobes to fall on her. But why was she in an open plaza? she asked herself. Because she was preparing to take part in a religious procession.

Pursuing the analysis further, she arrives ultimately at her lifelong fulfillment of ritual obligations as the reason for her survival. Because of that, God saved her. Thus, having begun with an immediate, empirical reason for why she was spared—that she was in an open space—she ends up with a remote, supernatural explanation of what led her to be in that open space. The empirical reason was not satisfying enough for her. It addressed only the immediate circumstances of her escape. There had to be something that would address the ultimate questions of her life and give meaning to her survival.

It is often said that supernatural explanations are assigned to phenomena that we cannot understand and, above all, control. Witchcraft beliefs, for example, elucidate events that otherwise elude empirical knowledge. Speaking of the great Chilean earthquake of 1835, Darwin pointed this out in his journal. Survivors in the town of Talcahuanco thought the earthquake had been brought about by an old woman who, two years before, had been offended and in reprisal had stopped up the volcano of Antuco. "This," wrote Darwin, "shows that experience has taught them to observe that there exists a relation between the suppressed action of the volcanoes and the trembling of the ground. It was necessary to apply the witchcraft to the point where their perception of cause and effect failed."

It is true that where science has laid bare fewer causal mechanisms, human beings swing toward remote or supernatural causation. However, no culture relies on one type of explanation exclusively. All peoples engage in some scientific activity, experimenting, trying to verify hypotheses. And, contrariwise, the laymen, certainly, of all cultures take on faith the word of practitioners in possession of esoteric information. To the uninitiated, germs or seismic subduction are just as invisible and impalpable as witches or divine providence.

For most of humanity, scientific answers, whether uncovered for ourselves or taken on faith, never quite suffice. Human beings seek more meaning than science divulges and demand a more rational and accountable world to live in than the world actually is. Anthropologist Clifford Geertz refers to the myriad hypotheses about the world that are constantly being made to explain phenomena and goes on to say, from his fieldwork experience in Java, that his informants were little attached to any particular hypothesis but were "all too ready to abandon it for some other. . . . What they were not ready to do was abandon it for no other hypothesis at all: to leave events to themselves."[5]

IN general, survivors were not content with objective explanations of survival. A beam's falling on someone or missing someone else by a hairsbreadth were not considered enough to account for a person's survival or demise. And when it came to understanding the devastation of the valley, the physical process of an earthquake was deemed inadequate. It was of little consequence to survivors to know how many adobe bricks had buried Huaraz or how fast the ice and rock had descended upon Yungay.

An Indian peasant is weaving at his loom in a hamlet on the slopes of Huascarán. A boulder strikes him. Why this collision of events, a man weaving and a boulder hurtling down into the valley? Why this man and not some other, the man mere yards away who is bending over the upturned soil, picking up stones to prepare his plot for planting? Czech mountaineers are in the avalanche's tracks and perish, while a mere mountain crest away, Japanese climbers watch, safe. Can this all be mere chance?

This chance element is what burdened people. Callejón survivors labored at dispelling the uncertainty through inquiry into the reason for the survival of one and not another. In the following chapters, we look more closely at this preoccupation with chance as it touched individuals and groups within the valley and will see that survivors were ultimately asking why, of the thousand glacial valleys in the world, the shaking earth and shattering glaciers should tear asunder *their* valley.[6]

FOR those ensnared in the valley on May 31, 1970, chaos reigned. After the earth settled down, they became impatient to rebuild their world, incorporating the trauma that afflicted it. In their rush to understand, to find meaning, the disaster entered the realm of metaphor. The more survivors talked about it, the more they attached symbols to it. The Huascarán avalanche came to have the power of the wings of a condor; the adobe collapse of Huaraz, to embody the hand of God. The event was at one time a cataclysm, at other times a blessing or a lesson or a proof of some impression, only tenuously held before, about the way life is. It was a punishment, just or unjust. And at times it was all those things at once.

Even the "facts" surrounding the earthquake became clouded in the perception of it. For example, many survivors recalled the hours before as having been dark and cold. In contrast, the North American monks, situated high above Huaraz, more aloof from the event, reported that they had looked down upon a warm and sunny day. One man saw the avalanche that thundered down Huascarán as a huge red ball, another as a fire of white lights. Looking down upon the "explosion" of the valley from their purchase on the Cordillera Blanca, an Indian couple suspected that the two great mountain chains, the Negra and the Blanca, were at war.

In sum, events come to take their shape inside the individual and are molded by the trajectory of a lifetime. Insofar as the earthquake was a communal event, a communal tragedy, it was sculpted also by the life history of the whole valley and of its barrios, towns, and hamlets. The "objective" event, minutes after it occurred, began to undergo an almost instantaneous transformation by human consciousness bent on comprehension.

Despairing of getting at "the event in itself," of seizing upon it as a singular motive of change, even of grasping in some immediate way what had "actually" happened and what was happening all around me in the aftermath, I came to realize that only by piecing together people's perceptions, feelings, and meanings would even a sense of the totality of the disaster emerge. The survivors themselves had led the way. They were engaged, when I arrived, in the same enterprise, comparing impressions, taking note, exchanging ideas, changing their minds, seeking to structure the whole.

Eight

DESIGN IN THE UNIVERSE

If there were any plan in the universe at all, if there were any pattern in a human life, surely it could be discovered mysteriously latent in those lives so suddenly cut off. Either we live by accident and die by accident, or we live by plan and die by plan.

Thornton Wilder,
The Bridge of San Luis Rey

ONE OF THE THINGS that struck me most when I arrived in the valley and began to listen to what people were talking about was that, even sixteen months later, they were still intensely reliving the earthquake and their part in it. They were engrossed in setting the stage for the event by locating everyone on that Sunday afternoon, May 31, 1970, as if a first step in comprehension could be taken by discerning some pattern in who died and who survived.

The first days after the disaster, people asked each other where they had been when the shaking began, what relatives they had lost, and where the ones who were lost were at 3:23 that afternoon. "No one talked about anything else," said Reyna, my assistant and friend. "It was the most natural thing to hear that two or three of someone's family had died. The most extraordinary thing was to hear that no one of someone's family had died." Down through the months, the survivors' stories were told and retold, to each other, to outsiders, and to me.

"My nephew, if he had not been in front of the school, would have been in some other part of the Plaza de Armas," a man told me. "Then he would have knelt down in the open plaza and would not have died."

That Sunday, the Mexico-Russia soccer game was blaring out over a transistor radio in an open orchard in the barrio of Belén in Huaraz, where a family had gathered for a picnic lunch. "I was running back and forth across the road to bring food from the house," the señora said. "If I had been in the house, I would have been crushed. But I was in the orchard. My youngest son had climbed up on a little burro, and my husband said, 'Ay, I'm not going to miss this,' and he took a photograph. Then, all of us accommodated ourselves in front of the camera. 'Now you take our picture,' I said, and everyone looked into the camera. We were all positioned for the photo when the ground began to feel like it was sinking. Since the movement started slowly, we all said that it would pass. Then, in that moment, it began with such fury that it seemed like the whole earth would roll over, and the sky filled with dust." After placing her ear to the ground to listen for signs of an avalanche from one of Huaraz's glacial peaks, the lady moved quickly to the hospital, where she brandished eucalyptus branches through the corridors to forestall a flu epidemic.

A mother reluctantly left two of her daughters at home when she went to a gathering in a building near the plaza. Five minutes before the earthquake, her daughters set out for the baths at Monterrey and were crushed in the debris. The mother was spared, though the building she was in collapsed. If only the girls had stayed in the house or if she had forced them to accompany her. She went to Lima, but her memory only grew more vivid with time, and she kept coming back "to see" her daughters, buried at Los Pinos. There were so many "if onlys . . ."

The owner of a stationery store in Centenario said she froze in the doorway as her house fell in. The lintel supported the ruins for some hours as she stood under it thinking the earth would open up and she would drop into hell. "What will it be like?" she asked herself.

There was the doctor who lost all his family, who were out walking along Calle Belén, while his house was one of the handful in Huaraz's center that remained standing. "What an irony of fate!" people commented. Afterward, he would go nightly to the Tabarís, a bar at the corner of Raimondi and Centenario, drink himself into a stupor, and crying, stumble across the ruins in the early hours of the morning.

Juan Manuel, the English teacher, was at a luncheon in the center of Huaraz that Sunday. It got to be 2:00 P.M., and lunch still had not been served. So he went back home to attend to his nieces and nephews. "When it is not one's hour . . ." he said. In the house where the luncheon was held, all were killed, whereas at his house in the barrio of Centenario everyone stood by a wall that fell away from them. That night, Juan Manuel went to visit his friend Teófines in Centenario. The friend's wife had not returned home, and never did. She had been feeding someone's cat in a two-story house on Jirón Sucre, in the center of Huaraz.

A man from the hamlet of Huanmarín was in jail on the coast for pothunting in an indigenous grave site and didn't learn for months that he had lost his wife and all his children.

From many, I heard of the woman who didn't want to use her good dishes that Sunday afternoon and claimed she had lost the key to her china cabinet. Of her houseful of guests, she was the only person injured.

In the Café Chavín in Centenario, a lady spoke of the two American Peace Corps women who had returned from Lima the morning of the earthquake. She recalled that when they walked into the café that morning, she had a premonition that something would happen to them. "Could it be only by chance that they should return to Huaraz that Sunday morning and lose their lives that afternoon?" she asked.

There was Chepo, who had set off from Yungay with his truckload of pigs, his wife having urged him to leave without her. And Benjamín, who for reasons he could not explain to himself kept tearing his mother away from Yungay, keeping her from buying a special bread she loved in one of Yungay's bakeries. He had not gone to the Sports Club or lunched in Chancos or stayed for the *pachamanca* in Caraz or enjoyed after-lunch talk at Los Claveles or even talked to the geophysicists in the Yungay plaza. Rather, like the doves the priest was feeding in the patio of the archaeological museum, he had taken flight. Consequently, Chepo with his pigs and Benjamín with his family were already on the road to Carhuaz when the earthquake that loosened the glacier began.

When the shaking started, a grandmother in a house in Hua-rupampa barrio would not leave her room until a trunk had been opened and she could salvage a rosary and a favorite shawl from her youth. One woman limped barefoot across the rubble over "unrecognizable streets." Besides her shoes, she lost her jacket, which only rested lightly across her shoulders.

No details were spared. Rather, thousands of little facts were painstakingly cataloged in the minds of survivors and recited at any opportunity.

IN retrospect, everyone agreed that there had been signs of impending disaster. "Even people of ideas, educated people," a woman told me, had seen spirits. And in the cathedral tower, right there in the center of Huaraz, where people lived close by and cars passed, the population of screech owls had grown. A couple who customarily stayed late at night in their store on the Plaza de Armas would hear them singing "E-tooo-tu-ooca." "How odd!" the wife recalled saying to her husband as they walked home near midnight. "Owls singing here in the middle of the city. There will be many deaths."

Besides, in the days before, huge black butterflies had fallen to the ground like a night rain. Bats had also multiplied in the cathedral tower, flown over the plaza, and entered people's houses. Cocks had crowed before ten at night, and cats had coupled in strange ways. The day before the earthquake, dogs had barked loudly and, like roosters, much too early, before 10:00 P.M.

One old woman had seen a black bird with yellow feet; it had screeched shrilly. That, too, had been a bad omen. And students, when they compared notes later in their "classrooms" under the eucalyptus trees, found that in the months before the earthquake many had smelled a skunk or seen three cats fighting on a rooftop.

Vague olfactory premonitions were reported: an odor of death, like a cadaver in decomposition. One would suddenly come upon this odor in certain places in Huaraz's center. It was "the soul beginning to separate from the body," people said.

Perhaps all these signs should have been heeded.

It was common that dreams or premonitions directed people to one place or another. Reyna's mother told me, those many months after, that she had awakened on that Sunday morning with an intense feeling that her daughters should not go on a picnic to the Llanganuco lakes, as they had planned. Reluctantly, they honored her wishes and so were at home on the outskirts of Huaraz's center instead of in the direct path of the Huascarán avalanche.

Down the valley, near Yungay, a few weeks before the earthquake, a woman dreamed she saw her children floating on top of an alluvion. She awakened her husband to tell him of her dream. A few nights later, when she had the same dream, she insisted the family go down to Lima. Her husband resisted, and she left with the children. Just a few days before the disaster, her husband joined them in Lima.

On the eve of the disaster, a woman dreamed that a barefoot girl had taken her by the hand—she felt in her dream the warmth of the girl's hand—and brought her to a door. The door opened by itself, revealing a field of corn. The golden grains were falling from their cobs. The next morning she recounted her dream to a neighbor, who told her that a member of her family would surely die. The woman tried to put the dream aside. She found herself turning it into a good sign, telling herself that it meant that in the family *chacra* on the mountainside the corn had already been harvested and was very beautiful. Thus, although it was her custom to wash and iron on Sundays, she persuaded the family to walk up to the field that Sunday afternoon. There, in the open, they were all spared. Now she knew that the corn grains falling to the ground in her dream had presaged the death of "all the family of Huaraz."

In the months preceding the disaster, Don Juan of Secsecpampa, a hamlet in Huaraz's orbit, had dreams and revelations, too. His heart grew sad as he saw himself walking and shouting, then running in desperation. "You are sleeping too much," his niece consoled him, and he tried to forget these nightmares. But as he was traveling down by bus to work on the coast before the earthquake, he began to imagine that one day soon he would be walking up those same mountains, in agony, hungry, desperately trying to reach his family. And it did come to be that he made that arduous trek with other men, through the pass at Callán, over the Cordillera

Negra, and down into the valley, not knowing what he would find in Secsecpampa.

Had Don Juan been in Secsecpampa when the earthquake struck, he would have seen his aged mother-in-law running from the house with a bar of soap in her hand, as she had been arranging to go to a stream to wash clothes. First, though, she searched for her hat, but an adobe brick had smashed it. Once in the patio, she saw her grandson fly through the air like a stone. So did one of their little pigs. A falling rock crushed a guinea pig. When they were finally on the open slope, she and the children embraced her daughter, Don Juan's wife, who had been gathering ears of corn in preparation for the saint's day of one of her children. One of their lambs had followed them, bleating softly, and ate up all the tender ears of corn. When the shaking subsided, the family checked on the small statue of the Virgin Mary that stands in the patio of their house and saw that she had lost a hand. Next, they went to the hamlet's chapel, where they found the small image of the Lord of Solitude crushed, suffering the cold of the sudden dust-laden darkness. They returned to the mountainside, where all through the night Don Juan's wife cried inconsolably for her husband on the coast, not knowing that he was safe and had already decided to lighten his load by abandoning his heavy sierra blanket, which he had brought with him to the coast, and to join the younger men in their crossing of the Cordillera Negra.

MANY pursued, deep into their pasts, the motive for their having been at one place or another. Recall the lady who asked herself why she had escaped and reasoned that a religious ritual had brought her to an open space where buildings did not fall. At the time of the earthquake, Doña Delia was in the plaza of Belén preparing to accompany the Virgin Mary Helper ("María Auxiliadora"), on the statue's return from the Belén church to the Huarupampa chapel. But why was she there and not at home or strolling along one of the narrow streets in the center of town? Because she was fulfilling her obligation to the Virgin. Penetrating further, she drew on her earlier attendance at Corpus Christi, a ceremony that had been neglected by many *Huaracinos* that May 31, 1970. Gradually, she wove the threads of her lifelong observance of ritual, which made it probable that she would be in that open plaza. Then she projected her life into the future, vowing that from then on she would always bring a candle to María Auxiliadora, thus reinforcing those aspects of her life that accounted for her having been "saved."

Since the rescued statue of María Auxiliadora came to be housed downstairs in the house where I lived on the pampa, from the balcony I often saw Delia make her way through customers waiting in our patio to buy bread from the oven, enter the living room, and light her candle by the Virgin.

There were so many lives to be examined. Why was someone here and not there when the earth shook? I began to see how disaster freezes people for that moment in the memories of survivors. It was as if the world had stopped for those forty-five seconds. Like the interlocking plates of the earth's crust, fates were interlocked. Private lives became related to each other through the event, and to a large extent all lives came to be oriented around it.

The extent of this orientation took a course that surprised me. Survivors not only placed the living and the dead, they also placed a third category of people at the time of impact, those who had died before the earthquake. That is, even illnesses and deaths that had occurred prior to the earthquake were reexamined in light of the disaster: Where would someone have been that terrible Sunday had he or she not died before? A young woman said of her father: "Had he not died two years before the earthquake, surely he would have been at the movies. He used to go every Sunday afternoon, and people were trapped there. . . . It is better he died two years before."

A woman told me that when she was a child, she had dreamed that Huascarán would explode. At the time, an old man had commented on her dream: "These mountains are savage," he told her. "One day they will devour us all. My eyes will not see it, though, and my heart will not cry." Now, these many years later, the woman recalled her childhood dream and the old man's interpretation.

IT was not just people but saints' images, and even certain structures like the churches, that had to be pinpointed at the moment of impact and their history examined in light of the event. Why had certain ones stood and others not? Why had the Centenario church only cracked, while Soledad had crumbled? In Yungay, not an image was left except for the Christ on the cemetery hill. In Huaraz, bits and pieces of the saints' images were found, limbs ripped from torsos. Some few came through unscathed. All of this needed to be explored.

One day, in a little cane hut on the pampa, just back of the temporary structure that served as the Belén church, I found a cache of images. The sacristan of Belén had built the hut to protect them from the inclemencies. He lived with them there on the pampa, in a shack just in front of the hut. For eight years, the sacristan told me, he had been the keeper and protector of the saints, but most of all of *La Belenita*, the Virgin of Belén.

"She is so powerful," he said, "don't you see that nothing happened to her in the earthquake. I found her with two beams crossed on top of her, protecting her. Even the Lord of Solitude, they found him in pieces, but her, the Virgin, the same, the same, the same, I found her."

The cane hut was too low for either of us to stand up straight, and as we stooped over, the sacristan named all the images for me, giving something of their history, where they had been located in the church, where they were found afterward. His daughter sat nearby on the mud floor, playing with her baby.

"I was in the sacristy when the movement began, and María Auxiliadora was at the door in front of the church," Norabuena, the sacristan, said. "Everything was covered, obstructed. I escaped out back. The earth cracked, like lightning, into gullies. I was cut off back there. I thought, The world has ended. Will others have lived through this? Because if not, why should I escape? And the *Belenita*—where can she be? When I found her, it was so miraculous, and so much had come down on her! I can't leave her now. I can barely go to my *chacra* on the mountainside. I come back, running, right away, because she doesn't let me leave her. There are thieves now on the pampa. Oh, so often they have tried to steal her crown."

With a face out of a Goya painting, Norabuena moved around as if touched by a madness that sharpens things to a point we are not used to. I visited him often, and only in brief moments did the madness seem to depart from him. Once, as I was leaving, he stood by the little doorway that leads to the images, smiled, and said

Above: *The frozen puna, over 14,000 feet above sea level* (R. Carneiro). Below: *The Río Santa cuts its way between the Cordillera Negra and the Cordillera Blanca.*

Facing page, top: *The twin peaks of Huandoy;* bottom: *ascending to Lake Parón on the Cordillera Blanca* (R. Carneiro). Above: *Lake Parón, a glacial lake, with the Pirámide de Garcilaso in the background.* At right: *Suspension bridge over the Santa.* Below: *A mountain hamlet.*

Facing page: top, left: *Fallen church bells*; center: *Huaraz's cemetery—the earthquake unburied the dead* (F. Sotomayor); top, right: *the communal cross in the Huaraz cemetery, where thousands were buried*; bottom: *survivor camp in Caraz—the "beehives" Germany sent, still being used in 1980* (R. Carneiro). At left: *Survivor camp in Nicrupampa in the Huaraz foothills.* Center: *Domitila, "Edwincito," and his friends in Nicrupampa, 1980.* Bottom: *Huaraz "before"* (A. Minaya).

Below: *Huaraz: adobe upon adobe, stone upon stone* (A. Minaya). At right, top: *The cathedral on the Plaza de Armas on May 26, 1970* (F. Sotomayor); center: *"Now Huaraz is only a pampa."* Bottom: *Grass begins to grow on the pampa, and sheep graze.*

At left: *One of the few houses left in Huaraz's center; the barrio of Centenario in the background; and beyond, the foothills and the glacial peaks shrouded in clouds.* Center and bottom, left: *Christmas of 1971, under the cupola* (F. Sotomayor). Bottom, right: *Provisional shops, including a barbershop, built of canes, along Fitzcarral. An Indian woman shares the road with CRYRZA's bulldozer.*

Top: *The Ríos family has marked out their land on the pampa of Huaraz.* Center: *Salvation Army truck sent from New York City "with love."* At right: *My room in the Espinoza home on Nueva Granada, on the pampa.*

matter-of-factly, "Sometimes, in the afternoons, I do go to work in my field."

When Indian peasants from the mountainsides recounted the event, they, especially, included in the toll not only the dead but the images that had fallen. For example, no sooner had I arrived in Marián, a beautiful idyllic hamlet above Huaraz, than I was led to see Saint Michael, who was "very miraculous and who was saved from the earthquake!"

Rarely, but it did occur, a few survivors mused ironically on the whereabouts of God that Sunday. Audaciously, Humberto de Jesús wrote:

Tell me, Lord, what were you doing on May 31, 1970, at 3:24 [*sic*] in the afternoon? Perhaps, the answer is that God rests on Sundays and for that reason he didn't realize the earth was trembling. Trembling like a wounded animal that curls up its back, trying not to let death's grin show.

PERHAPS no one has dealt more vividly with the drama involved in the convergence of persons and events at a point in time and space than Thornton Wilder in his story—laid, too, in the vastness of the Andes—of five lives swept away when the bridge of San Luis Rey, on the high road to the ancient Inca capital of Cuzco, fell into the gorge below. Going beyond the immediate circumstances that brought people and bridge together at the moment of its collapse, Wilder has Brother Juniper pursue the question back through time. This notion of seeking to lay bare within the life history of an individual the reason for his having been at a certain place at a certain time is scattered throughout my field notebooks. I found little evidence for the stereotypical fatalism attributed to both Indians and Latins in South America. Even those who used such phrases as "When it is not one's hour"—as Manuel, the English teacher, did—pursued the issue further, to ask, "Why was it not my hour?"

As I collected story after story of people spared and people killed, I realized that the scene of the earthquake had in some sense turned into a laboratory for probing the age-old question of design in the universe. Survivors were engaged in the debate as to whether we are in the world by design or by chance. The notion of pure chance seemed to satisfy no one. Virtually all were trying to expose the hand of a creator at the bottom of it all, to unmask some pattern in human life that might have led to the sudden cutting off of lives that Sunday afternoon. Whatever pain or guilt this probing produced might be eased by evidence of some plan that would diminish the terror of lives taken, or preserved, willy-nilly.

Are we but flies killed by boys on a summer day, or are we like the sparrows who do not lose a feather that has not been brushed away by the finger of God? In my room on the pampa, by candlelight, as I read again, after many years, Thornton Wilder's words, they took on a life they had never had for me before.

Nine

CORRIDOR OF DEATH

Now, pushed to the edge of desolation, we know that pain is collective.

Hugo Ramírez,
Ancash, Vida y Pasión

URING MY STAY in the valley, many survivors shared their grief with me. More turbulent than fatalism, yet quieter than rage, grief went beyond the questioning of personal tragedy—Why me?—to the questioning of collective tragedy—Why here? Why now?

I soon became intensely aware of a feature of the tragedy of the Peruvian earthquake that is not present in private tragedy, namely, the *simultaneity* of its impact on *everyone*. There is a way in which the death of any similar number of people, dying their individual deaths, is not so great as if they died together. The whole is more than the sum of its parts.

In private tragedy, time and space are not constant. Misfortune strikes us at different times, in different places. But time was an absolute in the earthquake. It was literally one minute at 3:23 in the afternoon of May 31, 1970, when the force was discharged that touched *everybody*. Moreover, the valley's being so tightly circumscribed by two great mountain ranges gave an edge to the word "everybody." Shrouded in dust, its communication with the rest of the world summarily severed, the Callejóns containment was complete. Answers to the insistent Why? would have to account for everyone and everything in the valley.

With that moment—3:23 in the afternoon—constant, there ensued a kind of whirlpool effect. People felt the disaster first as individuals. Then, like ripples from a chunk of ice that plummets into a glacial lake, the waves of catastrophe spread out in circles to the distant shores until they swamped *the whole valley*. Yet all those contained in the valley had not died. The mantle of death, while it fell on all, fell more heavily on some than on others.

This required reflection: Why did I escape and my neighbors not? Why was the barrio of Soledad so hard hit and not Centenario? Yungay had disappeared, and Huaraz had been reduced to rubble, but in Caraz buildings still stood. Why were Catholics and townspeople struck down more than Protestants and peasants? How can we explain the loss of ten gentle nuns on holiday, crushed inside the small train weaving its way through the Cañón del Pato, when prisoners in jail escaped? Categories of people within the valley confines—like Catholics and Protestants; peasants and townspeople—seemed to crystallize under the cloak of disaster and their differential survival in it, though everyone also knew that in one way or another all had suffered.

IN the last chapter we saw some of the ways in which people considered their individual survival, attributing it to the correctness of their lives, to dreams and premonitions that had served as warnings, or simply to fate. Whatever the reason, though, there was not much rejoicing in one's own survival. Rather, it was clear that somewhere inside of everyone was the pain of survival, as if one's life had been spared at the expense of another's death. Earlier we saw evidence for this "survivor guilt" in the way Reyna and the old woman commiserated with each other on the pampa, their conclusion being that it was worse to survive than to die, for survivors must live out the suffering of so many deaths. And recall the troubled survival of the Oliveras, who almost two years later could not bring themselves to usher in the New Year because they had lost "so many relatives." And Chepo, who was drinking himself to death in Yungay Norte over the loss of his entire family and for having set off in a truck with his pigs, leaving them in the wake of the Huascarán avalanche. A kind of remorseful omniscience overtook survivors, as if they could have known and done better.

The following account of All Saints' Day, November 1, 1971, reveals the way guilt for sins as well as for merely having lived when others died, besides being felt by the individual himself, might suddenly be called forth in conversations with fellow survivors.

All Saints was a long celebration in the valley, lasting an entire week. The Huaraz cemetery, on the hill in Pedregal, had been hard hit, and as I walked through it, I occasionally had to avoid a coffin upturned in the earth or shaken from its niche. So many graves bore the date May 31, 1970. Passersby placed flowers on the two large communal graves, marked by tall bare wooden crosses, with nothing written on them. German nuns from Centenario were playing guitars and singing folk songs. They were followed from niche to niche by some twenty-five or thirty people.

By Tuesday, November 2, more and more people were walking up the hill to the cemetery, carrying small wooden crosses painted black. Along the Pedregal road, stands had been set up to sell *chicha*, the corn beer, and food. I went into a little hut where a woman was preparing tamales and sat down at a table with her husband and three friends of his. They were in the process of recalling the names of those who had lost their entire family. The woman spoke up from behind a counter. She said she was working in the hospital when the earthquake struck, but her husband was there in the house when the roof caved in, killing their two small daughters and her sister.

At the table, the men began to talk about sin, how we have sins we are not aware of. They looked at the woman's husband and said he must have many sins he didn't know about. Carlos, the husband, was uneasy. But then everyone seemed uneasy, seated around the wobbly wooden table, looking at each other, each perhaps feeling unworthy to be alive, with so much death around. The men had begun to drink heavily, and I walked out onto the road and decided to make the climb once more to the cemetery before

it got completely dark. Except for one man who was just entering
the gate, the cemetery was empty. On the road again, a big truck
stopped, and the driver offered me a ride back across the pampa.
As night fell, candles flickered along the Pedregal road, and people
huddled together over bonfires in the cold Andean night, eating
and drinking, remembering and sobbing.

PEOPLE were troubled about the children who had died, for everywhere children are felt to embody innocence. Children and innocence was a common theme in the aftermath. I remember Reyna
telling me that she did not cry until the day after the earthquake,
when she encountered Don Raimundo. Clutching a scarf wrapped
around his face, he came toward her, walking over the ruins. When
he released the scarf, his face looked as if it had aged a hundred
years since she had seen him just a few days before. He told her
he had lost his wife and two daughters, one of whom was Reyna's
best friend. He lost grandchildren, too, except for one, a toddler,
who had clung to the end of a flagpole for many hours before he
was rescued. At that moment, Reyna said to herself, If all this could
happen to innocent children, how could there be a God?

In their reflections, people would recall the circus in Yungay,
where indeed many children were spared from the avalanche. But
then, how might that be reconciled with what happened in Huaraz,
where as many as 400 children attending festivities in a convent
school perished?

It was the birthday of the directress of the religious high school,
the Colegio Santa Elena, located near the Plaza de Armas, and
hundreds had been invited to the celebration. All the seats were
filled. With the first tremors, fear spread among the audience of
parents and brothers and sisters watching the children perform in
plays and skits in honor of the mother superior. Thinking they
were only passing tremors and wanting to prevent panic, the mother
superior told everyone to sit quietly, and then she locked the doors.

Huaracino teacher, poet, and novelist Marcos Yauri Montero
and his family were trapped inside that building. Yauri lost two of
his children, Carlota and Ramón. After many hours, he, his wife,
Elba, and their remaining child, Illich, were rescued from under
the rubble. He began to keep a journal, published in 1971 under
the title *Tiempo de Rosas y de Sonrisas . . . Tiempo de Dolor y de Muerte.*

The first entry is July 15, 1970. While walking through the Patay encampment, Yauri sinks into memories of the night of May 31. He and his son Ramón are trapped under a wall. At the moment Ramón stops breathing, Yauri bellows:

> He is dead through all eternity! I begin to hate the world. To hate the world, to *hate* the world. I beat against the ruins with my elbows, I scratch in the earth. . . . For what crime? Why have we been abandoned? I calculate a space of only some 10 cubic centimeters in front of my face. . . . Soon I too am going to die, to die, to die forever.

Hours pass. Finally, Yauri hears footsteps above him. With the little breath left in him, he calls out and then waits a long time before the hand of his student, Cremonini, reaches him.

> They worked until a quarter to one in the morning, removing in buckets the earth that buried me. At intervals, I would ask after the rest of my family, and Cremonini would say, "They're all right, Illich is playing with his little lamb." I believed him and it eased me. Or I would ask about Huaraz. "Nothing remains but stone upon stone," Cremonini would answer, and I did not believe that. When they got me out, they carried me on a poncho to the Plaza. I saw the flickering light of bonfires. Friends came and bathed my face.

Still in July 1970, Yauri, alone in his tent 300 meters from the ruins of Huaraz's center, tries to sleep as winds lash the frail canvas. Finally, he lights a candle and writes:

> Silence swallows me up, and memories drench my heart. . . . They laid me down on the grass in the Plaza de Armas, and covered me with a blanket. I asked for my Carlota. "She is buried," Elba answered. My head hurt and my legs felt broken, and Elba tried to make me more comfortable. . . . My mind wandered between wakefulness and sleep. Don Víctor came and threw himself at me and cried. His wife and young daughter were buried under the Cathedral towers. . . . I remember the wailing, I remember that Illich curled up on my feet like a ball of yarn. . . . [When I awoke], I felt a heaviness in my head, in all my body. . . .

My eyelids were swollen over my pupils. . . . I saw something
unfamiliar like tall strange buildings, and asked Elba where we
were. "In the Plaza." I asked what were those strange buildings.
"There's nothing," she sobbed. My eyes wouldn't open, but I
didn't want to see anymore. Inside, my soul shouted, and the
future opened up before me like an immense deserted avenue. . . .
All around, the voices persisted, pleading, crying out, cursing.
A thick mist veiled the air, hiding the sky and the mountains. . . .
In front was Santa Elena, converted into a column of rubble,
from which the bodies of children didn't stop coming. The world
was empty. . . . We had died a thousand times. We were all
dead.

It was not easy for people to absorb the tragedy of Santa Elena,
precisely, I think, because it touched so many children. The lady
in the Belén plaza, for instance, about to take part in the procession
of María Auxiliadora, not only asked why she was spared but why,
simultaneously, not far away, so many died at Santa Elena. Everyone knew the empirical reasons for so much loss inside that
building—that it was packed, that the doors had been locked, that
there was panic. Still, the "sense of it" had to be determined, by
Delia and other survivors of Huaraz. There had to be a way to ease
the pain of it.

It happened that a young priest was passing by Santa Elena
when the tremors began. He could have escaped, people said, run
the other way, but instead he found a way into the building even
as it was falling apart. He was last seen giving absolution to the
entire stricken assembly. Therefore, people reasoned, all those inside Santa Elena were also saved, at least in a spiritual sense. Since
it was believed that souls not absolved by such priestly action might
remain on the pampa, restless and vexed, for a year before being
released from earthly ties, it was comforting to imagine that the
victims of Santa Elena, especially innocent children, had gone directly to heaven.

An elderly priest, himself badly traumatized by the event, both
physically and psychologically, told me the story of that young
priest, his nephew, in Santa Elena:

Padre Claudio was passing the corner of the Plaza de Armas.
Instead of being somewhere else, he was walking around reading

a book near the Plaza. When he is exactly forty steps from the Plaza de Armas, in front of the Colegio Santa Elena, the dreadful earthquake occurs. . . . Women and children fall on top of each other against the huge main door, which has been locked, and the fierce shaking continues, and my beloved nephew, my poor nephew, runs to save those persons. He goes inside in that moment of violent shaking. He had no fear. Padre Claudio died rescuing many women who had fallen down. He carried out seven, eight, ten, women and children, and then he went back inside when the earth shook the strongest to absolve them, hundreds of people, children, men, women who were dying in the Convent of Santa Elena. You see, being a priest, he tried to fulfill his sacred obligation to save spiritually, to absolve all those people who were dying. In that instant, in less than two seconds, he pardoned hundreds, and then adobe bricks struck his head.

When I asked what would have happened to the souls of those at the celebration without Claudio's absolution, the old priest answered:

Without the absolution, those people would have asked in a split second, "Lord, forgive me. Mercy! Save my soul!" In that moment they would have obtained salvation, like all my fellow countrymen, thousands and thousands who died and who begged God in an instant, they were saved. Only God knows for sure if they asked, if it was that way. But with that clamor of those at Santa Elena, and my nephew there, their absolution complete, the salvation of hundreds was complete. . . .

Santa Elena was the most tragic event in Huaraz spawned by the larger disaster. Other schools that had been destroyed reopened eventually with desks and benches that had been salvaged and placed under eucalyptus trees on the fringes of the pampa. Plans were made to rebuild them. But no temporary Colegio Santa Elena was set up, nor were there plans to rebuild it.

ANOTHER instance, this time of group survival rather than loss, that had achieved a certain notoriety in the environs of Huaraz was that of the Evangelical luncheon guests in Marcará. I first heard about the luncheon from a blind man who had come to Huaraz for an

Evangelical prayer meeting. Like almost everyone I met for the first time, the man told the story of where he was when the earthquake struck. He said that 107 Evangelicals were having lunch at his home in Marcará that Sunday, just after a baptism ceremony had been held nearby in the Río Marcará. When the house collapsed, only one of the 107 people was injured.

The man told me that almost immediately after the shaking diminished, the Catholics of Marcará began to throw stones at the Evangelicals, blaming the earthquake on their "pagan" ceremony in the river. Then the Catholics realized that the earthquake was widespread, and they stopped. The survival of the luncheon guests, he said, was testimony to the rightness of their religious beliefs. After all, a companion of the blind man pointed out, look at all the Catholic images that did not withstand the quake.

Months later, in a bus passing through Marcará, another Evangelical convert exclaimed loudly, "It was a miracle that none of us died here. God was with us!"

One of the immediate responses was to assign blame. Recall Yauri's "For what crime?" uttered as he beat his arms against the rubble that buried him and his son. A young American mountain climber, a longtime resident of Huaraz, said he ran to the Plaza de la Soledad, along with so many others seeking open space. Suddenly, he began to feel uneasy and then wanted to hide during the first days, as insinuations were made that the presence of foreigners in the valley might be the reason for the disaster.

Indeed, one of the first raging waves to explain the disaster was to suspect the presence of foreigners in the valley. North American Mormon missionaries were run out of the towns. Even Peruvian Protestants long established in the Callejón were suspect.

RESPONSIBILITY, it seemed, must be assigned to account for deaths, both individual and in clusters. One category of people was pitted against another—foreigners and natives, Catholics and Protestants—and guilt and conflict flourished as survivors searched for reasons. A major source of discord was the differential survival of townsmen and peasants.

The shaking had barely subsided when the cycle of questions and answers began. In the days that followed, as the realization slowly grew that the disaster had extended beyond the town one was in, or the road one was on, that Yungay was gone and the canyon that led down to the sea had caved in, the full awareness of the magnitude of the event brought forth a corresponding increase in the magnitude of the explanation. Understanding eventually must encompass *the whole valley*.

Besides, given the complex relationship of sierra people to their natural surroundings, their personal feelings toward nature and tender affection for animals, all of their natural world—even the mountains that had shattered and spat down boulders—became subsumed under the category of *the whole valley*. "What were the sun, the wind, and the desolate peaks of the Andes saying? They were sharing our sorrow . . . the wild boughs of the mountains like thousands of waving handkerchiefs soaked with our tears," a teacher from Yungay told Zavaleta, the poet from Caraz who compiled responses in the early days of the aftermath. "Even the birds were somewhat sad," an Indian from one of Huaraz's hamlets told me.

It was May everywhere. In the clarity of the sky, the moon shedding its brilliant light on valley, pinnacles, and hillocks. In streets silver-plated by the moon, where people walked. In church bells that rang out in the moonstruck silence of a late Callejón night. It was May in the Ancash sun dancing on rooftops and in the gentle shadows cast by tall trees over the valley afternoons. It was May in the sky and the earth, in love, in longings, in almanacs. In children's notebooks and in the confines of thought and hope. In this vein, Recuay poet Hugo Ramírez wrote about the "*all*" that disaster so consummately struck.

EXPLANATION went beyond accounting for oneself and other selves, for things and animals. It sought to account for the ties that bound them all together. Amid the torn fabric of their community, survivors began to question their institutions and the nature of the bonds that had cemented their life together in the valley, the framework that supported the flow of life.

This may be true in all cases of crisis to a collectivity. But the fact that Andean cosmology and ontology give strong emphasis to "community," viewing it not as God-given but as created by human beings—the ancestors—to be nourished through all time, made the breaks in the structure of life in the Callejón, I think, especially threatening. In the Quechua belief system, which forms the sub-

stratum or bedrock upon which other belief systems in the region
have had to build, the dimension of time is the only thing that
differentiates human from divine. "There is an eternal earthly family, all related with the people, the *runakuna*," an Indian explained.
"The only difference is time. The *aukikuna* ["wise old men"] of the
eternal family are our ancestors. They are the same people of the
community, perhaps the first men."

Despite almost 450 years of domination by others and the
intense infusion of Christianity, Andean populations, mainly the
Indians, still feel themselves connected to their earliest ancestors,
the *aukikuna*, these first men who formed and gave to them the
legacy of "community."[1]

Given this heightened sense of community, inquiry into why
the earthquake happened to *the whole valley* almost had to contain
at least a covert questioning of the structure of community life. Did
we bring calamity about through our social structure? Was there
something wrong with our political organization, our religious
structure or practice? And when it came to the broader question
of why *their* valley, all segments of society—Indian peasants, mestizo townspeople, and the small elite class alike—appeared to experience some sense of *communal* responsibility. Two years after
the disaster, on the eve of May 31, 1972, as if trying to gather the
frayed edges of the sundered community about him, a local bard
recited over Radio Huascarán: ". . . Huaraz is naked. I ask pardon
for this nakedness."

Thus, at the level of *the whole valley*, attempts were made to
sweep away conflict generated at lower levels, where one group
might lay responsibility at the door of another. Ultimately all would
be guilty, or all would be innocent. Likewise, the sovereignty of
the collectivity was such that, through the months after, the ex-
planatory process involved finding a way for everyone to be "saved,"
if only spiritually, like the children of Santa Elena, while at the
same time substantiating the suffering of everyone, even those physically spared. The dead were alive; and the living were dead.

As the event came to engulf the entire community, valley and
tragedy coalesced. I remember the day I became conscious that
event and place had merged in a disaster identity. It was early in
my fieldwork. I was walking in the foothills of the Cordillera Blanca
with the old priest who had been feeding his doves in the patio of

the archaeological museum when the earthquake began. After exploring the ruins of Wilkawaín, he took me to a less well known ruin, Ichiquilka, which means "small sacred place." He explained that even before the Inca came, it had been a ceremonial temple. He had found ancient burials in it. It suddenly got very cold, and as rain turned to large chunks of hail, we took refuge inside the ruin. As we sat on our haunches in the dark, peering out through a small opening, the priest mused, "Now they call this whole valley the Corridor of Death (*Callejón de la Muerte*). Even the reconstruction people don't want to come here."

Ten

CHINESE BOXES

*History dissembles the fact that humanity
goes on living and working like the silent
sea over which the waves of cataclysm
break.*

Miguel de Unamuno,
En Torno al Casticismo

BEING IN THE CALLEJÓN gave me strong and conflicting sensations. When I stood on the Yungay playa, hearing only the softest breeze, or on the Huaraz pampa, amid its silent sea of dust, I felt as if I were in the most remote place on earth. At the same time, I was aware of the impact that outsiders from the coast and distant nations was having on the valley. This gave me the feeling of being in the hub of the world's tensions, fears, and dreams. The Corridor of Death was strangely alive. I tried to reconcile these contradictory feelings.

Geologically, the earthquake afforded an instant glimpse of the tremendous natural forces operating within the earth. Then, recorded and transformed by human perception, it also made vivid the social and cultural forces that, as silent and constant as the bottom of the sea, were at work in the Callejón. The valley seemed injected with some phosphorescent fluid that threw into sharp relief contours of belief and behavior that had before lain obscure in the twilight of ordinary life.

Conversations and dreams were recalled in minute detail. Sermons listened to only desultorily in the months before the earthquake were recollected and repeated. Corpus Christi of May 31, 1970, was not just another feast day, forgotten like those of past years. Rather, people sifted back through the ceremony for peculiar ways in which it had been celebrated, noting lapses in the performance of the rituals.

A statue of the Virgin Mary at the doorway of the Belén church, ready to be carried through the streets in procession, was nothing out of the ordinary. Yet, people said it was a miracle that the Virgin had been in that doorway, protected by its lintel. The occasion even passed into verse and was recited during the second anniversary observances:

> *It was 3:23 in the afternoon,*
> *Jesus Christ was in the Plaza of Belén,*
> *And the Virgin at the temple door . . .*
> *Oh, Huaraz!*

BESIDES the highlighting of everyday incidents, other things were going on in the Callejón that also emerged from the shadows when disaster struck. In 1970, like many parts of the Third World, the valley found itself at the nexus of several major trains of events, some global, some national, some religious, some secular. Atomic power had been unleashed, and since 1966, France had been conducting a series of bomb tests in the Pacific Ocean, due west of Peruvian shores. Vatican Council II had plunged the Catholic Church into the turbulence of contemporary social upheaval; the 1968 Conference of Bishops, held in Medellín, Colombia, had clearly voiced sympathy with the radical transformation of Latin American society, and an intensely Latin American formulation of Catholic Reform, which would become known as the "theology of liberation," was being shaped by Peruvian Gustavo Gutiérrez. The dissemination of the Bible by both Evangelicals and Catholic reformers, translated into everyday language, along with increasing literacy in the valley, had opened up Matthew, chapter 24, which

speaks of earthquakes as a sign of the Apocalypse. And the Revolutionary Military Government of Gen. Juan Velasco Alvarado
had begun promulgating agrarian reform and social mobilization of
the Indian masses.

These events were represented only latently in pre-earthquake
Huaraz. Like a cloud, they had hovered tenuously over the valley,
and when the disaster struck, the cloud burst, and the ideologies
underlying these global and national events rained down on the
native soil and began to take root. The disaster, having left a kind
of tabula rasa, served to precipitate many of these latent forces into
overt social action. The long and hard-won post-Conquest equilibrium, a synthesis of native Quechua and Spanish Catholic worlds
that had prevailed for centuries in this sierra community, was now
in danger of being undermined.

A great deal of confusion resulted from the confrontation of
changing times and the disaster. The incipient pre-earthquake
changes became double-edged swords. Survivors were uncertain
whether the disaster had occurred because their social relations and
religious practices had begun to change or because they had not
yet changed enough. Perhaps, for example, they had resisted too
much the agrarian reform, already in progress by May 1970. On
the other hand, agrarian reform was upsetting the old social order.
Ironically, it was an Indian who barely spoke Spanish who told me
that the peasants were saying that the changes in land tenure had
brought about the disaster: "The things announced by the government are bad, because it is thinking very high, but God does not
want this. Even the skin of the potato they are controlling. They
are measuring everything. This is fatal, don't you see?"[1]

THUS, large movements that might have followed a more measured
pace and small incidents, otherwise unremarkable, were suddenly
charged with meaning. The earthquake had sparked a magical
worldview, where everything seemed to matter and signs and symbols were everywhere. Late one afternoon, in a hamlet on the
Cordillera Blanca, I watched a peasant prepare a huge rugged
wooden cross for its traditional yearly visit to the churches of
Huaraz. There, in normal times, it would have been blessed and
returned to the mountain peak to protect the hamlet from rains and
landslides and crop failures. But these were not normal times, and

since the earthquake, the *campesinos* had been forbidden to bring the mountain crosses down to Huaraz. Still, the man labored over the cross that lay in the muddy patio spanning almost the width of his house. He knelt over it, meticulously attaching to the cross special plants that grow only in certain places on the Cordillera Blanca. Later, he would coat the leaves with a silver paint. The man's small daughter, who was watching him from the doorway of the house, suddenly fell down and began to cry. He picked her up and said, "You see, my little girl has fallen. This is a punishment for not taking the crosses down to Huaraz. The Catholic Reform had already begun to take our customs away before the earthquake, and, well, perhaps for that reason, the earthquake happened."

In the heightened awareness, the valley was rendered vulnerable. Winds were no longer just winds, nor tremors merely the pulsating of the earth. Whirlwinds of dust had intent, religious processions were imbued with significance they had not had before, and people's acts were measured by the yardstick of the event. The period after the disaster was a long one of watching and waiting. New events and changing circumstances as well as the illumination of their predisaster past might give some clue to *Why?*

The date itself, May 31, would never be just another May 31. An ominous atmosphere preceded its recurrence in the year 1972. A young girl told me that "an old man they call a wizard" had called out to her and her friends, "It will happen again, the same hour, the same minute." It was the same two years ago, she went on, when an old woman in black had come to a store and told the shopkeeper that "Huaraz within hours will come to an end."

On the eve of the second anniversary, a group of friends and I were returning from a visit, walking across the pampa toward my house. We were all silent. I was conscious of the cold and the dark and the wild, broken hulks of the mountains enclosing us in the pit of the valley. Finally, someone said, "It was a night just like this before the earthquake."

During the course of my stay, such disparate phenomena from the grand and minor scales of life as land reform, the expulsion of two missionaries from the valley in 1965, the rains and landslides of 1972, a five-megaton bomb exploded beneath an island in the Aleutians in July 1972, and a child's fall all found a focus in the earthquake. Past and future, even in their most trivial detail, seemed to tumble headlong out of the disaster, providing grist for the mill of explanation.

In the aftermath, the outlines of what really mattered in the social and religious structure and practice of the people, and of their deepest beliefs, fears, and sentiments, were etched in as by acid. A schoolteacher in Huaraz put it this way: "Many have defined themselves, their philosophy of life, of death, all the essential. Because, really, most of us, we don't know what we are living for, do we?"

True, survivors were not transformed overnight into philosophers bent on unraveling the riddles of life. There were many moods. Life did go on. At times, in part because of the surrealness of the setting, the strange juxtaposition of things, people, and places—like pigs lolling under the imposing skeleton of the cathedral's cupola—it was the ordinary that seemed the truly extraordinary. I marveled at how the many small daily activities that make up a lifetime had resumed and routinely were playing out their course.

IN me, the deep Andean past of the valley, its myth, history, and intimate daily life, all aroused by the disaster, coupled with the intrusion of new ideas from the larger world, created that sense of paradox that grew stronger over the months of my stay and made me feel that I was in one of the most remote places on earth while simultaneously at its very center. Huaraz, although only 270 miles distant from a capital city of 3 million people, at 10,000 feet higher than that city, was ecological and cultural light-years away. Yet so many from even beyond Lima had gathered there at the edges of the destruction, with so many ideas about world building, it seemed that surely all eyes from outside, from the "intact" world, must be focused on this spot. Unrealistic, but so it seemed.

It is the insistent sensation I had of being far away, yet at the center of the world, that had to be reflected in some way in order to render the disaster and its aftermath as faithfully as possible. The secret to understanding the event might be found in the way it became tethered to interpretations emanating from the local, national, and world backgrounds. Consequently, in the following chapters, we unravel the story of the aftermath by opening successive "Chinese boxes." First, we see survivors grappling with making sense of the disaster in light of the world and national scenes, then in light of valley belief and custom, and finally, in the inner-most box, we find the image of the Soledad Christ. From those larger spaces where it seemed to me all eyes must be upon the valley, we will have moved to a corner of Huaraz, in Soledad barrio, where it seemed no one from outside was looking.

Part 3

THE WORLD AND THE VALLEY

From distant lands men come
Waving flags of brotherhood.
They have left behind their bombs,
Their death machines.
> Román Obregón,
> *Cuaderno del Damnificado*

Eleven

BEAUTY AND DANGER

*God has given us the best of nature, and
also phenomena that destroy us.*
    a man from the barrio of Belén

P ERU, along with other nations of the circum-Pacific, is part
of what has been called the Rim of Fire, where most of
the world's volcanoes rise and its earthquakes occur. High
seismic activity, youthful mountain chains, volcanoes, and ocean
trenches especially characterize the Peru-Chile arc. It is believed
that this belt of pronounced seismicity results from a progressive
underthrusting of a slab of the Pacific Ocean floor beneath the South
American continent.

The history of earthquakes in Peru from pre-Columbian times
down to May 31, 1970, is impressive. Spanish chronicler Cieza de
León remarked in the sixteenth century, "They say it is very certain
that the earth trembled in such a manner that many mountains
caved in, falling upon the valleys." The Peruvian viceroy dispatched
to the king of Spain the "True and Particular Relation of the Dread-

ful Earthquake . . . of 1746." In modern times, we have Thornton Wilder's hyperbolic statement:

> . . . for in that country those catastrophes which lawyers shockingly call the "Acts of God" were more than usually frequent. Tidal waves were continually washing away cities; earthquakes arrived every week and towers fell upon men and women all the time.

We get the impression of a country in constant geophysical upheaval. Yet, despite this history of repeated temblors, it is estimated that the 1970 disaster took more than double the toll of all of Peru's previous five centuries of earthquakes.

However, although many large earthquakes have been recorded throughout Peru during this century, the highland area struck on May 31, 1970, had been free of destructive shallow-focus shocks. Only the barely perceptible intermediate and deep shocks, with hypocentral depths below 70 and 300 kilometers, respectively, have been registered with any frequency in the Callejón.

Only one serious earthquake is known to have struck the Callejón de Huaylas before 1970. On January 6, 1725, violent shaking caused an alluvion from a glacial lake in the Huandoy gorge to sweep down the Cordillera Blanca, razing the town of Ancash and taking 1,500 lives. In 1956 and 1963, minor quakes occurred, the first shaking Carhuaz and its satellite hamlets, the latter damaging buildings in small hamlets on the Cordillera Negra.

In contrast to earthquakes, icefalls are a common occurrence. In the late 1940s geologists observed that small icefalls take place several times a day and major ice avalanches occur every few months or few years. The large talus slopes at the base of the unstable peaks of the Cordillera Blanca suggest that repeated ice-and-rock avalanches have occurred during Holocene times.

THROUGH the centuries, the earthquake has only reluctantly yielded its secrets to the probing minds and instruments of scientists. Though enigmas still surround the cause of earthquakes, the new science of plate tectonics, building on an older theory of continental drift, has contributed much to our scientific understanding of them. The tectonic view holds that the earth's land masses sit on giant rock plates that float on a partially molten layer of the earth's interior. According to this theory, earthquakes are due to the friction generated by the sudden sliding of one huge rock slab under another and are related to the same movements that have elevated mountain ranges and depressed trenches under the sea.

For hundreds of years before the rise of geology, the Aristotelian theory, which ascribed earthquakes to the pressure of winds imprisoned in the earth seeking to escape from underground cavities, had prevailed. These subterranean winds, in turn, were attributed to a fire raging at the center of the earth. Aristotelian theory thus tied earthquakes to volcanic explosions. However, observation of earthquakes distant from active volcanoes required some further explanation and led eventually to the tectonic theory. Although earthquakes occur in areas without active volcanoes, like the Callejón, tectonic and volcanic activity are generally associated, for plate disjunctions ultimately are due to the upwelling of molten rock from deep within the earth.

Investigations in the Pacific Ocean in the 1950s and 1960s revealed that three enormous slabs of the sea floor were exerting pressure against the drifting American continents. Pacific-floor studies also demonstrated that the separation of the three interlocking submarine plates was due to intrusions of wedges of expanding molten rock. It is presumed that the plunging of one of these oceanic plates, called the Nazca Plate, beneath the Peruvian coast was the cause of the 1970 earthquake. In response to the stress exerted upon the earth's crust, great seismic waves radiated through the valley, and the Cordillera Blanca fractured. Later, on the basis of microscopic examinations that disclosed signs of internal movements in the crystallized rock, geophysicists determined that the Cordillera Blanca may have risen a few feet that day in May.

The world scientific community had an explanation for the disaster. Now the survivors would weave this explanation together with their own notions of geophysics, their assessment of the landscape as both glorious and tortured, and their own telluric sensibility. They would rework the seismological thinking about the event to bring it closer to the beliefs they already held.

Before we look at people's perceptions of the earthquake as a seismological event, there is another scientific factor to consider. It is that the severity of an earthquake for its victims depends not only on structures and processes deep inside the earth but also on the condition of the surface layers of the soil. The floor of the Callejón consists of unconsolidated and partially consolidated fluvioglacial and mudflow deposits that in certain areas attain a thickness of up to several hundred meters. Much of this debris, which readily slides downhill when the mountains shake, originated from the bursting of glacial lakes and from ice-rock avalanches in the Cordillera Blanca. Nearly all the cities, towns, and villages in the valley were built on this type of alluvial material. However, geologists called attention to an "erratic damage distribution" in the disaster of 1970:

> In some places, damage to structures is clearly related to foundation failure, whereas in others the pattern of damage is somewhat variable and seemingly unrelated to geologic foundation conditions. For example, some villages were almost totally destroyed, whereas nearby villages of apparently similar construction and geologic foundation show only moderate damage. Similarly, parts of Huaraz were leveled, whereas other areas were only moderately damaged or undamaged. We have no explanation for the cause of these striking variations.

After the disaster, helicopters filled with scientists from many countries flew over the scene. They soon realized that what they were seeing was a major geologic event in the world's history. Transistor radios and newspapers that entered the valley spoke of the event in geophysical terms. What did survivors say about the disaster in these terms? What was their understanding of the seismic process? Had they expected that one day an earthquake of such magnitude might occur? Or that Yungay might disappear? What did it mean for them to live in the Callejón de Huaylas? Had they perceived the risks?

From the outset, I was gripped by the geomorphic drama of the valley. I was caught up in mixed feelings of peace and uneasiness stirred in me by the ensemble of a campestral valley wedged between the dark folds of one cordillera and the ice-draped peaks and glacial lakes of another. Early in the fieldwork, I learned that the Santa Corporation had for several years been located in Huaraz. The name of Benjamín Morales, its chief, became familiar to me.

Under his able leadership, the Santa Corporation had stood watch over the morainal lakes, draining them when necessary and keeping track of weaknesses in the glaciers that might threaten the valley.

During those early weeks of my stay, I found I could not keep my eyes off the glaciers or my mind from wondering if some crevice, still imperceptible to the naked eye, might be sinisterly menacing the delicate balance of forces. Driven by a desire to know more about the dangers involved, I went to see Benjamín Morales in his office in the barrio of Centenario. Sitting uneasily on the edge of my chair, I thanked him for keeping the lakes up there in their places. He smiled, the tension was broken, and we became friends. I was to learn later how much the Santa Corporation meant to the people of the valley.

Survivors praised the beauty of their valley. Their land was abundant, a land of grains, honey, and animals. The air was pure, in contrast with the fetidness of the jungle towns of the eastern lowlands and the pollution of the coastal cities. As I walked with them along the narrow, winding footpaths, someone might name a certain pinnacle in anticipation of our seeing it around the next turn.

Their awareness of the beauty was sometimes poignant. When conversations about the disaster were edging toward the borders of despair, it was not uncommon for someone to say, "But we must look up toward the peaks, *alzar la vista*" ("lift our eyes"). The ghostly memories that haunt one while crossing the pampa are not so bad during the day, someone said, "when we can look at the landscape."

But people's perception of beauty was tempered by an awareness of the danger that lay in that beauty. Ambivalent feelings of attraction and disquiet toward their physical setting were often close to the surface. Often the disquietude itself was felt to be enticing. A carpenter who had come from Trujillo to Huaraz as a young man remained in Huaraz, he told me, because the landscape awakened unrest in him, making him more meditative. To a townsman of financial means, which allowed him to live in Lima after the earthquake, "the enigma of these mountains which has no key" kept compelling his return to Huaraz. A townswoman said of the icy peaks, "They make me afraid. But I would never want to leave here, because they seem unattainable."

Inspiring both fear and respect, the glacial peaks were often the subject of contemplation and conversation. Indian women might tip their hats to a pinnacle, and I heard men speak of not turning their backs on a particular mountain. Muleteers crossed the high passes of the Cordillera Blanca with caution, for the mountain summits are still imbued with the religious overtones that made them the *Apus* of pre-Columbian times, when the highest mountains were divinities. An old priest remembered when Indians still spoke of *Apu* Huascarán. And even now, just as their pre-Spanish ancestors did, they placed stones at the passes. These piles of stones, called *apachetas*, are sacred (*huaca*), and travelers added offerings of coca or straw or worn-out *llanquis* (sandals made of rubber tires) to the *apachetas* to ensure their safe passage across the Cordillera.

To describe both themselves and the landscape, people used images of silent forces that suddenly erupt. "This landscape softens our character," one man said. "We do not explode so easily when we live in this paradise. We endure like water dripping slowly into a gourd. Then suddenly we explode." In like manner, the mountains also endure the earth's internal stresses, and ice-melt seeps slowly down through hidden crevices at the summits. Then suddenly the mountains explode, and the glacial peaks fly apart.

Early in my stay, I became aware that people spoke of "our nature" ("*nuestra naturaleza*") as if in contrast to Nature ("*la naturaleza*"), viewed in the abstract. No word for Nature exists in Quechua, and when I would ask Quechua speakers to respond to the Spanish word, they would begin by naming the mountains of the valley. "Our nature," it appeared, comprised the specific nameable entities of the Callejón.

I would sit on the Huaraz pampa and get people to identify the peaks, straining to learn them by their shapes and delighting in the litany of names. Cayesh, the dagger-shaped pinnacle; Vallunaraju, like a two-humped camel; San Cristóbal, its hump, as they would say, like a baby being carried on its mother's back. The tortured landscape had inspired myths and legends, which, much like people's statements to me then, combined a sense of peace, disquiet, and sorrow.

Huascarán was sometimes called a prince watching over the beautiful Huandoy. Although today Huascarán (from *huasca*, "rope," in Quechua) is thought of and referred to as masculine—*el Huascarán*—an ancient myth depicts the mountain as a lovely maiden. The Cordillera Blanca and the Cordillera Negra began as one mountain chain. The fair Huascarán was wed to Canchón, by whom she had thirty-two children. Canchón was unfaithful, and in a fit of jealousy Huascarán abandoned Canchón and his illegitimate children, who remained dressed in mourning as the Cordillera Negra. She marched to the other side, stationing herself above Yungay, flanked by her children, all turned into the snowy peaks of the Cordillera Blanca. The tears of unfortunate mother and children formed the high lakes of the Cordillera Blanca and the rivulets that flow down into the Santa. The bifurcated peaks of Huascarán are sometimes called the mother carrying her favored child. But I also heard them explained as male and female, like the two lakes of Llanganuco.

The feeling of containment one has in the valley is therefore real from many points of view: visually, geologically, and mythologically. Indeed, the intensity of the earthquake was augmented by the fact that it resonated between the two cordilleras. The enclosure of the valley contributes, perhaps, to the people's perception of "our nature," in contrast to Nature, abstract and unconfined.

Of all the familial geomorphic entities of the valley, Huascarán, especially, is personified, commanding awe, hate, and respect. It is "traitor," "villain," but also "the sovereign." After the disaster, ballads were composed about the relationship between the people and the mountain. The words of one begin, "Huascarán, you are at fault, / all your children have admired you . . ." Once, when we were approaching the gorge between Huandoy and Huascarán and a dense fog concealed the stone face of Huascarán, my companion suddenly shouted: "You are a murderer! You are ashamed, and you hide yourself now in the mist. Yes, it is right that you are ashamed." In imaginations, the killer mountain loomed even higher than it does in reality. "It is said that Huascarán can be seen from Europe," an Indian woman told me.

Despite Huascarán's villainous transcendence, the valley's greatest mystery and danger are clearly perceived as locked somewhere inside the deep gorges, *quebradas*, that penetrate the Cordillera Blanca. In these gorges nest the treacherous morainal lakes, and there, too, are found archaeological sites where the *ahuilos*, the "grandparents"—mummified ancestors—are buried. From time to time, out of these great gullets, destruction has poured. Water, mud, rock, and ice have erased hamlets and larger towns: Huaraz in 1702, the earliest landslide of which there remains any account; the town of Ancash in 1725; portions of Caraz in 1870; a part of Huaraz in 1941; the Cañón del Pato in 1950; and Ranrahirca in the 1962 avalanche from Huascarán. In 1945, debris sped down the eastern flanks of the Cordillera Blanca, destroying the town of Chavín de Huántar and settling over large portions of the famous ruins of Chavín.

Prior to 1970, the two worst disasters in the Callejón, which together took 10,000 lives, were avalanches: The first one was in Huaraz in the early morning of December 13, 1941, when Lake Chúrup spilled down Cójup gorge into the Río Quilcay, creating a wide avenue of mud and stone. I walked this "avenue" among the boulders, some of which lay cradled in the forking branches of a tree or served to buttress makeshift shelters of 1970 survivors. The other avalanche occurred at 6:18 P.M. on January 10, 1962, when Ranrahirca disappeared.

Besides these larger avalanches, landslides—called *huaycos* in Quechua—have on frequent occasions carried off some isolated hamlet, someone on a path, farmers in a field, animals grazing. Don Alejandro, the guardian at Lake Llanganuco, no doubt had this in mind when he said of life on the Cordillera Blanca: "One does not know if or when he will return to his house."

No wonder that survivors of the 1970 earthquake, huddling in tents and lean-tos, listened tensely through the long nights to the rock slides that rattled in the deep throats of the high mountains, any one of which might herald an avalanche.

Because of the combination of glaciers and lakes and the history of tragedy that has issued from it, the greatest threat to the well-being of the Callejón is seen as the Cordillera Blanca. Even thunder and lightning, people said, are fiercer over the Blanca than the Negra. The Cordillera Negra, though not lacking its own treachery, is perceived as gentler, more benign. It is also experienced more as a whole. Its summits are not readily singled out, nor are such strong bonds between individual mountains and people formed. High on the Negra, in the town of Huaylas, I tried to get a man to talk about the two cordilleras. Looking across to the Blanca, he named the peaks we saw: Huandoy, Santa Cruz, Alpamayo, and, of course, Huascarán. He said that the foothills and folds of the Negra, in contrast to the Blanca, are able to contain avalanches and that when water flows it is only to give life to Huaylas. Though he could not name the mountains of the Negra, when I asked which cordillera he felt more sentiment toward, he answered: "Here I was born. My race inclines me more toward the dark than the light. I get lost in nature. [*Yo me confundo con la naturaleza.*] I appreciate, I live, that is how we feel."

Though invisible from the valley floor and never seen by many, especially townspeople, who say they would never venture up through the gorges, the morainal lakes of the Blanca are nevertheless vivid in people's imaginations. "We live constantly aware of those lakes," one townswoman said. "Every day I think of them, that one could come down." People do not get too close to the lakes, for tantalizing treasures, supposedly lying on the lake bottoms, are said to draw one irresistibly into their depths.

Full of minerals and thus magnetic, the mountains likewise are believed to pull one toward them. To be too near the mountain is to risk debilitation because the minerals suck out one's blood and one grows cold. At Llanganuco, Don Alejandro told me he was sure Huascarán is enchanted because it contains so much mineral. It is even more fatal than other peaks. Black stones from its rock face plunge down to the Río Santa from time to time, because they need to suck blood. "The mineral grows and sprouts, and the more it does, the more lethal it becomes. Yes, it is a killer, Huascarán, but we are accustomed." As he spoke, I remembered other imagery I had heard, of rocks that break open and "blossom like a flower blooming." I tried to imagine these malignant outcroppings of black stones, alive, growing, irresistible beauty on a rampage drawing one to his death.

"Huascarán has to suck blood," Alejandro repeated. "That is why those who live near the mountain are pale. It makes some of us somnambulant, like ghosts. It weakens one. I, when I was young, was warm. Now I have grown cold up here. I suffer much from the Cordillera Blanca. Yes, Huascarán sucks at you like a magnet. One is walking and is suddenly frozen dead in his tracks, turned to stone. But there are herbs that protect you so that the rock does not suck blood," he allowed. "The place itself has its own remedy."

Besides the danger of the magnetic Cordillera Blanca, other hazards were described to me. A vapor, called *huayra* in Quechua, emanates from the mummies, the ancestors of the pre-Columbian burial sites. This vapor can make one ill. In the high reaches, too, phantoms and souls of envious people who have been converted into malevolent spirits may attack one. The complex of diseases contracted in these awesome places is subsumed under the heading *mal sitio* ("bad place"). One is said to suffer from *mal sitio*.

Thus, the lakes, peaks, and gorges of the Cordillera Blanca, in both their objective and subjective realities, represent a combined beauty and danger. The imagery of "drawing one in" (*jalar*), as the lakes are said to do, and of "sucking" (*chupar*), attributed to magnetic peaks, metaphorically expresses the attraction felt to the Cordillera Blanca, to a beauty so immense, perhaps, that it hurts.

THE rhythm of disaster in the valley, then, was the cadence of avalanches and, in a minor key, of landslides. In Huaraz, even during the shaking on May 31, 1970, people had screamed, "The *laguna* Chúrup is coming!" as the memory of 1941 loomed large. As that first long night set in, survivors looked to Cójup gorge. Some described putting their ear to the ground; others spoke of trying to get a whiff of a certain odor that would warn them that the lake was coming down.

The general feeling of intimacy with alluvion, but not with earthquake, contributed to the feeling on the part of the people that the earthquake was an "unnatural" disaster. An occasional tremor might be felt here and there in the Callejón, but the valley was not thought of as "a place of earthquakes." The more informed compared the seismicity of the valley to other areas like Arequipa or Cuzco or Lima, saying that the Callejón had never been called a "seismic zone."

A townswoman from Huarupampa barrio explained:

> If we thought about dying, it was by an alluvion, which is some-
> thing we always expect, a natural thing. I would have taken it as
> something natural. But not an earthquake. Who could imagine?
> We would at least have prepared ourselves in spirit.

If an earthquake was not anticipated, neither was a cataclysmic avalanche. A wall of debris as high as a ten-story building that would destroy Yungay, the "jewel of the Callejón," was not considered within the realm of possibility. Valley inhabitants had always counted on that 600-foot ridge to protect Yungay from Huascarán, just as it had in 1962. In the hours and days that followed the earthquake of 1970, people who viewed from afar the darkness over Yungay and felt the encroaching cold from ice that buried the town could not believe what their senses told them had happened. Though many *Huaracinos* had not seen the Yungay playa and said they could not bear to go to see it, the mere knowledge of its presence contributed to an already enormous sense of the extraordinary that the violent shaking of Huaraz had engendered.

CRUCIAL to understanding survivors' comprehension of the "extraordinary" seismological event is a knowledge of the significance they give to the elements of water, wind, and fire. Wherever it is found—in rivers, streams, and trickling waterfalls—water is possessed of life and meaning. Water is the hiding place of fantastic creatures, like the *ichicolqo*, a small and alluring blond being who inhabits bubbling brooks and beckons one into them. One must take care in crossing streams, especially in the dark. People were also conscious of which springs were gushing forth and which ones were drying up. Danger threatens when water gets out of hand.

In relating the history of Huaraz, people recalled that a whirlpool in the barrio of Soledad had gushed forth at the opposite side of town, in Huarupampa. Huarupampa (a Quechua word) was named for the tree trunks that acted as bridges over its watery marsh. Water is thought to connect places, close and distant: Soledad to Huarupampa, for example; and Rataquenua to Huascarán; and Huascarán to Chavín in the adjacent valley of Conchucos. Rataquenua and other lower foothills, as well as the higher mountains, are thought to be volcanoes of water. "There is a thin layer of earth," an Indian *campesina* said, "and underneath is water." People described their region as consisting of "volcanoes of water" formed by the glacial lakes, by water just beneath the earth's surface, and by the mountain summits.

I was perplexed by the notion of "volcanoes of water." Benjamín, the glaciologist, also had noted the prevalence of the idea that the Callejón is studded with volcanoes of water, but he could not explain it, either. There is volcanic rock in the valley, but there have been no active volcanoes for perhaps millions of years. He conjectured that the mudflows are confused with lava flows. To the people, their mountains, draped in mantles of ice and snow, "erupt" explosively, like volcanoes.

At any rate, putting the elements of fire, water, and wind together, people hypothesized that the disaster was caused by winds that penetrated the concavity of the earth. "It is mysterious how this happens," one woman said. "It must enter through one of the earth's poles. The earthquake started with a noise. This was the air getting into the hollow of the earth," she reasoned. The winds clashed beneath the earth's surface, and where the crust was weak, air and the fire that burns at the center of the earth sought to escape entrapment. The ice peaks, which act as lids on the volcanoes, blew off, and Huascarán, the mightiest volcano of water, "exploded."

Their descriptions of what occurred seismologically are reminiscent of the Aristotelian theory of the volcanic origin of earthquakes. Popular for many centuries, this theory must have come to the valley with the Spaniards. A townsman of Belén analyzed the event in this way:

> It is true the Callejón has seismic waves and is volcanic. We know it is volcanic because of the mineral waters of Olleros, Chancos, and Monterrey. There are no craters on the volcanoes. The cold of the snow-capped peaks cuts them, acts as a vent. It is like a pot with water boiling. The snow peaks act as a top on the pot. They lower the heat. If you add cold water, the boiling pot doesn't have the same force. But if you add more energy, the top flies off. The snows cannot hold back the force of the central fire. The Callejón is like a flattened orange, closer to the central fire. Where the crust of the earth was weak, it exploded. Yes, this earthquake was a telluric phenomenon.

Next time, someone said, Huascarán would not only finish off all of the valley but would explode so high that it would jump the Cordillera Negra and "go to sit" in the Plaza de San Martín in Lima.

Survivors spoke also in the language of tectonics. They pointed out that the Cordillera Blanca had risen and sunk during the earthquake and forecast that one day it might slide beneath the Cordillera Negra. Some recalled that Lima's patroness, Santa Rosa, had predicted that Lima would someday sink into the ocean and disappear. "The trench in the Pacific is so deep that the continent is moving from east to west to fill up the abyss in the sea," a townsman said. Just as over a century before, Darwin had marveled at finding a seashell on a mountain peak in Chile, an Indian woman reported to me her astonishment at hearing that a seashell had been found on Huascarán. She called Huascarán "the beginning of the sea." A man exclaimed, "How it must have been when the whole cordillera emerged from the sea!"

Thus, three major lines of perception merged in survivors' seismological comprehension of the event: (1) their appraisal of the Callejón as rather precariously balanced on water and studded with volcanoes of water that can explode; (2) their assessment of the valley as volcanic in the medieval plutonic sense; and (3) their tectonic sensibility derived from their communion with the highly sculptured relief of their valley and a keen awareness of its shifting features, drawn, perhaps, from their familiarity with *huaycos*, the mudflows that are like moving continents in miniature.

At times, the language of geophysics shifted into metaphor. The earthquake, a consequence of the inevitable and natural evolution of the earth, became a result of the overripening of the earth. The earth was "spoiling" (*pudriéndose*). Or, absorbing elements from some deep mythological past, some saw the earthquake as the effect of "too much existence," overpopulation, which increased the weight of the earth. In an explanation reminiscent of a Mayan myth of four gods that shoulder the world, grow tired when the population increases, and shift their burden, causing the earth to shake and people to fall off, one man told me that God, who holds the earth in the palm of his hand, had clenched his fist, causing the earth to shake, thereby lightening his burden by ridding the world of people.

IN spite of survivors' feelings about the "unnatural" and extraordinary quality of this disaster, they do carry inside them the equation that "the greater the beauty, the greater the danger." Their understanding of the disaster, from a geophysical point of view, was consequently fraught with ambivalence. Their beloved yet treacherous setting had brought them catastrophe. But they managed to resolve the ambivalence, and in so doing, to absolve, ultimately, the valley physiography from its part in the tragedy.

Their thinking followed this course: The inhabitants of the

Callejón believe that certain components of their landscape are threatening because they are *chúkaro*, a Quechua term best translated as "raw nature." The *chúkaro* is that part of nature that has not been touched by human beings, which people have not yet tamed, nature still wild, strange, aloof, and unsociable. It is like the wild horse, not yet broken. "The mountains which we don't tread are *chúkaro*; they can eat you," a woman said. "There are demons and phantoms and bad spirits in these *chúkaro* places," another added. Lake Ahuac, above Huaraz, was thought to be still very *chúkaro*: "It draws you in, like it did one man who went there and reached in to get a hot chile," one of the elusive treasures believed to tempt one from the depths of the lakes. A woman shook her fist at Huascarán, saying, "How arrogant you are, Huascarán! You are *chúkaro*. You do not let yourself be seen; you don't like people. You are savage, antisocial!"

Within the Callejón, tamed and untamed nature coexist. Raw nature, which has not yet been subdued, may perpetrate hostile acts upon man. Yet, in such a contained environment, human beings could not live with bald hostility, and a web of intimacy is spun around even the most *chúkaro* characters. There is a joking relationship between people and Huascarán, and the outsider who joins in criticism or name-calling can be cut off with "Yes, but we love it. So much power!" Though one bard sang, "Beautiful Huascarán, you are at fault . . ." another intoned:

> *Huascarán, don't hide yourself,*
> *Because if of blame we are speaking*
> *Today more than ever,*
> *Not you, nor the earth that throbbed*
> *Unrestrainedly*
> *Are accused, but rather,*
> *Nature's telluric fury.*

Recall that Don Alejandro followed his statement "I suffer from the Cordillera Blanca" with "but the place itself has its own remedy" and went on to name herbs to counteract the debilitating effect of the high, untamed reaches. The landscape provides the clarification, the light, as well as the suffering, darkness, and danger. The beautiful mountains that devastate can also make things all right if one will only *alzar la vista*, "lift his eyes" to them.

To mitigate the feeling that the Callejón's physiography—"our nature"—was to blame, people worked out an interpretation that a more generalized nature had staged its battle inside their valley, using as its instruments the marvelous and treacherous features of the Callejón. Thus, while at the intimate, ethnoseismological level, the *chúkaro* parts of the valley were at fault and Huascarán was the principal villain, in the broader scope, the event was seen as having been perpetrated by an abstract Nature—*la naturaleza*—external to the valley. As survivors formulated supernatural explanations of the disaster, this abstract Nature was perceived as having been controlled, set free, or, finally, abandoned by God.

This helps to explain why the catastrophe was believed to have injured people, mountains, birds, and animals alike. "It carried off Christians, animals, and birds," as Don Alejandro had said. Often people pointed to fissures in the mountainsides, calling them "wounds of the earthquake." An Indian woman said, "The mountains have felt everything and have suffered enormously. As they are mineral, they cannot talk, but they are alive and they breathe. They feel because they have life."

Though some of the wealthier people left, went to Lima, most survivors, to the dismay of outsiders, remained in the valley. This was not foolhardy fatalism. Rather, there was a sentiment that one could not abandon a bruised and injured place, be it town or landscape. A townsman of means, who could easily have begun a new life elsewhere, put it eloquently:

> It is going to be difficult for me to fly to heaven. I like to live in this place. My dear ones died here. It will be hard to get me out of here. . . . Before the earthquake, I liked to go away from Huaraz, to see new things. After the earthquake, I have just one thought, not to go away. My heart and soul are happy here. I look at the landscape and feel I am the happiest man in the world. . . . Every morning I can see my Huascarán, my hills, my snowy peaks. The real reason I can't leave is that if I go away, Huaraz is going to suffer a little more. Huaraz needs people.

In a sermon, a priest said, "Huaraz is like a mother, tender and wounded. We must be at her side until she is well." An old woman told me that she could not leave Huaraz alone now. Moreover, she was glad she was in Huaraz when the earthquake struck. She had

been in Lima for the four months before, and impelled by the feeling
something would happen to the valley, she returned ten days before
the disaster. "I have pain for this region. I shall never leave it," a
woman from Belén said.

This is what I managed to write down from a local poet reciting
on Radio Huascarán:

> . . . *the hail of February*
> . . . *tender ears of corn, fresh cheese*
> *Diaphanous dawns*
> . . . *sweetly intoxicating*
> . . . *So much beauty!*
> Ancashinos *of pure blood* . . .
> *Millions of earthquakes can come.*
> *There will not be sufficient alluvions to*
> *Tear us from the valley.*

Huaraz needed people because the town, and the whole valley, had
become dehumanized by the lash of a savage "external" nature—
the nature of plate tectonics and world seismology. Beauty had
erupted into chaos. All had been made *chúkaro*. The valley needed
the civilizing hand of man to restore the lost harmony, the structure
of community, which, here in this valley, includes not only human
beings and their institutions but the physical relief of the landscape
itself. An Indian woman described the end of the world as when
"all would be flat; there would not be any mountains." That would
be the ultimate structurelessness.

Recall the local bard who recited, "Naked is the landscape; /
naked are the people." The contrapuntal strains of the theme of
nakedness, I was becoming aware, would run through various interpretations of the disaster. Few other phrases would better describe the feeling of the aftermath.

Twelve

THE BOMB AND OTHER PROVOCATIONS OF THE UNIVERSE

. . . and the sun will not consent.
Jesusa of Secsecpampa

WHILE SURVIVORS generally embraced the world's scientific explanation of the earthquake, although sifting and refining it according to their sentiments about their landscape, they also constructed other interpretations of the event that depicted it as a manifestation of science gone haywire. Human beings were seen to be engaging in questionable activities, which survivors phrased as "man provoking the universe."

Such a provocation was the landing of human beings on the moon. Esther, a townswoman, said:

. . . And human beings are going to the moon. They are provoking the universe. Before, people lived happily. The *campesinos*, especially, are angry that men have landed on the moon.

Just as I was leaving the house of another townswoman, at the edge of the pampa, she suddenly blurted out, "What a world! No one is happy." We had just spent a lazy afternoon knitting, and I looked at her questioningly. She spoke of the 1941 alluvion, then said there had been tremors in the Callejón but never an earthquake. "Could it be that man himself is bringing disasters about?" she asked. "Could we be venturing too far out into space?" Two years before the earthquake, she had seen flying saucers spin down the Río Santa toward Caraz. Might they have had something to do with the disaster?

On another occasion, a young boy, having just described the weeping of the first night, added, "It is all because of the scientists. What can we do?"

It was Jesusa, Don Juan's sister-in-law, a *campesina* from Secsecpampa, who gave me the most complete list of the technological signs of the Final Judgment, of which she saw the earthquake as a harbinger. She said her grandfather, over forty years ago, used to tell all the children that the Final Judgment would come:

When there were planes flown by human beings, Christian people.

When a machine carrying fifty or sixty people would walk upon Huaraz and only one man would make it move upon the streets.

When a machine would be built that would fly alone without a pilot.

When the earth grew weak. No longer would there be nourishment from the earth.

When wheat should go up to 500 *soles* a sack. Long ago it was 450, and now it is up to 480 *soles* a sack.

When suddenly foreigners, the big people, the scientists, are going to be able to go to the moon; afterward, they are going to want to approach the sun, and the sun will not consent.

Though human beings can humanize space, bring order into nature, tame wildness, there is always a risk that in the process the reverse may occur. Human beings may be thrown into chaos. People told me that to plant a flag on a mountain summit, as the climbers do, humanizes the mountain a bit, makes it less *chúkaro*. But they had also taken part in too many burial ceremonies for mountain climbers and known of too many wayfarers vanished while traversing the high passes to ignore the dangers of penetrating the *chúkaro* places. It was felt to be presumptuous of man to think he might humanize the moon and the ultimate travesty that he should approach the sun. The sun and moon, Inti and Q'uilla, were the sacred god and goddess in ancient Andean religion. Perhaps this sense of the arrogance of human beings in exploring space is in some way comparable to our Western notion of the insolence of Adam and Eve's desire to be equal to God.

TO survivors, however, by far the worst of man's affronts to the universe is his assault upon the earth by dropping atomic bombs. That the earthquake was caused by nuclear tests in the Pacific became one of the most important and widespread interpretations of the disaster. "To drop a bomb is to disturb the underpinnings of the earth, to leave a hole which must be filled," they explained. The same man from the barrio of Belén who analyzed the volcanic propensity of the Callejón wove the bomb theory into his argument. Since houses had sunk on the coast of Ancash during the earthquake, he reasoned, this proved that a void that had to be filled had been left in the earth by a bomb.

During my year in Peru, innumerable reports of protests against French atomic bomb tests on the Pacific atoll of Mururoa, 4,000 miles due west of Lima, appeared in the national press, in newspapers from the official *El Peruano* to the popular tabloids. The latter predicted imminent and alarming consequences, such as plagues and the beginning of a new glacial age. Protests had begun as early as 1966, with France's first Pacific explosions, but in August 1971 the Peruvian government began threatening to break relations with France if another nuclear test was conducted. Joined by other Andean nations and by New Zealand, Australia, and Japan, Peru took the case to the United Nations in June 1972. In spite of a UN concordance with the Latin American condemnation of atomic tests, France continued to detonate bombs in the Pacific. These tests were often carried out secretly, as during June and July 1972. The Peruvian government sent telegrams demanding "immediate suspension" of the tests for the sake of the "health, security, and survival of the Peruvian people."

Finally, in July 1973, Peru severed diplomatic relations with

France, claiming contamination of the atmosphere and the sea as well as a relationship between the frequency and strength of earthquakes in the Andean mountains and the tests (*New Orleans Times-Picayune*, 15 July 1973). Though this last contention has not been scientifically proved, it has been a matter of heated debate in the press.

In May 1970, France exploded four nuclear bombs in the Pacific: on May 1, May 15, May 22, and May 30. It was conjectured that a causal relation might exist between the bomb detonated at three o'clock in the afternoon on May 30, 1970, and the earthquake of May 31, 1970 (*La Prensa*, Sunday supplement, 25 June 1972, p. 5). The strongest statement came from journalist Carlos Miano Piqué in a little book published in June 1972 entitled ¡¡*Basta*!! (*Enough*!!).[1]

It was November 8, 1971, when I first heard the disaster explained as the consequence of the French bomb tests, and specifically the test carried out on May 30, 1970. I had gone to visit a *campesina* living in a tin shelter on the roadside near Tingua. She had just heard on her transistor radio that the United States had exploded a bomb a few days before, on November 6. This was a five-megaton bomb detonated beneath Amchitka Island in the Aleutians. She had no idea where this was, but she was frightened. "Since we heard that," she told me, "we are waiting to die, we have not slept. There will be another earthquake, and perhaps the world will end."[2]

The Indian peasant woman went on to speak of the disaster of 1970, when the bomb had been dropped in the Pacific. The disaster had been forecast, she said, in a dream her sister had had three months before. In the dream, an old man was eating an enormous gourd filled with stewed corn. "He had a tremendous quantity to eat," she said, gesturing with her arms. The old man said that upon finishing the huge portion, he would go away, and then Huascarán "would come to sit in the plaza of Yungay." Then she told me that the 1962 avalanche had also been caused by a bomb, only that time it was dropped from a small white plane "manned by gringos, perhaps North Americans." The plane had flown over Huascarán, dropping a bundle. Mysteriously, the bomb did not explode right away. But when it did, it produced the avalanche that buried Ranrahirca.

I had been hearing snatches of conversations about bombs

dropped on the mountains and planes drawn into the magnetic Huascarán, but I had not connected these stories with nuclear tests. Now here it was again, this time made explicit in the context of the fear attached to the Amchitka bomb test.

Driving back through the valley that November night, I felt stunned. It seemed preposterous to me that there, in the clear, thin air of an unusually rainless November evening, an Indian woman was telling me about thermonuclear bombs, and furthermore, a specific bomb exploded 6,000 feet under the earth thousands of miles away in the Aleutians, a bomb I had not even heard about. I experienced those strong contradictory feelings of isolation and centrality. A major world issue had surfaced on a roadside in the Callejón. Besides, the old man eating stewed corn from a gourd, in the woman's sister's dream, has mythical overtones. This meant that a far-distant past and the nuclear age were being compressed into one time period on that same roadside of a remote valley. Most important, though, Amchitka and Mururoa having coalesced in my mind, as in theirs, I would feel uneasy when survivors blamed the disaster on France's tests in the Pacific.

"How could they face us?" one man asked, talking of the French relief workers who came after the earthquake. When I or someone would point out that earthquakes occurred before the invention of the atomic bomb, people would reply something like "Yes, but not so strong." They would say that since 1966, when France began testing in the Pacific, there had been more earth movements.

Now, in early November 1971, people waited to see the earth's response to the Amchitka test, and again, before I had heard on the radio or read anything about it myself, they told me:

> It has been felt in Japan. And also here. The reaction from the bomb took fifteen minutes to reach here. It showed up on seismographic charts. Surely the French bomb is what carried so many to their deaths in 1970.

A young student said:

> The French bomb was exploded just a few days before the earthquake. And now the United States has exploded a bomb, and it caused an earthquake somewhere. Was it South Africa? This cannot be coincidence.

The Amchitka test of November 6, 1971, had clearly reawakened talk of bombs and their effect upon the earth, and my notes are full of fear of the bomb. A *Huaracina* told me she had heard the news of Amchitka the night before. "And look at the winds we've had today," she said. "In 1970 it was a French bomb set off in the Pacific. What we suffered was more than an earthquake. It was a cataclysm, like Hiroshima." A fourteen-year-old girl said she was afraid there would be another earthquake because of these American tests. A *campesina* in the marketplace, recalling 1970, which she believed was the punishment of God, mused nevertheless: "They say that some gringos dropped a bomb. And Huaraz was finished. Can that be true? The bomb finished off Huaraz, they say."

The next period of acute anxiety over nuclear bombs occurred in July 1972, when it was revealed that France had resumed tests in the Pacific. I remember it vividly. On Tuesday, July 4, when I returned home across the pampa, it was later than usual and already dark. As soon as I entered my room, I switched on Radio Huascarán, a local broadcasting station manned, almost heroically, from one tiny room by a young man named Peter. He worked hard to keep news and music coming out over the airwaves from his crippled transmitter, which had been locked in a position marked "Emergency" since the day of the earthquake. It was Peter who had found the record "Los Cubanos" in the rubble and played it round the clock for two days following the disaster.

Every night at 8:00 P.M., Peter did a science-fiction program called "Strange, Very Strange." What I heard when I switched on the radio that Tuesday night was Peter saying, "Don't be frightened; it's all over. It was a bit strong, but everything is tranquil now." I was struck by his words and the tone of his voice, but since I had not felt anything, I thought it was part of the story he was telling that evening. Later, in the middle of the night, on shortwave, I heard that France had carried out a test "sometime on Sunday or Monday, secretly."

The next morning, before I got up, there was a temblor. It was evidently lighter than the one the night before, which I had not felt because I was walking or because it had shaken only parts of Huaraz. My landlord called up to my room: "You see, twenty-four hours exactly after the test, just as it was in 1970. It's bound to influence the earth." Throughout the day, people asked me if I had felt the strong tremor of the night before and the one that morning. And they compared this instance to the Mururoa bombs of May 1970 and the earthquake and avalanche of May 31.

IT was not just the possible connection between bomb tests and shifts inside the earth that weighed heavily upon survivors. They were troubled by deep and pervasive feelings of contamination from these bomb tests. They felt their climate had been altered and attributed health problems to fallout from the explosions. Some remembered that on May 24, 1970, a radioactive cloud had passed over Peru.

It happened that the 1972 Andean rainy season was the worst, some said, in a hundred years. Newspapers called it the worst since the rains of 1925. It felt as if the mountains were literally sliding down into the valleys and onto the desert coast. The bridge over the Santa at Ranrahirca was washed away four times in three months. Twenty-eight kilometers south of Huaraz, waters raged through the camp at Ticapampa. Fifty already earthquake-struck families had to be relocated, amid their mourning for three children drowned in the floods.

Huaraz was isolated from the coast for days at a time, once for nearly a month. Frequently, we could not pass from one Callejón town to another because a landslide had obstructed the road. Trying to reach Llanganuco one day, we saw a landslide of mud and rocks fall just in front of our jeep. A jeep just ahead of us, now on the other side of the landslide, continued up to the lakes, where its occupants were stranded for two days before the road was cleared. Either one of our vehicles would have been flattened by the slide.

During this rainy season I had to go down to Lima to arrange for a visa. My memories of the Pativilca road are of a sea of mud, of looking up the mountainsides to rocks tenuously poised. On our first attempt down the road, we drove for hours without seeing a car coming in the opposite direction. The head of a slaughtered bull lay half-buried in the mud at the edge of the road. Cows waddled in mud drifts. The women in our jeep commented that as the cows looked so sad, something must be wrong. The men were silent. We continued on despite evidence that we would not be able to get down the mountains, the unspoken rule being that one proceeds as far as one can. Finally, reaching a place where the road was choked by a mud slide, we turned back. Setting out a few days later, the driver, at one stretch, gunned the jeep through the mud sea. Then, slowing, we slid alarmingly close to the edge, if there was an edge. Everything was rounded and melting in torrential sheets of rain. Finally, we came out into the light of day onto the bright coastal desert. Our vehicle was the last one to get down for many weeks.

Having accomplished my errands in Lima, I was desperate to return to the valley. I had absorbed the survivors' feelings of not wanting to be away from an injured place. Assailed by the rains, Huaraz seemed to be calling me back. The FAO engineers and I made an attempt to go back up the mountain but got only as far as Supe and had to return to Lima. It was impossible to travel on the ground. On March 30, I finally got a flight to Anta, the airstrip outside Huaraz. From the plane's windows I could see the mudslides, like finger paintings down the mountainsides. The plane turned at Conococha and flew up the valley, between the two ranges. We were so low I could see clearly the cupola of the cathedral and my house on the pampa. As the towns went by beneath us, I thought we would never turn around. We appeared to be flying straight into Huascarán. Time seemed interminable until the pilot turned us around and landed at Anta alongside the Río Santa.

It was Holy Thursday. With so few vehicles on the roads, Huaraz was even more ghostly, and all the talk was of rain and of food shortages, for the roads, which are a lifeline to the coast, had been closed for so long. People were also talking about the young engineer from the Ministry of Agriculture, on his first assignment, who had been struck by lightning in Olleros. He had set out on horseback because there was no gasoline, and some recalled that he had said he felt safer on horseback than in his jeep on the roads. He was in a hut when the flash "split him open to the heart," they told me. The funeral had been on Wednesday, and he was buried in the Huaraz cemetery, with *campesinos* from Olleros singing in Quechua over his grave. Not long after, the head of the Cuban contingent, which was building two clinics in the valley, went over the side of a cliff in a *colectivo*. When the Pativilca road to the coast finally reopened and the first big trucks rolled in, people lined the roadsides, greeting them as if they were a liberating army.

During the year, too, the winds were strong. They would rise predictably in the early afternoon. If I was lucky enough not to have gotten caught in them, I would watch from my window as the dust swept across the pampa, often carrying tin sheets or other debris and once toppling the tattered circus tent that men were struggling to secure as if it were the mainsail of a ship in high seas. When I did not make it to shelter before the winds came up, I was covered in dust, my eyes caked, my face stinging. Out on the pampa there was nowhere to hide from the dust, and relief workers and I would ask ourselves, "Why are we here swallowing dust?" "*Tragando polvos*," as they would say.

It rained late into what was normally the dry season, and the rains came again precipitously in mid-August. Survivors remarked on the "changing climate," saying that radiation from the bomb was causing the unusual rains and winds. Benjamín, of the Santa Corporation, said he thought it could be responsible for these climatic effects, which were extreme even in a zone familiar with striking meteorologic phenomena.

One night in July 1972, Reyna and I walked along Centenario. The night was dense with an unusual kind of vapor. Was it fog or smoke or both? we asked ourselves. Along the way, people commented, "It's the bomb. Huaraz will be enveloped in contamination." These pronouncements at times blended into others, of "men going to the moon" and a generally tampered-with and menaced universe.

Stories circulated about new diseases. Esther, of San Francisco barrio, said:

> The earthquake? It was the bomb. Don't you see there were tremors, too, with this last test? And a new disease has appeared. They call it "guitar" because one scratches and scratches, like things are crawling on the skin. It's like *sarna* ["itch," "mange"], but *sarna* is an ancient disease. Now pimples with pus are coming out. No doctor can figure out what it is, and they say it's the bomb. They can't find a cure.

Survivors also attributed symptoms of tiredness and dejection to the bomb. Its noxiousness was said to sap energy. Taintedness seemed to affect everything: "Times are bad, rain until now, and everything is artificial. Before, potatoes were good, and milk was pure. Our grandchildren won't live to be fifty. Before, we were strong until ninety-two," a man said.

The immediate and horrible experience of pollution from the thousands of bodies left after the earthquake in a concentrated area was reinforced and prolonged by this feeling of radiation contamination. Fortunately, countervailing beliefs in the innate healthfulness of the sierra air and of the soil were there to be seized upon.

IT is hard to estimate exactly when survivors began to connect the French bomb with the earthquake. The bomb appeared in none of the many accounts I recorded of what people were talking about that first night nor in accounts of the days immediately following. A priest at the only church that remained standing, Centenario, who was in the thick of early emergency measures, told me it was only after relief workers got into the disaster area that survivors spoke of the bomb tests. However, he remembered that on the very day of the earthquake a Santa Corporation engineer was saying that it was caused by the bomb.

Besides the emotional anxiety I shared with survivors over the bomb tests in the Pacific and the anger I felt toward the superpower technology that produced anxiety in people with no control over that technology, the bomb explanation left me suddenly with an unanticipated intellectual surprise. Not only did this explanation create nagging doubts, since a connection between bomb tests and earthquakes has never been disproved, but I had not considered that interpretations of the disaster would involve man-made catastrophe. I had not counted on hearing so often allusions to Hiroshima: "It was like Hiroshima," or, "We are going to die at the hands of man, not of God." The specter of the dust cloud rising 18,000 feet over the Callejón after the earthquake fused with what had previously been for me another distinct mental image—the mushroom clouds of Hiroshima and Nagasaki.

IN ordinary times, people in the Callejón are close to meteorologic phenomena. The sky offers an ever-changing panorama. A day transpires in infinite shadings of light and shadow, mountain peaks are spawning grounds for clouds, and people say things like "We shall arrive just as the sun reaches that cloud." Now, in the aftermath, the tectonic drama, bomb tests, ideas of human beings venturing too far into space, all enhanced the meteorologic consciousness and, together with the unusually severe rains and winds, produced a sense of world transformation. Climatic phenomena were amplified, imbued with meaning, drawn into the orbit of intensity of the extreme event itself. In the everyday quickened sensitivity to nature, the subject of climate was minutely examined. When it was cold, foggy, and drizzling in May, people said, "Never, never before in May." A thunderstorm in June and a warm sunlight through which large chunks of hail fell on Huaraz one July afternoon were viewed with dismay. People spoke of the winds and rains as "crazy." "We do not know what to expect from them since the earthquake." In a *módulo* in the Nicrupampa camp, Ana pulled her shawl close around her shoulders, saying she was afraid a "hurricane of air" would carry away the fragile shelter. Frequently, I heard the simple statement "There is a new wind in Ancash." Some commented that since the earthquake the earth had grown very cold. Others foretold a new glacial age.

Rhythms of world change were felt to be accelerating: "Our grandparents did not talk so much about these things. There were always traces of past calamities. We see the boulders, but the world is really changing now. These things will happen often from now on."

Concomitant with the sense of world transformation was the strong feeling that the valley was alone, that it had been singled out for the manifestation of these larger world phenomena. The Callejón would herald the new glacial age. Or, where the focus was on world decline, on events abroad that made the whole world suffer, there was the suspicion that the valley was the victim of these world events, like bomb tests, that it would have to endure them alone in order to show the world the devastation they could cause.

After all, they said, were not outsiders afraid to be in the valley? Had they not begun to call it an Alley of Death? Survivors were alert for signs of fear in outsiders, which would corroborate their impression of being "different" since the earthquake. One night I took a friend from the States to meet Esther, in her hut at the edge of the pampa. Esther stooped to come out the little door and in the pitch dark felt for my friend's hands, held them, and asked, barely audibly, "Are you not afraid to be here?"

Thirteen

PEACE ON EARTH . . .

"Our Tragedy Unites the World"
El Correo, a Lima newspaper,
June 5, 1970

S CIENCE HAD EXPLAINED *how* it happened that the earth moved
as it did in the Callejón on Sunday, May 31, 1970. Survivors
could take the scientists' word that plates grind against each
other and that a huge slab of the ocean floor had slid beneath the
continent. They could suspect that nuclear bombs detonated in the
earth might cause shifts in its subterranean structure. But science
did not even pose the question of *why* the earth's crust should be
fractured like a giant eggshell into plates that move about on a
viscous mantle, sometimes plowing into each other, or why the
Callejón should have borne the brunt of such a tectonic encounter.
To close this gap and ease the sense of victimization, a grand metaphor was constructed that cast the destroyed valley as the architect
of world peace. Through the tragic gathering of diverse peoples in
the disaster aftermath, the world would learn a lesson of love and

brotherhood. This would give purpose to the suffering. In this way, hope for the valley and the world was wrested from the tragedy. The metaphor was elaborated over time.

At first, reports of the destruction in the valley stunned Lima into disbelief. When radio contact was finally made with the capital in the early hours of June 1, after survivors in Centenario had broken into the Santa Corporation office to gain access to its transmitter, the receivers of the news thought it must be grossly exaggerated. Lima's radio stations closed down that early morning in confused silence over conditions in the Callejón. Gradually, from the monks at Los Pinos, who had radioed their parent monastery in Indiana, and through continued desperate pleas coming out of the Centenario radio, Lima began to accept the tragedy. But as late as June 2, in the first news conference held after the quake, a Lima official stated: "God grant that this [the reports] won't be actually confirmed, because it would be the most frightful tragedy that any country in any part of the world has suffered from an earthquake" (*New Orleans Times-Picayune* 3 June 1970). Finally, after a few days and several unsuccessful attempts, helicopters managed to penetrate the dust cloud and confirm those early frantic attempts of survivors to convey the proportions of the disaster.

Once known, the event began to be called one of the world's worst natural disasters, and the world began to respond. Condolences, materials, and people poured into Lima. Physicians in California, Argentina, and Russia met to plan mercy missions. The hospital ship *Hope* was dispatched to Chimbote. The United Nations declared the event bore the mark of "Universal Tragedy" and was thus the world's responsibility. In Geneva, an emergency fund was agreed upon by the Red Cross. Engineers from UNESCO and FAO convened in the valley. Some seventy countries sent aid.[1] Survivors recalled that the mere news of the world's response, which reached them on transistor radios long before any of the materials themselves, assuaged their sense of aloneness and abandonment.

As gifts and representatives from many nations flew into Jorge Chávez Airport at Callao, a subtle transition began to take place. The bridge between the stricken valley and the rest of the world provided by tidings of help on its way was taken up by survivors as their own personal mission. The heralded relief was cast into symbolic language. Material goods and foreign emissaries began to be seen as messages and envoys of love, and survivors began to demand the spiritual counterpart of material help.

Phrased in the national revolutionary language and adapted to local valley history, this bridge between world and valley was lifted to visionary status, with survivors and Peruvians in general as draftsmen of its meaning. The idea took hold that although the nations of the world have different politics, which causes conflict, a shared sentiment and care for imperiled fellow members of the human race dissolves their differences. The mission was no less than that peace on earth should result from the ruin of a heretofore little-known spot on the globe. The catastrophe would not be in vain. The convergence of peoples from every corner of the globe in the aftermath must set an example for the whole world. A black band covered the June 5, 1970, edition of the Lima newspaper *El Correo*. It was a day of national mourning. The headlines read "Our Tragedy Unites the World."

The event began to be referred to as "the earthquake of world solidarity." A sign stuck into the alluvionic debris of the Yungay playa read "Sanctuary of International Solidarity." ASPA, the national airline, termed its fifty-two flights to pick up sixty tons of foreign donations "Operation Solidarity."

The icons of world solidarity became concentrated in the narrow valley: a monument to seventy Russian doctors, en route to the Callejón, whose plane went down in the North Sea; empty five-gallon cooking-oil cans marked "From the People of the U.S.A., Not for Resale," now serving as vases for flowers on the provisional altars of Huaraz; two small but streamlined Cuban clinics; cooking utensils sent by China; signs along the road reading "Thanks to the People of the United States" for the temporary dwellings—the *módulos*—sheltering 15,000 survivors; Russian and Peruvian flags planted side by side on the summit of Huascarán Norte. Even the *chúkaro* villain-mountain would be humanized and brought into the world community.

Meanwhile, as survivors slept in rain-drenched tents in October 1970, in death-defying pomp and ceremony, Spain's greatest bullfighters offered a corrida in Madrid on behalf of victims of the earthquake. And five of Mexico's most famous bullfighters flew to Lima to fight in the bullring for the same cause.

Given the historical self-image of the city of Huaraz, it is not surprising that *Huaracinos* should see in the disaster's aftermath the opportunity to demonstrate to the world the power of mutual generosity and fellowship among peoples that should ultimately contribute to peace in the world. The disaster had stirred up the story of how Huaraz had welcomed and helped the liberators José de San Martín and Simón Bolívar, leading in 1823 to the proclamation of Huaraz by the first Congress of the new republic as the "*Muy Generosa Ciudad*" (the "Very Generous City"). An old man of the barrio of San Francisco in Huaraz spoke of the great joy that Bolívar had felt upon arriving in Huaraz, how after dining sumptuously in the house of a poor Indian, the general had stood up and proposed a toast to the "*muy generosa ciudad de Huaraz,*" how even now wise and learned men refer to Huaraz in this way.

In this same spirit, hospitality to foreigners, to relief personnel, was rendered in the aftermath amid not only poverty but devastation. People felt that, like Bolívar, those of "noble heart" would accommodate to the hardships and through this mutual cooperation the destroyed "City of Liberation" would become a monument to world peace. It was imagined that as the spirit of reconstruction radiated out to the world, people from everywhere, in some future time, would arrive in Huaraz at an "International Airport of Human Solidarity" to see for themselves the crystallization of this dream of peace. A *Huaracino* proposed to the national assembly that May 31 be proclaimed the "Day of International Friendship."

This was "survivor mission,"[2] a way of giving a positive meaning to the people's feeling of having been singled out to bear the brunt of nature's havoc or the folly of the modern world's technology. This was also a way of alleviating the encounter with mortality. Many members of the community had been lost, but the ideological community, through this mass encounter with death, would achieve immortality: "Huaraz has been and will be, through its own destiny, a majestic presence in time and in eternity. And more, in centuries to come, it will be immortalized in the universal soul." In a hand-lettered sign placed on the crude altar on Yungay's playa, citizens of Arequipa proclaimed that the noble Yungay would return from nothingness to immensity, "*de la nada a la inmensidad.*"

AT the same time that the survivor community reached out to the world, enjoining it to learn a lesson from the event and the aftermath, they also recoiled from having to burden the world with the disaster, not materially but psychologically. The world must be spared such blows. This sentiment was expressed in statements like "When the awful tragedy was confirmed, the Revolutionary Military Government had the unenviable but unavoidable duty to let the world know what had happened." Shortly after the disaster, the president of the Civic Committee of Huaraz implored survivors to heed the advice of technicians, who, "as painful as it may seem," may even want to move their towns so that should another earthquake occur, inhabitants would be more protected and "the losses not astonish the world, as did the cataclysm of the last day of May." Feelings of survivors were projected onto the world. Yauri wrote in his journal: "The world was alone. . . . the world was empty. . . . We were all dead."

Though they recoiled from having to inflict upon the world the knowledge of their tragedy, survivors felt their only redemption lay in the world's recognition of the extremity of the event. By the time I arrived in the valley, most of the emissaries of earlier months had departed, and the people were again alone. The desire to jog the world's memory had already begun to assert itself. It took the form of rustic paintings, poems recited over the local radio stations, ballads (*huaynos*), composed and sung in the valley and over national airwaves, the drawings of schoolchildren, and a symphony, *Apocalyptic Overture*, by composer Manuel Rivera, performed by the National Symphony Orchestra in Lima for the first time on February 27, 1972.

Zavaleta Figueroa's pamphlets had begun to circulate in the valley. In one, he wrote:

> . . . I present myself before you, my beloved readers of the Callejón de Huaylas, of Peru and of the world, bringing the sad missives of many survivors. . . . This tragedy is for the history of Peru and of the world an unspeakable event, for its intensity, and the magnitude of economic, social, biological and moral destruction. It has left in its path psychological and spiritual devastation in the majority of us who remain.

I, too, became a vehicle for messages to reach the world. I was made acutely aware of this very early in my stay, when, during a polite social gathering with music, food, and drink, there occurred a sudden and totally unanticipated emotional breakdown that spread instantly to everyone in the room. The next thing I knew, the host was shouting at me: "This is what we are really living. Do you see how we are? You must carry this to your country." In its abrupt shift from normal existence to this hysterical outburst, from form to formlessness, this incident seemed to mirror the event itself. In spite of the fact that life was going on, it was a life dominated by the event, by the intimate knowledge of chaos that survivors had shared. Perhaps if the world were made to participate empathetically in their encounter with chaos, its impact might in some way be diminished. It could be endured if the world knew, and remembered.

No, the world must not forget. The unspeakable had to be spoken. The event had to make its mark in history, even, perhaps, determine history by bringing the peoples of the earth closer, making the planet a more humane place—less strange, less *chúkaro*.

A few days before I left Peru, a clerk in the immigration office in Lima asked where I had been living during the year. When I answered, "Huaraz," he said, "Ah, Huaraz is a small wound for humanity."

Part 4

THE NATION INTERPRETS: REVOLUTION AND REFORM

*To destroy is to change, nothing else.
. . . In destruction is the thought of
what one longs to be. To destroy is to
change; to destroy is to transform. In
the world in which nothing is annihi-
lated, in the world in which nothing is
created. . . . to destroy is to change; to
destroy is to transform. In the volcano
that rises in the midst of the ocean, in
the island that sinks into the sea, in the
wave that evaporates, in the cloud that
is condensed into rain. . . . To destroy
is to change, to destroy is to transform. . . . Pale images of human
thought, brutal explosions of inert material: you are equally destructive, you
are equally creative. To destroy is to
change. No, something more. To destroy is to create.*

Pío Baroja, *Paradox Rey*

Fourteen

PLAN INCA

Upon the traces of this immense tragedy . . .
General Juan Velasco Alvarado

I ARRIVED IN THE VALLEY in October 1971 to find the center of Huaraz—now called the pampa—scraped clean. The scathing "removal of ruins" had taken place on the first anniversary of the disaster. Bulldozers had crawled up the Pativilca road, worked feverishly, even at night by torchlight, and departed. The national government had paid the caterpillar operators by the cubic meter to remove the rubble. An old man said, "These men carried off in an instant stones that I brought with my own hands over the years."

About a week after I arrived, I traveled with a few Peruvians from Communal Development, a small government contingent that remained in the valley. Coming to a stop in the central plaza of a hamlet, José jumped from the jeep and asked the Indian peasants who had gathered around to "pass the word; we want to talk to everyone." When about twenty-five people had assembled under the arches of a public building, José, using posters, began to instruct them in how to build houses more resistant to earthquakes. The lesson completed, he turned to a discourse on the injustice abroad in the land. The rich and powerful lived on the coast, he said, while poverty and ignorance reigned in the sierra. The peasants could help bring injustice to an end by organizing themselves. They could begin by cooperating in the construction of a canal to bring water to their hamlet. An Indian smiled in recognition and said yes, they knew about cooperation. They called it *minka*. *Minka* is a Quechua word that refers to a practice of mutual assistance among Indians that has persisted from pre-Columbian times. Through the long disquisition, I squatted in a corner with the women, who giggled into their shawls, and watched the pure gold light bathe the countryside.

Those early days, everyone was talking about CRYRZA, whose principal act so far had been the "removal of ruins." Why were they now nowhere to be seen? Why had nothing been done? Not a house had been built. Could it be that they were planning to redistribute the land, that people would not get back their lost land? When I first visited the survivor camp, Nicrupampa, a young woman from Lima associated with "Operation Roof" proudly told me that everyone in the camp was "equal." At a meeting of a cooperative formed some years before the earthquake, townspeople recalled a woman who would not share her land. "We can't blame her," others said. "We can't even blame the earthquake for the lack of cooperation now." A woman laughed nervously, saying that many members of the cooperative had died in the earthquake, and besides, how could they locate members now with everything destroyed? A man accused me of being from the CIA, but after some debate it was agreed I could remain at the meeting.

One day at noon an unusual fanfare broke the silence of the midday heat. I went out to the plaza to find a band playing the national anthem, loudspeakers blaring, and the bicolored Peruvian flag being raised. Oil had been discovered in the Peruvian jungle. A tribute was made to the Revolutionary Military Government, which, within days after taking power in 1968, had seized the American-owned International Petroleum Company. This celebration seemed out of context miles above both Lima and the jungle, in the center of the empty pampa, which showed, as yet, no signs of regeneration. Only a handful of people stood cheerlessly around the plaza.

Verbal and visual icons of revolution dotted the disaster landscape. I noticed that signs designating different zones within the survivor camps bore the names of Inca Manco Cápac and insurgent Túpac Amaru. In hamlets I saw posters proclaiming the slogan: "*Campesinos*, the Landowner Will No Longer Eat the Bread of Your Poverty." Indian peasants themselves spoke of Pedro Pablo Atusparia and Ushcu Pedro, the great Indian leaders, who, in the name of social justice, led an uprising in Huaraz in 1885.

One night at about seven o'clock, as we passed through deserted Carhuaz, a throng of angry Indian peasants surrounded our jeep. "Gringos, something for the *campesinos*," they said, heads crowding through the open windows. We managed to work ourselves free, and, unsettled, we drove on through the dark.

During those first weeks I spent sipping herbal teas in cold and damp makeshift restaurants, along with the remnant relief personnel and the earliest envoys of the reconstruction unit, I became conscious of certain phrases, "changes in mentality" (*cambios de mentalidad*) and "changes in structure" (*cambios de estructura*), which they constantly used. On the mountainsides I would hear the same words from Indian women bent over a cooking fire and men hoeing their fields. Don Juan of Secsecpampa, my principal Indian informant, would slap his knee and chuckle. "Peru has decided to 'humanize' us *campesinos*."

Early on, too, the charismatic priest of Soledad preached from his rustic pulpit, "There should be no diversion; these are times of war." By the middle of 1972, I understood this. The "war" was between the coast and the sierra, between an ideology of change and a deep longing for restoration and continuity. It was not a war between right and wrong. There were no good guys versus bad guys. And there were no bullets. Confusing, sometimes ill conceived, and at times glorious, the war was the Peruvian "revolution" testing its mettle in the destroyed valley.

THE Peruvian revolution began on October 3, 1968, when armed officers under Gen. Juan Velasco Alvarado hustled President Fernando Belaúnde Terry from his quarters to a plane bound for exile, thus ending his constitutional government (1963–68). That bulletless coup significantly altered the face of the Latin American military. "Revolutionary Military Government" even seemed a contradiction in terms. The military in Latin America had traditionally been on the side of the ruling oligarchy, preservers of the status quo. In contrast, the military government of General Velasco took as its "profoundly moral purpose" social, political, and economic reforms that would integrate the marginal sierra culture of Indian peasants into the coast-dominated national sphere. Poverty would be conquered, and a brotherhood of the nation achieved.

The uniqueness of this Peruvian enterprise was repeatedly stressed. According to General Velasco Alvarado, Peru would establish its independence from all foreign domination, especially that of the United States, and set itself apart from the world. Its ambition was no less than "to make possible a new human morality" based not on the models of either communism or capitalism or any other than "our own way of conceiving our reality." The new government's model was Inca socialism. Having many of the characteristics of nativistic and millenarian movements, the Revolution set about to resurrect its Indian past, elevating figures like Túpac Amaru to national heroes, while at the same time it engineered the demise of a mighty oligarchy whose wealth, linked to the outside world, exploited the labor of the Peruvian masses. "We are in the midst of a revolutionary process which implies redoing all the reality of the world in which we were born," the general proclaimed.[1]

The nation's goal to overturn the old hierarchical structure and create a new egalitarian state built upon "human solidarity" on a national scale found fertile soil in the leveled valley. Velasco Alvarado seized upon the disaster as a springboard into his visionary future. The event had had an impact on the nation. Now the nation would have an impact on the event. Change and transformation might be tried anywhere at any time, but creation is perhaps only the other side of destruction.

The military regime was not the only revolutionary force beginning to stretch its limbs in the immediate predisaster years. The Catholic Church, also, had undergone a radical change during the sixties, resulting in the reforms of Pope John XXIII and Vatican Council II. Even as the earthquake struck, a Latin American interpretation of the Catholic Reform movement was being constructed by Gustavo Gutiérrez, a Peruvian priest and theologian.

Gutiérrez described his philosophy, which he called a "theology of liberation," as a "political hermeneutics of the Gospel." Its heavy Marxist component called for a transformation of the world. The Catholic Church, which, like the military, had been traditionally aligned with the wealthy and powerful, came out squarely on the side of the oppressed.[2]

The strength of the Peruvian Revolution and Catholic Reform lay in their interpenetration. At the same time that the Church spoke in secular terms, the Revolutionary Military Government used religious language. Its "most sacred cause" was the illumination of every man. In their joint messianic mission, society became sacred and religion secular.

Even before the disaster, the seeds of reform and revolution had been sown. Reformers had begun to filter into the Callejón. The sweeping Agrarian Reform Law, passed on June 24, 1969, had already begun to eat away at giant Utcuyacu hacienda, near Recuay at the south end of the valley, and other smaller holdings were crumbling. Catholic Masses in some of the valley churches were being modernized. All over the world, the Mass was to become accessible to everyone, and toward this end, modern languages replaced the conventional and universal Latin. In the Callejón, more and more frequently, Masses were being said in Quechua and Spanish. Breaking other age-old traditions, they were being held in the evenings as well as mornings and were accompanied by *criollo* music of the coast and guitars and folk songs that were becoming international symbols of the Reform movement. Some valley priests had already begun to prohibit *costumbres*: native dances, fireworks, processions, all that bore upon the ancient Peruvian past, including many aspects of pre-Columbian religion that had for hundreds of years survived intact within Catholicism.

Amid the new thinking and tentative groping toward change, the earthquake occurred. In the aftermath, the disaster came to be seen as a providential mandate for further redesigning all that had been.

THE dust cloud had barely dissipated before the Revolutionary Military Government snapped up the valley by placing a moratorium on all transactions concerning the exchange of land. In Huaraz's urban center, no one could buy or sell land, occupy his own land, or rebuild upon it. On July 28, 1970, General Velasco informed the nation that "upon the traces of this immense tragedy, we will all see rise a piece of the New Peru. . . ." Reconstruction of the "Affected Zone" became known as the "Revolutionary Reconstruction."

Even before CRYRZA had established its offices in the valley, it made its objectives known:

> The revolutionary orientation of the Government and the magnitude of the disaster signify a juncture propitious for striving for, through all available means, the transformation of the structures which reigned in the Zone before the cataclysm, accelerating in this way the process of change on which the country is bent.
>
> This objective is in perfect accord with the Revolutionary Government of the Armed Forces, which has proposed to structure a more just and united society, in which privileges are excluded and in which there is no room for any type of economic, social, political or cultural marginalization or discrimination.
>
> . . . CRYRZA considers that the politics to be followed in fulfilling its specific function most certainly do not consist in a mere physical reconstruction, but on the contrary its goal must be . . . to structure the necessary bases for the operation of a new social model, more just, that may assure social peace. . . .

In the countryside, where the moratorium on rebuilding did not apply, I was struck by the new types of buildings around the central plazas. In the hamlet of Llipta, for example, an adobe structure on which were painted the words Agrarian Cooperative of Saint Augustine had taken its place beside the chapel. In some cases, these cooperatives were built even before the chapels were repaired. These agricultural production cooperatives were the purest examples of the concept of "social property," the major commitment of the Revolutionary Military Government. In these cooperatives, all means of production were to be jointly held and worked, and the profits equitably shared. Based on the indigenous unit of land tenure, the *ayllu*—simultaneously a system of communal labor—the cooperatives embodied the government's search for native socialist pathways, a search they called Plan Inca.

During my early months in the valley, when little was happening, these cooperatives, the signs, the posters, the slogans, the talk in the temporary restaurants, and the occasional group of peasants such as the one we encountered on the road through Carhuaz, were practically the only manifestation of the Revolution. But from time to time a refugee from one of the survivor camps would come down to the pampa and try to figure out where his land was. With all landmarks erased, if not by the earthquake, then by the removal of rubble, it was not easy to determine where one's property had been. The refugee would begin to build his house on "his" land. Within a day, sometimes overnight, the frame would be dismantled by the Civil Guard. In the early-morning hours of November 6, 1971, with tension mounting over the lack of activity on the valley floor, as CRYRZA's plans for rebuilding the towns remained on the drawing boards in Lima, some twenty or twenty-five refugees came down from their hillside encampment. They staked out their property by drawing white chalk lines in the dirt, printing their names in the dust, and planting tiny Peruvian flags. Their attempt to reclaim their land didn't last the day. Everything was removed, and the pampa was restored to anonymity.

In January 1972, CRYRZA finally moved its full operation from Lima to the valley. Even then, however, as they began to build rather luxurious quarters for themselves in Vichay, near Monterrey, it seemed to survivors that CRYRZA was still in retreat from the main scars of the disaster, that rhetoric was the mainstay of the Revolutionary Reconstruction.

On June 24, 1971, the Social Mobilization Law had legislated into existence an indispensable arm of the Revolutionary Military Government, SINAMOS, the National System of Support for Social Mobilization, which was intended to establish a dialogue between government and people. This highly centralized agency was designed to ensure that the stimulation and channeling of citizen participation in the reconstruction was controlled by the national government, that the dialogue never got out of hand or was never usurped by private interests.

It was not until April 1972 that SINAMOS was put into operation and the "social promoters," who were to play a major role in the reconstruction, began to arrive in the valley. Just as on the first anniversary of the disaster the frenzied removal of rubble took place, its aim being to quell the rising unrest among survivors, so, too, near the second anniversary, momentum picked up, and the revolutionary rhetoric began to flow more steadily. CRYRZA put out a paper stating: "The earthquake of the 31st of May 1970 confirmed the unequal and unjust socioeconomic and political order existing in the Affected Zone, a situation that as revolutionary Peruvians we have the obligation to change through the tasks of Reconstruction and Rehabilitation."

By May 1972, CRYRZA, finally settled in its Vichay quarters, would try to convince the town of Huaraz that its *Plan Regulador* was the best way to reconstruct Huaraz. A new aspect was added to the plans for rebuilding: The reconstruction must bring not only a new social order but, at the same time, modernization. SINAMOS workers, calling themselves "consciousness-raisers," had begun to organize, and now, on Tuesday, May 16, in a building in the barrio of Belén, the first of a long series of meetings between CRYRZA, SINAMOS, and the survivors took place. These meetings brought townspeople and Indian peasants out of the camps and down from the mountains, together with coastal people, to engage in the process of building "a new world."

By May 16, the determination of CRYRZA not to permit the rebuilding of adobe brick houses on the old sites having become evident, delegations of the four main barrios of Huaraz had met clandestinely to form Committees for Defense of the Barrios, one for each, San Francisco, Belén, Soledad, and Huarupampa. Therefore, even though the coastal authorities had sought to stage the meeting so that nothing would get out of hand, it was tense and confusing, with many undercurrents emanating from these still-secret committees of the sierra survivors.

I remember feeling squeezed in the midst of the crowd that filled the building on the pampa. Indian women with long braids and mestizo women with short permanented hair intermingled. Two Indian women sat on the sidelines spinning wool. *Campesinos* in shabby tufted woolen pants stood side by side with townsmen dressed in their "best" suits, old, dark; for us, from another era. I saw many people I knew: Don Antonio, the shopkeeper of Centenario, Señor Morán, a former mayor of Huaraz, Esther and her sisters, the little girls Consuelita and Machi, who lived nearby when I first came to the valley. The archaeologist-priest was there, as well as people "no one recognized," some said. It was not expected that such a crowd would gather there. Earlier that day a CRYRZA official had told me they had "advance information" that people would boycott the meeting. Instead, everyone was there, and ironically they represented all the cultural differences in the valley that the new social order and modernization would seek to obliterate.

The meeting began with CRYRZA officials giving speeches, in order to "clarify points," as they said. They tried to set the survivors' minds at ease by saying they would be allowed to participate in the reconstruction. But they must "see the truth." The "communal aim" must be to discern correctly the "reality" of the times. Simply to give back Huaraz to survivors, to return all the land now held in moratorium, and to reconstruct the "old reality" would be both "antijustice" and "antitechnology." Instead, a "human revolution" must take place.

Besides the quantity of land to be allotted to each survivor, two other main issues were discussed: (1) place: where things were to be—this struck at the deep and pervasive sierra concept of *terruño* (literally, "piece of ground"), the belief that one's birthright was to live and die in "one's place"; and (2) technology and modernization: how things were to be.

A huge map was unveiled that displayed distinct areas for residences and for commerce. Areas of "public utility," for schools and health centers, were also designated. Rumbling dissension spread through the crowd. Such arbitrary separations had not before existed in the sierra. Furthermore, they meant that one could not count on being able to return to one's *terruño*.

The rumbling continued as CRYRZA began to describe the houses themselves and the manner in which they could be acquired. All around me I heard phrases like "Such small rooms!" "No windows to look out on Huascarán!" "A house to be paid for in installments!" "Long-term loans—how can this be?" "Insurance, in case the head of family should die!" All of these things were unfamiliar, mind-boggling concepts. Whenever "the Huaraz of 1990" was mentioned, the murmuring reached a crescendo. Clearly, two radically different concepts of "time," so intimately cultural in its dimensions, were butting heads.

Furthermore, the CRYRZA people alluded to new laws, actually decrees, since constitutional government had been suspended, and they hinted at a possible urban expropriation of the lands held in moratorium.

"How is this helping us?" someone spoke up. "You say you will pay us for our lost property, but you will deduct from the price the damage done by the earthquake, all the damage to the 'infrastructure'—the services of water and electricity and sewage. Is it our fault that there are no more services, that all the infrastructure was destroyed? And then you say we must pay for these tiny new concrete houses and for the land they are built upon in a place the government wants to put them? And we must pay over a period of twenty years and pay interest? How does this help us? How can we do it?" "I am old now," another man said softly. "How can I begin again and pay over twenty, thirty, years? I have built my house with my own hands already, and it is gone."

"You have not given us anything," a young man shouted. Then another man rose to speak. He said he wanted to outline the points arrived at by the Committees to Defend the Barrios at a meeting they had held the Sunday before. Since these committees were not the controlled form of participation that SINAMOS sought, and operated underground, a CRYRZA colonel begged him not to do so, but the crowd shouted, "Let him speak."

> Give us back our lots and let us build our own houses. This has come as such a shock, this decree law you allude to. We thought eventually we would have our land back. We can form our own cooperatives and make our own bricks, and we will follow your antiseismic codes for building.
>
> Don't make us pay for the infrastructure when you will not pay us for the services lost in the earthquake.
>
> Those who want the concrete houses can have them, but put them outside the center of Huaraz and let the government pay this interest you speak of for the purchases.
>
> Please begin the infrastructure soon. We are living without running water, electricity, and sewage for two years now.

He ended with something that made me feel uncomfortable:

> We want to declare the imperialism of these loans you call BID [*Banco Internacional de Desarrollo*, "International Development Bank"]. You say this international bank is telling us where to put the houses and how to pay for them and that if their conditions are not acceptable to us, then the money they have loaned will

have to be returned. It will go to Colombia or to Ecuador. The worst imperialism of all is that of the United States.

A lady asked, "What is development?"

The colonel replied, "It means to elevate the standard of living of a people to a better life."

"And what is BID?" someone else asked.

Then the former mayor of Huaraz appealed to be heard. I had once, in early November 1971, wandered into the patio of the ravaged house in which he now lived above the barrio of San Francisco. Seeing I was a gringa, he invited me to listen to the evening news with him on his shortwave radio. When I was leaving, as we stood on the hill overlooking the center of Huaraz, he looked out over the pampa and said, "Huaraz is asleep; people should demand their lots, put an end to this CRYRZA that rules our lives from Lima."

Now, at the meeting, he spoke in the fashion of an eloquent Latin American statesman. He had carefully written out definitions of reconstruction and rehabilitation, which he begged to read. These definitions did not include "change," and much less "creation of a new reality." After reading his definitions, the elderly mayor pleaded, as if baring himself before all the world, "Here you see me, my Colonel. I am dressed up because I have found an old suit and a tie to wear to this meeting, but this doesn't represent my reality. The reality is that we are all like cornered animals, abandoned, neglected. I have nothing. Where am I to go?"

When the answer from behind the table at which the CRYRZA and SINAMOS dignitaries sat came back, "Let's hear something constructive," a sharp pang of embarrassment for the ex-mayor shot through me.

A man asked, "When will you begin to put in the sewerage and water lines?"

"That is constructive," the colonel said.

But then another man shouted, "We are already so hurt."

Then a townswoman, poor, I knew, took up the theme of the *damnificados* ("the hurt ones"; "the damaged ones"). "We are already hurt, and we will be more hurt still," she said. "You will take from us our *chacras* to make everyone equal. What you ought to take away is the property of Doña Anatolia, the richest woman of Huaraz, all of it!"

My mind slipped into another memory, of the afternoon not long after I had arrived in the valley when I had met Doña Anatolia, who was not at this meeting. An old woman now, she had broken into tears remembering her piano, which had been destroyed along with all her possessions. As she sobbed, her husband spoke: "What have they done, these people who have brought us 'aid'? They have given us supplies, salt, and cooking oil. And the Indians have taken them, and now the Indians think that to do any work one must pay them with something. The *campesinos* no longer want to work for us. I am left with a small pasture and one peon to look after it. The others have come down to Huaraz to live in the free *módulos*." His face clouding suddenly, he finished by saying, "We with our whiskey, the Indians with their *chicha*, it's all the same. We do not know how to work, either."

My reminiscence was interrupted by another voice at the meeting, a new voice, speaking now in a very different tone from the voices before. In a speech as eloquent as that of the former mayor of Huaraz, this middle-aged man was praising the Revolutionary Reconstruction. "We must try to quell our egoism, our selfishness, our individualism," he was saying. "I had property right on the central plaza, but I happily give it up. We must let the poor into the center of Huaraz." Applause broke out.

But then another man whom I recognized, the baker in San Francisco, said, "But I have calculated the cost of these concrete houses after twenty or thirty years. With the interest on the loans, their cost will be double, triple. You people of the Revolution speak of marginalization, but is it not a fact that not one poor person will be able to afford to live in the center of the capital of the Department of Ancash?" People cheered this also, and I found myself wondering, Which is true? Will the proposed *Plan Regulador* open or close Huaraz's center to the poor?

The meeting broke down into the persistent themes of where, out of so many millions of *soles* in the budget for reconstruction, has all the money gone and what was causing all the delay. "Two years have passed" was the chorus from the people.

The response from the national authorities was "There had to be studies. We could not reconstruct the old reality, the same city. You have not grasped this fact. Don't be dense." Saying this, the colonel rested his forehead in the palm of his hand. Again, rumbling shot through the crowd. Looking up tiredly, the colonel almost

whispered, "There will be no more delay." He asked that the sur-
reptitious barrio committees be suspended until another big meeting, this time with General La Vera—CRYRZA's chief—could be
called.

The meeting had lasted several hours. As everyone silently
filed out of the now dark interior of the building, that rose-colored
glow that bathes the valley as the sun sinks behind the Cordillera
Negra enveloped the forlorn and confused survivors and the uneasy
and exhausted reconstructionists alike.

Two days before the anniversary, on May 29, 1972, after two
years of moratorium on all urban land, by Decree Law No. 18974,
some 2 million square meters of Huaraz's urban center were officially expropriated (*El Peruano* 29 May 1972; *La Prensa* 30 May
1972). This was the first urban reform attempted by the Revolutionary Military Government anywhere in Peru. It was now clear
that the meaning of the earthquake from the vantage point of the
nation was the mission of seeing a new Peru, like the phoenix, rise
out of the rubble. The Law of Expropriation read:

> Upon the ruins of the cities and the dust of the earth today faded,
> we will construct a part of the New Peru of our children.

Anticipating the law, a CRYRZA official had remarked at another
meeting of survivors the day before, "The earthquake has permitted
us justice."

In a special broadcast on the eve of the second anniversary,
CRYRZA's Gen. Luis La Vera Velarde emphasized that an unjust
society must not be rebuilt: ". . . property cannot be an absolute
and egotistical right; it must fulfill a social function of the first order
in benefit of the collectivity. . . . It is a matter of not reconstructing
the previous reality, unjust and discriminatory. . . ." Rehabilitation, he went on, must not be "merely physical" but rather "more
ample and more human . . . and upon the base of spiritual rehabilitation, we will build the new cities that will serve as a dwelling
for a worthy, just, and collectively responsible society." Distrust
of CRYRZA, of General La Vera, of rhetoric, and perhaps most
of all, of what the new "reality" would be like, was mounting, and
the day before, I had noticed that several guards surrounded the
general's quarters in Monterrey.

During the day of May 30, on the pampa in front of my house, children were doing a dance named after the last Inca emperor, Atahualpa. They twirled around, waving branches of eucalyptus, using old cardboard cartons and sticks for drums. Fifteen or so Indian peasants from Paria were crossing the pampa. One man carried a small image of Christ on a platform that rested on his shoulders. At 6:00 P.M., I switched on my radio. The local poet was reciting: "It was 3:23 in the afternoon . . ."

About seven o'clock that night, I walked up to a *módulo* near the hospital, where people were sitting around listening to the radio. There I recorded La Vera's speech. Everybody was talking about CRYRZA when the priest from Soledad came in and called Ernesto, the occupant of the *módulo*, aside. I overheard the words "This speech will kill CRYRZA." Pacing back and forth, the priest began to speak out loud about the agitation in Soledad that night, how it was getting harder and harder for him to maintain order. "There is another reality from the one that CRYRZA paints," he said. He reported that during the religious procession of the Señor de la Soledad that took place on May 10, the townspeople had threatened an uprising against CRYRZA. He had been able to calm them then, saying that such protests should not be mixed with religion. But now, with the anniversary of the disaster the following day, how could he contain them?

Ernesto had made what he called an "underground film," which he and the priest were planning to take to the National Palace in Lima. Maybe they would take it all over the world "so that everyone will know the truth of what is happening here." Ernesto tried to get a projector going to show his film, but the generator failed. The Soledad priest left, and everyone began to disperse.

Four of us walked back together across the pampa. Rosa María said her husband had told her that the model concrete houses CRYRZA had recently built at the edge of Belén would blow over in a strong wind. A wall had already fallen for no reason at all. Big adobe bricks were much better than concrete in the sierra, she said. For me, it was so unreal, the small gathering around the radio, listening to a vision of a totally new world, the priest's visit, the talk of taking a film to Lima, and even abroad. Reality was the black sky, with stars shining over the dark and empty pampa.

I had absorbed all the cold of the rainless night and the tense expectancy about what would happen tomorrow—May 31, 1972

—and slept fretfully. Would there be an uprising? Would restless refugees descend from the camps and try to breathe life into their benumbed city? Would they oust CRYRZA and reclaim their lands? I felt more like a reporter at the front, on the eve of a battle, than an anthropologist. How could I "cover" tomorrow? If an uprising occurred, would it come from the discontented survivors of Soledad barrio, with their reputation for insolence and their fierce claims on their land; from Indian peasants from the district of Carhuaz, known to be easily moved against any figures of authority; from some group of hamlets above Huaraz whose residents feared the revolution would destroy their religious practices; or from the handful of "true" Yungay survivors, exiled from their buried town and feeling the threat of peasants from satellite hamlets taking over their positions as district leaders? How could I go everywhere and see everything?

AT about 7:00 A.M. on May 31, 1972, just after Radio Huaraz broadcast a telegram from General Velasco in Lima to General La Vera in Huaraz, I went out to the plaza for the raising of the flag. Commemorative ceremonies had been planned, and a program of events published in the Huaraz daily newspaper, which was being printed again in a shed at the edge of the market. However, only a few guards were standing around the plaza, and nothing was happening. As the day wore on, I realized that the program of events would not be carried out. I learned later that CRYRZA had worked behind the scenes to prevent the ceremonies, which would have drawn large gatherings of people, from taking place. But, from early in the morning until night fell, there was an endless stream of people walking up to the cemetery in Pedregal, high on the rim of the pampa. Uniformed schoolchildren formed long segments of this stream.

About 8:00 A.M., I left the central plaza and went to buy flowers in the market. "You must be the wife of one of the Czechs," the vendor remarked. The wives of the climbers lost at the base of Huascarán had been flown over to attend a ceremony between the Llanganuco lakes. Next, I left some flowers by the altar in my house in memory of the nephew-priest of my landlords, who had been killed at Belén, the man whose room I occupied.

Then I made my way up to Soledad, where, at about nine-twenty, a Mass was in progress in honor of the teachers lost in the earthquake. Dressed in dark suits, the remaining teachers of Huaraz filed in with a huge wreath to be blessed before taking it to the cemetery. As sheep bleated outside, the Soledad priest, Padre Espinoza, so wild and intense the night before, gave now the softest sermon I ever heard him give. "Whoever knows how to speak from the soul cries," he was saying as an Indian woman walked right up to the altar to place a candle. I thought how at home the Indian peasants feel at Soledad.

After the Mass, I went by the Oliveras', the family that had lost five children. No one was home. They must be at the cemetery, I thought. I took flowers to Angelita at her little store in San Francisco barrio. She was not feeling well and had decided to stay in all day. Only a few pieces of round, crusty bread were in her showcase.

I walked back to the plaza. Now troops were there, about fifty soldiers. Some people were lying on the grass of the plaza, where bonfires had burned that night two years ago. By now we all knew that there would be no ceremonies here on the pampa. As I walked around, chatting among the people, who seemed to be lost, waiting in vain for the events that would not occur, several remarked, "They are afraid that we *Huaracinos* will rebel. But what can we do? We can't do anything." The prefect—governor of the Department of Ancash—passed in his jeep, followed by SINAMOS personnel in another jeep.

I walked over to look at the few model houses at the edge of Belén. A lady was coming from a Mass held at San Antonio. "When will the aid all the foreign countries sent us reach us?" she asked me. As we walked together up to the cemetery, she said CRYRZA didn't know what it was like for the survivors.

At the tall wooden cross marking the communal grave, the mayor and then the priest of Belén spoke. I was too far back in the crowd of mourners to hear them. Then, as the priest from the barrio of San Francisco began chanting in Latin, people went forward to lay flowers beneath the cross. A group representing the hospital placed a wreath at the grave, and the nurses sang. The floral spray from CRYRZA was prominent at the grave site, but no one was there from CRYRZA. A fresh white coffin, a child's, lay nearby. A *campesino* dressed in tattered black woolen pants and poncho began

to play the violin next to the cross and to sing softly in Quechua.
I saw Flavio and Elena, who had lost their two daughters. Abraham,
their new baby, was plump and beautiful in his mother's arms.

The mourners began to disperse from around the communal
grave and to visit other graves. Among the small group that remained near the Indian who was singing in Quechua was a stately
woman dressed all in black, wearing a hat that would have been
more appropriate on the streets of Paris in the 1920s. Instead of a
woven bag or a basket, which townswomen as well as *campesinas*
used, this woman carried a pocketbook. She was near seventy,
perhaps. She took hold of my arm and began to tell me about the
day of the earthquake. She had owned a big house with a patio in
the center of Huaraz. She had reached the patio by only four steps
before her house collapsed. "Now I rent a room in Centenario, and
I eat in these restaurants they put up for the foreigners," she said.
"I have a thermos in my room, too, for hot drinks. So much sacrifice
in life, and then everything ends in a moment."

We walked to a little place called Posel, with battered tables
amid tall eucalyptus trees, to have some lunch. Strips of meat,
called *charqui*, hung from lines, drying in the sun. As we ate, the
old woman told me how she had suffered from *susto* ("fright") after
the earthquake. She could not sleep at night. She went to Lima for
three months but could not stay away from Huaraz. "This atmosphere tones one," she said, looking up at the trees. "These trees
give oxygen by day, though at night they are poisonous."

Her face began to dissolve into memories. In 1914 she had
fallen in love with a handsome French doctor who had come to
Ticapampa to care for the miners. Then they called him away to
a war they were fighting over there, she said. He promised to send
for her but never did. "He must have died in that war," she said
sadly. "I kept waiting for a letter, and so I never married." She
had not lost any family in the earthquake, because she had no
family. I should have inquired, for it is unusual indeed not to have
family in the highlands, to be so alone. But I just drifted in the
noonday sun, eucalyptus branches swaying overhead, not doing
fieldwork, just accepting. When I did think for a second, it struck
me that of all the friends I by then had, who had lost so many
relatives, I was spending these moments of May 31 with a stranger,
a rather mysterious woman who had lost no one in the earthquake,

who had waited all her life for a Frenchman who never came. My day had taken a strange turn, into a loneliness beyond the bounds of disaster.

Brightening, the old woman said, "Let's go to visit the Lord of Solitude. I always go to visit the Señor de la Soledad. We will rest there a little and then go home." At Soledad, two *campesinos* were bent over candles on the dirt floor. We sat on the crude benches. Next to me was another *campesino*, his hair shaved almost to the top of his head, and next to him a townsman in a dark coat and tie. After a while, each of these men went up to touch the Christ through the plastic that protected the image. The townsman laid a flower on the alter. The Indian went behind, lifted the plastic, and kissed the feet of the image. We stayed for a long time. Sheltered from the midday sun, I watched the candles flickering, the image, the people. Soledad was cool and immensely quiet, like the center of a storm.

By the time my watch marked 3:23 in the afternoon—two years to the minute—my companion and I were seated in the central plaza, resting from our walk in the hot sun down from Soledad. The only movement was among the silent tiers of mourners filing across the pampa up to Pedregal. The parting words of the old woman were "I have an idea there will be another earthquake." I never knew her name, and I never saw her again.

I returned home to find my landlords talking about the ex-propriation. "The decree law has taken from the Río Santa to José Olaya and from Raimondi to the Río Seco," Don Alejandro said. "This means CRYRZA can take this house from us, throw us out. But who knows when it will be? What can we do? We must continue living." In their little kitchen, we talked into the dusk, having coffee and bread, the guinea pigs starting to chirp in the patio. A sudden chill in the air extinguished the heat of the day. I was exhausted from the sierra sun and from the suppressed emotion and frustration that lay under the surface of the day. What dignity human beings are capable of, I thought, as I fell asleep that night. Death is survivable.

Fifteen

THEOLOGY OF LIBERATION

*. . . what looks like tragedy is in fact the
threshold of triumph.*

the Apostle John

THAT DEATH IS SURVIVABLE—the message of the
Resurrection—was the cornerstone of the Catholic Reform
movement. Its even deeper message was that life must be
livable for every person, not just a privileged few. In this, Catholic
Reform echoed the message of Velasco's revolutionary enterprise.

Following the Latin American Bishops' Conference held in
September 1968, in Medellín, Colombia, the bishops of Peru, in a
document entitled *Justice in the World*, stated their understanding
of the new role of the Catholic Church. First, the Church must
review all its property and begin to "live the Gospel poverty." It
must denounce exploitation, break with old structures, and foster
the creation of new values, behavior, and beliefs. It must work
toward making the oppressed aware of their circumstances and the
injustice under which they lived, decrying this "situation of injus-

tice as a situation of sin." Radical self-awareness, through *conscientización* ("consciousness-raising") became the principal task of Reform Catholicism in Peru. "*Concientización* means the development of an awareness of one's existential situation. . . . The essential point is to get a man to reflect on what he is, where he is, and why."[1]

It awaited, however, Peruvian priest and theologian Gustavo Gutiérrez to synthesize the thought of the Catholic Reform movement and the politics of social change in his consummate treatise *A Theology of Liberation: History, Politics and Salvation* (1973; first published in Spanish in 1971), a major contribution of Latin America to world theology. In his book, Gutiérrez explores the idea of a risen Christ who will free people from both external and internal bondage.

Consequently, symbols of hope and world renewal in the Callejón aftermath were not only those of the Revolution—Túpac Amaru and Atusparia—but also the risen Christ. The Catholic Church in Latin America had always emphasized the worship of the crucified Christ and looked to justice only in an afterlife. Now it had stepped down from its transcendental posture, legitimizing revolution and change. The postdisaster valley was ripe for dramatizing the transition from an emphasis on the wounded, dying Christ of medieval Spain to the triumphant risen Christ of the Resurrection, to whom the new Latin American church now turned its attention.

The new theology sought a deeper meaning in Christ's Crucifixion, of synchronous endings and beginnings, of darkness turned to light. The disaster that had darkened the valley on May 31, 1970, found its symbolic translation in the hours of Christ's agony. The Apostle John's interpretation of the Crucifixion came to describe also the disaster: "What looks like defeat is in fact a victory, and what looks like tragedy is in fact the threshold of triumph." The zeal of a young revolution, seeing the chance to catapult the mountain society from one stage to another, had its own apostolic version: "In the life of towns there are moments that signal simultaneously the end and the beginning of different stages."

The ideology of hope sprung from disaster was far-reaching indeed. Not only survivors but a new Latin American humanity would emerge from the chaos: "If among the rubble of a society which has suffered a great earthquake, one must resurrect Latin American man, faith in the Resurrected Christ will give a new meaning to everything, rejuvenating marginalized humanity. This, the new liturgy of the Church will call 'the liberation of the oppressed.' "

The Revolution and the theology of liberation came together as two messiahs whose mission was to direct change and effect progress that the earthquake had "permitted." Just as the Revolution saw an opportunity to move beyond agrarian reform and expropriate urban land of the leveled towns, the Church saw the chance to move beyond mere changes in ritual that broke with traditional Catholicism, changes that had already been tentatively introduced in some of the valley churches even before the disaster.

The instantaneous poverty of everyone had created a setting of people much like those described by Jesus and Marx. At the same time, the aftermath had brought to the valley outsiders versed in the more theoretical aspects of the new radical Latin American Church, whose starting point was a Marxist analysis of society. Thus, while the Revolution, for which justice was its "most sacred cause," spoke of "spiritual rehabilitation," the Church, turned millenarian, took up the cause of justice upon this earth. One of its more radical spokesmen, a priest who had come to the valley in the early postdisaster months, spoke of the "human promotion" that must now take place within a framework of Marxist ideology.

There was no need even to "review Church property"—one of the proposals of the Medellín Documents—since the steeples had fallen, the churches had collapsed, and the religious images, the *santos* ("saints"), lay strewn in the rubble. The Reconstruction's "removal of ruins" had dealt a final blow to these material representations of religion as it existed in the valley prior to the disaster. A CRYRZA official told me one day, "People talk about the bulldozers that knocked over altars and plowed through the saints. They say there have been two disasters." The earthquake and the "removal of ruins" made it possible for the new Church to ask: "What world shall we reconstitute, a world with images or a world without them?"

The official Church language, which was changing all over the Catholic world, developed a special poignancy in the disaster aftermath. Words and phrases like "alienation," "exploitation," "social

justice," and "liberation" were prominent, and "God," "sacraments," "prayer," and "ritual" were less audible in the new code.
"Sin" and "morality" in the old sense were missing entirely in the
new language. Ivan Illich, Paolo Freire, and Gustavo Gutiérrez,
the new Catholic spokesmen, had replaced them with "growth,"
"consciousness," and "expansion of the personality." "Sin" became
subsumed under the word *injustice*.

In November 1971, a new bishop was installed in Huaraz. A
ceremony marking his new tenure was held on the pampa on November 21. Indian bands from Atipayán and other hamlets came
down to play their crudely hewn instruments and sing in Quechua.
Alongside these bands, nuns from Lima, who, in the aftermath,
had become a new contingent of the progressive church of German
priests at Centenario, sang international folk songs and played guitars. I sat on a rock in the hot noon sun, amid all these cacophonous
elements of the old and the new, and tried to write down verbatim
the bishop's words as he addressed the crowd. Upon the landscape,
in his words, in faces, everywhere, the earthquake was present:

> This is a town that has suffered a terrible misfortune, a hard test.
> There are material, spiritual, and social problems. Socially, we
> must break with the old structural truths, pass from them to new
> ones. Injustice existed. Upon the ruins, we have to construct a
> more human, a freer, society. Some of you desire the same society
> of before, with its oppressions, its injustice. What is it worth to
> us if we build wide streets without conversion in our hearts? Let
> us do miracles and transform everything, create a world of justice.
> Faith and love are the only things that can transform us. We ask
> the Church to realize its role as liberator, to free us from every
> kind of exploitation and domination.

A truck bearing the name of Indian leader Atusparia passed near
the cupola, and a lady commented to me, "Huaraz is purely *campesinos* now."

I recalled the ceremony held here on the Plaza de Armas, with
trumpets heralding the discovery of "native" oil in the Peruvian
jungle. As the months passed, ideology seemed to be exerting more
and more pressure that religious rites that took place in the shadow
of the cathedral ruins be secularized, and in turn secular rites, like

the discovery of oil, had the markings of religious rites. As the destroyed Huaraz became a laboratory for the joint forces of revolution and Catholic Reform, both bent on the utopian goal of social justice, the secularization of the Church and the sacralization of society were intensifying.

Christmas on the deserted pampa was an occasion in which religion and revolutionary rhetoric coalesced. As there was no money for gifts the Christmas of 1971, the Church presented to the children a gigantic nativity scene staged under the shell of the cupola of the destroyed cathedral. The Holy Family, the Wise Men, and the shepherds were real people and the sheep, goats, pigs, and donkeys that wandered about on the pampa provided the animal actors. Bands and costumed dancers came down from the hamlets to welcome the Christ child. Wearing ponchos and with woven sacks flung over their backs, Indians danced up to the manger, bowing, retreating, dancing closer, bowing again. Opening their sacks, they laid potatoes and other produce at the foot of the manger. A dancer clutching a hen approached the manger, and handing it over to Padre Quintana, the Spanish Franciscan who played Joseph, he shouted, "Beloved Baby, the father will show you the hen."

Scrawled in large black letters on the curved dome of the cathedral were these sayings:

Christ is not divided.

Christ is for the poor and for the rich.

Peace and justice were harmonized in Christ.

In Huaraz all was lost except faith and joy.

Priests and politicians sat together behind wooden tables at the edges of the nativity scene. General La Vera of CRYRZA, the prefect, the mayor of Huaraz, and military personnel were there. Hamlet leaders wore signs announcing their newly founded cooperatives and "Committees pro-Works." The crowds gathered on the pampa were mixed, townspeople and *campesinos*, though there were many more Indian peasants, setting the pampa ablaze with color. An old woman with a badly deformed foot, who slept in a tent on the plaza of San Francisco, hobbled up to the manger.

Others went up to lay bouquets of yellow flowers near the crib of the squalling baby. Standing behind the manger, a little girl from the town clasped to her breast a red-haired plastic doll that had survived the earthquake.

CATHOLIC Reform in the Callejón launched its main attack against the ancient customs, the *costumbres*—Indian dances and bands, religious processions, fireworks, "worship of the saints"—practices the reformists considered false, sinful, and dangerously linked to the native Andean religion. "Progress" meant that native Andean religion, which for centuries had coexisted with Catholicism, must finally be extinguished. The *costumbres* were seen as keeping the Indian "backward" and superstitious, unable to break into full national life. In other words, the ancient customs fostered injustice in the valley.

The principal spokesmen for doing away with traditional religion, besides the temporary religious personnel who had come to work in the aftermath, were the German priests of the Church of the Sacred Heart in the barrio of Centenario. And, according to a Maryknoll priest, "between the German priests of Centenario and the old-time Peruvian priests who allow, even encourage, the native practices, every point of view in between is represented. The earthquake has agitated the conflicts."

Indeed, underneath the prevailing ideology of Catholic Reform, a wide range of Catholic belief and practice was present in Huaraz, from the most radical to the most conservative. As time went on, I found Huaraz to be a microcosm of everything that was going on in the universal Church.

On a Sunday morning in mid-November, I went to Mass at the Convent of the Barefoot Fathers, also called San Antonio, in the barrio of Huarupampa. This church of the Spanish Franciscans was now a large prefabricated pasteboard building, the biggest of the makeshift churches during the aftermath. It had a concrete floor and wooden benches. Remnants of the stained-glass windows, recovered from the rubble, had been inserted into the sidewalls. The church was filled with *campesinos*, Indian women in their multiple skirts of vivid hues—oranges, purples, reds, and blues—and Indian men in black, wearing rubber sandals over feet thickly coated with clay. The townswomen covered their heads with lace mantillas, while the Indian women removed their wool hats.

A townswoman was kissing the feet of an image as the three Franciscans intoned in Latin. Padre Quintana delivered his sermon about world wars, pestilence, and earthquakes, which, he said, announced the end of the world. "But this is not the end of the world," he stressed. "Our destroyed city and the ruins are like sinful man, his virtue broken. But we can build it up again. . . . Christ can cleanse it all, and it will become whiter than the driven snow."

The next time I saw Quintana, witty, articulate, so very Spanish, was late in November, when, for the first time, I went to Mass at Soledad. Quintana was standing in for the priest of Soledad, Father Espinoza. His sermon this time was filled with allusions to conflicts concerning the Reconstruction, conflicts still at that time largely obscure to me. "We are getting ourselves into a chaos that not even penicillin will save us from!" the Spaniard declared.

From time to time as the year went on, I would go to talk to the Franciscans at night, and we would sit around a table having a glass of wine. "There have been many 'earthquakes' here," Padre Hidalgo said one night. "First, *the* earthquake, when everything fell and the material world was lost; then a 'human earthquake,' when values were lost, people were at odds, and a great psychic unhinging occurred; then an 'economic earthquake,' when money poured in and has been so poorly managed." Some got what they had never lost, he said, and then to "a family of seven they would give two eggs, five potatoes, a pinch of salt, and one blanket, and that after a week of standing in line." Padre Efraín spoke of the census takers, who "spent all their time with numbers until finally they would have to toss spoiled chickens into the Santa." One night, when the statistics stalkers had awakened survivors in tents grouped around the ruins of San Antonio for the umpteenth time, Efraín went out and forbade them to proceed: "Let them sleep tranquilly at least one night!"

Quintana interjected, "This was a chance to really change things, but the Revolution is a lie. Revolution is not a mechanical thing, not a thing of numbers, but instead of sentiment, and they come with institutions and organizations." Believing in "real work," the Franciscans had started a brick factory in their patio. They would make adobe bricks even if they could do nothing with them for the time being. One of them pointed with pride to the stained-glass windows they had salvaged and pieced together. My eye fell

on the piece of stained glass that said Bank of Credit, which, in
their enthusiasm to rebuild, they had wedged among the religious
scenes.

These occasions were filled with Spanish humor, indignation,
and lament. I remember Efraín holding forth about the measuring
of the streets that was going on, streets that were to be wide and
beautiful avenues, the likes of which had never been seen before
in the sierra. "They have painted the streets in all colors, it rains,
and they paint them again," he said. "They are measuring these
streets more carefully than the railroad to the old American West
was measured."

"Ay!" Quintana sighed. "Even Saint Peter would not be able
to straighten all this out." When the going got tough, we would
talk of lighter things, musing over topics like whether it would be
worse to be lost in the jungle or in the glacial gorges. I would walk
home across the dark pampa thinking that the Reform had not really
touched San Antonio yet. Nor were these Franciscans like the old-
time Peruvian priests. The American Maryknoll had called them
"Spanish reactionaries."

The Spanish Franciscans had all come to Huaraz after the
earthquake, because they belonged to an Order, which had quickly
replaced those who had endured the trauma of May 31. Likewise,
the German priests of Centenario had external support from an
Order. In contrast, the elderly *Huaracino* priests had gone through
the disaster itself. Not belonging to any Order, these priests could
not be replaced from outside, and they were short on finances.
Many had been physically injured, or had "become nervous," as
people said. Without the financial backing of an Order, their
churches destroyed, they considered their parishes to be "orphans"
in need of help from CRYRZA. Yet this help was not forthcoming,
because the plan, even of the secular revolutionary forces, was to
"change religion." And by and large, these priests of the pampa—
of San Francisco, Belén, and Soledad—adhered to the old Catholicism and were sympathetic to native practices. Because of its
image of the Lord of Solitude and its charismatic priest, however,
in many ways, Soledad stood alone.

Sixteen

SENTIMENT AND IDEOLOGY

*One's own being makes him stay, return-
ing for the night to the same place.*
a man from the barrio of Soledad

THERE HAD BEEN no uprising on May 31, 1972. But as we inched toward the middle of that year, a storm was gathering in the valley. The radio was announcing with frequency: "Huaraz on the march, the task that history has set for us." CRYRZA was moving out from its headquarters in Vichay onto the battleground, which was no less than the pampa of Huaraz.

The actual acts and proposals of the Reconstruction as it cranked into gear were more threatening than the sense of abandonment of the previous years. The despair that had grown as the gap widened between the idealistic rhetoric and the actual performance in those first two postdisaster years now turned into more overt conflict between the Revolutionary Military Government, represented in Huaraz by SINAMOS and CRYRZA, and the earthquake survivors.

After the Decree of Expropriation, Huaraz was virtually in the hands of CRYRZA. However, for many reasons and difficulties of its own, involving international loans as well as internal problems, CRYRZA could not begin to build. It became a matter of staving off survivors until their *Plan Regulador* could be initiated.

The plan was to redistribute the land of Huaraz's center equally. No matter what someone had owned before, he would now be allowed 300 square meters. If this lot fell in a section in which the concrete houses provided through long-term loans were to be built, he would have to sign up for one of these houses or leave the center of Huaraz altogether. The vastly broadened avenues, the public places, the parks—called "lungs" by the people from Lima, signifying areas of fresh, pure air—and the new commercial streets also meant it would not be likely that one could live again "in his same barrio."

The overriding objective of survivors in the disaster aftermath was "to return to one's place." This sentiment—"to be in one's place"—could not be quantified. *Huaracinos* I knew who had owned more than 300 square meters were quite willing to relinquish the excess if their lot could be located on their former spot or near it or at least in the same barrio. And, again, some who had lived in the center could not return there at all if they could not sustain the long-term loans for the projected concrete houses, houses that at the same time appeared to them to be *casas ajenas* ("foreign," "different," literally, "houses of others").

So the majority of survivors from Huaraz's urban center did not balk at the *quantity* of land that would be parceled out to them. But they wanted their allotted share of land to be located near where they had lived. And they wanted to be able to put up their own houses, conforming, of course, to a building code for seismic-proof construction. It looked now as if none of this would be possible. Distress lay not so much in reduced wealth as in not being able to return to the land on which one grew up and live in a house of one's own design.

People knew that scientists had called the earthquake an "adobe disaster." I can think of no one who did not attribute, at an empirical level, so much devastation to the fact that the towns of the Callejón were a trap. Built of earth, the towns returned to earth, "adobe upon adobe," as they would say. They admitted that from time to time in the past they had felt a vague anxiety about the durability of the timeworn, closely clustered dwellings. And after the earthquake, with the first influx of technicians, the magic words "aseismic" and "noble" material (concrete) did gain currency. The marketplace was flooded with "aseismic" plastics.

But the vision of Huaraz as an exemplary city of the future, comparable by the year 2000 to some of the world's most important cities, with spectacular avenues up to twenty-eight meters wide, did not stick. It would be a concrete city, and concrete was "foreign." Windows in the concrete houses would be small and vertical, not horizontal, as in the adobe houses of *antes* ("before"), they would say, and worst of all, they would not face Huascarán. "The earthquake has been a real shaking up in everything," a man told me, "in our thought, in the idea of what a room is and what it should contain, in what a window is. . . ."

People sneered at the "lung" areas, since they think of the whole Callejón as being filled with healthy air. They snickered at the spacious avenues and wondered where they would keep their guinea pigs and other animals, with no corrals and patios.

They pointed to a four-story school building of reinforced concrete and brick that *did* collapse during the earthquake and to the few well-built adobe houses that resisted the shaking. News that the concrete wall on one of the new model houses going up by May 1972 had been blown down by a strong afternoon wind spread quickly. Also, since valley dwellers perceive the main threat to be from avalanche and listen to an internal rhythm that tells them that earthquakes happen only every several hundred years, they felt no urgency for "noble" material. Clearly, science and technology were bridled by the immense sentiment of *land* and the aesthetic will of the sierra.

The unreality of the envisioned future, with its "foreign" aesthetic, lessened the impact of the "adobe disaster" and turned survivors not toward that future but to reminiscences of pre-Columbian times and the wisdom and technology of the Inca builders. The Incas located their towns on hilltops out of the path of landslides and farmed the more fertile and more dangerous valley bottoms. An aroused mourning for the lost stone empire, with its scattered settlements of thatch-roofed houses, merged with the mourning for the ill-fated, vulnerable, yet charming colonial town of Huaraz.

However, despite survivors' nostalgia for the Inca past, as anthropologist Richard Patch remarked, it would have taken all the power of the Inca Empire to force valley-bottom towns to safer sites in the higher mountains.

Most of the larger battles over relocation of the towns themselves had been fought and won by survivors during the first year after the disaster. Huaraz itself had been designated as unsafe, but after many threats by the national government to move it, it was finally determined that geologic conditions did not preclude reconstruction at its present site.

Even the handful of survivors from Yungay, which so obviously lay in the deadly path of Huascarán, were strained and taut over their proposed relocation to a hillside on the Cordillera Blanca north of their buried city. But this was at least close to the playa, and more amenable to them than more distant sites, like Tingua, with which they had been threatened.

In July 1972, when I went to visit Cirila in Yungay Norte, she took me up into the Atma foothills to where they had begun to put up a model house. Russia had sent prefabricated wooden dachas for the new Yungay. The construction of the model house was stalled, however, because the instructions sent with the dachas were in Russian and no one could read them. But roads were being bulldozed up the mountainside.

Cirila joked that the houses cost 75,000 *soles*, which she could not afford, but which was only three months of a CRYRZA engineer's salary. "With those salaries, why should they hurry up with the reconstruction?" She laughed and continued to escort me around a place she knew she would never live in. We made our way down to the plaza of the proposed Yungay. "How big and beautiful!" Cirila exclaimed. "Who knows what important people will be living here on the plaza!" The new site of Yungay was indeed a spectacular setting, with clusters of eucalyptus swaying in the afternoon breezes. From different points, we viewed the snowy peaks. Huandoy loomed magestically above us, over the northern slope of Atma.

In spite of the tacit agreement about Yungay's new location and these beginning efforts to rebuild there, *Yungaínos* were starting to talk of preserving fewer acres of the alluvionic area as the cemetery and of edging back toward the playa. Cirila even began to dream about moving back onto the playa itself. This desire of *Yungaínos* to return to the playa, the alluvionic cemetery itself, to live "where one's dead are buried," to "live with the dead," was poorly understood by the coastal people. They tended to interpret it as negative passivity rather than a positive choice. But it was choice. In a *colectivo*, as we crossed the playa one day, I overheard someone say:

> This is where we want to be. We are accustomed to dying, to losing family. One dies everywhere. Huascarán will keep on. We are strong-willed. We want to be here, to die where we were born.

At one of the many meetings held in Huaraz during the dry season of 1972, an old man stood up and said, "I want to live where I was born, where I grew up, where my own history has been enacted." And on a path in the hamlet of Secsecpampa, a young boy told me, "Here we were born; we are going to die where we were born."

The pull of the land was stronger than the desire to be "safe." The sierra, after all, is never safe, but then, as they would say, nowhere else is, either. This seemed especially true as survivors grappled with the idea that a bomb test might have caused the earthquake and thought about the ways in which human beings impinge upon nature and on fellow humans. Walking across the playa with Cirila and Rubén one day, discussing the possible sites for the new Yungay, I found myself pointing to a place on the mountainside. "Is that strip of land over there safe?" I asked.

Serenely, Cirila answered, "The sierra is never safe."

Rubén added, "There is no security anywhere. If you're in the United States, then the Russians or the Chinese come."

"Where can one be safe?" Cirila challenged me. I had to admit I didn't know.

Besides, places that were called "safe" by outsiders were known by the natives themselves to be dangerous. For example, survivors from Pedregal, on the edge of Huaraz's center, were scheduled to be moved to Vichay. CRYRZA tried to force them out by not providing any services—no water, no electricity. Voicing the view of many, a woman from Pedregal exclaimed, "They wanted to send us to Vichay, to the mouth of the wolf, with the lakes on top of us!" Vichay had caught the tail end of the 1941 alluvion, and now CRYRZA was installed there.

Misunderstanding due to different assessments of the valley environment were never so strident as when, in August 1972, a ministry in Lima, short of funds because they were being put into roads, threatened to close down operations of the Santa Corporation. Overseeing glaciers and lakes, draining lakes about to overflow, reinforcing moraines, the corporation was truly the technological backbone of the whole valley community, practicing precautions that even the Incas recognized as important. Control of the glacial lakes was perceived by everyone in the valley as the one indisputable technological necessity.

As word of the proposed shutdown of the Santa Corporation leaked out, fear swept Huaraz. Of all the faux pas of the Revolutionary Reconstruction, none was deemed worse. For the first time, survivors were moved to unambivalent, concerted action. Benjamín Morales was dispatched to Lima. We all awaited the outcome over several anxious days, and no one spoke of anything else. "It is for all; all live or all die," people said, "no matter what kind of houses we have, adobe or concrete." Facing the minister in Lima, Benjamín asked, "What value are new roads, new houses, if the whole valley disappears?" From President Velasco himself, the order reached Huaraz: "Remain in operation."

LAND and technology, property and modernization, words and action, justice and longings—all these themes spun around through the dry season of 1972.

The meeting of May 16 had concerned mainly those who had owned property in Huaraz's center. These property owners were the ones who had formed the Committees in Defense of the Barrios. But there were also those who, before the earthquake, had rented houses or rooms in the urban center: the *inquilinos*. These "renters," or "non–property owners," as they called themselves, had been settled, too, in survivor camps, the majority of them in Nicrupampa, on land that had been taken over provisionally by the Revolutionary Military Government from Doña Anatolia, known as "the wealthiest woman in Huaraz," and a few other landowners. The Nicrupampa area had been declared emergency land, as part of CRYRZA's Operation Roof, and in September 1970 the owners of Nicrupampa were prohibited from collecting rent for two years.

First, tents had dotted these hilly flanks of the Cordillera Blanca above the barrio of Centenario. When the prefabricated *módulos* arrived in September 1970, they were allocated mainly to the "renters" from the center of Huaraz, but also to property owners and to many Indian peasants who had come down from their mountain hamlets to partake of the new "urbanization" and of provisions that were distributed after the disaster.

Although the Nicrupampa *módulos* were supposed to be only for former renters who could provide a rent receipt or a light bill as proof of their having lived in the center of Huaraz, in practice this was almost impossible to enforce. How could everyone be expected to have salvaged such documents from the ruins? Besides, the fervor of Operation Roof, with its slogan Here We Are All Equal, soon began to override all other considerations. So, all in all, some thousand families—renters, property owners, and peasants—had been settled in Nicrupampa.

When the former property owners had begun to form their Committees in Defense of the Barrios, the renters formed the Association of Non–Property Owners. Their aim was to have a permanent urbanization built right there in Nicrupampa, where they had at first pitched their tents. In order to effect this, the Nicrupampa acreage had to be expropriated from its owners. Being outside the center, Nicrupampa did not fall within the land expropriated under the decree law of May 29, 1972.

I followed especially one family who had rented a house in Huaraz's urban center when they came down years before from the Cordillera Negra hamlet of Pira, where they still retained a *chacra*. In their Nicrupampa *módulo*, Señor Menacho and his family had set up a tiny store where they sold bread, sugar, rice, candles, and other basic items. I would sit in the store for hours talking as small children came in with their *soles* to buy a few matches, or vermicelli for an evening soup.

Early on, Menacho said, "I am in favor of the equal distribution of land. Why should some be renters and some property owners? These property owners want to stop Huaraz from being made a modern city with broad avenues. To the danger of all of us, they cling to their land and would have again narrow streets." When I asked his thoughts about the peasants who had come down to take *módulos*—who before the earthquake had been neither property owners nor renters, not urban at all—he explained that one could no longer get ahead on the land. There were no schools, and besides, all the ancient wisdom of that land had long ago been lost, destroyed by the Spaniards. After all, years ago they themselves had left the mountain flanks to become urban.

Late one night I went to visit the Menachos. Only one candle, which kept blowing out in the wind, provided any light. Señor Menacho gave me a piece of bread and began to speak of the "Invasion Plan" that had not worked. The property owners had gone to General La Vera eight days before the May 31 anniversary to tell him that if CRYRZA did not begin work, they would invade their land, take over the pampa. The expropriation of Huaraz's center was in the works, and that threat, Menacho said, had propelled La Vera to Lima to speed up the enactment of the decree law expropriating the urban center of Huaraz. The renters had wanted to present a united front with the property owners. "We wanted to help them unselfishly, demanding that CRYRZA hurry up, but they accused us of taking advantage of the earthquake to obtain a lot, our own houses, so we backed down, and then they did not invade," he told me. Now some of the pieces of the puzzle of that period around the second anniversary were coming together for me.

"This government is worse than an ordinary government," he went on, "because it raises hopes and then dashes them. It works on deception, and they use more sand than cement in those concrete houses and place the bricks in a line instead of on their heads. . . ."

As September 1972 drew near, the occupants of the Nicrupampa camp grew more and more apprehensive. They had heard that the owners of the land were ready to begin charging them rent as soon as the two-year emergency moratorium was up. They had even threatened to take back their land, which would have left many of the 5,000 or so occupants of Nicrupampa homeless again. Those non–property owners who lived in the camp wanted CRYRZA to expropriate the land and build them houses, however modest, on the site of their present *módulos*.

A meeting of Nicrupampa residents with CRYRZA and SINAMOS was called for the night of July 6, 1972. It was held in the communal *módulo* in front of a little marketplace that never really functioned. A banner tacked to a post read: "Pro-Dwellings for Non–Property Owners of Huaraz Who Suffered in the Earthquake." Peter announced the meeting on Radio Huascarán.

Typhoid had broken out in Nicrupampa. Peter also gave reports of the many children dying in the camp. The hospital in Huaraz was filled to capacity. This was not surprising, for the level of sanitation in the camp was appalling. Six privies had been provided for the 5,000 occupants. People used the tiny streams that flowed down through the mountains, which served as irrigation ditches. Water, too, was drawn from these rivulets, and dishes were washed in buckets of this cold water. Only a few spigots in the camp worked.

July 6 was the night that a strange vapor had hung in the air and people spoke of nuclear contamination. I remember the night as the coldest and darkest of nights. Everything was dark: the epidemic, the fear of contamination, the night itself, the cold. The meeting was dark. Two dim electric light bulbs flickered in the *módulo*, threatening to go out entirely. Víctor Figueroa, one of the leaders in Nicrupampa, was there, in a dark old army coat. Men were there in dark ponchos. All in all, about a hundred people crowded into the dark *módulo*.

We all sat quietly in the cold and dark waiting for the meeting to begin. So far, no officials had come. Finally, a man said, "We *Huaracinos* have lost our character. All our will is gone. We say we will do something, and we don't do it." After about an hour or so of waiting, the "social promoters" of CRYRZA arrived and took their places at a table in front of the group, and the meeting finally got under way.

A man from the camp spoke first. He said they wanted housing that was affordable for those with so few economic resources. To save costs, they would help each other in house construction. Property owners should not be able to remain in Nicrupampa and should return to the center of Huaraz. *Los bajados* (the *campesinos* who had come down from the heights) could remain and be entitled to a house if their fields were far up the mountainsides. If their *chacras* were close by, they should build their houses near their fields.

Another man spoke of the lawyers and teachers, former property owners, who had taken *módulos* in the camp. "For nothing will they move," he said. "And one of them, who is the president of one of our organizations, is the only person with the key to a latrine.

The rest of us, only God knows what we must do. We all keep quiet. You people," he said, directing himself toward the CRYRZA promoters, "have closed off the way for them. With your *Plan Regulador*, many of them cannot move back to Huaraz's center."

Still another man pleaded with CRYRZA: "You people don't know the truth of things here. Get inside the minds of the *Huaracino*. You don't see the reality. You don't let yourselves see it. You must acquaint yourselves with the misfortune of each person. You have not done this. I beg you to come to visit us in Nicrupampa."

One of the social promoters answered: "CRYRZA, it is true, up until now, has been very distant from you, but that stage is over now."

Another official said: "Of some twenty survivor camps, there are those which are made up of only ten or twenty families, like the one near La Unidad. There are over a thousand families here in Nicrupampa. You must organize yourselves, surmount your idiosyncrasies. If the owners of this land try to charge you rent, don't pay."

Then the familiar phrases of "consciousness-raising" streamed out: "*You* must be conscious of your problems. *You* must know your own needs. We must all perform a social function."

One of the leaders of the various sectors of Nicrupampa, seated at the table with the social promoters, conceded tiredly, "Yes, what we lack is consciousness of our needs." I could hardly contain myself. The needs were so profound, so many, so blatant—the need for warmth and dryness from yet another rainy season, when the whole camp creaked under the wet sierra winters; the need for clean water.

From the audience, the dim mass of a hundred people in the fragile *módulo*, a man said simply, "Nothing has been done."

Another added, "We have been living in this state of emergency for over two years, in provisional housing. When will there be something definite?"

A young woman asked, "When will the expropriation of this land take place? Others before you have come to organize groups. Groups and more groups have been organized, and still nothing happens. When will we emerge from the crisis in which we are living?"

Then the aim of this particular meeting became clearer. The

social promoters explained that CRYRZA could not do things for them. They were only there "to coordinate." "We cannot be everywhere at once," they said. "We cannot effect the expropriation. You must become aware of your problems. You people do not flourish. You want to live oppressed. We cannot foster paternalism. You are accustomed to paternalism. You yourselves must plan and find a solution. You must form a group to ask for the expropriation."

"Like in Patay," a man in a black poncho ventured, "we knew that with CRYRZA we would get nowhere. So we got the posts ourselves to put up electric lights, and then you wanted to charge us for the installation!"

At this point, the president of Zone D of Nicrupampa read a petition, dated June 21, from one of the owners of the land the camp occupied. "You entered violently upon our land, calling it Operation Roof. Now the two years are up."

A CRYRZA person answered, "The owners cannot order you from this land. Until December, the property of the zone affected by the earthquake is held in suspension. CRYRZA can dispose of whatever property it wants to for public benefit." He advised the president of Zone D to see the assessor of Zonal Office No. 7. Thus dismissing him, the official continued: "We must create a metamorphosis in the valley, a system where there are no oppressed or oppressors."

From the assembly, a man dressed in the worn and tattered clothes of the oppressed said, "SINAMOS calls Nicrupampa a 'zone of social expansion, of public need.' If this is so, why, then, have you not expropriated this land? You know that not even with a second earthquake will the landowners withdraw. We ask not for paternalism but for a demonstration of strength, for action."

The official answered: "We don't know how many people are going to live in Nicrupampa. We must know how many families there will be in order to determine the quantity of land. The first step is for you to ask for expropriation, and then to form groups."

A Nicrupampa leader said: "We need to see a plan of the streets, lots, blocks. We need technical assistance. Show us some model of a house. Everything is so provisional. Look at the marketplace; it serves no function. And the medical post, millions of *soles* and it is all provisional. Oh, how money has been wasted!"

A serious and thoughtful man whom I knew well and had often

visited in the camp said softly, "We are not against the government, but perhaps your institutions do not fit us."

Then came a more anxious call from the back of the dark assembly. "Do you know the inclemencies we suffer? And the word has passed that you will not begin here until after you have finished reconstructing the center of Huaraz."

Ignoring the question, the official finally stated CRYRZA's message of that evening loudly and strongly: The survivors themselves must work, must organize. If they can build wattle-and-daub huts, why can't they organize? Why can't *they* expropriate the land?

"How?" a voice asked feebly from the back of the room.

I could hardly believe what followed. A CRYRZA man, acting as secretary for the meeting, was seated behind an old typewriter. He said they must begin by forming a committee of people who would take it upon themselves to learn how to make a document of expropriation and learn how to type so that they themselves could complete all of their own paperwork. Once they had learned how to wrest the land from the owners and to fight for their rights, CRYRZA would lend a hand. It would put in water and sewerage and create a storehouse of materials from which people could draw. CRYRZA would lend them the money to buy these materials, and they could pay it back over twenty years at 4 percent interest. CRYRZA would furnish a plan for the type of house they must build. "Remember, Huaraz must take on the physiognomy of a city, which means uniformity," the official said, again ignoring the aesthetic will of the people. Finally, all the officials concluded that if the survivors could build shacks from whatever materials were at hand, they could certainly learn how to type and to create a document of expropriation.

After brief and halting efforts among the people to try to decide if, that very night, they should attempt to form the committee to effect the expropriation and halting discussion of how they might learn to type and where they would acquire a typewriter, they agreed to call another meeting. Word would be passed through the camp of when the meeting would take place.

It was nearly eleven o'clock and extremely cold. As we left the *módulo*, people held their ponchos and shawls up to their mouths so as not to breathe in the frigid night air. During the meeting, there had been a lot of coughing. People were sick with respiratory ills, and they were exhausted. Two years of living under terrible conditions had passed, and now despair stalked outside as we all dispersed along the rough paths of the camp. The message had been that they must learn to organize, to type, to fight. But their stomachs were empty, and it was too cold, and they were too tired.

"I wonder if my oven could remain in the same place as my *módulo*. They say commercial areas must be separate," I heard an old man say almost in a whisper.

As he walked back up the hill, a Nicrupampa leader was saying, "Since the day that CRYRZA installed its offices, it is as if it were the enemy of the people."

They had pleaded for help, and they had received advice and criticism. As I walked back to my room on the pampa that night, the purest and most isolable emotion within the sense of confusion I felt was fury. The center of Huaraz, which had belonged to so many, had been expropriated. Why not Nicrupampa, which belonged to a handful of the richest landowners? I felt like a teacher who knows you cannot teach children who are cold, hungry, and sick. This did not seem like the right time for talk, instruction, "consciousness-raising." It was not a time to carry out the Revolution but, rather, a time to bring all forces that had not suffered the disaster and its aftermath of two long years to bear upon the reconstruction. It was a time to build, not talk, I was thinking, yes, even, in this case, to build *for*. I imagined the army thronging into Nicrupampa and building houses, antiseismic houses, in a style congenial to survivors. Then they could have the Revolution, move to abstraction, try to create the dreamed-of utopia.

In my sleeping bag, I tossed and turned. I decided that the very next morning I would take a *colectivo* down to Lima, go straight to the palace, and tell General Velasco about the meeting in Nicrupampa, tell him about the typhoid and the mud, and the soft-spoken assemblage of camp dwellers in tattered clothes, waiting, hoping, despairing, bewildered. My resolve, spawned in the utter stillness of the black night and the strength one feels when operating inside the imagination upon which there are no practical restraints, was gone by the light of day. Like everybody else, I simply went on, piecing life together with droplets of water, and bread and kerosene, the warmth of the quiet flames of hope inside of people that flickered but never went out, and the utter beauty of the landscape, which was inviolable.

I remember the dry season of 1972—June through August—as an intense period, in ways the most difficult of my whole year of field work. It was difficult for me not just because I was struggling to understand all the issues within a foreign political setting but because I had to do a kind of tightrope act. I was openly for the survivors, who for the most part were deeply enmeshed in their immense sense of loss for their "old world" and their longings for its restoration. Yet I was also for the principles of equality that were the ideological fuel of the Reconstruction.

On a practical level, too, I knew I could not alienate the members of SINAMOS and CRYRZA and other Revolutionary Military Government representatives with whom I came in contact. That could have meant the end of my work or the confiscation of my field notes. I had a padlock on the door of my room and would count my field notebooks, hidden in the well of my table, each time I returned to my room during those months of May through August of 1972. At the many meetings taking place between the Reconstruction forces and survivors during this period, I always tried to make myself as inconspicuous as possible. But I was known. Once I was asked to report with identification to the PIP, equivalent to our FBI.

During all this period, I never lied, never said anything I didn't believe. There were instances, I know, that I refrained from saying things I did believe. These were confusing times, with no clearly drawn lines, no clearly identified villains, no clear right and wrong. Rather, the "truth" seemed to shift, and doubt prevailed. My experience of these shifts reflected the way CRYRZA and survivors felt themselves. On each side, there was incertitude and vacillation. At times, the Reconstruction people hesitated over their own plans, and survivors agonized over the correctness of their own needs and wants. All of this reflected the awesomeness of the task: the opportunity to create a new world.

I never became close to any of the coastal people, CRYRZA or SINAMOS officials and social promoters, except one—a high-ranking CRYRZA official from Lima named Cagliostro. I met him early in 1972 when a friend brought him to my room on the pampa.

Through this man I came to feel the turmoil that was going on within the minds and spirits of the coastal Reconstruction contingent itself.

On several occasions before he introduced me to Cagliostro, Abel, one of the surviving members of the small predisaster "high society" of Huaraz, had sat in my room on stormy nights in February, reminiscing about the Huaraz that had been and contemplating the one that would be rebuilt. Shorn of worldly goods, the "empire" his father had built in the Callejón, Abel was freed to roam in that never-never land that only those who have experienced apocalypse are permitted to enter. Abel was in Lima at the time of the disaster and had come walking up from the coast to find nothing left of the family businesses and homes. Now, he said, he no longer wanted to build an empire. Perhaps he would run away to a Portuguese village and spend his days beachcombing. He didn't want *things* anymore. But he felt disconcerted in the topsy-turvy world of the aftermath. The streets, the houses, banks, restaurants, all the landmarks he had been accustomed to, were no longer there to guide him through the day. In memory, he caressed each barrio and told me what each was noted for, the cold of Belén and the strident wit of Soledad. He dreamily recalled the balconies, the flowers, and the music that had poured from windows out onto the narrow streets of Huaraz.

Abel had struck up a friendship with Cagliostro, the CRYRZA official, based on mutual interests in literature and knowledge of that "other world" that was Lima. One night he brought him to my room. A big hulk of a man, Cagliostro lounged on my cot, obviously feeling my room to be a safe place in which to speak from his heart. It was that night that I learned from him how the idea of creation had caught fire in the National Palace just after the disaster. "We will make Ancash an experimental state," General Velasco had said. "We are at zero in the Callejón. We can create a model state of the Revolution." As the months passed, Cagliostro came to visit me from time to time and revealed his doubts and spoke of all the things that were going wrong. Why were things so askew? he would wonder aloud, when all the "correct" motivations for the reconstruction were there.

One night a CRYRZA sociologist came with Cagliostro. By now we were into June, and the lack of action had begun to take its toll in the growing dissension among survivors. The sociologist said that the man in charge of the reconstruction budget had told him that the money was there, waiting. But organization was the problem. The ministries that had been moved into the Affected Zone were used to working alone, and now they must coordinate with each other. It was chaotic. They were trying, but when money was not used, according to a schedule that had been designed much earlier in Lima, the money had to be returned to Lima. For example, $30 million in the World Bank had been set aside to build the Pativilca-Huallanca road. But the construction was held up in studies. Perhaps Pativilca should be abandoned and other routes explored. I was getting a glimpse of the frustration that reigned inside the Revolutionary Reconstruction forces also—as well as among survivors—a frustration exacerbated by the "good face" CRYRZA sought always to show to survivors. I wondered if it would not have been better to reveal the doubts, the frustration, to join survivors instead of maintaining an omnipotent and omniscient air in front of them.

On one of their visits I learned something that startled me beyond belief and led to many uneasy nights when I didn't sleep much. The sociologist said that, after all, the long delays were not due to lack of money. He had heard it intimated that perhaps some long-range decision had been made that everyone, all the valley survivors, would be better off on the coast, anyway! If the reconstruction were delayed until conditions became so unbearable in the sierra, then people would move down to the coast. "Perhaps," the sociologist said, "these are not opposing ideas—the Revolutionary Reconstruction and such a migration. Maybe this *is* the Revolution. Revolution cannot be carried out in the mountains. This way, the masses needed to carry it out would come together on the coast."

Cagliostro speculated, "Perhaps someone has put a bug in Velasco's ear."

This was the tenor of those conversations in my room. They were full of hints, doubts, and intimations. No one actually *knew* everything. At any rate, no one was telling everything. I never revealed any of these talks, all of which took place in my room by candlelight, shadows falling across the whitewashed gypsum walls, to the people who were the subjects of the "experiment." I didn't know to whom to reveal them or how to reveal them or if I should. It went beyond any moral dilemma I had ever faced before as an anthropologist. The more I learned, the less sure I became of anything. No one had a complete picture. There *was* no complete picture. It was all groping. One night, when the sociologist and Cagliostro had gone and I was alone with my thoughts, I recorded in my notes: "Are we all involved in a dance of death up here?" My feelings swung from exhilaration at the idea of world building to despair over what everywhere loomed as the human limitations on "creating a new world."

The summer of 1972 was the time of the U.S. elections. Often, not sleeping soundly these nights, I would listen to campaign speeches broadcast on the Voice of America. But, always, closer voices in the blackness of my room would drown out our own political rhetoric. "Perhaps the delay *is* the Revolution," I would hear. Then a survivor's voice would boom in the dark, "What they are doing is delaying in order to earn more money for themselves. We will not have a place in which to drop dead." A new verb, *terremotear* ("to earthquake"), had been invented, and these sleepless nights I would hear, too, a familiar chorus of voices chanting about CRYRZA: "They have earthquaked more than the earthquake!"

One night in July, late, Cagliostro came alone to my room. I had returned that evening after spending the afternoon with an old woman at the edge of the pampa, in a hut, talking of the wind and the dust and the hardship and suffering. As on the night after the Nicrupampa meeting, I was feeling the sharp reality of people's pain, and I was not much in the mood for intellectualizing and for the abstractions of Revolutionary rhetoric. I found myself taking a stronger position with Cagliostro than I ever had before.

That night Cagliostro began by pondering the fact that he could not identify with the people of the Callejón. He could identify more in Cuzco and Puno, the southern highlands, he said. "There are so many Perus." Bursting with his own conflict, he went on; "The people here are so distrustful, so suspicious of us. Why don't they rebel?"

"Their hands are tied," I answered simply.

"It's not legal . . ." His voice trailed off into a long silence.

"What's not legal?" I asked finally.

"The law of expropriation is not legal, but anyway, since when does one respect the law here? They rushed the Supreme Resolution through as a trick to stall for time, to prevent the invasion of the center of Huaraz on May 31," he explained.

"I don't understand. It's not a constitutional government. Can't they do what they want to?"

Cagliostro elaborated on the intricacies of Peruvian law. I poorly understood them, but he seemed convinced that the decree law of expropriation was not legal.

We were both quiet for a long time. Even from across the room, in the flickering candlelight, I could tell by the look on his face that what he was about to say would be important. "Where are the lawyers from Huaraz?" he asked. "Why aren't they speaking up?"

I knew I was being tough with him when I said, "At the same time you want rebellion, because you sympathize with the plight of survivors, you and CRYRZA do all you can to deceive them in order to forestall their rebellion." He answered at length with all the complications they were encountering, with abstractions and intellectualizations about the valley and its place in Peru, and Peru's place in the world.

"It's more profound than deceiving or not deceiving," he said finally. "We want to bring a better life to the people up here. We don't want them to die in the huts they could build for themselves. But these people are so strange. They want, for example, the churches to be in the exact same place. You and I know that is ridiculous."

I winced. After a long pause, he sighed. "The truth is CRYRZA doesn't know where to go from the model houses, what to do next. These people are used to living in big rooms. They're going to feel like they're in a cage in these little concrete houses. SINAMOS is failing. CRYRZA is failing."

"Do you know what bothers the people most, more than the size of the rooms or the concrete?" I risked. "What bothers them is the air of coastal superiority, the patronizing voice in which CRYRZA and SINAMOS people often speak, and the clothes you wear, the salaries you earn, and the lodgings you've built for yourselves."

Cagliostro drew his collar around him, this big man who

seemed now so small and vulnerable in his big black overcoat. My heart began to loosen inside of me. There are so many different kinds of pain, I thought.

"Sociologists were here in advance," he said. "They knew what these sierra people were like; they knew they'd be meek and we could push through our plan without truly consulting them."

"If you have a friend less strong than you in your terms, a friend who has suffered a great tragedy, do you walk all over him?" I asked, remembering a Belén man's lamentation, "To put up with what *they* want for us is our fate."

Cagliostro was angry now. "All you need is your *pollera* [the skirt Indian women wear]," he said, getting up to leave. "Why can't I talk to you as an anthropologist instead of as a native of Huaraz?" What did he want from me? Praise? Criticism? I did not know, for he was tossing about on waves, now the hero, now the villain. The Revolutionary Reconstruction was good. It was bad.

I followed him down the stairs with a flashlight. As the dark pampa enveloped us, he suddenly put his arms around me and held me tight. "I would prefer violence or perhaps to leave CRYRZA or to give these unfortunate people something I have," he whispered, and left.

I saw him only one other time. He had been injured, and when I learned this, I went to visit him in the hospital. Nothing was mentioned of our talks.

The morning after Cagliostro's last visit to my room, I awoke feeling depressed. Reyna came and was transcribing tapes in the workroom we had set up next to my room. I had long ago decided that I would say nothing to anyone of whatever was revealed to me in confidence by Cagliostro or the sociologist, or by Abel, who had their confidence. But during our morning's work, I asked Reyna simply, "Where are the lawyers of Huaraz?"

"They are dead. Some have gone to Lima. Some who are still here are very old now." She mentioned names. I returned to my room. A little later, Reyna came in. My simple question had opened up a Pandora's box of things she had not been telling me. She said some of her neighbors had been called in before CRYRZA and cited for beginning to construct houses on their lots at the edge of Huaraz's center. CRYRZA had threatened to put one woman in jail for twenty-four hours. "They're concealing so much of what is going on from the people. This is not *aid*, it's a *struggle*," she said. "There is no more trust."

After relating several other incidents—a wall someone had built that CRYRZA had promptly knocked down; CRYRZA's use of a widow's land to park their cars—she named a *Huaracino* lawyer who she said had intimated to some survivors of Huaraz's center that property-rights legislation still existed and therefore the Supreme Resolution of Expropriation might be illegal. The government was simply "taking advantage of the earthquake."

"He said CRYRZA could expropriate land for public benefit, for schools or hospitals, but not for houses," Reyna reported. Still I said nothing. I was thinking how houses were going up, houses were being knocked down, bursts of inert material, the labor pains of creating this new world. "He says he must try to work from inside CRYRZA," Reyna went on. "The *Huaracino* is so innocent in his mentality, but now we are becoming aware of what is going on."

"What will happen?" I asked.

"Everything will collapse," she answered. "What has CRYRZA *done*? They keep changing personnel, and each time they redo all the studies. So many studies! Who knows where this will all end?" Looking out over the empty pampa, I thought how ironic her saying that everything would collapse was. Destruction upon destruction.

As Reyna left my room to go back to the workroom, she expressed what was always so clearly troubling to the people: "Their salaries! They lead the high life, and they call *us* anti-Revolutionary!" Quoting Peruvian poet César Vallejo's "There are such fierce blows in life!" she closed the door behind her.

IN contrast to longings for reduplication of the lost world, the disaster had also produced, townspeople said, a "detachment from things" (*desprendimiento de las cosas*). The theme of detachment from things arose time and time again, often within the imagery of nakedness: "When our things were destroyed, we were not interested anymore in things. Conceived inside the mother, naked, without anything, naked I shall return," a woman said. When the things were enumerated, they ranged from all the material accoutrements of life—utensils, clothes, furniture—to things imbued with a great deal of sentiment, like photographs and souvenirs. One man who had been writing a book said that even the loss of notes and drafts of chapters for his book no longer mattered. I discerned a sense of freedom, of release, that this loss of possessions had produced. Freed from "things," people could enact their dance of survival unencumbered, like children in a primeval valley, as yet unformed.

Desprendimiento struck a contrapuntal chord to the strains of loss and despair. At times I even wondered whether there was not some deeper peace in this having nothing that unconsciously kept reconstruction from getting under way. Perhaps all the arguments, doubts, and conflict over the reconstruction were only the edges of a whirlpool whose quiet center was really governing the aftermath. Though on the one hand permanent housing was desperately wanted, at the same time, there was still such fear of being inside any structure. Perhaps a period of time was necessary in which "houses," of whatever type—pleasing or displeasing to sierra tastes—must exist only in the imagination. I would consider this when every night, the first months I was there, I saw a crippled old lady leave her adobe house, which had withstood the earthquake, at the edge of San Francisco, hobble down a hill to an open space, and crawl into a small tent, where she slept, perhaps less fretfully than in her own house. Esther and her sisters, as well as others, had houses they could go to, but they clung to shacks and even tattered tents that had already endured two rainy seasons. Maybe the knowledge that nothing could fall on them made life for everyone in the prefabricated shelters a bit less gruesome. To have nothing was to have nothing to lose.

But *terruño*, one's place, one's land, was never a "thing," never an entity outside one from which one could become detached. The disaster was a release from all but the land. Everything was severed but a deep cultural connection to one's place. This sentiment of *terruño* was the real opponent of modernization, change, and technology. From the very beginning, a nun told me, people had clung to their ruins, then to tents, and resisted resettlement anywhere.[1]

Now, in the dry months of 1972, the word "barrio"—neighborhood—filled the meetings between the Reconstruction forces and the refugees. SINAMOS tried to use the words "neighborhood units" (*unidades vecinales*), but neighborhood units were not the same as barrios, survivors said. " 'Barrio' means people who have the same ideals, the same habits and activities. 'Neighborhood units' are simply blocks of houses." At one meeting, a woman pointed out, "If I as a *Soledana* must go to Huarupampa, I can't say 'my barrio of Huarupampa.' I shall be a stranger."

Another person from the barrio of Soledad tried to explain: "One's own being makes him stay, returning for the night to the same place."

Still another asserted:

> We have known each other. We have lived off the bread, *chicha*, chickens, and pigs of the barrio. Now if we cannot join the housing program, we must leave. We are already hurt, and now we will be hurt still worse. Huaraz has always been forgotten. Why now do you remember us?

The man's rhetorical question made me think of how often I had been told that after the 1941 alluvion in Huaraz no aid had come. The world was embroiled in war. President Manuel Prado made a brief pilgrimage to Huaraz right after that disaster, and then the town was left to its own devices. "There was not this world publicity of the event," a man who remembered it well told me. "The government didn't come, no aid came, but President Prado came the very next day. This meant so much to us, spiritually." At one meeting, a young man, his tongue loosened by *aguardiente*, shouted angrily, "Velasco didn't come after the earthquake. What problem would it have been for him to fly here? And all those millions in foreign aid came, for what, to build these cardboard houses we live in?" Many called the aid "a bombing"—*un bombardeo*—that had created the rubble of dissension and brought little real solace.

THE more the deeply cultural connection to "one's place" was interpreted by the forces of modernization as greed and egotism, the more the schism between coast and sierra widened. "They are people from outside who do not know our reality," a *Soledano* said. "They will destroy the barrios. . . . They think that mountain people don't know anything. They live in complete isolation from us."

It was in fact the isolation of the Reconstruction forces from survivors that created the feelings of alienation and helplessness. While preaching against the reinstatement of a privileged class, the Reconstruction unit had itself become a privileged class. Bureaucracy had swallowed up the New Society, and the promulgated participation of refugees in the restoration of their world—the "dialogue"—was in fact a monologue. After long months of claims that property should serve a social purpose, "Now," as a journalist who passed through the valley put it succinctly, "everything is owned by CRYRZA."

With ideology and action thus engaged in such a deadly duel, it is no wonder that acceptance of the national interpretation of the disaster as an opportunity to create a just and egalitarian society was at best ambivalent. Compounding survivors' ambivalence was the fact that the Revolutionary Reconstruction had linked together the politics of social change and technological modernization. Therefore, to speak out against modernization was to recoil from justice, to be anti-revolutionary, an untenable position. Justice was laudable, but modernization, though intellectually appealing since it might bring a modicum of physical security to the valley, was not psychologically compelling. Sierra people had long become adapted to the insecurity of their mountain environment. Their deepest longing was to "return to one's place"—*al sitio de uno*.

The greatest weapon the coastal reconstructionists held against the mountain survivors was to call them anti-Revolutionary, or reactionaries. Survivors' efforts to avoid this epithet engendered a great deal of suppressed mourning for the tangible physical world of the sierra, lost in the earthquake, and now in further jeopardy —a world they felt was never understood by the larger nation in the first place. The stress lay in not being able to mourn openly, to long with impunity for the familiar physical domain of before. Survivors winced under the "anti-Revolutionary" epithet, for they, too, despised injustice. Yet they grieved for their valley as it had been. Consequently, they suffered the contradiction inherent in the mourning of a world that had been declared unjust. They suffered the conflict between the earthquake as extreme adversity and the earthquake as "a stroke of luck" for the Revolution.[2]

Many townspeople, regardless of their former socioeconomic status, pondered the reconstruction in the same vein as this man from the barrio of Belén:

There are unique things happening here. The government had said it was not going to do the urban reform. It is a little hard to have that reform in these very bad times. But perhaps there is not going to be another opportunity to do the reform, a good one or a bad one. . . . But how are they going to take from the people everything we had when the earthquake itself took so much? And where is all the money and machinery from afar? This is the other face of what we are living. They are doing things in a way that seems terrible. God has given them the best opportunity of any government to do a good work. But they should be more conscious of their honorability. They go very slowly. . . .

Through my remaining months in the Callejón, CRYRZA publicly continued to take the stand that they were providing so much to an ungrateful people. They continued to speak in terms of "truth" and "reality," but it was clearly their truth and their reality. The problem was not so clear-cut as they phrased it: "The socialist mentality versus the personalistic and egotistic mentality." Rather, two cultures—sierra and coast—were confronting one another. CRYRZA and SINAMOS made the problem quantitative, saying that their plans were not accepted because sierra people did not have "enough culture" to see the benefits of the new scheme of things. But instead of *"enough culture,"* the issue was qualitative. It was a matter of different cultures, and coastal personnel had little or no awareness of *different cultures.* In this, sierra people were the wiser, knowing that they were now balanced precariously at the edge of a different culture—maybe neither better nor worse than theirs but *different.* In their meek way they tried to hold at bay the coastal culture that sought to invade them, carrying the stress of being in the twilight of one world and the dawn of another, for the most part, inside.

Seventeen

TOWNSMAN AND COUNTRYMAN

After all, in tragedy, we're all the same.
We're all cholos.

member of Huaraz's
"high society"

I N THE CENTURIES prior to the disaster, the valley population
was polarized into two large social groups: mestizos and Indians. The mestizos were dominant, the owners and managers
of agricultural lands and commercial establishments. Urban, oc-
cupying the valley towns, they carried out almost all bureaucratic
functions. Economic, political, religious, and social power was in
their hands.

The Indians constituted the dominated sector. Those not attached to haciendas lived off small agricultural plots, their *chacras*,
and animal husbandry, pasturing their animals on high puna lands.
This was not sufficient for basic well-being, and to supplement
their mode of subsistence, they entered into the mestizo world as
wage earners in the towns, doing menial jobs, coming down to
work as masons in construction or as servants. Or they tilled the

chacras of mestizos, for almost everyone, even the urbanites, had some plot for planting on the mountainsides. Indians were readily identified by their dress, their almost sole use of the Quechua language, by place of birth in the upland hamlets, and by close affinity to their ancient customs. They were, by and large, a rural proletariat.

Town mestizos lived off their small businesses and the surplus produced by Indians on haciendas and smaller farms. Indians sold produce from their own diminutive lands as a way of obtaining money to purchase, in the towns, manufactured articles like soap, candles, and medicines. In the marketplace, they sold to mestizos and bartered with one another. The interdependence of town and country, Indian and mestizo, represented a centuries-long pattern. Joined by economic and social ties, town and country, mestizo and Indian, formed a symbiotic union.

In many ways, in the Callejón, town and country were not rigidly demarcated. Town houses had their corrals for animals, and it was an adobe world from the valley floor up through the hamlets to the snow line on the eastern cordillera and to the tablelands of the western puna. There was a cultural continuum of dress, language, and customs, all becoming more *Indian* the higher one went on the mountain slopes. This sheer physical dimension of altitude was no doubt the single most important measure of differences in way of life. In all of Peru, actually, factors such as what crops are planted, what dress is worn, what language is spoken, and what beliefs are held are linked to the altitude at which they are found. *Verticality*, then, was also the natural dimension denoting town (valley bottom) and countryside (valley uplands), mestizo and Indian.[1]

Besides being economically subordinate, Indians were discriminated against in the predisaster Callejón in a myriad of ways. They were obliged to act in a servile manner, were placed in the rear of churches during ceremonies, were kept standing during negotiations in public offices, and were seated in the most uncomfortable seats in buses, though they paid the same fare as mestizos did.

It is therefore not surprising that the valley towns stirred ambivalent feelings in the Indian population of the surrounding countryside. While the town was seen as the center of all authority, of commercial activity and services, the point from which buses departed, the apex of civilization, it was also a place where Indians felt uncomfortable and wary. An anthropologist who worked in Hualcán, above Carhuaz, wrote: "A trip to town appears to be more dangerous, in many respects, than journeys to the puna or *huaca*."

In the immediate predisaster years, with their seedling ideologies of social reform, we begin to see a shift away from cultural descriptions—like dress and language—for defining social categories to new criteria. The major dichotomy becomes exploiters and exploited. By the end of the 1960s, the poignant markers of the Indian category had plainly become the criteria of poverty and helplessness, based on marginality from the mainstream of Peruvian national life.

In 1968, in what Dwight Heath called an "exercise in social reform by semantic decree," the word "Indian" was officially stricken from use and replaced by the more neutral *campesino*— peasant, farmer, or simply "countryman." Also, through the late sixties, the term *cholo*—which had designated a group transitional between Indian and mestizo and had been almost as derogatory as the word *indio*—began to lose its static and deprecatory connotations. *Cholo* came to be used in different ways best understood in the verbal concept of *cholification*. It took on political overtones indicating social mobility, the integration of the rural Indian masses into the national sphere.[2]

THOUGH before the earthquake an antagonistic relationship born of the mestizo/Indian opposition existed between Huaraz and its indigenous hinterland, there never was anything like an effective caste system. There had always been the free, at least daytime, flow of mestizos from the town to their *chacras* in the foothills. In the daytime, too, Indians before the earthquake had come down into the town to sell and trade in the market and conduct their business in municipal offices. On Sundays, they would visit the images in Huaraz's churches and socialize in the canteens along the narrow streets. So the vertical flow up and down the mountainsides was an everyday occurrence, while Sundays, feast days, and market days brought *campesinos* down in even greater numbers. At night, though, the two main social groups assumed their places on the flanks of the cordilleras and on the valley floor.

The earthquake shattered this design. The patterned flow of

life up and down the mountainsides was interrupted. Indians were no longer settled for the night in the surrounding mountains, and mestizos on the valley floor. Many Indians moved down into the valley to occupy the deserted ruins of a town house or to avail themselves of free shelter and provisions being distributed. "We are all mixed up now," a young girl said. "Before, people had their places."

Several factors produced this occupation of the valley floor by *campesinos*. For example, mestizos and Indians were often bound by ritual kinship ties, the *compadrazgo*, which allowed them to take advantage of each other's assets. Indians, by choosing mestizos as godparents for their children, could gain access to education for them in the town and help with legal matters they had to negotiate in Huaraz, like marriages or burials. In exchange, mestizos enjoyed the privilege of being able to call upon the services and produce of their mountain neighbors that godparenthood conferred. Many of these ritual ties had now been severed by death or loss of property, and, for instance, where Indian children could no longer live with godparents while attending school in Huaraz, an Indian family might take a *módulo* in a camp in order to send their children to school. Conversely, some mestizos, having lost everything in town, moved up to their fields where they might already have had a small adobe house or where they could easily build one, since the moratorium prohibited rebuilding only on the valley floor.

The predominant movement, however, was from the top down, Indians descending into the decimated towns. To do so did not entail their giving up their minuscule holdings on the slopes. To *campesinos*, this downward movement meant, no doubt, access to what had been perceived to be the wealth of the towns, to goods, services, and entertainments, things that ironically no longer existed except in memory. "The disaster has presented an opening up of the towns to the *campesinos*," a priest observed. "They have always come down because of the churches and the images and because it was prestigious to come to the city to buy their salt and their sugar. They would change their thick woolen hats and come on Sundays in fine cloth hats."

The descent meant perhaps, also, access to national political life, for with CRYRZA, SINAMOS, and government ministries set up in the Callejón, in a way "the nation" had come to the valley.

Moreover, the consciousness-raising by Church and state was making the *campesino* aware of his exclusion from full participation in town life. And the towns provided at least a tenuous link to national life in Lima. From the beginning of the aftermath, emergency contingents, working within the ideology of Plan Inca, had fostered the descent of Indians onto the valley bottom.

IN the months after the disaster, as people moved outside their normal social contexts, visual identity of any individual—through dress, hairstyle, habits, the whole range of stereotypical cultural cues—took on renewed significance. For example, Indian workers, who normally take a morning and afternoon coca-chewing break, sitting on a hillside, now could also be seen seated on the ruins of what had been Huaraz's only traffic signal, at the corner of Raimondi and Fitzcarral. The makeshift churches were filled with *campesinos*, who no longer occupied only the rear of these buildings. It seemed all one saw was the bright color of Indian women's dress in Huaraz. The mourning black that mestizo women would wear for years after the disaster contrasted with the color of the dress of their Indian counterparts. When I commented on this to a townswoman, dressed in black, next to whom I sat on a rock on the pampa at the bishop's ceremony, she retorted, "You think those clothes are pretty. I don't. They're not street clothes, not for the city." Where are the streets? Where is the city? I thought, gazing across the empty hollow.

Mainly, everyone along the continuum of predisaster socioeconomic statuses was compressed into the survivor camps in the lower foothills encircling the deserted and government-preempted urban center of Huaraz. Geographically, this was a position midway between the valley floor and "the heights" (*las alturas*), where Indians traditionally have lived. In the largest camp, Nicrupampa, a doctor and three lawyers lived side by side with teachers, merchants, preachers, and Indian farmers from "the heights." A shoemaker from the urban center, who opened a shop at the entrance to Nicrupampa, said: "All the *campesinos* have come down. They are here with those of us who had our businesses in the center."

A young teacher remarked: "Yes, we are all here. The government is trying to make us all equal."

Two women from the Ministry of Housing confirmed: "There

are all social classes represented, *campesinos* and merchants, a doctor. Economically, the earthquake leveled them. Perhaps prejudices were strengthened, however. Some argued, 'Why should a *campesino* have a shelter just like mine?' But Operation Roof upheld the tenet of equality."

The disaster, the Revolutionary Reconstruction, and camp conditions spawned new postdisaster categories that now imposed themselves on the basic mestizo/*cholo*/Indian dimension. The disaster categories were *damnificados*, those who had sustained losses, and *no-damnificados*, those who had not lost material goods. Among the *damnificados*, a further division arose between those who had been renters and those who had owned property in Huaraz's center: "property owners" and "non–property owners." Vis-à-vis the rest of Peru, all these categories collapsed into the inclusive term *sobrevivientes* ("survivors of the disaster"). The area itself had become known as the Affected Zone.[3]

Since townspeople considered the Indians to have had nothing and therefore to have lost nothing, *campesinos* comprised the newly generated label *no-damnificados*. A man from Huarupampa barrio, who said he had lost everything, commented, "The Indians, what have they lost? Pots that in total are not worth more than a few *soles* . . . a bed. They were able to go out into the open spaces." In other words, *campesinos* had always been "detached from things." Why now should they want them?

In fact, material losses had also been sustained in the satellite villages. Entire Indian hamlets in the path of the Huascarán avalanche had been erased. But adobe and stone houses in the heights could be repaired or rebuilt right away. There simply was no scar in the countryside comparable to the pampa of Huaraz or the alluvial burial ground that Yungay became.

Both the economic and social stripping were visible in the survivor camps. In contrast to predisaster colonial Huaraz, with its whimsical house decorations and doors painted in colors indicating one's barrio affiliation, now only a letter and a number—G-4 or F-10, for example—marked in black crayon on a cutout pasteboard door provided identification. This number identified an individual or a family and contained no message about the social attributes of the occupants. In this absence of facade, in the total lack of privacy in the overcrowded camps—where voices were audible through paper-thin walls—and in occupations and chores suddenly shared by all, people experienced a sense of exposure. Bereft of social structure, refugees frequently evoked images like that of the doctor or lawyer and the *campesino* side by side carrying buckets of water along the camp paths or across the pampa. In this empty space, there being no more colonnades, corners, adobe walls, all could see the commingling. On the eve of May 31, 1972, over Radio Huascarán, the local bard had recited, ". . . Huaraz is naked, / I ask pardon for this nakedness."

In the camps, then, suddenly everyone, from monolingual Indian peasants of the heights to bilingual mestizo professionals and merchants of the valley towns, was living together in similar circumstances of economic distress and social confusion. With all classes aggregated now on this horizontal plane, the old linguistic indicator of monolingualism in Quechua most helped to preserve the unique Andean dimension of *verticality*. While language was the most certain criterion of the old categories, the long braids and multiple multicolored skirts of Indian women, and the rubber sandals, wool pants and hats, and solid black ponchos with a single stripe down the center of Indian men remained, also, as cultural markers to identify people whose economic and social places were now in disarray.

Townspeople commented, "Huaraz is purely *campesinos* now." One lady told me, "Before, only 100-percent *Huaracinos* lived here. The people of the county lived in the country. Now, it's all *chacra*."

"Where are all the *Huaracinos*?" lamented another lady at a religious ceremony held at Soledad. Pausing only for a second, she herself replied, "They are dead or they have gone." Acquiescing in the pattern of devastation they saw around them, townspeople would shake their heads. "Yes, it has been the towns that have suffered."

BY 1971–72, in revolutionary Peru in general and especially in the destroyed valley, the process of *cholification* had acquired, it seemed, still another aspect. It not only meant upward mobility, incorporation of the masses into a higher class, but the concomitant dissolution of that higher class, whose members, downwardly mobile, were likewise becoming *cholos*.

In the disaster-aftermath settlement pattern, *cholification*, as a

process of elevating one social class while lowering another, occurred quite literally, geographically, in the meeting of mestizo and
Indian—townsman and countryman—in the survivor camps in the
foothills around Huaraz, a setting in between the traditional mestizo
and Indian worlds.

In the new ideology, to be *cholo* was the best one could be.
While on a national scale it became good to be *cholo*—the best
battery one could buy was La Pila Chola and signs read "*Cholo
Power*"—in Huaraz, when used among surviving members of the
"high society," it appeared to have the added meaning "After all,
in tragedy, we are all the same. We're all *cholos*." Within the revolutionary aftermath, *cholo* came to embrace at times not only mestizos and Indians but also *criollos* and *serranos*—coastal and mountain
people—in other words, the nation. Beyond this, *cholo* was even
used to address foreigners working in the valley aftermath, and
along with the Marxist, Evangelical, and Catholic Reform terms of
Brother and Sister, it most inclusively summoned a feeling of world
community.

Certainly to the eye alone the disaster had erased economic
classes in Huaraz. But for the rare exception of a house left standing,
even members of the small predisaster "high society" were left, at
least for the time being, as homeless and resourceless as the poor.
It is true that better-off *Huaracinos* were able to go to Lima and
begin new lives there. But of these, many returned, preferring to
live among the ruins than to experience the feeling of having abandoned their injured homeland.

I knew also of instances where the formerly rich were, in the
aftermath, worse off than the poor. For example, a woman who
had been a landowner and who, besides losing possessions in the
earthquake, had had her farm taken in the agrarian reform, told of
standing in line for provisions and being refused them by workers
who knew she had been rich and thought she must "of course" have
access to blankets and utensils, though in fact she had nothing left.

The few who had owned large tracts of land around Huaraz's
center had had the land taken by the government, and refugees
settled on it, as in the large holdings of Nicrupampa, which eventually were to be expropriated. The handful of *Huaracinos* who had
owned a block's space within the center lost this land in the instantaneous moratorium and eventual expropriation. Movie houses,

hotels, restaurants, businesses, and other sources of wealth had all collapsed. The concern of surviving owners, both as creditors and debtors, was how to handle outstanding debts. Mostly, they were canceled. In the aftermath, one simply did not see riches. In this sense, the earthquake was an efficient leveler.

Paco, who had been a member of Huaraz's "high society," which he called "the group," summed it up this way:

> First it was the earthquake, then the reform. They didn't kill me as a man but as a symbol, a symbol of capitalism, of free enterprise. Before, there were the Indians and the group. The group was well-off, the Indians pretty bad. Now they did away with the group, and the Indians are worse. But they don't have someone higher than they, and that is good. Well, there's no one to lift them up now, though. What is in place of the group are the military and the engineers. But the group was a symbol, and that is gone. We used to sit in the plaza getting our shoes shined. That is gone.

Paco's parents had owned the big hacienda called Utcuyacu, a cattle ranch, and he had acted as manager. After the earthquake, when agrarian reform took over, he moved down to the coast, where he started a chicken farm. I met him one day in January, and then suddenly, on an early Saturday morning, he appeared at my room on the pampa. He was in the Callejón to get some personal items that had remained at Utcuyacu and asked me to accompany him. This was to be his first visit back to the hacienda in over a year, since the agrarian reform personnel had moved in.

Though he was eager to see what the *campesinos* had done with the ranch in a year, as we drove along, Paco was tense, approaching the hacienda as if it were a hot burning coal on the mountainside. "I don't hate the *campesinos*," he remarked. "I pity them. They won't know what to do with Utcuyacu."

Halfway there, we stopped for lunch at the *módulo* of an elderly woman who had also lost her home in the earthquake and her hacienda to agrarian reform. Sitting there in the pasteboard shelter, which Doña Eugenia had tried to fix up with tattered lace curtains salvaged from her home, the two of them, the young man and the old woman, spoke of the past and the uncertain future. "I am so

crushed by the disaster and the reform," she said. "After the earthquake, I didn't ask them to give me tools to work the land, only
that they lend me something to work the land. But no, and it's all
gone now. It doesn't matter."

Dressed in black, Doña Eugenia sat like a sovereign, serving
us a tea of *yerba luisa*. She spoke of her husband, whom she had
buried, and of the lovers of her youth. I thought what a catalyst
an extreme event is in people's lives, how it lifts the past to consciousness. "I want to die here," she said finally. "I want them to
build me a mausoleum on this mountainside."

She was thin and gaunt, and at one point Paco leaned over
and whispered to me, "Can't you see that she is starving?"

As usually happened on a first encounter after the disaster,
they told each other exactly where they were and what they were
doing when the earthquake struck. "I was in Chosica [near the
coast]," Paco related. "I saw the waves in the land coming from
the north. Maybe it is Ancash, I thought. The next morning I flew
to Chimbote. They were looking for tractor drivers to clear the
roads. I turned my coat inside out and became a tractor driver. By
Wednesday, I got to Carhuaz. I stayed drunk on pisco. You saw
so many things you had to stay drunk. Those were marvelous and
horrible days at the same time. By Thursday night, I arrived at
Utcuyacu. The *campesinos* were huddled in the patio. The earth was
still trembling. They were afraid."

Around three o'clock in the afternoon, we left Doña Eugenia,
who waved good-bye from behind a lace curtain that covered the
cutout windows of her *módulo*.

Utcuyacu comprises some 33,000 acres, climbing right up to
the snow line. As we inched our way higher in the mountains,
curving, doubling back along the narrow shelflike roads, I caught
glimpses of Huantsán sending its sharp spire into the sky. At the
entrance to the hacienda, I could see the murals of Atusparia and
Túpac Amaru—the iconography of revolution—and the words
"House of the Peasant" (*Casa del Campesino*) were painted on the
walls of the main building.

As our truck came to a stop near the central building, *campesinos*
poured into the patio, laughing with delight to see Paco, covering
their mouths with their hands as they do, shaking hands with Paco
and me, hands roughened and encrusted with earth. A man sat

nearby in a wheelchair, waiting his turn to greet Paco. A toothless old woman sat on her haunches, tipping her felt hat. From that moment on through the duration of our visit and the journey back to Huaraz, strange feelings, something magical, seemed to be carrying me, as if I were suspended in the high, thin air. To what were they due? Was it the man coming home, the loser, who in his loss had won the great affectionate outpouring that greeted him then, the affection of those who had benefited from his loss but who acted now as if they would give up their souls to him?

The foreman, Héctor Zúñiga, came forward to invite us in for coffee. This had been Paco's home, but now it was he who must be invited to enter it. We sat in a little room, and Héctor lit a candle. Looking up, he said to me, "Don Paco used to pay me a salary and give me meat, and something extra each year. Now they pay me a higher salary, but I don't get meat. I work harder. My spirits are not really elevated."

When Héctor left the room to get the coffee, Paco said, "It is better now. The year before the reform took over, they couldn't look me in the eye around here. They felt guilty, maybe; they knew what was happening. Now they look me in the eye. Maybe they pity me. They know that today I am leaving for good."

As we started back for Huaraz, we could not pass through the big hacienda gates. About a dozen *campesinos* were in the middle of the road with a huge bull. Our truck came to a stop, and they gathered around. A man stuck his head through the window and smiled broadly. "That's my bull," Paco said, laughing.

"Yes, Don Paco, we're moving him to Caraz to sell him. He's a mating bull," the man said.

"Good," Paco replied, and they cleared the road for us. As we drove off, Paco turned to me and said, "It gives me pleasure to see they're doing with the bull just what I would have done." There had been many reports of *campesinos* on newly taken ranches slaughtering bulls and eating them, profiting in the short run only to lose in the long run.

The gold of a Callejón sunset suffused the countryside as we wound down the narrow road onto the main Pativilca road. With good reason the Inca worshiped the sun and treasured gold, I thought. Their mountain outposts at sunset became enclaves of muted gold, created by the great disc that, having dropped behind the Andes, could no longer be seen. We didn't talk much on the way back. Once, Paco said simply, "The reform can't touch you inside," and I did not ask him to say more. It was dark by the time we rounded a curve in the Río Santa for the last kilometers into Huaraz, and a lumbering Expreso Ancash bus almost bullied us off the road.

I learned much later that Paco had moved back to the Callejón and, distraught, was living in a hut at the edge of the Santa in Carhuaz.

WHILE momentum for social change had been building even before the earthquake occurred, in the aftermath something ironic began to happen. The same forces—the disaster, the Revolutionary Reconstruction, and Catholic Reform—that were closing the ranks of the prevailing social structure by the leveling of rich and poor and through *cholification*—that process whereby Indians and mestizos would converge—were reopening them along the lines of town and country, *pueblo* and *campo*. Consciousness-raising aspired to lift up the *campesino* by making him aware of his exploitation. In doing this, he was contrasted with the townsperson, who was depicted as having had everything before the disaster. Thus, two disaster-generated worlds emerged: the destroyed one, unjust, the land of exploitative townspeople and exploited *campesinos*; and the new visionary one, where justice and equality would triumph.

In contrast to similar efforts by Church and state in the rest of Peru, where modification of ideals might be expected over time to foster behavioral changes, in the Callejón the disaster had already forced behavioral changes. Now consciousness-raisers undertook to justify those changes and thus ensure, through a restructuring of the belief system, their persistence. The disarranged social configuration of the aftermath must not only be tolerated but deemed right and good. A SINAMOS social promoter said, "Beliefs change slowly. Such ancient beliefs exist here. Social relations may have changed, but beliefs, the mental part, that does not change so easily."

This campaign to make lucid the exploitation of *campesinos* left in its wake among survivors the rationalization that the valley towns were destroyed because townspeople treated *campesinos* unjustly.

Survivors had taken the seismological information that entered the valley from the world setting and, based on their unique perception of their valley and its hazards, had fashioned it into an interpretation of the disaster as a geophysical event. Likewise, survivors took the national interpretation of the disaster as a chance to create a new and just world and carved out an explanation of the earthquake as a sociohistorical event. Social injustice, proclaimed by both the Revolutionary Military Government and Catholic Reform as the highest sin, became the chief ingredient in the survivors' reasoning that the disaster occurred as punishment to the valley towns, to mestizos, for their mistreatment of the Indian *campesinos* of the valley uplands. The pattern of destruction, which left the towns decimated and inflicted the greatest mortality rate among mestizos, played into the hands of this reasoning. Death as the great leveler was its thematic core.

This interpretation of the disaster was not intentionally promoted by SINAMOS or Catholic reformers. Rather, it evolved slowly as a by-product of their consciousness-raising. Wearing plain clothes, sitting in her *módulo* in Nicrupampa, a Reform nun who had come to the valley shortly after the earthquake explained the way she worked to me: "I never talk about religion or the Church, but about values. We do not give the values, but rather initiate a search for values among the *campesinos* themselves." Speaking out of Freire and Gutiérrez, she said that *concientización* was the method "to make the Indians aware of their reality," so that in a growing "critical sense of their existence" the social changes wrought by the disaster would be indelibly engraved on "their mentality," and still further change would be demanded. Consciousness-raising was therefore aimed at awakening the *campesinos*, who were seen by Catholic Reform and the Revolutionary Military Government to be slumbering in the heights of Peru, unaware of their true misery.

I saw the good of this, for I was keenly aware of sickness, untimely death, and hardship in the hamlets. I knew Don Juan's struggle to feed his family of ten in Secsecpampa, that he tilled his small plot, that for pittance wages he came down to Monterrey to clean out the cubicles where people from the valley towns bathed in the thermal mineral waters. He went down into Centenario looking for odd jobs and even had to find periodic work on the coast. He was already old, and in spite of his always good humor, he was bone tired most of the time.

But I would cringe whenever I heard the words that were the slogans of both Catholic Reform and Revolution: "to humanize" the Indians; "to culturize" them. Daily, Radio Huascarán broadcast: "Culture, more culture, until we evolve man!" It was as if the Indians were not already human, as if they did not already have culture.

Campesinos themselves would speak of "becoming human beings," though I suspect at least in part they placed this "humanizing" mission within the perspective of a deeper wisdom. A glimpse of this wisdom came one day when Don Juan, his eyes twinkling, laughter in his voice, compared former years of traditional Catholicism and old political structures with the new movements. "Before," he said, "they dealt with us as burros! Now they say we must become human beings."[4]

The next time I saw the Reform nun was in Lima. Disillusioned because the bishop in Huaraz was not taking a firm enough stand for Reform, she had left the valley. Having protested the expulsion of priests working in Recuay who were feared to be communists, she felt her position in the valley no longer viable. Nostalgically, she said, "There is really no revolution going on. The inequality there was before between mestizos and Indians disappeared in the earthquake. But now I don't know. Maybe those who dominate will remain the same, under another mask. . . . It is a pity. Up there, it is a pleasure just to wake up in the morning."

THE German priests of Centenario were laboring diligently at consciousness-raising. Centenario was in a good position to influence the *campesinos* since these priests had begun to work in the countryside even before the disaster. Founded in 1951, this Order of the Sacred Heart always had more priests and nuns than the churches of the center of Huaraz, and they could devote a lot of time to the Indian population. By 1971, the German priests were working in twenty hamlets as well as in Centenario proper and had also extended themselves to Jangas up the valley. After the earthquake, the many survivors and entrepreneurs from outside the valley who had established themselves in this sole intact barrio had also swelled the numbers of those who came to Mass at Centenario.

On a December afternoon of 1971, Father Auscario recalled how the idea emerged after the disaster that the earthquake had created an opportunity for many of the changes advocated by the new Catholic thinking. "But changes should come slowly," Auscario said. "We are perhaps not as extreme as some of the religious personnel who have come after the earthquake, who do not know the sierra."

Nevertheless, the Germans were serious about "fomenting philosophical reflection," the essence of *conscientización*. In order to do this, they first had to teach *campesinos* to read and write so that they could study the Bible. During the literacy training, they would try to pick out some person or persons from each hamlet who would be designated as *catequistas*, the native consciousness-raisers who became leaders and teachers of the rest. The plan was that gradually, over two or three years, groups would form who could work alone, independently of the clergy. The locus of even the formal "religion" thus began to shift from the barrio church to the hamlets themselves.

A geographic move was not the only change. More significantly, the substance of this "religion" shifted. The group teachings included hygiene, civics, "all the things a man must know to become truly responsible and independent. The dependence of the *campesinos* on the town, on the lawyers, is horrible," Auscario said. "They must learn not to fear the forms they need to fill out, that are part of the town and civil life and necessary to their own development."

Since the theology of liberation and Marxism appeared to me to share so much, in their focus on the new human being, free from bondage to others and from alienation from land and work, I asked Auscario how they differed. "They are very much alike," he replied, "except that at the end of the road the Christian makes that leap to faith, to Christ."

After many months, already into 1971, the explanation that the earthquake had been a punishment to the townspeople for their oppression of *campesinos* began to circulate, fueled by the rhetoric that social injustice was best left to die buried under the ruins and ignited by a sierra sense of sin and punishment. Father Auscario told me how elements of the Church that were actually trying to quell the idea of the disaster as punishment unwittingly played a part in the unfolding of this interpretation. He described what happened this way:

Look, that opinion that the *campesino* is giving now, that "the urbanite did not accept us, therefore God punished him by the

earthquake," that's only recently, last year. Perhaps the Church
has some blame in that interpretation, because we have called
upon to help solve our problems social workers, anthropologists,
sociologists, to give talks, to focus new work after the earthquake.
We had to totally reorganize the Church. Therefore, all the new
ideas came. The organization that existed was undone. There
weren't priests, there weren't sisters, nothing! . . . And the
Church in Lima offered sisters and priests for the early times to
the end of 1970, and with them came the new ideas. . . . The
differences between the *campesino* and the city dweller began to
be focused upon, and then it began to be asked why there are
those inequalities, and the groups that were working began to
discover one cause after another. Then came another group,
which worked directly with the country people, and again they
talked of the differences between townsperson and *campesino*, and
they made the *campesinos* see in what situation they really were,
what the relationship really is between the urbanite and the countryman. Then the normal reaction of the *campesino*, in his way of
thinking, is "Ah-ha, then if it is that way, if this is our reality,
therefore the townsperson was punished." We see that the
consciousness-raising is still not sufficiently profound, because
the *campesinos* ought not to arrive at that conclusion.

Thus, at the same time that the proponents of modernization were
painting the towns as repositories of culture into which the *campesinos* must be drawn, the predisaster towns were also depicted by
CRYRZA and Catholic Reform as having been arrogant and oppressive. In retrospect, town survivors, too, began to feel the guilt
of their ways and to contemplate whether the earthquake had not
indeed been a cosmic confirmation of their mistreatment of Indians.

What might have been just an emboldening of the Indian in
his transformation into *campesino*—now "noble" and "human"—
became encumbered with the symbolism of the earthquake. We
may wonder whether the ideology of the Revolutionary Military
Government would have coincided so brilliantly with the disaster
had it not been for the pattern of destruction. Would the Callejón
have been so prime a target for transfiguration into "an experimental
state" had, for example, more of the Indian countryside been destroyed and the towns left intact or even had the cleavage between
destroyed towns and intact countryside not been so clear?

Eighteen
THE PARABLE

My campestral love descended barefoot
to your doorstep,
Proclaiming centuries of heartache.
Marcos Yauri Montero, *Poema V*

ONCE IN LATE NOVEMBER, when I was walking up through Nicrupampa, a man beckoned to me from the door of his *módulo*. Dressed as a *campesino*, yet with clear green eyes shining from a face lined with deep crevices, he identified himself as Clemente Quispe, a native of Huanmarín, a hamlet on the Cordillera Negra. He had some pre-Columbian *huacas* in a corner and asked if I wanted to buy any. The *módulo* was dark except for one burning candle, but I could see the outlines of an old bedspring that rested on adobe bricks. Señor Quispe had been to the Quilcay to wash his clothes, which hung now on ropes above us. He sat down on the spring to resume mending his thread-bare clothes and invited me to sit down on a little wooden bench. He showed me a bag he was weaving out of puna grasses. I looked at the *huacas*, which were distinctively from Chancay, a site near the town of the same name on the coast.

Señor Quispe seemed eager for company. He had heard that I wanted to know all about the earthquake, and he was ready to tell me his experience. Speaking in a mixture of Quechua and an untutored Spanish, he said that when the earthquake struck, he was in jail on the coast for digging ancient grave sites. Three days after the quake, he was transferred to a jail in Huacho, where he remained for three months. With his one year of schooling, he said, he could read the headlines in a newspaper he found in the cell at Huacho: "Huaraz Is Finished." All my family has died, he thought. Some time later, a letter from his brother confirmed the death of his wife and three children. They had been in Huaraz that Sunday afternoon. "Yes, my wife and three little daughters are gone, only three, why should I lie?" he said. A poncho his wife had woven for him covered the spring on which he slept.

He became animated as he fell into a long reminiscence about his hamlet, all the wonderful things it contained—a chapel, images of saints, flutes and drums that would lead processions in which a religious image rode on the back of a donkey—and all the hardships. His father had died in the 1941 alluvion in Huaraz, leaving him, as the eldest son, to do the plowing. "I was crying, and I was falling down behind the oxen," he recalled. Still, compared to the coast that he had come to know in recent years—the coast that wielded so much money and where there was so much robbery—the sierra was so beautiful. "What can anyone rob here?" he asked.

Before the earthquake, he would come down to Huaraz to work as a mason. "There was always something to do, but now there is no work." So he was making grass bags to sell in the market, and last week he laid a little piece of pavement in the camp, he said, and got some food in exchange.

His house in Huanmarín had been destroyed, but he wanted to go back there, and he wanted to show me the hamlet and the beautiful images that remained. This was one of so many times I felt touched by people's endurance, their ability to make do, to see beauty in their mind's eye, even, as Quispe did, from inside a dark *módulo*, seated on a rusting bedspring, displaced and very much alone. I said I would return, that I would like to walk up to his hamlet with him. "Sí, *nunata respitanki karu pitah.*" He explained that this meant that we would become friends and a respect would exist between us. "We know each other at a distance, respectfully."

During a subsequent visit, I asked him what he thought had caused the earthquake, and he answered this way:

Jesus, Little Papa, walked upon the earth as a poor man, an old man. He was wearing a poncho full of lice and fleas. His pants were in tatters, all ripped and torn. He went from house to house. He even went to the jail. No one would help him. They said to him: "Go away, you are dirty and all full of fleas." There used to be some very rich people in Huaraz. And that old man came, with his poncho, old, torn, full of holes. Well, two or three months afterward, the earthquake happened. Then it was said that it was Jesus Christ who had come to the earth as a test. When God permits the punishment, everyone dies. All are equal. There are not so many rich ones now.

When he had finished, I asked, "Does God cause or only permit evil?"

"He permits the downpour, the earthquake," he replied concretely. My eyes fell on the timeworn poncho his wife had made for him that covered the old spring, supported above the damp earth floor on adobe bricks, and on his tattered pants. I remembered him mending his clothes by candlelight that first November afternoon.

FROM time to time, from varied sources, both townspeople and *campesinos*, I would hear the explanation that the earthquake had destroyed the towns because they spurned the *campesino*. It was often phrased in this kind of parable, of a poor man, a beggar, who came to Huaraz and was turned away, and then some months later, the earthquake occurred. Then it is learned that the poor man was Christ. This parable is reminiscent of Matthew 25, verses 42–46:

For I was hungry and you wouldn't feed me, thirsty, and you wouldn't give me anything to drink; a stranger and you refused me hospitality; naked, and you wouldn't clothe me; sick, and in prison, and you didn't visit me. Then they will reply, "Lord, when did we ever see you hungry or thirsty or a stranger or naked or sick or in prison, and not help you?" And I will answer, "When you refused to help the least of these my brothers, you were refusing help to me." And they shall go away into eternal punishment.

Matthew 25 is the cornerstone of the theology of liberation, in essence a "theology of the neighbor." Christ becomes identified with the poor and oppressed in the new theology, which insists upon "a love which is manifested in concrete actions." Preached from the pulpit of Centenario, Matthew 25 was also a common text of Reform catechists who were active in the mountain hamlets.

The wellspring of the parable of the earthquake may reach deeper into the past than Catholic Reform's popularization of Matthew 25. The theme of the "unknown one," the threadbare wanderer who turns out to be a god, appears in several versions in Andean mythology. No one offers the beggar respite, and punishment ensues: ". . . the stranger, who arrives at the town . . . to whom no one offers a plate of food. He is the god Tonapa. . . . The ungrateful town is flooded as a punishment." In another myth, men failed to recognize Viracocha, the creator and supreme being of the Incas, when he went in the guise of a beggar: "This Cuniraya Viracocha, in most ancient times, walked, wandered around, in the disguise of a very poor man, his cloak and his tunic worn to shreds. Some, not recognizing him, whispered, 'miserable flea-bitten beggar.' This man Viracocha had power over all the towns." Another version of the myth concerns the deity Pariacaca:

> And when they were well into their cups, Pariacaca arrived at that town. But he did not make himself known; he sat at the far end of the place where people were assembled, as if he were a very poor man [and] during the whole day, no one invited him to have anything. . . . The townspeople continued drinking without fear or shame. Then Pariacaca climbed a mountain in the high parts of Huarochirí. On that mountain, Pariacaca began to grow, and making red and yellow hailstones fall, he dragged all the townsmen and their houses to the sea, without pardoning even one of the towns.[1]

A *campesino* who had moved down from the heights above Huaraz some years before the earthquake and who had a permanent stall in the market reasoned this way:

The earthquake was punishment, wasn't it? That's what I believe. People from outside were not given a kind welcome. People from Conchucos and from the hamlets are not like people from the coast who can stay in a hotel. No one wanted to give anything to the *campesinos* from the heights. The earthquake was punishment to the town because they didn't want to give to the people of the country. When they come down now, we give to them. There could be another punishment.

The theme of the hoarding town appeared in another version of this interpretation of the earthquake. The *campesino* couple who told the story—Jesusa and Nicolás, Don Juan's relatives, who had become catechists in Secsecpampa—recognized its biblical origin (Luke 12, verses 16–20):

NICOLÁS: Don't you see, in the Bible it says there was a rich man who gathered up all his seed and kept it in a house so he could rest. . . .

JESUSA: All his food.

NICOLÁS: Then he said, "I have enough so that I can rest for at least five or six years. I have everything!"

JESUSA: "I am going to be tranquil," he said to himself.

NICOLÁS: Then the Lord said, "Well, you intend to rest, but tonight you are going to die, and for whom will all these things remain?" For the same reason, of course, the Lord has disposed that all the town [Huaraz] should die.

A townsman brought out still another instance of the theme of the evil town, then countered the explanation with reasoning that frequently accompanied interpretations of the disaster containing the notion of punishment:

The *campesinos* say that God has punished us of the town. They believe the town has disappeared because we were more corrupt, more false, than they. But if that were true, wouldn't God have punished only the adults, the worldly men?

In a myth collected in the Cordillera Blanca hamlet of Hualcán, Adam places a curse on his son Baltazar for having shown disrespect toward him. Until the Final Judgment should remove that curse, Baltazar and all his descendants must serve mestizos. Baltazar becomes the ancestor of all Indians. This myth of inequality between Indians and mestizos, viewed as intrinsic in the nature of the world, was severely challenged by the earthquake, which was taken as a judgment, even the Final Judgment during the moments of shaking and the hours that followed. "All are equal; everyone dies," as I heard so often.

Following the earthquake, some *campesinos* came down to sack the ruins of the center of Huaraz. Many town survivors described the plundering with a tone of resignation, as did a woman from Huarupampa barrio:

> They came with ropes. Right after the earthquake, the *campesinos* were entering with ropes to carry things off . . . and they passed by our side with typewriters, adding machines, trunks, and even telephones . . . and we could not even say, "Look, don't steal that, that's not yours." No one had the energy to speak, and we only witnessed it.

I heard tales of horror, of fingers sliced from cadavers in order to steal rings. Guards were assigned to the center and ordered to shoot anyone among the ruins after dusk. Still, many survivors clung in silence to the remains of their houses by night and moved about only by day.

When, in the early aftermath, *campesinos* were apportioned corrugated tin slabs to build shelters in the camps, some tarried only a few days on the valley floor, and then the "shelters" walked away. A nun laughed as she told me how strange it was to look up into a mountain fold and see tens upon tens of the tin slabs glittering in the sunlight as they "marched" up the slopes, their human carriers invisible from the valley floor.

That many items, like telephones and gas pumps for filling the tanks of vehicles, for which there was no practical use in the countryside, were taken contributed to a philosophical perspective among some townspeople. "What will they do with a gas pump on the puna?" a man mused aloud, and a young *Huaracina* analyzed the sacking this way:

> . . . the *campesinos* have always been a submissive class, thought to have to obey the townspeople. Not only with the earthquake but already with social evolution, the form of thinking of the *campesino* was changing. A certain rebellion had emerged. . . . Then, with the earthquake, they looked for, how does one say, an "escape valve." They found it with the earthquake. A form of revenging themselves on the townspeople was to come to plunder the town, perhaps not because they really wanted to do this, but as a liberation of their spirit.

On February 12, 1972, in the first official event opening the pre-Lenten carnival season in Huaraz, townspeople released theatrically and with great mirth some of their own pent-up feelings of having been hit, while down, by both the Indian and the coastal populations. Men dressed up like knights rode across the empty pampa on horseback, ridiculing both the sacking of the town and the then still-incipient reconstruction. A band of musicians and a swift-moving crowd followed the riders, who stopped from time to time to read from a long scroll. One such proclamation made fun of CRYRZA, which had "come to finish the destruction of Huaraz": "All the money has been spent, and everything—hospitals and avenues—is written down on paper; 'KIRSA' [as they called the Reconstruction unit in bare disguise] moves so slowly that they might barely be ready for the next earthquake." When the cavaliers stopped in Huarupampa barrio and the crowd gathered around, the following text was read from the scroll: "I hope that all you upstart *campesinos* who have come down to Huarupampa will come to the fiesta to show us the jewels you have pothunted in the rubble after the earthquake while we lay wounded."

This was a joke on themselves, too, as fun was always made of "jewels." Survivors scoffed at any sign of wealth in the aftermath. Months earlier, when Consuelo Velasco, the first lady of Peru, had come to view the ruins, a townswoman had ripped a necklace from her neck. People said this incident was instrumental in the move, finally, of CRYRZA to Huaraz in January 1972.

No *campesino* ever admitted to me having taken part in the

plundering of Huaraz or tried to justify it in any way. Rather, they attributed the sacking to "wizards" (*brujos*), the same ones that were said to cause illness. These wizards hauled things away from the pampa by night, their identity concealed in darkness. Don Juan took me out to the path in front of his house and said, "They took radios, cloth, shoes. They passed by here on this very path by night. They are *brujos*, those people, yes, *brujos*, aha!" Frequently, *campesinos* cited the Inca commandment *Ama suwa, ama llulla, ama quela* ("Don't steal, don't lie, don't be lazy").

The pillaging of the towns as well as the instantaneous economic leveling of the disaster itself had led to that state of mind townspeople called *desprendimiento de las cosas* ("detachment from things"). In general, the consensus that the disaster had been "worse for the rich" brought with it the sweeping tone, expressed by one man this way: "Now to have or not to have, it's all the same. Those who did not have lost nothing. If you don't have, it won't be taken away."

THE detachment from things had its counterpart in the "social nakedness" experienced in the anonymity of life in the survivor camps, where identification of one's *módulo* was by a letter and a number. The bereavement for the old social structure people felt was the negative side of the coin. On the positive side were feelings of release or liberation from its bondage. For instance, a young woman from a family who had been quite well off became so adapted to camp life that she refused to better her lot. She expressed a kind of exhilaration in the uncertainty and hazards of camp conditions. This quiet reveling in the chaos was a countercurrent to the distress of exposure to rain and cold and to the many daily encounters with the unexpected that took place in the aftermath.

This undercurrent of elation in freedom from structure is akin to what anthropologist Victor Turner describes as *communitas*. Its defining feature is a vision—no matter how transitory—of society as unstructured, undifferentiated, "whose boundaries are ideally coterminous with those of the human species." *Communitas* engenders a sentiment of unity, where structural categories, roles, statuses, and social hierarchies are dissolved away.

I see *communitas* as a deeply longed for sense of oneness with others, a kind of wholeness. Structure, rules, and order weigh heavily upon us, and we seek to break out of their constraints in a variety of ways, in ritual and ceremony and ideologies of perfect freedom and brotherhood. One of the paradoxes of the human condition, however, is that society is of necessity structured, and yet human beings have this vision of total harmony with others. In the process of social life, the two models—of society as structured and as ideally undifferentiated—are in conflict.

In the postdisaster years, the Callejón was engaged in acting out the conflict of the two models, a conflict intensified and made overt by the tragedy. I felt the ebb and flow of structure and structurelessness. The landscape itself seemed to reflect it. Mountainsides slid down on the valley and beyond, as if disintegrating, and then once again the valley stood up, settled for a time, in a new shape. The sacking of the towns and their "invasion" by *campesinos* can be seen, perhaps, as rituals of status reversal, dramatizing the tensions of rich and poor and seeking to bring "social structure and *communitas* into right mutual relation once again." Many townspeople, though, felt that the earthquake, together with the plunder of the towns and the Revolutionary Reconstruction, had been more than a leveler, that they had brought a reversal of classes. At any rate, the consensus was that relations between the towns of the Callejón and the countryside would never be the same again. Even if *campesinos* eventually abandoned their *módulos* and newly found lodgings on the valley floor and returned to the mountain slopes because "they cannot live without planting," still, the old ways, the old mistreatment of *campesinos*, that could not return.

THE tearing apart of town and country implicit in the interpretation of the earthquake as the result of social injustice and in the sacking of the towns was rewoven by that overriding sense of the collectivity, of everyone being contained within the valley. The feeling predominated that, in some final analysis, the disaster hurt everybody, even the physical valley itself, the mountains, birds, and animals. This immersion of the whole valley in the event made everyone guilty or everyone innocent of whatever offenses might have brought about the disaster.

The rendings produced by tales of horror were repaired in stories of heroism of *campesino* and townsperson as they came to the aid of one another. Townspeople cited social rapprochement as a value that had emerged from the disaster. They asserted in many ways the Indianness of the valley and their own "sierraness," taking pride in the qualities of mountain people. They recalled the common heritage of mestizos and Indians and said that, after all, they all shared the dark Mongoloid spot, which they call in Quechua *kolyusiki*, at the base of the spine. For their part, *campesinos* spoke of feeling at times sympathetic pains with the dying in Huaraz's center, of arms and shoulders that troubled them still because of blows victims had sustained in the town on May 31, 1970. All these things, it seemed to me, were ways to set things right again, to reintegrate town and country and reaffirm the valley community.

Also, the mere presence in the Callejón of CRYRZA and SINAMOS and Catholic Reform workers from the coast tended to blur Indian/mestizo differences and foster unity in the valley. More of life's circumstances and more cultural traits were shared by Indian and mestizo of the highlands than by mestizo highlander and someone from the coast. When confronted by the outside contingent from Lima, Indians and mestizos became one, *serranos*, mountain people. Antagonism toward the new coastal sovereignty engendered a pride in the sierra, including the Indian.[2]

In addition, reaffirmation of the valley community took place in ceremonial interludes that seemed to dissolve away all the social categories into which people might be divided. One such jubilant occasion took place on June 24, the Day of St. John, when a schoolhouse was dedicated in Mataquita, a hamlet high above Jangas on the Cordillera Negra.

CARE had financed the project, and Peace Corps volunteers and villagers had built the structure. The dedication date had been set some weeks earlier, and as I traveled by truck with the volunteers and a CARE representative, they wondered whether the people of Mataquita had remembered the date and whether they would be waiting for us with horses in Jangas. When no one was waiting, we debated turning back to Huaraz, but it was decided that we should plow on as long as the road was passable. Where the road ended, a *campesino* from Mataquita was waiting for us. He flashed a big smile and said they had been working on the road all night long, *a pulso* (literally, "by pulse"). That's why there was no need to take horses down for us. Materials we had carried in the truck for the schoolhouse were loaded on the Indian's back, as only he could have carried them, using a tumpline, which fits over the forehead, sustaining the load in back. A forty-five-minute climb on a narrow, winding path was still ahead of us, and we set out one behind the other. When I could take my eyes off the precipitous path, I would stare back into the face of Huascarán across the way. Fields of wheat billowed beneath us.

When finally we emerged over the rounded curve of a knoll, suddenly the hamlet, of which we had not caught even a glimpse during the trek, lay before us. Not only had the villagers not forgotten the date, but they had prepared regally for the occasion. They were all dressed in their most beautiful clothes, making the flat, almost puna, land radiant with color. A band began to play with great spirit, announcing our arrival, and we could smell the lamb and potatoes roasting in a *pachamanca*. Caldrons of delicious lamb soup and great buckets of *chicha* had been prepared, and we shuddered to think we had almost turned back when we found no horses at Jangas.

The women of the hamlet and I crowded together on the floor of the new schoolhouse, where a German priest from Centenario said Mass. The men stood along the walls or peered in from outside. Dogs that misbehaved during the Mass were smacked, and crying babies were jounced in their shawls on their mothers' backs.

In the highlands of Peru, even material objects have godparents. I was asked to be the godmother of a window, still just a cutout with no glass. I made my way to the front of the schoolhouse and stood by the window. A prayer was said over the window, and I contributed 100 *soles* to its upkeep. Officially, I am responsible for that window, and from time to time I have wondered if it has withstood the rain and hail.

After Mass, we all went outside for the secular part of the ceremonies. The teacher in charge of the one-room schoolhouse spoke eloquently, saying this new building was a tribute to progress. It was "a little piece of the New Peru." He gave the history of the school. The old adobe structure had been leveled in the earthquake. Don "Somebody" from below in the town had owned the land, but the villages had taken it over and placed a flag upon the ruins. Then the teacher contacted the Peace Corps and CARE. Villagers made adobes, but they were not aseismic, and they had to make them all over again. This they did joyfully, the teacher said, for it was a miracle to see the New Peru rise from the ruins of their tiny hamlet.

The band of flutes, drums, and violins broke out in lively *huaynos*, and then the *teniente gobernador*, the major political figure of the hamlet, spoke. He said that Mataquita had been so forgotten until the earthquake. Then he called forth a child to recite a poem he had written: "My beautiful little school . . . your new windows . . . my little heart opens . . . my countryside, my land . . ." When the boy had finished, very small children began to dance. Dressed like a tiny adult, each girl carried something on her back and wore a hat sassily perched on her head and draped with a scarf. I still remember one little girl, almost a toddler, who wore on top of her many skirts and taffeta blouse a green-and-white-striped apron.

And then, two young boys, about eight years old, trained by consciousness-raisers, presented a skit. One boy was dressed in his full Indian attire, poncho and wool pants and rubber sandals; the other in Western garb, smoking a cigarette like a *gamonal* (a term used for the wealthy, with a connotation of "city slicker") from Lima. The skit ended with the boys dancing off as the band played, embracing each other with the following words:

INDIAN BOY: . . . there is no superior or inferior race.

CITY SLICKER: Ay, well, if that is true, that merits an embrace and a drink!

A euphoria was swelling in Mataquita, and after eating the food baked in the underground oven, we all danced to *huaynos* inside the schoolhouse. The *chicha* flowed, and I recall the countryside swirling outside as I danced, seeing it through the cutouts where the glass windows would eventually be placed. Still, as always, the earthquake was present. Pulling me aside, a *campesino* recounted, "I was in a cornfield when the earth began to tremble. I threw myself down into a pile of tender ears of corn. Then I knelt to pray. Tiles flew off our houses, nothing more, why should I lie? . . . We are hoping to get a new bell for our chapel. After the earthquake, our bell no longer rings. We will have to send to Lima, but it could be robbed on its way to us. But we will try to get the bell by the Day of the Cross, September 14. Our patron saint is the Holy Cross."

Night began its sudden fall, and a round moon rose. It was hard to get away. Villagers followed us with the buckets of *chicha* for one last toast to the school, to Mataquita, to the valley, to the New Peru, to Mother Earth. We knew the fiesta would continue through the night, people from the town below and *campesinos* celebrating together this new piece of the nation. As we scrambled down the knoll onto the path, a villager shouted in Quechua: "Come back, and next time, don't forget the doors and the windows!"

It was dark by the time we got down the footpath to where the truck waited. I climbed in back of the truck and lay down, drunk with altitude, the mountains, *chicha*, music, and the emotion of *communitas*, dizzy with the idea of constructing one's world— just and egalitarian—that permeated the schoolhouse dedication. The truck bumped along as I lay on my back, eyes half-closed, looking up sleepily. Overhead, the moon bobbed in the immense cold black sky.

IN a ceremony conducted on May 31, 1972, beneath the snow line on the shoulder of Huascarán, the net of inclusiveness was cast even farther, beyond Indian of the heights and mestizo of the valley towns; beyond *serranos*, mountain people, and *Limeños* of the coast. This ceremony commemorated the Czechoslovakian mountain-climbing expedition swept away in the avalanche set loose by the earthquake. The Czechoslovakian ambassador and other dignitaries; the wives of the lost climbers, flown from their homeland; and Peruvian military representatives and mountain climbers were gathered between the two glacial lakes of Llanganuco.

A Mass was in progress when suddenly truckloads of people from the valley below, having left their own ceremony on the Yungay burial ground, began to arrive at the scene unexpectedly. One by one, the survivors of Yungay came forward to deliver impromptu funeral orations. They spoke of the friendship that had developed between the members of the expedition and the town and recalled the events of the last days before the catastrophe. They expressed sorrow that such a terrible thing should happen to those who had come from so far away. Telling me about this ceremony, which I had not witnessed because I spent the anniversary on the pampa of Huaraz, Benjamín remarked that something special, unnameable, unites people on a mountain, "something that is beyond all the things of below, the things of the land, the things of the cities. . . . When one is on the mountain, what one's name is— Pérez or Toshino or Petrov—doesn't matter." Huascarán itself, villain that it was, seemed to mediate the antagonistic oppositions generated below, shedding down its steep flanks categories that separate people.

It was fitting that one of the most spontaneous and effervescent rites of healing, of *communitas*, to emerge from the event of May 31, 1970, should take place on Huascarán, where the differentiations and contradictions of the world below were literally and symbolically transcended. I find recorded in my field notes, also, the genuineness of the ceremony at the schoolhouse dedication in Mataquita—the skit depicting the equality of Indians and non-Indians—performed as it was, high up near frozen tablelands. Below, the battle to come to grips with disaster, with what it meant and how to reinstate relationships among people living amid the folds of the two great mountain chains and on the valley bottom, was still being waged.

Part 5

INSIDE THE VALLEY: PUNISHMENT AND PROPHECY

Teitanchiqmi mandamushqa jei tem-blorta. Jeipa castiqunmi. ("Our Father has sent us this earthquake. It is his punishment.")

campesino in Huaraz

Nineteen

THE ROOTS OF PUNISHMENT

Viracocha, Creator of mankind . . .
What is the sin that makes me suffer?
an Indian in the
sixteenth century

ANY SAID that in the long minute of the earth's shaking, there was no thought. Self-preservation alone had gripped them, and in the minutes and hours that followed, concern for kinsmen and neighbors had occupied them. But even during the void of thought, the words *Castigo de Dios* ("Punishment of God") had escaped from their lips. Through the first night, the next days, months, and years, these words were repeated over and over again.

I heard the phrase *Castigo de Dios* hundreds of times. It was uttered with varying shades of meaning and feeling, and at times with no meaning at all, just a pronouncement that surely the earthquake was punishment. If I asked "Was it the will of God?" perhaps they would say, "*Sí, la voluntad de Dios.*" But I did not often hear that phrase uttered spontaneously, and I did not feel the resignation, peace, or hopelessness it implied. The ubiquitous word was *castigo* ("punishment"), and the sentiment, guilt.

Others said that in that minute of shaking, they "thought" of punishment and reported that they or people nearby had asked God why he was punishing them or begged him to stop the punishment. A young man from Huaraz told me: "In that moment, I thought of God. It was the punishment of God. I couldn't stand up on the ground because it was shaking so. I started to cry, and everyone began to cry on their knees, shouting and pleading with God in that moment."

Some said that even during that brief minute they had assumed some blame, or heard others do so, screaming confessions into the darkening sky. A few gave accounts that seared my mind. Protestants in a small town were said to have shouted, "Punish more, punish more!" as the "pagan" Catholic earth beneath them shuddered.

A shopkeeper in Nicrupampa told me how the minute of shaking had confirmed for him God's existence. "In the moment," he said, "it was as if I had fainted. I was seeing everything, but I was not thinking. I was speaking, asking God why he was bringing this punishment to us, but it was not like thinking. Then, when many hours had passed, I began to think about God, but I was mute. I thought about my family, about my wife, who had gone to wash clothes in the stream, and my children, who were in Patay. And I thought about God, how the earthquake was punishment for something. It could not be nature alone. God controls nature."

The spontaneous and pervasive utterance of "¡*Castigo!*" sprang from the native soil of the valley. The sins believed to have brought this punishment were not sins of injustice or disharmonious social relations but rather sins that came from deep within the native system of belief. These were sins that the social revolutionaries of Lima, or even the spokesmen for the new Catholic Reform, knew nothing about or did not fully understand.

In this religious sphere, survivors faced the same predicament they confronted in the secular arena. The disaster had struck amid changing times, and they debated the merits of their old social order versus the new vision the Revolutionary Military Government provided. In the religious sphere, their quandary was over what was right and what was wrong about modernizing religion. Did the disaster strike because Catholic Reform was moving too fast or too slowly? Had the new beliefs and new rituals incurred God's wrath, or was it the persistence of the old in face of the new?

The interpretation of punishment addressed the ultimate cause of the disaster. The "How?" it occurred had been answered seismologically. It had also been addressed in the anxiety over France's bomb tests. And the nation had furnished messianic rationalizations for the disaster when it propounded the new egalitarian society that could now be created. The "Why?" demanded a religious answer.

Passion suffused this search for an ultimate cause. Because religious change struck at customs that touched the deeper religious core of the valley, bewilderment over the message of the disaster at times became acute. The debate over ultimate cause was conducted at many levels. It seized upon interpretations that pitted different religious groups within the valley against one another. And it pondered the possibility that the whole valley might have been singled out for punishment. In this reasoning, the valley was seen as a scapegoat, suffering for the sake of the whole world:

A man said:

> This has been a punishment in order that all the world believe in God. I have more faith than before. My faith had been weakening, and this should not be. Punishments must take place in different places in order to show the world. They happen where there is much disbelief in God.

When Lima newspapers referred to Huaraz as "a punished town," it appeared to mean no more than "an injured place." Even the words "cruel punishment" seemed nothing more than a journalistic metaphor. Thus, an issue of the national magazine *Nueva* was dedicated to Huaraz, "which has been harshly punished by nature." In the Huaraz newspaper, the word *castigo* appeared daily, and it even appeared in the scientific treatment of the event.

But among the *campesinos*, and even a preponderance of the mestizos of the valley, *castigo* meant something much more literal and more intentional. It meant everything from God's wrath for grave wrongdoing to a warning or lesson. The teachings of the Spanish Inquisition were passionately alive in the valley. This *cas-*

tigo, invoked by the catastrophe, overflowed with a sense of sin, guilt, judgment, and retribution. And everywhere in the valley, *castigo* was shouted, cried, discussed, and whispered.[1]

THE pervasiveness and intensity in the Callejón of the interpretation of the disaster as divine punishment suggest that concepts of sin and retribution reach deep into the Andean past, even predating Catholicism. Many of these ancient concepts influenced survivors' deliberations on the ultimate cause of the earthquake.

Our knowledge of the pre-Spanish past comes largely from chronicles written by Spanish priests and soldiers in the throes of conquest and in the decades and century that followed. These ethnohistorical sources must be interpreted cautiously. The early Spanish missionaries and adventurers tended to see the indigenous culture from their own ethnocentric perspective. Nevertheless, correcting for the biases of these early writers, contemporary scholars of Andean ethnohistory have given us a clear picture of a pre-Columbian religion of an ethical character in which concepts of sin and punishment were deeply rooted.

John Rowe has synthesized from the chronicles a description of Inca state religion at the time of Emperor Pachacuti Inca Yupanki, who reigned from A.D. 1438 to 1471, the period during which Quechua speakers moved out of the valley of Cuzco and far beyond. An ancient creator god, Viracocha, was believed to have created Inti, the Sun, tribal god of the Incas. As the Incas' conquests spread, Inti became the god of the empire. The emperors, *Sapa Incas*, were thought to be descended from Inti and to share his divinity. Inti was worshiped along with Mama Q'uilla, the moon goddess, Illapa, god of thunder, and the morning and evening stars. Sweeping over the Andes, the Incas not only spread their own sun cult as a means to securing political unity but also adopted local and regional gods. This tolerance of local deities made it easier for the Incas to subjugate entire provinces without the loss of a drop of blood.

Rowe tells us that sin, penance, and purification were important Inca concepts. Serious sins were murder, especially by poisoning or witchcraft; stealing; carelessness in worship and neglect of ceremonial duties; fornication and adultery. Sin was punished both in this life and in the next. Confession was practiced. All the people of the land made public confessions, accusing themselves of not having venerated the sun or the moon or of having spoken ill of the *Sapa Inca*. The practice of medicine was a priestly function, with disease seen as punishment for sin. Other scholars report that severe penance and punishments were inflicted for not honoring religious festivals or showing proper reverence for *huacas*, sacred stones and places, and that sin and all unlawful conduct were considered to harm not only the individual but also the community.

These were Inca beliefs, but it is presumed that notions of sin and punishment existed in the Andes even before the expansion of the Inca in the fifteenth century, as part of the popular religion of the conquered peoples. These peoples were said to be concerned with "the powers of springs that furnished their water, the stones that watched over their houses, and the mountains that brooded over their land." Beneficent and baneful manifestations of nature alike—rains and frosts, lightning and thunder—were seen by ancient Andean peoples as vital phenomena sent by supernatural beings who, in this way, communicated with them. These phenomena were cryptic messages whose meaning had to be interpreted.

When fertilizing rains turned torrential and were accompanied by hail and lightning, they were interpreted as a curse. When the gods were angry, they sent yellow and red rain as punishment. Pachacámac, the oracular coastal deity, sometimes manifested his ire by stretching himself, thus shaking the earth. When that occurred, Inca soldiers and sinful commoners alike perished, because earthquakes destroyed simultaneously the good and the wicked. Chronicler Cabello Valboa writes:

We have been told by witness given from father to son down the line that one day the world suddenly quaked and shook. The sun . . . became totally dark. Stones hurled themselves against one another and broke into pieces. Graves of many people dead many years opened. Among the animals of the world there came a great disorder and confusion.

In a manuscript entitled *Gods and Men of Huarochirí*, written in Quechua in the sixteenth century, we are told that because of a certain sin—false worship—"a great rain occurred that carried everybody, including houses and llamas, to the ocean."

Many of these calamities were said to be punishments sent by the Creator, Viracocha. It is he who was believed to have sent the great flood. After the flood waters receded, people who were to form the *ayllus*, or ancestral communities of ancient Peru, emerged from a *pacarina*—a lake, a rock, a cave, or the trunk of a tree. These first people were turned into stones—some say into condors and other birds and animals—by Viracocha. Each group worshiped its stone "idol" as the ancestor of the community and offered sacrifices to it.

Andean cosmic myths resound with ideas of cyclical world destruction and rebirth. In one tradition, Peru, which had existed since the act of Creation, takes further shape after the universal flood subsides, carving out valleys beneath towering ranges of the most frozen snows. Other ages follow, but each ends in disaster. Another indigenous tradition divides time into four periods of a thousand years, each governed by a different sun. These four Andean worlds were destroyed by cataclysms—plagues, fire, flood, earthquake—after mankind had become lustful and the ancient customs corrupt. Then, in this myth, the Incas arose and inaugurated the fifth sun.

Anguished by the changes the Spaniards made in the early days of the colonial period, Indian chronicler Guaman Poma pondered these ancient notions of cyclical time and of *pachacuti*—total upheaval—fearing that the disappearance of the traditional Andean world might bring with it, too, once again, the end of life.

DESPITE its pomp and ceremony, Inca imperial religion was dominated by the same concerns as those of the remotest village, and it shared beliefs and rites common to the majority of Andean peoples well before their unification into a single polity. The village religion was strongly agricultural in character. Pachamama, the Earth Mother, no doubt a unifying principle, was invoked in daily rites throughout the kingdom.

Eclipses were viewed nervously as a sign of imminent and severe chastisement. Divination entered every aspect of life. Evil omens abounded in the form of rainbows, foxes, spiders, and snakes. Omens that cast a pall upon the immediate pre-Conquest years, during the reign of Huayna Cápac, were said to be comets, earthquakes, the moon girdled by rings of multicolored fire, thunderbolts, and hawks chasing eagles in the sky.

Since rural as well as Inca state religion was deeply animistic, a *huaca* (holy object) could be a mountain, a plant or a rock crystal, a stone idol or the *pacarina* from which it emerged. A recurrent mythical element is the metamorphosis of figures into personified rocks and mountains. Sometimes, becoming agitated like mere mortals, certain mountain peaks also behaved like sovereigns, utilizing their omnipotent powers. Stones that clash in the air and tumble down to crush sinners, "pursuing them as if they were llamas," is another common mythical theme.

Huacas were also old tombs and funerary urns where the ancestors—the *ahuilos*—were buried, deep in the mountain gorges. Ancestors were likewise presumed to exist within the mountain—*Ucu Pacha*, the "world of within"—and ultimately, with time, to become the mountain. These were the *Aukis*, wise old ones within the mountain, and the *Apus*, the mountains themselves.

So much of the world was sacred—*huaca*—that in 1590 Jesuit José de Acosta was moved to write that witnessing the "perdition" of the Peruvian Indians was enough to drive one mad: "They adore rivers, springs, gorges, boulders and rocks, hills and the mountain peaks. . . ."

Besides the *Aukis*, the stone *huacas*, rock crystals and holy places of origin, the world teemed with evil spirits and supernatural monsters. Flying heads planted their teeth in their victims' necks and sucked their blood, and fiends fed on the fat of people surprised on paths in the night. Chroniclers speak, too, of a personified evil principle, called *supay* in Quechua. This "devil" appeared in various guises, the least fearsome being the tiny creature called an *ichiqolco*, who wore a long braid down to his feet, with which he played coquettishly. On especially misty nights, the *ichiqolco* lurked in streams enticing women and children.

WHATEVER concepts of sin and punishment may have existed prior to the Conquest in 1532, it is certain that with the coming of the Jesuits in the late sixteenth century and their *visitas* to the far-flung Andean valleys to "extirpate idolatry," the punishment of God was superimposed on those concepts of supernatural retribution that were already a part of the Indian mind. The Catholic "extirpators" sought to give even greater amplification to the concept of evil. The native concept of *supay* was seized upon and said to be a manifestation of the Christian Devil. And in cultivating the need for confession, the Jesuits took pains to keep alive and to enhance the pre-Conquest consciousness of sin.

However, against the visible emblems of Indian religion, the Spanish friars led a concerted attack. The stone idols—*huacas*—became for them synonymous with paganism. Actually, it is because of the ruthless pursuit of the *huacas* that we learn more about their worship than about any other aspect of Indian religion. As older priests retired from their work, they wrote guides for their younger colleagues. These treatises, together with sermons denouncing popular "superstitions," give us priceless details of the beliefs and practices of Andean villagers.

Even after the death of Atahualpa, the last Inca emperor, and the demise of the official religion of the Inca, the cult of the localized *huacas* remained more alive than ever, fueled no doubt by the extirpators' zeal to extinguish it. By the early seventeenth century, the campaigns to wipe out idolatry had reached a virtual paroxysm. Father Pablo José de Arriaga, whose assignment was to expunge the idols from the central Peruvian highlands, describes the task in vivid detail.

Bemoaning the difficulty of uprooting idolatry from the Indian world, particularly in the highland valley of Huaylas and other parts of what is now Ancash, Arriaga says that were he to tell what happened in that valley in all its fullness, it would "make a long and sorrowful story . . . To uproot the *huacas* from their hearts, a second and third plowing will be required . . . and they have been warned by punishment." The *huacas* of Huaylas, Arriaga tells us, had the faces of men and women, and some the Indians called the sons, wives, or brothers of others. The Indians confessed to their priest, the *soncocamayoc*—"keeper of the heart, life's center" in Quechua—believing that their misfortunes were due to having incurred the anger of the *huacas*.

Andean villagers, perceiving the Spanish representation of saints to be the *huacas* of their conquerors, accepted them in the same way they had accepted the state pantheon of their Inca conquerors. This, Arriaga found amazing. He wrote that it was a common error for the Indians "to carry water on both shoulders, to have recourse to both religions at once," and he cited the following example: "I know a place where a cloak was made for the image of Our Lady and a shirt for their *huaca* out of the same cloth. They feel and even say that they can worship their *huacas* while believing in God the Father, Son, and Holy Ghost. Thus, for the worship of Jesus Christ they generally offer what they offer their *huacas*," thinking "their lies compatible with our truth and their idolatry with our faith."

"The dissimulation and boldness of the Indians have reached such a point that during the feast of Corpus, they have slyly hidden a small *huaca* on the very platform of the monstrance of the Holy Sacrament," the friar remarked with astonishment. *Huacas* were even found "in the hollow niches of the saints in front of the holy altar!"

Thousands of *huacas* dotted the highlands of Peru. They were worshiped as ancestors of the *ayllus* and as guardians and protectors of the villages. The Indians asked them for health, food, and long life. Making the arduous journeys to the tops of the mountains, the extirpators destroyed the places of worship and the stone idols and placed large wooden crosses where the *huacas* had stood. On rare occasions, a trusted Indian convert was allowed to replace the *huaca* with a cross. Arriaga relates that on one such occasion, an Indian went up the mountain with a cross, and as he tried to implant it, a great wind came up. The wind blew so hard that the cross broke. Frightened, the Indian descended the mountain to tell the friars that such extraordinary gusts of wind scarcely ever occurred in that area.

Once the crosses were finally situated on the mountaintops above a village, the missionaries departed, moving on to another village to replace idols with Catholic crosses. On return visits to the villages, though, they often found that the *huacas* they had removed had been buried beneath the crosses. In a town of Huaylas, Arriaga reports, on the site where a cross had been put on a previous visit, suspicious friars dug down about a meter and were about to give up when they came upon evidence of sacrifices and found three *huacas*.

JUST as the "confusion" of Catholic crosses and statues of the Catholic saints with native *huacas* was inimical to the extirpators, so, too, did the manner in which the Indians celebrated the festivals appear to violate some "natural" distinction between the sacred and the profane. Their dismay at the revelry that accompanied Indian worship echoes down through the years of extirpation. Amid Indian confessions, there was music, dance, and song. *Chicha* was brewed in large pots, consumed by the celebrants and offered to the *huacas* along with coca and guinea pigs that had been sacrificed. Arriaga observes that such were the bacchanalian proclivities of the Indians that when reciting the Apostles' Creed in their language, instead of saying *hucllachacuininta*, meaning "communion or gathering of the saints," they said *pucllachacuininta*, meaning "jest or merriment of the saints."

The early missionaries warned that sins of revelrous idolatry as well as sins of adultery, incest, and witchcraft would bring severe punishment upon the land. One friar told of an "almost unbelievable" avalanche that in the year 1581 fell upon a town steeped in idolatry.

The ancient popular religion and daily practices remained more firmly entrenched in the sierra fastnesses than on the coast. Here Indians viewed the zeal of the extirpators, and of the priests who followed, as aggressions against their native beliefs and resisted them both openly and secretly. Though the stone idols might be broken and crosses and saints' images put in their places, the entire sacred world could not be destroyed. Arriaga himself remarked, "Some of the *huacas* are hills and high places which time cannot consume."

Faced with accusations of idolatry and the negation of their culture, Andean peoples brooded over their loss. The decision whether to embrace or to resist colonial society, with its new religion, clouded their days with doubt and confusion. "The world is upside down," wrote Indian chronicler Guaman Poma at the beginning of the seventeenth century. With the Inca gone, the world had sunk into chaos. The sufferings of the Indians, their increasing mortality due to epidemics and to abhorrent working conditions in the mines, were themselves considered by the Andeans to be punishments.

Throughout the colonial period, Sunday sermons threatened sinners with earthquakes, and those that did occur were attributed to the wrath of God. Perhaps Spain's relative freedom from earthquakes made it easier for Spanish priests to see earthquakes as divine punishment for idolatry rather than simply natural phenomena. At any rate, God's judgment was thought to have prevailed during the great earthquake of 1746, which destroyed Lima, whose inhabitants were "unbelieving, contumacious or corrupt." In processions following that earthquake, penitent survivors carried the Lord of Miracles through the rubble, flogging themselves and holding aloft signs reading, "This is the justice that the King of Heaven sends down upon vile sinners." Prelates' shouts of "Lima, Lima, your sins are your ruin," resounded through the streets.

HARDLY anything I have said about what the chroniclers and early Catholic missionaries recorded of the religion of the Andean peoples they encountered in their conquest and proselytizing failed to turn up in some form in my field notes. The failure of the Spanish campaigns to eliminate Andean beliefs and practices revealed itself daily in many ways.

When I accompanied Clemente Quispe, who was then living in Nicrupampa, to his hamlet, Huanmarín, on the Cordillera Negra to visit his beloved San Isidro, we passed a small cave in the side of a cliff. He told me that late one night, as he was passing this cave, a pig came out. Later he asked himself, Was that Christ, or was it an ancestor in the form of a pig?

All along the way, he pointed out important hills—Queshkipunta, Purukuta, and others. On the path, we passed a huge wooden cross with fruit tied to it. As we cautiously balanced ourselves on a plank bridge high above a stream, Quispe gestured toward a big rock in the water. A little girl had been pasturing her sheep near the stream when she disappeared, he said. The villagers held a wake over the rock for three or four months, for surely some power within the rock had drawn her inside it. Once again on the path, a snake slithered between us, and he said it was a sign that one of us would soon die.

When we got to Clemente Quispe's village at noon, we found it almost deserted. The villagers were at work in their fields. Only a few women were spinning, and a little girl was playing in the mud on the plaza. We sat on the steps of the chapel. "At night, San Isidro comes out of the chapel and plows one's fields, to help," he said. "He wears boots. But we cannot take him out of the chapel in procession because when we do, it hails." Stretching out his arms wide, turning himself into a cross, he spoke of the fine cross he would construct, of huge wooden posts, to carry down to plant on the coast.

On another occasion, an old priest was speaking of the witchcraft and superstition that reigned in the countryside. The *campesinos*, he said, believe in the Devil, who appears in the form of a donkey, or sometimes as a tiny humanoid creature, the *ichiqolco*. To my surprise, he added, "But, you know, once when I had a bad thought, a little illuminated face, the face of a monster, appeared at my window. I think it was the Devil." This was not the first time the Devil had peered at him through the windows of his church. And long ago, he said, one of the first priests at San Francisco had fought with the Devil in the shape of a donkey.

When I was bitten by a dog in a small settlement off the main valley road and went late in the day to search for the animal, the villagers kept me inside a little store where *chicha* was sold. At night, on a path, they said, a *ñaka* or *pishtaco* might waylay me to extract the fat from my body. From early in the Conquest, the Indians feared that churchmen were *pishtacos* who would render their fat to make candles for the church. Nowadays their fear was that human fat would perhaps be used to grease the tractor of a wealthy landowner. Half believing, half not believing, they told these stories, and others, about manifestations of the *supay*, who lurked in caverns, water, and on dark paths.

Whenever dark was descending as I got ready to leave Don Juan's house in Secsecpampa, he would pray for me beside a large wooden cross that rested in his patio. There were rivulets to ford on my journey down to Huaraz, and *ichiqolcos* might entice me into the icy water.

Inextricably mixed with medieval Catholicism was the belief in *almas*, souls and apparitions of the dead. In pre-Conquest times, the dead were visualized as "living corpses," without any real distinction between body and soul. "They left their old familiar places with regret," fearing loneliness and trying to take some relative along with them for company. In 1971–72, when I traversed the pampa with survivors at night, they often said they saw the "living corpses" and quickened their step, lest they be tagged.

I cannot count the times that *chicha*, or even Inca Cola, was poured upon the thirsty earth and a toast made to Pachamama. Much of the intimate native religion, such as beliefs about the rainbow, *pacarinas* and other *huaca* places, holy lakes and springs and stones, was still alive high on the flanks of the Andes. Divination with guinea pigs was still practiced to diagnose illness, and prophetic dreams and other omens still served as guides for living. The crosses and saints' images of the twentieth century had "relatives" just as the ancient *huacas* had and were worshiped with the same revelry of that ancient time.[2]

In the Callejón, there is a Quechua word for "sin" (*hutsa*; *hucha* in Cuzco Quechua), and as in many parts of Peru, the Quechua *muchuchiy* ("to punish") has been replaced by the Spanish word *castigar*, with a Quechua suffix: *kastigay*. The idea of punishment persists still in legends collected in recent years in the valley. In one such story, a crime is punished by avalanche. In others gathered in the countryside by *Huaracino* Yauri Montero, the Sun God punishes lovers; and Mama Q'uilla, Mother Moon, punishes villagers who disobeyed the Virgin's plea to build her a temple.

ONCE, I asked a townswoman to recall as much as she could of what was preached from the pulpits of Huaraz about punishment before the earthquake, through the course of her growing up. This is what she told me:

> Before the earthquake of May 1970, the sermons delivered in the churches at Sunday Mass did not announce an earthquake as punishment for sins but, rather, a series of epidemics, hail storms, lightning, excessive rains, frosts. . . .
>
> In order that the faithful behave well and live morally and come to church to fulfill their obligations as Christians, priests threatened us with calamities that God would send as a *castigo* to all who in one way or another had offended him.
>
> For example, when much hail fell, they said that a mother had harmed her child and that heaven got angry and sent a *castigo*. Sometimes it happened that a dead child was found, or a buried fetus.
>
> There is a very strong wind in this zone called the *shucuquí*, like a crazy wind that lifts up everything and comes suddenly,

frightening people. Then it was said that a child had raised his hand against his mother or father. . . .

Excessive rains coincided often with a crime or when the cadaver of a person who had fallen into the river was found.

Droughts and frosts are *castigos de Dios* for having wasted food, even giving it to animals. . . . The priests said God gets disturbed because we are giving "his face" to the animals. When one gives wheat to the pigs or throws it to the ground and the pigs step on it, they say God cries, because the wheat is his face, his body . . . and he will punish people with droughts.

Generally, priests threatened with these things of nature the people of the country, of the *chacra*, the *campesinos*. The towns-people believe these things, too, but not so strongly as those of the country. The priests threatened townspeople with great cat-aclysms, hell, purgatory, and the condemnation of the soul when one dies. . . .

They said that to behave badly, immorally, was to nail one more nail into Jesus. . . . At the noon Mass, which was more solemn and frequented mainly by townspeople, the padre would say that the end of the world was near because people each day got closer to evil and the *castigo de Dios* was coming in wars among nations, floods, and epidemics. . . .

The priests used to say: "God will show his anger with this town, sending us a series of plagues, catastrophes, alluvions. You of the town ought to give to your brothers of the country, what-ever they need, but you of the country ought to be good and faithful to your patrons because they give you food and a roof. You men of the town, help your *campesino* brothers, because they are, just like you, children of God. . . . You, *campesinos*, you shouldn't be lazy, drunkards, because *Papachito* ["Little Papa," "God"] will punish us. He won't give us food. He won't give us rains. . . . We are going to eat dirt as a punishment of God if we squander food. . . . Don't fight among yourselves, because God will get angry and will punish us. . . .

All of the rhetoric and activity of Revolution and the Catholic Reform movement, the barrio meetings and the meetings in the survivor camps, the talk of creation and change and modernization, rested upon an ancient base of history and myth. The apprehension of survivors about the meaning of the disaster of May 31, 1970, echoed earlier forebodings surrounding cataclysms, real and mythical, of the Andean past. The struggles over the saints, the *costumbres*, the crosses, the nature of the sins, and the fear of apocalypse that fill the following pages, all resonate with the ancient religion, with traditional Catholicism, and with the "*castigo*" that for centuries, perhaps millennia, has sprung so readily to the lips to explain calamity.

Twenty

CUSTOMS, OLD CUSTOMS

Customs, old customs
You don't let the world get on with it
Customs, old customs . . .
Reasons without foundation
Roads that must be traveled
Want to or not, just because
They are the ways of yesterday.
Man is in chains from the day he is born,
Invisible chains you wear, like it or not . . .
And the day you want to be free, to fly,
You remember the customs and
Return to the same yesterday.

ballad played by Peter
on Radio Huascarán

I N THE AFTERMATH, the universal Catholic Reform movement butted up against beliefs and practices of pre-Columbian religion that had remained intact within Catholicism and other indigenous beliefs and rituals so inextricably bound up with traditional Catholicism as to defy separation of the elements.

These Andean beliefs and practices, whether "pure" or bound to colonial Catholicism, were perceived by the new Latin American theologians as millstones around the necks of the oppressed, from which they must be freed in order to achieve true liberation and equality. Politically conscious Latin American Catholic Reform also viewed native religious practice as inimical to "progress," which meant entrance into the modern, technologically sophisticated world stream. An equal footing in the world community would, in turn, mean freedom from bondage to "First World" powers.

Those native practices that were regarded by modernizing Catholicism as most irreconcilable with social justice and "progress" fell into two principal categories: the "saints" and the *costumbres*. Reformists argued that there should be fewer statues of the saints, and those that would be allowed should be clearly understood only as representations, symbols of the Church's mystics and martyrs. They should be seen for what they are, plaster or wood, inert material, rather than as flesh and blood.

Costumbres literally means "customs," or "habits," but within its Andean context, it is a word full of sentiment toward one's ways of doing things, ways that are experienced strongly in the present and at the same time are infused with a deep nostalgia for the ancient past. In many aspects, *costumbrismo* (the practice of *costumbres*) had become synonymous with merriment and pageantry in worship. Huaraz was especially famed for its *costumbrismo*: processions with bands and dance groups that came from towns and hamlets all over the Callejón and even beyond; saint's day celebrations with fireworks that lit up the sky; even unique giant ornamental candles that filled the churches on special days.

When the earthquake of 1970 struck and Catholic Reform seized the moment, the word "idolatry," muted for some 400 years, since the Spanish friars had burned and broken the Indian "idols," was once more heard with frequency in the valley. After all, religious change was, in the aftermath, no longer principally a matter of shifting belief. Rather, at the level of iconography—of religion as tangible, concrete objects and visual performance—a clear choice could now be made. Indeed, decisions had to be made about whether to reconstruct the icons and reinstate the pageantry. In few circumstances is so much power invested so suddenly in clergy and worshipers themselves. So, out of a long intimacy with the idea of punishment for errors in worship, survivors began to debate the message of the earthquake. Was it a confirmation of their "idolatry," or, conversely, was God perhaps angry because, in the immediate predisaster years, some people were no longer honoring the *costumbres*, performing the rites as they used to be performed?

Early in my fieldwork, I was faced with the two conflicting positions. In a town plaza, teenage boys tried to explain to me that the earthquake had occurred because of the innovations in the Catholic Church, like changing the Mass from Latin to Spanish or Quechua and celebrating it with modern music. As I recorded in my notes of October 19, 1971, "They say it also happened because the padre prohibited their *costumbres*, the fireworks, dances, drinking, and use of coca." Not long afterward, in another town, a man spoke to me of the impotence of the saints in the disaster. This appeared to him to uphold the new ideas of Catholic Reform: "Many people have forgotten the saints. Why? Because the disaster was a punishment, and the saints did nothing to contain the earthquake."

In this way, accusations of "idolatry" and "paganism" had begun to alternate with accusations that the valley, in even tentatively accepting the changing times and new ways, had fallen from grace. In this view, it was not idolatry that had occasioned divine punishment but rather abandonment of the saints.

ALL things conspired to challenge those religious beliefs that were embedded in iconography—the "religion," as one lady put it, "that enters through the eyes." In Huaraz, the cathedral and all barrio churches but one, Centenario, had been completely destroyed. Statues of saints were crushed, and the big church bells lay on the ground. Then came the earth movers of May 31, 1971. As people spoke of the destruction of images, the way they lay shattered in the rubble and the way the machinery swept up the pieces they could not salvage in time, I was reminded of Pablo de Arriaga's statement about the ancient Andean *huacas*: "To uproot them from their hearts, a second and third plowing will be required."

"The saints have died" was the way survivors often described the broken images. In Yungay, there simply were no more images. They were all buried under the alluvion. The only visible vestige of religion in Yungay—besides the enormous Christ of the cemetery knoll, the rustic altar at the site of the buried cathedral, and handhewn crosses on the playa—was one long *módulo*, completely bare, even of benches to sit on. Only a rough wooden cross rested against the pasteboard wall. Reform Catholicism was quick to point out that it was better that way, that that part of religion "that enters through the eyes" was best left buried in the ruins.

Reformists, many of whom had entered the valley from the coast in the early aftermath, began to focus also on the matter of the sacred and the profane. They distinguished between these two modes and sought to prevent their intertwining. The big wooden crosses that stood on the hilltops surrounding Huaraz, no doubt similar to the crosses the extirpators had placed there four centuries earlier, were forbidden entry into Huaraz at carnival time for their customary Mass and blessing. It was argued that the profaneness of carnival—the drinking and the playing with flour and water— should not be mixed with the sacredness of the cross.

It was an opportune time for Catholic Reform to make an all-out effort to eliminate *costumbrismo*. A moratorium had been placed on all festivities in the entire country for the year following the disaster, a year of official mourning. During the second year after the earthquake, the Church decided that now was the time to attack profane practice by preventing its resumption.

In brief, if the Revolutionary Reconstruction was experienced by many as a "second Conquest," there was something of another extirpation of idolatry in the proclamations of Reform Catholicism, an "extirpation" phrased locally by many survivors as "They are trying to kill the true religion."

ASSAILED by those clergy in Huaraz who sympathized with the determination of the Reform movement to uproot the saints and eradicate the *costumbres*, the old religion sought reemergence with renewed vigor. This was true for the mestizo town as well as the Indian countryside. "Saints" and *huacas* had long ago fused. Whether carved stone or wood or plaster, images were endowed with power and sacredness. After all, the Catholicism of extirpation had exhorted the newly proselytized Indians to own images of the saints and had distributed the statues among them as prizes for knowing the doctrine. And the fact that some Spanish Catholics of the Conquest era viewed the saints' images as real flesh-and-blood beings had made it easier for the Indians to accept the new religion.

My notes are filled with vivid details of the controversy over the meaning of the destruction or "salvation" of saints' images during the earthquake. Like people themselves, the statues were viewed as individuals, and survivors asked after their whereabouts and welfare in much the same manner as they inquired about the well-being of a person or a family. Largely, a sense of the miraculous prevailed. That any saints at all had survived seemed to carry the message of their rightful existence. With varying degrees of devotion, people "rescued" their images from the wreckage, repaired them, and sheltered them within the bosom of their families or in temporary dwellings until proper churches could be built. The words employed gave away their "human" qualities. The saints were deemed "healthy" or "saved," "dead" or "wounded."

The saints were familiar markers of time as people moved through the religious calendar year, from saint's day to saint's day. In the end, the saints were companions through life. They may not always have answered one's prayers, but they *responded* in some way. To be without images, though it might simplify life, carried with it too high a price.

ONE day in February, as I was walking up toward the barrio of San Francisco, from a distance I saw what looked like a person standing on the pampa. Four people were fussing over the still and erect figure, which wore a long robe that was blowing in the afternoon wind. As I got closer, I was startled to see that the motionless figure was not a person at all but a religious image. A woman was directing three men in disrobing the statue. As they removed each garment, she carefully placed it on a pile on the ground. I stopped, and the woman said, as if introducing me to the image, "This is San José. He was wounded in the earthquake. He has lost an arm. I had a dream last night in which San José appeared to me and said, 'Have you forgotten me? How long are you going to allow me to be put aside in a corner? You must see to it that I am fixed up.' There is a sculptor who is going to repair him. It will take about a month."

Then, ignoring me, she turned to the three men, and they began a spirited conversation about other images that had been damaged and what needed to be done to repair them. San José now stood on the pampa disrobed except for an ordinary man's hat, which was rumpled and dirty. The woman lamented the misshapen hat and began asking the men if they knew who could restore it to its original shape. One of the men said he knew someone capable of doing this, and she told him to take the hat and she would pay for it. He carried off the hat; a second man, the clothes; and the third, the statue of San José. As the woman hurried away, she looked back at me and shouted, "I am also caring for the Virgin." This had all happened so fast that I didn't get to say a word and was left standing alone on the site where this flurry of activity had taken place.

I had to go down this staircase (at left) *or climb down the ladder* (above) *into the patio.* Below: *Jesusa, with her mother and daughter outside my room.*

Top: *Here I pose with Jesusa, Nicolás, and family in Secsecpampa, 1980* (R. Carneiro). Center: *Padre Soriano, the priest-archaeologist, and I standing by pre-Columbian* huacas. Bottom: *At Mataquita, where I became the godmother of a window.*

Clockwise: *A Callejón woman; the Yungay Norte market—the man is shaving ice carried down from Huascarán, "avenging himself" on the villainous mountain; aerial view of the avalanche off Huascarán, taken on June 13, 1970, by Servicio Aerofotográfico Nacional.*

Top: *Huascarán and the avalanche scar.* At left: *Severed hamlet on the slopes of Huascarán* (R. Carneiro). Above: *Terraced cemetery of Yungay, where ninety-two people gathered after outrunning the avalanche.* Facing page: top, left: *May 31, 1970: "Daughter, let go of me and save yourself";* top, right: *the sixty-foot statue of Christ erected atop the Yungay cemetery in 1962 after the avalanche that buried Ranrahirca;* bottom: *the Yungay playa, where thousands were buried alive, and only the tops of four palm trees that had stood on the town's central plaza remained.*

Above: *May 31, 1972, on the Yungay playa* (E. Olaza). At left: *This monument, which reads "Holy Ground—Yungay," was built for the ten-year commemorative ceremonies on the playa.* Below: *Crosses at the edge of the playa, 1980* (R. Carneiro). Facing page: *Dying palms and mound with a rustic altar that covers Yungay's cathedral, 1980* (R. Carneiro).

Top, left: *Anthropologist Anthony Oliver-Smith, Rubén, and Cirila in the doorway of her restaurant in Yungay Norte, December 1971.* Top, right: *Cirila behind her restaurant.* Center: *On May 31, 1980, Cirila, holding her grandson, stands by her sons' crosses marking the place on the playa she judges the avalanche caught them on May 31, 1970.* At left: *Topiary snake appears to attack Huandoy from the plaza of Matacoto, a hamlet on the Cordillera Negra. Here villagers found in their midst a huge chunk of ice cast all the way across the valley from Huascarán on May 31, 1970* (R. Carneiro).

I went about my business that afternoon, but slowly, over the next days, I realized I wanted to find the woman and to know more about the fate of San José. During the next months, from time to time, I would ask about sculptors. I went in search of one, in a little shop off Centenario, only to find his door padlocked. When I finally located his brother, also a sculptor, he said he knew nothing of the image.

In early April, I had occasion to visit an image maker whom people called Pilatos, who worked in a shop in the Pedregal section of Huaraz. His shop was filled with small personal images that had been kept in private homes. Many needed repainting and limbs replaced. When I asked after San José, Pilatos said that he was a large statue that belonged in the San Francisco church. But he knew nothing of its present whereabouts. He did, however, give me information that eventually led to my finding Claudia Suárez, the woman whom I had seen directing the men on the pampa that February afternoon.

Finally, on May 18, I found her in her *módulo* in Pedregal, not far from Soledad barrio. When I entered the door, Claudia was kneeling on the mud floor in front of San José and a Virgin, saying the rosary. A table in front of the two large images held religious pictures and bits of candles and flowers. As if no time at all had elapsed since our encounter on the pampa, Claudia pointed out to me that San José now had his new arm, and that his clothes had been cleaned and his hat blocked. The Virgin had also lost an arm, she said, and the restoration of the two images had cost her 1,600 *soles*.

Just then a woman came into the *módulo*, part of which Claudia used as a small grocery where she sold a few food staples. The two women commented on the high price of potatoes and onions. "What a blow this earthquake has been," said the shopper. "My house fell down, and if there is no house, even if one has twenty-five pounds of potatoes, where can one keep them?" She filled her small basket and left. I told Claudia I wanted to know everything about San José and the Virgin.

Claudia began by telling me that on the day of the earthquake she was seated alone in her small store in her house in Soledad barrio. She said to herself, Instead of just sitting here alone, it's better to go to visit my friend Señora Josefina. As the two women sat chatting, the trembling began, slowly. But then, by the time they decided to move, the house collapsed around them, and they "were blown around as if we were packages." A maid and her child were buried, the child already dead. Señora Josefina lay facedown under a beam. Claudia was bathed in blood and encrusted with dust, with two big cuts on her head and various fractures. Why have I come here? she thought. This house is older than mine. All houses are not equal. With a strength she did not imagine she had, she lifted up the huge beam, freed her friend, and then carried her "as if she were a child."

Making her way across the ruins, she was shocked to find her house and store leveled. My death was certain had I remained at home, she now thought to herself. I am alive because of the Virgin in Señora Josefina's house, because my friend is so devoted to the Virgin, and I used to help her to find people to give money for Masses for the Virgin. With a bottle of San Mateo mineral water, found intact in the rubble of her store, she began to wash her wounds and those of her friend.

Months later, the priest of San Francisco told Claudia that the damaged image of San José was in a patio under an overhanging roof up on the hillside above the barrio. He suggested that perhaps she would have it mended. When she went in search of San José, she found, propped next to him, the Immaculate Virgin, also lacking an arm. "Her dress was all torn, and she was without hair. Her crown was gone, her beautiful crown of fine stones. . . ." Claudia realized she must rescue the Virgin along with San José. "I have such faith in her," she said. "You see, I have the idea that she saved me from death; by a hair I was saved."

Finally, that February day, her dream of the night before spurred her into action. Upon awakening, she said to herself, Ay, how can it be? If a person has a broken arm, how desperate we would be, and look, here are *Mamacita* [the Virgin], and San José here for months without arms. Once they had been restored, she brought the images to her *módulo* because there was no room for them in the tiny chapel of San Francisco.

Claudia told me that the Virgin was the same now as before the earthquake except that her face had a little more color before. "I buy her lilies, and with the ones you have brought, that makes thirty-five *soles*' worth of lilies, and with the carnations, twenty-five *soles* more. I can't explain it, but I have so much faith that I have spent all my savings to restore her, to have her safe and sound with me," she said softly. Then, becoming animated, she turned to San José and his hat. "He always wore a hat, you see. Now he is here at my side, too. Who would have thought I would ever have the Virgin and San José here at my side?"

MARIÁN, with its 1,500 inhabitants, is about an hour's walk along the Quilcay up from the edge of Huaraz. It spreads over the foothills in bucolic splendor, framed by the snow peaks of San Juan and Huantsán. San Cristóbal, Huaraz's nearest mountain, casts its shadow over Marián, where corn and potatoes grow amid adobe houses. Above, in higher hamlets, amber fields of wheat sheathe the mountain slopes.

A ninety-year-old man came out to greet me as I arrived in Marián. Speaking in Quechua, he told about his father, who had been a companion of Atusparia, the Indian leader who led the 1885 uprising in the valley, whose birthplace was this idyllic hamlet. The man led me to the tiny chapel. A large wooden cross rested against the outside next to the entrance to the chapel, now closed by a tin slab door. Inside, there was only a crucifix. All the niches for saints' images were empty. By now a small group of villagers were escorting me. They pointed to the broken windows and cracks in the chapel walls. "Air and dust enter, and so we have taken the saints to be lodged in our homes," one man said. "There used to be more authorities, including one who oversaw the chapel, but now they are dead."

They spoke of San Miguel, their patron saint, and decided to take me to visit him in a nearby house. Touching the image tenderly, San Miguel's keeper said, "Our patron is very miraculous. He was saved from the earthquake! We have much faith in him. He is a person like you. He comes to us in dreams and tells us what to do. We work with spirit because of him. We will build him a bigger and more beautiful chapel."

Another man said that there used to be a big cross that stood on a hill overlooking the hamlet. The bishop had had the cross removed, saying the people had lost respect for it by taking it down in procession and drinking along the way. Now Marián must depend on San Miguel for all its protection. "He is the one who most cares for us, watches over us. We have much veneration for him. Faith makes us think about him. You see his sword. He has over-thrown demons."

They told of the danger from "volcanoes of water," like Ra-taquenua, from which an alluvion had leapt in the last century, "in the time of the grandfathers of the grandfathers." They said they worked to drain the lakes, Llaca and Palukocha, above them, but the protection of the saints and the crosses was also needed. It was not enough to drain the lakes.

Just then some small boys who had been hunting birds and viscachas came in, and all together, in the amassing group, we went to visit other images quartered temporarily in the houses of Marián.

AFTER the earthquake, the old *Huaracino* priest of San Francisco had first held Mass in a prefabricated building the bishops of Chile had sent. Finally, he was able to build a tiny provisional adobe chapel and to whitewash it. He was still staving off CRYRZA, fighting to keep the land and to rebuild "on the very same place" as his beautiful church that had been destroyed.

One night, in an alcove in back of the altar of his tiny chapel, we talked for a long time. He believed the Catholic Church to be in the midst of a tremendous crisis. New currents of a materialist bent were telling the people that fiestas, processions, and the saints' images, dressed in wonderful clothes, were wasteful, he said. "They tell the *campesinos* that the rich have exploited them. They disparage the sacraments and say that we native priests are drones who believe in images which are just assemblages of wood or gypsum."

We walked to the front of the altar to look at Our Lady of Sorrows. He switched on a fluorescent light to reveal the beautiful robes the image was wearing. "Before the earthquake," he said, "we used to put on these robes only for fiestas. Now, one never knows, everything is so temporary that I have her wear them every day." On the right side of the altar was San Juan, also dressed up, holding a skull, and in the center, between the Virgin of Sorrows and San Juan, was the Child of Prague. I noticed that this image was wearing only its blond wig. The day before Christmas, when I had gone to Mass at 5:00 A.M., the image wore a dark-haired wig over the blond one. On that cold, rainy morning, the padre had sent a small boy to bring me to the back of the altar where he was preparing the *Niño de Prague*. I had taken it to be a saint, but he corrected me: "It is Jesus himself. Don't you see that he is a Jew? All Jews are gringos." With that, the padre had lifted up the long dark wig to reveal the blond curls.

The padre thought that all the new phrasings of the Church were in the end just new terms for saying the same thing, terms that Christ had never used, so why should they invent them now? In a sudden burst of optimism, he said that all this would pass and the *costumbres* would again be respected. As a precautionary measure, he added, "After carnival, though, I'll go up into the hamlets to collect the *cánticos* ["poetic songs" the *campesinos* sing in Quechua for Lent]. They should not be lost."

DOWN on the pampa of Huaraz, few houses remained in which saints could be sheltered. The house I lived in, in Huarupampa barrio, was one where every day I could observe the affection with which the big statue of the Virgin Mary Helper was treated. Some images had traveled to the outskirts of the pampa, like Claudia's San José. At almost the geographic center of Huaraz, in Belén, the intense sacristan, Norabuena, was giving refuge to many images, in a hut built for that purpose alone. There he was zealously guarding the treasured Virgin called *La Belenita*. Other images were in the ateliers of craftsmen and image makers.

No images were simply discarded. In both towns and hamlets, they were sequestered until the day they could be returned to newly built chapels and churches. In some cases, survivors subjected themselves to more risk in the aftermath than they would allow their images to endure. For example, in the town of Aija, I was told, an engineer had instructed the people to tear down their church because they were endangering their lives when they entered it. Refusing to destroy their church, they said they would keep using it until another was built. Nevertheless, they had removed their patron, Santiago, and other images to their homes.

Many instances demonstrated the individuality with which the saints were imbued. In one case, a small Virgin that had occupied a niche in a public building in Centenario had been packed up for the duration of the reconstruction. When a *campesina* came down with flowers for this particular Virgin, it was suggested that, instead, she take the flowers to a chapel and offer them to the Virgin there. She went away crestfallen, because it would not be the same.

Challenging the sense of the images as flesh-and-blood individuals, a priest, I was told, cut off the braid of one of the saints in a chapel he was visiting in the countryside. "You think these things are alive," he admonished. "They are only images." The worshipers went after him, took over the chapel, and ran him out of the hamlet. "Such," a churchman commented to me later about this incident, "is the resistance to Reform in the Church."

WHEN I first entered the Centenario church, the parish of the German priests of the Sacred Heart, I was struck by its austerity. Except for cracks in the concrete walls, it had remained intact. Dominating the rear wall behind the altar was a gargantuan crucifix, cubistic in its form. There were no other images or paintings, only the stark Christ figure on the cross.

After some twenty years at Centenario, the German priests had a comprehension of native religion that contrasted with the naive fervor of Reform personnel who had come after the earthquake to destroy with one blow all vestiges of *costumbrismo*. Though sympathetic to Reform, these Germans worked more slowly. Holy Week in the Callejón had always been elaborate, with many processions. Now Centenario, which took the lead in organizing Holy Week of 1971—the first after the earthquake—planned that there be only two processions. Above all, the procession of the Holy Sepulcher, in which Christ was carried solemnly in a coffin to the sound of drumrolls and a funeral dirge, should not be held. "The mystery of Christ does not end in suffering and death," a nun at Centenario told me. "We must take away all that foments a spirit of suffering."

The German priests planned a simple celebration for Palm Sunday. Beginning in Nicrupampa, they blessed the palms, and then a procession proceeded to the church in Centenario. Along the way, people stopped from time to time, singing and praying for the Reconstruction, reciting all the marvelous intentions for Huaraz. This was new, the first time such secular commentary had taken place within a Holy Week procession.

In the center of Huaraz, however, the Holy Week plans broke down. Rubble still mounted high, worshipers cut paths for processions. "All the images were broken, and still they carried them. That caused me great pain," Father Auscario, the German priest I knew best, told me.

And Holy Week of 1972 was almost like those before the earthquake. Again, the Germans blessed the palms in Nicrupampa, but this time, when the secularized procession arrived at Centenario, it was met by a group of *campesinos* who had come from Patay with a band of musicians and a man riding on a donkey. The old and the new met head-on. Despairingly, the nun said, "It is just a symbol. The *campesinos* don't have to come every year with someone actually mounted on a donkey."

During the first part of Holy Week, 1972, I was still stranded in Lima because of the excessive rains in the sierra. It was noon of Holy Thursday before I could get back by plane. On the road from the airstrip at Anta to the pampa, we saw men dressing a *chuncho*, an image representing a Roman soldier. Talking excitedly in the *colectivo*, the passengers commented on the different images that appeared during Holy Week, wondering where they were lodged and whether they would be able to take part. Over the following days, I would overhear comments like "Oh, it must have been lost in the earthquake!" when a certain image did not appear or "That is the image from Belén. Usually the one from San Francisco comes out now." In the aftermath, even the saints were seen to be behaving strangely, emerging from unexpected places or not emerging at all.

On the night of Holy Thursday at Soledad, the Lord of Solitude was draped in black, and the atmosphere was that of a wake. "It is presumed that the Lord of Solitude is now the Lord of Nazareth," Reyna said. An image of the Lord of Nazareth stood on an *anda*, a large platform on which images are carried in procession. His hands were tied in front of him with a rope. "Usually his hands are tied with a chain," someone commented, "but it must have been lost in the earthquake."

Near the Lord of Nazareth, on another platform, was the Virgin of Sorrows, which I remembered from San Francisco. Two other *andas* held images of Mary Magdalene and of John, the Apostle. Worshipers stopped to kiss their robes. In a quiet vigil, mainly *campesinos* sat huddled on the ground around candles burning on the dirt floor.

Finally, Padre Espinoza, in his black pants and black turtleneck, began to speak. "This is the night of the abandoned and forgotten Christ, the Christ of Soledad," he was saying. I was distracted by whispering about the padre and CRYRZA. Like the

Spanish Franciscans, Espinoza believed in "works" and had started to make his own bricks to rebuild his church. Apparently there had been an altercation—some said it had come to blows—between him and CRYRZA.

By now it was getting close to midnight, and the procession from Soledad to San Francisco was to take place at about 3:30 A.M. Since I did not want to miss it and was exhausted from the abrupt change in altitude, I went back to my room to get some rest.

I awoke to the sound of what seemed to be the low drumroll of a funeral march. Looking out onto the patio, however, I could see candles flickering in the room below and the men kneading the dough for the morning's bread. It had been the rhythmic kneading I'd heard.

It was biting cold at this hour. I hurried over to San Francisco, to which the procession had already arrived. The images that had been at Soledad were on their *andas*, which were covered and resting in front of the tiny whitewashed chapel. *Campesinos*, in their heavy brown wool ponchos, were asleep on the ground next to the platforms. Small groups stood over fires making punch to warm those who were keeping the all-night vigil. Townspeople conversed quietly about the images—which ones had been "injured," which ones were "missing," and which "had died" in the disaster. As dawn broke over the moonlit, frozen pampa, the ice-blue contours of Huascarán were sketched upon the iridescent sky.

About 7:00 A.M., I went back to my room to wash and make coffee and prepare for the activities of Good Friday. Radio Huascarán announced that the Association of the Lord of Solitude, "in order to preserve our *costumbres*," was inviting the civil and military authorities to the day's processions.

At about 10:00 A.M., the procession of the "Judged Christ" began to march from San Francisco. I spotted Doña Angelita, frail beside the Virgin's platform, shielding her eyes from the bright sun. Next came a huge *anda* on which Christ was surrounded by all the *chunchos*. Some twenty-five bearers, mainly *campesinos*, staggered under the weight of the platform. Bands of Indian musicians played. It was a slow march, with many interruptions. Finally, as three o'clock drew near, the retinue rounded the central plaza and headed up to Soledad. "There," a lady near me remarked, "they used to nail Christ to a cross, but no more. It is not so real now."

Feeling dizzy with heat and altitude, I again returned to my room and didn't set out until 7:00 P.M. At Soledad, the images were placed as they had been the night before. This time, Padre Quintana was preaching, reprimanding the *anda* bearers for having gotten drunk. He went on to tackle the gossip and dissension over the reconstruction that he felt were consuming everyone. He announced Mass for Saturday night, and the crowd dispersed, people asking each other about the procession of the Holy Sepulcher. They missed most this procession, during which they would weep over the dead Christ. "Before the earthquake, it was incomparable!" a townswoman exclaimed. "There was nothing to match it anywhere. People came from all over, from Yungay, Caraz. At Soledad, they would unnail Christ from the cross and put him in the coffin and carry him through the streets of Huaraz. It is very different now."

At Soledad that Saturday night before Easter, Padre Espinoza was preaching: "From out of the ruins, the new city of Huaraz will arise. All of the barrios will live again: Soledad, San Francisco, Belén, and Huarupampa." It was as if Centenario did not exist. It was midnight, and a light rain was falling as I walked over to San Francisco. The tiny chapel was filled with clergy. The American Benedictines had come down from Los Pinos, and the bishop had come. Quintana and the other Spanish Franciscans were there. Only the two polar extremes of Catholicism in Huaraz were missing: the priest of Soledad and the Germans of Centenario. When I left the chapel, in the early-morning hours, the clouds had moved beyond the moon, and the pampa, with its few ghostly ruins, shone in the moonlight.

By 9:00 A.M. on Easter Sunday, the procession was coming down from Soledad toward the plaza, Christ down Bolívar and the Virgin down Calle Sucre. Bands preceded the platforms, which were enveloped in eddies of incense. People poured onto the pampa. At the central plaza, the two *andas* confronted each other. First, the platform bearing the Lord of the Resurrection swayed and retreated, simulating Christ bowing to his Mother. Then Mary's platform did the same. Doves, placed in a basket beneath her gown, were released at this moment. "What joy!" exclaimed a woman standing next to me. Others near me murmured that it was a pity that the Virgin, in her encounter with her Risen Son, was still wearing her mourning clothes. They speculated that her beautiful white veil had been destroyed in the earthquake.

As the *andas* began their journey back to Soledad, a holiday air filled the plaza. "Ice creams Los Andes!" shouted a vendor. The prefect sat nodding to the crowd on a little balcony attached to a building that had been split down the middle, a strange half-building where you could see the rooms inside, like a doll's house. Boys perched in the trees like birds to watch the festivities.

It was a gentle, sunny day. Just the day before, the roads to the coast had opened, and the sweet smell of gasoline was in the air. I ran into my good friends, Teófines and Juan Manuel, and we decided to celebrate by taking a ride in Teófines's truck, nicknamed *La Guinda*. He slid a cassette into his tape deck, and as we bounced along the road toward Monterrey, "Jesus Christ, Superstar" blared out upon the valley.

Twenty-one

THE CATECHISTS

We ourselves are the images of God.
Jesusa of Secsecpampa

Most of the more radical Catholic workers had left the valley, discouraged by the complexities they confronted in the sierra. Some had been recalled for being too leftist. Four of these were priests who worked in Recuay who were labeled "priests connected to Peking." "They don't want to hear anything about the saints, the images, or churches," people said. "They dress in shirtsleeves."

The Centenario Church of the Sacred Heart took upon itself the task of bringing down the *costumbres*. It is not surprising that the Reform movement found its most ardent sympathizers among the German clergy of Centenario, inasmuch as this parish was already "without images." Knowing, though, the religious practices of the valley, as the recent outsiders had not, the Centenario priests proceeded with prudence. Nevertheless, the process of Reform—

conscientización—was not accomplished without taking its toll of confusion, doubt, and uncertainty among the *campesinos*.

I began to feel the turmoil over the endeavor to rid the valley of "deformed religion" as I got to know well two catechists of Secsecpampa, Jesusa and Nicolás, Don Juan's sister-in-law and her husband, who were being trained in consciousness-raising at Centenario. That Don Juan was pulling in opposite directions from Jesusa and Nicolás over what constituted "the true religion" caused some strain among them. Yet Don Juan was very dependent on them and on Jesusa's mother—his mother-in-law—to help him care for his eight motherless children. And they did this lovingly. When we were all together, religious topics were usually avoided. I learned of the tensions in private talks with Don Juan and with Jesusa and Nicolás at their own house in Secsecpampa or during the many occasions when they visited me in my room on the pampa. Though cautiously feeling their way through the new religious instructions themselves, they nevertheless were trying to influence Don Juan.

I first got to know Jesusa and Nicolás at Don Juan's house in Secsecpampa. Jesusa, who is a curer, was frying guinea pigs over a fire in the patio in preparation for the birthday meal of Don Juan's son, Heliodoro. Her mother, the *abuela*, was spinning yarn, and the children were washing their faces in basins of water in the patio. Before I left, Jesusa offered to mix me just the right combination of herbs that would take away the heartache I must be feeling, being so far from home. Over the remaining months of my stay, I became very close to them and listened to their confusion over the new ideas of Catholic Reform.

One Sunday afternoon, when I found Don Juan's gate barred, I continued up to Jesusa's. She told me that Don Juan had gone to Mass at San Francisco, and then to buy a piglet. He never attended Mass at Centenario. As she sewed colorful borders on a *pollera*, she talked about curing, her methods of divination using a guinea pig, and of the herbal tonics that were especially effective against the "pain of the heart," a kind of deep nostalgia and longing that is prevalent in the valley. Laying down her sewing, she showed me a tiny piece of magnetic rock, kept to attract any envy that might enter the household, protecting the occupants against this significant cause of disease. "Just a little piece of magnetic rock will help," Jesusa explained, "but, for example, the Huascarán is too much of a magnet. It sucks your blood, and you can die rapidly."

"What do you think caused the earthquake, Jesusa?" I asked out of the blue.

"They say it's the bomb or a punishment of God. Maybe God is warning us of the Final Judgment," she replied.

At this point, Nicolás came in and sat down on his haunches against the stone wall. The house was damp and cold, and he pulled his wool cap down over his ears and began to voice his concerns about the fate of religious images. "We believe in images since the Conquest," he said. "The German priests don't know the history of Peru. They don't know about the Spaniards. Our great-grand-fathers, the Incas, did not know about our images either. But we have known that God exists through our images. We know that God died through our image of the Lord of Solitude. The German priests perhaps don't know that God has died." Pointing to a small wooden cross made by his grandfather, he added, "It is the same, the same as people."

"What is the difference between the crucifix of the Centenario church and the Lord of Solitude?" I asked Nicolás.

"The German one is without dress, and there are no wounds. The Señor de la Soledad is Christ himself. We are the same as he is. We do not know death without the image. We dream of the cross of Soledad. The Señor comes to us, perhaps to announce a misfortune."

They began to rhapsodize about the way Holy Week used to be before the earthquake. " 'Mourning' is what they called it," Nicolás said. "There were huge candles, ten feet tall, adorned with black paper, and we kept the all-night vigil near the crucified Christ. Now, since the earthquake, the priests prohibit these things."

"You see," Jesusa interjected, "everything our ancestors said would happen is happening."

"What did they say?" I asked.

"That no longer are we going to recognize images, not God, or where he lives. We are going to live just tranquilly, like animals. They said that no longer is one going to say that God exists or doesn't exist, but rather that we have been born just because. People are wondering if there is a God or not, or do I live for myself and nothing else? Is this possible, Barbara?"

I was often put on the spot in this way. Perhaps people felt that I, being from so far away, might have answers not readily evident in the crossfire of beliefs that prevailed in the aftermath.

Their son had told me that they spent weekends at Centenario, even sleeping overnight during catechism training sessions, and I asked what they were learning there. Nicolás answered that they were told that there were communists around who were materialists who worked without God. Christians, on the other hand, must not deny Christ but must know that he is in heaven. His image is only for the purpose of being acquainted with Christ, not to adore. "It is like a photograph of our mother," he elucidated. "We cannot talk directly to her photograph. It is just a reminder. And they say other images should not exist, nor fireworks and bands, because that is not devotion. The money for them vanishes in the air, and the poor remain."

Jesusa burst out, "Did you see the fireworks for the Virgin of Fatima?" Yes, I remembered being awakened in the middle of the night by bands playing. I looked out of my window to see the most astonishing fireworks I had ever witnessed. Sparks swirled round and round against the black sky, exploding into ever larger canopies of color that drifted slowly down, emblazing the empty pampa.

"Wasn't it beautiful, all the colors!" Jesusa exclaimed. "It is for the people—the eyes of people are made happy—but they want to do away with the fireworks."

She asked if there were images in my country. I said yes, but we did not take them out in procession. "Ah-ha." Nicolás nodded with recognition. "That's exactly what the priests want now, that we leave them in their chapels."

By July 1972, Jesusa and Nicolás were more deeply involved in the consciousness-raising enterprise. Two of five catechists in Secsecpampa, they had garnered the support of some 30 of the hamlet's 100 adults. The split between the catechists and the traditional Catholics, which erupted over the disposition of the mountain crosses at carnival, was becoming more pronounced. One of the Centenario priests had been stoned and since then had refused to say Mass in the chapel in Secsecpampa. Rather, he came once a month to say Mass at Jesusa and Nicolás's house. To protect the priest, they would meet him at Monterrey and then, after the Mass, walk him back down the mountain. "Catechists believe in loving each other," Jesusa said, "and we want to have fiestas without drunkenness. We can tell jokes, laugh and be happy, and even dance quietly, but then go home at a certain hour. The noncatechists are falling down drunk, fighting each other."

The division between catechists and noncatechists had also made inroads into the ancient system of contributing one's labor to public works. The catechists had refused to help the noncatechists in the repair of a road. The authorities had leveled a fine of 200 *soles* against them. But then, the traditional Catholics had not assisted in the digging of an irrigation ditch. "They call us Evangelicals," Jesusa said, "but we are Catholics and know how to speak, and we are fighting against that fine. After all, our irrigation work canceled out their road work."

On July 18 the couple dropped by my room. They seemed more confident about their instruction at Centenario. "We ourselves are the images of God," Jesusa said. "There is no need for other representations." Yet, never completely free of conflict between their traditional beliefs and the new ideas of Catholic Reform to which they were exposed at Centenario, they began to waver. Jesusa said it was true that the images were like family members. One encounters friends and family in dreams, and the images also appear before you and talk to you in dreams. It is the spirits or souls of friends and family that come in dreams, and therefore, the couple reasoned, the images must likewise have their spiritual counterpart and not be merely inert matter.

"For example," Jesusa recalled, "during one period of my life I had a terrible sadness; I walked around crying all day. And then one night I dreamed of Jesus of Nazareth, alive, walking toward me, a beautiful arch of flowers over his head. I stopped and greeted him. 'Lord,' I asked him, 'why can't I die and go with you?' And he told me, 'Don't cry. Why are you crying? Why are you suffering so? Hush, you *are* with me.' That's the way he spoke to me; I remember so well. When I woke up, I felt tranquil. I said, 'Lord, if I am with you, must you not be here in your images? You are in heaven, and you are on earth, too.' "

"But, of course," Nicolás said, "the images do not do miracles." When they would explain this to the villagers, however, they would call Jesusa and Nicolás Protestants. "They don't understand," Jesusa said. "They tell us we are kissing the ass of the devil. Even Don Juan calls us Evangelicals. Who knows where he will end up in all this? And he, who is a man who can read! They say we live by the explanations of the priests. The Protestants are the real materialists! They don't even agree that there *are* saints."

I learned that day that the matter of the communal labor on

public works had not been resolved and was tearing the hamlet apart. The chapel in Secsecpampa had been padlocked by the catechists so that the noncatechists could not enter. Then the noncatechists seized the man with the key, tied him up, and locked the catechists out of the chapel.

Nicolás enumerated a number of hamlets in which similar events were occurring: Aclla, Chúrup, Chontayok, Chicnay, Ukru, Paccha, Unchus, wherever there were catechists. "They do not understand us." Jesusa sighed. "They spend all their time drinking, and in one hamlet they spent eight thousand *soles* on fireworks for one night."

They told me that soon Padre Auscario of Centenario, the bishop, and the subprefect of Ancash would come to Secsecpampa to hold a meeting in the plaza. "They want to see why all this hate exists," Jesusa concluded, and we turned to other subjects.

WHEN the new bishop, a Jesuit from Arequipa, arrived in Huaraz in November 1971, the task he confronted was not easy. He had to attune himself to all the strains of Catholicism as well as the new religions that came in on the coattails of the disaster. He must embody the theology of liberation while not alienating a valley steeped in ancient indigenous belief as well as the Catholicism of the Conquest. As a representative of the newly politicized Latin American Church, he was also expected to be a spokesman for the "sacred" mission of the Reconstruction. He had to mediate the differences among the four traditional barrios of Huaraz and the conflict between those barrios and the progressive outlying barrio of Centenario, which had ascended to a certain preeminence upon the destruction of the central core of Huaraz. His constituency comprised the smallest hamlets in the heights and the destroyed towns of the valley, monolingual Quechua-speaking *campesinos* and mestizos, as well as the politicians and military personnel from the coast.

It was fitting that the new bishop chose to occupy a compound of *módulos* within the survivor camp of Nicrupampa, in which diverse predisaster social and economic classes now commingled. In the religious sphere, also, Nicrupampa sheltered survivors from all the barrio churches, *campesinos* from the surrounding hamlets, and converts to the new Protestant sects, most of which had established their houses of worship in *módulos* in the camp.

After attending the inauguration of the bishop on the pampa in November 1971, I made an attempt to talk with him in December, but he was traveling in the province of Yungay at the time I called at his *módulo*. The priests I found that December afternoon in the humble episcopate in Nicrupampa seemed to span the centuries since their counterparts had made the first calls at the newly conquered Indian hamlets. They were persisting in the task of conversion begun then, only now with a kind of melancholy recognition of the immensity of their endeavor. The vicar, second to the bishop in religious authority, was especially articulate. "We warn the *campesinos* not to enter their chapels, the ones that are dangerously falling down after the earthquake, but they go, anyway. They go because of their images."

Leaning over his desk, the vicar confided, "Their religiosity is profound, but it should not be confused with Catholicism. The religious man believes in whatever satisfies him. Our missionaries have never really effected the work of conversion."

Imagining the missions of the sixteenth century, the vicar reconstructed a scene he felt must have been typical: "The early missionary asks the Indian, 'What does this idol do?' The Indian answers, 'It saves me from frosts and hail.' The friar, replacing the idol with a crucifix, says, 'Christ also protects.' Then the friar adds another factor: 'Your idol has not died for you. Christ has died for you.' But for the Indian it is not Christ but *that particular* Christ, and for him there are as many Christs as there are crucifixes."

The vicar compared the attempt to convert the *campesinos* to a "true" Catholicism to the political movement. "Like the agrarian reform," he said, "it crushes, but only superficially. It does not really arrive at the core of the problem. In religion, it is even more difficult. We don't arrive at their souls."

After that visit to the episcopate, I made no attempt to talk to the bishop until the end of July 1972. On the basis of remarks I would hear about him, reports of things he had said, I felt we were in some way engaged in the same process, of trying to see the big picture of the aftermath. I remembered Pilatos, the image maker, saying, regarding the plans for Holy Week, that the bishop had declared, "It is not necessary to take away from the people tradition in one blow." Now it seemed it was finally time for me to compare notes with the bishop.

So, on July 31, late in the afternoon in his darkening *módulo*, we finally spoke. He began by telling me the immense impact that coming to the destroyed valley had had on him. He wanted to know the whole valley well and had traveled far and wide, up and down. He projected the years ahead, when he might penetrate more deeply into the beliefs and sentiments of the *campesinos*. He had already learned, for example, that the shepherds near the puna of Chiquián place a small stone sheep among the potato plants to ensure an abundant harvest.

Caught up in the saga over the crosses at carnival, he had thought much about the mingling of the sacred and the profane. "Here, more than elsewhere in Peru, they 'play' in front of the cross, and here, too, the personification of religious images is more pronounced. They treat the image as if it were the saint. They give it a personality, and they do not tolerate that one image be substituted for another." He cited a recent instance in which a priest had sent to Lima for "beautiful artistic" images of San Antonio to replace the "frightfully ugly" and broken images of the saint the people carried in little baskets to Mass for a blessing. But the new images were rejected.

In the hamlet of Huata just the day before, the villagers had spoken to the bishop of their patron saint and specified its "brothers" and "cousins" that were located in nearby hamlets. My mind drifted to the seventeenth-century treatises on the extirpation, where missionaries reported with dismay that the *huacas* of the Indians had brothers and other relatives. I, too, heard so often of the brothers and sons and even grandfathers of a certain image. Perhaps this sense of the "concrete" has become even more vibrant, I was thinking, with the destruction of the physical world. Perhaps, too, the genealogies, the connections of one image to another, have been enhanced, just as survivors have counted their relatives and renewed their bonds to others.

"How should all the changes in the Church take place?" I asked the bishop.

"I think there have been grave errors committed," he lamented, "by the priests and workers who have come after the earthquake and have tried to impose the changes. They want to change everything violently. And that has produced a reaction. The opposite of what they want has occurred. Change must be a very slow process, that will take us many years, and it must be carried out with much

affection." I had never precisely put those two words together—
affection and change (*cariño* and *cambio*)—as the bishop was doing now.

"For example," he went on, "the other day we were talking in
a hamlet. The villagers wanted all the prayers to be in Latin. And
my vicar asked them, 'How did you come up to this hamlet ten
years ago?'

" 'On a donkey or on foot,' they answered.

" 'And how do you come up now?'

" 'In trucks.'

" 'Then you have changed your custom, no?'

" 'Yes, Padre.'

" 'Well, the Church, too, is changing.'

"We must make very concrete comparisons, taken from the
world in which they live. This presupposes much affection. . . .
To speak to them and to achieve change, there must be love, and
they must perceive the affection. Then they can change. . . . All
of this means much patience, many hours. I am not in a hurry."

I brought up Secsecpampa. The bishop felt that the Centenario
catechistic enterprise was too harsh. "Our people are very sensitive,
wounded easily by even a raised voice," he said. "We must be more
patient." Then, smiling, he added, "And the catechists can be a
little puritanical, too. If I go, I will take a drink with the villagers.
It is important, because drinking from the same cup for them is to
participate in their joy, to be a member of their family . . . and
dancing, too, is for them a sign of the soul's joy."

As I left, the bishop said he planned to go to Secsecpampa on
August 8 to try to bring together the two factions, the traditionalists
and the catechists. I told him I would be there.

WHEN I arrived in Secsecpampa on the morning of August 8, I
found the paths leading to the central plaza decorated with arches
of lilies. During the colonial period, the paths were lined with
flowers, too, but then the Indian authorities would kneel and kiss
the hands of the priests. Now, of that custom, only the floral arches
remained, and the bishop took them as a sign of affection.

As I stood in the plaza, I saw the bishop and the subprefect
walk down the path beneath the arches and into the little chapel.
The men of Secsecpampa sat in the front of the chapel, and the

women and children crowded into the back. It was noisy, babies crying and the women chattering in Quechua. The subprefect was calling for the unification of the hamlet, promising to cancel the fines to the catechists for not helping with the road work and not to speak of them again. There should be no need to if everyone worked together amicably.

Then the bishop spoke. "Don't insult each other," he was saying. "Unite. The way your priest talks to you, the way he explains things to you, is good."

A man shouted, "Yes, Padre Auscario is trying to make of us one body." Others grumbled.

"We must try to accept the changes," the bishop continued. "They are not happening only here. The Church is changing all over the world."

When we all knelt down on the earthen floor to say the Lord's Prayer, silence finally prevailed. In this tiny chapel in the Andes, the edicts of Rome, the new equality and brotherhood of men on earth, sought to take root in the momentary silence.

But as soon as we were all on our feet again, the bickering began anew, rumbling through the group. Looking sad, the bishop raised his voice to be heard, promising to come to Secsecpampa again to say a solemn Mass only after he heard that everyone was united and treating each other like brothers.

Afterward, I went with Don Juan to his house for lunch. He didn't think the meeting had resolved anything. Nothing would change, he said, his voice full of resignation. Margarita, his two-year-old, played in the patio, her cheeks chapped with the cold and sun and encrusted with earth. Shanti's hair had been cut. The *abuela* was gay and playful as usual. Swishing her skirts in the manner of a cancan, she danced out of the patio, saying she wished I would marry her seventeen-year-old grandson, Heliodoro, and live with them forever. The time for my departure was drawing near. Wondering how I would ever be able to leave the valley, I tarried this time at Don Juan's until long after dark.

The next day, Jesusa and Nicolás came to see me. Commenting on the meeting the day before, they reasoned that in such a small hamlet there simply could not be two opposing groups. "We have to be united in order to work peacefully together. But they keep calling us Evangelicals." Jesusa sighed, throwing up her arms.

"And, in the end, none of us really fulfills our obligations, not the catechists or the noncatechists or the Evangelicals."

"Fulfill obligations?" I asked.

"Yes, somehow none of us really knows how to love one another as we should. We don't know how to love our fellow human beings, and now the Final Judgment is near, and we must try to understand how to do this."

Twenty-two

THE CROSSES

*The Indians worshiped them [*huacas*] as guardians of the town. These* huacas *were disposed of like all the rest and crosses were put in their places.*

Pablo José de Arriaga,
in the year 1621

Uno no puede estar desamparado del todo. (*"We cannot be completely forsaken."*)

campesinos of Secsecpampa, 1972

THE FIRST INDICATION I had of the importance of belief in supernatural protection against the environmental hazards of the valley came early in my stay, from the old priest-archaeologist Padre Soriano. He said that in February, during carnival time, the Indians from the surrounding countryside would bring down into the valley towns their big mountain crosses, which during the year stood on hilltops above their hamlets, defending their *chacras* from hail and landslides and ensuring plentiful crops. They would take them to the churches for a special Mass, during which the crosses would be blessed by the priest, and then return them to their places of vigil on the mountaintops for another year. The bearers and followers of the crosses would get drunk, throw flour and water at each other, and in general participate in the license of carnival. For 400 years, it had been this way in the valley,

the crosses making their journey to the town centers for their blessing and back again to the mountains. "These are their *costumbres*,"
the padre said.

Before the Conquest, he explained, the Indians celebrated with
great merriment in front of their idols. No doubt, I thought, some
of the stone images in front of which the Indians had celebrated
were the very ones the padre had described as dancing on the
gelatinous earth as the doves took flight on May 31, 1970; the same
ones that now stood outside in his patio. After the Conquest, the
friars substituted crosses for the stone-idol guardians of the hilltops,
and the people began to feast these crosses.

The early Spanish missionaries threatened with divine punishment the revelry that took place around both crosses and saints'
images. They especially exhorted their new converts to commem-
orate the Holy Cross with solemnity on September 14, the day of
its exaltation. This day, every year, they said, would mark the
triumph over idolatry. During the colonial period, however, the
Festival of the Cross was shifted to coincide with the universal pre-
Lenten carnival, which, in turn, fell about the time fiestas had been
held before the ancient *huacas*.[1]

Padre Soriano's scholarly exposition did not fully prepare me
for the weeks preceding carnival of 1972, as Catholic Reform made
its influence felt and sought to wrest the cross, once and for all,
from its connection to carnival. Using as a springboard the moratorium that had been placed on all festivities for the year following
the disaster, the Reform, backed by the civil authorities, forbade
that the crosses leave their mountain enclaves to enter the valley
towns.

All had been quiet during the year of moratorium, but now,
the second year after the earthquake, it became clear that the disaster and the year of official mourning had only temporarily subdued the *costumbres*. Carnival day, the day before Ash Wednesday,
the beginning of Lent, fell on Tuesday, February 15, in 1972. By
the end of January, the carnival season was well under way. My
landlady told me the mountain crosses would descend for their
church blessing on the Sunday before carnival day. They would
then return to their hamlets for their *colocación* ("replacement"). On
carnival day, the big town crosses would be carried across the
pampa, where they would meet in the Plaza de Armas.

"Already they are playing with water," she remarked, having seen balloons filled with water burst in the market. Buckets of water used to be thrown on passersby from the balconies of Huaraz. "Of course, we don't really know what will happen this year," she lamented. "Nothing is definite anymore. We used to know when and where things would take place."

On February 2, two weeks before carnival, I got the first sign that the crosses might not descend. I was visiting Unchus, above Huaraz. A villager was telling me, "Already the festivities were slacking off even before the earthquake, and afterward, even more. Now the priest only comes up here for a payment of 600 *soles*, and he spends all his time scolding us." For carnival, he said, they used to begin to keep watch over their crosses days ahead of time, burning candles in front of the crosses in the hamlet chapel, to which they were brought from the hilltops. But this year the priests had locked the chapel doors. "Then we would take our crosses down to Soledad so that Padre Espinoza could give them their Mass and bless them. But last year, and now again, the padre has said he would not bless them. He might even lock them up until the 'real' day of the cross in September."

Back down in Huaraz, I mentioned what I had heard about the crosses to Don Antonio, in his store on Centenario, where I used to buy some of my staples. "Yes," he said, "people say the earthquake was a punishment because our festivals, even carnival, were being criticized, but I believe it was nature." I walked to the market, which was beginning to look very festive. Sheep's heads for soup graced the stalls, cutout paper decorations hung overhead, and a band was playing that would continue late into the night.

By Sunday, February 6, the market was full of *campesinos* carrying armfuls of *machitu*, a plant that grows only between rock slabs high up on the Cordillera Blanca. Customarily, the leaves of this plant are painted silver and used to decorate the mountain crosses before their journey. Burros laden with *machitu* nudged their way through the market and onto Avenida Centenario. I overheard a group of *campesinos* speaking in Quechua:

"Let's go to decorate the cross," one said.

"Let's do it," another agreed.

"Come, and we will prepare a meal," a third added.

I had decided to explore the hamlets on the slopes in back of the Hotel Monterrey and headed out to Monterrey in a *colectivo*. All along the road young revelers splashed us with muddy water tossed from buckets through the car's windows. This was to be my first visit to Secsecpampa and the day I would meet Don Juan.

Secsecpampa is half an hour's walk up a narrow, winding path behind the Hotel Monterrey. At a small clearing on the hillside, called Huicos, I ran into about a dozen *campesinos* who were clearing the path of stones and leveling it. When I asked why they were working on the path, they answered that it was their *costumbre* to repair the path on the Sunday before carnival weekend in order that the crosses might descend without incident on the following Sunday. They quickly added that the crosses would probably not pass on the trail this year, as they had been prohibited from taking them to Huaraz. The terrain was very steep there, and one of the men pointed to a huge wooden cross high above, atop a hill that served as Secsecpampa's cemetery. The man who seemed to be in charge of the work crew said they were readying the path whether or not the crosses descended. Perhaps they would simply carry the crosses up and down on the path if they could not go to Huaraz with them. "The priest said he would not come to Secsecpampa to bless the crosses either, though perhaps he will come," the man added. At any rate, they would carry on, and he would begin to decorate one of the crosses early on Thursday morning.

On the hillside at Huicos were the ruins of an adobe chapel that had collapsed during the earthquake. One of the work crew, a young man, seventeen years old, said his father was the *dueño* ("owner") of San Miguel, who had occupied the chapel. This boy introduced himself as Heliodoro Durán and invited me up to meet his father in Secsecpampa. This is how I came to know Juan Durán, who became one of my main *campesino* informants and a faithful friend whom I respected without reservation and whose entire family I grew to love. Out of this respect and affection, I always called him "Don" Juan.

As Heliodoro and I proceeded up the path, I asked him why they were working on it when in all probability the crosses would not come down. He answered that they were doing it "in order to imitate the "ancient ones" (*los antiguos*), and then he began to speak of the *costumbres*. Their musical bands, their dances—these things replicated the "customs of before," recalling the ancient times. I asked him if in his heart he really believed in the crosses and the saints, or was it just tradition. Without hesitation, he replied that in his heart he believed. "The German priests of Centenario want to take away our saints. They want us to go directly to Jesus Christ. They say the saints can't do miracles, but they *do*. They answer our prayers."

Upon arriving at Don Juan's house, a compound of adobe rooms surrounding a muddy patio, Heliodoro introduced his father to me as the *teniente gobernador*. This meant Don Juan held the most prestigious office in Secsecpampa and served as liaison between the hamlet and the Huaraz authorities. Inviting me into the patio, Don Juan introduced himself as "a true Catholic." What would happen over the crosses was evidently foremost on his mind, and as we sat on big rocks in his patio, the sixty-four-year-old man spoke mainly of this:

> We want to carry our crosses to Huaraz so that the padre can say a Mass for them. Or, at the least, let the padre come here to say a Mass. We want to do this because it is our *costumbre* since the Spanish Conquest, since the time of the Incas. This is the first year that the Church prohibits this. It didn't happen last year because of the mourning, but by now we should be "normalizing." This is the cross of Our Lord, where his blood was spilled. . . . If they say that we profane the cross, let the padre come early before the fiesta to say Mass so that our little ones can hear it. These priests are crushing the true religion, carrying us into paganism. It is all right that they upbraid us, but they are trying to make us forget the Christian religion.

Don Juan's earnest lament suddenly turned into quiet laughter as he fondly recalled the old days, when the priests would come to reprehend them for drinking. "They would compare us to donkeys, and we would all 'convert' on the spot! How beautiful it was!" His brow furrowing again, he said that things were more serious now. The priests refused to come, and furthermore, they made laws that forbade the *costumbres*.

He told me that the lieutenant governors of all the hamlets above Huaraz had agreed that morning to protest the prohibition on the descent of the crosses. They would first register their complaint with the mayor of Huaraz and the prefect of the Department of Ancash, and then, if that had no effect, they would go all the way to Lima, demanding that the monsignor order the valley priests to say Masses for the crosses. The protest in Huaraz would be made at four o'clock on the following day, just six days before the crosses were scheduled to come down.

"Maybe the authorities of the other hamlets will let me speak for all of them," Don Juan wondered aloud, showing me the diploma that Secsecpampa had won on Christmas Day for the Dance of the Angels they had performed beneath the cupola in Huaraz. "This dance shows the way the angels tried to be in contact with God," he said, and only then did we turn to other subjects.

Don Juan's wife had recently died, at age forty-one, leaving him with eight children, one of them two-year-old Margarita, who was playing nearby. She wore a little apron over her tiny *pollera*. She was covered with mud and from time to time would fling her small arms across Don Juan's knees. His wife had worked very hard, he told me, and it was probably the carrying of a heavy load of alfalfa down to Huaraz that had made her ill. His wife's mother, whom I came to call "grandmother" (*abuela*), was eighty-four years old and came every day to help look after the children.

Don Juan took me into his room, where he and all the children slept together on a wooden platform, "embracing one another" against the cold, beneath heavy woolen blankets. In the dark room, he showed me a small cross and a small image of the Virgin. The Virgin would perhaps grant that he find work in Huaraz the following day. And then soon the villagers of Secsecpampa would have to bring down the big crosses from the hilltops, decorate them, and begin the candlelight vigil over them in the chapel. As I left, knowing I would return time and time again to Don Juan's house, he said, "After all, the crosses stop up the glacial lakes" ("*Las cruces tapan las lagunas*").

ON February 8, I went to ask the Spanish Franciscans in Huarupampa what they felt about the prohibition of the crosses. "There should not be this union of carnival with the cross," one of them said. "It blasphemes the cross. The *campesinos* can celebrate the cross on September 14. And from now on they must hold their fiestas in the hamlets. The crosses cannot come to Huaraz anymore.

The custom was broken last year, and it must remain broken."
Padre Efraín explained that the ancient Peruvians used to pile stone
upon stone on the mountaintops and fete their ancestors in front
of these cairns (*apachetas*). The early missionaries inserted crosses
into the *apachetas* and turned the celebrations into a thanksgiving
for good crops. That had given the ancient fiestas a "modern sense,"
and now the Church was trying to "modernize" them further.[2]

At noon on Thursday, February 10, in the building where the
Soledad priest lived, I happened to sit next to an old woman from
the hamlet of Killesh, who had come to get a copy of her birth
certificate. As we both waited for the padre, she leaned over and
confided that the priest of San Francisco had agreed to go to Killesh
on Saturday to say a Mass for the crosses. When Padre Espinoza
came out, he would not talk to me about the crosses, saying only
his familiar "There should not be diversion in times of war," referring to the tensions between the people and CRYRZA over the
reconstruction.

From Soledad, I took a bus out to Monterrey and walked up
to Secsecpampa. When I arrived, Don Juan was in his patio, dec-
orating the smaller crosses that belonged in his household. He had
just finished "arming" the one that had belonged to his wife. The
children were handing him pieces of *machitu*, and he admonished
them to hand him only healthy and fat fragments of the plant.
When he had finished lashing the *machitu* to his wooden cross, he
tied tufts of rosemary at either end. The grandmother, who spoke
only Quechua, sat nearby on the ground, spinning yarn.

Don Juan said that the lieutenant governors of the hamlets had
not been able to make their protest in Huaraz the preceding Monday, as the municipal agent had been off working in his *chacra*.
Resigned, he said with a sigh, "The Holy Cross, may God's will
be done. . . . Perhaps God does not want the crosses to go down
to the town. . . ." Instructing me, he said the next step was to paint
the *machitu* leaves with a silver paint made from a very fine powder.

Heliodoro asked if I would like to visit the principal crosses
of Secsecpampa, the ones that had been brought down from the
mountaintops. I happily agreed, realizing I was being swept into
the drama of the crosses, becoming more and more determined to
follow every lead and learn as much as I could of the events and
sentiments surrounding them.

Heliodoro and I climbed higher up in the vertical hamlet, to the house of Calixto Campos. In his patio, an enormous wooden cross, twelve feet long, lay across two wooden frames. Bent over the cross, Calixto was meticulously attaching clumps of *machitu*. Small children were playing in the mud, teasing a scrawny dog. Campos's wife peered from the doorway of their small house, which was dwarfed by the big wooden cross lying in front of it. Against the house stood another large, unadorned cross, with only a small bunch of flowers tied at the bottom. The cross Campos labored over had replaced this one, whose "arm," he said, was broken.

No sooner had Heliodoro introduced me than Calixto Campos said, "The three big crosses of Secsecpampa shielded us from the earthquake. They are very miraculous. They *must* be blessed." I passed on the news I had heard at Soledad about Killesh, that the priest at San Francisco had agreed to go there to bless the crosses. Instantly, Calixto and Heliodoro began to plan how they might carry Secsecpampa's crosses to Killesh for their blessing. The paths upon which they would pass seemed very important to them. They could not carry the crosses along roads that had not been properly prepared. Also, it was significant that the *vestido* (the adornment—literally, "dress") of the crosses be blessed. The "body of the cross" had received many benedictions, but its adornments were renewed every year.

Lashing the last bits of *machitu* to the huge cross, Calixto said he had a small cross inside, which was "the child" of the big one. Little by little, I was learning of these familial relationships among crosses and saints' images. Don Juan had also spoken of the "brothers" and "children" of the crosses, told where each one was located, and he did the same for the *santos*. The image of San Cayetano, the patron saint of Secsecpampa, he had told me, had its "brothers." Some of these "relatives" occupied the same hamlet, others nearby villages, and a few even resided in distant coastal towns.[3]

"These crosses reveal things to us in dreams," Calixto said. "If you lose something, by asking the cross you may find it. And they tell us if someone wants to rob our houses." He always says a prayer to the old cross that stands in his patio before he goes down to work on the coast, and he returns home safely. "But they must have music. We must play our flutes in front of them and dance."

Just then a villager passed by. He stopped to ask Calixto what they should do if they could not get the crosses blessed in Huaraz and the priest refused to come to Secsecpampa. "The cross is protecting us from the rains," the man observed, oblivious of my presence, and then he suggested that the *Secsecpampinos* themselves could perhaps say a rosary in front of the crosses. "Your uncle was a priest. Couldn't you say the litany?" the man asked. "It's not the same," Calixto answered. "The crosses should have many Masses. The more the better."

Then the two older men and Heliodoro began to speak of the dangers of the glacial lakes on the Cordillera Blanca. "It is not Huascarán, but *under* Huascarán that is the most dangerous," the passerby said. Now including me, he explained, "And above us, you see, is Acuacqucha. It is a magnet. It draws us in if we get too close, or it comes down on top of us." The crosses, they said, offered some measure of protection against these hazards. Heliodoro interjected, "Perhaps with so many engineers now, they will dominate Huascarán."

"*Shapinko* [the Devil] appears in the waterfalls from the cordillera. He wears a pointed hat and has a tail," Calixto Campos went on as the three elaborated upon the perils from which blessed crosses safeguarded them. "One must kneel before the cross and say, 'Little Papa, accompany me to my house so I do not see the Devil.' " He recounted a dream he had had when he was a youth. Goats with horns carried him off as a band played. The goats may have been the Devil. The next day, he prayed to the cross, was sprinkled with holy water, and confessed five times.

Walking back down to Don Juan's, Heliodoro told me that when the priests began coming up to Secsecpampa to say Mass, the Devil had disappeared. "Well, somewhat, but nights are still risky," he quickly added.

It was dark and raining hard by the time I got down to the Monterrey Hotel. The path that the work crew had cleared had turned into pure mud. I went into the bar to have a drink before traveling back to my room on the pampa. A CRYRZA official, sitting nearby, put his feet on the table. As I mulled over all I had heard and seen in Secsecpampa, unconsciously I stared at his cream-colored corduroy, sponge-rubber-soled shoes.

THE next day, Friday, February 11, I went to talk to the priest at San Francisco, who I had been told would disobey the Church's orders and go to Killesh to bless the crosses. Padre Maguiña said he wanted to go because that was his birthplace and his elderly mother still lived there. But the German priests of Centenario had asked him not to go, since Killesh belonged to their parish. The Germans had decided to go to all their hamlets to say Masses over the crosses, beginning on February 20, after carnival. On February 29, Father Auscario planned to be in Killesh. In this way, the crosses could be separated from the profanity of carnival.

"But that won't work," Padre Maguiña asserted. "You see, it is all a communal effort. People are needed to carry the crosses, to make the *chicha*, and to form the bands and dance groups, and everyone is involved in this *now*." It would not be the same at just any time. Perhaps, he proposed, the Church might manage to connect the blessing of the crosses to the rites of May 3 for the Lord of Solitude, when again people would have set aside time to prepare the festivities. As we sat talking, a *campesino* looked in and asked if there would be a Mass for the crosses at San Francisco, and the padre answered reluctantly that there would not be. "But there is already one cross in the chapel," the man insisted. "Can I not bring my small cross?"

"Well, I have no objection," Maguiña relented. "Go ahead and bring it."

Before I left, I looked into the chapel. Already two small adorned crosses rested against the side wall. Walking back to my room, I ran into a young boy I knew. "You'll see," he said. "The crosses will come down on Sunday, anyway, even if there are no Masses for them. The *campesinos* will come to play with water and talcum powder."

Later that afternoon I returned to Secsecpampa. The *machitu* on the crosses in Don Juan's patio had not yet been painted. The children said he was working in his *chacra*. I went up to see Calixto Campos, this time carrying my tape recorder. I asked him who put the crosses on the mountaintops originally.

"That was so long ago, in the time of our great-grandfathers."

"Before the Spaniards?" I probed.

"It must be," Calixto replied. "The ancient ones placed them there." The huge cross still lay in his patio. He had just finished painting the leaves silver.

In Quechua, his wife said, "The cross has a name. Tell her."

"This is Uchcupat'sa," Calixto complied. The name meant that it customarily stood on land called Uchcu.

"Uchcupat'sa punishes severely," his wife added. "When you don't want to do something, it punishes."

It was then that their daughter fell out of the doorway and began to cry. Calixto grabbed her up in his arms and handed her over to his wife, who carried the child off to a field to comfort her. He then unraveled the incident. "Don't you see, my little girl was punished because we are insulting the cross by denying it its festival." He related the earthquake to the Church's early attempts to cut away their ancient customs. "That's why at least we must pray over Uchcupat'sa, kneel in front of it, bring candles. Have you noticed that practically everyone who passes by leaves a candle? We must care for it and never *propasarlo*."

Lo is the masculine object, while "cross" is feminine, *la cruz*. I wondered if the cross was He—*Él Señor Cruz*. I was lost completely about what *propasarlo* meant and asked.

Talking all at once, everyone in the patio explained that the cross moves by itself through the air, as if it had wings. "We are carrying it, and it is as if it weighed nothing. But if it is angry and doesn't want to move, it weighs a ton!" Calixto said, excited. "Then it may fall on top of us, the bearers, and crush us." I understood now that they were worried that this might happen as they carried the crosses back to the hilltops, crosses that were angry and didn't want to move until they were blessed. *Propasar* meant to take too much liberty with the crosses by not following the customs exactly.

Then Calixto recounted that when his wife had gone to get the powder to paint the *machitu* leaves that morning, the cross was so angry that it made the basket in which she carried the powder jump from her back, spilling its contents onto the ground. "Don't you understand?" he pleaded. "We are denying the cross, talking about it so much, arguing among ourselves over what we will do now that we cannot carry out our fiesta as before, that He [*Él*] has gotten bitter."

If not before, at this moment I became acutely aware of the fear that the prohibition of the descent of the crosses was producing in Secsecpampa. I also got an inkling of the dissension that it was causing in the hamlet. Feebly, I said, "But it seems to me you are trying to do your best by the cross."

"Yes, more or less, señorita," Calixto Campos answered sadly.

In Quechua, his wife started to relate things that over these days were beginning to ring in my ears from the *campesinos* of Huaraz's satellite communities: "We work in our fields tranquilly after praying to the cross. . . ."

Calixto picked it up in Spanish, in what sounded like the litany of the cross that carnival season, 1972: "I go to my fields or to the coast, tranquil, having asked the cross for my safety. I work in his name, tranquilly. Nothing happens, and I feel happy. The cross shields us from everything—hail, downpours, frosts. From everything he protects us. But we must remember him. . . ."

"You speak of the cross as if it were a person," I said.

"Hah, hah, ay, the same, the same!" He brightened at my comprehension. "It only lacks a mouth to speak."

"But it does speak in dreams," his wife amended. "Yes, yes, in dreams the cross is standing at your side, but a man speaks to you. That's the way it is."

The women were beginning to prepare a soup over a fire in the patio. Calixto's wife put in some potatoes and asked her neighbor to add some rice. I took some delicious bread baked in Huaraz out of my bag and laid it down. "They are talking in Huaraz," I said, "that perhaps the crosses could have their Masses later, around February 20."

"No, we can't wait," Calixto replied firmly, "because by next Tuesday they have to be carried back up to their cairns. If we keep them in the chapel all that time, there will be no one to defend us from hail, the rains. . . ." And then the recitative "*Uno no puede estar desamparado del todo*" ("We cannot be completely forsaken").

His wife added, "We will bless them with holy water and pray over them. They must be planted again in their places. We cannot give in to the priests." Of course, I thought, realizing that as long as the mountain crosses were in the chapel, or in houses, the hamlets were not protected.

"It has to be Tuesday," Calixto said emphatically, and then with some joy they began to discuss the activities that would take place on that day, inviting me to be there. "We will first take this big cross, Uchcupat'sa, to its place, then Perejil—no, then the cross called Panteón ["cemetery"], and then the smallest one, Perejil."

"What is the name of your cross?" he asked me.

"Cross," I answered simply, in English, feeling somewhat at a loss.

Then Calixto's wife related a dream she had just before the earthquake. In the dream, she saw her house collapse. "My house has become a pampa," she said to herself in her dream. But in that moment the three Lords (the three mountain crosses) appeared, saying to her, "Your house is all right. The walls have only cracked a little bit, and some tiles have fallen from the roof." And that's the way it was. She and her husband and children had grabbed one another, huddling together in the *chacra*. The earth parted. Her husband called above to the crosses. Not one of the three crosses of Secsecpampa fell. "Only one villager died, and he was in Huaraz."

"There being so many crosses here," Calixto Campos explained, "with the small ones, which we keep in our houses, and the big ones on the mountains above us, no one died."

"The more crosses, the more protection?" I asked.

"Of course, they all help," he affirmed. "Just like people. If I help, and he helps, and another helps . . ." Because of their crosses, Secsecpampa did not suffer much. They did not even need to take the food provisions that were distributed. "We are full every day. From our land we get the food we need," a neighbor added.

It was only now, with this crisis over the crosses, that they were beginning to feel uncertain. Before, it was all so clear. In December they would go to pick the *machitu* in the high passes. Then, six days before the Sunday when the crosses traveled to Huaraz, they would take them down into their homes to be decorated. Majordomos, elected the previous carnival day, were the ones in charge of removing the crosses from their pedestals and adorning them. Men, widows, and unmarried women served in this capacity. Each cross would spend one night in the house of each majordomo. On these nights, much money was spent, because feasts of guinea pig, potatoes, and *chicha* were offered to the villagers, who gathered to celebrate and burn candles. On the Friday before carnival day, the crosses were placed in the chapel.

Now it was Friday, and Calixto Campos was the majordomo

of Uchcupat'sa, but no one would come tonight, he felt, to take Uchcupat'sa to the chapel. He would sit alone, watching over the cross. Perhaps some neighbors would come, but there would be no food and drink. Before the earthquake, these pre-Lenten evenings had been so beautiful, with food, dancing, and drinking. The year following the earthquake, there was nothing. He had not had even one drink, but he had brought the cross down and adorned it, since he was elected majordomo the carnival before the disaster. Now he would finish out his time. At least on carnival day itself there would be big pots of food, *chicha*, and a *cajaplauta* (a band of drums and flutes). Before, there had been more instruments; still, it would be a nice day. And if the crosses could have their Masses, how wonderful it would be! "I don't know why the priests don't want this anymore," Calixto said, his face clouding up again. "After the earthquake, they just don't want to bless the crosses, and for two years now, they do not bless them. And they are the only thing we have, our refuge. They shield us from everything . . . rain, hail . . ."

His voice trailed off, and I could feel his tiredness now and knew that I should leave. As I was about to, his wife suddenly picked up an old rusty bucket that was lying in the patio and plopped it on his head. Laughing, she asked me to take his picture. The outrageous sight of Calixto Campos standing by his cross in this bucket headdress made me think of the barber's basin that Don Quixote had worn, thinking it a shiny helmet. I snapped the picture and promised to return on Tuesday for the repositioning of the crosses on their mountain outposts.

ON my way down the winding paths of Secsecpampa, I peeked into Don Juan's patio and found him discussing the cross situation with a man called Francisco. Though Don Juan often dressed like a mestizo, now he was wearing a black poncho and rubber sandals and looked more Indian. He appeared dejected and reiterated that the priests were driving them into paganism. "On the cross, our Lord suffered. He suffered too much, and we must care for him," he said.

Don Juan asked me if I would take a letter about the crosses to the archbishop in Lima. Like the night with SINAMOS in the Nicrupampa camp, this was another time I felt perturbed and had a kind of sinking feeling. I was sure that those who were dictating the changes in ritual did not fully understand the anguish these changes were producing. The civil authorities and most of the religious personnel who were trying to enforce the changes never pursued the issues closely in the satellite communities themselves. If indeed they ever came to the hamlets, the people treated them with awe, a respect that masked their deepest sentiments. The *costumbres*, if not viewed as wrong by the outsiders, were seen as routine and senseless acts, outworn tradition, and the emotion behind the rituals was not duly regarded.

I frankly cannot remember what I told Don Juan, but I knew I could not go down to Lima with a letter. This interlude with the crosses was only one facet of the sprawling aftermath. It was inextricably bound up with revolution and reform, with development and modernization, and the toughest thing of all, with the goal of justice and equality that it was believed could best be achieved without the old traditions. For me, the episode of the crosses could only pose the questions of religious sentiments versus the pragmatic side of life. I had no answers. It was true that the *costumbres* diverted energy and resources from useful pursuits. Yet I knew that ritual was useful, too. Was I not witnessing its meaning and use at every turn during these days preceding carnival? What I knew most profoundly was that in my heart I was pulling for some "miracle" that would turn the whole thing around in these last remaining days so that the crosses could be properly blessed before regaining their places on the mountains.

As I listened to Don Juan and Francisco, I learned more about the factions that existed within Secsecpampa itself and began to understand why Don Juan acted so beleaguered. He was telling Francisco that they should go ahead with everything and do their best. They should even select majordomos for the following year. The ex–lieutenant governor, from whom he had taken over the office, had become a Protestant and was inciting the villagers not to proceed with even the curtailed preparations.

"There are just a few Evangelicals in Secsecpampa," he explained to me, "but they speak so unkindly to us Catholics. They should talk nicely to us. But even the Catholics—we are arguing among ourselves about how to carry out our festival of the crosses." This discord further clarified for me what Calixto Campos had said about the anger of the big cross that lay in his patio.

Another man entered the patio to ask Don Juan what they should do. Together, he and Don Juan decided to hold a vigil over the crosses in the chapel the following day. "If we say the rosary well, perhaps it will be of as much value as a Mass," Don Juan said unconvincingly.

Down at valley-floor level again, I got a ride back to the pampa with former residents of Belén. Now they lived in a shack at the end of Tarapacá. Lamenting the dust and mud, the woman said she no longer tried to wear stockings or any decent clothing. Would the valley towns ever be rebuilt, and how, in the end, would Huaraz look? These days of almost daily excursions into the hamlets always brought such contrasts. I moved back and forth between the extreme fear over the crosses in the countryside and the fears about the outcome of the reconstruction of the towns. Wherever I looked, in the end, I always struck some core of hardship and hurt.

OFTEN in fieldwork one has to make difficult decisions about where to be on a certain day when significant events are to take place. Will you learn more at the designated place of the ritual, for example, or somewhere behind the scenes? This was magnified in the aftermath, where everything was in the throes of confusion and indecision. As people often said, "Nothing takes place anymore at the expected times or in the expected places."

I wondered where I should be on the Sunday before carnival Tuesday, the day the crosses traditionally came down to Huaraz. I decided to attend Mass at Soledad. Though the priest of Soledad had refused to talk about how he would deal with the crosses, by this time I already had a feeling about the importance of Soledad, that this church and its barrio formed a strong bond between Huaraz and the *campesinos* in the heights.

Outside the large wattle-and-daub building that served as Soledad's church stood a group of *campesinos*, all carrying ponchos over their shoulders and wearing rubber sandals. They were discussing *La Santísima Cruz* ("the Most Holy Cross"). "The padre went to say a Mass over the crosses at Huánchac yesterday," one disclosed.

"At San Antonio in Huarupampa, the priests didn't want to hear about the crosses," another reported. "They showed us the Bible. Before, only the Evangelicals had the Bible."

"And the Germans are like Protestants. They say Mass like the Evangelicals and have no images," another added.

An old man informed the group that in Recuay the priests were allowing the crosses to come down. "They are charging twenty to thirty *soles* per cross there. What profits the crosses are earning them!" he exclaimed. "But still, it is better. All our crosses will remain without their Masses, and we will have to put them back in their cairns unblessed."

"Our *costumbre* cannot be saved," a young man said with resignation.

"It will not be our fault, though," the old man retorted. "The priests will be punished. First, they began to say Mass in Spanish. And there was punishment, the earthquake. Now there is no Mass of the cross."

"That is why God has punished us all, for not believing in the cross, for changing things. There could be more earthquakes," still another *campesino* reasoned.

As Mass began, we all entered the church. On a wooden bench, a blind *campesino*, dressed in ragged clothes, sat playing a mandolin and singing softly in Quechua. *Campesinos* were kneeling on the dirt floor, digging little holes in the dirt with their fingers and placing candles. The words *Tayta* ("Father") and *Mamee* ("Mother") escaped their lips.

Padre Espinoza walked to the wooden table that served as an altar. Wearing his black pants and black turtleneck sweater, slowly he began to put on his robes. As he did so, a *campesino*, serving as the explicator that morning, was telling the congregation, "Our dances and drunken sprees are like nails in the hands of our Lord. We come down bearing the cross, and flour and water is thrown on the cross."

I overheard a man nearby whisper, "We never threw things at the cross."

"It is better this way," the explicator continued, "that there not be a Mass for the cross. We will not offend it any longer."

The priest then began to speak, very slowly and deliberately, in the Quechua of his native Abancay. As his dialect is close to Cuzco Quechua, which I had studied, I could understand much of what he said. Referring to the Lord of Solitude, which stood behind him, he began, "Our Lord, wounded, destroyed in the earthquake, for so long no one came to repair him. And our church—we are still here in this poor hut. There is gossip about me, and our Lord is full of the arrows of ingratitude. We are all involved in a war of misery." He spoke of the aid that had never reached Soledad. I knew his insinuations were aimed at CRYRZA, which, I was learning, saw him as a threat to modernizing reconstruction and religion. Yet, in his own contradictory way, he appeared to be on the side of the prohibition against bringing the mountain crosses to Huaraz when he announced, "There is no time for fiestas." His sermon finished, he blessed the host and the chalice and called for communicants. No one stepped up to take communion.[4]

Just as he was pleading, "Is there no one to take communion?" the tin slab door at the entrance to the church was flung open, and three *campesinos* struggled inside with a cross so large that they could barely get it through the doorway. Staggering under its weight, they finally let it fall with a thump, so that it lay propped on a wooden bench just inside the building. The silvered leaves of the *machitu* glistened in a ray of sun that entered the open door. The exhausted men stood facing Padre Espinoza, the whole congregation between them at the door and the priest at the altar. During the dead silence that ensued, everyone looked from the priest to the *campesinos* by the fallen cross and back to the priest again.

Finally, Padre Espinoza said softly, "It will be damaged." He called over two young boys who were assisting him at the Mass and whispered something to them. They walked to the back of the church and whispered to the three bearers of the cross. Together, with great effort, they stood the cross up, resting it against a wooden beam just inside the door. Silence fell again as the priest studied the cross now confronting him. The tension increased.

At last, Padre Espinoza raised the chalice and, extending it toward the cross, began to sing, "I adore you, Holy Cross." Audible sighs of relief spread among the worshipers. As he sang *"Yo te adoro, Santa Cruz,"* another large cross was shoved under the lintel, and then there followed several smaller ones, so that soon the back of the church-hut was filled with a dozen crosses in all, adorned in gold-and-silver-painted leaves.

The padre kept singing, his voice growing louder and louder. A lady near me murmured, "The crosses will have to remain for their blessing since they did not hear the entire Mass."

Finishing the Mass, the padre walked to the entrance and stood before the crosses. "You know that this was prohibited," he said to the *campesinos* who had borne the crosses.

"Little father, *Papachito*, we know, but we have not come with drink. Please bless them," a spokesman pleaded.

"With affection, I do it," he replied, and he sprinkled the crosses with holy water. The bearers lifted the crosses onto their backs again and began their trek across the pampa back up to their hamlets.

It was a warm, dusty, windy afternoon. In Nicrupampa, people were splashing each other with water, and a few drummers and flute players wove their way among the *módulos*. During the rest of the day, I saw an occasional cross being carried across the pampa, but everyone said it was not like before the earthquake, when hundreds of crosses had descended into Huaraz the Sunday before carnival.

ON Monday afternoon, February 14, I returned to Secsecpampa and found Don Juan up at Calixto Campos's house. Uchcupat'sa had been taken down to the hamlet's chapel, along with Panteón Cruz ("Cemetery Cross"), which "defends the cemetery against evil spirits." Don Juan took me down to the chapel to see them.

Age had eroded the whitewash of the fine plaster on the outer walls of the chapel, exposing crumbling adobe bricks, but it had not been badly damaged in the earthquake. There were a few holes in the roof. Don Juan, who was proud that Secsecpampa managed on its own after the disaster, said the former authorities of the hamlet had made the holes themselves in order to receive food aid in return for repairing them. But no aid ever came, and the holes remained.

It was pretty inside, its adobe walls painted white and blue, and there was a colorful retable behind the altar, with primitive paintings of birds and angels. Don Juan pointed out all the saints, which stood in their niches: San Cayetano, the Lords of Nazareth and the Exaltation, and a Virgin of Sorrows. When I asked him what INRI, appearing on a crucifix, meant, he answered that INRI was "the father of Jehovah." He even spoke of the grandparents of Jehovah. *Abuelos* are very important in the valley, and it was fitting that even God not be bereft of them.

After reviewing the images, we sat down on two of twelve

chairs that he had obtained from the Popular Cooperative of the New Peru for the festivities of carnival day. He began to tell me about his activities of the preceding days, since I had last been in Secsecpampa.

On Friday night, he had gone down to visit the bishop in Nicrupampa. He put it to the bishop, telling him he simply could not follow through with the prohibition. "Sacrifice me," Don Juan told him, "but not the people." With those words, he won out, and the bishop agreed to have one of the old-time priests from Huaraz—a *padre suelto* (a priest not connected to any Order or to a particular church)—go to say Mass in Killesh.

Relieved, Don Juan arranged everything for Sunday. He bought two bottles of alcohol and a basketful of bread. Followed by forty persons from Secsecpampa, drum and flute players, he led the way to Killesh, carrying the big Uchcupat'sa on his shoulders. "I don't know where I got the strength to carry it," he reflected. Perejil and Panteón Cruz also traveled to Killesh. The padre charged sixty *soles* to bless the three crosses.

Warming to his description, Don Juan told of their triumphant entrance into Killesh. The authorities there had greeted the pilgrims, saying, "Señor lieutenant governor of Secsecpampa, you honor us by coming to Killesh." And, upon seeing Don Juan leading the group, bent almost double under the weight of the enormous cross, the priest had proclaimed, "Who is this señor? Let him enter, for he is a true Catholic!" Giving his characteristic humorous twist to even the most serious matters, Don Juan chuckled when he told me, "The padre should have said, 'Who is this old man, ridiculous in his misery?' "

After the crosses were blessed, Don Juan looked into his little basket of bread and saw how meager a feast it was for so many people. But the priest blessed the bread, and it and the alcohol turned out to be more than enough. "In this way, I managed to get our crosses blessed," Don Juan concluded jubilantly.

Later, on Sunday night, the *Secsecpampinos* held a candlelight vigil over the crosses, which now leaned against the side walls of the little chapel where we sat. "We recited the rosary with respect. Everything was tranquil. And then I said, 'Now it is time for everyone to return to his house.' There was no drinking."

Time passed, and as dusk came outside, we sat there, just the two of us, Don Juan telling me one Bible story after another, some laced with threads of native myths. He prided himself on how, no matter where he was, on the coast, in the hamlets, or talking to churchmen of Huaraz, he could win arguments about the Bible, even "against the great materialists of the world and the great Evangelists."

When finally I left him at his house that Monday night, he confided that he had asked for two civil guards to be in Secsecpampa on the following day, "just in case." Obviously, he was anticipating that there might be trouble as they carried the crosses on high once more. From whom? I asked myself. The Evangelicals? Perhaps the catechists?

TUESDAY, February 15, 1972, carnival day. I was up very early and arrived at Don Juan's house by 10:00 A.M. He seemed nervous and wondered if the civil guards would show up. Holding Margarita, who was crying, on his lap, he spoke of the vigil in the chapel the night before. When the child was comforted, he went into his room to get his shoes and, sitting on the big rock, changed from his sandals. He, Heliodoro, and I then went up to a house across from Calixto Campos's, where the feasting would be held.

In a large room opening onto the patio were some fifteen women, all dressed in their best *polleras* and fancy taffeta blouses in brilliant blues, purples, yellows, and reds. The women's braids hung down from under their hats, and earrings dangled from their ears. With their babies asleep in shawls wrapped around their shoulders, the women squatted on the floor, beginning to peel mountains of potatoes, tossing them one by one into a giant boiling caldron. Cabbage and bits of lamb were cooking in another big kettle. Some of the women were skinning guinea pigs to be roasted in a hot red-pepper sauce. I spotted Señora Campos, who had a leaf plastered to her cheek, perhaps to draw out the pain of a toothache.

Outside in the patio, a drummer and a flutist played from time to time. About a dozen men stood drinking an almost pure alcohol rum, passing the bottle from one to the other and also dipping out ladles of foaming *chicha* from kettles on the ground. The children were having a great time, chasing each other around the patio and throwing flour at one another. Silently observing the activity from a passageway sat an old woman, her skin coursed by deep lines from a lifetime under the parching Andean sun.

The men stationed themselves in front of Perejil, the smallest of Secsecpampa's three mountain crosses, which stood against a wall in the patio. They were "playing," as they say, talking animatedly and pushing each other. After about an hour and well into their cups, they began to argue about what the "proper" behavior was in front of the crosses on carnival day. Heliodoro took an avid part in the argument. Don Juan, whom I did not see drinking at all, was more reserved. Calixto Campos and a few others were getting quite drunk, and Don Juan ordered them out of the patio. The argument then turned to whether Lord Perejil was the cross after or before Christ was crucified on it.

About eleven-thirty, the men headed down toward the chapel. I tagged along. Suddenly, the group stopped along the winding path, and another argument ensued. A boy came running up to the men to say Calixto Campos was drinking in a house where the key to the chapel was kept. They told the boy to fetch the key and continued their controversy. As well as I could understand, they were disagreeing over whether to go ahead and choose majordomos for the following year or not. At one point, Heliodoro shouted, "They cannot take our *costumbres* away. Man lives by his sentiments. The ancient ones used to do this."

Slowly, I was coming to decipher the factions in the hamlet. Don Juan, Calixto Campos, and their followers were essentially together. They were the "true Catholics." But a rift had developed between them over the demeanor that should prevail during the rituals. Don Juan wanted all the rites to be performed without what he considered to be the excessive drinking and frivolity that were taking place. Second, there was another Catholic group, which consisted of the catechists training under the wing of the Centenario church in Huaraz. During the arguing, I gathered that they were to become the new authorities in Secsecpampa, who in the future would try to dismantle the complex rituals of the crosses at carnival. It is they who did not want to elect new majordomos for the following year. Later, I was to learn that this group was led by Don Juan's own sister-in-law and her husband, Jesusa and Nicolás. Finally, there was a small group of Evangelicals who wanted to abolish the rites altogether.

As I was struggling to figure out exactly what was happening, the key was brought, and we all proceeded down the path and onto the dirt plaza, bordered by houses and the chapel. By this time, villagers were walking down the various paths that converged at the plaza. The group of men I was following, who were in charge of the festivities, entered a house off the plaza for a drink. I knew I could not go inside with them and waited outside with the women and children. I was told that the "shield" of the new authority was in the house, and that was the reason for the toast. I suspected it might be Don Juan's shield, the one he had shown me when I first met him, which signified the office of *teniente gobernador*. I later learned that this was so, that the shield had been taken from Don Juan's patio early that morning. Since he had not mentioned any of this to me, as the day wore on I began to realize that this had been a rather abrupt change of office and to understand better his tribulation during the day.

Finally, the villagers entered the chapel where Uchcupat'sa and Panteón Cruz stood. One by one, they knelt in front of the crosses and kissed their bases, near the tufts of rosemary. One woman was crying and shouting loudly. Don Juan explained that she was a widow, all alone, and was presenting her grievances to the cross. Then the crosses were carried outside and propped against the chapel. Uchcupat'sa was as tall as the chapel itself.

I remained with the women, who squatted in front of the houses facing the plaza as the men, with some formality, took seats on wooden benches in front of the crosses in order to elect the majordomos for the following year. They debated a long time before coming to a vote. At one point, they walked over to a group of women, "to consult them," I was told.

The children were playing hard now. They were coated in flour and talcum, and from time to time I got dusted, too. It was the girls against the boys. The little girls got sticks and began chasing the boys with them. Amid this jollity, the band came down from the house where the cooking was taking place, playing loudly.

The sun was hot that day, and about 1:30 P.M. I went back up to the house to take refuge from the heat. In spite of the bubbling caldrons, the dark kitchen area was cool. I just sat there quietly eating a boiled potato as the women stuffed more and more cabbages into the kettles. Looking out a small window, which framed the almost painfully bright day and the eucalyptus trees swaying in the hot breeze, I daydreamed, shutting out for a while all the events and the nuances I was trying to piece together. The band had returned and was playing again loudly in the patio as people drifted in again from the plaza.

I must have dozed off, for I woke with a start, realizing the music had stopped and the household had almost emptied of people except for the few old women who were tending the caldrons. When I went out into the patio, Perejil was gone, and afraid I had missed the relocation of the crosses in their cairns, I ran down to the plaza.

Now the men, too, were all covered with flour and had multicolored paper streamers wound around their necks. Calixto Campos, especially, looked like the perfect clown. He was almost in a stupor from liquor and *coca* but still had enough of his wits about him to hold back a man who was shouting in Quechua and trying to strike Don Juan. It seemed fights would break out all over the place as the men tussled, pushing and pulling at each other. From time to time a woman would cautiously approach them, tap a husband's shoulder, and admonish him.

This went on for quite some time, until finally Don Juan and Heliodoro were pushed off the plaza and down a path. Their shouts of "Tranquil!" and "More respect!" rang in my ears. Perpetua, Don Juan's eight-year-old daughter, sat clinging to me. After about a quarter of an hour, Heliodoro came back and whispered to me, "There was no reason for them to push my father off like that." Then he told me that the new lieutenant governor had come early that morning to take Don Juan's shield away from him. Heliodoro left Perpetua and me there in the plaza and went off to be with his father, who had returned, dispirited, to his house.

Flour battles continued. A bell was rung to signal to the people that it was now time for the men to take up the three crosses—Uchcupat'sa, Panteón Cruz, and Perejil—resting against the chapel wall. One man tried to lift Uchcupat'sa, but he fell, others catching the cross before it hit the ground. Finally, after various attempts, Calixto Campos, who had painstakingly decorated the enormous cross, managed to get it up onto his shoulders.

Men and crosses leading the way, the women and children tagging behind, we went straight up the mountain, at almost a forty-five-degree angle, through the *chacras* on the steep slopes. The ascent was so astonishingly swift that it seemed, just as Rodríguez and his wife had described, as if the crosses were indeed flying of their own accord.

At the very top of the mountain, Calixto Campos plunged Uchcupat'sa into its pedestal of stones, proclaiming, "Here I leave my old one!" ("¡Aquí dejo mi viejo!") Several men helped now to make the cross stand straight and secure. Then everyone knelt down on the mountain slope beneath the cross and began to sing and chant plaintively in Quechua, interspersed with the Spanish words "Santísima Cruz." I ventured to look down and saw the Río Santa winding like a snake far below.[5]

For half an hour they sang, led by Calixto Campos, who was kneeling directly in front of Uchcupat'sa. He was impressive, his face white with powder, the wind blowing the colored streamers wound around his neck. As I crouched on the slope with the women, looking at him, I thought of the day of the disaster, when, in Yungay, circus clowns with whitened faces presided over the circus at one end of the town while the enormous Christ statue commanded the cemetery at the other.

When the chanting stopped, one by one people wove their way up to the cross to kiss it for the last time this year. I did not follow, but remained on my spot, I thought, quite alone. Unable to resist a photograph of Calixto beneath the giant Uchcupat'sa, stealthily I risked removing my camera from my bag and snapped the shutter. Before I knew what was happening, two drunken men were trying to grab my camera. Since I was somewhat apart from the main group and there had been so much drinking, anyway, I knew there was no one to call upon. Instinctively, I said to Perpetua, who still clung to me, "Run, get Heliodoro," and she darted away. The men now had hold of my arms and were trying to push me from my tenuous purchase on the slope. I remember looking back, considering how far I would fall if I lost the struggle.

We wrestled in this way for what seemed interminable minutes, until Heliodoro came running. In his youth and soberness, he was able to detach the men's hold on me, and they staggered off. I slumped down for a moment, shaken, but decided to catch up with the throng, which was now climbing laterally across the mountain to leave Señor Perejil in its place in the middle of a chacra. Heliodoro stayed by my side for the final steep climb to the cemetery, where, with the same singing and chanting, we left the cross called Panteón. Then he returned to Don Juan.

With Perpetua and another young girl, I returned to the house where the food was being prepared. The male villagers had not yet arrived at the house, and I felt secure with the women, all in good humor and quiet much of the time. Children played out back with water, their laughter filtering into the patio. The women served me a big plate of cabbage, lamb, guinea pig, and a tin cup of *chicha*. It all tasted delicious, there in the sheltered dark kitchen, and I relished these moments before everyone would return.

Soon enough, I heard the approaching band. The flutists and drummers played on in the patio as dusk came, everyone eating and drinking. At one point, the old flute player asked, a twinkle in his eye, "Shall we pardon God for the earthquake? We should forgive him, shouldn't we?"

It was still fairly early, but I had to get down before the light faded, as the path was not easy to travel after dark. When I passed Don Juan's house, all was quiet, no one was in sight, and the patio had been swept clean. I supposed he was asleep, that he felt shamed by the wresting of his authority, by the way the day had turned out. But it was he who had carried the cross on his back to Killesh, who was responsible for the fact that all three of Secsecpampa's crosses now stood in their places, blessed, ready to defend the hamlet for still another year. I decided not to bother him and continued down the path.

Back in my room, I found hunks of meat wrapped in newspaper on my table. My landlord said a friend had left the meat for me. I knew it was Abel, who hunted deer on the mountain slopes, and smiled, feeling tired and ecstatic at the same time, so very far from cellophane-wrapped steaks and so very close to the hunt.

A week passed before I returned to Don Juan's house. While we sat on the big rocks in the patio, Nicolás arrived and drew Don Juan aside. They spoke in Quechua about the crosses. The women—Jesusa, her mother, the older girls, and I—strained to hear, and eventually it was revealed that the Centenario priest had gone to the bishop to complain about the Mass that had been conducted for the crosses in Killesh. "I just can't understand," Don Juan said, "after the bishop knew about it, how he could change his mind." Nicolás had learned that the *Huaracino* priest who had held the Mass in Killesh was to be defrocked, a fact I was later able to confirm.

This was why Don Juan had lost his authority so peremptorily on carnival day. Some catechists—not Nicolás, though I could sense his discomfort as Don Juan spoke—had gone to the secretary of the subprefect to accuse Don Juan of taking the crosses to Killesh. "They no doubt took chickens and little potatoes and gave him his drinks," Don Juan now surmised. Nicolás had also learned that the bishop's vicar would try to help Don Juan regain his authority as *teniente gobernador* of Secsecpampa. "There are so many projects I have in mind to make Secsecpampa better," Don Juan said. "I want my authority back."

After this, the afternoon turned back to its previous mood of joviality. Don Juan took out his reader from the time he had attended primary school for a few years and, seated again on his big rock, began to read stories to us. One story was about Pido, a cat that lived with an old woman. When she became ill, they both had nothing to eat. So Pido went to the church and rang the bell. The priests, seeing how hungry and sad Pido was, followed him back to the woman's house. They brought her to the church and gave her a good meal and the last rites.

"What a great thing that this should happen before she died!" Don Juan exclaimed. "Pido was a good, smart cat."

BECAUSE the *costumbres* had long provided a network of festivities anchoring town to countryside, divisiveness over the restoration of the old customs did not occur along mestizo-Indian lines. Townspeople, too, lamented the fact that the hundreds of mountain crosses did not descend into Huaraz that carnival season of 1972. And they themselves had their own crosses to honor. From my window, on Ash Wednesday, the day after carnival, I saw sporadic clusters of small crosses pass as well as an occasional large mountain cross.

Carnival was laid to rest on Wednesday afternoon. It was one of those afternoons when, at 10,000 feet, we seemed to be in the vortex of all the atmospheric pressures of the world. Since it had not rained for a few days, the earth was dry, and an icy wind lashed us with dust. Overhead, warring hordes of clouds moved in the sky. Spectators lined the banks of the Quilcay, waiting for the "coffin of carnival."

Finally, the carnival actors, wearing huge papier-mâché masks, came across the bridge over the Quilcay. Scattered among them were the "KIRSA men," who were mimicking the incessant surveying of the pampa. As the coffin was tossed into the river, carnival's widow wept profusely, and onlookers threw stones at the coffin as it plummeted over the rocks jutting from the rushing waters of the Quilcay.

An old woman at my side pointed in the direction of Huaraz's principal crosses: toward Pumacayán, a knoll above San Francisco barrio, where the cross, since its shrine had fallen, now occupied a *módulo*; toward a hill above Nicrupampa, where the *Calvario de Auki* ("Calvary of the Old Wise One") stood; and down toward Calicanto bridge and the hermitage of *Tayta Cruz Calicanto*, which they called *Papa Aukiteeta* ("Old Father"). Even in Huaraz, the guardian crosses were viewed as being old, more like *huacas* than the way we perceive the cross of a young Christ. When the woman had finished locating the crosses for me, she sighed with nostalgia that since the earthquake Calicanto and still another guardian, Rataquenua, had not met in the Plaza de Armas, as was their custom. Before, there was so much life in everything, and now "everything is dead."

On Sunday, February 20, five days after carnival had been "laid to rest," the cross of Pumacayán was given a Mass at the Franciscan church in Huarupampa. The cross, about nine feet tall, was "dressed" in plants embroidered with gold threads; to these was attached a picture of Jesus. The church was filled with townspeople, and *campesinos*, who crowded in at the back.

The Spanish priests began the Mass by saying: "Now that carnival is over, the cross can no longer be a reason for frivolity, but for meditation. We must liberate ourselves from the drunkenness and the stupidity, the gossip and envy."

The tradition of dancing and drinking around the cross was scarcely less prevalent in the town than in the countryside. Guilt over this frivolity, for which the priest had just chided the congregation, was probably the reason that no one came forth to receive communion. Indeed, at the very moment the priest elevated the Host, firecrackers exploded outside. A band began to play just as the cross was carried out of the church. We followed it across the pampa. The entourage was composed mainly of mestizos, and about every 100 feet they would stop and, as the band struck up, dance *huaynos*. Bottles of *aguardiente* were passed around. I overheard people commenting, "We continue dancing and getting drunk with the crosses."

A townsman wearing a beret, who referred to himself as a "troubled painter," joined me and some little boys who had taken hold of my hands. He lamented the fact that the procession paled in comparison with those of former years, when much larger crowds had followed the cross and people watched from their balconies, when it had all taken place amid the jocularity of carnival. "You see," the painter said, "they take advantage of the destruction of Huaraz to liquidate our paganism, to destroy our *costumbres*. For the *campesinos*, the *costumbres* are pure rites. They have no dogma. Maybe we do, though the paradox is that the Indians have been able to mystify the religion of the whites."

It seemed to me that the main difference between town and country was in the sentiments that motivated the ritual of the crosses. Among townspeople, I did not feel the same urgency behind the rituals that existed in the hamlets, the extreme apprehension that had pervaded the countryside over what unblessed crosses might cause. Throwing up his hands, unable to complete his analysis, the painter concluded, "But in the depths of people, nothing changes; only in the outer form."

Twenty-three

THE NATURE OF THE SIN: COMMUNAL FLAW

> *What punishment could it have been*
> *To a noble town that fought for*
> *Independence with Bolívar, and*
> *Raged with Atusparia . . .*
> *If we are pure of heart?*
>
> Diario de Huaraz,
> May 31, 1972

ON THE AFTERNOON of July 18, 1972, a special kind of wind, called the *shucuquí*, arose on the pampa. A mother was accused of mistreating her children, and a priest was called. Another day, a vendor in the market told me that he had become gravely ill with fever because he refused to have an arch made for an image in honor of the saint's name day. "Images punish when one does not fulfill his duties toward them," he said.

These kinds of individual transgressions cause illness and minor disturbances like the *shucuquí*. Grave community flaw, however, must have brought about the earthquake, because people, mountains, animals, and the saints themselves suffered. Like the vendor's neglect of his small image, but on a grand scale, faults or omissions in worship were among the possible communal sins invoked to explain the earthquake. "People have forgotten God," survivors would say. That only a handful of worshipers had participated in the Corpus Christi noon celebration of May 31, 1970, was much discussed in the weeks following the disaster and was still recalled when I was there.

"What thing has this town done for you to punish us so? Forgive us our sins," a young townswoman shouted to God in the throes of the shaking. Jesusa and Nicolás were high up on the Cordillera Blanca, working in a relative's *chacra* when the earthquake struck:

NICOLÁS: I was preparing the ground for a new seeding. She was at my side gathering potatoes. . . . There it caught us both.

JESUSA: In that moment we said it must be the Final Judgment, we were going to die. . . .

NICOLÁS: Dust, dust everywhere. Then it was all black, but Cátac below was pure red.

JESUSA: Every place has a different-color earth. . . . There in the *chacra*, dawn came for us.

NICOLÁS: The rock is strong. All during the night it made noise, *cak, cak, cak*!

JESUSA: Each time the earth moved, *cakst, cakst, cakst, chuk, chuk, chuk*. . . .

NICOLÁS: During the night we said it must be the punishment of God. We kept speaking of that.

JESUSA: It must be the sin that we have . . . all the people . . . the sin of humanity.

All sectors of the valley society intimated the communal nature of the sin, whatever it might be. A priest told me that throughout the first weeks after the disaster "the opinion kept growing that God had punished the Callejón de Huaylas." Sometimes it was simply "*castigo*," and the sins were undefined. But, more often, survivors talked about sins, trying to uncover them, to fathom what had gone wrong. The "social sins," the inequitable relationship between Indians and *mestizos*, which was raised to consciousness by Revolution and Catholic Reform, and the strong words "idolatry" and "paganism"—Andean sins—were common community accusations.

These charges were blatant. But brewing under the surface was the suspicion of incest in the community. This accusation became more threatening with the introduction by Catholic Reform of changes in the sacrament of baptism. It was a long time before I fully understood what was meant by "the sin of humanity" that Jesusa and other Indians talked about. Gradually, I realized it referred to sexual sins, mainly incest. It was still longer before I put together the ritual change in baptism and the growing preoccupation with what *campesinos* called *convivencia entre compadres* (literally "the living together of co-parents").

Idolatry and the devotion to old customs might have brought the earthquake, but incest, "the worst sin," was even more ancient. *Campesinos* said incest had reached a high incidence just prior to all the disasters (mythical and real) that through the centuries had struck the valley. Since incest was "almost unspeakable," it took time to be able to discuss it, though I was hearing about it in the euphemisms of "there is no respect" or "the sin of humanity." The first time it was made explicit was at Jesusa and Nicolás's house one day. "There is no longer respect," Nicolás said. "Like before, when the Deluge destroyed the world, there were relations among family members, brothers and sisters. Here there are relations among *compadres*."

"And then, as one can take the whip to a child," Jesusa added, "there can be a lashing of all the people, if they live like animals."

Campesinos believed that *convivencia* with one's *comadre* or *compadre*—co-mother or co-father, that is, the godmother or godfather of one's children—was even worse than incest within the biologic family. They believed that incest occurred in both towns and hamlets, though in the towns people tended to "cohabit" mainly with members of their biologic or "true" family.

Townspeople themselves only rarely mentioned incest. Rather, the sexual sins they perceived as predominant in the towns were other forms of "not having respect": young people cohabiting out of wedlock and adultery. In lighter moments, they liked to tell the story of a priest who stood at the pass of Punta Callán on the

Cordillera Negra, looked back, and said, "Good-bye, Huaraz and its walls. Of one hundred married couples, there are ninety-nine cuckolds."

The institution of "co-parenthood" (the *compadrazgo*) is central to Andean life. In contrast to our conceptualization of godparenthood, where the important bond is between godparents and child, in the Hispanic and Indian world, the tie between the biologic and the ritual or spiritual parents forms the most significant bond. Strong *compadrazgo* ties unite the hamlets on the flanks of the Andes into networks of reciprocity. Through these networks, agricultural products, grown at varying altitudes, as well as the grazing land of the puna, become available to people who otherwise would be dependent on a limited ecological zone. The *compadrazgo* also links town to countryside, again in a network of exchange of agricultural land or labor for the educational and commercial resources of the towns.

The ritual aspect of the *compadrazgo* is the sacrament of baptism. As performed in the valley for centuries, baptism consisted of the godparents presenting the baby before a priest, who, in the ceremony, cleansed the baby of original sin and welcomed it into the Church. The biologic parents were never present at this ceremony. Rather, they waited at home for the child to be brought back, and then the new bonds were celebrated.

Once, when I asked Jesusa if people tried to figure out what sins had brought the earthquake, she was quick to exclaim, "Of course! It was the sin of humanity. Living with your *comadre* or your *compadre* is the mortal sin. One goes directly to hell forever." The *ahuilos* had committed incest, she said, and their punishment was a shower of burning hailstones. They took refuge on the mountaintops, placing large, flat stones on their heads. "As all of them did not die, they sinned even more. And then came the Deluge, which destroyed all the *ahuilos*. Perhaps some escaped, living in caves or making rock houses deep in the snows."

When incest between co-parents takes place, Jesusa went on, the community is alerted by the howling of dogs at night and the sounds of birds that go "*chic-chic-chic*." Sometimes the *comadre*'s head separates from her body and is seen flying at night, making the sound "*qeqeq qeqeq*." "It flies on high, what an enormous fright! It even shakes the earth. . . ."

I was able to understand *campesinos*' thinking that the sin that brought the disaster was incest, but I was slow at grasping why they were so sure that incest among *compadres* was spreading now and their fear of a new disaster because of this spread. I had learned from the clergy that on April 18, 1971, under Catholic Reform, worldwide changes were instituted in the rite of baptism. Principally, the godparents were no longer to present the child for baptism; rather, the biologic parents would do so. But I could not imagine that this change was having such repercussions, especially in the countryside.

Perhaps the guarded way in which people spoke of this made me miss the connection between the changes and the growing fear of further calamity. They would say they did not like the new baptism rite, that it made them uneasy. They said it was not "like before" and mentioned subtle differences in what was done with the oil and salt as well as the fact that "now the parents must hold the child." They would tell me that before, "the baby's parents, at most, peeked in at the ceremony from the church door." But because this change was discussed along with other changes in ritual, I took the apprehension to arise simply because the new rite represented a break in tradition.

It was only during my last six weeks of fieldwork that incest and the fear of the new baptism rite came together for me. Not surprisingly, it was Jesusa who clarified it. One day, in my room, she said, "But if Nicolás and I have a child and we hold the baby for baptism, we cannot sleep together anymore." Suddenly it dawned on me that in their minds the new rite was making *compadres* of biologic parents and creating a situation of that most grave sin of incest between *compadres*! If they stood together holding the baby, Nicolás would be both husband and *compadre* to Jesusa. And she would be both wife and *comadre* to him.

"Everyone is asking now," she went on, "how can it be when we ourselves baptize and then we will be sleeping with our *compadre* husbands?" She said that the Centenario priests had explained that they, the parents, had brought the creature into the world and that they must present it to the Church and take responsibility for the new child, not putting their obligations off on *compadres*. "Some understand and some don't," she sighed.

Jesusa's daughter, Julia, told of a recent case in which a couple had their baby baptized at Centenario. When the ceremony was finished, though, they carried the child to an irrigation ditch and washed him, thereby removing the baptism. Then they had the godparents take the baby to the Spanish Franciscans, who performed the rite in the old way.

Jesusa's mother, speaking in Quechua, exclaimed, "Only the father and mother will look after the child? And then with your *compadre* you are going to have more and more children!"

"In all nations, the Church is changing, the bishop said," Jesusa reminded us. "Everything is changing. There will be no more drunkenness, and we shall not kill bulls any longer." The latter referred to the landowners' criticism of agrarian reform, that the *campesinos* did not know how to breed bulls but would eat them, depleting the stock.

"We have enough to eat with guinea pigs," the grandmother said, laughing. "When will you come back to eat with us?" she asked me, knowing I was leaving soon. "We'll be waiting with your little guinea pig, perhaps even a little chicken." She wondered if I would have guinea pig in my country, and when Reyna said there were no guinea pigs in the United States, she concluded, "Aha, they must eat only rats there."

Jesusa smiled. "Huaraz is sweeter, isn't it?"

Suddenly, the grandmother burst out again with indignation against the new baptism rite: "It turns your child into your godchild, and later, in the afternoon, you sleep in the same bed as your *compadre*, making *qeqeq qeqeq*."

Not long after, Don Juan, too, finally became explicit about the new rite:

> This new rite is very bad! Before the priests invented it, I named a distant person to be the godparent for my children. She carried the child, and my wife and I waited at the door of the church. And now the mother herself has to carry the little creature, and the father if it's a boy. They are doing this against religion. What a sin! Yes, with this modernization, it is a sin that we are committing. The parents can no longer have more children. They can't even sleep together. They are *compadres*. This has been completely prohibited since long ago.

JUST a few days before I left the valley, in a little shop in Caraz, a painting hanging on the adobe wall caught my eye. The painter, an elderly man, told me that he had entitled his work *The Sin of the Compadres*. It depicted a legend, he said, that *campesinos* tell about the origin of the beautiful Lake Parón, nestled among the jagged peaks above Caraz. The story goes that two *compadres* were traveling together and stopped in a gorge to have lunch. A little bird appeared, singing, "*Shapill, shapill, compa. . . .*"

"The bird is calling us to the carnal act," the woman said. Her *compadre* answered that the god of the gorge would punish them. But he gave in. After they had intercourse, the roar of thunder was heard, the buttresses of the mountains began to move, and great boulders fell on the sinners, who were turned to stone. The boulders obstructed the gorge, and Lake Parón formed from high waterfalls and glacial melt.

"Until one hundred and fifty years ago," the painter added, "the stones of the *compadre* sinners could still be seen, water gushing from their genitals."[1]

Driving back that night to Huaraz, I kept turning over in my mind the legend and what I had learned in the last few weeks. The *campesinos* described the *ahuilos* as *chúkaros*, wild and uncivilized. They were the first people who sinned, bringing the Flood and the dissolution of the ancient valley community. I thought again of that underlying sense of being stripped of culture that the disaster had left in its wake. Sins having been exposed by "public punishment," one felt naked. The poem recited on May 31 kept coming back, "Naked is the landscape; / naked are the people. / I ask pardon for this nakedness."

Earthquake and new rite, objectively unconnected, were nevertheless reinforcing a subjective, timeless truth. Because co-parenthood represented important links in "community," perhaps people perceived a threat to their community life in the changes taking place in this institution. In fact, a variety of tensions arising out of modernization may have found expression in fear of the ancient sin of incest, which above all else violates "community" and cannot be tolerated.

ALSO more submerged than idolatry and the sins of social injustice was the fear that witchcraft and what follows from witchcraft— hate, envy, anger, and unruliness in living—might have brought the punishment. More prevalent in the hamlets, where witchcraft can be a sufficient cause of illness and misfortune, it is also familiar to the towns, where people, besides relying on Western medicine, may seek the services of *curanderos*. A diagnosis of witchcraft, usually made by dissecting a guinea pig, means that someone envies the person who has fallen ill. The patient is then said to suffer from envy as well as hate and anger.

This complex of evils was perceived as existing in the valley, more in some towns or hamlets than in others. Witchcraft, like incest, was always discussed vaguely, under a cloak of suspicion, with a great deal of hearsay. A *Huaracina* reported, for example, that "they said that people were bad in Yungay, that they were idolaters, that there were many witches, and that many led disorderly lives there."

I was told about cases of individual illness and death that had been caused by witchcraft and envy. Don Juan's daughter, Rosa María, believed that her mother died bewitched because she was envied for her progressive ways, including the fact that she could speak Spanish fluently.

The disaster, though, was not seen as the result of any one act of witchcraft. Rather, the practice itself was inculpated. The valley must be cleansed of witchcraft just as it must be cleansed of idolatry. Catholic Reform, which had played a role in the development of the idea that idolatry incurred God's wrath, also lifted to consciousness the evils of witchcraft.

One afternoon, Jesusa and Nicolás tried to make me understand the old and the new ideas about witchcraft. They said that witches, very bad people, existed. They attributed, for example, the plundering of the destroyed towns by *campesinos* to witches in their midst.

They went on to describe how witches can implant the notion that even your own family members are trying to do you in, which creates envy and hate and dissension within families. "But it's all a lie," Jesusa said, "and we are failing to believe God's Word when we believe witches." She made it clear that witches existed, only they lied. Jesusa still found signs of envy in guinea pigs she dissected.

"Then 'envy' still exists for you?" I asked.

"Yes," she answered. "A little bit of poison may be put in your food by someone who envies you. This poison is the evil in the dust, the bones, and the skin of the dead."

"They do this to you to make you fail," Nicolás said, "to make you lose your job or a friend. Once this happens, people look at you as if you were already dead."

"But there are herbs and remedies," the benevolent curer Jesusa quickly added.

We had come full circle, and I was confused. "But if you no longer believe in witchcraft and that someone's envy can make you sick, does it still exist?" I persisted.

They agreed it did, because *others* still believed. Furthermore, the two of them were now being envied, they feared, because they no longer believed in envy! Their new beliefs had fed right back into the traditional lines of accusation. Witchcraft was being practiced against them because they no longer believed in it.

In normal times, witchcraft always belongs to others. It is "others" who practice it. No one admits to being a witch. The extreme event, though, had acted as a catalyst to bring the practice of witchcraft itself to public repudiation. At the same time, the shared event made public use of it. Witches and wizards were accused of being the plunderers and, also, believe to be the soothsayers who announced further impending calamity.[2]

THE sins of immorality that were talked about in the aftermath were largely sexual sins: incest, abortion, adultery, and sodomy. These were the sins the seventeenth-century extirpators of idolatry had been careful to point out among the conquered people. These priests also accused their new flock of calculating their degree of guilt on the basis of the extent of the "punishment" they received.[3] Now a townswoman from the barrio of Belén was telling me: "I wonder why this punishment, such a huge punishment. I believe that it's because of the things that were happening here, abortions and lack of respect. . . ."

Frequent imagery was of the Callejón grown heavy with sin, sin at times extended to the world. Jesusa was eloquent on this:

All the world, all nations, the whole earth is rotting. It is like an orange, an avocado, or a banana that is rotting. It is becoming ripe, and at the last hour it will finish undoing itself. The winds are such now that they will come and punish, carrying the house to the mountain. The Lord himself must not be the one who punishes, but we ourselves seek the punishment. With our sins we are aging the whole world. . . . We are ourselves rotting and calling down the punishment. Human nature, and the earth, too, is producing a fruit that is going bad. The punishment is inside of us, and the sin is its cause. A mother can take the whip to her children if they do not fulfill their obligations. The same with the Lord. Only the whip is not the hands of the Lord. It is the hailstorm or the strong rain. In that form one sees the punishment of the Lord, and we ourselves ask for punishment.[4]

When sins seemed to weigh heavily upon people, I would usually say something about how the sins they spoke of existed in many parts of the world. Once, speaking with a woman from Belén, I pointed at random to places like New York and Tokyo. "But those places are more extended," she quickly responded. "Here all the sin is concentrated, and if it continues for some time in a concentrated place and they are public sins, like drunkenness, then there is public punishment." Again, I was reminded of the geologic opinion that the seismic waves were more deadly because of their resonance between the two great mountain chains encasing the valley.

IN spite of all the talk of sin, other chords were struck that sought to chip away at the pervasive sense of sin and punishment. One of these was that the earthquake served as a *prueba*, a lesson in patience and fortitude. Christ had suffered, and we should learn how to suffer as he did, with serenity. We should imitate him. This use of *prueba* recalls a medieval meaning of *castigo* and reminds us, too, of Job. It borders also on "ordeal," as when the bishop called the disaster *una prueba dura* ("a stiff test").

At times it meant the earthquake was sent to strengthen one's faith, as if this should be the natural outcome. At other times, the event was seen as God's way to determine the strength of one's faith. A townswoman said, "God is trying to test our faith, to see how we would react."

Another townswoman put it this way: "It is to test the spiritual strength of people . . . to make clear our decision . . . some to move away from religion, others to accept it in a better form or try to comprehend better."

Another strain running counter to guilt and punishment was an evolutionary one: The world was in the process of transformation, at times seen as "perfecting itself," but mostly as declining, "growing old," "maturing," or becoming overpopulated. One day I dropped into the Belén chapel just as a ninety-two-year-old priest, long retired, was deciding that he wanted to say a Mass. Belén's priest and Norabuena, the haunted guardian of images, had gone to a hamlet. Only the blind man who sang responses in the cemetery was there, and myself, and just the two of us listened to the Mass.

Afterward, I asked the old priest if the earthquake had been a punishment. He said no, that human beings, good and bad, are the grains of God, who is the master reaper. From time to time, when God sees that his grains have matured, he harvests his crop of wheat, taking us into the great sky granary of heaven. God's sickle can be an earthquake or an avalanche. Its swing is swift and harsh, yet in a way gentle, too, the padre went on, "because death is gentle." God also employs the Devil to harvest his crop, but for that he makes use of human beings—murderers—not nature. When God uses nature, as in the earthquake, he is harvesting a bumper crop. "Perhaps," the old priest concluded, "he is purifying his house, as if he were sweeping."

THERE were, of course, chords of disbelief, talk of God's injustice and, much less frequently, his nonexistence. Most people pointed out that the mere fact God's name was called in the minute of the earthquake was proof that he exists.

Feelings of God's injustice or of his nonexistence came mainly in reports about others. It was rare to hear someone say directly, "I no longer believe." What I heard mostly were statements like "Many no longer believe in God. They say how can there be a God if the earthquake could happen."

Reports of disbelief often accompanied stories of extreme loss. For example, a man who had lost his mother and sisters in the 1941 alluvion, and his father, brothers, wife and children in the earthquake, had despaired, they said, and no longer believed in God. "How can I believe in a God who punishes so harshly?" he had asked a friend.

From Yungay, where losses were most often extreme, came the strongest statement of disbelief in God, even hatred of God. The mayor of Yungay described the scene of a group of survivors on the hill of Aura overlooking the devastation on either side:

People spoke of another disaster happening in order to finish off life once and for all. Many were completely dejected. . . . Still others denied the existence of God, saying that no God would let this happen to innocent people. I lost my faith. We did not pray. We did not hold Mass. We did not have faith. God had sent us the disaster. We hated God. Many said that the disaster had been a punishment, but I disagree because my five little children had not done anything for which they should have been punished in such a way.

In Yungay, Ramón had connected his disbelief to the destruction of the images. "All of the saints have been buried. How could they save themselves, being only representations, like a photograph of a brother?" he asked me one afternoon as we sat around Cirila's oilcloth-covered table. "I no longer believe in anything. I have seen so much. . . ." His friend Chepo, who was enduring the extreme loss of his entire family—parents, siblings, wife, and children—reasoned this way:

After the avalanche, I arrived at this conclusion: If God had existed, children, who are without sin, would not have died. God has punished beyond necessity. In the beginning we all protested vehemently against God, shouting our complaints in this way. Later, I thought it was the evolution of nature. Those of us who reflected thought this. Children can die of anything. It was a transformation that we who were living in Yungay got caught in. And the punishment is for those of us who continue living the tragedy. We live now to offer prayers for the dead. Every night I say my "Our Father" for my dead ones. We get up, we drink, we sleep. . . . In Europe, men punish each other with wars. Perhaps God does not punish. Perhaps only nature harms us. And men punish each other. Nature is regulated by certain forces. Is it God? But God does not exist. No one has seen him. Men have invented him so that he may bring order into our conduct, so that we do not slap our children. Such a being as God does not exist for me, but to that being I pray, to that being whom I myself have invented. . . . Life is not eternal. Man was born to die. It can be on the horns of a bull or perhaps asphyxiated. . . .

Up at Los Pinos, a young priest who spent the first five months after the disaster in Yungay told of the immense confusion of belief survivors felt. The priest said Mass every day. One man, who had lost seven children, came every day, confessing over and over again that he had not been leading a good life. Another, in his extreme loss, didn't want to have any more to do with the church. Mainly, the priest said, he listened, and survivors cried. "When you are down, way down, what else can you do?"

IN the valley, not to believe in God was seen as truly a position of despair. More common than God's nonexistence or his injustice were suggestions of his absence. God had abandoned the valley that Sunday afternoon. He was shirking his duty, or maybe he was sick that May 31—"If God was ill that Sunday . . ." (*Diario de Huaraz*, 31 May 1972; p. 6)—or then again, perhaps he was simply elsewhere.

One of Latin America's greatest poets, César Vallejo, was born and grew up in Santiago de Chuco, a town just north of the Callejón. A boardinghouse in Centenario was named for his first book, *Los Heraldos Negros*, published in 1918. This notion of God's truancy is similar to one of Vallejo's verses: "I was born one day that God was gravely ill."

On May 31, 1972, the German priest Auscario, in a sermon delivered in front of the massive cubistic Christ of Centenario, recalled the blasphemy heard in the moments just after the disaster:

> Huaraz suffered so much. The whole town was sunk in a deep despair. Perhaps in those moments of blasphemy and anger at God you said: "My God, if you had been man, today you would know how to be God." That was justified, for those are the words of a poet and of a town that was aching.

Auscario was quoting this verse by Vallejo:

> *My God, if you had been man,*
> *Today you would know how to be God;*
> *But you, who were always so fine,*
> *You feel nothing for your creation.*
> *Man is the one who must endure you:*
> *He is the God!*

The strains of disbelief in God were only that. Catholicism had so thoroughly embraced the miracle that the overwhelming emphasis was on the good that prevailed, the miraculous "salvation" of so many, on God's protection in calamity. Evil was the punishment itself, and survivors looked within the community for reasons for it, though at times they formulated counterarguments to attenuate the valley's guilt. A young woman from the barrio of Huarupampa did this:

> People everywhere said it was punishment, that the Callejón had become pagan. In Lima they said this, too. Maybe we were pagan with our idolatry but not in our morals, as this is a small town and everyone knows everyone. People do more bad things in Lima.

Huaraz, the "generous city of Bolívar," always open-hearted to strangers, was invoked to diffuse the guilt so that it would not be concentrated in valley inhabitants alone:

> Sometimes I think there were many from outside, not *Huaracinos*. They came from all over, Pomabamba, Huari. . . . This is generous land; it receives many people, who may do bad things. We offered lodging to the pilgrim, but they came perhaps with a lover. We women have lived very much sheltered. I can't imagine my grandmother ever left her house. . . .

Some said that many strangers had come to the valley just before the earthquake, only on death's eve.

ON the afternoon of May 24, 1972, I went to visit an elderly *Huaracino* priest. He had been badly injured in the earthquake, never really regained his strength, and died a year or so after I left the valley. In the aftermath, he was laboring to purge the disaster of the idea of punishment. That afternoon, he explained to me:

> Nature, like man, is free. God is not going to tell the mountaintop to fall. . . . Just as with a kettle of water that is boiling, the boiling itself makes the kettle jump and move. It moves, and no one can stop it. So, this earthquake has been an unforeseen thing. God could not contain it. God would stop being God if he were to say: "There, no more, no . . ." He created nature free. He created me free, and also you. Like the boulder, the rolling stone that

comes down from above, or the water, like the lake that came down in 1941, they are free! They are free! One must not say for anything in this world that the earthquake of Ancash is a punishment of God.

Just that morning, Padre Guimaray said, he had traveled on horseback up to a hamlet on the Cordillera Blanca to bury an old woman. When he arrived in the hamlet, a man came up to him and asked: "Is it true, Padre, that the earthquake was the punishment of God, that God has punished Yungay and Huaraz because we are sinful men?"

Then and there the old priest decided to give his funeral oration on the subject of punishment, and he repeated it for me:

In Quechua, I explained to them very nicely, with examples, that God is our Father. Being a Father, he cannot punish us in such a horrible way. He loves his children too much. . . . And so God leaves us free, all of us, and he also leaves free all natural things, and in that freedom the mountain peak comes down. God cannot snatch in the instant the rocks that are rolling, rolling. Mountaintops come down freely because of their weight. And the earthquake came freely. But God in his goodness has saved us. . . .

Seven days later, on May 31, 1972, standing next to the communal grave in the Huaraz cemetery, Padre Guimaray delivered his memorial sermon. Again, he spoke of freedom and of how the earthquake had not been punishment.

MY original quest—to find out whether there was more or less religion, whether people turned toward or away from God after the disaster—was doomed from the start. There was no definitive answer. Survivors did both. Some told of having more faith, others of less. People saw in their fellow survivors "bad people converted to saints" and "saints made bad and blasphemous." Faith was said to be weakened by the idea of God's punishment or strengthened by it. "I say it was a punishment, and I believe more in God," a market vendor told me. Often the same people vacillated between doubt and faith. Moreover, the moratorium on religious festivities and the iconoclasm of Catholic Reform were responsible for many effects on religious belief and practice.

The fact of reflection itself was the important thing. Religion, embedded in life, was lifted out of its matrix for questioning, along with other facets of life that were disentangled in the aftermath. "The earthquake gave us occasion to reflect," a Nicrupampa leader said simply. Answers changed with the questions that emerged, and the questions were what stood out. There was evidence enough to back up any hypothesis survivors put forth for themselves or to confirm any observation, whether it was that the disaster brought religious revival or religious rebellion.

I remember a small granary being constructed in one town. People said it was only camouflage. The "granary" was really destined to become a chapel, only its builder "didn't want his religiosity to show." In contrast, many of the small chapels I saw being built in the hamlets, people said, were not born of "true religion" but out of the desire of workers to receive goods being distributed in exchange for labor. In the reweaving of religion, people had the new political weft to integrate.

What is certain is that religion had become "luxuriant," as my young schoolteacher friend Cucha put it—"*bien frondosa.*" The disaster had forced people to "define themselves," and in the defining, different religious and philosophical currents unfolded. Chepo of Yungay himself had called this process a *hilación*, a spinning, a reasoning, a connecting. I thought of Spanish poet Antonio Machado's "*Caminando se hace camino*" ("By walking, we make the road"). Chepo might have said, "By talking, we spin the ideas." Father Auscario of Centenario believed that "religion is discovering reality."

The term itself—*religion*— was defined and redefined. To my friend Domitila, it was "something for us to keep close and to respect." For an old-time priest, it was "to love God, and for this we don't need to know, only to feel." Another person called it "a way to cultivate moral qualities and live better in human groups," and still another said that whereas once it was "devotion," now it was "a social compromise." To a market vendor, it was "passion."

Religions and religious beliefs had undergone a branching. "Now there are several religions," Claudia, who had rescued San José and the Virgin, said, "whereas before there was one." Besides every shade and interpretation of Catholicism, there were now, in the aftermath, many Protestant sects of fundamentalist persuasion in the valley.

These non-Catholic groups did not feel that it was the whole valley community that, because of sinful acts or disharmonious social or religious relations, was at fault. They did not extend salvation or guilt to the collectivity. Instead, the fundamentalists saw themselves as innocent, a "chosen people."

Twenty-four

EVANGELICALS

"Let's break just the little finger of your image, and you will see that it is pure plaster."

Evangelist to Domitila,
in the 1940s

THE DIVISIONS THAT AROSE between traditional and Reform Catholics over the restoration of the old customs and the saints' images were only part of the story. Beliefs of Protestants already in the valley were strengthened by the earthquake, which, at the same time, drew more personnel and several more sects into the valley. As the schoolteacher Cucha had said, religion was growing "luxuriantly."

The bishop's vicar himself compared the proselytizing of rival creeds after the disaster to the Conquest and the Catholic extirpation of idolatry. "Now, the Pentecostals, the Seventh-Day Adventists, the Jehovah's Witnesses—they have all come to say the earthquake was sent by God to finish off all the bad. The way the Protestants use the earthquake as something that has brought an end to all the evil of before is religious exploitation, just as Catholicism in the colonial period was exploitation. The Church had so much land, so many *chacras*!"

If the Revolutionary Reconstruction and Catholic Reform saw in the disaster a chance to create a new world of social justice, it was the Protestants who seized the opportunity of chaos to speak out on behalf of what they perceived to be the more peaceful, ordered, and moral world of evangelicalism. No effigy would adorn this Protestant world. Perhaps a plain wooden cross might occupy a house of worship, but no images, not even a crucifix, should exist as an intermediary between man and God. Whereas with Catholic Reform the matter of the saints was one of the number of images and their interpretation, for Protestants, images must be eradicated altogether, once and for all.

Without images and *costumbres*, moral integrity would prevail. Beyond this, for some interpreters of the Protestant faith, economic progress might ensue, to thrust Peru into the forefront of nations. Alongside the rhetoric of the Revolution and Reform, however, the Protestant idea of earthly progress paled. The Protestants seemed to see themselves more as apolitical innocent children in a pagan land. Moreover, since they looked for the imminent appearance of Christ, of which the earthquake had been the prophetic precursor, an earthly future did not matter very much.

There were Protestants of long standing in the valley. I heard stories of conversions going back twenty and thirty years, and I know that at least in one hamlet on the Cordillera Negra, Protestants were established as far back as 1935. In the early days, the sects were largely ministered by North American missionaries. By 1970, although connections to faraway mother churches still existed and North American clergy made sporadic visits, most ministers and missionaries in the valley were Peruvian. At least one sect had deliberately severed itself from foreign influence, calling itself simply the Peruvian Church.

The term *Evangélicos*—"Evangelicals"—embraced several sects: Assembly of God; Church of Christ; Pentecostals; the Peruvian Church; Baptists; Seventh-Day Adventists. Excluded from the comprehensive "Evangelicals" were the Jehovah's Witnesses, who believe Christ was only a prophet, and the Mormons, for what many felt to be their aberration from Christianity as it is generally understood. The Baptists and Adventists, at least, and probably other offshoots, entered the valley only after the earthquake. Many missionaries from the United States, belonging to all the sects, were also there in the early aftermath.

Most of the new wave of fundamentalists settled in the Nicrupampa survivor camp. I counted at least six sects, whereas there was only one Catholic chapel, attached to the bishop's headquarters. "Here the population was concentrated after the disaster. Therefore, all the missionaries have come here," a camp leader told me. The new sects took *módulos*, distributed food and clothing, proselytized, and by 1972, counted some 600 members among Nicrupampa's roughly 5,000 people.

Catholics in the camp claimed that "conversions" were bought with aid given only to those who would accept the sect's faith. Echoing the vicar, many priests called the missionary activity "religious imperialism." Another camp leader, who said he followed no orthodox religion, took a rather dispassionate view:

> The Protestants have evangelized a lot since the earthquake. The North American preachers are more practical. There is mutual aid, friendship, Christian charity. And they have the economic pocketbook. People feel protected. They begin that way. Then they accept the rest of the sermon because of the security they feel.

Most of the Protestant missionaries and ministers reported that their numbers were growing, especially in the countryside. In one hamlet, membership in a congregation near the Quilcay grew from four to twenty-five after the disaster. One young missionary told me the Catholics were powerless to detain the Gospel, which was "climbing the mountains into the heights of the valley." Perhaps, I thought, *campesinos* are more accustomed to "extirpations of idolatry" or more adept at feigning acceptance of new beliefs.

But not always. I remember running into an Evangelist, his Bible tucked under his arm, who was on his way to Secsecpampa. Don Juan told me later of the verbal battles they had fought that afternoon. "The Evangelicals do not teach about Christ and how he walked and how he suffered. I shall have to die with this Catholic religion and not embrace another," he said. There were no more than a handful of converts in Secsecpampa.

It was difficult to assess the depth and tenacity of conversions to Protestantism, and I often wondered whether the religious landscape of Huaraz, when it was rebuilt, would be vastly different or whether the rival creeds would prove as temporary as the *módulos* that housed their growing congregations. Several converts I knew well confided that they nevertheless continued in the sacraments of the Catholic Church. At the very least, they had their babies baptized by a priest. After all, later, as adults, they could always be baptized again.

THE staunch bulwark of Evangelism in Huaraz was the Assembly of God congregation, which everyone called simply *el culto* ("the cult"). Started by North American missionaries over three decades before the earthquake, the Assembly of God had as its temple a building that, like Centenario, withstood the earthquake.

The cult was located next to the house I lived in on the pampa. Almost every night there were services and meetings of various groups, one called Ambassadors for Christ. Far into the night, I often heard the singing of hymns, familiar Protestant tunes, and speaking in tongues. It was strange to hear these sounds pouring out onto the dark and desolate pampa as I passed coming back at night, or to awaken in my room to this manifestation of the Holy Spirit, as the glossolalia was described to me by Manuel Torres, the pastor of the cult.

A man of *campesino* upbringing in the large village of Pampas Grandes on the Cordillera Negra, Torres was new in Huaraz. When I first visited him, like most Evangelicals, he began by giving me his "testimony," telling me the incidents that led to his conversion in 1948 in Pampas, one of the first settlements on the mountainsides to which the Gospel had arrived. Seeing the futility of alcohol, *coca*, and *costumbres*, he told me, he accepted the Gospel as a transformation of his life that would make him different from others. Then, one Sunday, praying along with other Evangelicals, something like an electrical current entered his body. Ecstatic, he began to speak in tongues.

The cult numbered some 200 members in 1972, *campesinos* and townspeople, with the numbers swelling, Pastor Torres said. In his native Pampas, the majority of survivors had become Evangelicals. He felt this was because they had experienced the punishment of God when the large colonial Catholic chapel turned into a hot oven during the earthquake and then seemed to explode. Like so many people over the course of my fieldwork—both old and new converts to Evangelism as well as Catholics—Torres pointed out that the cult building in Huaraz had remained intact. And not one Evangelical in Pampas had been lost in the earthquake, and not even one in all of Huaraz. "God protects his children, those who truly serve him," the pastor said, pronouncing a theme I was to hear at least a hundred times.

In the cult temple was a plain wooden cross. "Images have eyes and ears and noses and lips and even feet," Torres remarked, "but what can they hear? They can't hear you. God is present in spirit, and he is listening to all we ask." Catholics had deceived his Inca ancestors, he said, by bringing the images and saying they were alive. Observing that now even the priests had begun to preach against the adoration of the saints, he told of one who had gone to Pampas, and, confronted with the salvaged images of Santa Rosa, Magdalena, and another Virgin, he had challenged the people: "Which one of these are you going to serve?" Torres concluded that in this way people were becoming aware that there is only one God.

Indeed, if Catholicism had "entered through the eyes," the energized Evangelism was bent on entering through the ears. On his free days, Pastor Torres traveled to the hamlets of Rivas, Macashca, Olleros, Chura, Anta, and Unchos, preaching the Gospel. In Unchos alone, he reported, there had been 220 conversions, "because they have realized that these punishments come from God because of our immorality. In my Bible, I read, according to Saint Matthew, chapter 24, that there will be earthquakes, famines, pestilence, wars, and rumors of wars, that it has to be that way. . . ."

As I got up to leave, the pastor commented that I seemed to be a religious person but that I should manifest my sentiments by serving Christ, the only God. Suddenly jerked from my suspension of disbelief—that safe place the anthropologist occupies—I muttered feebly, "But in many parts of the world God is not called Christ."

"Think things out well and arrive at reality," he answered, smiling with that utter imperturbability I had begun to recognize in Evangelists and to become intrigued by.

Because of its Pentecostal leanings and its close, though now unofficial, ties to the United States, two groups had split off from the cult. One night Reyna and I went to visit the pastor of the offshoot located in Centenario, next to the lone gas pump on Fitzcarral. Almost without preliminaries, I asked him what he thought about in the moment of the disaster. "In the fulfillment of God's word," he replied without hesitation. As the earth shook, he said, "Thank you, Lord. You know why you are sending this," and serenely went to check on the whereabouts of his family. He didn't feel frightened or desperate. "The Bible tells us these things will happen." Next, he looked for other "brothers and sisters," his fellow Evangelicals. Not one had perished in all Huaraz.

The pastor described the way in which, two weeks before the earthquake, at Sunday services, his congregation, guided by the Holy Spirit, had reconciled the differences that had been causing dissension among them. They had repented and forgiven each other and were thus prepared for the disaster. At Sunday morning services, the day of the earthquake itself, a premonition had come over the congregation. Then, experiencing a special feeling of blessing, they had all cried.

Not right away but as the days passed, the brotherhood began to recall a Bible study, led by the director of the Bible Institute in Lima, which took place some weeks before the earthquake. Gripped by the Holy Spirit, the director had remarked upon the disbelief that pervaded Huaraz and pronounced these words: "Huaraz will suffer." Some members recalled a priest who stood in the doorway listening to the director and laughing. "I don't know if this priest is still living," the pastor said with a smile.

"What was the disbelief in Huaraz that brought such disaster?" I asked him.

"The superficiality of Catholics who worship saints when the Bible says, 'Do not make images. . . .' "

"You don't believe in the saints?" Reyna asked, incredulous.

"I believe in living saints, made because of their faith and obedience."

He and Reyna engaged in a long discussion about saints and God and how one imagines them. "I don't know if Christ was tall or short, fat or thin," the pastor declared.

"How can it not matter?" Reyna asked, distraught.

"God is invisible; he is spirit, but, well, more or less he must be like men," the pastor conceded.

Out again into the cold, dry night, Reyna and I made our way to the *módulo* of the Baptist minister in Nicrupampa. There were only fourteen members, Mendoza, the soft-spoken pastor from Lima, told us. "Many more come to services, but they do not commit themselves. When we came after the earthquake, we found so many sects, and people are confused now about which is true." From their center in Nicrupampa, he conducted his "Radial Program," proselytizing in the sierra above Huaraz.

"The Catholics are mistaken with their saints and their *costumbres*. They sacrifice everything, family and the preparation of their children, to give a fiesta, and in the end it is bad for the community," Mendoza said. Though Baptists were not then in the valley, he, too, pointed to the salvation of all Protestants in the earthquake. Unlike Pastor Torres, though, he did not rejoice at the fulfillment of God's word: "That would be a lack of feeling for our fellowmen who suffered such misfortune." For him "it was simply recognizing that God's word was carried out."

ONE day I had lunch with Bill, a North American missionary who came to Huaraz after the earthquake. Finding "such a state of religious confusion," he decided to take up his work in the hamlet of Atipayán on the Cordillera Negra. I asked him why he thought the disaster happened.

> It was prophesied. It's a sign of the end of the world. And this fits with the scientific explanation of the earth's cooling and its crust buckling. Christ will return to bring God's creation back into order.
>
> Also, it was to make people not place hope in material things. It marks a weaning away from the things of the world to a dependence on Christ.
>
> And it was a chastisement. The Old Testament won't have any traffic with idols, remember? There is only a transcendent and personal God. It is sad to make God an object. Idols are only a fraction of Christ.

Bill told me that a big reunion of Evangelicals would take place in Atipayán, and late that same night, in his truck, we took a group from Nicrupampa across Huaraz and up into the Cordillera Negra. They sang hymns in Quechua all the way, interrupting them only to tell me that all Evangelicals had been spared in the earthquake. We left them off at a place where they still had a two-hour walk up to the hamlet. Bill would join them with another group the next morning.

On our way back, I told Bill about the fear in the hamlets over the crosses not being blessed at carnival time. "Cataclysm should bring people together. There should be a reconciliation in the cross," he said. "But with all these local crosses and all the Christ images and other saints' images, and one more powerful than the other . . . well, there is only dissension."

He attributed the growing numbers of Evangelicals to the fact that so many images were destroyed, to the new attitude of priests who had begun to encourage the reading of the Bible, and to the aid that the Evangelists distributed, sent by their churches in the United States. But, most important, he said, was the power of the Gospel to transform one's life. People were reporting a light in their dreams; it was the Holy Ghost. This was not the Holy Ghost that seizes one and has him sing in tongues, Bill explained. As a matter of fact, the "fanatical" speaking in tongues of the Pentecostals had divided the cult and led to the establishment of the Peruvian Evangelical Church, whose center was now in Nicrupampa.

THIS Peruvian Church had been one of my very first contacts with Evangelicals in the valley. I was in Nicrupampa, watching a work crew put up an open post-and-beam kitchen in back of someone's *módulo*. A woman who was shouting orders at the workers suddenly spotted me and beckoned me to follow her. She led me to the chapel of the Peruvian Church. The *módulo* was bare; the only hint that it was a chapel was a wooden stand with the Bible opened on it. The woman's first words to me were "You see, there are no saints here and no cross, only the living Christ. Since the earthquake, people are looking for their salvation. Now even the Catholics are selling the Bible! For them, it used to be a privilege to read the Bible, or a sin."

Then the woman took me to her own *módulo*. She turned out to be the wife of the minister, and I would go to visit them from time to time, to talk to her husband, and Samuel, her son, who was to follow in his father's footsteps.

Samuel attributed the rise of Protestantism almost solely to the mobilization of the Catholic Church after the disaster. "The Catholics used to make fun of the Evangelicals, the way we called each other 'Brother' in public. They called us *Aleluyas* because of our hymns. It has been a great shock for the people, when *they* themselves began to sing hymns and pray in Spanish and Quechua and call each other 'Brother.' People say they may as well be Protestant or nothing at all, they are so disconcerted. Really, they don't know what to do. The big error for Catholics is the Reform. It should have come more slowly, not all at once."

As Samuel spoke, I was thinking of a young Evangelical convert who described what was happening in his hamlet: ". . . few fiestas now. And the priest who comes preaches like the Evangelicals. Instead of Latin, he speaks in good Spanish and does not charge for Masses. He gives a good teaching. I even heard him say, 'We do not keep order here. We are evil, fighting among ourselves. The Evangelicals have a book that shows them order.' And besides the priest, North Americans come, too, preaching in our plaza."

I was thinking of the woman who whispered to me during a ceremony on the pampa that Catholics and Protestants were all alike now, "only Catholics have more fun." And of my Evangelical friend, Domitila, saying, "How I danced my *huaynitos* as a Catholic and wore earrings, for pure pleasure!"

I was thinking of the old man who told me, "There are so many Evangelicals now talking of morality, but one should never, never change. If we know how to manage ourselves, Catholicism can be very free and full of joy."

Months later, I heard even the bishop ponder over Evangelism. "They shame people so, insisting on the Final Judgment and on eternal punishment." How long would the new morality, "based on fear and a harsh rigidity," last? Perhaps it would last a long time. Perhaps Evangelists had a way to make people understand that Catholics could learn. "They do speak so beautifully about Christ," the bishop said.

Samuel called his church "antiforeign." But, in spite of this, they had received a lot of aid from the United States after the earthquake, and "the more we distributed, the more people filled our *módulo* for services."

ONE afternoon, walking through Nicrupampa, I came upon a group of women weeding a small garden. As they bent over the dry soil and the desiccated plants, their *polleras* tilted toward the sky. It looked like fun, and I began to help them. My digging companion commented, "We work together as a collectivity." A bystander retorted, "They do it for the president of Sector G because he gives them food."

One of the weeders, a large middle-aged woman, invited me to her *módulo*. An Evangelical since a few years before the earthquake, Leonarda spoke of the peace she experienced in her new faith. "As a Catholic, I walked around lost. Now there is no more dancing and drinking in my life." She called the earthquake a punishment to Catholics because of their images.

> The saints have no blood. In the earthquake, I have seen them hurled through the rubble, and then the tractors came and scooped them up. With the living God inside of us, nothing can happen to us. Not one of us was even wounded in the earthquake. We were all saved. When it happened, I said, 'Thank you, Lord, your word is fulfilled,' while the Catholics were dazed, mute, crazy. And afterward, the brothers helped us, gave us blankets, and always came to see what we might need.

At this moment, a woman entered the *módulo* and invited Leonarda to walk to Marián with a group of Evangelicals later that day. They would hold a prayer meeting and descend again by midnight. As soon as I saw this woman, named Domitila Rodríguez de Melgarejo, I knew we would become friends. Her hat perched on her head, with long braids hanging down from under it and a broad smile lighting up her wide face, she looked jaunty, and a little comical. She immediately began a half-joking kind of proselytizing of me. When I tried to get her to compare Catholic and Evangelical beliefs, she refused, waving her arms about and dismissing me with "But those Catholic beliefs are of no value." I promised to visit her another day and eventually became as close to her as I was to Jesusa of Secsecpampa. They were both *campesinas* to the core, though I would learn later that Domitila had been an Evangelical for twenty years, since 1951, when she was thirty years old.

DOMITILA was fond of talking about her girlhood on the puna of the Cordillera Negra, near La Merced in the district of Aija. Her first seven years were spent in an agricultural hamlet, but then she was taken to live almost continuously on the high tablelands, where she served as a shepherdess to her father's considerable livestock. "Three hundred sheep, thirty cattle, eight or ten milk cows. Sometimes three baby goats and ten lambs would be born each day," she recalled. She glowed when she spoke of the pure crystalline water and the fresh milk and cheese of the puna. "I was raised in abundance, in such abundance!" she would often exclaim—"*abundancia*," the word itself sounding round and full. It was not until many years later that she would know what it was to buy an animal or to see potatoes weighed and sold by the kilo.

But she was terribly lonely on the puna, her parents and brothers far below in their *chacras* growing *ocas*, potatoes, and barley. She slept alone in a tiny straw hut, feeling like "a little orphaned calf," all by herself with her six dogs to keep vigil over the flocks. By day she would sit on top of a boulder, singing to herself and playing her *rondín*. She made up a *huayno*, which she would sing, tears streaming down her cheeks, asking in her song how long she would be so alone on the puna. With the almost constant cloud cover, she couldn't even see the animals.

Not until the age of fifteen did she have her first taste of school, and not until she was nineteen did she study her second year of primary school, in Aija. Still speaking only Quechua when she was given her first books in Spanish, she devoured them "for pure pleasure alone," because she did not understand a thing they said. She married at age twenty and gave birth to her older children through the decade of the 1940s.

Domitila's first contact with Evangelism came when she was in her twenties, already with two children, when a man who did not reveal his identity as an Evangelist arrived in Aija. She had always kept near her, even on the puna, a small image of San Juan, which she had acquired in exchange for a sheep. Picking up the image, the man remarked on how much she seemed to love the figure and told her that by Judgment Day she would have collected more and more images, until her house overflowed with them.

"Well, if that's the way it is," she answered him, "what harm can it do?"

"Let's break just the little finger of your image," he suggested, "and you will see that it is pure plaster."

Gingerly, she poked the finger with her spindle, and fine dust streamed out. "It was true, it was plaster!" she exclaimed to me. "I thought it was a live image, because every year, on June twenty-fourth, we used to feast this image! But after that, I gave it to my little daughter to play with like a doll. It got broken in three parts, its head, its body, and its feet, and I saw clearly that it was only plaster."

"You became disillusioned, or what happened?" I asked her, feeling now, through this fine detail, survivors' conflict over images shattered by the earthquake.

"Yes, yes," she said, "because we used to call it *Tayta* ["Papa" in Quechua], San Juan and how could it be my God?" Not many years after, in 1951, Domitila "surrendered" herself to the Gospel. This was when, at age thirty, she finally learned to read and write, taught by an Evangelist who came to her hamlet on the Cordillera Negra. Her conversion strengthened her resolve to send her children to school so they would not grow up lonely and unlettered on the puna, and for this reason Domitila and her husband moved to Huaraz in 1958.

Protestantism had not completely eradicated prophetic dreams from Domitila's life. One day she related a dream she had had the night before. She was digging up huge black potatoes, high up on the puna, beneath a boulder that was drawing her into it. "Why were potatoes planted so high up?" she asked, saying her dream was a bad omen and puzzled because, since her conversion, she no longer interpreted boulders as potentially angry *huacas*. Her relatives, who had converted with her and then fallen away, appeared in her dream as worms boring their way into the big black potatoes.

Nor had Protestantism deadened her memories of the Devil, *supay*, who used to appear to her on the puna when she was a girl. She would hear his cries emanating from caverns and caves. In streams, tiny human forms with long blond hair would appear. Throwing a stone, Domitila would see, beneath the whirlpool produced by the stone, the Devil sitting playing a small drum. Peering down, she could hear the *tic tac* of its beat. One time, her grandmother had seen a man enter a river and dissolve.

"Was that the Devil?" I asked.

"Who else could it be? A real person would not dissolve, and it couldn't be God." Since her conversion, Domitila said, sighing, she rarely saw the *supay* anymore.

During the course of my stay, I spent endless hours in Domitila's *módulo*, cooking and eating, laughing and talking, often about the things I needed to know but often, too, about whatever came to our minds. Sometimes I would nap on her cot and awaken to the chirping of guinea pigs that scurried around her floor eating up the garbage and to Domitila lighting the kerosene stove out back to prepare our "*lonche*" of bread and coffee, a snack taken at about 6:00 P.M. and often the last meal of the day. On long, rainy afternoons, we would sit together, watching the downpour out of the cutout doors of her shelter, Domitila reading her Bible or knitting and I reading to her five-year-old son. Many afternoons brought a steady stream of her "spiritual sisters" to borrow a few drops of cooking oil or a can of kerosene, to discuss new information they had heard about the reconstruction, or simply to bemoan the cold and dampness and to ask together how long they would have to endure it in the skimpy temporary dwellings. Around five or six o'clock, Domitila's husband would return, having delivered bread on his tricycle to stands in the marketplace and along Centenario.

Caught by the cold night that crept stealthily upon us as the sun fell behind the Cordillera Negra, I often made my way back to my room on the pampa wrapped in one of her shawls. On a few occasions, sickness and despair overtook even Domitila's indomitable spirit, and I brought up medicine late at night and sat with her.

Once, she summoned me to help her decide what clothes to take on her first trip down to Lima, to visit her eldest son, who was studying at the Bible Institute there. And I made sure to be waiting at her *módulo* when she returned to hear her impressions. She was disenchanted with the big city, which for half a century had been only a distant dream to her. She found life boring there. They baked the bread in the wrong shape, and one had to go around cooped up in a car or a "tiny windowless room" that climbed mechanically to the top of buildings. Above all, one could not turn a path and suddenly catch sight of the peaks of the Cordillera Blanca. If it were God's will that she go again to Lima, she would, but not otherwise.

When the earthquake struck, Domitila was washing clothes in

the Río Quilcay. Two small girls clung to her as she said, "Lord, your will be done, you live in me and I in you." Her older son was at home, distracted in the painting of a canvas for a school project. Just before their rented house in the center collapsed, God roused him from his canvas, saying, "Get up and go now." Her whole family, as indeed all Evangelicals in Huaraz, had been spared, she told me. They took a tent in Nicrupampa, then the *módulo*, and hoped one day to be allowed to build a permanent dwelling there.

MANY survivors I knew, especially in Nicrupampa, were on the fence about conversion. Clemente Quispe, who had taken me to visit his beloved San Isidro, was, like Domitila, impressed with discovering that the saints were "pure plaster." Helping people dig their belongings from the ruins, he had uncovered arms and legs of images. Though he remained faithful to San Isidro, from time to time he would go to listen to the Evangelicals in the camp. "They preach so beautifully, but one must know how to read so you can verify what they say for yourself. Since I do not know how to read, I listen to them, and also to the Catholics."

Clemente seemed to fear Domitila, which I never quite understood, except that he felt pressured by the Evangelicals and in conflict over what he should do. He didn't want her to know I knew him, and he would ignore me if we should all meet on a camp path. Perhaps he thought that if she knew we spoke, she would try to find out his true feelings about Evangelism. Or maybe he feared I would tell her he kept a few *huacas* in his *módulo*.

On one occasion, I went inside a *módulo* to ask if anyone had seen Domitila. In one small space were crowded a man, a woman, her father, and six children. The younger man, who had obviously been drinking, was sitting on the mud floor sculpting birds out of bulls' horns to sell in the market. Thinking I must be a missionary, he looked up at me with sad, imploring eyes. He wanted to repent, to "surrender himself to the Gospel." His wife said she was still wavering between her Catholic faith and Protestantism but would become an Evangelical if that would stop her husband from drinking.

Señor Menacho, from Pira on the Cordillera Negra, who was one of my main sources of information on the non–property owners of Nicrupampa, was also searching his conscience. I sat in his little store many afternoons and evenings as children trickled in to buy rice, bread, and candles. Menacho was one of the few sympathizers with Evangelism who was political. He was not committed yet, but rather, as he put it, "in a state of acute reflection." He saw Protestantism as a way for Peru to progress and become like other protestantized nations.

"I like to investigate all religions," he told me. "I am in such doubt. They bring me pamphlets and say I'll find something, and I look for it and it's not there." A woman who had come to purchase rice suggested that that was because all the Bibles were different.

"That's true. The Mormons say that God was white and that Jesus appeared here in America, that America is Christ's other sheepfold," Menacho offered as an example of the different bits of information he was grappling with. "There are so many contradictions, I can't really believe in any religion, though I have a desire to pray."

"Do you feel anything when you look at an image?" the woman asked.

"No, nothing, it's only the work of a sculptor," Menacho replied. "The saints were finished with the earthquake. Only the Lord of Solitude has been saved. Now the priests are speaking against the saints and the *costumbres*. I agree that in countries where there are processions and fiestas there is backwardness. Imagine all the money spent on fiestas! There can be no progress that way. The saints, crosses, and *costumbres* will not survive. But this should all happen more slowly, over time. The old customs can't be taken away so quickly, because one can die, just as the body can die from the sadness of not eating."

Señor Menacho believed that the earthquake was a punishment to warn of Christ's Second Coming. "How else would we know?" His faith grew with the disaster. It had been diminishing, and he felt he was lucky to have made it through the earthquake, for "those of us who have remained, it is because we believed. Those who disappeared did not believe."

"What about children?" I could never help asking.

"Well, it could be the fault of their parents," he answered.

The woman commented that it was being said that *Yungaínos*, especially, were idolaters and that they led a disorderly life.

"It's possible," Menacho replied, shoveling some rice onto a scale. "God does not consent to idolatry, and he controls nature." In his native hamlet of Pira, he reported, twenty-eight people had converted to Evangelism because the earthquake had heralded the fulfillment of prophecy.

Menacho and the woman then turned to the deep trenches CRYRZA had begun to dig on the pampa. "One never heard that people got lost in Huaraz!" the woman exclaimed. "Now children, even adults, are disappearing into these trenches, never to be found. Just today a twenty-eight-year-old man was lost!" As I walked home, the beam of my flashlight bouncing among the trenches, I threaded my way. It was true. CRYRZA had begun to turn the pampa into a giant mazeway.

High above Nicrupampa, in the big hamlet of Unchus, another man, like Menacho, was undecided about converting. I remember him well, because fastened to the side of his house was an enormous dead condor, its wingspan perhaps ten feet. On a bench in the patio was the head of a sheep with a pincushion tied around it. This was to ward off evil, the man told me. He said that the Evangelicals were working hard in his barrio of Llupa. They had put up a hut that they used as a meeting place. "Here in Unchus we used to have such big celebrations for the saints," the man said, "with two cows slaughtered for each feast, and *chicha* and fireworks, but not anymore since the earthquake. There is no money for anything. And the Evangelicals tell us it is a waste." Without the *costumbres*, he felt he might just as well become a Protestant.

"But I can't decide whether to convert. I shall see." He smiled, his silhouette framed by the vast wingspan of the condor.

BY June 1972 I was going up into Nicrupampa at some time during almost every day, trying to get the feel of life in the survivor camp. One day I ran into the Jehovah's Witness from Lima, who had set up a *sala* (room) in Nicrupampa. I recognized him easily, for he and a friend had actively tried to convert me. On New Year's Eve, they came to my room and remained for two full hours. Always "persecuted, yet fearless," they were carrying their message that the disaster was natural in this "unnatural" life, which is ruled by Satan, with God's indulgence.

This was a period of a lot of sickness in the camp, typhoid and other intestinal infections. When I commented on this, the

Witness smiled serenely and said, "It was written there would be much sickness and pestilence." Some twenty-two Witnesses preached in his *sala*, he told me, and forty camp dwellers attended meetings. Most of the converts, he said, were townspeople, as one must be literate to be a Jehovah's Witness.

The Witnesses, along with the Mormons and the Seventh-Day Adventists, were the most adamant that the earthquake had been a punishment to Catholics because of idol worship, ignorance, and other sins. A *Testigo* townswoman reasoned that Yungay disappeared because of so many "bad people," though she conceded there must, undoubtedly, have been some good ones, too. But, in this present world, the Devil and injustice reign. The disaster was all part of a larger plan. She longed for the end of the world, which she said had been carefully calculated to occur in 1975, when the just reign of God would prevail.

After my encounter with the Witness in Nicrupampa, I felt dejected. The camp looked more ugly than ever to me. It was hot, absolutely still, dry, and dusty. Pigs lolled on the almost desertlike paths. As I walked around aimlessly, here and there I would come upon an overturned latrine. Dogs were barking, and children kicked buckets in the dust. A man and a woman urged a donkey along. A big bull suddenly charged down the path, weaving among the *módulos*. The door of one *módulo* was half cut away. On the remaining half the word *Family* was scribbled in black crayon, just *Family*, no name, not even a number.

I was happy to see Domitila swishing along a path in her *polleras*. She had gone to draw water from the spigot. Motioning me to follow her, she went scurrying up the paths to her *módulo* church. We sat for a long time on the plain wooden bench and looked around at the simple pasteboard walls and up at the tin slab roof. She took me up to the front to examine the wooden lectern, carefully removing its cloth covering, which she had embroidered. When we came out, dusk had come, and we hurried back to her *módulo* for *lonche*.

We lit candles in Domitila's kitchen area, a space enclosed by corrugated tin slabs, and she primed the kerosene stove and put water on to boil. Both her sons came in. One had been preaching in Trujillo on the coast. The other was trying to get work with SINAMOS, but in the end, someone from Lima always got the job. Domitila, removed from her *campesina* upbringing, did not believe in sitting on the ground, and we gathered around a wobbly wooden table.

They began to discuss the recent death of one of the early Evangelists in the valley, Emiliano Cano. His body had been brought back for burial in Huaraz. The wake would take place that night in the cult. "When Pastor Cano first came to Huaraz," Lucho, Domitila's son, who was studying for the ministry, said, "Huaraz was so rebellious. No one wanted to accept the Gospel." I often heard stories of "rebelliousness" from Evangelicals in not very veiled connection to the earthquake and other disasters. Ministers spoke of the "toughness" and "incredulousness" of the valley. They went as far back as 1918, when a missionary arrived in Yungay, only to be expelled. And they cited the occasion in 1961 when, on Christmas Eve, some Evangelicals passed through Ranrahirca and were told they had better not stop because they would be stoned. Then, of course, in January 1962, the avalanche buried Ranrahirca.

"Now," Lucho went on, "there are signs of Evangelism all over."

"I got my husband to pasture sheep with me back in 1940," Domitila, who was not much given to analysis, said, changing the subject. "But he was a man of the *chacra* and didn't know the puna like I did." She teased her husband about his lack of skill at being all alone with the animals on the puna. And she teased me about my dark eyes, so much less pure and delicate than the blue eyes of the Indians of the Chavín valley. As she tossed her head back with laughter, in the flickering candlelight I could see her long braids and her almost toothless mouth, and I thought, My God, how much I love her. Domitila, Jesusa, and Cirila of Yungay inspired in me the same feelings of admiration. I wanted to be like them.

As I was making my way down through the camp in the dark, the daughter of the minister of the Peruvian Church came running after me. She was on her way to Cano's wake at the cult. "The Gospel is spreading," she said as we walked along. "When Evangelists first came to the Callejón, they were stoned." Then she told me the story of the "salvation" of all the Evangelicals at the house of the blind man in Marcará, a story I had heard so many times before.

When we arrived at the *culto*, the wake for the old Evangelist was already in progress. The Salvation Army truck, which normally stood over by the Plaza de Armas, was parked outside. I was too tired to stay and went up to my room. But long into the night, all the next day, and into the following night I could hear the preaching and singing before the burial.

LATE one day, a long and fruitless search for a man from Atusparia Zone in Nicrupampa led me into the market just as it was closing. I found myself inside the hut of a couple who sold ponchos, mattresses, and cooking utensils. The man was sewing together a mattress that had been stuffed with straw. They said the person I was looking for had gone to live in Carhuaz. I was too exhausted to set out immediately and slumped down on the dirt floor and, with no preliminaries, asked something that came out of weariness.

"What is religion?"

"It is to adore images," the man answered, barely missing a stitch. "The Evangelicals say otherwise. They call themselves the voice of hope, and they preach very prettily, but I shall not change. I am a Catholic."

They were *campesinos* who had left their hamlet on the Cordillera Negra before the earthquake and built an adobe house near the market. Their house still stood, but they were afraid to live in it and slept huddled together with their eight children in this hut beside their market stand. The hut was crammed with huge baskets of wooden spoons, graters and other cooking utensils, and piles of straw for the mattresses.

"They say the *campesinos* robbed," the man volunteered, "but they have taken nothing from me. Only CRYRZA has destroyed all that remained. Oh, yes," he said, as an afterthought, "someone did rob a door from me."

"I have been so nervous since the earthquake, and many have become crazy," the woman added.

"We used to feast our saint," her husband said, turning again to my original question, "but no more. Other religions are coming, preaching. They are gaining. Perhaps it is because of the economy after the earthquake. We are even poorer now. Before, for carnival, all the crosses coming down . . . Now everything has changed."

"And your faith?" I asked.

"My faith is stronger."

Within a few days of that conversation, outside the church at Belén, an old-time priest from Huaylas, Padre Max, was speaking informally about the way images revealed the "reality" of religion. For him, images did not go far enough to portray this reality. "Christ bled in all his body, though the crucifix only presents the bleeding in the front of his body," he explained to worshipers after a Mass.

And a few days later, at 7:30 A.M. Mass at Belén, the parish priest, in his sermon, was admonishing the congregation: "In our militant life on earth, we must fight against evil. For this, the saints act as our intermediaries. We are not such pure spirits to come directly to God. There are those who say we are materialists because we worship saints. But we are materialists if we forget the saints." Alluding to the Reform and to Centenario, he went on: "They speak of consciousness-raising, the liberation of society. They forget sin to speak of poverty. And people say the Catholic Church is turning against the images, that they may as well become Evangelicals. But I tell you that devotion to the saints is necessary. True, there are those who go to an extreme, and that is idolatry."

Next to me I heard a woman whisper, "Yes, the Evangelicals call us idolaters, saying that no church remained standing in the center of Huaraz, and that is true . . . only the cult."

Two days later, the catechist Nicolás said to me, "There are true Evangelists who do not believe in images. We evangelist Catholics believe in images."

And at dusk, at the end of July, passing the Belén church, I heard music. I looked in to see Norabuena all alone, in the dark, playing the rustic organ. Not stopping, he looked up from the keyboard and smiled at me. "I must protect the Belenita. I can't leave her," he said. I nodded and left.

Twenty-five
APOCALYPSE

Everyone said it was the end of the world because the earth woke up trembling. I was thinking, It's going to be Judgment Day. No longer will there be living beings.

Catholic boy in Nicrupampa

You see, the Bible says there will be earthquakes, and then will come the end of the world.

Evangelical in Nicrupampa

WITH THE FINAL HEAVE of the earth and in the hours that followed, during that moonless and cold night in the rubble, cut off from contact beyond the valley, survivors considered the possibility that the world was ending. When this proved not to be so, the earthquake was taken as a sign of the impending end of the world. This sensation of Apocalypse, sometimes related to punishment, existed also in a free-floating way. It was pervasive, contagious.

Perhaps this apocalyptic spirit was another form of *communitas*, another way of dissolving categories and being part of all humanity. If the world was going to end, anyway, then the survivors in their valley outpost were not alone. In the grand scope of things their suffering really didn't matter.

This overpowering apocalyptic sensation was no doubt a sum-

mation of the confluence of events and beliefs that came together
in the aftermath: the indigenous notion of a cyclical buildup of evil
and world's end; bomb tests and man's capacity for blowing up the
world; remembered Catholic sermons preached in the years before
the earthquake. To these themes was added a biblical Judgment
Day imagined in fundamentalist terms and made supremely conscious by the Evangelicals.

It was essentially from Matthew, chapter 24, that the prophecy
of world's end stemmed:

> "What events will signal your return, and the end of the
> world?" the disciples asked Jesus.
> ". . . The nations and kingdoms of the earth will rise against
> each other and there will be famines and earthquakes in many
> places. But all this will be only the beginning of the horrors to
> come. . . . The sun will be darkened and the moon will not give
> light, and the stars will seem to fall from the heavens, and the
> powers overshadowing the earth will be convulsed. And then at
> last the signal of my coming will appear in the heavens and there
> will be deep mourning all around the earth."

However spontaneous the feeling of the end of the world may have
been immediately following the earthquake, as time passed, it was
this chapter of the Bible, interpreted and preached by a small
though growing number of Protestants, that gave survivors, whatever their religious orientation, a textual basis for their apocalyptic
fears.

The Bible did not belong to Protestants alone, of course. Yet,
only with the Reform had it become a book for Catholic laymen.
Evangelicals took it to be "their book," and they were using it to
their advantage in the aftermath. Their mission was singular: to
spread the Gospel, to make known Matthew 24, which, in light of
the disaster, they felt, could not be questioned.

In the hamlets, missionaries read the Bible to *campesinos* in the
Quechua language. In Nicrupampa and other meeting places in the
barrio of Centenario and at "the cult" on the pampa, Matthew 24
was proclaimed to clarify the valley's plight. Among the Protestants
I spoke to, no matter who they were, no matter which sect they
belonged to or the context of our discussion, sooner or later they

all arrived at Matthew 24. More than once when I went to visit someone in a hamlet, at a camp, or on the pampa, he or she would say. "They have just been here. They say the world is going to end soon."

Occasionally, I was asked to read aloud from Matthew 24. One day I arrived at Leonarda's in Nicrupampa at lunchtime. She was cooking a wheat soup over an open fire. Potatoes boiled in a blackened pot. Along with her daughter and grandchildren, we sat on the mud floor around the boiling pot, eating the potatoes right out of it. Suddenly, Leonarda reached behind her and handed me an old Bible filled with underlinings. She directed me to read from Matthew 24. I did as she asked, and when I closed the book, she said, "You see, the Bible says there will be earthquakes and then will come the end of the world." There followed all the familiar themes of punishment, idolatry, and a life of Catholic diversion in contrast to the "tranquil life" of the Evangelicals. And there was the unfailing allusion to the way Evangelicals were spared and how their numbers were swelling—300 now at her church on Fitzcarral.

One Sunday morning, on dusty Avenida Raimondi, near the marketplace, I stopped to listen to a Peruvian Evangelist from outside the Callejón. He was preaching to a sizable group of *campesinos* and townspeople gathered around him. Holding up the Bible, after citing Matthew 24, he said that this was the book read by a man called Nixon of "the great power to the north." Then, informing the gathering that astronauts had landed on the moon on a day called Thanksgiving Day in that powerful country, he asked rhetorically, "And what is the first thing they did as they stepped from their spaceship? Did they think first of the famous North American turkey? No, no. They read from the Bible, the book that went to the moon."

Not many days afterward, on that very same spot in the market, a shaman up from the brow of the Amazon lowlands spread out his needles, bits of glass, and other charms on a cloth at his feet. With his bare, muscular body and long black hair, he contrasted sharply with the highland Indians, clad in layers of wool, and the preacher in his threadbare suit. A young woman nudged me and said that both the witch doctors from the jungle and the "Evangelists who shout" frightened her.

IF Matthew 24 kept alive the fear of world's end and conferred validity on the idea that the earthquake was a "sign," for Protestants, in turn, the disaster itself became the validation of Matthew 24 and further "proof" that the Bible was an inspired document. As Domitila snatched one guinea pig after another from her kitchen floor, scraped them, skinned them, removed their innards, and dropped them into a pot of boiling water, her son Lucho was explaining, "The earthquake was like a letter that a father sends to his children. It was a message from God. Did it not say in Matthew 24 that near the end of the world all these things would come to pass?" Consequently, the brotherhood of believers had embraced in the ruins, crying and thanking God that he had protected them all, shouting, "Thanks to God, your word is fulfilled!"

"We were happy, though sad," Lucho went on. "We were tranquil. Maybe we were afraid, but not surprised, because it was a prophecy, all written in the Bible. We saw that this was the precise moment to preach to people. We all slept together those first nights, and we preached. We recalled the time when Evangelicals were baptizing converts in the Río Paria and were stoned, the incident incited by a priest who warned that if baptizing in the river went unchecked, the river would dry up, and Huaraz would lose its source of water. But that did not occur."

Some to whom the "brotherhood" preached after the earthquake turned against them, blaming the Evangelicals, but many recognized the sin that existed in Huaraz, Lucho said, the way no one wanted, really, to listen to the Word of God. "Then they heard the message of the earthquake and repented." Yungay had been sinful, too. The lamentable thing, he said, was that after the earthquake, when many may have been ready to repent, the avalanche came down and took everyone. "So we can say that either the disaster was a consequence of the sins or that it was to teach us that we must all be prepared to die at any hour. . . . In Huaraz and Yungay and other towns, people were not prepared. Death surprised them, and they died forever."

As Lucho spoke, another guinea pig was plunged into the water, and I picked up one of Domitila's missionary books. Ironically, on a scrap of paper pasted on the back cover was a famous anonymous Spanish sonnet of the seventeenth century: "I am not moved, my God, to love you by your promise of Heaven or the threat of Hell. . . . I am moved by seeing your wounds."

Later, Domitila took me to meet Víctor Figueroa, a tinsmith, who was president of the José Carlos Mariátegui sector of Nicrupampa. Dressed in an old army jacket, hammering out objects as we spoke, he expressed a not unconflicted sense of joy:

> When Jesus Christ was on the earth, it was said that so many things had to happen on this earth when it grew close to his Second Coming. So then, of course, this earthquake was not a sadness. Of course, as flesh, as human beings, we have felt sorry, but on the other hand, we have rejoiced. God always proves his teachings to his children in different ways. And we believe that God exists, because the Scripture itself affirms that the prophecy had to be fulfilled to the letter. What is prophesied in the Bible is fulfilling itself, and we know that God has not lied to anyone.

Without exception, Protestant ministers and laymen alike reported experiences during the earthquake itself totally different from those of non-Protestants. All said they felt calm and secure. The tinsmith Figueroa recalled that although the earth had opened and closed twice beneath his legs, he was not afraid, but simply gave thanks to God. As they sang hymns through the first night, counting twenty-eight movements of the earth, Catholics joined in. Some were converted during that first long night, he told me.

Also, invariably, all Evangelicals said that in Huaraz none of them had been harmed. "All saved!" was the cry that went up as they counted their numbers. In the retelling, "Not even a child" (*ni una criatura*), was the expression used. The story of the house in Marcará, where 107 Evangelicals survived, was told and retold. No one considered the minuscule proportion of predisaster Evangelicals within the overwhelmingly Catholic valley. Yungay, of course, was the Evangelicals' nemesis. Some twenty Evangelicals were buried in the avalanche. It was conceded that "in Yungay, there was no escape." The North American missionary reasoned, "God never promised that his people would not suffer. He said we'd be like sheep before the slaughter. Things happen to Evangelicals, too, but it does seem that there was miraculous protection of the Evangelicals."

Mostly, the reason given for the sparing of Evangelicals was the power of the Gospel to transform one's life. Accusations of paganism and idolatry among Catholics mingled with those of punishment for their immoral lives and declarations of the moral superiority of Protestants. "The Gospel is power. There is not this power of transformation in Catholics," one minister said. And then, with the fine detail of a raconteur, he related an incident that had recently taken place. He was invited to a function at the Catholic secondary school, which his daughter attended. A tray of cocktails and crackers was passed around. "I took only some little crackers but not the cocktail. The priest, then, also refused the cocktail. He looked at me. I looked at him, and we both smiled."

It did appear that in this notion of "chosen people" there was some breakdown of that overwhelming sense of collectivity I experienced in the Callejón. For Catholics, whether *campesinos* or townspeople, some communal flaw was to blame for the disaster. And it was always seen as having harmed all living creatures and the landscape itself. To a direct question of "Whose sins?" had provoked it, they would answer, "The sins of all." Pressed further, they might say, "The sins of Catholics and Evangelicals alike." Individuals accused themselves and extended the sins to others or accused others and extended the sins to themselves. Evangelicals did not do this.

Something in the Baptist minister's "testimony" of his conversion from Catholicism is perhaps a clue to the apparent breakdown of "community" among the valley's Protestants. "When one is Catholic," he said, "one thinks Jesus is *our* Christ, that he died for *our* sins." As the Baptist friend who was trying to convert him was speaking one day, though, he "suddenly realized Jesus was a personal Christ, that he was *my* Christ, that he had died for *my* sins."

In the course of long discussions, however, many Evangelicals eschewed blaming the Catholics for the disaster and directed their full fervor toward the explanation of the earthquake as prophecy fulfilled. Some said that the peace that knowledge brought them made it possible for them to help others after the disaster, even Catholics. One man recalled he had run to the movie house on the Plaza de Armas to help remove the stricken, though he knew that he would not find Evangelicals at the movies, surely not on the Sabbath.

For the Jehovah's Witnesses, Seventh-Day Adventists, and

Mormons, however, belief had hardened into "truth," an absolute certainty that the disaster was a punishment because of, and to, Catholics alone, and that it validated the apocalyptic admonitions they had preached. The Adventist minister, who had been in Huaraz only since March 1971, spoke harshly of the valley, which he saw as full of sins of all varieties, from idolatry—Huaraz, with only five churches, had celebrated 400 fiestas a year, whereas his native Ayacucho celebrated many fewer fiestas and had thirty Catholic churches—to witchcraft, and the worst of all, sodomy. In the towns, especially, sodomy had always been rampant, he noted. Had not Huaraz already been hit by an alluvion in 1941? Did not the remnant boulders on either side of the Quilcay trace a "belt of sodomites" that had existed in Huaraz? he asked.[1] And, citing Job, chapter 28, verses 25–26, he pointed out that "God has reserved the snow in order to punish." That's the way it happened in Yungay.

The Mormon church, too, saw "the Lord's hand" imprinted upon the valley in the disaster of May 31, 1970. A document entitled *Earthquake*, released by the mother church in Utah, stated that "the significance of the earthquake for the members of the Church of Jesus Christ of Latter-Day Saints is far greater than just another happening in the course of nature." Their prophet, Nephi, speaking 550 years before Christ, had warned that all the nations of the earth, Gentiles and Jews, would become "drunken with iniquity and all manner of abominations . . . and when that day shall come, they shall be visited by the Lord of Hosts with thunder and with earthquake, and with a great noise, and with storm, and with tempest, and with the flame of devouring fire."

"We must be considered the chosen of God," the "elders," two boyish American Mormons, told me, in their room in Huarupampa. People in Yungay had said, before the avalanche, that the mountain would come down if the Mormons were not driven out of the town, and in early May 1970 they had indeed run the Mormon elders out. Without a shadow of doubt, this was why Yungay disappeared, they said dispassionately. And the whole valley, notorious for its sins and periodically punished by disasters, had been struck with the thunder and the earthquake prophesied by Nephi.

From time to time I would see these two young men, who stood out in their blondness, their pressed suits, white shirts, and ties as they walked along the dusty, chaotic streets of Centenario and across the pampa, and think how uneasy they must feel to reside in this strange land, at this time, when Mormon missionaries were no longer welcome. But they did not show it.

OFTEN threaded into interpretations of the disaster as punishment or as biblical prophecy fulfilled was another prophecy—actually more a premonition—that Huaraz would one day come to a disastrous end. Limited to Huaraz and environs, this premonition was no doubt a long-standing oral tradition. Survivors traced it to the early part of this century. It was often their grandparents who had told their parents, who, in turn, had told them when they were children. The prognostication was attributed to a Padre Palomita, or Palomino, so named because he was "humble, simple of heart, and noble." It was never told with great detail, and its simplicity gave it a certain dramatic impact. For example, the padre is supposed to have predicted that "one day these towers will fall," referring to the cathedral, or, again, that one day people would arrive in the valley to say, "This was Huaraz," or, "This had been a city."

A townswoman related it this way: "On one occasion, Palomita traveled through the streets of Huaraz. Stopping at one of them, he announced, 'One day Huaraz will be left in ruins.' He died as a saint, perhaps eighty years ago." A *campesino* recalled that Palomita had predicted that Huaraz would be destroyed by the "volcano of water," Rataquenua, above the barrio of Soledad. Then "wayfarers would arrive in the valley and say that Huaraz must have been very pretty, that it must have been quite a big, beautiful city."

Another version predicted that the inhabitants of the adjacent valley of Conchucos would swarm over the mountains, only to find Huaraz in ruins. A priest told me that Palomita was not a priest at all but a geographer, who, upon seeing how conceited *Huaracinos* were, announced: "Huaraz, how you boast! I hope you are not destroyed one day."

Weaving various threads together, an old man from San Francisco barrio said: "I don't think this earthquake was a punishment. The word *castigo* is an adornment. These are things prognosticated by God, prognosticated by Palomita, taken from the Bible. . . . The earthquake has arrived like its moon. [*El sismo ha llegado como su luna.*] Its moment came. It had to be that way. . . ." On that same night we spoke, for many hours in a shack up in Pedregal, he also said that just after the earthquake "I tried to dissimulate, to conquer all the bad and evil, but in my insides evil stirred, and to this date it torments me."

Perhaps, though, he reflected, some good would come from all the destruction and Huaraz would, within a century, be a great city. "How beautiful it will be, how strong!" he predicted, grinning, his face etched in a thousand lines. After all, life was change, he went on, pointing out that the great Sahara was now desert where once it was a sea, that the world was embattled, growing old, its boulders leaping from their mountain perches, water jetting from its interior, oceans forming and receding. "Everything comes and everything goes," he said, and I thought of Santa Teresa. "*Todo se pasa.* . . ." No, the world was not ready to end yet: "Just now we are beginning to arrive at the practical, becoming civilized, having only recently plucked the feather from our Inca heads. All these changes, the good Padre Palomita predicted."

JESUSA and Nicolás recalled that when they were children, *los viejos* ("the old ones") would cry from time to time and say that all these things—winds, earthquake, alluvion—would come to pass in Huaraz. "Long ago they told us of the *patsakuyun* [earthquake]." With sound effects and gestures they relived for me the apocalyptic fury of the cordilleras that May 31, 1970:

> Boulders ejected from San Cristóbal on the Cordillera Blanca buried Callán on the Negra. . . . Flying through the air, they fought, immense boulders, striking one another. . . . The sky thundered, and we all shouted each time they collided in the air. . . .

The old ones said that afterward strangers would arrive in the valley to find only emptiness, pampa. "And hasn't it happened?"

"This has been so everyone would repent, but they continue in the same sins, and punishment will continue to come," Jesusa said, now animated. "Punishment and more punishment! A fierce wind will come and destroy everything, all the mountains . . . and when people continue with the same sins, then will come another stronger earthquake, and the earth will open up and swallow all the people."

One morning Nicolás told me that he had not slept well the night before, because while walking in the Quilcayhuanca gorge above Secsecpampa, he had dared to peek into the "house" (pre-Columbian burial site) of the *ahuilos*, the pre-Christian ancestors. These "people of before," he said, lived in the snow and were *chúkaros* like the mountains, and when he passed their tomb, he had neglected to give them some *coca*. Consequently, all night, as he tried to sleep, he felt the *ahuilos* tugging at his shoulder. "They are so bothersome. They died in the flood."

"What flood?" I asked naively.

"In the water, the universal Deluge," he answered impatiently.

"They were punished," Jesusa explained, "for the same sins we see now—envy, people lacking respect with one another, the way the young men and women speak to each other by daylight, with no shame. That's the way it was before. Like animals they lived, and God got angry and let loose the water. . . . And now it is the same with the earthquake."

Even among *campesinos* and townspeople I scarcely knew, the story of repetitive calamity was the same. The events might be different, the emphasis, the gestures, but the themes of death and renewal, of the building up of sin, event, release, and regeneration were ubiquitous and spontaneous. I once stopped to talk to one very old woman who was seated in the shade of a tin roof in Nicrupampa. I remember I stopped because of her face. Its deep lines were encrusted with the dust of the camp, like an ancient and beautiful map. She had lived in Huaraz for thirty years. I sat down on the ground with her and did something I rarely did, just asked outright why the earthquake had occurred. She answered simply, "Papa Jehovah punished us. . . . He had punished the whole world before, with the Deluge."

On another occasion, a *campesino* answered the same way and then elaborated on the flood:

The *ahuilos* were the first inhabitants who lived on this earth. They were men like us. They made the drawings and the gold and silver and jewels we call the *huacos*, which people look for to this day. The *ahuilos* were finished off in the flood, the punishment of God. They forgot God and did many sinful things. They had many, many sins.[2]

The earthquake had stirred both mythical and real events. Sometimes I lost track of whether people were speaking of the disaster of 1970 or of some distant past when boulders had collided in midair,[3] angry mountains had tumbled down, or water had washed away the contents of the valley. The proportions of the 1970 disaster for the Callejón were fully revealed when I realized that survivors classed it with that other transcendent event of their cosmos: the universal Deluge. Sin was believed to have reached high concentrations at both these times, bringing on both events.

To sit and hear people talking with such conviction and such immediacy about the Deluge, or boulders rebounding from one cordillera to another, filled me with feelings similar to those I had when survivors talked about the French bomb tests. Bombs, earthquakes, worldwide contamination, and the "end of the world" had been for me largely abstractions, in their essence not very different from the legendary universal Deluge. Now, in the aftermath, these abstract "ideas" were being filled out with the detail of real and enormous events that had caused and were causing now real anxiety in real people. Apocalypse was possible.[4]

Perhaps it was even appealing. A world's end was truly the cosmic leveler, antistructure par excellence. In the extremity of the aftermath, the tension between the human need for structure and the simultaneous longing to break its bonds and transcend it was almost palpable. Apocalypse was both feared and courted. I can still bring back my feelings that year of being somewhere on its edge.

Part 6
THE SOLEDAD
CHRIST OF HUARAZ

Life is doubt,
And faith without doubt is only death,
It is death that sustains life,
And doubt, faith.
> Miguel de Unamuno, *Poesías*

Twenty-six

HISTORY, LEGEND, AND CIRCUMSTANCE

Legend and history have interwoven to make the image of the Señor de la Soledad live.

Pilatos, image maker of
the barrio of Soledad

AS DUSK SETTLED over the valley each day, the neon cross that stood on the foothill called Rataquenua would be illuminated. By dark, its beam hung below the outline of the massive sculpted peaks that rose from the valley's edge. When I was late heading home from Nicrupampa or Centenario, the cross served me as a beacon on a black sea.

Early in 1972, I climbed Rataquenua. At turns in the path, looking down, I could see the pampa, flat and empty. As I got close to the top, I felt as if I would be swallowed up by the deep gorges between the peaks of the Cordillera Blanca. Finally, at the very top of Rataquenua, the neon cross loomed a hundred times larger than it seemed from below. On its cement base someone had painted the words "Sinner, in these heights, where the cross shines, forget your bitterness." Some six feet behind the neon cross, obscured by it, stood a big wooden cross, fashioned of rough timbers.

Below, beneath Rataquenua, lay the barrio of Soledad. I could see the rustic church and knew that it contained the most significant cross of all, which bore the image of the crucified Christ of Solitude, whose fame had spread beyond Huaraz, and even outside the valley. Other saints and other crosses were swept into its vortex. The story of this Andean Christ brings us close to some driving local truth that lies deep inside Huaraz and its surrounding countryside.

People said that the inhabitants of the barrio of Soledad— *Soledanos*—were "frightful in their haughtiness" and that the bells that pealed from the church's twin towers before the earthquake were the saddest in the world. Afterward, there were no more towers, no bells to toll, and Soledad became the humblest of all the makeshift barrio churches of Huaraz: a cane-and-mud structure with a dirt floor and a corrugated tin roof. Wind whistled through the cracks, consuming the candles surrounding the figure on the cross, the Señor de la Soledad, Lord of Solitude. The image was wrapped in plastic to protect it from the inclemencies of the lowly temple, which was perched on a hillock that did not belong to the church. "The Lord," as Soledad's charismatic priest would say, "lives *en chacra ajena*," on a plot of land that does not belong to him.

Originally, this image, which dates from the early days of the colonial period, was of finely carved wood. Before the earthquake, the Christ, adorned in fine robes covered with silver "miracles" in the shape of hearts that the faithful brought in gratitude for favors granted, had enjoyed long seasons of splendor. These periods of prosperity were disturbed from time to time by various catastrophes that befell the Soledad Christ and led to outbreaks of doubt and confusion. By the time I came to know the image, it was no longer made entirely of wood, since, in part, cloth stuffing and plaster had been used in a series of restorations, the most far-reaching of which took place after the disaster of 1970. His face was not right, people said, and since the earthquake, he was really poor. "He hardly has any clothes left."

THERE are two main versions of the legendary origin of the image. One I heard for the first time from Flor, the eight-year-old girl from San Francisco barrio who would lead me up the path to my first room with the same candle she burned at night by her lamb, who Flor believed could not sleep without light. She told me that long ago three priests were living together. One asked to be left alone to carve a crucifix. When the other two returned in about a week to bring food to their companion, they found he had disappeared. There was only a beautiful crucifix, and they concluded that the priest-sculptor himself was the Christ on the cross.

Up to this point, this is similar to other origin legends of crucifixes in Peru, like the Captive Lord of Ayabaca. The Soledad legend, however, goes on to reveal that the crucifix, found on the outskirts of town, was brought to the church in the center of Huaraz, a more fitting setting for such a beautiful image. But, mysteriously, the Christ returned to his hut in the lonely reaches of Huaraz. Again and again, people brought him to the center of Huaraz, only to find the next day that he had returned to the hut.

The second version of the origin of the Soledad Christ tells that a lady went out into the swampy countryside on the edge of Huaraz to pick grasses for her guinea pigs. There, in that remote part of town, the bleeding crucified Lord appeared to her. She ran back to town, where everyone rejoiced at her news and hurried to bring the Christ in procession to the cathedral, where the crucifix was placed in a special glass case. But the next morning he wasn't there. He had returned to the marsh. Every day they brought the crucifix to the cathedral, and every night it returned. Finally, the woman asked Christ why he didn't want to be in the cathedral, and he answered simply that he liked being in that remote spot. It was "his place."

So they built him a hermitage, and as his place was so sad and solitary, they called him the Señor de la Soledad. Volcanoes of water made the land marshy, so they put a chain from the Christ's feet to a stopper that sealed a well believed to be the mouth of a volcano of water. Gradually, the land of what then became the barrio of Soledad dried up, although people still believed that the Christ saw to it that the volcano of water inside Rataquenua did not erupt.

Everyone seemed to know these legends and delighted in telling them, with variations, but they always brought out the main themes of *soledad* and nostalgia for being in "one's place."

The Señor de la Soledad was not the official patron saint of Huaraz, though people called him that and were even beginning to say he was the patron of all Ancash. Huaraz's patron was San

Sebastián, who was located in the cathedral and, after the disaster, had been stored away. Hardly anyone ever mentioned San Sebastián, and I had the impression that the cathedral itself had relatively little meaning for the people. Its cupola was perhaps more significant as the stark and towering ruin in the center of the pampa than it had been as a living architectural feature.

PILATOS, the local artisan and retoucher of images, through whom I eventually located Claudia and the image of San José she had rescued, explained the importance of the Lord of Solitude this way: "Legend and history have interwoven to make the image of the Señor de la Soledad live." It was true that by all accounts, since its legendary beginnings, the Christ of Soledad and those who had come in closest touch with the image had endured a turbulent history. A brief recounting of this stormy past will help to understand the role the image played immediately before, during, and after the tragedy of 1970.

There are several stories about the Señor de la Soledad during the time the Chilean army occupied Huaraz around 1880. One relates that the night before the Chileans planned to burn the city, a man on horseback, with a long beard, appeared before the Chilean general, instructing him to leave immediately with all his troops. No one could identify the bearded rider, but the *Huaracinos* said it must have been the Señor de la Soledad. To prove them wrong, the general entered the church on his horse, brandishing his sword at the image. Horse and general were instantly struck down. The Chilean army, convinced of the power of the Señor de la Soledad, departed Huaraz that same night.

Another version claims that the Chileans, aware of the valor the Lord of Solitude instilled in the people, tried to kidnap the image, shouting, "We will rob the *Huaracinos* of their sorcerer!"

Next, the image figures in episodes of the indigenous uprising of 1885, led by Pedro Pablo Atusparia against public officials because of their inhumane treatment of the Indians. Amid turbulence in Huaraz, the Señor de la Soledad was taken out in procession. During the procession, the image's crown fell to the ground. Since the fate of the image has, through time, been ardently linked with the fate of the people, this mishap was taken as a bad omen. Sure enough, just as the procession was about to end and the image restored to its place in the church, cannon fire was heard from the north, and that night Huaraz was strewn with dead in a terrible slaughter.

"We have that faith," Don Alejandro of San Francisco barrio said, "that if something happens to the Señor de la Soledad—if his crown falls, for example—some misfortune will occur to us. And it appears true. Something always happens."

Sometime around the turn of the century, the left arm of the image was burned by one of the tall candles for which Huaraz was famous and which the devout always tried to place close to the Señor. Don Alejandro's face lit up with delight as he recalled these immense candles of his youth. *Campesinos* would carve them into flowers and all kinds of imaginary figures. "They were four, six meters tall, brilliant torches! What a sign of the Indians' devotion!" But the burning wax would melt the paint of the image, and it would have to be retouched. On this occasion, furor over the restoration erupted. People wanted only that arm repainted, using earthen dyes that would match exactly the color of the rest of the image. Pilatos told me that was an impossible task, but the faithful had nevertheless harassed the artisans of that time, who tried to persuade them that the color could not be matched exactly and the entire image had to be repainted.

Some years after this incident, the parish priest of Soledad, Amadeo Figueroa, found himself in Lima among the most eminent political and religious figures, the president of the republic, senators, and canons of the Church. The president asked him to deliver a funeral oration. Being a humble man, Figueroa declined, saying he was not prepared, but the archbishop of Lima ordered him to mount the pulpit. Offering a silent prayer to the Señor de la Soledad, the provincial priest began to speak. As he spoke, "not even the flies could be heard buzzing," a woman told me, from all she had heard of the affair.

"Who was that?" the dignitaries of Lima asked in astonishment.

"Amadeo Figueroa of Huaraz" came the answer.

From that moment on, the modest priest became known as Pico de Oro ("Golden Tongue").

When Pico de Oro died in Soledad barrio in 1914, the Indians descended from the foothills and intercepted the funeral procession that was bearing Figueroa to Huaraz's cemetery. Shouting that they

did not want him to be buried in the cemetery, they seized the
coffin and, against the bishop's orders, buried the famous orator-
priest at the feet of the Señor de la Soledad. According to Don
Alejandro, who was old enough to have seen it firsthand, townspeople joined with the *campesinos* against the authorities. In the
skirmish, the walls of the temple were blood-streaked, and the
bishop declared it unworthy to be used any longer. He removed
the sacred Host and chalice and left Soledad without a priest.

The image of the Señor de la Soledad remained, though, "all
alone, and all the people, we were in pain," Don Alejandro's sister
added. They pleaded with the bishop that the Host be returned,
and as they were so forlorn, after some fifteen or twenty days he
relented. Pico de Oro remained buried at the feet of Soledad. "The
people overcame"—Don Alejandro smiled—"and, there, after the
earthquake, we found Pico de Oro's remains, pieces of the coffin
and patches of cloth from his robes."

Many stories tell how the Soledad Christ tried to alert Huaraz's
sleeping population of the alluvion that swept out of Cójup gorge
one December morning in 1941. Finally, as the waters neared the
city, a dove flew out of the church of Soledad, deflecting the descending avalanche away from the old, heavily populated center,
saving many lives and preserving especially the barrio of Soledad.[1]

PEOPLE themselves did not distinguish between myth, legend, and
history in telling these stories. But there was one event, a real
historical event involving the image, that stood out above all others.
The big fire that took place at Soledad in 1965 was frequently and
vividly recounted to me.

The sacristan, upon retiring for the night, left a lighted candle
near the robe of the Virgin of Sorrows, who flanked the image of
the Señor de la Soledad. The robe caught fire, and the glass case
in which the Christ was kept exploded, flames enveloping the image.
Barrio people rushed into the church in their nightclothes, led by
the mayor of Huaraz, who managed to wrest the burning image
from its case. But in the process the mayor severed his jugular vein
on the broken glass. As he descended from the altar with the burning image, he fell unconscious and died as he was being taken to
the hospital.

Huaraz awoke the next morning not to the expected *huaynos*

played on Radio Huaraz and Radio Huascarán but to somber fu-
nereal music and the announcement that there had been a great
tragedy. The charred image lay in the church prepared as for a
wake. Many people who were skeptical before, upon seeing that
the image was like burned flesh, not wood, were finally convinced
at that time that the image was indeed Christ himself.

Word was passed that the bishop intended to send the image
to Lima for restoration, as no one in Huaraz was competent to make
such extensive repairs. Then rumors began in the barrio that the
fire had really been part of a plot between the priest and the sacristan, joined in, or perhaps instigated by, the bishop. Under the
guise of the fire and the image's absence during restoration, they
would sell the Señor de la Soledad to another country, perhaps
Spain, which "collects miraculous images," or to "a rich country
like North America." They would try to deceive the faithful by
replacing the "real" Señor with another similar image.

Actually, a few years before the fire, between 1961 and 1962,
there had already been talk that the bishop wanted to sell the Lord
of Solitude. At that time, the rumors grew around a dispute that
arose between the bishop and a much beloved priest of Soledad,
Padre Romero.

The story unfolds in this way: Padre Romero was accused by
the bishop of an immoral act. Some parishioners thought this accusation was merely a pretext to remove the priest, who was young,
recently out of the seminary, and somewhat rebellious against
Church authority. He seems to have been only one of a number of
Soledad parish priests who set their ministry above Church juris-
diction. Watching the present cleric of Soledad in the aftermath, I
gradually came to understand the way in which the Soledad clergy
developed a strong identification with the Soledad image. Through
this identification, they considered themselves to be, as the Soledad
Christ himself, beyond reproach.

However, Romero got wind of the bishop's accusation and was
indignant. The bishop decided that the young priest might well
profit from a few years away from Soledad and decided to send
him away—some said to Rome, and others to a minor parish called
Ocros—where "he might learn a little more obedience." Padre
Romero contrived to have his new orders handed to him during
Mass. When he read them aloud, pandemonium broke out. Wor-

shipers shouted, "You are noble, you are a saint, the bishop will see!"

Over the months, the controversy brewed, and as tension mounted, parishioners began to suspect that the bishop might really want to get rid of Romero in order to clear the way for the sale of the image or for its exchange for another. With clubs hidden under their ponchos, *campesinos* began to sleep on the steps of the church, ready to strike whoever might attempt to carry off the image.

"It was like a rolling ball," a townswoman told me. "Everyone, townspeople and *campesinos*, all of us, we were like in mourning, frightened. When the bishop finally ordered the priest to leave, the Indians came down with stones and clubs and surrounded the temple."

"Thousands, all the countryside," another told me, "descended from their hamlets with rocks and sticks to defend the parish priest, and thus the Christ," from the sinister designs of the bishop. Don Juan of Secsecpampa counted the throng that came to "protect the Señor" at 40,000, even from as far away as Vicos. "We came as if possessed," he said.

No priests were safe on the streets. The *campesinos* attacked them, accusing them of being "the same as the bishop," of wanting to throw out the Soledad priest in order to clear the way for selling the image. The clergy of Huaraz took refuge in the nuns' quarters, but even the nuns were menaced, I was told. The military arrived with tear gas, Padre Romero was dispatched, and another priest was put in his place.

When the fire occurred in 1965, the new priest was believed to be an accomplice in the bishop's plot to sell the image of Soledad. After the fire, the whole town rose up once more against the bishop, and once again *campesinos* pressed into the city, the men carrying sticks in their shoulder bags, the women stones in their skirts, shawls, and market baskets. The whole area, from Avenida Tarapacá across the city center and up to Soledad, was strewn with stones, and the police again had to use tear gas. Several townspeople told me that the *campesinos* were ready to kill the new priest, the bishop, and the sacristan who had been careless with the candle. The sacristan disappeared, and the priest and bishop hid out, some said in the church of the Spanish Franciscans, others said in the basement of the hospital. Disguised in women's clothes, the priest was smuggled out of Huaraz. Don Alejandro told me that he had learned that the priest was buried in the Yungay avalanche. The bishop rode out the tide of discontent and eventually died in the earthquake.[2]

ON the same afternoon of the uprising after the fire of 1965, a priest named Espinoza, from the region of the Río Apurímac in the southern highlands, happened to be in Huaraz on sick leave. By his own account, he felt a strange and sudden identification with the image of Soledad. The challenge of restoring order in the town captured his imagination, and he vowed to himself that day to leave his native Abancay and become the parish priest of Soledad. It was this man, charismatic and controversial, who headed Soledad at the time of the earthquake and who was still presiding there in the aftermath.

Over the months after the fire, things settled down. The bishop placated the people by agreeing not to send the charred image away for restoration. He sent for a sculptor from Spain, who, joined by an artisan from Lima, restored the image as it rested on a table in the middle of the Plaza de la Soledad. The two craftsmen worked in full view of everyone and under the watchful eye of the newly installed priest from Abancay. A twenty-four-hour guard was placed around the Señor de la Soledad, composed of both *Soledanos* and *campesinos* from Huaraz's satellites, each hamlet taking its turn at watching over the image, once again placed on the church's altar. From that time on, except during the first days of utter destruction after the earthquake, when all one could see was rubble, someone always slept next to the image.

Though they existed before, suspicions that the Soledad Christ had enemies who wanted to get rid of him appear to have grown more frequent after the fire.

Twenty-seven

THE CHRIST OF MAY

The Señor de la Soledad was warm,
The Señor de Mayo, cold.
   campesinos and townspeople

T HE LEGEND AND HISTORY of tragic events that had befallen
the image of the Lord of Solitude and the speculation about
subterfuge leading to its being kidnapped, or sold, and
then replaced by another image were complicated by the fact that
the Señor de la Soledad had a double. This effigy was referred to
as "*su paso*" ("his step"), or, less frequently, "his double." The double
was the Señor de Mayo, the Lord of May, so named because the
saint's day of the Señor de la Soledad is May 3.

The May Christ received little direct veneration. This image
was believed to be merely the representation of the Soledad Christ,
who, in turn, was the representation of Christ, or as I came to
appreciate fully only with time, the "real Christ" himself. In order
to distinguish the two images, people referred to the Lord of Solitude as "the real" (*verdadero*) Señor de la Soledad.

The real Señor de la Soledad was rarely removed from the temple for fear that something might happen to him and, as a consequence, misfortune would befall Huaraz. This is what had occurred in 1885 during the Atusparia revolt, when the crown fell off and Huaraz was decimated. In the ordinary course of festivities, at Easter, or during the May feast-day celebrations, the Señor de Mayo was carried in procession—hence, the designation *su paso*.

However, the Señor de la Soledad was taken out in procession in extreme circumstances, like excessive rains or drought. One such occasion was the drought of 1969. The image was carried through the streets of Huaraz. The crown fell off, and, in retrospect, this was said to have foreshadowed the earthquake. I was told that when the crown fell, people began to murmur that some terrible thing would happen, and "no sooner said than done, the earthquake finished us off."

Although the two images were supposed to be identical, people had noticed subtle differences, in the inclination of the head, for example, or that the May Christ had features slightly coarser. Some said that to the touch the Soledad Christ was warm and the May Christ cold. Nevertheless, two virtually identical images existed down to the time of the earthquake.

During that minute at 3:23 on May 31, 1970, many people called out "Señor de la Soledad, have pity on us, forgive us!" One man said, "Here in my town, one didn't hear 'My God, Jesus Christ!' Everyone cried out to the Señor de la Soledad."

PILATOS had grown up as an altar boy and sacristan at Soledad. But, he told me, since the time he began to work with images, his faith had waned, because as he handled the materials he saw them for what they were. He described what happened involving the Señor de la Soledad in the first days and weeks after the earthquake:

> When the Señor was found—it was some three or four days afterward when they got it out from under the rubble of the church—the image was all torn apart, the feet crushed, and in the heat of the earth, the paint had peeled. And the people cried as if it were a living being. The Christ was broken here and there . . . but they covered him with flowers and carried him to a little hut they built. They laid him on a table and put sweet-smelling

herbs and lilies on him. Imagine the faith in this image! In spite of their seeing that it was wood and paint, they covered it with their tears, with flowers, with perfumes.

A nun who had come from Lima to help after the disaster said that they "waked" the Señor de la Soledad in that way, covered with embroidered cloths, until November. At that time, in one of the first concrete actions of CRYRZA, a sculptor was brought from Lima and the image restored at a cost of 26,000 *soles*, about $600.

Meanwhile, the search went on for the Lord of May in the debris of the Santa Rosa chapel, next door to the Soledad church, where the double had been kept. Not a trace was found of the May Christ, no piece of cloth from his robes or even so much as a splinter. Again, the clouds of doubt over the authenticity of the surviving image began to gather, this time fomented by the fact of the double's total and "mysterious" disappearance.

Survivors speculated that the real Señor de la Soledad could have been sent away—perhaps in one of the first relief trucks that carried provisions to the valley, someone said—and the restored image covered with plastic in the cane-and-mud temple could be the Lord of May, the double.

I came to know all of this and to realize its importance rather slowly. When I first arrived in Huaraz, May was a long time away. Still, the first reference I had to the Señor de la Soledad was in a discussion I overheard about his feast days, which occur in early May. The feast used to be very gay and last a whole month, the people were saying, with *campesinos* descending into Huaraz to perform their dances, but "no more" would this take place.

Early on, too, I heard reference to Soledad from Esther, a woman I visited often, in her shack at the edge of the little plaza of San Francisco. As we drank coffee and ate the delicious bread from the Robles oven, she spoke of the tents she and her sisters lived in before they put up the shack, how she could never leave Huaraz, and of the French bomb tests in the Pacific. Finally, almost casually, she mentioned that there had been two images of the Señor de la Soledad, but one had disappeared. "They carried it off," she said, "and the other was badly hurt." An artist had come from Lima to repair it, but "the Señor just doesn't look right." All this meant very little to me, since I was not attuned to the idea of a double and because, from my first days in the valley, it was common to hear about the fate of various images as well as of people.

True, the Soledad image was often singled out: "All the saints were finished off in the earthquake. Only the Señor de la Soledad was saved," or, conversely, "Even the Señor de la Soledad could not save himself." I noticed that even those devoted to a certain saint—as Claudia was to San José—seemed to put Soledad above all others.

During those early days of fieldwork, I would often strike up a conversation with someone who was crossing the pampa, on his or her way "to visit the Señor de la Soledad." On one of these treks I encountered an old woman who could barely walk. "They call me 'great-grandmother' [*bisabuela*]," she said, grabbing on to my arm and calling me alternately "Little Mother," "Little Girl," and "Little Gringa." Without any further comment, she began to point out the crosses of Pumacayán and Rataquenua to me and then said suddenly, "I want to go to visit the Señor de la Soledad. We have been born of him. Him only have we known. His temple, well, there is no more temple, will it be open, *Mamita*?" Still trying to absorb the sheer impact of that vast empty pampa with its ghostly ruins, on this occasion as on others when I met someone on the way to Soledad, I veered off, leaving the old woman to her mission. So, though from the beginning I got inklings of the power that the Señor de la Soledad exerted, I saw it as nothing beyond veneration for a patron saint.

It was Sunday, November 28, before I first got around to attending a Mass at Soledad. In the dusk of the evening Mass, I could barely see the image beneath the folds of plastic. Padre Quintana, the Spanish Franciscan, preached. I felt very much the outsider, for there were many allusions to "gossip" and "troubles" at Soledad and to events of the image's past history with which I was not yet familiar.

"You must look after the Señor de la Soledad, love him," Quintana was saying. "He is not mine, not the bishop's, not Padre Espinoza's. He is yours; he is of the people." Whispers were heard among the taut assembly. "If you don't stop murmuring, I shall speak no longer," the Spanish priest reprimanded.

Walking back to my room, I spoke to a woman who had been

at the Mass. She told me that Padre Espinoza had been stoned because he had "seized some land and was beginning to work." He was recovering from the blows, and that's why Quintana had preached, she said. "All the saints have died in the earthquake," she remarked softly as she drifted off toward Huarupampa and I climbed my hill behind San Francisco.

So many of these allusions to Soledad and its priest were just that, veiled and vague remarks. As my first field notebook closed, and I outlined questions and issues, I still had not singled out Soledad as being of particular importance. On the contrary, I had made the note: "Where I look for religion, I find revolution."

Twenty-eight

THE PRIEST OF SOLEDAD

Slim of body and rebellious of soul.
Marcos Yauri Montero

ON THE COLD AND RAINY Christmas Eve of 1971, Elena, who lived in back of the house in the barrio of San Francisco where I had my first room, went to fetch water at the spring gushing outside the temple of the Señor de la Soledad. For days there had been no water in any of the few functioning spigots in Huaraz. Making the best of the dismal evening, I boiled potatoes in the spring water, and Elena roasted over a wood fire a turkey she had gotten drunk, decapitated, and defeathered. With her husband, Flavio, and their children and relatives who came from Pedregal, we ate under an open archway, the cold rain dripping from the slanting roof. The feast over, Elena suggested we go to midnight Mass at Soledad. She and her family had been Evangelicals for a long time, but they always went to Soledad on important occasions, and baptized their babies there.

Only two bare low-wattage electric bulbs shed light in the dark sanctuary. Candles usually burned on the mud floor, but there was no room for them, as the building was packed, mainly with mestizos in dark clothes. Padre Espinoza was already preaching when we crowded through the doorway, his striking dark *cholo* face animated in the shadowy light. He was declaiming against "false pride," contrasting the attitudes of survivors who tenaciously tried to cling to their former holdings to the "simplicity, poverty, and humility" of the Christ of Soledad, visible only as a plastic bundle in the inky recesses of the temple. He bewailed the slowness of reconstruction, that for a second year the Christ would still be *en chacra ajena*. Then he attacked the new ways—men with long hair, women wearing pants—that had filtered into the valley with all the newcomers from the coast.

As we were returning home across the pampa, black and muddy on the starless night, I spotted a middle-aged American Peace Corps volunteer. He had a certain fame in the valley for his drinking and for the way he bragged about being able "to use the authorities" to accomplish his ends. He was something like Padre Espinoza, rather quixotic, battling the windmills of all the currents of the aftermath. He was very much a loner, and now, drunk, he was staggering back to his room in the sepulchral ruin of the Gran Hotel, where he was the sole occupant. And we ran into Doña Angelita, from whom I bought bread in San Francisco and who usually went to Mass at her barrio church. She had gone to Soledad, though, for Christmas to pray for all the survivors of Ancash.

On New Year's Day, as tiny groups of Indian musicians moved across the pampa up toward Soledad, a townswoman told me the legend of the image's origins. "Within this tradition, perhaps reality is hidden," she said. "It could have been a miracle. Perhaps the Señor did appear all by himself." She reasoned that the artist, or the artist-turned-Christ, must have been famous, because the Señor's features were so sharp and well-defined. "I have faith. If I am in difficulty, I always pray to the Señor de la Soledad." Almost everyone called the image "miraculous" and said that the Señor de la Soledad "had been wounded" in the earthquake and that he now lived *en chacra ajena*.

In this way, I was slowly working my way around Soledad, and it was not until early February that I decided to try to speak to the priest himself. He invited me to have lunch with him, in a building behind the sanctuary-hut where he lived, along with children orphaned in the disaster and aged survivors who had no remaining family.

We ate boiled potatoes and rice, and drank herbal tea in the bare dining room, the padre wearing his black turtleneck sweater. In my notes, I recorded the "revolutionary ambience" of the austere setting and described the priest in words that came to me first in Spanish: "*quejumbroso, histriónico, martirizado*" ("complaining, histrionic, and martyred"). In spite of these adjectives, I liked him and found it hard not to be caught up in the magnetic spell he cast over whatever he touched or spoke about.

"We have not received help from *anyone*," he said, "*no one, no one, no one*," enumerating all possible sources from which aid might have come—the Alliance for Progress, the Russians, the OAS, and so on—thus establishing his stance of aloof abandonment. "Only Quintana helps me," he went on, referring to the Spanish priest of Huarupampa. He began to attack CRYRZA. "The Peruvians are the worst. There is no true revolution. I am my own revolution! Three to four thousand *campesinos* come down to hear me preach. . . . Nothing is happening here. *Huaracinos* do not love their land the way my people of Abancay do."

Though still sickly from injuries he received in the earthquake, he said, he worked hard and was defending the parish virtually single-handedly. He had set up what he called his Citadel of Children, comprised of the waifs who had found no one to take them in after the disaster. He had also started a cement brick factory near a stream in Pedregal above Soledad. Bricks were being made, though there was no way to know whether or not he would ever be allowed to use them to rebuild the sanctuary of the Señor. His taking over the land for the brick factory had brought about CRYRZA's attack on him in late November. At least, though—he sighed—the work kept the older boys of the Citadel occupied.

Try as I did, I could not get Padre Espinoza to speak of religious matters. He ignored my questions about the images of Soledad and the Christ of May, and he fended off my inquiries into the disposition of the mountain crosses, which I was avidly pursuing at the time, with carnival approaching. Or else he fielded them with his "manifesto": "There should be no diversion in times of war."

Anxious for me to see his brick factory in Pedregal, he hurriedly finished his meal and beckoned me to follow him. As we climbed hastily over the foothills, he was alternately scurrilous and sociable, at one moment passionately attacking all elements at work in the aftermath and in the next, laughing, tousling the hair of the boy-workers who ran toward us down the hills. He gathered up the smallest one, Shanti, in his arms and carried him during our tour of the "factory." As we moved among neatly arrayed stacks of cement bricks, the padre began to speak about his enemies in the clandestine style I was beginning to recognize. I can still recapture the strange elation I felt on that windswept sierra afternoon, being led up the mountainside and escorted through the stockpiles of bricks by this man in whom madness and wisdom met.

SOON after that occasion, I walked up to Soledad early one morning. At this point, I was thinking that if I could just sit in the quiet of the temple, looking at the image, perhaps the secret that would explain the magnetism of the place, its priest, and the power of the image might reveal itself.

I found Padre Espinoza baptizing two infants. On a wooden bench were seated three *campesinos*, one the blind musician. Their carefully folded ponchos rested on their shoulders, and their mud-encrusted feet, clad in rubber sandals, tapped the packed dirt floor. Propping against the bench the stick he always carried, the blind man took up a mandolin and began to sing in Quechua:

> *I would like to buy myself new clothes,*
> *And come to die at the cross of our Lord,*
> *Señor Jesus Christ, you have died for us,*
> *Without any fault of your own. . . .*
> *Now we come crying our sins. . . .*

A young woman I recognized from previous times at Soledad was darting around the temple. Emaciated, wearing a ragged dress, her hair stringy and unkempt, her expression forlorn and crazed, she always seemed busy with some pursuit known only to her. I came to know her later as Marianela, one of the afflicted and hapless ones whom the padre had gathered into the bosom of Soledad.

When a child began to fidget noisily during the baptism, Marianela shushed her, and referring to the image of the Señor de la Soledad in the familiar way as *Papacito* ("Little Papa") she admonished the child: "Be quiet. *Papacito* is going to get upset."

The girl responded peevishly. "He doesn't see me because he's dead."

"No, *Papacito* is alive. He's still warm," Marianela shot back.

The music played on, the blind man singing: "We have sung at the cross, where our *Tayta* ["Father," in Quechua], Padre Cristo, has died. . . ." My growing sense of this Christ as old was reinforced. *Campesinos* began to filter in, greeting each other, "*Teetee*," "*Mamee*" ("Father," "Mother"), and placing their candles in the earthen floor.

An argument ensued between two of them. One was saying, "*Papacito* knows the good and the bad of all of us. The priests can fail. But *Papá*, no, he is the only one."

The argument may have had to do with whether or not the Señor de la Soledad only performed miracles of benefit to people or whether he also punished—a controversy I had heard before—because Marianela interjected, "If one does not follow a straight and narrow path, *Papacito* punishes."

The blind man finally put a stop to the dispute, saying, "You should not argue in front of our *Papacito*. Let's go outside." Then, muttering, "Our Creator, our Father of Solitude," he felt his way out of the church with his stick.

The Evangelicals were in full swing as I passed their church on my way back to my room on Nueva Granada. *Campesinos* overflowed the entrance. Loud singing and preaching poured out over the pampa, contrasting sharply with the soft strains of the mandolin and the melancholy song of the blind man in the Soledad sanctuary.

Perhaps I had gotten a fraction closer to understanding Soledad. But its priest was still an enigma.

Twenty-nine

FAITH AND DOUBT

From so much believing in something, one comes to doubt.

townswoman of Huarupampa

A FEW DAYS LATER, as Don Juan and I were seated facing the altar in the tiny Secsecpampa chapel, talking about the carnival crosses, he pointed to a small image of the Señor de la Soledad. The bishop had wanted to take this image away, Don Juan said, but he challenged him: "Kill us all, but don't take him away from us. . . . I am ready to shed my blood in order that he stay."

Don Juan told me the image had been in their chapel since 1904, having appeared either "by himself or brought by angels or made by a sculptor. It is not known which." What was known with certainty was that the Virgin was the Mother of the Señor de la Soledad and that after the Crucifixion, "on the third day, the Señor de la Soledad appeared." The historical Christ, the large image in Huaraz, and the small one in Secsecpampa, all three, seemed to fuse in his mind, and I am not sure which image Don Juan meant when he spoke of the bishop's wanting to take him away. Often in my discussions with Don Juan I had that dizzying feeling of sliding back and forth among different kinds of "realities," which I kept neatly categorized but which he did not. When I asked him the difference between the large and small images, he said simply that the Huaraz image was "the real Señor de la Soledad."

I was becoming more attuned to the theme of the "reality" of the image of the Christ of Solitude. I often heard statements like "One can't look too long at his eyes, he is so real." And I began to take every opportunity to stop for a moment at the rustic sanctuary, where, at any time of day or night, *campesinos* and townspeople could be found sitting quietly, lighting candles, or softly addressing the plastic-wrapped image on the cross.

One afternoon, as violent winds battered the temple-shed, dust and air penetrating to ruffle the plastic, I sat down behind two kneeling townswomen and overheard them whispering to each other:

— What do you think? Is it the Señor himself?

— I don't know, it doesn't seem to be. The Señor was more olive-skinned, darker.

— And look at his hair. He had more hair. And his expression is coarser. The Señor was more delicate.

— Yes, it must be his double, the Christ of May.

— Yes, yes, it's only his double.

— And the Señor himself? Do you suppose he was lost in the earthquake? Or was he just injured?

— I think the priest has the Señor himself. He must have put him away somewhere. That priest! But I don't know; perhaps it is the Señor himself.

— Yes, perhaps, but look at his arm. . . .

— And they're going to expropriate Huaraz, you know.

— Ay, yes, they're throwing us out of our places.

Very late one night, about 11:00 P.M., I decided to walk up
to Soledad, hoping the tin door would not be padlocked and I might
be able to enter and, for once, study the image without distraction,
perhaps even look under the plastic covering. The door was ajar,
and I slipped in. Only a few candles burned near the table that
served as the altar, and as there seemed to be no one in the temple,
I cautiously approached the image. Behind the altar, asleep on a
blanket at the foot of the image, was Marianela, the deranged young
woman whom I had often seen in the daytime, arranging and rear-
ranging flowers, candles, and admonishing worshipers. Rousing,
she flinched at the sight of me. As she got to her feet, I babbled
something about coming to visit the Señor while in her pressured
high-pitched voice she began to harangue incoherently about how
she had to protect the Señor from his many enemies. She told me
that since the fire of 1965, except for the nights succeeding the
earthquake, before they dug the Señor out, she had always slept
beside the image. Thwarted again, I quietly left and walked back
to my room.

During the early months of my fieldwork, I was also hearing
veiled suspicions about Padre Espinoza, like the one I overheard in
the church. Another time, an image maker in Centenario, after
explaining the existence of the double, the Christ of May, asked if
the priest had told me anything about it. When I said no, that he
wouldn't speak to me about the May Christ, the artisan remarked,
his voice pregnant with implication: "It is very curious that no
remains whatsoever have been found."

Espinoza himself, in his sermons, alluded to those who "call
me a thief, who criticize me, slap me in the face, when I came here
from afar to do something for this Christ. . . ."

IT was only after five months that the pieces of the Soledad puzzle
began to fit together. Nicolás, Jesusa, and I were sitting one afternoon in their house in Secsecpampa, discussing a wide range of
subjects. All at once Nicolás brought up the Señor de la Soledad.
"When we needed rain, we of the hamlets would make a Mass for
him," he said, "and by afternoon the clouds would begin to ac-
cumulate. If it didn't rain for a long time, then we would take the
Señor himself out in procession."

I remained silent, merely listening, as he went on rather

circumspectly—seated on his haunches, his wool cap pulled down over his forehead—to relate the following:

> They say—frankly, we don't know for sure—that our image has been sold. The bishop has sold it. It is not clear. Our grandparents said that the Señor was the work of angels. The Señor was like alive. It was our faith that he himself, Christ himself, lived in Huaraz. Long ago we used to guard the Señor, each hamlet. But the bishop prohibited this. And there was a punishment in 1941, but it was only an alluvion. People became demoralized when we were kept from guarding the Señor. We began to protest.
>
> In a sermon, before the fire, Padre Romero said that the bishop wanted to sell the Señor, and the bishop rose up against the padre. They say the bishop sold the Señor to a nation that collects miraculous images.

Still I said nothing, and Nicolás, proceeding cautiously, continued with a statement that, with brilliant logical coherence, linked the disaster of 1970 to the belief that the image had been sold:

> Now, we don't know if the Señor de la Soledad himself permitted himself to be sold—just as he permitted himself to be crucified—in order that there might be an earthquake; or if he got angry and sent the punishment because they sold him; or if it was nature, and the earthquake happened simply because our guardian was not here to protect us.

Nicolás went on to question, however, whether it really could have been merely a dispassionate nature or a cruel act of man, because, he asked, "Doesn't God control nature? And if it was the bomb, does God not permit the bombs?" The one certainty was his belief that, for some reason, Christ—the Señor de la Soledad—was not in Huaraz when the earthquake occurred.

Jesusa said that her grandmother's grandfather had told her grandmother when she was only ten years old that one day "people will pass through Huaraz and say, 'This was Huaraz.' It's going to be only a pampa."

"That's why," Jesusa went on, "they said the Señor de la Soledad was so powerful in Huaraz and the day that he should be absent, something would happen. It would be the wrath of God, and the punishment would keep coming. The earth would eat up the people. And still, people don't repent."

Later, Don Juan told me with equal certainty that "the earthquake could never have happened if the Señor had been in Huaraz. He would have contained it, just as he had contained the alluvion of 1941." Don Juan connected the absence of the Soledad Christ to the prophecy of Palomita: "These rumors began long ago. A Padre Palomita, in the early part of the century, predicted the earthquake would occur after the Señor had been sent away." Several people identified Palomita, or Palomino (which mean "dove"), as the parish priest at Soledad around the turn of the century, and I suspect that the gentle prophet was the famous orator of Soledad, Amadeo Figueroa—Pico de Oro—who had been buried at the feet of the image.

As time went on, I became more and more aware of the depth of the identification of the image of the Señor de la Soledad with the historical Jesus Christ, who, according to Christian belief, is both God and man. Right down to my departure, I heard many statements to corroborate this. Don Alejandro, just a few nights before I left Huaraz, in his reminiscences about the barrio of Soledad at the turn of the century, recalled that whenever the Host (which Catholics believe is Christ's body and blood) was lifted during Mass, a curtain would be lowered in front of the image of the Señor de la Soledad. "Why was that?" I asked.

He replied simply, as if I should have known, "In order that there not be two Gods at once."

This merging of image and the personage it represented was not unlike the people's feelings that other images, too, were real, of flesh and blood. But the threats against Soledad made the sameness of Christ and image more poignant. The absence of the image could mean God's absence from the valley.

IN the predawn cold of Good Friday morning, as hot punch was being prepared to warm those keeping the all-night vigil near the stretchers that bore the Señor Nazareno and the Virgin of Sorrows, another facet was disclosed: People had had dreams before the earthquake in which the Señor de la Soledad revealed himself. In these dreams, he asked to be rescued from abroad, usually Spain, lest there be catastrophe in the valley.

I learned this from a small group of townsmen as we stood in front of the chapel in San Francisco barrio. I had been drawn to the group because I heard them call one of the men Atusparia. The man told me that he had been named for his ancestor, Pedro Pablo Atusparia, the Indian leader from Marián. A dark, handsome man in his thirties, Atusparia was a lawyer who had studied at the University of San Marcos and for the last ten years had been living in Lima. He was in Huaraz on his annual visit to his aged parents, who had refused to leave Huaraz after the disaster.

Exhausted from my trip back from Lima and still dazed with altitude, at first I listened halfheartedly to their conversation. I found it hard to focus my attention and simply reveled in the dreamlike quality of the night, the moon striking Huascarán, punch bubbling in caldrons on the narrow strip of the San Francisco plaza, *campesinos* asleep by the platforms, and townsmen in their dark clothes, scarves wound around their necks or raised to cover all but their eyes against the frosty night. But my attention was suddenly channeled to Atusparia and his friends when a discussion arose among them on the "reality of the saints" and on "truth" versus "artificiality."

"We cannot compare this night with others before the earthquake," a man named Cáceres was saying. "This Nazarene Christ is on loan; he is not the real one from Soledad, which is in Lima for restoration. Those artists there will repair him with too much art."

"What difference does it make if he is on loan? What does it matter if this is the image that comes from Soledad, San Francisco, Belén, or Huarupampa?" Atusparia asked.

Cáceres replied that the Señor de Nazareno that came out in procession from Soledad was "prettier, and more real, because he was from Soledad." He explained, "This one [that rested now on the platform outside the San Francisco chapel] is permanently bent over from the waist. The Soledad Nazareno moved, and when he stumbled with the cross, he could rise up alone. And his eyes were very real, as was his passivity. . . ."

"As real as two bright stars that light up the evening sky," a third man interjected.

"Like the Holy Cross of Rataquenua that shines on us and which, it is said, controls the volcano," Atusparia added.

The conversation grew more surreal, like a stream of consciousness. "What is reality?" Cáceres asked, and answered himself, "Truth is reality. Without reality, there is no truth. . . . There, in front of us, on San Cristóbal, for example, we see a woman spinning and a bull," he said, alluding to the shape of the mountain.

"But it is only a legend that San Cristóbal is a woman and a bull," Atusparia asserted. He himself had climbed San Cristóbal with a friend from Lima, and they had eaten ice from the mountain. The ice was real. In Lima, everything was artificial.

"Here, too," Cáceres retorted, "for example, Popsicles." After a pause, he added, "But here we do follow our processions like the rushing waters of a river, like the Santa—"

"More like the Quilcay, which cascades," the third man corrected him.

Drawing me into the conversation, Atusparia turned and asked, "What do you think of these traditions of our beloved Huaraz?"

Soon he was talking about Soledad. Everyone was worried because there was still no proper basilica for the Señor de la Soledad. "Millions and millions of *soles*" had been donated, part of which had come from the cardinal of Peru, and still Padre Espinoza had not built the basilica. Atusparia grew adamant: "The moment will come when we professionals of Huaraz will make the *campesinos* see that the Señor de la Soledad is not the real one, who has been sold. I think that because of politico-religious affairs, the real Señor de la Soledad is not here but in Spain. We are going to rise up, all the people, against the padre and against CRYRZA."

"I respect your ideas, Dr. Atusparia," the third man said, "and I support you, especially with regard to CRYRZA, but the padre is helping us with his brick factory. He is working for society and the good of us all."

"What do you mean when you say the Señor de la Soledad is not the real one?" I asked Atusparia.

"There are some priests before the present one—and some conjecture that the present one also—who may have sold the image to a foreign power. The real Señor has been found through dreams. Many say he's there in Spain," Atusparia answered.

"But how do you mean through dreams?" I insisted.

"There are many very Catholic, very religious people, who morning and afternoon can be found praying in the church," he replied, now separating himself from those who had actually had the dreams, becoming their spokesman. "And they say, 'I have dreamed of the Señor de la Soledad, and he is not this image here. This is another one, and the real one is in Spain.' This problem arose before the earthquake, and people believe that because he was not here, because of the falsity of the Señor who is here, the earthquake occurred. It was because people did not concern themselves to bring him back. These are the beliefs."

"Among the people of the town and the countryside?" I asked.

"Yes, both," Atusparia replied, pointing out the complicating factor of the existence of the double. He confessed that he had spent little time as a youth observing the image, preferring to enjoy himself in other activities, so he could not detect the subtle differences between the Lord of Solitude and the Lord of May. "Therefore, they say all this, but I don't know if it is actually true or not."

"I have heard in the countryside that the *campesinos* believe that Christ himself lived in Huaraz," I said.

"Of course," Atusparia concurred, "that's why, when they would take him to the cathedral, he would always return to his place. His place was very swampy, but recently it has dried up, and people say it dried up because it is no longer the real Señor."

"When did it dry up?" I asked.

"During the time of the last bishop, before this one, when there was the great scandal."

I think it was at this point that I realized that the origin myth, the fire of 1965, and the earthquake had been joined together. In the confusion of the fire, the real Señor had disappeared; hence, the dreams people had in which the real Señor appeared to them from afar and, finally, the earthquake due to his absence.

"What does Padre Espinoza say about all this?" I asked, thinking I might finally learn through others the priest's thoughts about the disappearance of one of the images.

"I'm not much for conversing with priests," Atusparia responded, "but he won't say anything, and I think that he, too, is implicated."

Continuing to slip back and forth between his stance as outside observer—the professional living in Lima—and inside believer— the boy of Soledad barrio—Atusparia confirmed what Jesusa had said about continuing punishment: "People are uneasy now, because there could be another disaster if the Señor is not returned to his place." He went on to name the rival Protestant creeds that had emerged in the aftermath, reasoning that until the problem of the image was resolved, it was very possible that different kinds of religion could easily be introduced.

"If only it were possible to prove what the truth is," he said, "to verify if the disaster was the punishment of God or not."

"How might that be done?" I asked, feeling myself drawn deeper and deeper into Atusparia's own struggle with rationality.

"That is the problem," he lamented. "There are no convincing proofs that it was the punishment of God. The valley topography is very dangerous. The Ranrahirca avalanche of 1962, for instance, was caused by the rupture of a glacier from Huascarán. How can I think it was punishment? But, of course, at times I do begin to doubt, when I hear the whole town talking of punishment."

"Can you imagine what a proof of punishment would be?" I asked him.

"The appearance of Christ himself. . . ."

I let it go, and Atusparia began to talk of how he liked to spend time walking over the foothills, stopping in the hamlets, from Conococha to Carhuaz, trying to understand the *campesinos* and his heritage. "One must come to know them well," he said, "because they can be very delicate." His grandmother had zealously kept the beautiful staff of his famous ancestor, the rebel of Marián, but it was destroyed in the earthquake.

Walking home across the pampa in the early morning, the sun climbing over Huascarán—that other powerful entity in the Callejón—Reyna, who had heard our conversation, remarked, "It's true what he says. Without the Señor de la Soledad, everything is topsy-turvy."

ALONG about this time, I wrote to a friend in the States. Reading over a copy of that letter, I can feel my frustration over the Soledad affair. Now, too, I marvel at the way I approached the issue. Ironically, though, the more of the Western sleuth I became, the more I was suspending disbelief and beginning to see it all through the people's eyes.

> In 1965 there was a fire at Soledad. The mayor was killed trying to save the Señor. They held a wake for the image, and

Top, left: *The Lord of Solitude—or his double, the Christ of May—leaving the Soledad church in procession, sometime before the earthquake* (P. Doughty). Top, right: *On the Sunday before carnival Tuesday, in 1972,* campesinos *bring down their huge mountain cross to be blessed in the provisional Soledad church.* Above: *More crosses come to the pampa of Huaraz.* At right: *The path to Secsecpampa, hamlet on the Cordillera Blanca.*

At left: *On carnival day, 1972, Perejil, the smallest of Secsecpampa's mountain crosses, stands against the patio wall as Don Juan and the cross's majordomo prepare to take it to the plaza.* Below: *The crosses in front of the Secsecpampa chapel before their return to the mountain peaks.* Bottom, left: *The flute player who asked wryly, "Do you think we should forgive God?"* Bottom, right: *Don Juan.* Facing page: top: *The chapel in Secsecpampa ready to receive the bishop* (T. Cook); bottom, left: *the* abuela, *Don Juan's mother-in-law, preparing guinea pig (skewered against the wall) in Don Juan's patio;* bottom, right: *Rosa María, Margarita, and Shanti, Don Juan's children, wait as Jesusa and her mother prepare a meal in Don Juan's patio.*

At left: *Norabuena watching over his san-*tos. Below: *The Virgin, protected in the aftermath, at Soledad.* Bottom: *The Lord of Solitude being "waked" after the fire at Soledad in 1965; people said his face felt like charred flesh* (F. Sotomayor).

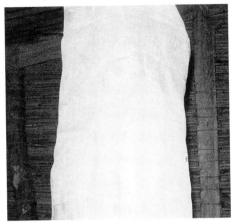

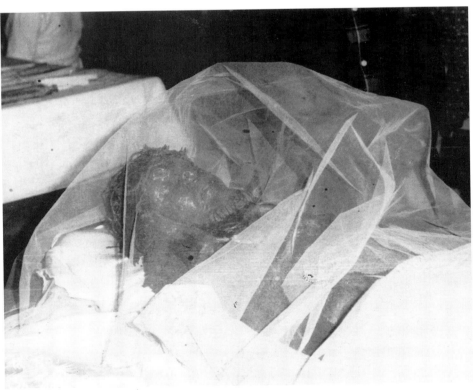

Top, left: *The Lord of Solitude, covered with plastic, in his rustic church.* Top, right: *The Lord of Solitude is carried in procession on May 10, 1972, the eighth day of the feast of Soledad. The image is preceded by the prefect, the subprefect, the CRYRZA general, and the bishop's vicar.* At left: *The Señor de la Soledad in 1980.* Above: *The Christ at Centenario.*

1980: Houses in Huaraz's center have been built; political graffiti have marked walls, boulders, mountains; television has come to the Callejón . . .

But the stairs still go nowhere.

as they saw the "blisters," they were convinced it was "burned flesh." Yet many believe it was a hoax to confuse everyone, replace the "real" Señor, and sell him to Spain or the United States, a plot between the sacristan, the priest, and the bishop. Hence, the earthquake, because the "real" Señor was not here. However, at the same time, people feel that it is not the real Señor *now*, because after the earthquake, only one image was found, which, they say must be the Christ of May. (The present priest says the Christ of May was destroyed and this one *is* the real Señor.) Anyway, now the double has disappeared without a trace, or one of the images has disappeared without a trace! So much for that; it is ten times more complex, and I go crazy trying to deal with it in Western rational terms: e.g., would the bishop have had the real Señor burned (the fire is a *fact*; everyone saw the charred image), would he have risked that, and *then* had him repaired and *then* sold him? Doesn't make sense. Now, it would make sense if the burned image were the May Christ (but then, they wouldn't have felt it to be "burned flesh"), they had sold the real Soledad, and replaced him with the Christ of May and burned that image so people would not notice the subtle differences. *But* the Christ of May existed right down to the time of the earthquake!

. . . It is so intriguing, I tend to try to live it as a detective story. Surely there must be some microscopic analysis to reveal once and for all whether or not the present image is the real Señor de la Soledad! But I *know* I cannot treat it in this way. A greater "reality" may lie in the hearts of believers . . .

NOT long afterward, my landlady's daughter, Cucha, then a teacher in Casma, came home on a visit. She helped me understand the complex of beliefs about the image of Soledad. One cold, windy afternoon, I sat outside, in front of the house, with the two women. My landlady had patches of candle wax on her temples to cure a headache, and we were all wrapped in wool ponchos. With just my mention of the Señor de la Soledad, they began to recount the past history of the image, beginning with its legendary origins. I told them I was hearing more and more frequently that the earthquake occurred because "they"—someone—had sold the image of the Soledad Christ. But, I added, despite people's conviction that the earthquake simply could not have happened had the image been in "its place," there were so many loose ends in the story of how this could have taken place.

Cucha explained, "Yes, people have a great preoccupation with the reality of the image. They say it has been sold, or exchanged for another. From so much believing in something, one comes to doubt. So strong is the faith in the Señor that any little disequilibrium makes doubt spring up. The more one knows something, the more one doubts.

"The Señor de la Soledad exerts a charismatic power over us," Cucha went on. "Even Huaraz's patron saint, San Sebastián, has been displaced by the Señor. Other images—their feast day is celebrated and then people forget. But the Señor transcends. He survives everything. Around him turns all the religious faith of this region. When *campesinos* came to Huaraz with their produce, their greens, their grains, they always went first with their candles and their flowers to visit the Señor de la Soledad."

Excitedly, my landlady began to recount past processions, where so many people thronged around the stretcher bearing the Señor de la Soledad that one could not walk but was swept along. She did not leave out 1969, when the crown fell and people began to worry. Sure enough, the earthquake came. The old woman was not certain the real Lord of Solitude was the one in the temple now. The expression on his face was not quite right, she said, and his features were slightly coarser, as those of the Lord of May had been.

"Now," Cucha concluded as we were driven inside by the night, "some are indifferent, but many still care very much." Her mother was one who still cared.

Climbing the treacherous staircase to my room, I pondered the Soledad faith and the cloak of doubt that seemed to ignite the faith rather than extinguish it. Even those who said the image now in the rustic temple was not the real Señor de la Soledad carried on as if it were. Had not Pilatos, the image maker, who no longer believed in a "real" or an "unreal" Señor, since all images were only material, anyway, said, "In spite of all I am telling you, there are moments, and always when I am passing the temple, when I feel a force, something from him, the Señor de la Soledad, that makes me think better, some force that makes me more human"?

It struck me that the haze of doubt surrounding the image was in fact an undercurrent of the allusions to God's absence during the earthquake that I had heard from time to time even before I became aware of Soledad. "Where were you that Sunday, God?" had its literal side. It referred, too, to the specific presence or absence of the Señor de la Soledad. If the image were only the Christ of May, or some other substitute, that could explain the failure of the Señor de la Soledad to allay the disaster. Possibly, I reasoned, the honor of the Soledad Christ, in this way, was preserved. I was beginning to understand that *Huaracinos* and *campesinos* looked after the Christ as much as he looked after them.

Thirty

THE FEAST OF SOLEDAD

Half I believe it, half I don't believe it.
Don Juan of Secsecpampa

P ADRE ESPINOZA, who felt the call to come to Huaraz from
Abancay after the fire of 1965, had avoided speaking to
me about the image itself. Indeed, he eschewed all religious topics. He was so commanding a figure that I did not approach
him with ease and had not sought him out since that day in February
when he took me to the mountain enclave that served as his brick
factory. Now I knew I had to get closer to him and make the effort
to break down his reluctance to address the identity of the image.

Toward the end of April 1972, people began to speculate on
how the feast of the Señor de la Soledad would be celebrated that
year. The Soledad feast day is May 3, and before the earthquake
there were eight days of celebration, building to a crescendo for
the *octava*, the "eighth day," May 10, when the procession took
place.

I had been hearing that Padre Espinoza was vacillating about whether the image would come out in procession or not. There had been no procession in 1971 due to the official year of mourning. The decision was crucial, since now there was only one image, which meant the "real" Señor de la Soledad would have to leave the security of the temple and risk some mishap.

On my way to visit the padre one morning, I stopped by Doña Angelita's shop in San Francisco. The latest news was that the procession would take place and that the Señor would go all the way to the Franciscans' church in Huarupampa, whereas before the earthquake he went only as far as the Plaza de Armas. "We have a blind faith in the Señor," Angelita said. "You know, of course, that his double has been lost."

A lady buying bread from Angelita added, "We are afraid to take out the real Señor. There are so many beliefs about what could happen to him when we take him out. My grandmother used to tell me all these beliefs."

"He could hurt himself," Angelita said. "They will have to take him out of the plastic wrappings."

When I finally reached Soledad, I found the padre indisposed. He was up, but he had a blanket wrapped around him and said he was not feeling well and didn't want to talk. Marianela confirmed for me that the procession would take place, leaving at 9:00 A.M. and not returning until 5:00 P.M. Dancers would come from all over the valley. She fretted about the procession but was even more disquieted by orders from CRYRZA to relocate the Señor de la Soledad after his feast days. "They are reclaiming this land," she said, agitated, "and now we must build a new hut for him."

On the following day, I returned to Soledad. The priest was feeling better and was in good spirits. Animatedly, he gathered together the orphaned children whom he sheltered, to perform for me. He introduced the performance by railing against those who, instead of "looking for something to feed the children and clothes to dress them in, came with their titles: 'I am Dr. So-and-So' or 'I am a consciousness-raiser for Don Pablo Freire . . .'" He went on, recalling those who came with their cameras to make films that they carried off to be shown in the churches of Europe. I felt a slight twinge of guilt.

The padre then attacked the Evangelicals, who, he said, had

turned away the orphans. Then he assailed the Catholic elements who had insulted him and gossiped behind his back. Next, CRYRZA fell under his sweeping scythe. Everywhere, it seemed, there lurked enemies—communists, liberals, conservatives alike— all seeking to prevent him from rebuilding the sanctuary for the Lord of Solitude. I realized that this was the priest's way of setting himself above all ideologies and movements, of seeing himself as alone and perhaps as pure in motive as the Christ of Solitude.

The earthquake had not been his fault, he went on, and yet he alone had struggled to care for the orphans and the old women who were left with no one, and to protect the Señor de la Soledad. The Señor, the orphans, the old women—they had all lived so long in tents dripping with rain, and no one helped. Yet he knew he must follow the example of Christ, who had himself been crucified by enemies who failed to understand him.

His harangue completed, the children then began, in sharp contrast, to sing in clear, high voices the praises of the Cordillera Blanca and the Cordillera Negra and then the song of Soledad: "My barrio of Soledad, / capital of Huaraz, / the sun rises announcing my solitude . . ."

As the pure, crystalline tones faded, an eerie, rehearsed dialogue between the priest and the chorus of children began. He asked if people loved them or insulted them, and their answer, in perfect unison, rang out, "They insult us."

"Yes, they insult us," Espinoza shouted, "the enemies of the children, of Huaraz, of our sanctuary. We work for the spiritual and moral rehabilitation of Huaraz, and they slander us!" This dialogue continued for a painfully long time, interspersed by the pure strains of the children's voices as they sang the songs of their valley and their barrio.

Back in the parish house, the priest and I sat again at the long table in the dining room. This time, I focused on a painting on the wall. It depicted Padre Espinoza in the midst of ruins, elevating the chalice. Two lambs stood nearby on the rubble. He told me that in 1967 he was on the verge of leaving Huaraz because of the people's lack of comprehension. Then one night he dreamed that the Señor de la Soledad appeared before him and told him he must not abandon Huaraz. Within a few years the city would be destroyed, and he would be the one to build it up again. Because of this dream, Espinoza desisted and decided to remain in Huaraz. At that time, he found an artist to render his dream in a painting, the one that now hung on the dining-room wall. The artist, he told me, had died in the earthquake.

In the years following his dream, he preached repentance more vigorously and even took the Señor de la Soledad himself to the Plaza de Armas in the procession of 1969 in order to save all he could. Just as now the *campesinos* help him more than the towns-people, he said, they were the ones who had repented, and hence more of them were spared in the earthquake.

Stunned by this unanticipated revelation, I could not find words to question him further, and so I left.

THE next day I visited Pilatos in his atelier in Pedregal, above the barrio of Soledad. He introduced a new twist to the story of Padre Espinoza's brick factory. Soon after the earthquake, according to Pilatos, the priest had pressed the *campesinos* into making adobe bricks to rebuild the Soledad church. By the end of a year, they had brought 20,000 or 30,000 adobes down to Soledad, each hamlet contributing 1,000 bricks. Then Espinoza told the *campesinos* that adobe would not be acceptable to CRYRZA and that he would sell the adobe bricks and begin a cement brick factory. The *campesinos* saw no profit from their labors except for an occasional small image the padre would present to a community. "He is getting rich on the faith *campesinos* have in the Señor de la Soledad," Pilatos said. "He can do anything, shielded by that image." Like others, Pilatos suspected Espinoza of the loss of one of the Soledad images. "Espinoza went into the rubble of the Santa Rosa chapel with a tractor. He should have done it carefully, and perhaps the Christ of May would have been found." It was curious, so curious, he felt, that no remains whatsoever had been found of an entire image.

MOMENTUM for the Soledad feast began to build. Mass at Soledad on Monday, May 1, brought many *campesinos* down, bearing candles and flowers for the Lord of Solitude. The trio led by the blind man were singing in Quechua:

Kamakok Yaya, La Soledad,
Nokallami charallamu,

haquiquiman ishquirishpa
Jutzallata huakarishpa.

(Creator Father, "La Soledad,"
I have come to kneel
At your feet for my sins,
I come crying my sins.)

Kamakokpa rantin Yaya,
Santa Cruzcho huanurishka,
Huekellanguan shuparishka
Yaguarllanguan taksharishka.

(Divine Son of the Almighty
Dead on the Holy Cross
Soaked with your tears
And bathed in your blood.)

Now naming specific persons in CRYRZA, the civil authorities, other priests, and even *Soledanos*, the padre spoke again in his sermon of his enemies. He read passages from the Bible that pointed to Christ's enemies and told how Jesus needed to be defended, even with one's life.

"Have you thought," he addressed the worshipers, "when you have heard things against the Señor de la Soledad, how you must defend him? How can you defend him if you are drunk? You must defend him with your work. . . . You must come to talk to him early, before dawn, saying, 'Papa, how are you? I have come to greet you, to embrace you, to give you my tears and the flowers of my heart. . . .' " Again came the plaintive and haunting strains of "*Kamakok Yaya*," the congregation now echoing the trio at the altar.

Outside, after the Mass, amid drums, flutes, and trumpets, *chicha* and shouting, the bell that had fallen from one of the church towers during the earthquake was raised. Hanging precariously from the makeshift wooden trellis and clapperless, the bell was struck with a rock by a *campesino*, who ascended the rustic belfry to ring it for the first time since the disaster.

Back at Angelita's afterward, she and a customer in her shop argued over whether the image was the real Señor or not. Doña Angelita said that she had "looked him in the eye, and he *is* real."

The head of the Christ of May had tilted slightly upward, the Señor de la Soledad's slightly downward, just as it is now.

On May 2, the eve of the saint's day, I walked up to Soledad and found the temple crowded with about 125 people. The padre was preaching in front of the image, which, for the first time, I saw without the protective plastic covering. "They have abandoned the faith, they have abandoned the Señor, they have abandoned Huaraz. They hate us, and they insult us. . . ."

As I left, I brushed against Pilatos, who was standing in the doorway, "listening," he said and planning his case against Padre Espinoza. "He uses the Señor to attack, and he uses him to defend. He creates enemies in order to be able to fight against them, doing business with the Indians," the young image maker whispered to me.

The dark inside the temple was relieved only by candles flickering on the earthen floor, and now, in the dark outside, ponchoed figures were dispersing, moving slowly down the hill.

THERE were two Masses on May 3, the feast day itself of the Lord of Solitude, one at 10:30 A.M. and one at 5:00 P.M. Between the Masses, worshipers came and went, cautiously threading their way among the candles, which now almost covered the dirt floor. A townswoman spoke of the glorious celebrations before the earthquake, how attached the *campesinos* were to Soledad, coming with their music and costumed dancers from as far away as Coronga and Piscobamba. "Now, how can we know when or where or even if the procession on the *octava* will really take place?" she asked.

In Nicrupampa that afternoon, people recalled the big fire of 1965, one man saying that it was a trick, when really the priest of that time and the sacristan had sold the Señor to a gringo who took him to Germany. "We loved him so much . . ." His voice trailed off.

"What is the difference now?" I asked. "The Señor is there. I have just come from the temple."

"Before he was warm; now he is cold," the man answered. "The earthquake happened because they sold him. It was a punishment. Now I put candles, but only for pleasure."

On May 4, I went up to Secsecpampa. It seemed important to follow the Soledad events through the eyes of Don Juan and his family, much as I had followed the events surrounding the blessing of the mountain crosses. I was disappointed to find that Don Juan was away, working for a few days in a mine in Tarica. The women of the household, Jesusa and Don Juan's older daughters, were in the patio roasting corn kernels. Again, just as with the crosses, they didn't know if the German priest of Centenario would come to say Mass for their small Soledad image in the Secsecpampa chapel. He was annoyed because people were calling him an Evangelical. Nevertheless, Jesusa said, there would be a procession in Secsecpampa, with dances and a band.

"Many nations wanted to steal the Señor de la Soledad at the time of the fire," Jesusa began to relate, filling in for me still more details. "Do you know why they wanted to steal him? Because he was so miraculous." To illustrate this, she told of the time in 1925 when the cloak alone of the Señor was taken to Casma on the coast and had calmed the heavy rains that were threatening the entire seaboard. "Even from Lima they came to adore the Señor. He was very miraculous in the past." This reflected her present doubt, and she told the story of the good priest, dispatched at the time of the fire by the bishop. "The priest warned us that the bishop would sell the Señor and that he had already received half a million *soles* from the Spaniards. For a long time, the Spaniards have wanted to steal our Lord!"

The grandmother came into the patio. Sitting on her haunches, her skirts billowing around her, she began to sing "*Kamakok Yaya, La Soledad . . .*"

On my way back home, I met townspeople who told me they had just been to a meeting of former property holders from Soledad barrio. As well as the *octava* of the Lord of Solitude, the second anniversary of the earthquake was also approaching, and people were becoming more vocal about the proposed reconstruction. "Communications" to President Velasco had begun appearing in the local newspaper. The big questions discussed at the meeting were whether survivors should reclaim their land on May 31, starting an uprising in Soledad, and whether SINAMOS, too, might turn against CRYRZA.

ON Sunday, May 7, I returned to Secsecpampa. Don Juan was back from his stint in the mines but was collecting firewood higher up on the mountain. I waited a long time for him in his patio, and when he finally came, we sat on wooden stools facing each other, in our formal way, as we always did when serious discussion was to take place. I asked him about the celebration of the *octava*. In vivid detail, he gave me an elaborate version of the image's legendary beginnings, how no one had seen the sculpting of the image, the bearded sculptor who had promised to carve the image having disappeared without touching even a morsel of the food that people left for him. Thus, everyone knew at once that the bearded man was Christ himself, who would sustain the people of Huaraz and its countryside. "When there was scarcity, or it didn't rain, and we could not plant, then we went with our flowers, our candles. We took him out to the Plaza de Armas, and when we returned him to the temple, rain would fall," Don Juan said.

He went on to tell me that during the presidency of Manuel Prado, North America had offered many millions of dollars for the Señor. This attempt to sell the image was thwarted when an old woman noticed the cotton attached to Christ's wounds in disarray and advised the *campesinos* that someone had already been trying to lower the image from the altar.

"Afterward, two more times we were able to save him," Don Juan said, recounting, for one, the incident of the big fire. That fateful night, though, remained in a cloud of doubt for Don Juan. Perhaps the real Señor did not burn. Rather, another image, sculpted in his likeness, was the one that burned. The face was so disfigured that no one could tell. According to Don Juan's interpretation, the fire was a cover-up because the real Señor had already been removed. Indeed, he had heard planes cross the valley through the night, which was most unusual, and it is possible that they were able to get the Señor de la Soledad out. Swept along in these fresh details of the planes heard during the night, I did not think to ask about the Lord of May. And Don Juan was providing still another detail of the great fire. The Soledad priest whom the bishop eventually removed and sent away to Rome had taken measurements of the charred image after the fire. As best he could, he had measured the feet and the thickness of the torso. In Rome, he would consult the pope and establish the authenticity of the image or unmask the bishop's treachery.

"But there it remained, in silence." Don Juan sighed. Nothing was proved, and the people quieted down. Many finally concluded, he said, that the image that burned was the real Señor. But he himself did not think so: "Before, the Señor had a face one could see; now his head is lowered, and his face is not so visible."

"Many of us Catholics," Don Juan went on, "we do not believe it is the same Señor as before the fire, because the real Señor has done so many miracles. With the Chileans, and he saved Huaraz in 1941, when the volcano of water rushed toward Soledad and the white dove flew out of the temple, deflecting the alluvion to Centenario. He has averted so many calamities. When we suffered misfortunes, we went with our candles, our flowers, and on the spot he made things better. No, this one is not the same. That's why the earthquake happened. . . . In the night, a voice was heard to say, 'When I am absent, when I go, when I no longer exist in Huaraz, you will see what will happen, misfortune upon misfortune,' that's what the voice called, loudly in the night."

"Was this in a dream, Don Juan?" I asked.

"No, no, persons heard, in the late hours of the night. Many persons heard, but they could not locate from where the voice came or whose voice it was."

"Do you think it was the Señor de la Soledad?"

"The Señor de la Soledad himself, yes," he answered.

I asked him about the celebration in Secsecpampa for their small Soledad image. He replied that he would not take part, fearing it would turn out badly, like the festivities for the crosses, with too much drinking and dissension. When I said I would not come to Secsecpampa if he were not going to be with me, he brightened. "Oh, if we go together, then, let us go to the pampa, where the Señor himself is!" I was immensely pleased, and we planned to spend the whole day together, following whatever festivities would take place on that day, the tenth of May—the *octava*.

Down on the valley floor, I got a ride back to my room with Benjamín Morales, the director of the Santa Corporation. He spoke of the political storm that was brewing as the second anniversary drew near. Might the two great bureaucracies, SINAMOS and CRYRZA, butt heads? But Benjamín was certain about one thing: The procession of the Señor de la Soledad would take place that Wednesday. "Soledad is synonymous with Huaraz. SINAMOS, CRYRZA—they won't let that feast go by. They may destroy our barrios, but they can't touch the Señor de la Soledad. That image is crucial to the recovery of Huaraz." The night had turned icy, and the stars seemed close to the touch, just beyond the windshield. As we fell silent, I had the momentary sense of seeing everything at once, the overlapping contexts of the aftermath, one shining transparently through the other.

I had promised to be in Yungay on the next day, Monday, May 8, to accompany Cirila when she went to the playa to observe the saint's day of one of her dead sons. The *colectivos* were on strike, and by the time I reached her restaurant in Yungay Norte, she had already left. I went running up the road that winds through the playa to meet her. The priest at Yungay had also been unable to be with Cirila, as he was called to attend to someone dying in the camp. I could almost not bear to see her alone as she came walking toward me, her black dress full of nettles, her stockings torn from the brush that was pushing itself up through the alluvial silt.

Yungay was different from Huaraz, the despair deeper, the handful of true *Yungaíno* survivors less engaged in religious activity. Yungay was barren of churches, even makeshift ones, and there were no images left. It surprised me when, as I was about to leave, Cirila remembered the feast of the Señor de la Soledad and gave me a candle to burn in her name at the foot of the image.

No vehicles were moving that night, and it was harder than ever to get back to Huaraz. After waiting for a long time on the road, I finally got a ride in the back of a truck. The truck was carrying a group from the Ministry of Agriculture who had been making surveys on the other side of the Cordillera Blanca. They had crossed the puna on horseback to ask the people what they usually ate. Whereas I was used to riding among sacks of flour or potatoes, now I huddled in the freezing sierra night, sheltered by big boxes of survey questionnaires. When the truck finally pulled into Centenario—it must have been near midnight—*campesinos*, dressed in costumes, dancing in the deserted street, suddenly appeared in the truck's headlights, and we had to come to an abrupt stop. This is just one of many surreal images I carry with me, the sudden touching, so late at night in the thin dark air, of the modern world of surveys and the timeless Indian world. These dancers, down from the mountainsides, were for me the first concrete sign that the procession of the Señor de la Soledad would indeed take place.

BY the eve of the *octava*, I began to feel the apprehension that was building over the fact that the Señor would be coming out of his temple in procession for the first time since 1969. During the day, I observed from my window groups of dancers descending on the pampa. Other groups from the hamlets and valley towns were arriving with shoulder platforms bearing small replicas of the Señor de la Soledad. Slowly, they would make their way across the pampa and up the hill to the church.

The sky was filled with pink clouds by 6:00 P.M. as I walked up to Soledad. Mainly *campesinos* were inside the temple, including many children and young people. The plastic covering had been removed from the image on May 3, and now men were just finishing changing the clothes of the Señor, putting on green robes in place of the purple ones, and were beginning to comb his hair. The padre, in his black turtleneck sweater, was preaching, in words now familiar to me, against the background of dancers advancing across the pampa, the sound of their flutes, drums, and the bells they wore on their ankles growing louder and louder as they neared the temple. Scribbling in shorthand in a little notebook, I caught his words:

> The dancers are coming to make the night pleasant, to bring joy to the Señor amidst the ruins of the wounded city, which will be reconstructed just as the sanctuary of the Señor will rise again. Tomorrow is a fiesta for all, *campesinos* and townspeople. Men will stand guard over the Señor all night, because his enemies are always alert, and there could be another fire. The Señor cannot be left alone for a minute. We must be always with him, our patron of Huaraz. Look at the Señor. His leg was wounded in the earthquake, but now it has been repaired. The Señor is sad, like you, and happy, like you. Like you, he is living in a shack on somebody else's field [*en chacra ajena*] with no place of his own. Only now, after the earthquake, will he go out to look for his children among the ruins. He will bless the souls. Before, in 1969, he went to bless for the last time all his children who were to offer themselves, some innocent, beneath the ruins. You have an appointment with Christ at ten o'clock tomorrow morning.

Outside it grew dark. In the Soledad plaza, people drank hot punch and said it used to be better, that there used to be electric lights and roast pig and fireworks. There were ten times more people, more dance groups. Still, they conceded, it was gay, anyway. Expectancy filled the air.

By 9:00 P.M. the mud floor near the altar was covered with candles, and the temple was packed with people, now more townspeople, dressed in black, though the *campesinos*, in their colorful apparel, outnumbered them. I heard one townswoman say, "Where are the *Huaracinos*? They are dead or they have gone."

A man near me asked another, "His crown, is it the same one?"

A lady commented, "The Señor has already advanced. He is ready to leave."

Group by group, the costumed dancers from the mountain hamlets entered the temple, dancing and bowing their way up to the altar: Ahuarunas, Huanquillas, Negritos, Atahualpas, Pieles Rojas. Beating drums and executing their steps, they bowed deeply before the image as they sang:

> *We are the Indians, the commoners,*
> *We come from the backwoods,*
> *Little Señor Soledano.*
> *What a beautiful altar you have!*
>
> *We come adoring you with flowers,*
> *Señorcito Soledano,*
> *You are on high,*
> *We the commoners.*
> *With sadness, we have adored you.*

As violins struck up, the dance groups moved backward toward the door, always facing the Señor and bowing,

> *With permission, Señorcito,*
> *Now we must leave your side.*
> *Tomorrow we shall return*
> *To accompany you, we, your friends.*
> *Good night, Little Lord . . .*

Another group would enter, singing the praises. "What a beautiful cloak you have, Señor, adorned with golden threads."

By 11:00 P.M., the temple was emptying, and people were again drinking the warm punch, listening to the music, the *cajaplauta* that played on into the night. When I passed the Evangelical church next to my house, inside they were singing Protestant hymns.

DON Juan came to my room promptly at 8:45 the next morning, May 10, the *octava*. He reported on the dance groups he had passed on his way. As we walked toward Soledad, he pointed out where, before the earthquake, all the beautiful buildings of Huaraz had stood. Spanning the centuries from before Conquest up to the present, he spoke with equal enthusiasm about buried Inca treasures under Pumacayán and the predisaster colonial city. I remember thinking it was a layered land, culture upon culture, stone upon stone.

By the time we reached the temple, *campesinos* and townspeople were pressing in. Many carried shoulder stretchers with small images and pictures of the Señor de la Soledad to be blessed. Don Juan and I could barely squeeze our way through. *Campesinos* and townsmen both were vying for positions around the large platform on which the image of the Lord of Solitude now stood. Padre Espinoza was having a hard time controlling the mass of worshipers, such was the desire to carry the Señor's platform, or at least to walk close by, within touching distance.

Speaking alternately in Quechua and Spanish, the padre gave instructions about caring for the Señor, admonishing the bearers to beware of enemies, to keep the lighted candles at a safe distance, to be orderly and respectful. "Now those who have gone astray will return to the side of our God," he was saying in Quechua, Don Juan translating for me.

Bent under the weight of the platform, the bearers lifted it, wobbling, onto their shoulders. The crowd sang "*Kamakok Yaya, La Soledad* . . ." Don Juan whispered, "They are singing that we are spilling our tears at his feet." As the procession was about to begin, everyone broke out in the verses, now sung in Spanish: "Pardon your people, Señor. Don't be eternally angry, pardon your people, Señor," repeated over and over again.

Espinoza, his eyes on the doorway, seemed anxious. Finally, silencing the singing, he said aloud, "So the authorities haven't come. It doesn't matter. We don't need them."

Just as he spoke those words, the prefect of Ancash, the sub-prefect, CRYRZA's General La Vera, and the bishop's vicar pressed their way in. Espinoza went on: It was a time of war. "We must work, fight, though they insult us, calling us thieves, to build the temple of our Señor, who has saved us from the earthquake. He must not remain any longer in this straw house."

Don Juan nudged me, "Do you see, the general, the prefect, and the subprefect have come. The subprefect is with his wife and all his children."

Like a giant, lumbering centipede, platform, bearers, and worshipers emerged from the temple into bright sunlight. A band played loudly, and dance groups—Shacshas, Pallas, Huanquillas —joined the procession, which made its way down toward the Plaza de Armas. Don Juan was delighted that there were ten dance groups when he only knew of five that were supposed to come. Before the earthquake, he said, many groups, perhaps thirty-five, came, some from as far away as Cuzco and Lima. Once, a group of Atahualpas from the coast had died of altitude sickness crossing the puna at Conococha, he recalled.

As we accompanied the procession, everyone seemed to be reminiscing about the way it was before, commenting on how the Reform and Reconstruction were trying to take away "the devotion," how the *campesinos* had fought in order that the procession go forth. "We will forget our devotion to the Señor when our eyes are finally closed," Don Juan remarked to a man walking alongside us.

"Yes, of course," responded the man, "but life changes many things."

"Ah, yes," said Don Juan.

Another man leaned toward Don Juan and asked him, "Is it, or is it not, the Señor?"

"It is another," Don Juan responded.

"No, I think it's he himself; he's just restored," the man countered.

Spotting the CRYRZA general, Don Juan pointed him out to me. "There he is, the general himself!"

Atahualpas, wearing peacock plumes and playing a harp, danced by us. I heard a man say, "The Señor is heavy. I've carried him several times, and he is very heavy."

"The Señor does not usually wear green in the procession," Don Juan commented. "Surely this robe has been loaned to him.

How beautiful that some group, some town, perhaps, has loaned him this robe!"

"The Señor used to be warm," he added, "and we all believed that he was alive. I used to anoint him with a little oil on a piece of cotton and carry the little piece of cotton in my pocket, and nothing bad happened to me. It was so nice. . . ."

He broke off to point out the Antihuanquillas dancing with bells on their feet. "Those are the ancient ones," he said, "representatives of the Incas." His face lit up as he saw the *Cuzqueños* come dancing by. "See, they have come, from so far! And we have all been afraid that dancers would not come and bands would not come, that they would modernize our town." He went on to tell me that at the last minute *campesinos* protested to the bishop, demanding the procession take place. "And he agreed. He had to agree. If not, he would have looked very bad."

"How did they arrange it all so quickly?" I asked.

"By word of mouth," he answered. "No circular was necessary; by word of mouth alone."

As we were nearing the temple once again, at the end of the procession, a *campesino* approached us and drew Don Juan aside. When he rejoined me, Don Juan reported what the man had said: "This man who was at my side has just told me that a gesture was made to ransom the Señor de la Soledad, from North America, and he has returned! This image we see now is the real Señor. A big sum had to be paid; all the aid money given to President Velasco after the earthquake has been deposited to rescue the Señor. That's what he told me people were saying."

"Don Juan, what do *you* believe? Do *you* believe this is the real Señor de la Soledad?" I asked, astonished, not so much at the news itself but at the tenacity of the issue.

"I don't know. Sometimes people talk to be talking. That's why only half I believe it, half I don't believe it."

Real or not, I breathed a sigh of relief when the procession ended without incident and the image was once again back safely inside the rustic sanctuary. As the platform that bore the Señor was gingerly set down in silence beneath the altar, loudly sung verses of "*Kamakok Yaya, La Soledad*"—"Creator Father, Soledad" —broke the tension of the day.

Abruptly, the mood changed, and Soledad leaders began handing out awards in the form of diplomas: one to a man who had gone down into the rain forest to gather palm leaves for Easter; one to a taxi driver who, in the first months after the earthquake, for only two *soles*, carried people to Soledad by skirting the edges of the rubble and going up through Pedregal; one to the bereaved father of Soraya, who had donated to the Señor a whole entrance collection to his makeshift movie theater.

The official ritual of farewell and collocation—the setting of the image in its place behind the altar—would take place the next day. All through that night and the following day and night, the sound of the drums and anklet bells of the dancers could be heard on the pampa. It was raining and cold when I walked up to Soledad on Thursday, May 11, where, at noon, the Mass of collocation was supposed to take place. On the way, I met a group of *campesinos* who called themselves the "Guardians of the Honor of the Señor de la Soledad." Outside the church, *campesinos* sat on the ground, the women still in the festive clothes they had worn for the procession.

When I entered the temple, I found about fifty people, mainly *campesinos*, sitting quietly, in the mood of a wake. The padre was nowhere to be seen, and it was obvious that Mass would not take place. Only Marianela wandered among the people, stamping out burned candles on the earthen floor, now almost sealed with melted wax. From a bench next to the altar, Justo Lázaro of Atipayán and Domingo Cuchaching of Vichay, both nephews of Don Juan, watched over the candles near the Señor, occasionally lighting one for someone who approached the image. Domingo encouraged his young son to kiss the feet of the Señor before the image should again be wrapped in plastic. People whispered, got up to go to touch the image, returned to whisper. A *campesina* started to argue in Quechua about the reality of the Señor. When I asked a woman about the Mass, she said it had been canceled so that the temple might be left "to the people, so that we may sit with and accompany the Señor."

Now the dance groups entered one by one. They wore woolen masks, holes for the eyes cut out. One group carried tomahawks, another bows and arrows. Some dancers wore peacock headbands, others long foxtails. Bending forward, then backward, they danced up to the image, singing verses of farewell. "Next year we shall return, if God gives us life. Next year we shall return, our Little Father Soledad." Townswomen with pictures of the Señor pinned to their black dresses carried baskets of flowers to set down at the foot of the image among the tall, thin candles, wasting away into strange, crooked shapes in the wind that howled through the cracks in the tin roof.

I finally left sometime after 1:00 P.M., not having seen the collocation, which I learned did not take place until the following day. On the opposite edge of the pampa, that night I tried to understand more. "What does *Soledad* mean?" I asked a townswoman.

"Tranquillity, to be alone." She spoke then of the glacial lakes that threaten the people and the volcanoes of water. "The Señor helps us by holding back the one under Rataquenua. He could make the whole world disappear if he wanted to."

ON May 12, I went to Secsecpampa, not expecting that they would still be celebrating the Soledad feast there. Don Juan agreed to go to the chapel with me. Their Soledad image had been placed in the center of the altar, which was decorated in blue-and-white tinfoil on which were pasted cutout bird designs. Only the small image of Soledad was in view. The other images were draped with cloths. Just as in the temple below the previous day, here now dancers were bowing and singing. Don Juan whispered that their image, like the real Señor, never leaves the chapel, though they took him out on the day of the earthquake.

Outside on the plaza a kind of comic dance-drama I poorly understood was in progress. A "Negrito" was pretending to scare the onlookers by snapping a whip at them. "It is raining. That's why I am crying," he shouted. A man pretended to try to decapitate the dancer. Then men Don Juan called "corporals" arrived with sticks to which were tied oranges and lemons, which they eventually gave to the children.

Washi, Don Juan's son, was beautiful, dancing in his costume. "He has wanted to dance since he was five," Don Juan said, "and I let him because they promised not to make him drink." The women sat around the edge of the plaza in their finery. Don Juan's mother-in-law was wearing her best blue taffeta skirts.

I learned that Padre Auscario of Centenario, not wanting to

say Mass for the small image of the Señor de la Soledad in Sec-secpampa, had locked the chapel and the trunk where all the clothes of the Señor were kept. Don Juan went to the bishop, who explained that it was only that Auscario wanted to say a night Mass, the way they do it in Germany. The bishop gave the *Secsecpampinos* permission to break into the chapel and open the trunk. In the end, Auscario reluctantly said a Mass, but in someone's house, wearing ordinary clothes and without the image.

"What does that Mass that Padre Auscario said in the house *mean?*" Don Juan and the two men who had joined us asked each other. "What can it possibly *mean?*" They spoke with such passionate disgust that I wrote the questions in large letters across my notebook page that night. As the dancers cavorted about the plaza, the three men lamented the loss of *costumbres*, the modernization of religion and of the towns, and the fact that Secsecpampa had been "ruined, divided by the earthquake and by the Reform movement at Centenario." One villager had even felt the need to hide her Evangelicalism from her neighbors; it was revealed when both Catholic priest and Evangelical pastor turned up to conduct her funeral.

My habit of going up to Soledad every day was hard to break. I was always afraid I would miss something, some further clue to the power of the image. But the political tempo was accelerating, telegrams going back and forth between President Velasco in Lima and the barrio representatives, headlines in the paper referring to the "Arrogant Attitude of the Bank of International Development," the big meeting between CRYRZA, SINAMOS, and survivors planned for May 16, and the constant rumors that *Huaracinos* would oppose CRYRZA and reclaim their land on the thirty-first.

The star of the Virgin of Fátima, the patroness of the market, had risen on the waning of the Soledad feast. Amid fireworks, she had been carried from the marketplace across the pampa to "visit the Señor de la Soledad." She was there when I went to Soledad on Sunday, May 14, for the last time in what would be a number of days. That Sunday, I saw the Soledad Christ once again securely covered in plastic.

Thirty-one
LAST VISITS TO SOLEDAD

Soledad, *that's what I have been searching for.*

Padre Espinoza, 1965

B Y MID-JUNE I was again returning to Soledad with some
regularity. The temple seemed larger now, with fewer
worshipers in comparison to the feast days. At Mass on
June 18, they sang in Quechua: "*Apu Yaya Jesucristo*" ("Lord Father
Jesus Christ"), *Apu*, the same word used by the Indians to address
the highest mountains, when mountain and deity were one. In
Spanish they sang: "I adore you, Holy Cross." The padre was
intoning the punishment of "*Papachito*," which would ensue from
the "closed heads and hearts" that impeded the building of the
sanctuary for the Señor de la Soledad, even as his bricks rolled out
of his factory. He avoided me after Mass.

By now, in contrast to my earliest months in the valley, everything was beginning to have meaning, and the threads of meaning
were beginning to intertwine. At the same time, I was growing

ever more conscious of time passing and more eager to grasp some whole, though that only happened in fleeting moments. During the nights, I would frequently awaken anxiously and turn on my short-wave radio for diversion. But, uncannily, events related to my work pursued me even by radio from afar. In Kait, Russia, near the Afghanistan border, an earthquake and avalanche, much like the Yungay event, had killed 20,000 people. The Andean Pact and France were still debating the French bomb tests.

Drifting off to sleep again one night, I dreamed I had a large book in which was inscribed the name SEÑOR DE LA SOLEDAD. Nothing more. The following night, I dreamed the *chacras* on the mountainsides were swatches of cloth. I pulled them off to paste them in a scrapbook.

I was also wanting to savor and store up every image of the valley. As the cold season set in, nights seemed to fall even more spectacularly, dust sweeping across the pampa, the eucalyptus trees swaying against the deepening layers of the two cordilleras, yellows, greens, and browns shading into purples. Then, crowning the Blanca, millions of ice crystals would begin to shimmer in the light from the rising moon.

On June 23, the eve of the Day of San Juan, I was walking up to Soledad at 7:00 P.M. with my tape recorder, determined to see the padre. It was an extraordinary evening, with a full moon, colder than moonless nights. Bonfires heralding St. John's Day burned on the mountainsides. I felt like a tiny speck in a hollow cavity of the earth aflame.

"Before the earthquake, we used to go into the countryside and drink purple *chicha* on St. John's Day," my landlord had commented as I set out. When I asked him about the bonfires, he said that people wanted to burn up all the old and make a fresh start. Earlier, a man up from Lima had told me that bonfires were lighted at this time of year even before the Conquest in connection with the Inca feast of Inti Raymi. When I reached Soledad, the padre said he had asked the *campesinos* why they built the fires but was given "foolish answers" like "to burn up the sins of the world."

Congenially, he led me into the dining room, where boys from the Citadel of Children served us a noodle soup. He seemed more willing than usual to discuss religion. What was the good of taking away the traditional processions and *costumbres*, he mused, only to replace them with "other purely pagan customs." For him, the guitars and folk songs of Catholic Reform were equally "pagan."

"I am not a traditionalist; nor am I a modernist," he said. He threw Protestants, Mormons, Marxists, Catholic Reformists all into the same pot. For him, in the aftermath, religion was becoming "simple political propaganda," and all who preached this propaganda were enemies of Soledad. Religion must be timeless, embedded neither in the context of ancient Andean culture nor the context of modern history. I felt always in him a "longing for the impossible," an *"anhelo por lo imposible,"* some "Absolute," that Spanish poets like Emilio Prados talk about. I thought to myself, For him, religion is myth, ahistorical, a timeless truth, and he has found this in the image of the Lord of Solitude.

He told me more about his life. Sick of body and spirit, he had left the Dominican Order in Cuzco in the early sixties. Rudderless for a few years, through a series of happenstances he found himself in Huaraz on the day preceding the big fire at Soledad. At that point in his life, he was looking for *un aparte*, a place of refuge and of "mystical solemnity." *"Yo buscaba mi soledad"* ("I was seeking my solitude"), he reiterated, "even before I came to Huaraz. Solitude in mystical form is what I wanted."

On that fateful afternoon in 1965, the bishop suggested they take a walk. "You are sad, and this beautiful landscape will do you good," the bishop had said, trying to animate the disheartened priest.

"Even my faith felt sick, though," the padre recalled. "My soul was crying and nothing seemed good to me."

He had never heard of the barrio of Soledad or the Señor de la Soledad. When he and the bishop entered the church that afternoon and he first saw the image, "It was something so big . . ." Words failed him, and I waited. "And then, during that night, the fire occurred, and the next day forty thousand *campesinos* came down to take possession of Huaraz," he went on.

It was when he saw the charred image—"It was like alive"—that he said to himself, "Soledad, Señor de la Soledad, that's what I have been looking for." He requested and was granted the post as priest at Soledad, replacing the cleric who had been accused of treachery in the fire. At once, Espinoza was thrown into the fracas over the restoration of the image, defending *campesinos* and townspeople who demanded that the image remain at Soledad and the best artist be summoned to Huaraz to restore it. He was thus embattled from the beginning.

The padre was healed of his infirmities through the image, he told me, and over time the Señor de la Soledad began to reveal himself to him in dreams. In these dreams, the Señor directed his every action, whether it was when to go to Lima at just the precise time so he would run into an old friend or to remain in Huaraz to save the people from the earthquake that would surely come if a true conversion did not take place in their hearts. To Espinoza, the earthquake was a punishment. The Soledad Christ, foreseeing the disaster, had told him in his dream that one day he would say Mass upon the ruins of Huaraz, as the painting there on the wall had predicted.

And now the padre said in a way that let me know our talk was drawing to an end, "I labor for the Señor de la Soledad, whom I love so much. When the sanctuary is built, I will finally be able to leave Huaraz."

"Is this the real Señor de la Soledad?" I asked awkwardly, feeling this might be my last chance to ask, yet not really wanting to.

"Were it not that it *is* the Señor, I would leave Huaraz now," he answered matter-of-factly. "The Señor lives. But faith is not real here. Faith here is a distraction."

It had grown late, and we were both weary now. The padre offered to drive me back to my room in his old broken-down jeep. He laid a blanket over my knees, and we bounced across the moonlit pampa, the bonfires still igniting the mountainsides. I asked if the Señor de la Soledad had appeared all by himself.

"Yes, all by himself he appeared. He was alone, abandoned. But first he appeared in human form. . . ." At that moment, it did not matter to me if he referred to the image or to the historical Christ or if he took it as legend or really believed the story of the sculptor-turned-image. And certainly there was no way I could bring myself to ask.

AFTER this talk with Padre Espinoza, I decided to try to get the German priest's understanding of Soledad. Visiting Father Auscario at the Centenario church, with its gargantuan modernistic

Christ, was a totally different experience from my visits to Soledad. Not long into our conversation Auscario was saying to me, "For you, as an anthropologist, religion is a projection of man himself, and there is no revelation." I replied that it had occurred to me that perhaps he himself believed that man invented God, though already I could tell that he believed in God apart from man's imagination.

"God exists, and he reveals himself," Auscario explained. "But man responds to this revelation. The Señor de la Soledad is one response of man, a response that says, 'I am alone.' This shouldn't be so in society. Man should not be alone. If he is not alone, he doesn't need to express himself with the Señor de la Soledad. We are trying to change religious behavior in order to change the social structure. In turn, we are attacking the social structure in order that the social body be able to express Christ better."

When I asked Auscario if Centenario was a stronger parish since the earthquake, he replied dispassionately that it was, but probably only because there were now more people in the barrio of Centenario. However, he went on, despite the fact that more people had died in Soledad than in Centenario and that the Centenario church had withstood the earthquake, Soledad was still sovereign in Huaraz. "For me," Auscario said, "the Lord of Solitude is a representation of the social body of Huaraz." That society, as he saw it, was "closed," and the revolution taking place, both in the religious and political spheres, had, in the end, only superficially touched the valley, and secularization had only barely begun.

DURING this time I was trying to distinguish between the faith of *campesinos* and that of townspeople in the Señor de la Soledad. I suspected that faith in the image was stronger among *campesinos* than townspeople. I found, though, that Soledad stirred deep emotions in both Huaraz and its countryside. A woman living at the edge of Belén barrio was quick to tell me that not just *campesinos* but townspeople, too, had hurried to see the image after the fire and to look for it after the earthquake. And, after both, they had refused to allow the Señor to leave Huaraz. Sculptors had to be found who would restore the image before their eyes.

She told me that both country and townspeople alike had confided to her that in dreams some days before the earthquake the

Señor de la Soledad had appeared before them dressed in street clothes, the clothes of a mestizo, and announced the end of Huaraz. She herself had had no such dream, but many had. She felt that God indeed does appear to people, though more frequently to those of good and simple heart. Education and sophistication make one fight off revelation, she said.

This woman had, however, had a premonition that some misfortune would destroy the altars of Soledad because Padre Espinoza had removed one of her favorite saints from its small niche and given the niche to another image. But when all the altars of Huaraz collapsed in the earthquake, she forgot her grievance against Espinoza for this reason: One of her first thoughts was that this was an opportunity for the priests to preach from atop the rubble, thereby creating more faith. But they didn't do that, abandoning instead their fallen churches, as ordered by the guards. All but one, that is. Padre Espinoza said Mass in the midst of the ruins of Soledad only a few days after the disaster—just as he had dreamed he would do three years earlier. "He was the only one valiant enough," the señora said.

At that moment of the Mass amid the rubble and in the next few days as the disaster-struck image was raised from the ruins, she had no doubt about the action that had to be taken: "We all knew that the image of the Señor de la Soledad had to be attended to immediately to avoid further calamity." And they laid the broken pieces of the image on a table and began to cover them with flowers.

AT Mass, on July 30, 1972, the padre invoked the *campesinos* to assist him in his mission to undertake the reconstruction of the temple without the permission or help of conniving townspeople, without the bishop, and without CRYRZA or any other organization. "After the earthquake we made adobes to build the temple, and CRYRZA's tractor came and made us pampa," he reminded everyone in his sermon.

Actually, from the beginning of the Mass, it was clear that something unique was happening. Whereas Espinoza often spoke in his native Quechua, without translation, on this occasion he took no risk of being misunderstood. He spoke loudly and distinctly in the Quechua of his native Apurímac region, but at the same time, a man stood formally at his side, translating into the Ancash Quechua of the Callejón. The priest would then repeat what he had said in Spanish.

At his embattled finest, he asked why the aid of the world had never reached the valley and why the Lord of Solitude was still cast away in the cane and mud shack "*en chacra ajena.*" In the face of constant delays and troubles upon troubles, he and the countryside—the *campesinado*—the "legitimate sons of this region," would ignore everyone and build the sanctuary of the Señor. Deriding everyone from the Revolutionary Military Government to the plotting and gossiping townspeople, he preached: "They have abandoned the faith; they have abandoned the Señor de la Soledad; they have abandoned Huaraz. . . . Now let us see if we can lift up with our own hands, in front of the Señor, his sanctuary."

Calling the Señor de la Soledad *Papacito*, the padre began to ask individual *campesinos* for their help. Some of them seemed confused and hesitant. Where would the money come from to build the temple? "*Allapa karum yacha*"—"I live very far away"—ventured one voice from the congregation.

Marianela, the faithful guardian of the image, appealed to the man, "There is no one. That is why the padre is pleading with the people of the countryside."

A *campesina* spoke up: "We must begin now. The rains will come again before long."

A sympathetic townsperson suggested sending notices to the authorities of the hamlets. "No, no longer will I write on paper," shot back Espinoza. "Too much paper has already been wasted."

There and then committees were formed. It was decided that in the ancient way word would be passed from person to person among the hamlets. Each Sunday, the *runakuna*—the people— would convene, until the sanctuary was built. "*Papasitunchis,*" a man addressed the padre, "we are so grateful for the reconstruction of the Sanctuary."

My last long conversation with Padre Espinoza took place after that Mass. He, Marianela, and I retired to the parish house, where the young woman in rags, like a deranged Ophelia, sang for me in a wispy, childlike voice song after song about the beauty of the valley and carefully repeated again and again the songs that the dancers had addressed to the image on its *octava*. A young boy came in to the dining room and began to sing: "Cordillera Blanca,

Cordillera Negra . . ." Mellow now after his fiery sermon, the padre hummed along.

But when Marianela and the boy wandered off and the priest and I were left alone, he again grew intense. With words, he painted for me the gravest of landscapes, the ruins of the sierra enclave among which survivors lived, where all, he said, had grown accustomed to cold and hunger. "At times"—he sighed, now appearing so vulnerable I felt uneasy—"I fear the dawn. I am afraid to wake up and more afraid still to go to bed if I have not completed some work." Theory, "pure theory," seemed to fatigue him most. But with his new plan to build the church with help only from the *campesinos*, he went on, the time spent in the ruins would turn into "a spatial flight, full of dangers and marked by great velocity."

Volatile, he was at one moment carried along by the momentum of his audacious stroke, lambasting everyone, and then, in the next moment, he would suddenly soften, becoming filled with compassion. The great shock sustained by survivors had left everyone "paralyzed, sick, dizzy. . . . This girl Marianela—before she was not right, but now she is much worse. My poor people—it gives me pain to see them.

"This town cannot complain about me," he concluded. "My faith is pure, and I have loved them. Were this not so, it would be better that I were dead." Reaching under the refectory table, he stroked a scrawny cat that mewed at his feet. "The only faithful one is this poor animal." No one could really comprehend the tiredness that gripped him so tightly until he could do no more than cry, he said.

We talked for a long time before his embattled weariness overtook him. I never quite understood his last remark to me. Spoken in a kindly manner, it nevertheless left me feeling a kind of pang. "You are happy with your interior world. That's the way it is, sister," he said as I was leaving.

YEARS after I left the valley in 1972, I read poet-survivor Yauri Montero's description of Padre Espinoza. He called him valiant, energetic, and rebellious. Over their "Coffee of Friendship," taken together amid the rubble, the padre told Yauri that he had removed forty-five cadavers from the ruins of the sanctuary. He had carried the dead to trucks and the sick to the hospital. He had taken in seventy orphans. He insisted that food, piled up in bags and only inciting hungry survivors to steal it, be distributed. He had suffered a severe leg wound, which got infected on the fifth day, taking him eventually to Lima. He returned to Huaraz quickly, not yet cured, having discovered that in Lima people believed that in Huaraz survivors were well sheltered and well fed because of all the aid that poured in from abroad.

"I know you could have left," Yauri told the priest, "for better paths on this earth, places they might have indulged you more. You preferred to remain and fight. Besides being a mystic, like St. Francis of Assisi, you are a . . . warrior."

Thirty-two

A PLACE TO MOURN

All was silence. Only the wind was whistling, its sound pouring out soledad. *It is a loneliness, that pampa.*
Pilatos of Soledad barrio

THE SOLEDAD FAITH can perhaps best be understood in contrast to that of the Centenario church, physically located at the other extreme of Huaraz from Soledad: Centenario, its Christ gargantuan, robust, austere, intact, abstractly cubistic, its priest embracing the theology of the Risen Christ, rock and folk music emanating from inside its concrete walls; Soledad, its Christ of delicate features, "wounded," in pieces under the rubble, its priest saying Mass first amid the ruins and then in a cane-and-mud temple, the strains of a violin and voices singing "*Kamakok Yaya, La Soledad*" piercing the quiet of the hill at the edge of the destroyed old center of Huaraz.

Centenario and Soledad cannot be construed merely as extremes of liberalism and conservativism. More liberal elements of Catholicism than Centenario were present in the aftermath: "imported" ones, like the Maryknoll Fathers, and certain radical priests who people said were "connected to Peking." Likewise, many of the so-called old-timers, the priests who belonged to no Order, as well as the Franciscans of Huarupampa, were more conservative and unquestioning of the church's traditions than was Espinoza of Soledad. The image of the Soledad Christ transcended its own roots of tradition, and the Soledad priest himself upbraided the *costumbres*. The contrast lies more in the response of survivors to the Centenario Christ and the Soledad Christ than in doctrine.

It was Soledad that inspired the deepest devotion, the "big, big faith," as people said. In the aftermath, there were few points of identification between survivors and the modern cubistic Christ of Centenario. Jesusa, though deeply involved with the consciousness-raising arm of the Reform at Centenario, told me that when she needed to unburden herself, it was to the Señor de la Soledad that she went. That is the *"fe de llorar, de decir todas las penas"* ("the faith of crying, of telling all one's troubles"), she said. After the earthquake, when she and Nicolás went to Soledad, she told me, they would cry and ask, "Lord, you are the most miraculous of all time, but, Lord, are you still here?"

The rumors and fears concerning the authenticity and safety of the Señor de la Soledad were unique to him. Other Christ figures in Huaraz, the Lord of Miracles or the Lord of the Resurrection, for example, did not inspire doubt. The venerated Señor del Nazareno, also of Soledad parish, had, without qualms, been sent to Lima for restoration.

When I asked Don Juan why this was, he answered that it was only the Señor de la Soledad that people wanted to take away in order to acquire the same power that Ancash, and especially Huaraz, had because of him. They only fooled themselves, however, he said, because the Señor de la Soledad could not perform the same miracles elsewhere that he performed in Ancash. "He has appeared for the salvation, aid, and protection of Huaraz, and he has to be in Huaraz." This is why, he explained, the *campesinos*, in spite of their passion for the Christ, never wanted to take him to the countryside. "He must be forever in Huaraz, where we can go with flowers and prayers," he concluded firmly.

I am certain that to *campesinos* the Señor de la Soledad was *huaca*. He was not a mere symbol but an embodiment of the qualities their Indian ancestors had attributed to their ancient *huacas*. He appeared to be old, not the young crucified Christ we think of. Calling him *Papachito* or *Aukiteetanchikmi*—"Our Wise Old Father" —*campesinos* unburdened themselves of the perpetual sorrows of the Andes, hail and drought, landslide and ruined crops.

Historian Luis Valcárcel has written of this ancient Andean concept of *huaca*:

> Spirits of the community . . . these constitute what is called a *huaca*: the highest mountain, which dominates the life of the town . . . is considered the residence of the guardian spirit of the community. It is the *Apu*, generally a snow-capped peak. . . . There are other spirits that have a greater jurisdiction, certain *huacas* that have much prestige, and to whom has been attributed decisive action in determined moments in which the common interest was compromised, not only of one community but of several within the valley. These are the *huacas* that achieve renown and have jurisdiction over a vaster area.

"Around the Señor de la Soledad turns all the religious faith of this region," Cucha, the teacher, had said. And the night, shortly before I left the valley, when the old man Don Alejandro of San Francisco barrio sang *"Apu Inca yarquellame"*—"Lord Inca, come"—I heard the same tune I had so often heard at Soledad, *"Apu Yaya La Soledad"*—"Lord Father Soledad."

The Inca armies, out of a calculated tolerance, sent the local *huacas* of the valleys they conquered to join their pantheon in Cuzco. Then, out of religious zeal, the Spaniards combed the mountains for the native *huacas* in order to destroy them and replace them with Catholic crosses. Like the ancient *huacas*, Soledad was perceived as constantly threatened with extirpation by those who might want to send him away or to destroy him. And, like the Indians who hid their *huacas* from the flames and clubs of the Spanish friars, their *campesino* descendants and townspeople alike have tried time and time again to "save" the Señor de la Soledad. Each threat to the Señor de la Soledad, each blow that struck the history-battered image, appears to have generated more and more belief in its power.[1]

As the early Spanish missionaries were quick to point out to the Indians, the difference between the *huaca* of the Andes and

Christ was that Christ died for everyone. And in the Señor de la Soledad, the crucified Christ had been rendered in a profoundly Spanish concreteness. The eighty-four-year-old grandmother of Don Juan's children spoke in Quechua of the first time she saw the Señor de la Soledad. A small girl, tender as a lamb, she was taken by the hand to see the image and, she said, forever after to remember in her mind's eye the Lord of Solitude: "spilling his blood, whipped, with his crown of thorns. That's why you cry and you say to him, 'What difference does it make that I am hungry, God? You are shedding tears for me, scattering them. . . .' That's what we say." Now, three-quarters of a century later, she recalled that in her youth, when she lay dying of typhoid, her soul went to heaven, walking on a very narrow road, "a road made for rats or thin needles." And there, at the end of the road, "standing on a pampa, pure pampa, was the cross, exactly like—*igualito*—the Señor de la Soledad."

The new bishop had noticed that worshipers changed their demeanor at Soledad. "When they are at Centenario, they have a different attitude, but when they go to Soledad, they adopt the same attitude of those of the barrio." To test this, he went to Soledad early in the morning on Ash Wednesday after carnival, when all of Huaraz and the *campesinos* pass through Soledad. "Even the cultured people," the bishop told me, "cried and recounted their worries aloud before the Soledad Christ."

He understood that Soledad and Centenario were two sides of the same coin, that death and life were both part of life. Amid the destruction, especially, he felt, both "faiths" were needed. From his seat in Nicrupampa, he tried to mediate between the faiths of Soledad and Centenario. "Until we change human structure," he said, "we cannot change religion. Perhaps we must try to change both at the same time. But as long as there is hunger and abandonment, we cannot change the religious aspect, because for the people to cry in front of the Señor de la Soledad is a source of peace. It is as though I look for a friend on a day I am sad and his presence alone makes me feel happy."

JUST as the ancient *huacas* included the ancestor of a community, who "symbolized the threads holding families together [and] was their *Kamak*, their Creator, who had made the laws governing their group," the Lord of Solitude united the barrios of Huaraz and tied the countryside, the satellite hamlets, to the town. *"Kamakok Yaya, La Soledad,"* dance groups would sing, bowing to the Señor. Just as the ceremony held at the the base of Huascarán on the second anniversary of the earthquake seemed to melt away categories that separated people, the image, too, dissolved all social structural categories. Belief in Soledad crossed all lines: city and country, *damnificado* and *no-damnificado*, property owners and non–property owners. And as I learned on Christmas Eve, when I went to Mass at Soledad with Elena and Flavio, staunch Evangelicals, they, too, found it hardest to cut their ties to Soledad.

One day, talking to a *Soledano*, I tried to determine the boundaries of devotion to the Señor de la Soledad. Upset, he shouted back at me, "Look, I told you that *campesinos* believe in their image; they believe a lot and adore the Señor de la Soledad, just like all of us from the town." It was as if I had challenged a definition of "community" that was coterminous with devotion to the image.

But perhaps like all powerful entities, or powerful beliefs, the image of Soledad could also be used to separate and to create as well as resolve conflict. Padre Espinoza tapped its power in his singular mission to rebuild the temple without the aid of the town and of all "outsiders." He drove another wedge between the town and the countryside when he attributed the greater devastation to the town to their not believing his dream and repenting, as had, he said, the *campesinos*.

Anyone acting in the name of the Señor de la Soledad was unassailable. The padre defied everyone in a way he would not have gotten away with were it not for his closeness to the image. Pilatos said, "That Christ is his shield and his weapon of attack at the same time."

Cucha called the Señor de la Soledad "untouchable," and the Reform nun at Centenario, expressing the same idea, told me, "If CRYRZA touches him, either the priest or the image, there is revolution in Huaraz."

The new bishop was keenly aware of this. "If today I tried to touch the Señor, it would be fatal," he confided. He recounted his first day in the destroyed town. On that day, he went to say Mass at Soledad. Finding civil guards all around, he confessed to thinking his visit must be very important. But after the Mass the guards told him they were there because people were saying that he had come to sell the Christ of Soledad. "If a person wants to create conflict, he doesn't say that someone is going to burn the Peruvian flag. He says that he is going to burn the image or steal it or sell it," the bishop said ruefully.

The power of the faith sometimes led to conscious manipulation. The image was used as a political vehicle to attack or to defend any cause. It was central to any movement. "If people want to throw out a prefect, they say he wants to harm the Señor, or if they want everybody behind him, then they use the Señor that way, too," Pilatos told me. Cucha, too, said that those who defended the Señor often emerged as political leaders. "One had to vote for them, believe in them, because they defended the Señor de la Soledad or perhaps a favored priest of Soledad."

It was not always clear when the Señor de la Soledad was being leaned upon for personal gain. The rumors and gossip about Padre Espinoza challenged his "true" motives. Of Espinoza, the bishop would say only, "That priest is the only one who can contain the *campesinos*. He has a special power in his manner of captivating people." I, too, sometimes doubted the priest, but I would remember that moment he raised the chalice to the mountain crosses and sang, "I adore you, Holy Cross." And then, after seeing him at his most vulnerable that last time, I could not believe he consciously used the image for his own ends. Something deeper than personal gain was driving him.

One thing is certain, though. Persons of note who entered the valley did not delay in appearing before the image. "Belaúnde [the president before Velasco], when he came, went to visit the Señor, the Aprista Carlos Alberto went to visit the Señor, and now, when the CRYRZA general arrived in the valley, he went first to visit the Señor," a *Soledano* reported. When the wife of Peru's president, General Velasco, came to the valley to view the destruction, she went first to Mass at Soledad. And the *octava* of the feast of Soledad created strange bedfellows when the head of the Revolutionary Military Government in Huaraz—which lashed out against *costumbres*—marched in the procession alongside the Señor de la Soledad.

The Revolution could not ignore the Soledad Christ because, more than the abstract "Risen Christ" of Centenario and the Reform, even more than the flag of nationalism, the Soledad image was the prime mover of the masses of Huaraz and environs. Though the Reconstruction forces tried to tie into the Centenario Christ, it was ultimately to Soledad that they had to bow. All elements, from the most conservative to the most revolutionary, had to connect to the one transcendent vehicle of meaning in Huaraz. Restoration of the image was the first act of reconstruction. Eventually, also, on the plans for the proposed reconstruction of Huaraz, the Soledad church and plaza were earmarked to be located in the exact same place where they had stood before the earthquake. This was not true for the other churches.

The hegemony of the image, its temple, its priest, and the barrio of Soledad were taken into account, also, in the choice of where CRYRZA and SINAMOS would hold their meetings and where reconstruction would begin. The unpopular housing program was begun in Huarupampa, which was not only topographically more level but also had the reputation of being *plano* ("smooth") in temperament. As tension over the program grew, the word went out: "They will stop them in Soledad."

One of the most important meetings between top officials of CRYRZA and barrio representatives was held in the San Antonio church of the Spanish Franciscans, in Huarupampa, on April 13, 1972. As I sat at this meeting, I wondered why it was being held in that particular church and discussed this afterward with the people. One townswoman reasoned that the meeting had to be held somewhere in the old center of Huaraz and that a church was chosen because people could not protest the reconstruction plans too vehemently inside a holy place. "It couldn't be Centenario," she said. "It does not have importance because there are no purely *Huaracino* images at Centenario." People had noticed that the Host at San Antonio had been covered for the meeting, leaving only the images of the *Cristo Pobre* ("Poor Christ") and the Lord of Miracles as "witnesses." "Perhaps," the woman speculated, "they held the meeting in front of the Poor Christ because he is humble and meek. CRYRZA should not have held the meeting in a holy place but in a place where we might have raised our voices." I could not imagine the meeting having been held at Soledad. The magic of Soledad would have competed too powerfully with the secular objectives of the Reconstruction.

"And Soledad?" I asked.

"Ay, no, Soledad is a focus of rumor; things can get violent there. It is a place of ferment, of revolution, if not of arms, then of ideas."

The importance of the Soledad image to the rehabilitation of Huaraz revealed itself in humble prayers, "May he give us health and life to raise up Huaraz"; in the rhetoric of the priest, "Under his eyes and from the ruins will spring the new city of Huaraz"; and in the clandestine voices of those who felt betrayed by the way reconstruction was being carried out, "If CRYRZA restored the image to keep us quiet, that same image we can use to raise ourselves up. . . . For Huaraz he is the only hope. . . . For that Christ, Huaraz has to recover, through him, because he is the means of uniting ourselves."

BUT there was something in the Soledad Christ beyond the power to unite the community, something unique, rooted in the image itself and the place itself as well as in the circumstances of the aftermath and the way these elements combined at that moment of time.

So many chords of identification of survivors with the Christ of Solitude—his legend, history, and circumstance—were struck in the aftermath. In the origin myths the Señor de la Soledad kept trying to return to "his place," just as now *Huaracinos* tried to return to the deserted old center of Huaraz and "their places." Through the years, the Christ had been the victim of deceit, had been betrayed. Those in high places were felt to take advantage of him— *se valen de Él*—for their own purposes, even to have sold the image for their own profit. Likewise, survivors had feelings of having been betrayed, "sold out" by the forces of modernization, both secular and religious, as reconstruction—trapped in the struggle between immediate, local, concrete needs, and long-range national ideological commitments—took so painfully long to get under way.

The fragility of their makeshift dwellings, their location *en chacra ajena*, some alien corner of land, and the inclemencies they had to endure were all there, codified in the present circumstances of the Señor de la Soledad. I remember Don Juan's daughter, Rosa María, only fourteen years old, saying, *"Papachitu Dios, Teeta Soledad*, pounded and beaten by fallen timbers, in a hut, suffering cold and heat, everything!" Even the doubt that beclouded the identity of the Soledad Christ reflected the doubt survivors felt about whether they could or could not answer the ultimate questions, account for where God was, know if there *was* a God, given such immense tragedy. Jesusa, remember, cried to the image, "Lord, are you still here?"

A still deeper meaning of the Soledad faith lies in the reciprocity of salvation that punctuates the history of Huaraz and its image. Through the years, *Huaracinos*, both townspeople and *campesinos*, had saved the Señor de la Soledad from fire, kidnapping, and again, after the earthquake, when they kept watch, placing flowers over the shattered image. As many survivors had never found their dead or had learned that they had been burned or buried hurriedly in a common grave, perhaps the long waking of the Soledad Christ after the earthquake served as a kind of communal Pietà, providing survivors with a rite of separation, thus adding another link in the chain of reciprocal caring between image and community.

Don Juan said that when they nailed Christ to the cross, rocks began to clash in the heavens, the earth shook, and animals bellowed. "I find myself so pained when I see the Señor maltreated . . . but he shows us how we must suffer, with patience."[2] Jesusa and Nicolás added that from the Crucifixion onward they had felt sorry for him. A *campesina* enumerated, "One takes care of the Señor de la Soledad, accompanies him, asks things of him, loves him, feels sorry for him."

I knew that empathy had been fed time and time again by the long history of the intertwining fates of town and image. Toward the end, though, I realized that it was not only the people who felt sorry for the Señor de la Soledad. The empathy was mutual. I often heard that "Christ suffered in the earthquake" and asked Don Juan about it, expecting him to talk about the physically damaged image of the Señor de la Soledad. Instead, he answered, "Surely he must have suffered for all those people who were honorable, who used to pray. On seeing them die, he must have suffered." Once again, I was struck by the completeness of the grief. People, mountains, saints, animals, birds, even Christ, grieved.

This Christ was vulnerable, very different from the God of Vallejo's poem, which the German priest had read at Centenario on May 31, 1972: "If you had been a man, today you would know how to be God. . . . You feel nothing for your creation. . . ." Soledad was more like the God of another Vallejo poem, the God who, along with man, weeps for his "fragile Creation."

That Christ's suffering was perceived as not only physical but spiritual made me realize that the image of Soledad represented that part of the passion of Christ when he was alone, betrayed by man, and finally forsaken even by his Father. It was the Christ of Gethsemane, and even more of those most lonely moments on the cross when Christ cried out, "My God, my God, why have you forsaken me?"

"Tell me, Lord, what were you doing the thirty-first of May of 1970 at 3:23 in the afternoon?" rang in my ears. Perhaps the words meant more than the absence of an abstract God or even the absence of the "real" Señor de la Soledad. Perhaps they were an echo of Christ abandoned by his Father. And if Christ, too, could be abandoned by God, what empathy for survivors must have spilled from the cane-and-wattle shack at the edge of Huaraz. I heard again in my mind Padre Espinoza preaching not only "Huaraz wounded and destroyed, our Señor wounded and destroyed" but "The Christ abandoned and forgotten [*el Cristo del abandono y olvido*], the Christ of Soledad." This is exactly what survivors were feeling, alienated and alone, anxious over the accelerated political and religious changes that sought to yank them too fast from their old ways. No bells tolled for their destroyed world. In the loneliness of an aftermath appropriated by ideology, only at Soledad could they mourn unrestrainedly.

Huaraz and the image fused so exquisitely in the aftermath. Yauri wrote in his journal of feeling "naked in the face of a tremendous physical and spiritual *soledad*." Private emotions of aloneness, evoked by the image in the "faith of crying," became transposed to a collective sentiment. The Señor de la Soledad became the quintessence of all the private dramas of the aftermath and, at the same time, of the drama of Huaraz and its countryside. Heavy with history, yet full of poetic timelessness, the image seemed to obscure the line between myth and history, to blur the boundaries between ideology and action, and to resolve in some measure, in the communal sentiment of *soledad*, the contradiction between the individual's essential aloneness and the fellowship of society.[3]

SOME months after the earthquake, Yauri left his tent and walked up to Soledad over rubble, mounds of dirt, and enormous roots of eucalyptus ripped from the earth. He encountered Padre Espinoza, who took him by the arm and led him into the first temporary hut that had sheltered the image. They walked up to a table through a haze of dust blowing between the reeds. Dozens of dripping candles illuminated the table. On a bench nearby sat a guard, an old man, and several children. Espinoza picked up two old nails, joined together, from the table on which the battered image, covered by a dusty mantle of red velvet, was lying.

"We found these while scratching through the rubble," he told Yauri, "and had them soldered in the form of a cross. Huaraz has been crucified. . . ." The priest lifted the mantle, revealing the image. "His face is chipped," Yauri wrote later. "It is the face of Huaraz, anguished, but valiant." The guard approached. He was crying and begged the priest to say a Mass for the Señor de la Soledad. Yauri left. Outside, he observed the rooftops, unhinged from their walls like bandages torn from wounds. On his shoulders he felt the same light rain that was falling on the pampa.

For me, the meaning of the image and the aftermath lay on the pampa that had been Huaraz. Both bore the imprint of *soledad*:[4]

I walked back across the pampa. Wind and dust were high. The last group of dancers that had gone to take their leave of the Señor filed down Calle Bolívar. A woman was crossing Belén. I went past the freestanding wall where only the painted word *Funeraria* remained, past the building split in half, where "Ice Cream and Pastries" had been sold, past the crumbling Gran Hotel . . . stepping on an exposed piece of tile flooring . . . and past the stairs going nowhere. (From my field notes, May 11, 1972)

Todo era silencio. El viento no más silbaba. Y de allí el son se desprendía soledad. Es una soledad esa pampa. (Pilatos of Soledad barrio)

Part 7

TEN YEARS AFTER

Thirty-three

THE YEARS BETWEEN

FIELDWORK DID NOT END when I left the valley. The year afterward I lived in the far Northwest, where it seemed as if I were looking only at the backs of mountains. There were no jagged spires to confront. Memories and dreams of that year "in the gravest of landscapes" pursued me with insistence.

I could still see Domitila laughing in the flickering candlelight and hear Don Juan whisper, as I walked with him in the Soledad procession: "Half I believe, half I don't." I could still see the Soledad priest gesticulating wildly in his mountainside brick factory, his straight black hair standing on end in the wind. I could feel Cagliostro's arms enfold me in the dark ouside my room as he revealed that CRYRZA could not begin the Reconstruction and was stalling for time.

The pampa of Huaraz became a lamination of memories engraved on my mind, image upon image. I saw women and children with their five-gallon tin cans streaming across it in a light rain to buy a few *soles* of kerosene. I could see little girls squatting, switch in hand, watching over their sheep, and women scurrying after donkeys. I saw cows passing and big trucks lumbering behind them. I saw fireworks exploding in the late-night sky and the moon on Huascarán. I saw the stairs going nowhere and the freestanding facades.

Whole incidents obtruded upon my everyday life, like the time the circus set up its tent outside my window and the tent collapsed in a high wind. The eerie wails of the circus trumpet and the piercing screams of the man they called "the crazy one," who, at night, took refuge in a ruin on the pampa, punctuated my nights the years after.

One night, I dreamed three images, in the form of a triptych: The Señor de la Soledad; the glaciers of the Cordillera Blanca, framed in an archway; and a coffin. I was conscious of death in the dream, but upon awakening, I felt tranquil, because I had seen once again those mountains.

Another way in which fieldwork didn't end was in the residue of regret over mistakes made. More than for failing to ask certain questions, for the inevitable blanks that confronted me in notes, I would feel sad that I did not go to see Don Alejandro at the end, when I learned he had gotten out his dance costume to wear for me, or that I once gambled with Jesusa's life, only sending her medicine when I could not muster the strength to go up to her. Overnight, I had flown back to another world, another sense of time, where there was no really satisfactory means of communicating with people in the valley. Whatever my hopes for future contact with them, when the plane took off from Jorge Chávez Airport, the separation felt all too final, with no way to amend faults and clear up misunderstandings.

MAY 31, 1980, would mark the tenth anniversary of the earthquake. I knew there would be commemorative ceremonies, and as the time approached, I felt more and more compelled to be in the valley on that day. The years that had elapsed since my departure from the Callejón in 1972 might have brought answers to the questions that remained hanging when I left. Still, motivated as I was by a desire to see what had happened over nearly a decade, my main reason for wanting to return was simply to be there with the people at that time.

During the intervening years, my only contact with the valley had been occasional letters, mostly from Reyna, but from Domitila and a few others, too. I had sent Christmas cards, never knowing if they had reached anyone, especially those living more remote from the center, like Don Juan. I longed for news of him and his family, of Jesusa and Nicolás. From my colleague, Anthony Oliver-Smith, who had worked in Yungay and revisited the valley during the decade, I received news of Cirila in Yungay. I knew that her companion, Rubén, had died of cancer in 1979. I knew Huaraz had finally been rebuilt, that it looked "modern," and that the Russian dachas in Yungay had been assembled on the lee of Atma Hill.

Reyna had written in 1974 that Abel, who on impulse would get into his jeep and tear down to Lima, was killed on the Pan American Highway. Through the years, I also learned that the old priest, Padre Guimaray, who had delivered the eloquent eulogy at a hamlet graveside and tried to dissuade survivors from the idea of the disaster as punishment, had died. And Padre Soriano, the priest-archaeologist who had spent his life digging and praying, had died.

To my astonishment, recent eyewitness news came shortly before I left for the valley. Abel's brother, Ricardo, who had spent years in the Canadian north country, happened to be living in Brooklyn in 1980, and a mutual friend put us in contact. Ricardo had not seen his homeland since before the earthquake and had returned to Huaraz for the first time in December 1979. For him, the new Huaraz was a shock. Only a few old landmarks remained from his childhood. Even more shocking to him was the omnipresence of the disaster. Spontaneously, the first thing friends and family talked about was the earthquake. He could not walk across the Plaza de Armas without running into someone who would talk for hours, recounting the event to him. "It was not voluntary; we *had* to talk about it. It was inside everyone. It was like a weight upon them. It was etched in their faces, and sometimes they would break down crying," he told me in my loft in Manhattan.

From Ricardo, I learned that Huaraz's four barrios and Centenario had grown from a population of some 25,000 before the earthquake to 100,000. German and French mountain climbers augmented the numbers. Many members of the "high society," to which he had belonged, had gathered in exile in Lima. Most left only as the concrete city finally took shape.

That night, after I talked to Ricardo, a kind of peace settled over me. My life once again had been cast into a larger framework. I was eager to be again in a place on top of the world, that opened out into the larger universe, excited to let the mountains come inside me once again and stretch the landscape of my mind. My return would not be without ambivalence, however. The valley of 1971–72 still burned in my memory. I felt both drawn to it and afraid to go. But I knew it was something I had to do.

Thirty-four

FIRST SIGHT

ABEL AND RICARDO'S cousin met me at Jorge Chávez Airport in Callao on Friday, May 23, 1980. Though we had never met, I recognized him instantly. As he came toward me, it was like seeing Abel again striding across the pampa. Walking through the airport, I felt the same elation I had the day in 1971 when I got my Peruvian carnet.

The next morning, I found the center of Lima in shambles compared to even eight years before. I walked around amid ribbons of black smoke emitted from buses overflowing with passengers. Scarcely one of Lima's famed wooden balconies was intact. All was tawdry, decaying. The beautiful old churches of downtown were marred by political graffiti. Gen. Francisco Morales Bermúdez had assumed command in 1975 when General Velasco fell ill, but the Revolutionary Military Government in Peru was nearing the end of its days. Elections had already been held, and Popular Action candidate and former president Fernando Belaúnde Terry, from whom Velasco had wrested power in October 1968, would take office once again on July 28.

The venerable old Hotel Bolívar seemed, too, of a bygone era. Only five of us were lunching in its ornate dining room while as many musicians played European waltzes on stringed instruments. In the evening, in the plaza in front of the hotel, the poor were cooking over open fires even as great mounds of trash from a lengthy garbage strike were being burned. Overlapping layers of old magazines, being sold for a pittance, were spread out on the plaza, and street urchins were everywhere.

On Sunday morning, May 25, I boarded the Empresa Luis Rodríguez bus for Huaraz. The coastal wasteland was unchanged, and at Pativilca the bus turned off the Pan American Highway and climbed rapidly on the newly paved but still serpentine road up into the Callejón. On the mountainsides, the names of Belaúnde and other candidates and parties were painted in large black and red letters. The venerable mountains, like the old venerable buildings of Lima, had been politicized. Lake Conococha was frozen, its borders blending into the dead-earth color of the surrounding puna. It was as if the lake had not stirred in all these years. There, at 14,000 feet, the first ice summits appeared, indomitable, they alone impervious to all the change that had occurred below.

My seatmate was a woman from Yungay, now living in Huaraz. "Huascarán could come down again," she mentioned casually. The only good she attributed to the Revolutionary Military Government was the completion of the sanctuary of Soledad—before any other church in Huaraz—and the building of a university for Ancash. "The Revolutionary Military Government has meant the downfall of Peru," she volunteered. "The cooperatives failed, and goods are scarce. You have to beg for sugar and other staples, agreeing to buy something you don't need."

We passed through Cátac, Ticapampa, and Recuay. They showed little evidence of the earthquake. Adobe houses had been rebuilt. I felt order and pattern in the houses and in the fields, quite the opposite from my first ascent nine years ago. Now I was coming from the decay and chaos of Lima to order and newness.

As the bus came to a stop on Avenida Tarapacá in the barrio

of Huarupampa, I heard the 6:00 P.M. church bells ringing in Huaraz. A boy on a tricycle took my luggage to the new Pensión Tumi in the barrio of Belén. From the balcony of my room I looked out onto a sea of small concrete houses. When night fell, it was not the sierra night of nine years before, long, still, dark, pierced only by the the chirping of guinea pigs, the howling of dogs, or from time to time, the mad wails of "the crazy one." Now lights burned dimly from lampposts around which children played until very late. The lights invaded my room, and rock-and-roll music on transistors that seemed to be everywhere, inside and outside the hotel, bombarded the night.

But the same incandescent Huaraz morning I knew from years before dawned, and I walked out onto the broad avenues. They were lined with shops—BATA shoes, Chinese restaurants, tourist agencies, even a photocopy place. Cars and motorcycles were parked on the streets, whereas all one saw in 1971 were jeeps, dilapidated buses, and occasional pickups. There were no empty spaces, no rubble, no swirling dust. A soft breeze stirred the eucalyptus branches on the edges of the town. Only when looking up to the same breathless Cordillera Blanca did time appear to have stood still, and then only because, I knew, I could not detect from below new cracks in the glaciers or the slow melting of ice cornices.

I could tell right away that the house in which I had lived almost a decade ago, which at that time had stood almost alone on the vacant pampa, would not now be easily located. I hesitated but decided not to ask directions. I would find it for myself. Maybe it had been torn down, after all. For a few days, I would simply try to absorb these new surroundings, strange now in their ordinariness. I felt disoriented in this ordered world, like a reporter who had covered a war and returned in peacetime.

A shopkeeper told me that as construction of the concrete houses began in earnest on the small plots of land apportioned to people after the urban expropriation, many *Huaracinos* left the valley, and people from Trujillo and Chiclayo moved in. Finding exile worse, many of those who left were returning now, but there were no more houses to be had. "These tiny houses do not fit our way of life," the woman said. "Where can guinea pigs and other animals be kept?"

On my walk this first morning, I learn that Pilatos, the image

maker, has gone to Paramonga. Almost everyone I talk to tells me
that Padre Espinoza of Soledad is gone. I see the barrio churches
being built of concrete blocks. They look like small factories.

I stop in at the Centenario church. All the German priests left
in 1976. Italian priests replaced them. "The Italians are tending
the seeds the Germans planted," the sacristan tells me. He is an
Indian catechist from a hamlet above Huaraz. I ask him if there is
competition between Centenario and Soledad, and he answers,
"Competition, no; fighting, yes!" The people have returned to *costumbrismo*, the sacristan says. At carnival, he went to Soledad and saw
the big mountain crosses lining the walls. Only Centenario carries
on the struggle to implant Catholic Reform in Huaraz. The Mormons have grown to number three hundred, but Evangelism has
paled. The "cult" alone remains as it always was, even before the
earthquake, its worshipers singing in tongues. I ask about the Christ
of May. Soledad and the May Christ are the same, he answers.
"No one talks about the double anymore."

I walk back to the Tumi along Avenida Centenario, stopping
to see Don Antonio, where I used to buy my supplies. He is filling
bags with coca leaves for the miners at Ticapampa.

The next morning I set out in the gathering heat of the day.
I go to the Plaza de Armas, bordered now by the new municipal
building, the court, a museum, banks, and the post office. Nearby,
the Gran Hotel stands erect once again. The skeletal cupola of the
old cathedral, which had purposely been left as a landmark of the
earthquake, has been blasted away, and in its place workers are
building the new cathedral. They beckon me over and announce
proudly that the saints' images are coming back to the cathedral.

I spot the photographer in the center of the plaza. We talk for
a long time. Since 1955, he has been on the plaza, looking through
the same old-fashioned camera, its hood covering his head. Through
the eye of his camera, he has seen so much, the "beautiful city of
before," he tells me, and then, on May 31, 1970, as he was taking
the picture of two little girls, he heard the tremendous noise, like
a locomotive bearing down on him, and saw the city falling and
the dust rising. Then silence, as he knelt, praying, and then he left
the old camera in charge of his small son as he ran to find his wife
at their house in Pedregal. Two daughters were dead under the
rubble. In the days and weeks that followed, when they were given

only a fistful of rice at a time, he and his diminished family faced starvation.

He soon went back to the plaza, little expecting that his camera would provide a livelihood any longer. But during those first months relief workers came to have their pictures taken against the background of the rubble, and at twenty-five *soles* a photograph, he stored up some money. In the first days, people even wanted pictures of the dead. Then came the years of waiting, survivors "dead in life," he said, when he was often alone with his camera, just as I had found him the first day I sat on the plaza in 1971. Now, again, he was busy, though with inflation the 500 *soles* a day he earned scarcely bought anything.

What does the eye of the camera see now, I asked.

Many people from outside. They are the owners of Huaraz now. *Huaracinos* died in the earthquake or left. Many have died through these years, of pain, of the sentiment that affects the heart. There are no more rich. The great landowners died or left. But the agrarian reform was not well done, and now the *campesinos* don't want to work, don't want to bring their produce to the market. And in my Peru, we have no machines of production. . . . We are only colonies of Russia or the United States. They are the same, Russia and the United States. We speak, but we never get anywhere. Perhaps Señor Belaúnde and the new government will do better.

The one great joy the Revolutionary Military Government had bequeathed the valley was their university, he said. Only through education might a society without interests and greed come about. Until that time, more and more social upheaval would come to the world.

I became caught up in this man, now sixty-four years old, who had spent so much of his life under the hood of a camera on Huaraz's central plaza. He called himself an Indian, who, though Christian, still had "a feeling for Viracocha." "My conditions are very bad," he remarked, "but I like to surmount my pain. And my facial features are bad, but my sentiment has a respectful quality." He invited me to visit him and his family later that day in their house in Pedregal.

In the foothills, wind lashed the eucalyptus trees, and the landscape from there was magnificent. The photographer's house was humble. The wind whipped a plastic curtain separating its two rooms. His wife wore a ruffled felt hat. "There are not even potatoes anymore," she said.

"What caused the earthquake?" I asked, forcing myself to focus on which interpretations of the disaster had survived these years.

"France was using a big atomic instrument on the island of Mururoa," the photographer answered.

"They still are," I said.

"France is a great power, and Peru is not a great power," he replied.

"What of the Señor de la Soledad?"

"The Señor de la Soledad is a means to teach respect," he answered.

I did not press him. Already I suspected that the doubt that had flourished in the times of chaos had subsided. I began to accept that I would never find out whether the image that stood in the makeshift temple after the earthquake was the "real" Señor de la Soledad or the Christ of May.

I had to keep reminding myself that May 31 was close at hand. Very much in contrast to the days immediately preceding this date in 1972, people were not talking about the anniversary. I heard nothing on the radio. A loudspeaker on a truck that cruised the city was announcing only that a big social dance would be held on Friday night, May 30. I asked the photographer what he would do on Saturday.

"I will go the cemetery to say my prayers for my two daughters. What else can I do? Try to forget."

It was dark, and as I made my way down the hills, I was as frightened of the dogs as I had been nine years before. "The dogs are here to bite," said two little girls, giggling as they skipped their way down to Huaraz on their way "to night school."

The next day I visited my old friend Teófines. He was drawn and tired from an accident that demolished his famous truck, *La Guinda*, in which we used to sail through the Callejón, listening to tapes. "The city is better now. We have shops and broad avenues and a paved road to Lima," he said, his enthusiasm tempered, though, with thoughts about the general decline of Peru, high prices, scarcity, hard times.

I continued up into Nicrupampa. The land had finally been expropriated. There were still many *módulos*, and people were in various stages of building their own houses. When I finally located Domitila, we sat close together on an old sofa in her partially constructed house and talked as if no time at all had passed. She and Edwincito, her youngest son, now a teenager, walked me back to the Tumi. Crossing the bridge over the Quilcay was just as before—women beating clothes clean against rock slabs jutting from the growling waters, the burnished-gold dust of sundown whipped up along the banks of the river in the hustle and bustle of people and donkeys going and coming from the market, and over our shoulders the ominous weight of the Cordillera Blanca, growing icier as night came.

STILL, nothing is said on the radio about the May 31 commemoration. Even before I left the States, I had decided to spend May 31 with Cirila on the Yungay playa, so it is not crucial that I know when and where the ceremony in Huaraz will take place. But memories of the anxiety in 1972 over the thirty-first and CRYRZA are with me still, and I find the contrast with people now going about their normal tasks strange. "Normality" here in the valley seems strange. I knew that over these years CRYRZA had metamorphosed first into ORDEZA—Organismo Regional del Desarrollo de la Zona Afectada (Regional Organization for the Development of the Affected Zone)—and then into Ordenor Centro—Regional Organization of the North Central Part. People say simply that in due time Ordenor Centro will announce the activities for the day.

Walking toward the Plaza de Armas on Wednesday morning, May 28, I run into Juan Manuel, the English teacher. He had heard I was in town and was on his way to the Tumi. Seeing him come toward me, dressed as he always was, formally, in an old suit, I think of Antonio Machado, the poet of Sevillian orchards and the plains of Castile. Like Machado, Juan Manuel is, "in the finest sense of the word, good"—*un buen hombre*. As we walk along, he points with pride to the wide streets. "Huaraz, before the earthquake, was stagnant. Now Huaraz has progressed." I ask about the dream of equality that had pervaded the revolutionary rhetoric. "The really rich exist no longer, but privileges have returned," he says. "The Revolutionary Military Government of General Velasco had a good idea. But the functionaries are a disgrace. Perhaps everywhere the bureaucrats don't really fulfill completely the good desires of governments. Progress does not mean there is true social justice."

"And the *campesinos*?" I ask.

"He who has nothing gets nothing."

The ill-conceived agrarian reform, together with a terrible drought in the last years—a drought Juan Manuel attributed to changes in weather patterns after the earthquake—had virtually brought agriculture, at least on the Cordillera Negra, to a halt. "With the earthquake and the aftermath, and now the drought, the route was opened for the *campesinos* to enter the cities. They come down to be itinerants, selling and doing odd jobs. And from here they go down to the slums that surround Lima. That is not good," my friend reports.

"What about their love of the land?" I ask.

"Yes, before they never left, they had such affection for their *chacras*. But with the passing of these years, they prefer to go to the cities and suffer the anguish of the *barriadas*." At the same time, Juan Manuel said, relations between *campesinos* and townspeople were better. "Before, they were ignored, as if they were invisible, unseen. But the difficulty is, who is going to plant?"

I ask him about religion. "It is the same as before the earthquake. *Costumbrismo* has returned, though the catechists are campaigning in the countryside. Townsmen and *campesinos* have great faith in images, in processions. One cannot change beliefs that are inherited from parents to children."

"What do people nowadays say caused the earthquake?" I ask him.

"The bomb," he answers. "I, too, think it could have had an influence. People still talk about the French bombs and the island of Mururoa. And people still talk about punishment. That is the belief, that we did not know how to treat each other well and the earthquake was a punishment of God. Townsmen and *campesinos* say that, and the bomb was the vehicle of God. . . . A positive change is that we treat each other better."

As we walk toward the mayor's office in the municipal building on the plaza, Juan Manuel says, "The earthquake has taught us to look at things with serenity. Our spirits are prepared for any accident that might occur. And we keep abreast of the phenomena of nature." A phenomenon that has been observed is that two stars that used to be close together little by little are getting farther apart.

At four-thirty in the afternoon, I set out for Cirila's. Tony was in Yungay earlier in the year and has told her I will be coming. I catch a fine bus, so different from before, when the buses were decaying or I had to hitch rides on trucks going through the valley. *Campesinos* get on and off, and children beg rides to the next town. Now there are few signs of destruction, and on the bus people talk matter-of-factly. I feel Huascarán above us, but dead silence does not fall in the bus, as it used to, when we cross the playa.

Cirila lives now on the outskirts of Punyán, north of where the survivor settlement of Yungay Norte was. Her house is adobe, with great wooden posts. I call. Finally, she appears, beautiful and strong as ever. She has endured such unrelenting tragedy, ridden out the crest of the avalanche that buried her sons, and then she lost Rubén, who helped sustain her, helped sustain everyone with his rough-hewn humor, making us laugh those afternoons and nights around the oilcloth-covered table at Cirila's restaurant.

I could see her strength in her broad smiling face, coming from every cell of her large body, striding toward me. We sat together on chairs on her veranda out back, facing her *chacra* and her cows. She supports herself from agriculture now, working all day on her land and collapsing with exhaustion at night. She is at peace, she tells me. Her daughter, Dina, moved from Lima to Yungay, and now Cirila has a grandson. We make plans to go together with them to the playa on Saturday.

As I am about to leave, she asks if I remember Llacta. That word *Llacta*—a green piece of land at the tip of the spit called Aura, between the two major lobes of the avalanche—struck the nerve of everything that bonded the two of us together, joy and losses.

Yes, I remembered. Nine years before, I had been lucky enough to be with Cirila and Rubén the day they decided to visit his land at Llacta, and I'd witnessed life well up in them again for one brief moment. Back then the three of us had stood in the hot sun, alone, surrounded by the avalanche and the cordilleras. They began to make plans, dreaming of orchards and a little house. But as always in Yungay then, the specter of death loomed so large all around that the enthusiasm that burst out was as suddenly sapped by the boulders and gray alluvial silt, where houses had once stood.

"Do you remember?" one would ask the other as we walked back across the playa to her roadside restaurant. "Here lived so-and-so."

Now I walk out to the road, realizing that her house, which she built together with Rubén before he became ill, looks right up into the glacial face of Huandoy. It is in the path of the avalanche that erased the hamlet of Ancash two and a half centuries ago. I can see only the lights of the new Yungay, south of Cirila's house, twinkling in the foothills of the Cordillera Blanca. I catch the Expreso Ancash. A young girl who lives in Mancos sits next to me. She says that landslides from Huascarán drop through the clouds, making a "shouting" sound. We turn off the main road up toward Llanganuco to pick someone up, and then down again. A full moon is rising over the icy peaks.

ON Thursday, I walk around Huaraz, now deliberately looking for people I knew. I find Doña Angelita sitting in her doorway. She looks old now. She sells only bread and mineral water. "Huaraz is all foreigners," she says. "I can walk through the market and not see anyone I know . . . but it's all right. The streets are broad." I ask her about Soledad.

"He is there. All the saints are in their places. The Señor could not have gone. He would have returned all by himself, as he always did when he appeared and they tried to move him to the center of Huaraz. No, no, he is real. He is there."

I begin to realize that people want to forget the earthquake now, and with those who are not my closest friends, I start to feel a little awkward. I also feel strangely anxious as I walk back to the Tumi. I sit in the dining room and have a cup of tea. The afternoon winds whir outside. I feel I can't bear to be out of contact with my home. How did I bear it that year? I feel so isolated, yet then I was much more cut off. Now there is a good road to the coast. But the long sierra nights close in on me. I think about an earthquake, about where I would seek shelter. The idea haunts me more than it did then, in the midst of destruction.

In all my wandering these first days, I have not found my house. I have not even been able to locate the street it was on, Nueva Granada. Still I don't ask. I don't want to be led there. I want to find it myself. Maybe I fear finding it. Maybe it's no longer there, or my landlords are no longer alive.

The next day I go to the Café La Fontana on Calle Luzuriaga for lunch. I sit at a little round marble-top table. A huge Italianate floor lamp in the form of a statue of a sparsely clad woman is at my back. The woman is holding a jar on her shoulder, and the stem of the lamp protrudes from the jar. Painted on the great ornate fringed lamp shade are a man and a woman embracing each other and a laughing nymph. Abstract plastic yellow flowers, like tubes, stand in a vase on a counter. A kind of circus music blares from a tape.

I look out of a long horizontal front window where Indian women are buying ice cream cones for their children. These women would never come inside. Their hats, covered by colorful cloths, are silhouetted against the mountains of the Cordillera Blanca. At mid-depth in the view from the window are the concrete houses of Huaraz, some painted in pastel colors. The circus music seems appropriate to this Fellini-like scene, where layers of different cultures—Italian, Peruvian coastal, mestizo, Indian—begin in the ornate café and are framed in the view from the front window. The woman from Lima who owns the café serves me, and then she changes the tape. Barbra Streisand is singing "The Way We Were." There is virtually nowhere one can escape popular music in Huaraz now.

Staring through the horizontal window, my eyes fall on the stairs going nowhere, the same stairs I could see from the balcony of my house on the pampa nine years ago, the same stairs that dogs would run up, freezing in a sudden stop at the truncated top. I have a landmark. Now I can find my house.

I am still not ready to go to the house. That night, a friend drives me slowly past it. It is completely surrounded by buildings, bars, shops, a restaurant. The dimly lighted street with its dimly lighted stores makes me melancholy. My old room is dark. The only light in the house comes from downstairs, where through the open door I can see tailors cutting out cloth on a long table and sitting at sewing machines. Before, donkeys carrying wood for the oven entered the patio through the broad doorway. And at night, downstairs my landlords would sit sipping the evening tea by candlelight in their kitchen.

My friend takes me to the house of a young woman. No one is home, and we wait outside in his car. The woman drives up on a motorcycle. She is wearing tight jeans, high-heeled boots, and a

ravenous smile. She invites us in for coffee and crackers with jam.
I miss the herbal teas. Her mother and sister return from the movies.
The young woman, perhaps eighteen, wants to become a tourist
guide. She loves Huaraz now, much better than before the earthquake. There is so much going on now. But there are also drugs
and thieves, she adds. One can't leave one's motorcycle on the street
unattended for even a minute.

I am surprised when the young motorcyclist says she is a
devotee of the Señor de la Soledad. She remembered the double
from her early childhood, but no one speaks anymore about the
Christ of May. "It's the real Señor," she says.

The family talks of hard times, the scarcity of potatoes. I look
around the house. It could have been anywhere in lower middle-
class Latin America. There is a television set—the valley now receives one channel—and the furniture is covered with clear plastic.
Indian "folklore" hangs on the walls, and plastic flowers are everywhere.

All evening I feel strangely eaten alive. They are not after
"things"—like the waiter at the Tumi, who wants my transistor
radio. Rather, they are after my *cultura*, my "culture"—my travel
and experience. I feel worlds apart from them. I never for a minute
felt that way nine years ago. Perhaps the feeling of being so different
comes now because all the trappings of "culture" are back. Before,
everyone was acting at a deeper, more purely human level. We
were all closer to something universal.

I return depressed to the Tumi. I remind myself it is not this
way with everyone. A window to the outside world has been
opened, but not everyone has swallowed down, undigested, the
popular world culture. Sounds of barking dogs, roosters, the ubiquitous rock and roll, and the dripping toilet wake me in the small
hours. I lie there imagining an earthquake. No, I did not do that
before. Is it a wish to shake things up again and have the pieces
fall more to my liking? Am I looking for clarity and "pure" cultures
when I know they do not exist?

FRIDAY, May 30. Juan Manuel picks me up at the Tumi, and we
walk past all the trekking shops to the Instituto Nacional de Cultura.
There a poster announces a poetry and music recital for tonight in
memory of the disaster.

Next, we walk up to Soledad. A large concrete church stands

on the site of the mud-and-laced-cane sanctuary of the aftermath. Soledad is the only church that has been completed. Padre Washi, now seventy-six years old, a big white-haired man who was the priest in Yungay after the disaster, now heads Soledad. He sits behind a desk, but I remember him saddled on a white steed, coming off the Blanca where he had said Mass in one of Yungay's hamlets. The Soledad bells ring the hour as we begin a long tape.

The Christ of May has never been found, he tells me, nor has there been any effort to replace that image. The mere mention of the Señor de la Soledad evokes a poetic eulogy:

> That marvelous wholeness that the artist has put in his face has made all the people love him so, for that tremendous beauty . . . eyes so deep. . . . If you are pained, you see him with pain, and if you are happy, you see him happy. If you are troubled, you see him troubled. A very strange thing has happened. When I was in Yungay, I always saw him pale. Now that I am here, I go and look at him and I say, "Señor, such a sweet death, I, too, am encouraged to die soon." He is an interpretation of eternity. . . .

Snapping out of his reverie, Padre Washi laughs robustly and tells about the recent procession on May 10, the *octava* of the Señor de la Soledad, which celebrated the inauguration of the new church. It was his idea that the procession go all the way to Centenario and that the image spend the night in that church. "They received him well, and then the next day he came back, sweeping along with him all the faithful, to the blessing of his new home. Sixty-two thousand *campesinos* came down, carrying hundreds of small household and chapel images, an endless stream of dancers and bards. There were even dancers on horseback!" the old priest exclaims, growing more and more excited.

Juan Manuel interjects, "I was on the bridge over the Quilcay, and I was astonished. Such a quantity of images and people like that day had never been seen before!"

"Then, his fame has grown?" I comment.

"A lot," the padre says. "In all the Callejón, and people came from Lima, Chimbote, Trujillo. In the Soledad plaza not even a needle could have been squeezed between the people."

The president of Peru, Gen. Morales Bermúdez, as well as

bands sent by the national government, took part in the procession. The general had come to Huaraz in 1976 and gone directly to visit the Señor. In front of the image, he knelt for fifteen minutes, and then he said to Padre Washi, "Old man, you are going to build the church for the Señor de la Soledad. The Señor cannot remain in this shed like an animal." He ordered ORDEZA to construct the church, and it was completed in three years and two months.

Turning to the ceremonies of the following day, May 31, the padre tells us he will say Mass at Soledad. Then, at 10:00 A.M., he will be at the foot of the communal grave in the cemetery. All Huaraz's priests and the authorities will be there. "I like to remember that we are of the earth," he says with a smile.

I tell him I will be with Cirila on the playa. Padre Washi recalls her ordeal after the avalanche, the way they strapped her between two trees in order to carry her. Before the disaster it had been his mission to go from hamlet to hamlet, instructing the children. After the avalanche, he was called to Yungay, and his mission then was "to console." "It was too sad, what else could I do?" Alone in his tent in Cochawaín, he said Masses, and by night listened, like all the survivors, to the crashing of landslides. On one occasion, when they were sure another avalanche was coming and he was broiling with fever, "miraculously" a small boy carried him on his shoulders, and then he knelt down and confessed to the boy. There is no end to the images from those times, which jar the mind, I thought. I change the subject, to the new Huaraz.

The padre seems to lift out of his body and laughs heartily. "Huaraz is very nice. We have the most wonderful drains now. Before, the heavy rains would enter the houses." But people want to forget about the earthquake now: "Time flows along, opening out onto the great beach of eternity."

His last words are ambiguous: "God has placed his charisma here for everyone." Is he speaking of an abstract God and the whole earth? Or does he mean the Señor de la Soledad in Huaraz? It does not matter. I'm sure he would say they were the same.

I leave and go by the Oliveras' house in Soledad. They are the family who lost five children. The older daughter quickly reminds me of this. Their house, too, is now filled with plastic flowers, and there is a television. The Señora prepares a lunch of macaroni soup, yams, and rice. The house is as heavy with grief as it was nine years ago. They live by distraction when guests like me come, she says. But I still feel as unable to distract, really, as I did then. Five is too many to lose all at once.

I return to the Tumi. Now, finally, the radio is announcing activities for the anniversary. At seven o'clock, I go to look for Señor Víctor Valenzuela Guardia, whom I did not know before. I have been told he has composed beautiful *huaynos* and that many are about the disaster. I find him in a little concrete house in Huarupampa. He tells me he lost his wife and daughter in the earthquake. Now he has a new family, a wife and two lovely little girls. "That's the way it has to be," he says with a quiet sadness.

Víctor takes me to the poetry and music recital at the Institute of Culture. We sit together in the amber light of the interior, waiting for the performance to begin. Young boys crowd into the back of the room, like hungry waifs awaiting a banquet of poetry. The readings begin, interspersed with ballads about the disaster, sung and played by the Grupo Alpamayo and the Grupo Musical Yaucer Tacuy. The poetic images are nostalgic, channeling all the customary "pains of the Andes" into the communal pain of May 31, 1970: the rain inside the soul; the dust-clouded tears of the aftermath; the grotto silence of love that has lost its object—"What do I do with this love, without you?"—the bells of solitude that toll inside the heart or deep in the throat. After the disaster, the outcry remains, a poet reads, "hanging from the eucalyptus, falling in the rain, ripening in the corn cobs, hardening in the new adobes . . ."

"All the valleys of the world shed tears," another poet recites. But close on the heels of this line are images of struggle, of a "revolution" swallowed up in bureaucracy. Reconstruction has been too slow, too complicated, buffeted by the "wings of plunder." Above all, their valley is "suddenly different forever."

Another poet compares survivors to those of far-flung corners of the globe, in Vietnam, Biafra, Palestine. I see that a characteristic of survival is that it *must* transcend time and place. Otherwise, one is too alone. "You lift yourself toward eternity," still another poet is reading.

But as I listen, what stings me is the brevity of the tears of other valleys, other cities, as the world plunges on with new tragedies, new crises, so many and so varied, so instantly communicated on "the nightly news." We become inured. "*El Perú no se compone*"—"Peru is not healed"—Víctor whispers to me, and I think, The world is not healed.

Finally, a poet who has taken residence in Lima recites: "I leave you my heart so that you can distribute it among my people if I do not return."

As the poets read and the musicians played, I felt a counterbalance to the popular culture of the modern world that I was finding so intrusive in the Callejón of 1980. This generation of Huaraz poets was bound to place and circumstances. They were politically conscious of exploitation, both native—a "Revolution" that had failed to articulate its goals with the reality of time and place—and by "foreign elements and foreign formulas." Above all, this poetic movement, which had gathered momentum in the last ten years, had the goal of decentralizing the cultural activity of Peru, carrying it from Lima to the Andes. As such, the new creativity must "palpitate with the epoch." The "epoch" had brought the disaster of May 31, 1970, and its engraving in image and song was central to the commitments of the poets. The disaster had been the source of a tremendous creative outpouring.[1]

I did not yet know Víctor Valenzuela well. He was then only a man sitting next to me in the amber light, a thin, dark man. I had not yet realized that he was the man who had spoken up so eloquently at the CRYRZA meeting on May 16, 1972, the one who had said, "We must try to quell our egoism. . . . I had property right on the central plaza, but I happily give it up." I did not know that he would become the mayor of Huaraz shortly after I left in 1980 or that I would carry tapes of his guitar compositions with me always, playing them from time to time, bringing back in an instant all the beauty and sadness of the earthquake-struck valley. That night, I only felt that beside me was a presence, sad and nostalgic, but at the same time wise and filled with hope. He was a man who, even as the poets read, seemed to foresee the aching dilemmas that the decade of the eighties would bring to the brooding Land of the Sun when he whispered to me, "*El Perú no se compone.*"

I went back to the Tumi feeling better than I had on previous nights. Though rock blared again outside my room until late in the night, the recital at the institute had put some of the deep Andean quiet I experienced those years ago back inside me once again.

Thirty-five
MAY 31, 1980

A T 7:45 A.M. I am waiting for the bus to Yungay to join Cirila. The bus fills up with so many people that they begin joking that it will collapse under its own weight. Many travelers are carrying bouquets of flowers. Some are survivors who have been living in Lima. One woman says that after so long at sea level, the cold has hit her hard. The mood on the bus is lighter than at any time I traveled to Yungay when I was here before.

The young man whom Cirila took in as an orphaned boy after the avalanche meets me at the new Plaza de Armas in Yungay. He takes me to her daughter and son-in-law's house. It is a humble structure, pieced together with slabs of corrugated tin and adobes. Cirila is dressing her sixteen-month-old grandson, Omar, smothering him with talcum and kisses. She is wearing a black dress, heavy stockings, and running shoes. A widow who had worked with her in her restaurant in Yungay Norte joins us and we all set out for the playa. We walk high above the new plaza and the Russian dachas with their glassed-in porches, passing through several hamlets, the great bulk of Huascarán hovering over us. We have to walk single file on the path. Laughter and joking are interspersed with long periods of silence.

Cirila's face is remarkable, wide, brash, frank, now grave, then breaking into a husky laugh, smooth, taut skin suddenly dissolved in wrinkles. She lunges along, carrying Omar, kissing him, then coaxing him to walk, scooping him up in her arms again. At streams, she bends over to splash his head and face with cool water. I carry the flowers and sometimes Omar, whose mother, Dina, is limping with a leg injury.

After the long trek, we arrive at the site of the old Plaza de Armas, where a Mass is to be held by the rustic lean-to chapel of lashed logs and palm fronds, on top of Yungay's entombed cathedral. I look out over the playa, now baked by hundreds of sun-filled mornings. Small monuments and large crosses have replaced many of the tiny wooden crosses that were scattered on the playa years before. Groups of mourners are gathered around them, people in the dress of Lima, in black mestizo dresses and suits and in the gala attire of *campesinos*.

As nothing is happening yet, we wander down across the playa toward the Cordillera Negra, where the big monument to the avalanche has been built. It is a large, rude adobe arch, stark in its ugliness against the incomparable beauty of the setting. Black letters painted on it read Holy Ground of Yungay. A man is selling snowballs made with ice from Huascarán. To the west is the cemetery knoll upon which stands the gigantic Christ image.

The pilgrims gather by the monument. Soldiers line up with rifles. Finally, a priest speaks to the few hundred people standing by the arch. "We stand," he says, "between two great powers, the traitor Huascarán who buried the living and the Christ who awaited Huascarán with open arms and who remains to bless the dead." Cirila chuckles and repeats his words several times. Next, the priest points eastward to the four lone palm trees of the buried plaza that jut from the alluvial crust. Their tops no longer green, they have died, too, he says, in a long agony, withering in the sierra sun.

One of the trunks looks charred, and some of the tiny wooden crosses on the playa are charred, too. A lady near me comments, "It's the Evangelicals who burned the crosses, and they stole a cross of mine, too." At the top of the pyramidal cemetery, near the Christ, clumps of dead cactus lie. The whole playa, with the green sproutings I had seen toward the end of 1972, seems now seared and inhospitable.

"What better place to be born and to die," the priest was saying, "here where Christ contemplates them day in and day out? Yungay has disappeared only materially. To the north we are building the new Yungay."

He called for a moment of silence. A pilgrimage of cars arrived from Huaraz and lined up on the road that winds around the playa. People turned to see who was alighting from the cars. Were there any signs of officialdom, or would only the soldiers with rifles represent the nation?

As we walked back to the site of the old plaza, Cirila's friend stopped at a monument. She blessed it with holy water she carried in a small yellow plastic bucket. This was not her monument, she said, but it would do. She had no money to build a monument, and besides, her family had run toward the road, and who knows where they were buried. She, too, had run, and escaped. She alluded to the terrible roar of the descent of the avalanche, but such a sense of the unspeakable filled her face that I could not ask her to describe it further.

The bishop had still not arrived by the time we reached the lean-to chapel, and Cirila suggested we go up to visit the spot on the playa where she had marked her sons' burial. The trek took us to the easternmost extreme of Yungay, in the direct path the avalanche had taken. We stood before the two crosses. She had built a small monument, which said simply, "From your mother." She scurried down to a creek to fill two rusty tin cans with water. She put the flowers I was carrying into the tin cans and then took the plastic bucket of holy water from her friend and drenched the monument. Then she laid her broad hand, palm up, on the monument and poured water over it. Dina and Santiago, Cirila's son-in-law, stood nearby. I left them all alone for a moment. Then Cirila took Omar up in her arms. Her face was tense, strong, and as we walked away, she muttered, "Life is sad."

We joined the Mass, already in progress. Everyone was packed together, touching. The sun beat down mercilessly. There was no cover anywhere, no place to which to escape. The bishop stood next to the rough wooden cross, which was embedded in a boulder that had come to rest where the cathedral's altar was buried. "Yungay is eternal," he was saying. "The world will disappear, but Yungay will remain through all eternity." The Mass was brief, and the thousand or so people began to disperse across the playa.

Cirila turned abruptly and trudged toward the hill-cemetery. Only I followed her, clambering up behind her to Rubén's niche. I remembered the day she had spoken of her love for Rubén and his one surviving son as we climbed the hillside to the site where the new Yungay would be built. "I know that one day or another they will leave. Life is sad," she had said then, almost casually.

Rubén's grave was near the top. This was the closest I had ever been to the Christ figure. Cirila arranged flowers in another rusty tin can, and then she stood for a while in silence. As we carefully made our way down the cemetery's terraces, she ran into an acquaintance:

"How have you been?" the woman asked her.

"Between good and bad."

"Yes, but what can we do?"

"Life is sad."

"But we have completed ten years."

"Yes, ten years. But for me it has been like a month."

As the two of us walked back to rejoin her family, Cirila, not yet fifty, whispered, "I am old now. When will God take me?" She looks worn out, and yet, at the same time, she is as strong as a bull. She is an immense presence in the world. Tragedy and strength have so perfectly coalesced in her, as if one fed off the other. When she cries, it is not out of sorrow but out of a complex mass of emotions that address the trade-offs of life, the risks and the inevitable losses. Joy and sadness are two sides of the same thing.

All together once again, we began the journey back through the hamlets above the playa, stopping for lunch in a cousin's mud patio, where pigs and dogs cohabited with the people. A huge plate of roasted pork skins, hairs standing up on the frizzled skin, was set before us, along with sweet potatoes and rice. Then a wheat gruel was served. We ate heartily and drank cool *chicha* from a plastic canteen. To be in the shade for those moments, out of the mauling sun, was such a relief. Omar was given his tin bowl of food, but before the toddler could eat it, a piglet gobbled it up. Dina washed the bowl in a bucket of water and served him again. Long silences overtook us. I began to try to think of things to tell them about "my country." I even drew a map. They welcomed whatever I could say. I was a distraction.

Replenished, we started out again for Dina's house. I invited them to sodas in a little tavern on our route. We all sat around a table covered with oilcloth. We sat for a long time, and then, moving from the tavern, we sat for another hour in the rose garden on Yungay's new Plaza de Armas. Only a few people wandered around the new Yungay. It did not appear to be an inhabited city; rather, it was like a movie set. At the edge of the plaza was a deep hole where they were sinking the foundations for the new cathedral. Finally, we reached Dina and Santiago's house, where after a few games of hide-and-seek with her grandson, Cirila left for her own house to feed her animals. I lingered on.

Night falling is an event in the Callejón, the final plunge of the sun behind the Negra, the winds turning to soft cool breezes and then to a cold stillness. We begin to put on sweaters, socks, ponchos. The talk turns political, and by 7:00 P.M., when Santiago is waiting with me on the road for some passing vehicle to take me back to Huaraz, he is saying, "Peru must decentralize. The central government controls us too much, censures us. We must have power."

The cold stings my sunburned skin. As we wait and I listen to Santiago, I fight feelings of hopelessness, not just about Yungay but about the Third World in general. It is a kind of pure, floating hopelessness. A *colectivo* stopped for me. It was dark, and a light drizzle was falling. We crossed the playa. No one spoke all the way into Huaraz. Only the rhythmic sound of the windshield wiper could be heard.

When I alighted on Huaraz's plaza, I walked past the stores, still open. A band was playing at the Belaúnde party headquarters, where, over a loudspeaker, a man was calling people to dance in the streets. No one came. It was dark, and the streets were sad to me—Third World streets upon which a popular culture drawn from the modern world sought to establish itself in the high Andean town. The atmosphere was especially mournful because this "popular culture" wasn't working, at least not today. No one came. In the Tumi a woman told me that all afternoon they had tried to get street dancing started, but no one came. Everyone was taking flowers up to the communal grave in Huaraz's cemetery.

In my room, I felt chilled and tired, but gradually the anxiety melted away. I lay on my bed wondering if Cirila was asleep yet. The main day was gone. The main reason for my return, May 31, 1980, was over.

Thirty-six

DAYS AND NIGHTS
IN THE CALLEJÓN

I GO TO MASS at Soledad on Sunday, June 1. On the concrete steps leading to the altar, a beggar is seated, his bearded face resting in his hands. He wears a shabby suit and shoes obviously too large for his feet, which make him look something like a clown. Padre Washi is preaching, painting a great cosmic picture of worlds in collision. Like Espinoza, he is given to drama, only instead of the cosmos, Espinoza held everyone spellbound with the earthquake, punishment, and enemies of the Soledad Christ.

Marianela is there, wearing the same threadbare coat of a decade before. I ask her if she still sleeps next to the Señor de la Soledad, and she answers no and then asks if I have noticed the pretty new doors of the church.

I walk back through the new city to take a bus out to Monterrey. I pass once again close to my house. I know, because I hear the Protestant hymns coming from the "cult." I still do not approach.

I have come to Monterrey to go up to Secsecpampa and look for Don Juan. The hotel, once my refuge, is run down now. The great living room is shabby, and it is hard to imagine a fire in the fireplace. I sit down in the bar to have a pisco sour. Flies are buzzing, and I have to bat them away from my drink and my face. Agustín, from the hamlet of Aclla, above Secsecpampa, is working in the bar. I ask about Don Juan. "He died two or three years ago," Agustín tells me. An immense sadness sweeps over me. To return to the field after years have gone by means wondering whom you will find and who will have left or died. Don Juan, above all, I so much wanted to see, to embrace, to thank him for so many hours spent together.

"His last years were good, and everything happened naturally, as one might expect," Agustín says. "He died of old age." The grandmother had died. This was not a shock, as she was eighty-four in 1972. Then I learn that Rosa María, too, had died, at age eighteen. Her bright, beautiful face, round, healthy, fills up my mind. All the other children are somewhere in Lima, in the slums, with Heliodoro. Jesusa and Nicolás still live in Secsecpampa. I write a note for Agustín to take to them. There is no way I can go up to Secsecpampa that day. I was not yet ready to pass the entrance to Don Juan's house.

As I am about to leave the hotel, I spot a couple who are staying at the Tumi. They drive me back. The man is a traveling salesman—marmalade. "The marmalade business is thriving since the earthquake," he says. "Traveling salesmen never came to the Callejón before, but now so many businesses use marmalade."

The next day I go to write notes in the Fontana, with its Italianate lamps and its horizontal window. A European hiker with long hair and a band around his head is passing; then a *campesina*, her *lliclla* draped from her hat; then a *Huaracina* with dark permanented hair. The chaos of nine years before was more coherent. Now so much assaults the sense of wholeness.

I go to the new post office and recognize the lady sitting at a table, writing in a ledger. She is the same woman who ran the dark wobbly post office in Centenario in 1971–72. We greet each other warmly. When I say that this time I am here only for a little while, whereas last time it was a year, she replies, "Yes, during that year we needed you." She struck one of my feelings. It is true. Now I am not needed.

I brace myself and walk toward my house. This time I must try to see if my former landlords are still there. I peer in, past the tailor who is working downstairs. The couple, now really old, beckon me in, and we all embrace. "Ay, gringa!" they keep repeating. We sit in the living room. Here everything is almost the same. The image of María Auxiliadora is still there, and they tell me that Delia still comes each morning to light her candle by the Virgin.

The Señor takes me to see my room. It has been painted, but otherwise it is the same. They have never rented it since I left. I look out the window, my view of years before now obstructed by buildings. Memories flood back. I look across the black pampa night to see the brilliant white light of Abel's Petromax lantern burning in his shop at the edge of the Quilcay. I remember the night it had not burned, and then he arrived at my room, late, damp with sierra rains, having shot up through the mountains from Lima, where he found he could not spend much time, even in sought-after distraction.

"Some two or three years after you left the valley," my landlord is saying, "a CRYRZA official came to ask about you, what you were doing here, and if I knew of anything derogatory you had written about the government."

We return to the living room, and they tell me that their *chacras* have been expropriated. The great drought has come, and worms have gotten into the potato crop. All this, they say, occurred after the earthquake and was due to the change of climate, which was in turn related to vapors from the bomb tests. Sending me off with a bag of fruit, cakes, and little round breads from the oven, they add, "And besides, people are lazy and given to vices now, after the earthquake."

I walk up through Nicrupampa to Domitila's. She is crocheting in her patio and quickly begins to prepare the early evening *lonche* for us. I have brought a Frisbee for her son. We play with it. Perico, a ten-year-old, joins us. I wonder what he knows of the disaster. He was an infant when it occurred, but as I draw him out, he is filled with stories his mother has told him. He relives it for me in detail: his cousin, who was struck by a sheep that flew through the air; the sounds of the helicopters that landed from who knows what country. . . . His memories spent, he turns to vivid descriptions of the monsters that inhabit the puna, strange creatures in the form of huge frogs.

Just as nine years ago, when Domitila and I settle down to talk, it is not of the earthquake but of her early years as a shepherdess on the puna and of personal feelings about children, love, and the events of our lives. I am happy to see her in such good health, to hear her laugh again. Some special connection always occurs between us.

Finally, the boys walk me back to the Tumi, and I prepare to visit the distinguished man who accompanied me to the poetry recital on the eve of the anniversary, Víctor Valenzuela Guardia.

I felt a peace in this small concrete house, with this new postdisaster family, Víctor, his wife, María, and their daughters. Víctor sat down with his guitar and played the purest of notes: a *huayno*, perhaps fifty years old, indigenous, played during his boyhood for the Festival of the Crosses. "This is no longer heard in the valley," he says. "It is music transmitted 'sound by sound' from fathers to sons. It was never written down. Now our music is disfigured by the sounds of radios, tapes, and record players." Like gifts for me, he played his own compositions, based on the mountain *huaynos* and Creole *valses* of the coast. María's voice, too, was clear and pure as she sang the words she put to many of Víctor's pieces.

We stop to talk, sipping hot chocolate, and María recalls the terror of the nights after their marriage in 1971, when Víctor would awaken trembling and she would calm him. . . . *"Ya pasó."* ("It's all over.") She recalls her first twelve days after the disaster, when she tended the wounded, containing her fear by day and shaking with a "nervous fever" by night. She laughs as she remembers the first plane trip of her life, in a small Canadian plane, accompanying three of the wounded to Chimbote. Once aloft, she observed the pilot peering at maps and then out of his little side window. Their route was to fly south to Lake Conococha, then west to the coast and up the coast to Chimbote. With the hundreds of glacial lakes beneath them, the pilot had become confused and asked her to direct them to Conococha. Mesmerized by the dazzling array of glaciers and lakes she was seeing for the first time from above, she, too, became confused as the plane threaded its way tenuously up the valley. Then she spotted the flat plain of Conococha and instructed the pilot to veer right, down to the coast.

In Chimbote, she ran into a strict control over the identity of adults and children. "You see," said Víctor, "there was an explosion of people after the earthquake, and many children became separated from parents who were still alive. They didn't want these children to wind up as servants in Lima."

Taking up his guitar again, Víctor played pieces he had composed about the disaster, and María sang the words. In one piece, particularly, entitled "Homage to Yungay," the words and music fit together so perfectly, both evoking deep waves of emotion in me and in María, who broke down into sobs several times before she could complete the song:

> *Yungay, city of memories,*
> *The remains of your dead*
> *Are the seedlings of your earth . . .*
>
> *Shameful Huascarán*
> *Spreads its beauty over you,*
> *Searching for your forgiveness . . .*
>
> *Oh, my Yungay, you will be reborn*
> *Great, and full of humanity,*
> *Without the privileges that wound you,*
> *Where the blood of all will be equal,*
> *After this lesson you will never forget.*

María read poems she had written, which summoned the beauty and fragility of the valley and the strength and compassion of mountain women, "tender as doves and shy as the deer of the high punas." The poems evoked, too, the torrential rains and intense cold of Huaraz.

Over more hot chocolate, we talk again, seated around a small table, wearing scarves around our necks in the late-night cold. "The most important thing now is to recuperate," Víctor says. With measured words—asphalt, university, cosmopolitan—he enumerates the losses and the gains of the new "modernism" that flourishes

now in the Andean wilderness. María is not measured. She longs
for the old familiar Huaraz. Finally, Víctor says, "Really, this new
world does not impress us, but it cannot be avoided."

"The old Huaraz will die only with the survivors," María says.

Víctor and María have adjusted, I am thinking. Many have
not, I have been told. They have "died of pain"—*shonqu nanée*—
with hearts too heavy with nostalgia, too shattered by disruption,
to beat any longer. But this man in the concrete house, who before
commanded a whole block on Huaraz's main square, who plays
indigenous music and endures, he is one kind of hero. Here in this
house are pain and courage, quintessential survival.

We speak of other things and laugh. I tell them stories. Just
as at the lunch in the hamlet with Cirila, here I seem to be a genuine
distraction. Like nine years ago, I am again needed. But then, I
had to be, for I was stirring up the memories. Here the memories
had been channeled into music and poetry; nevertheless, I was
setting them loose. Like the mountains themselves, I feel I am, this
time, in 1980, both the evil and the remedy. In 1971–72, there was
little but remembering, reliving. Now people needed to forget.

My throat was very sore from the cold, and Víctor and María
drove me back to the Tumi. The next morning, I awoke with a
fierce flu. As there was no room service, I made up my mind to
move to the Hotel de Turistas on the fringes of town, at the end
of Centenario barrio. I had worked hard for ten days, and I had to
get away now from the cacophony, the pastiche that was the new
Huaraz.

I already had most of my answers. I knew that the earthquake and
the Revolutionary Reconstruction had succeeded in opening a
wedge to popular world culture, an "import of the people who have
settled in the valley from poor coastal cities." They, along with
hikers, mountain climbers, and tourists, mainly from France and
Germany, accounted for 30 to 40 percent of the present population.
Another 30 percent of Huaraz's population was from elsewhere in
the valley—Carhuaz and the hamlets—and from the adjacent valley
of Conchucos. Only the remainder were "purely" *Huaracinos*. Other
Huaracinos had left only when the tide turned irrevocably to the
modernization of the *Plan Regulador*. Of those who did leave, around
1975, some were trying to come back now, but all the land and
houses had been redistributed, and they had lost their chance.

I knew that the failure of the Revolution in the larger Peru—or perhaps, ironically, its success in modernizing Huaraz—had brought problems not unique to the Callejón, problems shared by the entire modern world: drugs, consumerism, crime. Even those who accepted modernization felt that Peru, the whole country, was worse off.

I knew that nature, too, had failed them, bringing a severe drought that threatened further the agricultural underpinnings of the valley. I knew that people attributed the drought to bomb tests and that the bomb had remained the main vehicle—along with telluric fury—for the punishment of God, which persisted still in people's minds as the ultimate cause of the earthquake.

I knew that the doubt surrounding the image of the Lord of Solitude had evanesced, though undoubtedly it would reemerge in times of crisis. Religious *costumbres* had once again begun to flourish, even amid the secular and religious modernizing influences. Rather than with Soledad or the rightness of customs, people were now preoccupied with the drought, high inflation, and other more practical problems.

Thus, looking at the broad palimpsest interpreting the extreme event of 1970, I could see that in the deepest recesses of the cave, the image of Soledad had dimmed. The messianic zeal of the Peruvian Revolution had faded into resignation. The valley had not become a showcase of social justice for the nation, and the world remained ignorant of even the dream that the earthquake-torn valley would spark international friendship and peace. Only the punishment of God was still etched in the valley, shining through the topmost drawings that still depicted the folly of bomb-crazed humanity and the insensate hand of nature on a rampage.

I knew that *pena* had consumed lives, the pain of the disaster itself, along with bitterness and anger at the slowness and manner of the reconstruction. For some, the pain had turned their hearts into "heavy stones," and they lived with "nervous attacks," pervasive nostalgia, and grief. As they said, fear had turned into a hardened knot in the chest. I knew, too, that for others the disaster had opened a space to a creative outpouring, that from the sepulchral silence had sprung a decade of poetry and song.

Above all, I knew that I could not penetrate beyond the conflicting dialectic strands that were the tone of ten years afterward: the strands of serenity—born at times of the peace of death ("my breast is a cemetery") and at times of a true acceptance ("everything is a gift")—and of continued trauma; strands of tradition versus modernization, that praised the university and the new visibility of the Indian—"*campesinos* are no longer 'the unseen' "—but blanched at small concrete houses and the new "harshness" in the valley, that praised broad avenues and remembered picturesque narrow streets. I could not go beyond the dialectic oppositions of forgetting and not forgetting, of recovery and nonrecovery. But I could sense that a scar was forming. "That must be the way it is, a scar," a woman said. "To remember causes pain and sickness." And I knew I had to tread lightly on this scar.

I had three weeks left. I would begin a study of medical beliefs and continue my rounds of people I had known. I had to see Nicolás and Jesusa. But I, too, would begin to forget. The peace and beauty of the new Hotel de Turistas was a great comfort. I had spent my first night in 1971 there, amid piles of shattered glass, staring at tortuously cracked walls. Now I looked out of wide expanses of window onto the Cordillera Blanca. My fellow guests were mainly mountain climbers, trekkers, and traveling salesmen. The hotel, situated at the edge of Huaraz near the foothills, gave me back the quiet of my nights years before.

THE next days I spent walking around Huaraz, with no fixed route, absorbing whatever came my way. I stopped to see Peter at Radio Huascarán.

"Your transmitter—is it still stuck on 'Emergency'?" I asked.

"No, now it is correct." He grinned, the same Peter who had played "Los Cubanos" over and over again those first long days and nights.

"The yellow rain poncho you left me—it still lives!" he yelled as I walked away.

I stopped at Belén and asked for Norabuena. He came toward me, his face as Goyaesque as ever. He had remained faithful to the Belenita, who was now wrapped in plastic. I visited the doctor who had held the diminished hospital staff together in the first days after the earthquake. He attested to the many cases he had seen of *shonqu nanée*, that pain in the heart, which, he said, in Western terms is "anxiety neurosis." Some had gone down to Lima to consult physicians, but even Dr. Ramos conceded that *shonqu nanée* could not be cured by medical doctors. The *curanderos* in the valley, like

Jesusa, were best able to treat these nervous ailments. The doctor spoke also of the psychological trauma that teenagers were suffering, those who were children around five or six at the time of the disaster.

One afternoon I had a curious experience that took me back to conditions nine years before. I was looking for the priest of San Francisco and wandered into a patio behind the old makeshift church, still there in 1980. There I found two very old women in threadbare clothes. One was blind. They were living in a shack and said they had only what they could carry in a bag. They had been left without any family after the earthquake. Padre Espinoza had taken them in, and they lived with him there at Soledad until he was forced to leave. They had only praise for the priest and lamented the storm of accusation against him—that he was stealing the money meant for the new church of Soledad. With that money he was caring for the homeless, they said.

"Where is he now?" I asked.

"Some say he's alive. Some say he's dead," the blind woman answered. "Some say he was killed on the road from Lima to Cuzco."

A middle-aged townswoman appeared then with a bag of bread for the destitute old women. We sat on some stones and began to talk. The townswoman was suffering from *shonqu nanée*. "I have pain; I want to cry. My heart aches. I sigh, and then my heart swells and becomes hard like a rock. Then I have to cry. I have the desire to go far away, without any bearing [*sin rumbo*], to go away with the wind."

As the blind lady began to gather sticks to make a fire, the younger woman spoke of Soledad. She recounted for me the dream the padre had had before the earthquake, the dream that had prompted his having the painting made of himself amid the ruins. At Mass one Sunday before the earthquake, perhaps six months before, he had told the congregation of his dream. She recalled his declaring, "Huaraz will soon be destroyed, and the innocent will pay for the corruption that exists here." Some men wanted to snatch Espinoza from the altar, but they were restrained. The earthquake had been a punishment. She was sure.

I had fallen back through the years to that time of extreme hardship. A big mountain cross stood in that dusty patio. It, too, seemed to have been left over from years ago.

When I got back to the hotel, Rafael, Jesusa and Nicolás's son, was waiting for me. They had received my note and would be waiting for me in Secsecpampa the next day. I asked what Rosa María had died of.

"Pain in the heart," he answered. "*Shonqu nanée.*" She was only eighteen.

I have adjusted to the fact of Don Juan's death, and now the walk up to Secsecpampa brings a feeling of tranquillity. With Huaraz built, modern, there is a great contrast now between town and country. *Campesinos* are climbing the path, too, with cows, donkeys, pigs, and sheep. Except for the swish of *polleras* and the hooves on the dirt, it is quiet. A soft breeze moves the eucalyptus branches against the blue sky. Don Juan's house is abandoned. I cross the same dirt plaza, with its little chapel, remembering carnival and the talcum-covered faces of the children, the big mountain crosses resting against the chapel wall. I climb up through Jesusa and Nicolás's *chacra* of golden wheat.

We sit at the edge of the wheat field. I slip a tape in the machine. It records memories, laughter, good times, and the tensions of those years ago. Nicolás has been ill the last three years, and Jesusa, the curer, has taken care of him. His illness opens out a long discussion of the causes of illness and the ways of curing. I am becoming intrigued with the idea of the *chúkaro* soul. One becomes frightened —suffers *susto*—and loses his soul. It transmigrates into various animals. As the soul enters ever wilder and wilder animals—from dogs to sheep to deer to condors and eagles—the person becomes sicker and sicker. There is almost no hope of retrieving the soul from the condor, the most *chúkaro* of creatures, and the person may die. I relive the year I was there, the feelings of the whole valley as having become *chúkaro*, alienated from its soul, in need of curing, humanizing.

"What do the priests preach now?" I ask them.

"They talk of punishment, when we don't marry in the church or baptize our children, when there are many abortions." *Castigo* has lingered in the countryside as the main cause of the earthquake. With all these sins, there will be more earthquakes, they tell me, and the world will end. Each potato now has five or six big worms, the corn crop has failed, and this is punishment, too. In the hamlets they don't talk of the bomb so much anymore, Nicolás says.

"And the Señor de la Soledad?" I ask.

"He is the real Señor," Nicholás confirms.

Campesinos have completely rejected the new baptism rite in which the parents are supposed to hold the child. Not even the Italians of Centenario, the inheritors of the Germans' zeal for Catholic Reform, insist on the new rite any longer. Godparents again hold the child. Jesusa and Nicolás are no longer such enthusiastic catechists.

"What of your relations with townspeople?" I ask. They say only that they are "disunited," "demoralized." "People have become idle after the earthquake. *Campesinos* don't want to work on the roads. There's a lot of complaining."

Rafael escorts me back down the mountain. It is already dark. He says he never wants to leave Secsecpampa, but I cannot help wondering if he, too, like Don Juan's children, will end up in the *barriadas* of Lima.

The next day, Domitila tells me about the spirit that "dries up," becomes *chúkaro*, withdrawing farther and farther until it enters, finally, the wildest of creatures, the condor. Then only the most intrepid of witches, with enough courage to pursue the spirit to the high reaches of the cordillera, to the "bad places," may hope to retrieve it.

On the following day, I take an Ancash tour to the Cañón del Pato. I sit anonymously on the bus, listening to the guide talk about the earthquake, the way many people have become "mute," and about the avalanche and the "crazy ones" who remain in Yungay. We stop at a little tourist restaurant near Caraz, where we are shown a condor in a cage. Wildness has been contained now, transformed, I am thinking.

What has not changed is the natural beauty. On the way back from the Cañón del Pato, the tour bus goes around the playa, now dotted with monuments, and begins to climb the road to Llanganuco into the clouds. The stone slab faces of Huascarán and Huandoy still confront one audaciously, and the little cabin at the spot where Don Alejandro saw the avalanche pass "flying as if on the wings of a condor" is still there. Now it is occupied by two geologists who are in charge of watching over the lakes. On the table in the cabin, where I spent that fog-bound night when landowners were driving their animals over the cordillera to escape the encroaching agrarian reform, stand a candle, a can of Leche Gloria, and tin plates.

On the way down, rock slides ahead of us bring the screech of brakes. The driver is silent. At the playa, the tourists get out, and we walk in the deepening dusk on the silt that cradles Yungay's uncounted dead. We ford streams that have been channeled to control their flow through the playa. We are surrounded by the mountains, silhouetted now against the darkening sky, serrated peaks inch by inch losing their glow in the fading reflection from the sun beyond the Cordillera Negra, which looks like a great motionless bull falling asleep.

The next morning, the sacristan from Centenario comes to look for me at the hotel. He is full of the account of the Señor de la Soledad's night at Centenario. He used to think the Señor was alive, but now he knows it is just an image. Nothing could dampen the crowds that swarmed into Centenario during the procession of Soledad a month ago. Even the new bishop had stood next to him and whispered, "Can't you give me, Albinito, an herb to quench this Soledad faith?" And at carnival, that same bishop had gone from church to church, saying the mountain crosses were not to descend on Huaraz. On the Sunday, when they have for years appeared for their Mass, the bishop returned to each church. At Centenario there were no crosses. But Soledad was filled with mountain crosses, and Padre Washi just shrugged his shoulders at the bishop, who, according to the sacristan, shouted, "Let all who don't accept Vatican II go away."

"It will take another generation," the sacristan tells me. "The force of the *costumbres* is very great."

I had planned to take Cirila to see Lake Parón, high above Caraz, the lake that had its legendary origins in an act of incest between *compadres*. She had never seen Parón, and I had not gone when I was there before, either. I hired a chauffeur, and we picked her up at her house. She had Omar with her and had prepared a large picnic basket. Slowly, we ascended the mountains above Caraz, passing idyllic hamlets on the flanks of the mountains, up, up into the rock slabs, and then, suddenly, through an opening in the rock faces, Parón appears. Far more beautiful than Llanganuco, its emerald-blue waters spread out to the magnificent Pyramid of Garcilaso.

We walk single file on the narrow path around the lake toward the base of Garcilaso. Directly above us are precariously perched granodiorite rocks. Cirila and I take turns carrying Omar. The chauffeur and Cirila are uneasy. For some reason, I am not. I have never felt better, there in that perfectly clean, clear atmosphere, brisk and cold. Only the white chalk of political graffiti on a rock slab suggests the world below.

When we come to a rockfall in our path, Cirila decides we should not go any farther. We sit on the rocks and eat heartily of her guinea pig in a hot red sauce, with potatoes. She recounts a dream she had the night before. Seeing the avalanche jump from Huascarán and sail through the air, she knew she and her sons must run toward the center, but she could not make her legs move. Children were carrying their parents on their backs. She could no longer see but only hear the tremendous roar and people crying out, "Huascarán is coming!" And then in her dream she fainted.

"So few true *Yungaínos* survive," she said, nervous, eating hurriedly. I knew we had to get out of there, though I didn't want to leave. She spoke of people I had known, the *chupamaros*, the group of men who were drinking themselves to death in her restaurant in Yungay Norte. One of them had gone to Brazil and begun a new life. The crazed guard who had taken on the task of guarding the dead of the playa, was "a little more tranquil." We quickly packed up the basket and went back to the car, and down the mountain into Caraz, passing a spectacular high waterfall, surely one of the highest in the world, yet unknown outside the valley. The German "beehives," those black temporary shelters that marched up the hillside from Caraz, are all rust-colored and crumbling now. Cirila wants to stop at the Palmira, the tourist spot where I had been the day before, to show Omar the condor in the cage.

As we head back into the orbit of Huascarán, Cirila begins to talk about the "bell" that hangs from the villainous mountain and rings when the moon sinks. She has heard the bell, and the response to the bell from the other peaks of the Blanca. "Huascarán must be enchanted," she says. "What else could it be?"

When we drop Cirila and Omar off, I feel greater emotion at saying good-bye than eight years ago. I felt sure then that I would see her again, and now I have doubts that I will ever see her or the Callejón again. I am still choked up when Julián, the driver, says he wants to stop and walk on the playa.

Julián is silent. We don't utter a word as we climb the Christ-topped cemetery. We walk under the arch of the *Campo Santo* monument. It is so pathetic and garish that it stands out sorely in comparison to the majestic grandeur of the event and the setting. In the distance, I spot the words *Yungay hermosura* ("Yungay, beauty") carved on the mountainside. That night, back inside the security of the Hotel de Turistas, I feel the omnipresence of the event more than I have on other days. It hangs over me again, as it did over the valley a decade ago.

The feeling remains with me the next day as I go up to the Huaraz cemetery in Pedregal. The communal grave still has nothing written on it. But a new white plaster cross has replaced the simple wooden one. There are now monuments to the lawyers and teachers who died in the earthquake. The flowers placed near the cross and monuments on May 31, 1980, are withering in the intense sun, and dust is sweeping across the cemetery. I am filled with lethargy and sit without moving for over an hour, wondering how I managed to live so long in the dust, sun, and devastation of nine years ago.

On my way back to the hotel, I stop to buy film in the new shop of the woman who had fanned the hospital corridors with eucalyptus branches that first night. Her daughter has taken ill that day. "Before the earthquake, we were strong," the father tells me. "Now our nerves are very delicate. Perhaps that is why she is ill. We have been so traumatized, it is hard to know what causes what now."

"This woman has shared our pain, the cold, the dust," the couple tells the other people standing by the counter.

Even now, when everything is back together again, I have that same feeling of being pushed to the extreme up here in the valley, of lack of control, of being on an edge. Some of it is real, some of it is bred by the sense of mystery that exists up here, the talk of bad spirits and luminous beings in the "bad places" on the mountains. Perhaps the people's sense of mystery emanates from the uncertainty of the delicate balance of the land up here. It comes out of the depths of the deep gorges that are everywhere above us here on the valley floor. The dim street lights that begin to come on, even the neon signs of the shops, don't seem to kill the mystery.

When I go by Víctor and María's and we sit in the dim austerity of their living room, it is as if Víctor knows what is in my mind.

He begins to tally up a list of the disasters that have struck the valley, the years, the events, landslides, avalanches. "The Cordillera Blanca is perturbing," he says. I type out María's poems on an old manual typewriter as Víctor plays his marvelous compositions on the guitar. The ground has turned to frost by the time they drive me back to the hotel. I awaken during the night to the braying of donkeys. The gentle hamlet of Shancayán spreads outside my window to the foothills of the Blanca.

The themes of beauty and danger, of tranquillity struck by sudden disaster, surface time and time again during the next few days as I travel the Callejón with Juan Manuel, Teófines, and Julián. Juan Manuel has escorted mountain climbers to the high peaks and carried them down, dead or injured, off the mountains. Julián once turned a bend in the valley road, struck an Indian girl who darted in front of his car, and was nearly stoned to death by the villagers.

From time to time, luminous beings have beckoned the three men in the high reaches, and once Juan Manuel heard a strange music played on a harp on descending a peak. Perhaps these phantom spirits, in the end, are one's salvation, he reasons. "They keep us from going too far into the *chúkaro* places, because we fear them."

"The ice cornices deceive one," Juan Manuel says. "The snow is not tranquil. It changes, it does not sleep. . . . The cornices drip like the blood of human beings, making the rivers. Life begins in these high mountains, but death lives here, too. Life and death go hand in hand. We carry within our memories a beauty that we cannot externalize."

ONE day I walk up along the Quilcay to Los Pinos, the Benedictine monastery that had broadcast the news of the earthquake to the world. The monks I had known are gone. One, Hilario, had become intrigued with geology and earthquakes and had acquired a seismograph. Eventually, he left to study geology at the University of Colorado, bequeathing the seismograph to the new university in Huaraz. It is the only seismograph in the Callejón and, according to the new monks, is in disrepair.

At San Antonio, one of the Spanish priests I had known is playing an old Peruvian game called *Sapo* with a nun. As if I had been there just the day before, he barely looks up from his game as he answers my questions about the crosses: "We can't take away the popular religion," he says with resignation. "Yes, the crosses came to San Antonio last carnival, and we blessed them." He tells me that Padre Quintana, the spirited Spaniard who had helped Espinoza at Soledad, was killed by a thief in Old Lima shortly after I left in 1972.

I go to visit my first house, in the high part of San Francisco. Elena is still living in the back of it, and few improvements have been made. Rickety old wooden chairs stand unevenly on the mud floor, basins of water are scattered around, chickens walk freely about, and flies are everywhere. I remember the Christmas Eve of 1971, spent with Elena and her family, the potatoes cooking in the muddy water, the deep darkness of Soledad at midnight Mass. I am very uncomfortable now. All the Third World seems locked inside Elena's room, all the flies and dirt, depression and anxiety, and confusion over beliefs. The air seems filled with vague longings that can never be satisfied.

At the Oliveras', depression hangs heavily. The señora and her one surviving daughter seem always just struggling out of sleep when I come. Their home is like a tomb. It does not epitomize "Third World," like Elena's, but rather something akin to pure tragedy from which it will never recover. The señora pushes her hair back. Her sad eyes stare at me and then blink embarrassedly. She is so shy and so hurt.

We sit down, but I feel strained and uncomfortable. Unlike years before, the larger world I carry around with me separates us. There is nothing to say. The feelings underneath are there to be talked about, but they are too raw and have been for too long. On the surface, we share too little, and they won't allow themselves any joy. I feel stupid even suggesting distractions. They still cannot let go of their grief. Yes, five is too many to lose all at once.

I look for Esther, but there is no one home. I had seen her and her sisters once and, in a way, am relieved. Now there is no one else to see. A feeling of freedom comes over me, of being just myself in a beautiful valley. I go back to the hotel, the sky a deep orange pink, dying but still so full of life, sinking deeper and deeper into the gorges. I have never felt so totally alive as in that valley watching the sky.

It is the night of Monday, June 16. I am at the Valenzuelas'. The poet Abdón Dextre is there. I know a story of the disaster lies inside him—of his departure from Huaraz, his return, a decade of poetry. But I don't ask. I am suddenly feeling very ill and lie on a couch listening to Víctor's music, my mind drifting, knowing it will end soon, remembering nine years ago. What has brought me to this valley, this fountain of all my feelings? They seem to emerge here as in no place else. The valley unleashes them, fires them, and then quiets them again.

My last day in the Callejón, I just walk around, buying a warm wool sweater, some *llicllas*, and vanilla cookies for the trip down. At night, I close the drapes on Shancayán and pack. The last night in the valley, getting down the mountain seems formidable, though not so much as eight years ago. But it is always harder to go down than to come up.

Julián is going to Lima and will take me down via the road to Casma. This road intersects the Andean spine and crosses into the valley at the high pass of Punta Callán. He is at the hotel at 7:30 A.M. We begin the climb, up and above Huaraz, stopping to get out of the car to look down at the city. The gaping wound I had seen from this spot years before has been closed by the thousands of little houses. We pass through hamlets, which are awakening, the *campesinos* moving their animals down into the valley. We pass a man, walking alone, carrying a cross. Everything is drier here on the Cordillera Negra. There is no ice or snow, no sheer rock faces. Vast, but without ragged pinnacles, this range is more enveloping, less threatening than the Blanca. The Casma road will take us down to the wastelands, where ancient Peruvians built Sechín Alto.

At Punta Callán, the highest pass on the Cordillera Negra—14,000 feet above sea level—we get out of the car to take pictures of the Cordillera Blanca. The thin, transparent air at this altitude hinders depth perception, and the peaks of the Cordillera Blanca present themselves to us on a single plane, a panorama spread out before us like a cosmic mural. On this level stretch of puna stands a huge wooden cross. Julián circles the cross, running and jumping as if seized by the magic of the setting. He settles down and begins to tell me his story.

He is putting the key in the lock of his café in Casma when the earthquake begins. He rushes to his house for his wife and three children and shelters them in the patio as the house collapses around them. The earth opens and closes, black water oozing from the cracks. He looks up into the mountains, imagining he sees the horizontal waves of the earth catching one town of the Callejón on the crest of a wave, then sparing another. Cátac is destroyed, Recuay not so completely, then Huaraz, but not Carhuaz, then Yungay. He runs to the telephone-company office to call his parents in Huaraz, but the machinery lies twisted in the street.

Monday, June 1, 1970. Julián flags down a truck to Lima, trying to get to an uncle on the Rímac. He is encrusted with dust, and when he finally arrives at his uncle's door, the uncle doesn't recognize him, and no one knows in Lima what has happened in the Callejón. He returns to Casma for his wife and children and leaves them at the uncle's in Lima. By Thursday, June 4, he is ready to begin to walk up the Casma Road into the valley to search for his parents and siblings. There is no food, and hundreds are walking up the mountain. On long, dry stretches, they drink water from small irrigation ditches.

As they reach Punta Callán, they meet hundreds of survivors who are fleeing down the mountain. Around the cross, survivors and those ascending from the coast embrace. But at this point, several men from the coast, already weary and hungry after days of climbing on foot, with no food and little water, die as altitude sickness—*soroche*—overtakes them.

Julián makes it to the outskirts of the valley. At a control station that has been set up, he must get an inoculation against typhoid. Wearied as he is, he suffers all that night from chills and fever, wandering around the ruins of Huaraz, searching for his family. The next day—it is Sunday by now, a week since the earthquake—he finally finds them in the foothills behind Centenario. They had been spared, because on May 31 they had gone to take flowers to the cemetery. In the *Panteón*, they saw the dead jolted out of their graves. During the next days, they reburied the long-dead along with the victims of the disaster.

After spending some days in Centenario, Julián tries to get back to his wife and children. A convoy bearing blankets and tents is being driven in from Lima, through Junín and Huánuco, taking seven days, since the only direct roads from the coast—through Pativilca and Casma—are impassable. On the back of a truck, Julián is moving in the opposite direction from the convoy, and it takes them seven days, too, to reach Lima. Just as he arrives, the Pativilca road opens, and he brings his wife and children back up to live in the destroyed valley.

As Julián tells his story, I listen, but my mind is also on another man who made that trek up the Casma road, Don Juan. He is old, hungry, and tired, and younger men scratch potatoes from the earth for him. The punishment of God occupies his mind as he climbs, trying to reach his family in Secsecpampa. At the cross at Callán, though, he meets two nieces who are coming down. By then, another idea has begun to take shape in his mind. Of that encounter with his nieces, he told me: "Then, I was thinking to myself, in my imagination, and I told them my thoughts. 'Little daughters,' I said to them, 'reflect. This is not the punishment of God. This is the defect of scientific men.'" He felt this inside himself, though it was not until later that he learned from external sources about the French bomb tests. Yes, my mind is on Don Juan. I remember the day the big mountain crosses were put in their cairns. I twinge, feeling Don Juan's shame when his shield of authority was wrested from him. I wonder if many people came to his funeral and wish I had gone to visit his grave in Secsecpampa. I wonder if there is a special place for those who die in the cold of the mountains.

I will never forget these scenes that took place around that wooden cross on Punta Callán in the Andean wilderness. Julián never attempted to live outside the Callejón again. "There, my bones will go to the *Panteón*," he tells me now as we walk back to the car.

From the car window I see in the distance the multicolored skirts of Indian women driving cattle across the Negra toward compounds of thatch huts. *Campesinos* are harvesting potatoes on the mountainsides. "Scarcely any food, though," Julián says. "The Revolution has brought down the country." Before long, we pick up the Río Grande, which flows into the Río Casma.

Yupash, Pira, Colltau—Julián knows all the names of the hamlets nestled in the mountains. He has made this trip a hundred times when he drove a *colectivo* back and forth to Lima. At 12,000 feet, Indians are planting eucalyptus against erosion. The tiny trees, with their frosty gray-blue leaves, look drunk leaning at awkward angles from the mountainside.

At 8,330 feet, the Quebrada Chacchán appears, bold and rug-

ged. Out of the car's rear window, I look back at the Cordillera
Negra, an ascending tapestry of yellows, browns, blues, and purples. We pass the community of Saishac at 7,000 feet, and then at
6,500 feet corn appears for the first time, followed by bananas and
beans at 6,400 feet. At each level, Julián recalls a landslide or a
trickling stream from the ordeal ten years ago. The village of Pariacoto appears at 4,000 feet, and then soon we invade dryness, the
first signs of the arid coast. Manioc appears at 2,450 feet, and at
Yaután, we are in the valley of the Río Casma. The road veers,
leaving the banks of the river. We are in wasteland. By 1,930 feet,
as I follow on the altimeter, there is no longer a blade of grass.

Gloom overtakes me. We have left the Cordillera Blanca long
behind. I remember that last glimpse, when we lost the last peak.
I had been saturated with the Blanca, and now it is gone and I feel
empty. And only emptiness surrounds the car as we head down
into the ruins of Cerro Sechín. Then suddenly the sea comes into
view, and the world opens out ahead of us.

The heat is intense, and we are terribly thirsty. In Casma, we
down three Inca Colas apiece and a plateful of meat prepared in a
tasty sauce. There are six more hours to Lima, and this is the most
harrowing part of the journey, on the Pan American Highway,
narrow and in disrepair. Most of the traffic is produce traveling in
huge trucks that give off streams of black smoke. It is winter on
the coast, and black stubble outcroppings dot the desert. We pass
the cutoff to Huaraz at Pativilca. I want to tell Julián to turn up
and return to Huaraz. This is my last chance to recapture the
Cordillera Blanca. But we continue, entering Barranca. Our car
inches its way along, having gotten entangled in a funeral cortege.
A child has died, and children line the streets, singing "*¡Jesusito
Aleluya!*"

Night falls and the road begins to get really frightening. The
blinding headlights of oncoming cars and trucks dim completely as
drivers use a code I don't understand for passing on the narrow
strip. Compounding the hazard, fog rolls in from the ocean, mingling with the exhaust fumes of the big trucks. There is a strong
smell of fish. I lie back, trusting Julián, yielding to the roaring
highway. The Pan American, devourer of men. You have claimed
Abel, and Teófines's truck, *La Guinda*. Little crosses by the roadside
mark the traffic deaths.

Suddenly, we are in Lima. We move slowly through the traffic and street vendors around the Plaza San Martín. The plaza itself is swarming with vendors, hawking old magazines, silver medals, barbecued meat, clothes. Julián is nervous in the traffic and crowds.

When I come back out to the car, after checking in at the hotel, I see Julián trying to stop the bellmen from untying sacks of potatoes from the roof of his car, potatoes he is taking to relatives on the Rímac. Julián is dead tired from the long descent and the tension of driving the Pan American Highway. I feel sad to see him drive off.

Thirty-seven

TWO DAYS IN LIMA

HERMAN MELVILLE called Lima "the strangest, saddest city in the world." I open the drapes of my hotel room the next morning to this sad, strange city. The day is gray, and I look out on dusty buildings, water tanks, steeples, crosses, and clothes drying on rooftop lines—the mélange of Old Lima shrouded in mist. I have only two days, and so much energy must be drawn forth to accomplish so much in so little time. Besides all the ordinary little things I have to do, there are three important people I want to see: Benjamín Morales, who was head of the Santa Corporation when I was in the valley nine years ago; Marcos Yauri Montero, the poet-survivor of the earthquake; and Walter Leyva, the artist who restored the Señor de la Soledad in 1970. I have never met Yauri or Leyva. I have good addresses for Benjamín and Yauri, but only an old address obtained in 1972 for the sculptor.

I try the old telephone number for Leyva. No one at that number has heard of him. I try the National Institute of Culture, but he is no longer there. I find out that he now has an art gallery in Miraflores. I search through the telephone book, trying various numbers without luck. I give up for now. After making appointments with Yauri and Benjamín for the next day, I take a taxi to the Japanese embassy to try to get copies of the photographs taken by the mountain climbers who witnessed the Huascarán avalanche. Everyone is cordial, but there are no photographs.

I go to the National Museum of Anthropology and then have lunch at Las Trece Monedas, still a gracious restaurant in Old Lima. Walking back to the hotel, I stop to browse through the bookstore Estudium. That night, tired, I again try Leyva's old number, and this time someone gives me a new number for him. I reach him, and he says to come right over. I can hardly believe I've found him, and I begin to get butterflies in my stomach.

I ring Leyva's bell, still filled with trepidation, born, perhaps, of a disbelief that I am actually about to meet the sculptor who restored the powerful image, there in the valley, only months after the earthquake. The sculptor answers and leads me into a room with an immaculate tile floor. The room is filled with art objects and suffused with the aroma of fine woods. He offers pisco and tells me that the restoration was one of the greatest experiences of his life. I sit down on a sofa, place the tape recorder on the coffee table, and listen.

The work of restoration is both a science and an art, Walter says, speaking first as the scientist. The Señor de la Soledad was sculpted at the end of the sixteenth century or the beginning of the seventeenth century. A polychrome image made in Huaraz, it is, he says, a beautiful example of the finest native art. So, it did not come from Spain? I ask him.

He explains that the early Spanish catechists would arrive in a valley and order native artisans to fashion a copy of a Spanish image out of native material. The Señor was sculpted in indigenous maguey, a wood that when dried is light, almost like balsa wood. Because of the fragility of the maguey, it was covered with cloth and then sized with a gluelike substance, just like a canvas being prepared for painting. Leyva is certain that the image is earlier than the eighteenth century, because the eyes were painted on. They were not glass eyes, which appear in the Seville school only in the eighteenth century. He is certain the image was sculpted in Peru because of the type of wood used. Ample, even large in size—1.85 meters, just a touch over six feet—were it Spanish, the image would weigh about 180 pounds. But, in maguey, it weighs only forty-four pounds. He goes on to name other famous religious images of Peru made in this way.

Interested as I am in all of this, it is the personal story of how he came to be the one to restore the Christ of Soledad, and what it was like up there then, that I am most eager to hear. Leyva fills with emotion as he recounts it.

It was four months after the earthquake. Padre Espinoza came down to the laboratory of the Museo de Arte to ask for help. There he found Walter, who, in his "restless youth"—he was twenty-eight at the time—thought it would be a fascinating opportunity. He had never even seen the Señor de la Soledad. The priest told him he would have to go to Huaraz to do the work, and he pictured himself confronting the Andes, face-to-face with Huascarán. Espinoza returned to Huaraz, and no further contact took place between the sculptor and the priest until they met in the Callejón.

Late one night, Walter took a *colectivo* from Lima to Huaraz.

> I arrived at six-thirty the next morning, my first concern to see which of the snow-capped peaks was Huascarán. The dawn was exquisite, but I had never seen a town in such ruins. I asked someone for Padre Espinoza and was directed toward Soledad. Then I had a very strange experience. When I encountered the padre, walking toward me, he told me, "I knew you were arriving this morning. The Señor de la Soledad announced your arrival." How was I to believe that? Until now I don't think I can believe it. My family is religious, but that's it.

Walter answered Espinoza rather coldly. "The only thing that I want to see is which is the image and what it is I am going to do."

"Well, let's go to see him," the padre beckoned.

> There was no temple, there was nothing, well, only a little chapel, a hut [*quincha*]. But then I saw people, about thirty people, from young to old. Indians were crying. What I saw was a wake. I

thought I was looking for an image, but they were holding a wake for a dead person. This was the first impact as I approached. I thought there was a dead person there. The padre commanded the people to make room for me. He spoke in their language, Quechua. As the people made a path, he lifted up a sheet covered with a great quantity of flowers. And it was the image, destroyed. And everyone was crying, as if it were a dead man. When I saw that, I was so moved, I said to the padre right away, "Padre, I am going to spend a month here working." If it had been a person, that person could not be saved. You would have to bury him. Or, if it had been plaster, perhaps I would not have wanted to restore it, but it was a work of art. It would be a labor of magnitude, but I could do it! What I could not do was mend the people of Huaraz.

Leyva returned to Lima to negotiate with his superiors, even as Espinoza sent messages trying to convince them. He needed to get the time to spend in Huaraz, and he even wound up using fifteen days of his vacation.

And I returned to the valley with such enthusiasm. And I lived all the poverty and discomfort as I worked with the Señor de la Soledad. And such incredible things happened! Each lament, each person who came close to the image, educated or uneducated, professional or not, mestizo or Indian—they all came and they cried. And they treated me as if I were doing a miracle, as if it were the "resurrection," not the "restoration," of the Señor de la Soledad. I worked hard for some months, until I got sick there. . . .

About ten days before I finished, a lawyer came to visit the Señor. He was crying from head to foot, crying, kneeling down. He tried to give me five thousand *soles*, but I told him I would take no money. An endless stream of *campesinos* came with chickens, potatoes, offering them to me. . . . Finally, I felt so sick, I had to finish. My head was exploding, perhaps the pressure, the altitude.

Leyva finished the restoration and told the padre he planned to leave the next evening in the seven o'clock car down to the coast. In the morning, Leyva went to the thermal baths at Monterrey. When he returned to Soledad, he saw that the "resurrection" of the Señor was in progress. There was an immense number of people, thousands, from all classes, townspeople and *campesinos*. He was ushered into a Mass, during which the restored image was placed upright. Then everyone wanted to kiss the sculptor's hand.

> That experience can never happen again, something so spontaneous, so sincere. That day gave me the greatest satisfaction I have ever had in my work. I had come to identify with the people, to go deep down into them. Then and there, I understood their necessity to see their Señor standing. I understood their sorrows. . . . Their *Tayta* is the only one who listens to them, who looks after them, who can resolve their problems, their hunger. . . .

Walter served more pisco, and we looked at photographs of the destroyed image—decapitated, thorax crushed, arms and legs separated from the body. The feet had to be completely redone; only slivers of wood remained. Again, speaking as the scientist, the sculptor pointed to the different materials of which the image was made and called attention to the terrible restoration done by two Spaniards after the fire of 1965. They gave the image cedar arms, too rigid and too hard, weighing more than the whole image. They destroyed the ancient polychrome and made a grotesque nose, like a boxer's. And they filled the image with plaster.

When he mentions the fire, I make myself ask about the authenticity of the Señor de la Soledad. Walter says he heard the doubts, too, and, as a scientist, he felt he had to investigate. Near the image he had found three golden nails cast from some melted-down Peruvian ten-*libra* gold coins. With these nails, the image had been attached to the cross.

"Which image had the three nails made out of gold coins?" he asked the padre. "Soledad or the Christ of May?"

"Soledad," the padre answered.

An imprint of the likeness of an Inca appearing on the coin was found on the foot of the image that Leyva worked on. I didn't think to ask him how he could see the imprint on the fragments that remained of the feet, but he quickly added two other pieces of "concrete data." He had recognized the traces of the terrible restoration of the Spanish "adventurer-artists." He relives that time after the fire in 1965, when a dignitary from Huaraz called the

Escuela de Bellas Artes in Lima, asking for someone to come to Huaraz to restore the charred image. His teachers asked him to go, and he was ready to go, but then he was only twenty-three years old, and the dignitary refused, saying he was still "in his cradle," too young to touch the Señor de la Soledad. So the "gypsy sculptors" from Spain were sent to Huaraz.

Finally, Walter tells me his third piece of evidence confirming that the image was Soledad and not the Lord of May. Digging down, he had found fragments and ashes of what had been an image in the very same place where the Christ of May was kept.

Walter Leyva had returned twice to Huaraz to see how the image of Soledad was faring. As Padre Espinoza was no longer there, he spoke to no one and quickly returned to Lima. I asked the sculptor what he knew of Padre Espinoza. In the valley I had heard various things: that he was ill, dead, in Cuzco, in Lima, in his native Apurímac.

"He must be lost somewhere in Lima," Walter answers, "but I don't know where. He used to look for me here in Lima, but since I have the gallery, I've not seen him. He was a little delicate of spirit. He had suffered so much deception, in part of his own making."

Little by little, the sculptor opens up. The padre had called him one day, crying. He had left Huaraz in a psychological crisis, believing people thought terrible things about him, that he had stolen the SINAMOS money and the archbishop's money that had been designated to build the temple, that he had a transport agency in Huaraz and owned shares in a hotel. The padre felt everyone was against him.

He asked Walter to visit him at the Hotel Leticia. Walter found him weeping. Only once before had he seen Padre Espinoza that way, on the day he arrived in Huaraz to restore the image. Walter tried to convince him to go to the convent of San Francisco, where they would surely give him a room and care for him. Since that day in 1977, he had heard nothing from the priest.

He could change so quickly. He had so many facets. I was his friend, and I consider him a friend still. There was so much good about him. At two in the morning, with lamps, on nights of a full moon, I would work on the image, Padre Espinoza at my side. I got to know him deeply, and yet . . . there was a madness about him, a madness to raise that image. And he had his brick factory and the orphans and old people and his ovens, so many projects. He wanted to be everything! He lost the factory eventually, and many denounced him.

It is getting late. Walter tells me it is hard on him to remember those times. He had never tried to speak of them before. Now it was as if he were stripping off the pages of memories that had been stored away in an archive of his mind. I understand. I feel the same way. I wonder if I would try to look for Padre Espinoza in Lima if I had time. It is better perhaps that I don't.

As I consider how to get back to my hotel, the artist tells me that because of so many years surrounded by saints' images and paintings of the Old Cuzco school he has been restoring, he has never learned to drive. Nonetheless, he will try to drive me to a thoroughfare where I can get a taxi. We get into a pickup truck and bump along, starting and stopping, through a dark back street. He is right. He doesn't know how to drive. I get out on the avenue and thank him. I feel a bond with him.

I open the drapes on another gray morning, a soft drizzle they call *garúa* falling on Lima's rooftops. My appointment with Yauri is not until the afternoon, and I decide to try to see a medical anthropologist at the Health Science Museum in the 2 de Mayo hospital, on the Plaza 2 de Mayo. The area around the plaza is medieval, as if jugglers would soon appear or the plague would break out. I feel wrapped in domes and steeples, poverty, the wares, grime and fruit of street stalls. The taxi driver warns me to watch my purse. In a similar section of Old Lima, last night, when I put my hand into my bag, I felt another hand gripping my camera. A woman had slit the bag with a razor blade. She darted off into a shoe store.

The man I am looking for is not there, but I talk to some specialists in medical folklore. Then I go back out into that underworld, remembering that shortly after I left Peru in 1972, Padre Quintana, the Spanish priest of San Antonio in Huarupampa, had been stabbed to death in it.

I make my way to the National Institute of Culture. Yauri is working there now as technical director. As I am led into a big, dark, austere office, I feel the same awe I felt in meeting Walter Leyva last night. Yauri is sitting behind a small desk, typing on an ancient Underwood. Many other people are working in that office, and we go out to a passageway where we can talk. I sink down into a low couch, and Yauri sits on the arm. He speaks freely, streams of memories and thoughts—about what it was like before the earthquake, about the Huaraz of a hundred pianos, where one read Boccaccio, about his writing, about society and what Huaraz has become—pouring out of him. He is one of a colony of some 7,000 *Huaracinos* living now in Lima. Most of them came here around 1975, as reconstruction got under way. They could leave then. Before that, Huaraz could not be abandoned. The Old Huaraz unites the colony. Though tragedy is still reflected in all his writing, Yauri says he feels new energy, new life in himself. It has taken ten years. Now the group in exile is letting go of the disaster, even as they still mourn the old Huaraz.

I begin to see that Yauri is a complex mass of disparate feelings. He is a "socialist" who feels nostalgia for the "finer things"—the hundred pianos of Huaraz. He lives in the mythopoetic Huaraz of the past, his face a question mark of why the things of the soul and the material world must be so inimical to each other. He dislikes most the inroads of popular culture in the restored valley, the cheap manufactured goods, the modern music. He seems to be searching for a way to have justice and equality while preserving uniqueness. I have felt these same things in the Callejón this last time and am interested in these larger issues also. But there is so much I want to tell him. I want to let him know how I felt about the Huaraz of 1971–72, how I felt about his personal loss, his children. I want him to know I felt the power with which he described it in his book, *Tiempo de Rosas y de Sonrisas . . . Tiempo de Dolor y de Muerte.* I want him to know how much all he is saying affects me, but he allows no room for this.

IN restaurants and taxis, everyone seems depressed, skeptical about the future. They are talking about the uncontrolled inflation and how the country has been destroyed by the economic policies of the Revolutionary Military Government. When I finally see Benjamín after all these years, he is uplifting. He is so full of affection and memories. He seems physically bigger now than the vulnerable man who appeared at my house on the pampa in his jeep one afternoon eight years ago. Then, he had just come off the Hualcán. He was exhausted, his lips scorched and his face windburned, but he wanted to talk. Back then, as his jeep aimlessly traced circles in the dust, he recalled the way the pampa was on Wednesday, June 3, 1970, when he walked onto the Dantesque scene to try to find his house. He spoke of his infant son who had just fallen ill and of his worries about the future of Huaraz and the valley. He may even then have had an inkling that the national government would threaten to cut off the Santa Corporation from all support, in effect, close it down, leaving the valley even more vulnerable than it was.

Now I learned that a new agency, Ingeomín, had been set up to replace the Santa Corporation, and in 1977, General Bermúdez had called Benjamín to Lima to head it. Administrative duties took him away from the glaciers, though, and he didn't like that. He wanted to be there, seeing how they were responding to stresses in the earth. He tells me he misses Huaraz, but I can see it is not with the same nostalgic longing of Yauri. Benjamín is in exile from the Cordillera Blanca, not from the lost city.

With his wife and three children, we sip pisco sours and watch Sugar Ray Leonard fight Roberto Durán in a welterweight championship match beamed from Panama. My mind is on the contrasts among the three men who had been, each in his own way, so prominent in Huaraz: Víctor Valenzuela, who had lived well on the Plaza de Armas before the earthquake and who had adjusted to, perhaps even embraced, the new Huaraz. Víctor, who lived now in a tiny concrete house, composing exquisite music on his guitar and soon to become the mayor of Huaraz. Then there was Yauri, living in exile in Lima, pouring himself into his writing and tenuously holding on to the past beauty of the Old Huaraz. And Benjamín, intently watching the fight now, the man of glaciers, who belonged more to the snow peaks than to any human settlement, whose love of glaciers lifted him out of the earthbound issues of society.

Benjamín drives me back to my hotel. It is late, and I have to take a 7:00 A.M. plane. The next morning, I ride to the airport through a still-darkened Lima. In the next years, the city will be beset by kidnappings, riots, strikes, and bombs going off in banks. Rationing and curfews will curtail life. Factions left and right will jockey for power in Peru. The Túpac Amaru revolutionary guerrillas and the ruthless and secretive Maoist terrorists of the Shining Path—*Sendero Luminoso*—will engage in a mortal combat of ideologies with the government. In the strife between revolutionaries and the army, *Limeños* on city streets will be killed and Indians in mountain hamlets massacred. Military and security guards armed with machine guns will become part of the landscape. A flaming hammer and sickle—symbol of the Shining Path—will burn on a hillside overlooking Lima. More and more political graffiti will be etched on the mountainsides, and where some mountain crosses stood alone, I read that the hammer and sickle burns, too, in the high Andes. "My Peru is not healed," Víctor had whispered.

Not a month after I leave Peru, at the end of June 1980, violence is to strike the Callejón, when, on the shores of Llanganuco Lake, beneath Huascarán, close to the same cabin where I spent nights near the mountain, German mountaineers are robbed and decapitated.

It is mainly the south of Peru that has been inflamed in recent years by the Sendero's activities, but terrorists have also attacked the northern cities of Jaén and Trujillo and fought in the jungles of Huánuco province. I cannot help wondering if hamlets on the Cordillera Blanca or the Cordillera Negra will one day, too, be ravaged, and whether the hammer and sickle will burn on Rataquenua, where now the neon cross illuminates the barrio of Soledad. I do not know whether Jesusa and Nicolás are well in Secsecpampa. I am afraid to find out.

Peru has elected a new president, Alan García Pérez, of APRA, the American Popular Revolutionary Alliance. He took office on July 28, 1985, promising to lift the country out of poverty and inequality and rid it of the violence the terrorists have created.

Time passes, but the Callejón de Huaylas, which must surely rank among the most beautiful places on earth, remains undiscovered. When Peru's turn comes to stand in the spotlight on the world stage, perhaps the valley will again appear on the front page of every major newspaper, as it did when it shook so violently on May 31, 1970. Meanwhile, I can still close my eyes and see a glacial night. . . .

EPILOGUE:
REMEMBERING

"Why have they forgotten? Are they insensitive? Don't they cry for their dead!" asks María Colón, the heroine of one of Marcos Yauri Montero's novels, written since he left Huaraz after the earthquake. She had returned on a visit to Uco (Huaraz) to find people busy in their shops and fields. No one was speaking of the tragedy any longer. At the close of an earlier Yauri novel (1974), Rupaní (Huaraz) was destroyed by an earthquake. In mid-recitation of a poem, a little girl was tossed to the ground "like a falling petal." Husband and wife were separated by crushing chunks of adobe from a vaulted roof. Never could the tragedy be erased from the memory of the protagonist, this father and husband of Rupaní. It would remain "terribly unforgettable" for the rest of his life.

From a barrio in Lima, María Colón soliloquizes:

> *About forgetting, I haven't forgotten . . .*
> *They tell me, if you return, what will you find?*
> *You will see other people, other houses, you*
> *will no longer find what you loved . . . that*
> *will be another Uco; you will look at other*
> *rooftops, walk along other streets. I know that!*
> *It's something that can't be avoided, life is like*
> *that, nothing remains the same, not even*
> *oneself. . . .*

To forget or not to forget? When can one stop remembering not to forget?, María Colón seems to be asking. To endure is perhaps to live through the tension between forgetting and not forgetting.

"The important thing," Yauri's heroine says, "is to be where one must be, where the soul feels at home. The soul has a home."

I remember, too. I remember the rain-washed New Orleans streets during the winter of 1970, when my world shattered. And I forget to remember. Life is like that.

Yauri—novelist, survivor—travels back and forth to Huaraz, teaching in the new university there. Through falling autumn leaves, I see my son Brett, almost seven, playing in these New England woods. The soul does have a home, inside the heart.

POSTSCRIPT

While reading proofs and checking references, I came across a passage I felt must be included.

A bell *did* toll in the Callejón. Not from any belfry, but from a pole spanning the backs of two townsmen of Carhuaz. Themselves stunned by the disaster, *Carhuasinos* nonetheless recognized Yungay's even greater tragedy.

"How could such a peaceful and pleasant place be struck from the earth?" they asked.

Setting aside their own misfortune, they arranged a pilgrimage to the alluvial burial ground to conduct a requiem. The date was August 1, 1970. All along the road to Yungay,

> in brilliant sunshine a bell, hung between the shoulders of two men and struck by a third, tolled its mournful dirge . . . the ancient toll for the dead. One toll, silence. A slow double toll, silence. Another single toll, silence . . .

GLOSSARY

ABUELA : grandmother.

AGUARDIENTE: literally "fire water"; a clear high-proof alcoholic beverage.

AHUILOS: "grandparents," when referring to the non-Christian ancestors who are the mummies unearthed in the ancient pre-Columbian ruins; considered dangerous.

ALLUVION: used synonymously with "avalanche" to refer to mud, water, ice, snow, and rock flows.

ALMAS: souls and apparitions of the dead.

ANDA: platform on which religious images are carried in procession.

ANDE: a poetic word referring to the Andes.

APACHETAS: piles of stones (cairns) on the mountain passes that serve as shrines where travelers offer coca from their mouths, an eyebrow hair, an old sandal, etc., and pray for safe passage across the mountain. Garcilaso de la Vega, "El Inca," observes that the correct Quechua form of the word is *apachecta*, meaning, "Let us give thanks and offer something to the one who enables us to carry these burdens and gives us health and vigor to scale such rugged slopes as this." He further notes that "through God's mercy," crosses have been placed on the mountain peaks (*Comentarios Reales*, pp. 133–134).

APU: (Quechua) Lord, great, eminent; god of the ancient communities; a snow-capped peak.

ATILECIA: plant growing on the coastal desert.

AUKI: (Quechua) old, ancient one.

AUKIKUNA: (Quechua) plural of *auki*. Benign spirits who inhabit the inner core of the mountains.

AYLLU: (Quechua) a social unit of the Andes formed of persons bound together by territorial, kinship, and religious ties.

BARRIADAS: slums surrounding large cities, like Lima.

BARRIO: section of a city; neighborhood; in the second sense, the term is imbued with much sentiment.

BRICOLEUR (French): Handyman; one who arranges and rearranges things using odd pieces of disparate materials.

BRUJA, BRUJO: witch, wizard, who brings sickness or ill fortune to others.

CAJAPLAUTA: an Indian band, usually consisting of drums and flutes.

CALAMINAS: corrugated tin sheets.

CALLEJÓN: alley; narrow passage.

CALLEJÓN DE HUAYLAS: pronounced Ka-Yay-HONE-Day-WHY-Lahs.

CALLEJÓN DE LA MUERTE: Corridor of death.

CAMPESINOS: peasants; Indians; people of the Andean countryside.

CAMPO: country or countryside; rural, as opposed to *pueblo*, town.

CAMPO SANTO: Holy Ground; specifically, the alluvial burial ground or "playa" of Yungay.

CARACINOS: inhabitants of the town of Caraz.

CASCO URBANO: literally, "urban helmet"; the urban center of Huaraz.

CASERÍO: Indian hamlet.

CASTIGO: punishment.

CASTIGO DE DIOS: punishment of God.

CATEQUISTAS: catechists; native Andean consciousness-raisers who became leaders and teachers in the hamlets.

CERRO IMÁN: magnetic mountain.

CHACRA: (Quechua) a plot of cultivated land.

CHARQUI: (Quechua) meat cut into strips and dried in the sun; jerky.

CHICHA: (Quechua) maize beer.

CHOLIFICATION: a process of social mobility involving the integration of Indian masses into the Peruvian nation. In the early 1970s, it came to mean equality for all in Peru.

CHOLO: (Quechua) a person transitional between Indian and mestizo who participates in both indigenous Andean culture and national or mestizo culture.

CHÚKARO: (From Quechua *chukru*, meaning rigid, hard) surly, wild, aloof, untamed, unsociable.

CHULLU, CHULO: (Quechua) a soft woolen Andean cap with flaps that cover the ears.

CHUNCHO: (Quechua) image representing a Roman soldier; originally a term applied by the Incas to the "wild Indians" living in the rain forest east of the Andes.

CHUÑO: (Quechua) potatoes allowed to freeze and then trod upon to press out the water; a kind of "freeze dried" potatoes.

CHUPAMAROS: A made-up term applied to a group of Yungay survivors who drank a lot and hung out together.

COCA: (Quechua) a plant, *Erythroxylon coca*, which, when brewed as a tea, is a mild soporific. It becomes a mild stimulant when the leaves are chewed with ashes or lime, which releases the alkaloid. Indigenous use of coca has always been as a leaf chewed to still hunger pangs and relieve fatigue, never as processed cocaine. Coca leaves are also used in various rituals.

COLECTIVO: a collective taxi, usually a 1950s model car, carrying up to five persons, besides the chauffeur.

COLOCACIÓN: reinstallation of a cross or saint's image in its customary location.

COMADRE: literally "co-mother." See *Compadrazgo*.

COMMUNITAS: a mood or feeling of being freed from social-structural bonds.

COMPADRAZGO: literally, "co-parenthood." A system of spiritual kinship among adults through the ritual sponsorship of a child in baptism, creating networks of reciprocity.

COMPADRE: literally "co-father." See *Compadrazgo*.

COMPADRES: literally "co-parents"; e.g., the godfather and the mother of a child are "*compadres*." See *Compadrazgo*.

CONSCIENTIZACIÓN: consciousness-raising.

CONVIVENCIA: literally "living together"; sexual relations between *compadres*.

COSTUMBRES: the old customs, specifically, Indian dances and bands; religious processions, worship of images; any practice linked to native Andean religion.

COSTUMBRISMO: "traditionalism," the practice of *costumbres*, a word synonymous with pageantry and merriment in worship and infused with nostalgia for the ancient Andean past.

CRIOLLO: native of the coast; a person from Lima.

CRYRZA: an acronym for the Commission for the Reconstruction and Rehabilitation of the Affected Zone.

CULTO: Cult; name given to the Pentecostal church next to my house on the pampa in Huaraz.

CURANDERA, CURANDERO: a specialist, female or male, who practices non-Western methods of curing.

CUYE: (Quechua) guinea pig, eaten as a delicacy in the Andes.

DAMNIFICADO: one who sustained material losses as a result of the earthquake.

DESPRENDIMIENTO DE LAS COSAS: a detachment from things.

EN CASA (OR CHACRA) AJENA: literally, "in another's house or field"; in a place alien to the individual or not of his own design and/or construction.

EVANGÉLICOS: Evangelicals.

GAMONAL: a city slicker.

GARÚA: a soft drizzle, especially in Lima, where it never rains.

GRINGA: a female foreigner, especially from the United States or Northern Europe.

GRINGUITA: a little gringa.

HUACA: (Quechua) sacred; a term applied to pre-Columbian idols, shrines, ancestors, mountains, stones, caves, springs, lakes, whatever exerts a strange and mysterious force; the most fundamental and enduring religious idea of Andean peoples.

HUARACINO: an inhabitant of Huaraz.

HUARAZ: pronounced War-AHS.

HUAYCO: (Quechua) a mud or rock slide.

HUAYNO: (Quechua) an Andean ballad, sad or happy.

HUAYRA: (Quechua) a vapor emanating from mummies of the ancestors.

ICHIQOLCO: (Quechua) a small, alluring blond humanoid creature who inhabits streams. At times, a manifestation of the Devil.

ICHU: (Quechua) a grass growing on the puna on which domesticated animals graze.

INQUILINOS: renters, non–property owners.

JALCA: (Quechua) wilderness; puna.

LLANQUIS: rubber sandals made from old tires, worn by Indian men.

LLICLLA: (Quechua) a colorful cloth in which Indian women carry their babies and their purchases.

LONCHE: a light meal served at sundown and often the last meal of the day; derived from the English "lunch."

MACHITU: a plant growing high on the Cordillera Blanca and used to decorate the big mountain crosses; also called *machay*.

MALQUIS: (Quechua) ancestors.

MAMACITA: Little Mother; used to address the Virgin Mary and women in general.

MAMEE: Mother, or Señora (title of respect for women).

MESTIZO: a person of mixed Spanish and Indian ancestry, or an Indian who has abandoned Andean customs and adopted Western dress, speech, and ways.

MINKA: (Quechua) collective labor mobilized for communal tasks or public works.

MÓDULOS: the temporary modular shelters in the survivor camps.

MONTAÑA: the area of rain forest just east of the Andes where tropical plants such as coca, plantains, sweet potatoes, peppers, and sugar cane are grown.

ÑAKA: see *pishtaco.*

OCA: (Quechua) native Andean tuber.

OCTAVA: the eighth day after a saint's day, when a procession in the saint's honor is held.

OLLUCO: (Quechua) a native Andean tuber.

ORDENOR CENTRO: acronym for the Regional Organization of the North Central Part, successor to ORDEZA.

ORDEZA: acronym for the Regional Organization for the Development of the Affected Zone, successor to CRYRZA.

PACARINA: (Quechua) a lake, rock, cave, hill, or the trunk of a tree, from which the *ayllus* of ancient Peru are said to have emerged.

PACHAMAMA: (Quechua) Mother Earth.

PACHAMANCA: (Quechua) method of cooking food on hot stones buried under the ground.

PAMPA: (Quechua) an extensive plain; name given to the destroyed center of Huaraz after it had been scraped clean of ruins.

PAPA, PAPACHITO: Little Father; used to address the Lord of Solitude.

PENA: emotional pain, grief.

PENAS OF THE ANDES: the "troubles" of the Andes: hail, frost, drought, scarcity of food.

PISHTACO: an outsider, especially a white man, supposed to kill Indians and render their body fat to use for candles or, nowadays, as grease for machinery.

PLAN REGULADOR: overall plan devised to govern how Huaraz was to be reconstructed.

PLANO REGULADOR: the regulating map of Huaraz, showing how the town was to be rebuilt.

PLAYA: literally, "beach"; name given to the area that was once Yungay and which, with the avalanche, became the burial ground of its inhabitants.

PLAYA DE LOS MUERTOS: Beach of the Dead.

POBLANO: town or city dweller.

POLLERA: a full, bright-colored skirt; Indian women wear several at once, one on top of the other.

PUNA: (Quechua) a flat, windswept plain in the Andes, above 13,000 feet.

QUEBRADA: a deep U-shaped gorge.

QUELAMIHUAQARQAN: (Quechua) a phrase meaning the spirit is fragile and the body uneasy.

QEQEQ QEQEQ: (Quechua) the sound made by the head of a woman who has had sexual relations with her *compadre*. The head separates from the body and flies through the night.

QUINCHA: (Quechua) a hut having walls of intertwined canes plastered with clay.

QUINUA: (Quechua) edible grain that grows in the lower puna.

QUINUAL: (Quechua) tree that grows on the banks of the glacial lakes.

REMOCIÓN DE ESCOMBROS: removal of ruins.

RONDÍN: a musical instrument.

RUNAKUNA: (Quechua) human beings.

SANTO: a saint; saint's day; image of a saint.

SECSECPAMPINOS: inhabitants of the Indian village of Secsecpampa.

SEÑOR DE LA SOLEDAD: the Lord of Solitude; venerated religious image of Huaraz.

SEÑOR DE MAYO: The Lord of May, the double of the Lord of Solitude, but not as highly esteemed.

SERRANOS: mountain people.

SHAPINKO: (Quechua) another word for *supay*, or devil.

SHONQU NANÉE: (Quechua) pain of the heart. The heart is said to become "hard like a rock." Perhaps anxiety in Western terms.

SHUCUQUÍ: (Quechua) a strong, "crazy" wind.

SINAMOS: acronym for the National System of Support for Social Mobilization.

SOBREVIVIENTE: survivor.

SOL: sun; the Peruvian monetary unit, valued at approximately 43 *soles* to the dollar in 1971–72.

SOLEDAD: solitude, loneliness, aloneness; a lonely place; also one of the barrios of Huaraz.

SOLEDANO: an inhabitant of the barrio of Soledad in Huaraz.

SONQO or SHONQU: (Quechua) the heart.

SU PASO: literally, "his step"; the Christ of May, the double of the Lord of Solitude, who was usually carried in procession in the Lord of Solitude's stead.

SUPAY: (Quechua) the Devil.

SUSTO: fright. An emotional incident may disequilibrate someone who then, suffering from "fright," may lose his soul.

TAYTA: (Quechua) Father, Señor, Lord. Also *Teeta* or *Teetee*.

TENIENTE GOBERNADOR: "deputy governor," a political authority in a hamlet who is appointed by the subprefect and acts as liaison between the hamlet and officials in the town.

TERREMOTEAR: a made-up verb meaning "to earthquake."

TERRUÑO: one's piece of land, imbued with sentiment.

UCHCUPAT'SA: (Quechua) literally, "hollow or opening in the earth"; the name given the largest mountain cross in Secsecpampa.

VENADO: The white-tailed deer found on the higher slopes of the Cordillera Blanca.

VISCACHA: (Quechua) a burrowing animal looking something like a ground squirrel and abundant in rocky areas of the Cordillera Negra and the Cordillera Blanca.

VOLUNTAD DE DIOS: God's will.

YERBA LUISA: an herbal tea.

YUNGAÍNO: an inhabitant of Yungay.

YUNGAY: pronounced Yoon-GUY.

NOTES ON SOURCES

Here the reader will find references to sources used within the body of the text. References to sources given in the numbered notes to chapters are included within the footnotes themselves.

PREFACE

PAGE

xxxix   If, as some scholars think: Pfeiffer, *The Creative Explosion*.
xxviii   "recent descendants of Ice Age people": Pfeiffer, "Cro-Magnon Hunters Were Really Us," p. 84.
xxxix   "The landscape [was] alive": Pfeiffer, "Cro-Magnon Hunters Were Really Us," p. 82.
   xl   "vulnerability" of transitional societies: Torry, "Anthropological Studies in Hazardous Environments."
   xli   "Peru is not merely": Beals, *Fire on the Andes*, p. 432.
   xlii   In Mexico, people knelt and prayed: Jennifer Sibley Clement, personal communication.

CHAPTER 1

   3   Myth tells that long ago: Yauri Montero, *Leyendas Ancashinas*, p. 115.

CHAPTER 2

   26   the towns of the Callejón de Huaylas: Ramírez Gamarra, *Ancash, Vida y Pasión*, pp. 153–54.

CHAPTER 4

PAGE

41 "Conceivably, such an event": Ericksen, Plafker, and Fernández, *Preliminary Report on the Geologic Events*, p. 20.

43 "No one knows when": McDowell and Fletcher, "Avalanche!," pp. 878–80.

CHAPTER 6

83 . . . Cirila, with her two young sons: in part from Zavaleta, *El Callejón de Huaylas*, vol. 3, pp. 1–6.

CHAPTER 7

96 A nurse from Buenos Aires: from tape made by Jorge Prelorán.

96 "ranks high among the world's": Ericksen, Plafker, and Fernández, *Preliminary Report on the Geologic Events*, p. 1.

96 "almost unbelievable, possibly surpassing": *Bulletin of the Atomic Scientists*, p. 17.

102 "This," wrote Darwin, "shows that experience": Darwin, *Voyage of the Beagle*, pp. 310–11.

103 "all too ready to abandon": Geertz, "Religion as a Cultural System," pp. 15–16.

CHAPTER 8

113 "Tell me, Lord, what were you doing": Ramírez Gamarra, *Ancash, Vida y Pasión*, p. 13.

CHAPTER 9

123 "What were the sun, the wind": Zavaleta, *El Callejón de Huaylas*, vol. 2, p. 7.

123 It was May everywhere: Ramírez Gamarra, *Ancash, Vida y Pasión*, pp. 115–16.

CHAPTER 11

135 The history of earthquakes: Silgado, "Historia de los Sismos Más Notables."

PAGE

135 "They say it is very certain": Cieza de León, *El Señorío de los Incas*, p. 16.

136 ". . . for in that country those catastrophes": Wilder, *The Bridge of San Luis Rey*, p. 8.

136 Only the barely perceptible: Gutenberg and Richter, *Seismicity of the Earth*; Silgado, "Historia de los Sismos Más Notables."

136 The large talus slopes: Ericksen, Plafker, and Fernández, *Preliminary Report on the Geologic Events*, pp. 5–6.

137 It is presumed that the plunging: Ericksen, Plafker, and Fernández, *Preliminary Report on the Geologic Events*, pp. 4–5; Morales Arnao, *Revista Peruana de Andinismo y Glaciología*, p. 17; Dupuy, *Bajo el Signo del Terremoto*, pp. 230–31.

138 "In some places, damage": Ericksen, Plafker, and Fernández, *Preliminary Report on the Geologic Events*, p. 15.

141 Indeed, the intensity of the earthquake: Morales Arnao, *Revista Peruana de Andinismo y Glaciología*, p. 5.

CHAPTER 12

154 Though this last contention: Healy and Marshall, "Nuclear Explosions and Distant Earthquakes."

CHAPTER 13

165 "Huaraz has been and will be": Ramírez, *Ancash, Vida y Pasión*, p. 47.

166 "When the awful tragedy": Oficina Nacional de Información, p. 10.

166 "The world was alone": Yauri Montero, *Tiempo de Rosas y de Sonrisas*, pp. 50, 23.

166 "I present myself before you": Zavaleta, *El Callejón de Huaylas*, vol. 2, p. i; vol. 1, p. 8.

CHAPTER 14

174 "to make possible a new human morality": Velasco, *Mensaje a la Nación*, pp. 7–8.

174 "We are in the midst of": Velasco, *Mensaje a la Nación*, p. 33.

PAGE

175 "political hermeneutics of the Gospel": Gutiérrez, *A Theology of Liberation*, p. 13.

176 "upon the traces of this": Velasco, *Mensaje a la Nación*, p. 14.

176 "The revolutionary orientation": CRYRZA, *Lineamientos de Base de la Política*.

178 "The earthquake of the 31st of May": *CRYRZA en su Etapa de Realizaciones*, p. 26.

CHAPTER 15

189 Following the Latin American Bishops' Conference: Comisión Episcopal de Acción Social.

190 "*Concientización* means the development": MacEoin, "Latin America's Radical Church," p. 69.

190 "In the life of towns": *CRYRZA en su Etapa de Realizaciones*, p. 26.

190 "If among the rubble": Pastor, *Terremotos y Signos*, p. 46.

191 whose starting point was a Marxist analysis of society: MacEoin, "Latin America's Radical Church," p. 72.

191 Thus, while the Revolution: Velasco, *Mensaje a la Nación*, p. 5.

CHAPTER 16

200 . . . as anthropologist Richard Patch remarked: Patch, *American Universities Field Staff Reports*, vol. 18, no. 9, p. 13.

219 "Now, everything is owned by CRYRZA": Martin, "Aftershock in Peru," p. 17.

CHAPTER 17

223 "A trip to town appears": Stein, *Hualcán*, p. 169.

223 *Cholo* came to be used: Matos Mar et al., *Peru: Hoy*, passim.

CHAPTER 18

240 "a love which is manifested": Gutiérrez, *A Theology of Liberation*, p. 198.

240 ". . . the stranger, who arrives": Valcárcel, *Historia del Perú Antiguo*, Vol. 1, p. 70.

PAGE

240   "This Cuniraya Viracocha": Arguedas, *Dioses y Hombres*, p. 23; Krickeberg et al., *Pre-Columbian American Religions*, p. 133.

240   "And when they were well": Arguedas, *Dioses y Hombres*, pp. 47–49.

242   Baltazar becomes the ancestor: Stein, *Hualcán*, p. 303.

244   "whose boundaries are ideally": Turner, *The Ritual Process*, p. 132.

245   "social structure and *communitas*": Turner, *The Ritual Process*, p. 132.

CHAPTER 19

255   Even the words "cruel punishment": "Huaraz en la Hora," p. 18.

255   it even appeared in the scientific treatment: Morales Arnao, *Revista Peruana de Alpinismo y Glaciología*.

256   John Rowe has synthesized: Rowe, "Inca Religion."

257   Other scholars report that severe penance: Valcárcel, *Historia del Perú Antiguo*, vol. 3, p. 267; Krickeberg et al., *Pre-Columbian American Religions*, p. 141.

257   "the powers of springs": Rowe, "Inca Religion," p. 540.

257   When that occurred, Inca soldiers: Trimborn, "El Motivo Explanatorio," pp. 25–27.

257   "We have been told by witness": Trimborn and Kelm, *Francisco de Avila*, p. 250, n. 54.

257   "a great rain occurred": Urioste, "Sons of Pariacaca," p. 84.

258   In one tradition: Imbelloni, "La Tradición Peruana."

258   Another indigenous tradition: Métraux, *The History of the Incas*, pp. 44–45; Wachtel, *Sociedad e Ideología*, p. 190.

258   Anguished by the changes: Wachtel, *Sociedad e ideología*, pp. 221–22.

258   Omens that cast a pall: Beals, *Fire on the Andes*, p. 53.

259   Sometimes, becoming agitated: Valcárcel, *Historia del Perú Antiguo*, vol. 1, p. 69.

259   Stones that clash in the air: Valcárcel, *Historia del Perú Antiguo*, vol. 4, p. 477.

259   "They adore rivers": Acosta, *Historia Natural y Moral*, p. 144.

259   Flying heads planted their teeth: Métraux, *The History of the Incas*, p. 75.

PAGE

260   Father Pablo José de Arriaga: Arriaga, *The Extirpation of Idolatry*.

260   "make a long and sorrowful story": Arriaga, *The Extirpation of Idolatry*, pp. 19–21.

260   "keeper of the heart": Arriaga, *The Extirpation of Idolatry*, p. 49.

260   "to carry water on both shoulders": Arriaga, *The Extirpation of Idolatry*, p. 72.

261   "The dissimulation and boldness": Arriaga, *The Extirpation of Idolatry*, p. 70.

261   Thousands of *huacas*: Arriaga, *The Extirpation of Idolatry*, pp. 76–77.

261   Once the crosses were: Arriaga, *The Extirpation of Idolatry*, p. 82.

262   such were the bacchanalian proclivities: Arriaga, *The Extirpation of Idolatry*, p. 61.

262   One friar told of: Acosta, *Historia Natural y Moral*, pp. 87–88.

262   "Some of the *huacas*": Arriaga, *The Extirpation of Idolatry*, p. 114.

262   "The world is upside down": Guaman Poma de Ayala, *Nueva Crónica y Buen Gobierno*, f. 1126.

262   The sufferings of the Indians: Wachtel, *Sociedad e Ideología*, p. 224.

262   Throughout the colonial period: Dupuy, *Bajo el Signo del Terremoto*, pp. 262, 266, 297, 326.

263   At any rate, God's judgment: Dupuy, *Bajo el Signo del Terremoto*, p. 297; *A True and Particular Relation*.

263   "This is the justice": Basadre, *La Multitud, la Ciudad,* p. 80.

264   "They left their old familiar": Métraux, *The History of the Incas*, p. 75.

265   In one such story: Sueldo Guerrero, "Wankar K'uyci: El Arco Iris," p. 78.

265   In others gathered in the countryside: Yauri Montero, *Warakuy*, pp. 14, 35.

CHAPTER 20

270   "To uproot them from their hearts": Arriaga, *The Extirpation of Idolatry*, p. 21.

271   After all, the Catholicism of extirpation: Arriaga, *The Extirpation of Idolatry*, p. 111.

CHAPTER 23

PAGE

334 "People spoke of another disaster": Oliver-Smith, *The Martyred City*, p. 77.

335 "I was born one day": Vallejo, *Los Heraldos Negros*, p. 106.

335 "My God, if you had been man": Vallejo, *Los Heraldos Negros*, p. 92.

CHAPTER 31

430 "I know you could have left": Yauri Montero, *Tiempo de Rosas y de Sonrisas*, pp. 157–61.

CHAPTER 32

433 "Spirits of the community": Valcárcel, *Etnohistoria del Perú Antiguo*, p. 141.

434 "symbolized the threads": Métraux, *The History of the Incas*, p. 71.

439 "If you had been a man": Vallejo, *Los Heraldos Negros*, p. 92.

440 weeps for his "fragile Creation": Vallejo, *Los Heraldos Negros*, p. 97.

440 "naked in the face": Yauri Montero, *Tiempo de Rosas y de Sonrisas*, p. 16.

441 "We found these": Yauri Montero, *Tiempo de Rosas y de Sonrisas*, pp. 156–59.

EPILOGUE

502 "Why have they forgotten?": Yauri Montero, *María Colón*, p. 76.

502 At the close of an earlier Yauri novel: Yauri Montero, *En Otoño Después de Mil Años*, pp. 332–35.

502 "About forgetting, I haven't forgotten": Yauri Montero, *María Colón*, p. 77.

POSTSCRIPT

504 "How could such a peaceful": Patch, *American Univiersities Field Staff Reports*, vol. 18, no. 9, p. 10.

NOTES

PROLOGUE

1. An accurate count of deaths in the Callejón will never be known. One factor in the difficult task of obtaining reliable statistics is that an official census had not been done since 1961. It was estimated that the immediate pre-earthquake population of Huaraz was 65,000, including the city and its rural satellite villages, or "Huaraz *arriba*" (upper Huaraz), located on the mountain slopes. This corresponds roughly to our designation of, e.g., "greater Detroit." At the time of the 1961 census, the urban population was given as 20,345. This would be the urban center —the four main barrios—and would not include newer outlying urban "suburbs" on the valley floor. The accepted figure for fatalities in the urban center alone is 10,000, though survivors themselves often estimate a toll far higher. The figures published by the National Emergency Committee and hung in the government palace in Lima through August 1970, for the district of Huaraz ("greater" Huaraz) are the following: missing: 2,498; dead: 18,932; injured: 13,230.

Most sources, including newspapers and the U.S. Geological Survey, give high estimates of fatalities for the "city" of Yungay. The *Revista Peruana de Andinismo y Glaciología* (Morales Arnao 1971:68) says, e.g., that the avalanche "buried completely the city of Yungay with its 18,000 inhabitants." In his book *The Martyred City*, Oliver-Smith (1986) gives the surprisingly low figure of some 4,200 "true" *Yungaínos*, with possibly 2,000 others who were in Yungay that Sunday. The wide variation probably results from different definitions of "the city of Yungay." Yungay had a large agriculturally based peasant population and a number of "suburbs" on the fringes of the main grid of "old Yungay." Oliver-Smith is talking about the strictly urban center of Yungay, and I tend to follow him, while accepting the higher figures for total fatalities from the avalanche within the larger Yungay community. In his book, he gives the higher figures for "Huaraz" (16,000–20,000), while I have used the 10,000 figure for Huaraz's strictly urban center. The National Emergency Committee published these figures for the district of Yungay: missing: 2,009; dead: 16,071; injured: 680. These figures are out of a total population of 18,830.

Of the estimated 75,000 dead in Ancash, the number of deaths in the coastal area of the department was low, probably around 1,000.

CHAPTER 2

1. People used *aluvión* in Spanish to mean the mud, water, ice, snow, and rock flows. This is perhaps more accurately "avalanche" in English, though one tends to think of avalanche as masses of snow alone. In this book, by "alluvion," I do not mean simply flood or water but, rather, the mixture of ice, snow, rock, water, and mud, and use it synonymously with "avalanche."

2. The greatest part of Benjamín Morales's account comes from a tape I made with him on July 5, 1972, and from our conversations. It is supplemented, however, by his report in the special edition of the *Peruvian Review of Mountain Climbing and Glaciology*, edited by Benjamín's brother, César Morales Arnao (1971:63–71). I never met Casaverde. My description of what he and French geophysicist Gerard Patzelt experienced during the avalanche comes from the same journal: Morales (1971:89–92). This special edition of the *Revista Peruana de Andinismo y Glaciología* contains invaluable geologic data prepared by scientific missions from various nations as well as a few personal accounts by Peruvian scientists and mountain climbers who experienced the disaster.

CHAPTER 3

1. Some chroniclers of the conquest of Peru say "Huaraz" comes from the Quechua word *huarac*, meaning "it is dawning," and that this was the spontaneous utterance of the natives to the morning star Venus, when they observed its quiet brilliance at daybreak in Huaraz. Once, when I remarked to a child that I was planning to get up at dawn, he said to be sure to look for Venus in the north. Other chroniclers attribute the name of the city to the Quechua *huara*, meaning "short pants," which the natives wore at the time the Spaniards arrived.

CHAPTER 4

1. This account of what happened on the cemetery that night was given to Isaías Zavaleta Figueroa of Caraz, who published it in mimeographed form in three pamphlets entitled "Callejón de Huaylas, Antes y Después del Terremoto del 31 Mayo de 1970" (Ediciones Parón, Caraz, 1970–71). From time to time, I heard similar descriptions, as well as other accounts of that first night. Throughout this book, where I do not give references to printed material, such as above, what I record is what I saw or heard firsthand.

2. This utterance was made to my friend and colleague Anthony Oliver-Smith, who worked in Yungay the year following the disaster.

CHAPTER 6

1. This has implications for the theory of "survivor guilt," developed by Robert Jay Lifton in his book about Hiroshima (1967). That "the dead were better off" was also a theme in the Callejón.

CHAPTER 7

1. Seismographic data are from the Centro Regional de Sismología para América del Sur. See Oficina Nacional de Información—ONI—n.d.:67–71. Even the geophysical data are not as "concrete" as might be expected. The earthquake was registered at all the seismographic stations in the world, and yet some figures vary. See Morales Arnao (1971:16) for slightly different epicentral parameters. The parameter most at issue is the hypocenter. The U.S. Coast and Geodetic Survey places it at a depth of fifty-six kilometers; other surveys at twenty-four. Both twenty-four and fifty-six kilometers fall within the range of a shallow-focus destructive earthquake. Richter magnitude is given variously as 7.5, 7.7, and 7.9.

2. Major Peruvian newspapers are *La Prensa, El Comercio, Expreso*, and *El Correo*. Other popular reports of the disaster are: Blank (1970); "Death by Glacier" (1970); "Earthquake and Avalanche" (1970); "Infernal Thunder . . ." (1970); Phelps (1970). Dupuy (no date) is a compendium of earthquakes, with special attention to the Peru disaster of 1970.

3. My research prior to going to the field included the ethnography of the area: Stein (1961); Doughty (1968); Patch's various American Universities field staff letters and reports from the Callejón since 1958; Mangin (1955); Vásquez (1952; 1955); Holmberg (1960); Fried (1962). I had also surveyed the disaster literature, examples of which are Wallace (1956 a, b; 1958); Baker and Chapman (1962); Dynes (1970); Barton (1970); and

The Great Alaska Earthquake of 1964 (Committee on . . . 1970). Many disaster studies have been called "instant research" for their short-term duration immediately after a disaster. See, e.g., the report on the Managua earthquake (Kates et al. 1973). Most have been centered in theories of stress, role, and mass behavior and have dealt largely with disasters in the Western world. I was more influenced by works such as Wolfenstein's *Disaster, A Psychological Essay* (1957) and Lifton's *Death in Life, Survivors of Hiroshima* (1967). For social science material on the Peruvian earthquake of 1970, see Doughty (1971a, b); Dudasik (1976;1978); Oliver-Smith (1973;1977 a, b; 1982;1986); and Bode (1974;1977). The best description of the immediate postdisaster scene is Patch's "The Peruvian Earthquake of 1970" (1971). More recently, Torry (1979) has brought together the scattered pieces of information and bibliography on the anthropological study of disaster, and on anthropology in hazardous environments.

4. My use of "explanation" approximates in its comprehensiveness Lifton's term "formulation," by which he means a reinstatement of the destroyed world that can absorb the catastrophic event (1967:367–68).

5. Much has been written on man as a reflective and interpretive animal, avid to find more than meets the eye in the bare data of experience. Becker (1973) and Lifton (1967) have called man's quest for meaning and continuity the prime mover of human life. Some scholars see cultures themselves as edifices built to allay the chaos our untethered senses would perceive (e.g., Berger 1967:80). For Lewis Thomas, human beings make language and symbols together, and are as bound by them as "termites in a hill. . . . Culture is our word for our kind of hill" (1978:1456).

6. Based on his work among the Azande of Africa (1937), anthropologist E. E. Evans-Pritchard pointed out that there is no necessary contradiction between objective and mystical explanations. For instance, the Azande were perfectly aware that a man died because a buffalo gored him. But, they would ask, why should a charging buffalo's path cross the path of that particular man and not some other? For the Azande, witchcraft was the mystical or supernatural cause. The two explanations together— one objective, empirical, immediate; the other subjective, supernatural, remote—account for the conjunction of two trains of events in a particular time and place.

CHAPTER 9

1. The *aukikuna* are conceptualized as benign invisible spirits who inhabit the inner depths of the mountains. Some mountains themselves are viewed as *apus*, gods of the ancient communities. More recent ancestors, called *abuilos* ("grandfathers"), are the pre-Columbian mummies

unearthed in the ancient ruins. In contrast with the *aukikuna*, the *ahuilos* are palpable and may be dangerous if one comes in contact with them. The ancient Andean hierarchy, which persists to greater or lesser extent today, thus goes from the living, the *runakuna*, to the *ahuilos*, to the more distant ancestors, the *aukikuna*, to the *apus*, and finally to the eternal celestial family—the sun, moon, and stars. Even in pre-Columbian times, the celestial family was remote, and then, as now, the ancestors were close. It is they who have handed down what ought to be, according to Andean belief, an inviolable sense of "community."

CHAPTER 10

1. Change is perhaps always hard on the human spirit. It is said that back in Inca times, Túpac Cauri Pachacuti prohibited writing on *quilcas* (parchments or leaves), attributing to this new practice of writing various catastrophes that had occurred. From then on, only *quipus*, the knotted device the Incas used for counting, were used, and there was to be no writing within the Inca Empire (Valcárcel 1971, V:310).

CHAPTER 12

1. France ignored a ruling by the International Court of Justice to stop testing in the atmosphere. "The French government has said that for reasons of national security the tests cannot be halted despite protests" (*New York Times*, 4 November 1973). In 1975, France finally stopped aerial testing and began detonating nuclear devices underground. France has steadily refused to confirm or deny these tests on Mururoa (*International Herald Tribune*, 20 June 1980).

2. On September 6, 1972, the *Washington Post* reported that the Amchitka explosion had caused a change in the earth's magnetic field. Ironically, it was hoped that this observation might lead to the ability to predict earthquakes: "Earthquakes occur after changes take place in the stresses holding the earth's crust together. It's just possible that as these stresses change, we can see it magnetically."

CHAPTER 13

1. On June 11, 1970, the USS *Guam* steamed into Callao harbor carrying 15 helicopters, 3 medical teams, and a 60-bed hospital. The helicopters made fifteen trips a day to evacuate the most seriously injured to the hospital on the *Guam*. Among other supplies, the United States donated 34,448 blankets, 7,113 tents, 6,473 cots, 2,019 sleeping bags, 1

million doses of antityphoid vaccine, and 36,000 rolls of X-ray film. Total U.S. government aid was $16,441,000. Here is just a sampling of the response of other nations: Russia contributed prefabricated houses, material for a hospital, three kindergartens with their entire staff of teachers, bulldozers, food, etc. In Ecuador, each member of the armed forces, from the highest general to the lowest soldier, contributed a day's pay. Bolivia sent blood, and Canada a million dollars. Cuba sent a medical brigade and 494,200 pairs of plastic slippers; the Society of Nordic Churches sent 5 aircraft to conduct rescue missions; and Hungary sent 5,800 Vitamin C lozenges. Hungary also established fifteen university scholarships for students from the Callejón. Among Portugal's contributions were 10 crates of port wine and 500 kilos of children's toys (Oficina Nacional de Informacion, n.d.:94–111).

2. "Survivor mission" is Robert J. Lifton's term (1967). In *Boundaries* (1969:9), he writes, of the survivors of Hiroshima: "Inevitably they have had great difficulty coming to terms with their experience, giving it some acceptable inner form or meaning and placing it within what we can call a 'formulation' in the deepest sense of that term. To render their experience significant, survivors looked to some form of peace symbol—to an image of a world chastened and rendered wiser by the atomic bombings—and some have participated actively in peace movements."

CHAPTER 14

1. For analyses of the Peruvian revolution, see Campbell (1973); Harding (1973); Rankin (1974); Lowenthal (1975); Middlebrook and Palmer (1975); Chaplin (1976); and Philip (1978).

2. The influence of this world phenomenon, which has come to be called Reform in the Catholic Church, upon the Latin American political and social scene is described in the following summary articles: Einaudi et al. (1969); Drekonja (1971); Bruneau (1973); MacEoin (1973); and B. H. Smith (1975). The Reform was felt by some to be a turning point in the direction and history of Latin America. For the influence of Catholicism and other modernizing religions on politics in Third World nations, see D. E. Smith (1970;1971), who writes (1971:8): "The new Catholic left is committed to revolutionary social change and is quite prepared to make common cause with revolutionaries flying the Marxist banner." Bourque (1971) devotes a chapter to the radical Peruvian Church and the *campesino*.

CHAPTER 15

1. Consciousness-raising (*conscientização* in Portuguese; *conscientización* in Spanish) has become practically a universal household word. Also

a catchword of the Peruvian revolution, it is associated with Brazilian educator Paolo Freire. The process receives its greatest elaboration in *The Pedagogy of the Oppressed* (1973), which has appeared in eleven languages.

CHAPTER 16

1. Paul Doughty (1971b:8) pointed to other reasons that made relocation anathema to the people, e.g., distance from fields and possible loss of political and social status if the seat of a district capital were changed. Anthony Oliver-Smith (1977b) also stressed ecological reasons for rejecting relocation.

2. Perhaps, whenever revolution, modernization, or religious reform hover over a people at the time a great natural disaster occurs, unresolved mourning and ambivalence over which way of life is right—the destroyed or the projected—ensue. One such dramatic conjuncture of politics and disaster took place in the aftermath of an earthquake that occurred in Venezuela on March 26, 1812, killing about 14,000 people. Since the destroyed cities were those under control of the Independence forces, the disaster was taken as a sign of God's displeasure with independence from Spain. Royalist clergy exploited the disaster politically, calling it a punishment for rebellion against divine authority, and survivors begged forgiveness of King Ferdinand VII of Spain. Reportedly, though, Liberator Simón Bolívar stood upon the ruins and proclaimed: "If Nature is opposed, we will fight against it and make it obey us" (Madariaga 1959: 332–42).

CHAPTER 17

1. "Verticality" is an idea first developed by John Murra to explain economic adaptation to the varied ecological zones of the Andes. See Murra (1972); Fonseca (1972); Brush (1977), and Lehmann (1982).

2. For a more detailed analysis of social stratification in the Callejón de Huaylas and a survey of the literature on social structure, see Bode (1977).

3. It has been shown that new groupings of people arise in crisis situations, such as categories expressing degrees or quality of injury, often with an undertone of hierarchy in victimization. See, e.g., Lifton (1967: 165–72) for a discussion of victim status and identity in the Hiroshima A-bomb aftermath. Victim categories developed, too, in the Callejón. Perhaps the most poignant class was the "*sobrevivientes*" of the Yungay avalanche, for they were so few of so many. I recall meeting people from

Huaraz and Yungay on the coast, who established themselves as "survivors." Outside the valley, this term at times communicated a demand for special attention—like the best seat in a vehicle.

4.   Ideally, the term *campesino* is neither racial nor social nor cultural, but a simple declaration of where one lives and finds his material sustenance. This ecological perspective ought to have removed the sting of class. But the term *campesino*, historically, has not been free of its own negative connotations. The city/country dichotomy has deep Spanish and Latin American intellectual roots. A major work of Latin American literature, Argentinian Domingo Sarmiento's *Civilización y Barbarie* (1845), contrasted city and country. Cities were depicted as repositories of *cultura*, in the Latin American sense of "civilization," i.e., arts and letters. The countryside was seen as backward, devoid of all *cultura*, even ultimately of culture in the anthropological sense, as that which makes us human. No doubt, from these old meanings of city/country came the rhetoric of "humanizing" the *campesino* and of bringing him culture.

CHAPTER 18

1.   People told a similar story about the alluvion that swept down Cójup Canyon onto Huaraz in 1941. That story contained a feature I did not hear with regard to the earthquake, perhaps because the disaster of 1970 was felt to have spared no one. The added detail is that a few people, or a family, feed the stranger, who in exchange for their kindness rewards them by warning them to get to high ground because Huaraz will be destroyed within a few days. This also occurs in the Pariacaca myth. A woman invited the god to drink some *chicha*. He then told her the town would be destroyed in five days, and she and her children were able to escape.

2.   In fact, at the same time the negatively laden term "Indian" was giving way to *campesino*, the nativistic component of the Revolution was revitalizing the Indian. In the Callejón, sections of camps, cooperatives, and expropriated haciendas were named after famed Indian leaders and insurrectionists of past centuries—Túpac Amaru, Atusparia, Uchcu Pedro. In Lima, it became fashionable to fill the home with Indian crafts, blankets, pottery, woven wall hangings. Many of their owners had never traveled beyond Chosica or other foothill towns of the Andean range. The "Indian" was becoming an artifact.

CHAPTER 19

1.   Within the word *castigo* itself there is a wealth of nuance. The verb *castigar* enters Spanish from the Latin *castigare* around the year 900

with the meanings of "to admonish, to warn; to publish the banns of; to correct or to reform" (Corominas 1961:134). The *Valázquez Spanish-English Dictionary* lists the following definitions: chastisement, punishment, correction, penalty; censure, reproach. "Example" and "instruction" are given as obsolete, having been slowly replaced by the modern meanings beginning in the thirteenth century. *Castigo de Dios* is rendered as "God's judgment."

2.   French historian Nathan Wachtel writes that "despite the collapse of the structures of their society, the Peruvian Indians resisted the process of acculturation which was imposed on them by the Spanish, at least as far as religion was concerned" (1977:9). ". . . even though the state cult lapsed with the execution of Atahualpa, the ancient Andean cults (founded on the local worship of *huacas*, stars, thunderbolts, etc.) have survived throughout the centuries up to our own day" (1977:154).

CHAPTER 22

1.   According to the *Encyclopaedia Britannica*, carnival is a period of license that "represents a compromise which the Church always inclined to make with pagan festivals." Ultimately, carnival goes back to the Roman Saturnalia, during the time of Roman demagogue Saturninus, who was born in 104 B.C. The Church has always shown ambivalence toward carnival, various popes alternately making efforts to stem the tide of revelry and others serving as patrons and promoters of carnival. For example, Sixtus V, elected in 1585, set himself the task of seeing to it that carnival was celebrated in a more sedate fashion. He reformed the "evil custom" of throwing flour at passersby and permitted only flowers or sweetmeats to be thrown. The Spanish Franciscans in Huarupampa said that carnival probably coincided with a native festival that marked the time between the solstices, just about the time when the rains were beginning to slacken.

2.   Jesuit Pablo José de Arriaga observed that the Indians worshiped the *apachetas*, which they believed would take away their weariness and help them carry their load (1968 [1621]:69). On these piles of stones and sundry articles—a wad of *coca*, splinters of wood, straw—the Spaniards "hurried to plant a cross." When asked about the *apachetas*, the Indians said they "worshipped them like a *huaca*" (Métraux 1973:73–74). Likewise, the stone images that guarded the ancient hamlets were "disposed of . . . and crosses were put in their places" (Arriaga 1968 [1621]:157).

3 .   Compare: "In the town of Quichumarca, at the place where the cross had been during the previous visit, we again dug down about three yards, and we were about to give up when we came upon the evidence of sacrifices and three *huacas*. The largest they call Huari Huaca, and with

him were his two brothers, with such strange faces that they were horrifying to look at" (Arriaga 1968 [1621]:82).

4.   Arriaga (1968 [1621]:94–95) recounts that once when the Indians had been warned that they had better come to communion, the Devil raised such a noise and confusion that night that the surrounding hills seemed to be falling down. The Devil appeared to the Indians, saying the town would be destroyed if they took communion when they were not prepared for it. During my time in the Callejón, it was very rare to see anyone take communion, especially *campesinos*.

5.   Arriaga's treatise on the extirpation of idolatry during the sixteenth century contains careful descriptions of the ways in which the crosses were to be honored. He says, for example, that "the streets will be prepared." The Indians were then to assemble to carry the large crosses to the church for a Mass. The "sorcerers" were to go in a body with candles, wearing a cord around their necks (the colored streamers?) to symbolize penitence. At the conclusion of the Mass, there should be a procession, and the litany of the cross must be sung in the Indian language. The sorcerers were to march like penitents in front of the cross as it was borne aloft. "This spectacle will arouse in those who look upon it as they should much devotion and deep feeling" (1968 [1621]:132). Arriaga describes the following occasion: A priest, gathering together some Indians, set out to climb a rocky hill until they reached a place so steep that the priest, seizing the big cross he intended to raise on the site of the *huaca*, used it for a staff and ascended "in this way for more than a quarter of a league." During the ascent, they came upon a *huaca* more than six feet high, which the Indians told him was to keep the lake that furnished water for their fields from drying up. On the same ascent, they encountered a *huaca* in a cemetery. "The Indians worshiped them as guardians of the town. These *huacas* were disposed of like all the rest, and crosses were put in their place" (1968 [1621]:156–57). Four hundred years separated the ascent of the priest with the cross up the rocky slope and Calixto Campos's ascent with Uchcupat'sa. Yet Arriaga's description and mine are remarkably similar. Also strikingly like what I witnessed in 1972 are descriptions of the celebrations the Indians held in front of their *huacas* four hundred years ago: "*Chicha* was brewed in large pots, consumed by the celebrants and offered to the *huacas* along with *coca* and guinea pigs that had been sacrificed (1968 [1621]:61). The Indians would assemble in their *chacras* near the *huacas*, where their common bond was "to drink until they fall down" (1968 [1621]:71). On these occasions they made confessions, played small drums and trumpets, and everyone danced and sang songs telling "foolish things about their ancestors" and invoking the *huaca* by name (1968 [1621]:50). The dispute I lived through over the demeanor

of the festival also strikes chords from those early days of Conquest: "From now on in no case nor for any reason will the Indians of this town, whether men or women, play drums, dance, or sing and dance at a marriage or town festival, singing in their mother tongue as they have done up to now. For experience has shown that in these songs they invoke the names of their *huacas*, the *malquis*, and the lightning, which they worship" (1968 [1621]:170).

CHAPTER 23

1. An Inca myth depicts the union of the Sun God and the Moon Goddess as taking place on a high mountain slope, where the two were turned to stone after mating (Krickeberg et al. 1968:126).

2. Friar José de Acosta, in Peru during the sixteenth century, insinuates that a huge piece of mountain fell upon a certain town because much witchcraft and idolatry were practiced there (1954:87).

3. Jesuit Arriaga wrote: "It is their custom to do everything by community effort and the common bond of such groups is to drink until they fall down. It is from these sources in addition to incest and many other wicked practices that the idolatry of past centuries has arisen. . . . It is usual with persons of limited understanding to know and estimate guilt not in and of itself, but by the punishment it receives. . . ." (1968 [1621]:71). Sermons printed in 1585 admonished "how much adultery angers God and how he punishes it, and also how fornication with an unmarried woman, even on a single occasion, is a deadly sin, and of the other manners of lewdness because of which God punishes the Indian nation. . . . Above all these sins is sodomy. . . . Let it be known that I tell you from God's command that if you do not reform, all your nations will perish, and God will finish you, eradicating you from the face of the earth. . ." (Guerra 1971:241–42).

4. Chronicler Bernabé Cobo, a Catholic priest, born about 1580, spoke of the sins the Indians were eager to confess: "In external acts, they believed there were many kinds of sin. Those considered most were to kill one another away from war, or violently, with witchcraft or poison; to rob; to neglect the care of their *huacas* and places of worship; not to keep the feasts or celebrate them; to speak evil of the Inca, or not to carry out his wishes. Although they considered it a sin to take the neighbor's wife and to corrupt a virgin, this was not due to thinking that fornication itself was a sin, but it was to break the order given by the Inca, who prohibited this. They believed that all the misfortunes and adversities which came to men were due to their sins and therefore those who were

the greatest sinners suffered the greatest tribulations and calamities. . ."
(1956 [1653], vol. 92, p. 206).

CHAPTER 25

1. The Seventh-Day Adventists may have been familiar with chroniclers who reported that the valley of Huaylas had a reputation for sodomy
(Cieza de León 1959 [1553]:113). Garcilaso de la Vega "El Inca" writes
that the Inca subdued the province of Huaylas and "he punished very
severely some sodomites who very secretly practiced the abominable vice
of sodomy. As until then this sin had not been found or heard of among
the Indians of the mountains, though it was known in the lowlands, it
caused great scandal to find it among the Huaylas. . . ." (1968 [1609]:435).

2. There are many versions of the Flood myth, which is of utmost
antiquity in all parts of the Americas. The Deluge is at times depicted in
Peru as the "final moment of a period of corruption," which extinguished
a "profane, rebellious, and contumacious" humanity (Imbelloni 1944:62).

3. Reports of great clashings of boulders appear throughout the
chronicles, e.g., Cabello Valboa's statement that "stones hurled themselves
against one another and broke into pieces" (Trimborn and Kelm 1967:250,
footnote 54). See also Valcárcel (1971, IV: 477) and Urioste (1969:42).
Survivors and geologic reports alike describe the way boulders struck each
other in midair, setting off sparks, in the Yungay avalanche.

4. An explication of the sixteenth-century Huarochirí document
tells us the following: "In various stories of the myths of Huarochirí, we
can see and understand how the people lived in constant, seemingly sub-
conscious, fear of a threatened end of the world. They practiced many
rituals with which they tried to ward off . . . such a disaster. In the end,
however, after trying many different rituals, they were not convinced that
they could free themselves from this final calamity" (Trimborn and Kelm
1967:250–53, paraphrased from the German).

CHAPTER 26

1. Similar feats are believed to have been performed by saints
around the world. By accounts of Italian-Americans in Little Italy in New
York City, for example, their famed San Gennaro once stopped a can-
nonball with two fingers and another time ordered the molten lava of
Vesuvius to freeze on the outskirts of Naples before it could harm the
city.

2. At the end of my fieldwork, while discussing something else with
a woman who had had a photography shop on the Plaza de Armas, by

chance I was able to fill in more details on the fire of 1965. On the afternoon before the fire, the señora and her husband left at Radio Huaraz tapes advertising their business to be played on the following morning. Unaware of the events that took place during that night, they eagerly turned on the radio the next morning to hear their commercial. Instead, they heard somber classical music and thought the announcer must be making fun of them. Then came the news that the Señor de la Soledad had burned and the mayor was dead. That day, as *campesinos* began to descend into Huaraz, the señora and her husband feared reprisals against their business. Perhaps the *campesinos* would blame the townspeople for the fire. As *campesinos* surged through the town looking for the priest, vowing to kill him, the señora got a call from a nun in the chapel of the Santa Rosa school, next to Soledad, where the priest had gone to hide. The señora's daughter was a student at Santa Rosa, and it was agreed that the priest would don her school uniform and feign an attack of illness. In this way, they were able to get him out to the hospital, where he hid in the basement until he could escape from Huaraz.

CHAPTER 32

1. Parallels between Soledad and the ancient Andean *huacas* are abundant. Here are some examples: (1) The Incas often sent native *huacas* to Cuzco to take their places in their own pantheon (Valcárcel 1971, IV:324). Also, during the colonial period, an occasional "idol" was sent to Spain (Valcárcel 1971, III:172). Suspicions that Soledad might be sent away may stem from these practices. (2) Each *huaca* had "its own custodian, who might be an old man or an old woman of the village" (Krickeberg 1968:136). According to a 1612 document, Spanish priests discovered that an Indian woman kept constant vigil over a certain *huaca* (Wachtel 1977:155). This recalls the constant vigil of Marianela at the feet of Soledad, where she slept each night. (3) A double for a venerated image like Soledad (the Christ of May) possibly has its origins in the fact that *huacas* had their "look-alikes." For instance, the seventeenth-century "extirpator of idolatry" Friar Arriaga, in remarks on the proliferation of *huacas*, reports that in addition to a certain *huaca* he had recovered, "we removed the *huaca* Achay, which looked like the first one" (1968 [1621]:86). He also reports that the *huacas* had brothers and other relatives. When the priests found Huari Huaca, "with him were his two brothers. . . ." (1968 [1621]:82). Later, he instructs his recently arrived colleagues to ask, "Has the *huaca* a son made of stone and considered a *huaca* like him? Has he a father, brother, or wife? This question must always be asked, for there are fables about the principal *huacas* to the effect that they were men, had

sons, and were turned to stone" (1968 [1621]:118). On various occasions, I heard that the Señor de la Soledad had brothers. In Charumá, above Huaraz, I was told that "the Señor de la Soledad is in three parts, three brothers: the Señor de la Soledad, the Señor de Humántanga, found in the province of Lima, and the Señor de Chaucayán, in Cajacay Province. The Spaniards found him and divided him." Don Juan spoke of the two brothers of Soledad, naming the Señor de la Exaltación and the Señor de Chaucayán. Once, at Belén, I asked Norabuena who the image at the center of the altar was. He answered, "El Señor de la Buena Muerte [the Lord of Good Death], who aids the dying. He is the third part of the Señor de la Soledad." I did not devote much time to this and never got beyond the fact of three brothers. The Reform priest told me that when he made inquiries about this, *campesinos* would become suspicious and not know what to answer. "They say the images are not different, nor are they identical," Auscario said. (4) The "waking" of the Señor de la Soledad after the earthquake is like an echo from the distant past. Arriaga says that a Friar Francisco pulled down a *huaca* and burned it, "but the Indians repaired it." Another time when Friar Francisco "broke and burned the *huaca*, the Indians put the pieces together again and worshiped them there" (1968 [1621]:89). (5) Certainly, the suggestion of some strange force, what anthropologists call *mana*, fits for both the ancient *huacas* and Soledad. Alfred Métraux describes a *huaca* as "everything in fact, near or far, that suggested the presence of some strange force" (1973:70). (6) Chronicler Guaman Poma (1936 [1614]:f. 1126) says that for the Indians "the world upside down is a sign that there is no god, and there is no king." Wachtel interprets this as chaos brought about by the absence of the Inca (demigod), protector of the people: "Infinite absence: once the Inca disappeared, the universe sinks into chaos" (1973:224). Recall Reyna saying, "Without the Señor de la Soledad, everything is topsy-turvy."

2.   For a discussion of the notion of Christ as a model for suffering, see Richardson, Bode, and Pardo (1971).

3.   The Señor de la Soledad is of course a powerful collective symbol. Such symbols are sometimes called "multivocal" or "master" or "dominant" symbols. The concept is extensively treated in Turner (1969;1974;1978:246–49). The patron saint of Mexico, the Virgin of Guadalupe, is a good example of a dominant symbol. Devotion to this Virgin has come to "link together family, politics and religion; colonial past and independent present; Indian and Mexican. It reflects the salient social relationships of Mexican life, and embodies the emotions which they generate. It provides a cultural idiom through which the tenor and emotions of these relationships can be expressed. It is, ultimately, a way of talking about Mexico: collective representation of Mexican society" (Wolf

1958:39). "The ultimate force of symbols depends . . . on their power to stir the emotions, moving men to action and reaction. . . . Symbols and sentiments feed upon each other, and their fruitful interplay lies at the heart of social behavior" (Lewis 1977:2). Cohen defines symbols as "objects, acts, concepts or linguistic formations that stand ambiguously for a multiplicity of disparate meanings, evoke sentiments and emotions, and impel men to action" (1974:ix). Kurtz writes that "Symbols are important in ordering, interpreting, even reconstructing reality, and in permitting humans to forge links with the social structures and events in which they participate in order to reduce disjunction and resolve contradictions" (1982;203). Turner (1978:44,241), lists certain thematic similarities of major Christian images, e.g., their miraculous discovery; attempts to carry the image to a more comfortable place, and its return; and the holiest shrines tending to be located on the periphery of cities or towns, peripherality suggesting *communitas* and liminality, as against sociocultural structure.

The point that should come through clearly from my treatment of Soledad is that the more powerful the symbol—seen from the outside, from an "etic" point of view—the less it is a "symbol" at all for believers. Powerful symbols become congealed into real things or real personages. Soledad was not a symbol to the people. He *was* Christ, at least a certain Christ. He was not experienced in a conscious way as a codification of the essential themes of the aftermath. He embodied them. The "reality" of these dominant symbols makes them untouchable. For example, an attempt in 1834 to clean the smoke-blackened image of the Lord of Earthquakes of Cuzco brought a clamor of rebellion. How could a "white" Lord of Earthquakes possibly work miracles?

4. *Soledad* is a lyrical word, rich with meanings of absence, sorrow, longing, affection, and nostalgia. From its first appearance in Spanish in the Middle Ages, it had already absorbed all the nuances that began to adhere to the word *Saudade*, as it was sung by Galician-Portuguese troubadours. Through time even a lonely place came to be called a *soledad*. *Soledad* was adopted in Castile as a name for the Virgin Mary, the Virgen de la Soledad. This Virgin represents the desolation and fatigue the Mother of Jesus felt after his burial (Vossler 1946:12,26). Virgins of Solitude appear in Spain and Latin America, but several inquiries I made uncovered no other Christ of Soledad than the one in Huaraz. The vicar in Huaraz told me that a Virgin of Soledad was brought to Huaraz in the sixteenth or seventeenth century. A chapel was built for her, but as it was so removed and she was so alone, people requested that an image of Christ be sent from Spain to accompany her. This Spanish image, according to the vicar, was the Señor de la Soledad. Sometime through the

years, the Virgin of Solitude disappeared. No one ever mentioned her to me.

Chapter 34

1. The decade following the disaster saw the publication of several works of poetry and prose, and the composition of many more that were never published. Music, and even paintings depicting the disaster also flourished. Among published collections of poetry and prose are: *Ancash-31* (Jesús Cabel, ed., 1976, Lima: Juan Mejía Baca); *Literatura del Sismo* (Jesús Cabel, ed., 1972, Lima: Juan Mejía Baca); *Desde Mi Sangre* (Abdón Dexter Henostroza, 1973, Lima: Impresiones Generales); and *Rocío de Lágrimas* (V. Hernán Carballido Chávez, 1972, Lima: Editorial Minerva).

Historian Jorge Basadre (1929:79) writes that throughout Peru's history, the "transcendental character" of earthquakes inspired poetry, and cites a poem written by Barco Centenera after a temblor in Lima in 1582. Among the themes portrayed by Centenera was the moment, frozen in time, when people were caught by the earthquake, and, in their panic, poured out onto the streets:

> *Some in shirttails, their hair tousled,*
> *Others, screaming, clothes disheveled,*
> *Still others with faces but half-shaven*
> *Fainted dead away in front of doorways.*

BIBLIOGRAPHY

Acosta, Padre José de. *Historia Natural y Moral de las Indias*. Madrid: Biblioteca de Autores Españoles, Vol. 73, 1954 (first published in Seville in 1590).

Alberti, Giorgio, and Enrique Mayer, eds. *Reciprocidad e Intercambio en los Andes Peruanos*. Lima: Instituto de Estudios Peruanos, 1974.

Alvarez-Brun, Félix. *Ancash, Una Historia Regional Peruana*. Lima: Talleres Gráficos P.L. Villanueva S.A., 1970.

Arguedas, José María, trans. *Dioses y hombres de Huarochirí. Narración Quechua Recogida Por Francisco de Avila* (1598?). Lima: Museo Nacional de Historia and the Instituto de Estudios Peruanos, 1966.

Arriaga, Pablo José de. *The Extirpation of Idolatry in Peru*. Translated and edited by L. Clark Keating. Lexington: University of Kentucky Press, 1968 (first published in 1621).

Baker, George W., and Dwight W. Chapman, eds. *Man and Society in Disaster*. New York: Basic Books, 1962.

Bartle, Jim. *Trails of the Cordilleras Blanca & Huayhuash of Peru*. Lima: Editorial Gráfica Pacific Press S.A., 1981.

———. *Parque Nacional Huascarán*. Lima: Asociación Peruana Para la Conservación de la Naturaleza, 1985.

Barton, Allen H. *Communities in Disaster: A Sociological Analysis of Collective Stress Situations*. New York: Anchor Books, 1970.

Basadre, Jorge. *La Multitud, la Ciudad y el Campo en la Historia del Peru*. Lima: Imprenta A. J. Rivas Berrio, 1929.

Bastien, Joseph W. *Mountain of the Condor: Metaphor and Ritual in an Andean Ayllu*. St. Paul, Minn.: West Publishing Co., 1978.

Beals, Carleton. *Fire on the Andes*. London: J. B. Lippincott Co., 1934.

Becker, Ernest. *The Denial of Death*. New York: The Free Press, 1973.

Berger, Peter L. *The Sacred Canopy*. New York: Doubleday & Co., 1967.

Blank, J. P. "Earthquake! The Horror That Hit Peru." *Reader's Digest*, Vol. 97, pp. 77–83 (October 1970).

Bode, Barbara. "Explanation in the 1970 Earthquake in the Peruvian Andes." Ph.D. dissertation, Tulane University, 1974.

———. "Disaster, Social Structure, and Myth in the Peruvian Andes: The Genesis of an Explanation." *Annals of the New York Academy of Sciences*, Vol. 293, pp. 246–74 (July 1977).

Bolton, Ralph, and Enrique Mayer, eds. *Andean Kinship and Marriage*. Washington, D.C.: American Anthropological Assn., 1977.

Bonner, Raymond. "Peru's War" (A Reporter at Large). *The New Yorker*, pp. 31–58 (Jan. 4, 1988).

Bourque, Susan C. "Cholification and the Campesino: A Study of Three Peruvian Peasant Organizations in the Process of Societal Change." Ph.D. dissertation, Cornell University, 1971.

———, and Kay Barbara Warren. *Women of the Andes*. Ann Arbor: University of Michigan Press, 1981.

Bruneau, Thomas C. "Power and Influence: Analysis of the Church in Latin America and the Case of Brazil." *Latin American Research Review*, Vol. 8, No. 2, pp. 25–51 (1973).

Brush, Stephen B. *Mountain, Field and Family—The Economy and Human Ecology of an Andean Valley*. Philadelphia: University of Pennsylvania Press, 1977.

Bulletin of the Atomic Scientists. "Environmental Disaster—Acts of Nature and Man, The Peru Earthquake: A Special Study." Vol. 26, No. 8, pp. 17–19 (October 1970).

Cabel, Jesús, ed. *Literatura del Sismo*. Lima: Juan Mejía Baca, 1972.

———. *Ancash-31*. Lima: Juan Mejía Baca, 1976.

Campbell, Leon G. "The Historiography of the Peruvian Guerrilla Movement, 1960–1965." *Latin American Research Review*, Vol. 8, No. 1, pp. 45–70 (1973).

Carballido Chávez, V. Hernán. *Rocío de Lágrimas*. Lima: Editorial Minerva, 1972.

Chaplin, David, ed. *Peruvian Nationalism, A Corporatist Revolution*. New Brunswick, N.J.: Transaction Books, 1976.

Cieza de León, Pedro de. *The Incas of Pedro Cieza de León*. Translated by Harriet de Onís. Edited by Victor Wolfgang Von Hagen. Norman, Okla.: University of Oklahoma Press, 1959 (first published in 1553).

———. *El Señorío de los Incas*. Lima: Instituto de Estudios Peruanos, 1967 (first published in 1553).

Cobo, Padre Bernabé. *Historia del Nuevo Mundo*. Madrid: Biblioteca de Autores Españoles, Vol. 92, 1956 (first published in 1653).

Cohen, A. *Two-Dimensional Man: An Essay on the Anthropology of Power and Symbolism in Complex Society*. Berkeley: University of California Press, 1974.

Comisión Episcopal de Acción Social. *La Justicia en el Mundo*. Lima: Editorial Universitaria, 1969.

Committee on the Alaska Earthquake of the Division of Earth Sciences, National Research Council. *The Great Alaska Earthquake of 1964*. Washington, D.C.: National Academy of Sciences, 1970.

Corominas, Joan. *Breve Diccionario Etimológico de la Lengua Castellana*. Madrid: Editorial Gredos, 1961.

CRYRZA. *Lineamientos de Base de la Política de la Comisión de Reconstrucción y Rehabilitación de la Zona Afectada*. Lima, 1970.

———. *CRYRZA en su Etapa de Realizaciones*. Huaraz, 1972.

Darwin, Charles. *The Voyage of the Beagle*. New York: P. F. Collier & Son Corp., 1937.

"Death by Glacier." *Scientific American*, Vol. 223, No. 2, p. 46 (August 1970).

Doughty, Paul. *Huaylas, An Andean District in Search of Progress*. Ithaca: Cornell University Press, 1968.

———. "From Disaster to Development." *Americas*, Vol. 23, No. 5, pp. 25–35 (1971a).

———. "Community Response to Natural Disaster in the Peruvian Andes." Paper delivered at the annual meeting of the American Anthropological Association. Mimeo. (1971b).

Drekonja, Gerhard. "Religion and Social Change in Latin America." *Latin American Research Review*, Vol. 7, No. 1, pp. 53–72 (1971).

Dudasik, Stephen. "Community Response to Shared Tragedy: An Essay on the Disaster Utopia in North Central Peru." *Florida Journal of Anthropology*, Vol. 1, No. 2, pp. 9–15 (1976).

———. "The Socio-Cultural Effects of Natural Disaster in a Peruvian Highland Community." Ph.D. dissertation, University of Florida, 1978.

Dupuy, Daniel Hammerly. *Bajo el Signo del Terremoto, Los Sismos Ante la Historia, la Ciencia y la Religión*. Lima: Ediciones Peisa, no date.

Dynes, Russell R. *Organized Behavior in Disaster*. Lexington: Heath Lexington Books, 1970.

Earthquake. Mimeographed document prepared by the Mormon Church in Salt Lake City, Utah, 49 pages, no date.

"Earthquake and Avalanche: Peruvian Disaster." *Science News*, Vol. 98, pp. 94–95 (1970).

Einaudi, Luigi, R. L. Maullin, A. C. Stepan, and M. Fleet. *Latin American*

Institutional Development: The Changing Catholic Church. Santa Monica: The Rand Corporation, 1969.

Ericksen, George E., G. Plafker, and J. Fernández Concha. *Preliminary Report on the Geologic Events Associated with the May 31, 1970, Peru Earthquake*. Geological Survey Circular 639. Washington, D.C.: United States Department of the Interior, 1970.

Erikson, Kai T. *Everything in Its Path: Destruction of Community in the Buffalo Creek Flood*. New York: Simon and Schuster, 1976.

Evans-Pritchard, E. E. *Witchcraft, Oracles and Magic Among the Azande*. Oxford: The Clarendon Press, 1937.

Flores-Ochoa, Jorge A. *Pastoralists of the Andes*. Translated by Ralph Bolton. Philadelphia: Institute for the Study of Human Issues, 1979.

Fonseca Martel, César. "La Economía 'Vertical' y la Economía de Mercado en las Comunidades Alteñas del Peru." In *Visita de la Provincia de León de Huánuco (1562)* by Iñigo Ortiz de Zúñiga, Vol. 2, pp. 317–38. Huánuco, Peru: Universidad Hermilio Valdizán, 1972.

Freire, Paolo. *Pedagogy of the Oppressed*. Translated from the original Portuguese manuscript (1968) by Myra Bergman Ramos. New York: The Seabury Press, 1973.

Fried, Jacob. "Social Organization and Personal Security in a Peruvian Hacienda Indian Community: Vicos." *American Anthropologist*, Vol. 64, No. 4, pp. 771–80 (1962).

Garcilaso de la Vega, "El Inca." *Comentarios Reales: El Origen de los Incas*. Barcelona: Editorial Bruguera, S.A., 1968 (first published in 1609).

Geertz, Clifford. "Religion as a Cultural System." In *Anthropological Approaches to the Study of Religion*. Edited by Michael Banton, pp. 1–46. London: Tavistock Publications, 1966.

Guaman Poma de Ayala, Felipe. *Nueva Crónica y Buen Gobierno*, Vol. 2. Caracas: Biblioteca Ayacucho, 1980 (first published in 1614).

Guerra, Francisco. *The Pre-Columbian Mind*. New York: Seminar Press, 1971.

Gutenberg, B., and C. F. Richter. *Seismicity of the Earth*. Princeton: Princeton University Press, 1954.

Gutiérrez, Gustavo. *A Theology of Liberation: History, Politics and Salvation*. Translated and edited by Sister Caridad Inda and John Eagleson. Maryknoll, New York: Orbis Books, 1973. (Originally published as *Teología de la Liberación*. Lima: Editorial Universitaria, S.A., 1971.)

Harding, Colin. "Peru: Questions of Revolution." *Latin American Review of Books*, Vol. 1, pp. 185–94 (1973).

Healy, J. H., and P. A. Marshall. "Nuclear Explosions and Distant Earthquakes: A Search for Correlations." *Science*, Vol. 169, pp. 176–77 (1970).

Henostroza, Abdón Dextre. *Desde Mi Sangre*. Lima: Impresiones Generales, 1973.

Holmberg, Alan. "Changing Community Attitudes and Values in Peru: A Case Study in Guided Change." In *Social Change in Latin America Today*. Edited by Richard Adams et al., pp. 63–107. New York: Harper & Brothers for Council on Foreign Relations, 1960.

"Huaraz en la Hora de la Tristeza." *Nueva*, Vol. 25, pp. 17–30 (1972).

Imbelloni, José. "La Tradición Peruana de las Cuatro Edades del Mundo en una Obra Rarísima Impresa en Lima en el Año 1630." *Anales del Instituto de Etnografía Americana*, Vol. 5, pp. 55–94 (1944).

"Infernal Thunder over Peru." *Time*, Vol. 95, pp. 26–28 (1970).

Isbell, Billie Jean. *To Defend Ourselves: Ecology and Ritual in an Andean Village*. Austin: University of Texas Institute of Latin American Studies, 1978.

Kates, Robert W., J. Eugene Haas, Daniel J. Amaral, Robert A. Olson, R. Ramos, and Richard Olson. "Human Impact of the Managua Earthquake." *Science*, Vol. 182, pp. 981–90 (1973).

Koth de Paredes, Marcia, and Amalia Castelli, eds. *Etnohistoria y Antropología Andina*. Lima: Centro de Proyección Cristiana, 1978.

Kinzl, Hans, and Ervin Schneider. *Cordillera Blanca: Peru*. Innsbruck: Wagner, 1950.

Krickeberg, Walter, Otto Zerries, Hermann Trimborn, and Werner Müller. *Pre-Columbian American Religions*. Translated by Stanley Davis. New York: Holt, Rinehart and Winston, 1968.

Kurtz, Donald V. "The Virgin of Guadalupe and the Politics of Becoming Human." *Journal of Anthropological Research*, Vol. 38, No. 2, pp. 194–210 (1982).

Lehmann, David. *Ecology and Exchange in the Andes*. New York: Cambridge University Press, 1982.

Levine, Daniel, ed. *Religion and Political Conflict in Latin America*. Chapel Hill: University of North Carolina Press, 1986.

Lewis, Ioan, ed. *Symbols and Sentiments: Cross-Cultural Studies in Symbolism*. New York: Academic Press, 1977.

Lifton, Robert Jay. *Death in Life: Survivors of Hiroshima*. New York: Random House, 1967.

———. *Boundaries*. Toronto: CBC Publications, 1969.

Lowenthal, Abraham F. "Peru's Ambiguous Revolution." In *The Peruvian Experiment*. Edited by A.F. Lowenthal, pp. 3–43. Princeton, N.J.: Princeton University Press, 1975.

Lynch, Thomas F., ed. *Guitarrero Cave: Early Man in the Andes*. New York: Academic Press, 1980.

MacEoin, Gary. "Latin America's Radical Church." *Latin American Review of Books*, Vol. 1, pp. 67–74 (1973).

Madariaga, Salvador de. *Bolívar*, Vol. 1. Buenos Aires: Editorial Sudamericana, 1959. (English edition: *Bolívar*. Coral Gables: University of Miami Press, 1967.)

Mangin, William P. "Estratificación social en el Callejón de Huaylas." *Revista del Museo Nacional*, Vol. 24, pp. 174–89 (1955).

Martin, Everett. "Aftershock in Peru." *Wall Street Journal*, Vol. 50, No. 23, pp. 1 and 17 (3 August 1972).

Matos Mar, José, F. Fuenzalida, J. Cotler, A. Escobar, A. Salazar, and J. Bravo. *Peru: Hoy*. Mexico, D.F.: Siglo XXI Editores, S.A., 1971.

McDowell, Bart, and John Fletcher. "Avalanche!" *National Geographic*, Vol. 121, No. 6, pp. 854–80 (June 1962).

Métraux, Alfred. *The History of the Incas*. New York: Schocken Books, 1973.

Miano Pique, Carlos. *¡¡Basta!! La Bomba Atómica Francesa, La Contaminación Atmosférica y Los Terremotos*. Lima: Tagrat, 1972.

Middlebrook, Kevin J., and David Scott Palmer. *Military Government and Political Development: Lessons from Peru*. Beverly Hills, California: Sage Publications, 1975.

Morales Arnao, César, ed. *Revista Peruana de Andinismo y Glaciología. Edición Extraordinaria Conmemorando el Primer Año del Sismo del 31 Mayo de 1970*. Lima: Imprenta Colegio Militar Leoncio Prado, 1971.

Murra, John. "El 'Control Vertical' de un Máximo de Pisos Ecológicos en la Economía de las Sociedades Andinas." In *Visita de la Provincia de León de Huánuco (1562)* by Iñigo Ortiz de Zúñiga, Vol. 2, pp. 429–76. Huánuco, Peru: Universidad Hermilio Valdizán, 1972.

Oficina Nacional de Información. *¡Cataclismo en el Perú!* Lima: Imprenta Editora Atlántida, S.A., no date.

Oliver-Smith, Anthony. "Yungay Norte: Disaster and Social Change in the Peruvian Andes." Ph.D. dissertation, Indiana University, 1973.

———. "Disaster Rehabilitation and Social Change in Yungay, Peru." *Human Organization*, Vol. 36, No. 1, pp. 5–13 (1977a).

———. "Traditional Agriculture, Central Places, and Post-disaster Urban Relocation in Peru." *American Ethnologist*, Vol. 4, No. 1, pp. 102–16 (1977b).

———. "Here There Is Life: The Social and Cultural Dynamics of Successful Resistance to Resettlement in Postdisaster Peru." In *Involuntary Migration and Resettlement: The Problems and Responses of Dislocated People*. Edited by Art Hansen and Anthony Oliver-Smith, pp. 85–103. Boulder, Col.: Westview Press, 1982.

————. *The Martyred City, Death and Rebirth in the Andes.* Albuquerque: University of New Mexico Press, 1986.

Pastor, Manuel. *Terremoto y Signos de Esperanza en América Latina.* Lima: Centro Nacional de Evangelización y Catequesis, 1970.

Patch, Richard W. "The Peruvian Earthquake of 1970." *American Universities Field Staff Reports, West Coast South America Series,* Vol. 18, Nos. 6–9 (August 1971).

Pfeiffer, John E. *The Creative Explosion: An Inquiry into the Origins of Art and Religion.* Ithaca, N.Y.: Cornell University Press, 1985.

————. "Cro-Magnon Hunters Were Really Us, Working Out Strategies for Survival." *Smithsonian,* Vol. 17, No. 7, pp. 74–85 (October 1986).

Philip, George D. E. *The Rise and Fall of the Peruvian Military Radicals 1968–1976.* London: The Athlone Press, 1978.

Phelps, Flora L. "The Town That Was, Until . . . May 31, 1970." *Americas,* Vol. 22, No. 9, pp. 16–26 (September 1970).

Ramírez Gamarra, Hugo. *Ancash, Vida y Pasión.* Lima: Editorial Universo, S.A., 1971.

Rankin, Richard C. "The Expanding Institutional Concerns of the Latin American Military Establishments: A Review Article." *Latin American Research Review,* Vol. 9, No. 1, pp. 81–108 (1974).

Richardson, Miles, Barbara Bode, and Marta Pardo. "The Image of Christ in Spanish America as a Model for Suffering." *Journal of Inter-American Studies and World Affairs,* Vol. 13, No. 2, pp. 246–57 (1971).

Rowe, John. "Inca Religion." In *Reader in Comparative Religion, An Anthropological Approach.* Edited by William A. Lessa and Evon Z. Vogt, pp. 540–53. New York: Harper and Row, 1958.

Sarmiento, Domingo Faustino. *Civilization and Barbarism.* New York: Hafner, 1974 (originally published in Spanish in 1845).

Silgado, Enrique. "Historia de los Sismos Más Notables Ocurridos en el Perú (1513–1970)." *Geofísica Panamericana,* Vol. 2, No. 1, pp. 179–243 (1973).

Smith, Brian H. "Religion and Social Change: Classical Theories and New Formulations in the Context of Recent Developments in Latin America." *Latin American Research Review,* Vol. 10, No. 2, pp. 3–34 (1975).

Smith, Donald E. *Religion and Political Development.* Boston: Little, Brown & Co., 1970.

————, ed. *Religion, Politics, and Social Change in the Third World.* New York: The Free Press, 1971.

Spalding, Karen. *De Indio a Campesino.* Lima: Instituto de Estudios Peruanos, 1974.

Sofue, Tokao. "A Japanese Perspective: Japanese Reactions to Disasters as One Aspect of National Character." *Proceedings of Organizational and Community Responses to Disasters* (Japan–U.S. Disaster Research Seminar, Sept. 11–15, 1972). Columbus, Ohio: Disaster Research Center, Ohio State University (September 1973).

Stein, William W. *Hualcán: Life in the Highlands of Peru.* Ithaca: Cornell University Press, 1961.

————. "Countrymen and Townsmen in the Callejón de Huaylas, Peru: Two Views of Andean Social Structure." *Special Studies No. 51, Council on International Studies.* Buffalo: State University of New York, 1974.

Sueldo Guerrero, Rubén. "Wankar K'uyci: El Arco Iris." *Tradición*, Vol. 2, No. 2, pp. 73–87 (1950).

Thomas, Lewis. "Notes of a Biology-Watcher." *The New England Journal of Medicine*, Vol. 298, No. 26, pp. 1454–56 (June 29, 1978).

Torry, William I. "Anthropological Studies in Hazardous Environments: Past Trends and New Horizons." *Current Anthropology*, Vol. 20, No. 3, pp. 517–40 (September 1979).

Trimborn, Hermann. "El Motivo Explanatorio en los Mitos de Huarochirí." *Revista de Antropologia* (Universidade de São Paulo), Vol. 2, No. 1, pp. 25–36 (June 1954).

————, and A. Kelm. *Francisco de Avila.* Berlin: Gebrueder Mann, 1967.

A True and Particular Relation of the Dreadful Earthquake Which Happened at Lima, the Capital of Peru, and the Neighboring Port of Callao, on the 28th of October, 1746. Translated from the original Spanish by a gentleman who resided many years in those countries. London: T. Osborne, 1748.

Turner, Victor. *The Ritual Process.* Chicago: Aldine Publishing Co., 1969.

————. *Drama, Fields, and Metaphors: Symbolic Action in Human Society.* Ithaca: Cornell University Press, 1974.

————, and Edith Turner. *Image and Pilgrimage in Christian Culture: Anthropological Perspectives.* New York: Columbia University Press, 1978.

Urioste, Jorge. "Sons of Pariacaca: Myth and Cult in Huarochirí." Mimeo. Ithaca, N.Y.: Cornell University, 1969.

————. "Chay Simiri Kaymi: Language of the Manuscript of Huarochirí." Ph.D. dissertation, Cornell University, 1973.

Valcárcel, Luis E. *Etnohistoria del Perú Antiguo.* Lima: Universidad Nacional Mayor de San Marcos, 1964.

————. *Historia del Perú Antiguo.* Vols. I–VI. Lima: Editorial Juan Mejía Baca, 1971.

Vallejo, César. *Los Heraldos Negros.* Lima: Editora Perú Nuevo, 1959 (originally published in 1918).

Vásquez, Mario C. "La Antropología Cultural y Nuestro Problema del Indio." *Perú Indígena*, Vol. 2, No. 5, pp. 7–157 (1952).

————. "Cambios en la Estratificación Social en una Hacienda Andina del Perú." *Revista del Museo Nacional*, Vol. 24, pp. 190–209, Lima (1955).

Velasco Alvarado, Juan. *Mensaje a la Nación del Señor General de División, Presidente de la República, con Motivo del 149° Aniversario de la Independencia.* Lima: Oficina Nacional de Información, 1970.

Vossler, Karl. *La Poesía de la Soledad en España.* Buenos Aires: Editorial Losada, 1946.

Wachtel, Nathan. *Sociedad e Ideología.* Lima: Instituto de Estudios Peruanos, 1973.

————. *The Vision of the Vanquished: The Spanish Conquest of Peru Through Indian Eyes (1530–1570).* Translated by Ben and Siân Reynolds. New York: Barnes & Noble, 1977 (first published in France in 1971 as *La Vision des Vainçus. Les Indiens du Pérou Devant la Conquête Espagnole 1530–1570.* Editions Gallimard).

Wallace, Anthony F. C. "Human Behavior in Extreme Situations: A Study of the Literature and Suggestions for Further Research." *Disaster Study No. 1.* Washington, D.C.: National Academy of Sciences, 1956a.

————. "Tornado in Worcester: An Exploratory Study of Individual and Community Behavior in an Extreme Situation." *Disaster Study No. 3.* Washington, D.C.: National Academy of Sciences, 1956b.

————. "Patterns of Group Behavior in Disaster." Publication No. 584. Washington, D.C.: Walter Reed Army Institute of Research, 1958.

Wilder, Thornton. *The Bridge of San Luis Rey.* Harmondsworth, Middlesex, England: Penguin Books Ltd., 1971 (first published by Longmans in 1927).

Wolf, Eric. "The Virgin of Guadalupe: A Mexican National Symbol." *Journal of American Folklore*, Vol. 71, pp. 34–39 (1958).

Wolfenstein, Martha. *Disaster, A Psychological Essay.* London: Routledge & Kegan Paul, 1957.

Yauri Montero, Marcos. *Warakuy.* Lima: Ediciones Piedra y Nieve, 1967.

————. *Radiografía del Sismo del 31 de Mayo de 1970.* Lima: Editorial Imprenta Ultra, S.A., 1971.

————. *Tiempo de Rosas y de Sonrisas . . . Tiempo de Dolor y de Muerte.* Lima: Editorial Imprenta Ultra, S.A., 1971.

————. *Ancash o la Biografía de la Inmortalidad.* Lima: P.L. Villanueva, 1972.

————. *En Otoño, Después de Mil Años.* Havana, Cuba: Casa de las Américas, 1974.

————. *Leyendas Ancashinas.* Lima: P.L. Villanueva, 1979.

————. *María Colón.* Lima: P.L. Villanueva, 1980.

———. *Mañana Volveré*. Lima: Editorial Lasontay, 1983.

———. *Así Que Pasen Los Años*. Lima: Editorial Piedra y Nieve, 1985.

Zavaleta Figueroa, Isaías. *El Callejón de Huaylas Antes y Después del Terremoto*, Vols. I, II, and III. (Vols. II and III, mimeo.) Caraz, Peru: Ediciones Parón (1970–1971).

ACKNOWLEDGMENTS

When I decided to go to Peru, I had the trust and support of my professors at Tulane University, especially Robert F. Gray, who through the years has always been there for me. A sailor in his retirement, he at times kept me on course, and, at other times, with his "lateral" thinking, steered me in a new direction. His earthy common sense steadied my sea legs with practical advice, like "Buy a good altimeter," though I couldn't afford one when I first went to the Andes. And, ultimately, in his quiet wisdom, he set me adrift to chart my own course.

When I arrived in Lima, in 1971, I stayed in the home of Alfredo Ferreyros, my cohort in an intensive course in Quechua at Cornell University. During that first week in Peru, I watched intently as Pablo Macera, professor of the seminar on Rural Andean History at the University of San Marcos, with a cat perched on his shoulder, typed a letter introducing me to "the authorities" of the hamlets of the Callejón and sent me off with good wishes. In the valley, Alvaro Whittembury, of Communal Development, helped me settle into my first room and took me on my first excursion. Ted Cook, of FAO, and the other FAO engineers helped me immensely with their companionship and their jeeps. At the end of my stay, Homer Campbell, also of FAO, came to the valley to breed trout in a glacial lake. He and his wife, Meg, shipped things for me and have remained my friends.

I am grateful to Paul Doughty and Anthony Oliver-Smith, who displayed none of that "territoriality" that anthropologists are sometimes accused of. They had worked in Huaylas and Yungay, and Tony spent the year following the disaster with the survivors of Yungay. That year is recorded in his book, *The Martyred City* (1986). Our paths crossed for the first time in December 1971, when Tony returned to the Callejón, and we traveled together for a week distributing relief funds contributed by anthropologists in the United States. Tony was my link to Cirila and to Yungay, and long after he had departed the valley, when I went to Yungay, his presence was keenly felt there. Towering above the *Yungaínos*, to the children he had become a kind of legendary Paul Bunyan. Once, a boy in the camp at Yungay Norte told me that Tony had actually fallen off Huascarán and survived.

The gratitude I owe to Reyna Alberto Quito and to her family runs deep. As my assistant, she was invaluable to me for her skills, but even more, her friendship sustained me through the year. I hope one day I will, in some way, be able to explain to her how, five thousand miles apart, I failed her one snowbound night in New York years afterward. Two other close friends, Juan Manuel Ramírez and Teófines Martel, of Huaraz, were also collaborators. I met them one day as I stood, rather in a daze, on a dusty street in the barrio of Centenario; within an hour they had furnished my room on the pampa with a desk and chair.

There are no words sufficient to express my appreciation for all the kindness shown me by the people of the Callejón de Huaylas. I have never felt and perhaps shall never feel such a profound sense of community as I felt that year. Men, women, and children, townspeople and *campesinos*, poets, priests, and shopkeepers, with all their loss, in all their misery, gave me warmth and opened to me their minds and hearts. My landlords, the Espinozas, their daughter Cucha, Benjamín Morales, the late Padre Soriano, the Sotomayors, Florencia and Luis, the Salazars, these are but a few names. In 1980, a thirteen-year-old boy, Lorenzo Díaz, tender and wise beyond his years, shielded me from dust kicked up by stampeding trucks on the road to Chavín. Víctor Valenzuela has shared his music, Marcos Yauri Montero his writings, all of them their lives.

I found in Cirila Luna, Jesusa Marcelino, and Domitila Melgarejo models of womanhood—in the laughter of Domitila, the gait of Jesusa as she swished along the mountain paths in her bright skirts, in the indomitable spirit of Cirila. The late Don Juan Durán, the gentlest of men, tirelessly taught me about his culture, his history and religion, his way of looking at the world. I felt at home with him and his family.

A grant from Tulane University financed the original fieldwork, and Fordham University my revisit in 1980. When I returned from the field the first time, I benefited from talks about the work with Althea Tessier and Barbara Lynch. Much later on, Nina Swidler read parts of the working manuscript for the book. Miles Richardson and Hilary Hanumara read the entire manuscript, and I am grateful to them all for their comments and encouragement. My friend of twenty-five years, Lydia Dufour, although she did not read the manuscript, knows the story herself, having been there with me through the final weeks of the original stay. She helped get me off the mountain and later transcribed several tapes. Carroll Mace, also my friend of many years, read the last draft and gave me the gift of his exquisite sensitivity, both to the turn of a phrase and to a valley he once traveled long before the earthquake. His affection and faith in me have been a source of courage.

A special debt of gratitude is owed to my husband, Robert Carneiro. He accompanied me during the final few weeks of the 1980 fieldwork, taking the measure of the mountain, and feeling the impact of the great event on what he, too, came to recognize as an extraordinary place in a world he knows so much of. He saw the manuscript through various drafts, pinpointing problems and helping me to focus the sprawling pages, or to find just the right word. He contributed several of his own wonderful photographs and worked on the maps with me. He has given his unfailing support to a book that is so unlike his own work in this vast and rich field of anthropology that we share.

My son, Brett, brought me lemonade at critical moments and, even in his youth, seemed to understand what "making a book" was all about.

I must end with the valley people, knowing I will not have

named here all those whose courageous lives in the face of such tragedy have enriched my own life beyond measure. Many appear in the book, their names unchanged—only in a few cases, where I have felt the need to protect someone, have I changed a name. I trust I have done no injury to anyone and have dealt fairly with even the most controversial figures and conflicting forces that played their parts in this immense drama. I thank all the people of the Callejón de Huaylas, those I had the honor to know as well as those whose lives touched mine in unseen ways. It is with deep humility that I have tried to tell their story, recognizing that this narrative is but a pale shadow of those epic times.

INDEX